Peter Norton's®

Complete Guide to Networking

Peter Norton
Dave Kearns

SAMS

A Division of Macmillan Computer Publishing
201 West 103rd Street, Indianapolis, Indiana 46290 USA

Peter Norton's® Complete Guide to Networking

International Standard Book Number: 0-672-31593-9

Library of Congress Catalog Card Number: 98-89593

Printed in the United States of America

First Printing: October 1999

01 00 99   4 3 2 1

Trademarks

Warning and Disclaimer

Associate Publisher
Michael Stephens

Executive Editor
Don Roche

Acquisitions Editor
Angela Kozlowski

Development Editor
Robyn Thomas

Managing Editor
Charlotte Clapp

Project Editor
George E. Nedeff

Copy Editor
Bart Reed

Indexer
Rebecca Hornyak

Proofreaders
Aaron Black
Kim Cofer
Carl Pierce
Mary Ellen Stephenson

Technical Editors
Mark Hall
Brian Powell

Interior Design
Gary Adair

Cover Design
Aren Howell

Copy Writer
Eric Borgert

Layout Technician
Timothy Osborn

Overview

Contents

About the Authors

Computer software entrepreneur and writer **Peter Norton** established his technical expertise and accessible style from the earliest days of the PC. His Norton Utilities was the first product of its kind, giving early computer owners control over their hardware and protection against myriad problems. His flagship titles, *Peter Norton's DOS Guide* and *Peter Norton's Inside the PC* (Sams Publishing), have provided the same insight and education to computer users worldwide for nearly two decades. Peter's books, like his many software products, are among the best selling and most respected in the history of personal computing.

Peter Norton's former column in *PC Week* was among the highest regarded in that magazine's history. His expanding series of computer books continues to bring superior education to users, always in Peter's trademark style, which is never condescending or pedantic. From their earliest days of changing the "black box" into a "glass box," Peter's books, like his software, remain among the most powerful tools available to beginners and experienced users, alike.

In 1990, Peter sold his software development business to Symantec Corporation, allowing him to devote more time to his family, civic affairs, philanthropy, and art collecting. He lives with his wife, Eileen, and two children in Santa Monica, California.

Dave Kearns wishes he had had a book like this when he was first thrust into a network management job in 1985, but he had to learn by trial and error. He did it so well that, by 1989, he was helping others troubleshoot their networking problems as a founder of the Novell Support Connection (née: NetWire) on the CompuServe Information Service, for which work he was honored by the International NetWare Users group with its annual service award.

Dave continued managing networks (NetWare, NT, UNIX, and more) until 1995, when he left the daily grind to found Virtual Quill, an organization that writes, lectures, and consults about networks. Besides books such as this, Dave has written for *Networking Solutions* magazine and *PC World*, and he regularly appears in the pages of *Network World* with his "Wired Windows" column. He also writes the twice-weekly newsletters *Focus on Windows NT* and *Focus on Directory Services* for Network World Fusion (`http://www.nwfusion.com/focus/`).

Dave continues to volunteer his services to help new (and old, but confused) network administrators with the Novell Support Connection (NetWire) and ClubWin (Windows NT/2000). He'd love to hear your thoughts on this book, which he can do if you email those thoughts to him at `PNG2nets@vquill.com`.

Dedication

For my parents, Virginia and Dave Kearns, who encouraged me every step of the way.

Acknowledgments

A book as all encompassing as this is never the work of one or two people laboring in quiet solitude. Many writers, editors, illustrators, indexers, and others whose jobs I can only guess at have contributed long hours and hard work to prepare this book for market. I apologize in advance to those whom I don't mention: Please know that I still appreciate all the effort you made to bring this work to completion.

First, I'd like to thank David Fugate and Matt Wagner of Waterside Productions, Mike Stephens and Angela Kozlowski of Macmillan Computer Publishing, and Scott Clark of the Peter Norton Group, who (collectively) got this project rolling. David and Angela, especially, stuck with it until the end, alternately offering carrots and sticks, as I needed them.

The facts and words used in this book are the product of a large group of collaborators, notably Mark A. Sportack, Richard Peete, James F. Causey, Arthur Cooper, Theresa Hadden, James M. Spann, David P. Welk, and Tony Northrup. Collectively they have over 100 years of networking experience, which translates into a lot of sleepless nights installing and maintaining the sometimes-fragile computerized conglomerations we call networks.

Project editor George E. Nedeff, development editor Robyn Thomas, copy editor Bart Reed, and technical editors Brian Powell and Mark Hall all did an outstanding job of keeping this book on time and on topic. We had our disagreements at times but never lost sight of the ultimate goal—to produce an outstanding primer on computer networking.

Finally, my thanks to Novell's Drew Major and Microsoft's Brian Valentine—friendly adversaries who nevertheless have advanced PC networking to its position as the center of today's business computing.

Tell Us What You Think!

As the reader of this book, *you* are our most important critic and commentator. We value your opinion and want to know what we're doing right, what we could do better, what areas you'd like to see us publish in, and any other words of wisdom you're willing to pass our way.

As an Executive Editor for Sams, I welcome your comments. You can fax, email, or write me directly to let me know what you did or didn't like about this book—as well as what we can do to make our books stronger.

Please note that I cannot help you with technical problems related to the topic of this book, and that due to the high volume of mail I receive, I might not be able to reply to every message.

When you write, please be sure to include this book's title and author as well as your name and phone or fax number. I will carefully review your comments and share them with the author and editors who worked on the book.

Fax: 317-581-4770

Email: droche@mcp.com

Mail: Don Roche
          Sams Publishing
          201 West 103rd Street
          Indianapolis, IN 46290 USA

Introduction

I wish I had had this book when I installed my first network in 1986. Of course, at that time a complete guide to networking would have been only 50 pages or so. (The manual accompanying my NetWare 4.61a system was only 120 pages long!)

Today, of course, networks have become an essential component of Information Technology infrastructures. Barely a day goes by without the announcement of a new application, protocol, standard, or OS version. Keeping on top of this exponentially expanding wealth of information requires a strong grounding in the basics of networks and how they work.

Surprisingly, at a time when the number of credentialled network administrators and consultants is the highest its ever been, networks are, perhaps, less understood than they were 10 years ago. The proliferation of graphical user interfaces and installation "wizards" means that many of us spend our productive time filling in onscreen forms without really understanding the choices we're forced to make (or worse, *not* forced, because there's always a default choice made for us should we decide not to decide).

Peter Norton's Complete Guide to Networking is divided into four sections plus a glossary. Each section can stand on its own merits—in fact, each chapter can be considered a complete educational experience. Here are the four parts:

- **Part I,** *Network Fundamentals*   This section discusses the things you need to know no matter what sort of network you're running.

- **Part II,** *Building Local Area Networks*   This section organizes the information from Part I into a coherent strategy for networking your organization.

- **Part III,** *Building Wide Area Networks*   This section presents the information you need to construct a multisite network, including allowing individuals remote access to your corporate network.

- **Part IV,** *Operating Networks*   This section provides a look at the major network operating systems as well as an overview of the skills you'll need to install and run them.

You can use this book as a primer to help you become certified as a networking professional, but you'll also want to keep it handy as a reference to help you maintain, repair, and optimize the networks you administer.

I enjoy getting feedback from my readers. If there's anything in this book you feel deserves comment, send an email to dkearns@vquill.com. I won't be able to answer your specific troubleshooting questions, but I may be able to point you toward someone who can.

Dave Kearns

Austin, TX

8/1/99

PART I

Network Fundamentals

A Networking Primer

In this age of distributed computing, networks have become a ubiquitous fixture in virtually all work environments. A *network* is the mechanism that enables distributed computers and their users to communicate and share resources. Despite their widespread use, networks remain the most mysterious and unfamiliar of the information technologies.

In this chapter, we will cover the basics of networking, identifies the different types of networks, and demonstrates how their evolution created the need for industry standards.

Since networking standards are set by several different standards bodies, we will also cover these various standards bodies, their standards, and any interrelationships between them. One of the more significant of these is the seven-layer Open Systems Interconnect (OSI) Reference Model. In this model, each layer supports a distinct functionality set. This model serves as a marvelous tool for understanding networks by dissecting them into their various functional components. We will also present and explain the OSI Reference Model.

Evolution of Networks

Networks originally were highly proprietary connectivity solutions that were an integral part of an equally proprietary bundled computing solution. Companies that automated their data processing or accounting functions during the primitive days before personal computers had to commit to a single vendor for a turnkey solution.

Typical configurations included dumb terminals that were hardwired to device controllers. The device controllers provided a communal, or *multiplexed*, access to the communications facilities that provided connectivity to the mainframes. These communications facilities were aggregated in a front-end processor (FEP) at the mainframe side. The FEP allowed many communications facilities to share a single channel to the mainframe. Given the speed differences between input/output and the mainframe's processors, this represented the most cost-effective solution, and is illustrated in Figure 1.1.

FIGURE **1.1**
*Hardwired access
to mainframes.*

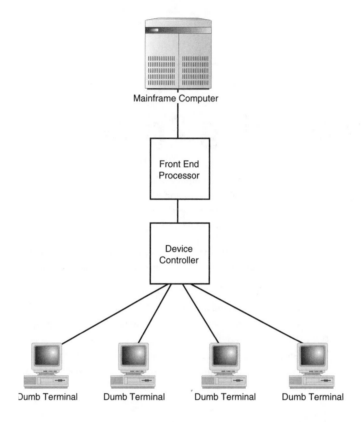

Otherwise, a low-bandwidth leased line was used to span the geographic distance to the mainframe. At that location, the leased line was linked to the mainframe's input/output (I/O) channel. This is illustrated in Figure 1.2.

FIGURE **1.2**
*Leased-line access
to mainframes.*

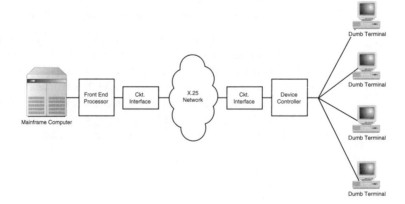

In these environments, the application software executed only on a computer supported by a single operating system. The operating system could execute only within the safety of the same vendor's hardware products. Even the users' terminal equipment and connectivity to the computer were part of the same, one-vendor integrated solution.

During the reign of the single-vendor integrated solutions, two different technological developments occurred that changed the future course of computing. First, the primitive ancestors of today's PCs began to appear. These devices were innovative in that they placed computational power right at the desktop.

Second, the scientists at Xerox's Palo Alto Research Center (PARC) began wrestling with ways to improve their own productivity. Specifically, they looked for a way to improve the sharing of files and data between their intelligent workstations. The existing method of sharing floppy disks was time consuming and problematic.

Their solution was the original local area network (LAN). They called it *ethernet*. It was a crude and simple LAN that relied on higher-layer internetworking protocols for much of its definition and behavior. The market potential of this technology was quickly realized. The original ethernet, now known as *PARC Ethernet* or *Ethernet I*, was superseded by a slightly better-behaved version. This version, developed by Xerox, Digital, and Intel, became known as *DIX Ethernet* or *Ethernet II*. Digital, Intel, and Xerox, in combination, set the "standards" for Ethernet II and produced its component technologies.

Together, intelligent user devices and local area networks would spawn a new paradigm: open, distributed, networked computing.

Standards Organizations

The success of Ethernets I and II demonstrated that the marketplace was tired of the proprietary approach to bundled networking and computing. Customers began demanding a more open environment that would enable them to build applications from mixed and matched products from different vendors. Interoperability would also, as evidenced by Ethernet, foster competition through technological innovation. Therefore, the interrelated goals of openness were as follows:

- Lower costs
- Greater capabilities
- Cross-vendor interoperability

Cross-vendor interoperability required the different platforms to recognize each other and to know how to communicate and share data. This necessitated the development of unbiased, industry-wide standards for every aspect of networked computing.

The need for standardization precipitated a flurry of standardization efforts. Today, many different standards bodies are responsible for defining national and/or international standards for different aspects of information technologies, including data communications and networking. Although frequently these standards bodies either collaborate or cooperate to ensure as universal a set of standards as possible, there can still be some confusion, although the overwhelming effect is positive. We will explore the more pertinent standards bodies and their interrelationships.

ANSI

The American National Standards Institute (ANSI) is a private, nonprofit organization. Its charter is to facilitate the development, coordination, and publication of voluntary national standards. ANSI standards are voluntary in that ANSI doesn't actively police or enforce its standards. Rather, through participation in global standards bodies such as the ISO (International Organization for Standardization), IEC (International Electrotechnical Commission), and so forth, noncompliance with its standards results in noncompliance with global standards. Such noncompliance is self-punishing in the age of open computing.

IEEE

The Institute of Electrical and Electronic Engineers (IEEE) is responsible for defining and publishing telecommunications and data communications standards. Its most significant effort to date (at least for our purposes) has been the definition of the standards for local and metropolitan area networks (LANs and MANs). These standards, embodied in a large and complex series of technical standards, are generically referred to as *Project 802* or the *802 series of standards.*

The intent of the IEEE is to develop standards that will be accepted by the American National Standards Institute (ANSI). This acceptance will result in a broader audience for the IEEE standards, because ANSI participates on global standards bodies.

The ISO

The International Organization for Standardization was founded in 1946 and is headquartered in Geneva, Switzerland. Certain reference sources identify this organization with the acronym *IOS*. Although, technically, this is the correct acronym, the organization eschews it in favor of a mnemonic abbreviation: ISO. This mnemonic derives from the Greek word *isos*, which means *equal* or *standard*. This is the appropriate way to identify the International Organization for Standardization, provided, of course, you don't want to use its full name. It's a voluntary, nontreaty organization that is chartered by the United Nations to define international standards. Its charter includes literally all fields, except for anything electrical or electronic.

Currently, the ISO membership consists of over 90 different standards bodies from around the world. Perhaps the single most important standard developed by the ISO is its *Open Systems Interconnection* (OSI) *Reference Model.* We will cover this model in much more detail later in this chapter, in the section titled, "The OSI Reference Model."

The IEC

The International Electrotechnical Commission (IEC), also headquartered in Geneva, was founded in 1909. The IEC sets international standards for anything electrical and electronic. Its current membership includes committees from over 40 countries. The American National Standards Institute (ANSI) is the USA's representative on both the IEC and ISO.

The IEC and ISO recognized that information technologies were an important area of potential overlap. They formed the Joint Technical Committee (JTC1) specifically to define standards for information technologies.

> **Note:** The Joint Technical Committee formed by the IEC and the ISO was the first such joint committee, so it is identified as JTC1. As of the publication of this book, there is still no JTC2.

IAB

The Internet Architecture Board, formerly known as the *Internet Activities Board*, governs the technical development of the Internet. It contains two working committees: the *Internet Engineering Task Force* (IETF) and the *Internet Research Task Force* (IRTF). As their names imply, they are functionally separate. The IRTF researches new technologies that may be of value to or have an impact on the Internet. The IETF is the recipient of the IRTF's research. The IETF is responsible for setting the technical standards for the Internet as well as the definition of new standards for Internet technologies, including the Internet Protocol (IP).

> **Note:** IP is a Layer 3 (or Network Layer) protocol. As such, it's inherently connectionless. It's also incapable of identifying packets that need to be retransmitted or performing any resequencing of packets that may have arrived in a different order than that in which they were sent. To make IP—or any Layer 3 protocol—more usable requires a Layer 4 (Transport Layer) protocol. Examples of Layer 4 protocols that use IP are TCP, UDP, and even the experimental TTCP. A slash (/) is used to separate the Layer 3 and 4 protocol names whenever they are used together (for example, TCP/IP and UDP/IP). This has the unfortunate effect of confusing the distinctions between Layer 3 and 4. Consequently, it's not uncommon to find technically proficient people using the term TCP/IP when, in fact, they really mean only IP.
>
> For more information on protocols that operate at Layers 3 and 4 of the OSI Reference Model, refer to Chapter 4, "The Network and Transport Layers."

The OSI Reference Model

ISO developed the Open Systems Interconnection (OSI) Reference Model to facilitate the open interconnection of computer systems. An open interconnection is one that can be supported in a multivendor environment. This model established the global standard for defining the functional layers required to support such a connection between computers.

When the OSI Reference Model was developed almost 20 years ago, it was viewed as radical. Computer manufacturers, at that time, locked customers into proprietary, single-vendor architectures. Open communication was viewed as an invitation to competition. From the manufacturers' perspective, competition was undesirable. Consequently, all functions were integrated as tightly as possible. The notion of functional modularity, or *layering*, seemed antithetical to any manufacturer's mission.

It's important to note that the model has been so successful at achieving its original goals as to almost render the model moot. The previous proprietary, integrated approach has disappeared. Open communications today are requisite. Curiously, very few products are fully OSI compliant. Instead, its basic layered framework is frequently adapted to new standards. Nevertheless, the OSI Reference Model remains a viable mechanism for demonstrating the functional mechanics of a network.

Despite its successes, numerous misperceptions about the OSI Reference Model persist. Consequently, we need to provide yet another overview of this model in this section. The overview identifies and corrects these misperceptions.

The first misperception is that the OSI Reference Model was developed by the Paris-based International Standards Organization (ISO). It was not. The OSI Reference Model was developed by the International Organization for Standardization.

> **Warning:** The International Standards Organization is frequently, but incorrectly, credited with the development of the OSI Reference Model. The model was developed by the International Organization for Standardization.
>
> For the purposes of any certification exam that might be lurking in your future, International Standards Organization is the "correct" answer. It's inaccurate but expected on the examinations.

The OSI model categorizes the various processes that are needed in a communications session into seven distinct functional layers. The layers are organized based on the natural sequence of events that occurs during a communications session.

Figure 1.3 illustrates the OSI Reference Model. Layers 1–3 provide network access, whereas Layers 4–7 are dedicated to the logistics of supporting end-to-end communications.

FIGURE 1.3

The OSI Reference Model.

OSI Reference Model Layer Description	Layer Number
Application	7
Presentation	6
Session	5
Transport	4
Network	3
Data Link	2
Physical	1

Peter's Principle: Pay Your Money, Take Your Choice

As someone once said, "The nice thing about standards is that there are so many to choose from." And so many standards bodies, too. For example, Arcnet (which you might come across in older network installations) is an ANSI standard, not an IEEE standard like Ethernet, Token Ring and FDDI.

Many standards also represent a "lowest common denominator" and are often extended in practice by various vendors. Protocol standards, such as HTTP, are often in this category.

You need to be familiar with the standards. You should make standards compliance a priority with the networking products you buy. Just remember that two similar products—both standards compliant—may not necessarily be interchangeable.

Layer 1: The Physical Layer

The bottom layer is called the *Physical Layer*. This layer is responsible for the transmission of the bit stream. It accepts frames of data from Layer 2, the Data Link Layer, and transmits their structure and content serially, one bit at a time.

It's also responsible for the reception of incoming streams of data, one bit at a time. These streams are then passed on to the Data Link Layer for reframing.

This layer, quite literally, sees only 1's and 0's. It has no mechanism for determining the significance of the bits it transmits or receives. It's solely concerned with the physical characteristics of electrical and/or optical signaling techniques. This includes the voltage of the electrical current used to transport the signal, the media type and impedance characteristics, and even the physical shape of the connector used to terminate the media.

Note: Don't fall into the misperception that OSI's Layer 1 includes anything that either generates or carries the data communications signals. This is not true. It's a *functional* model only.

Layer 1, the Physical Layer, is limited to just the processes and mechanisms needed to place signals onto the transmission media and to receive signals from that media. Its lower boundary is the physical connector that attaches to the transmission media. *It does not include the transmission media!*

Transmission media include any means of actually transporting signals generated by the OSI's Layer 1 mechanisms. Some examples of transmission media are coaxial cabling, fiber-optic cabling, and twisted pair wiring. The confusion seems to stem from the fact that the Physical Layer does provide specifications for the media's performance. These are the performance characteristics that are required, and assumed to exist, by the processes and mechanisms defined in the Physical Layer.

Consequently, transmission media remain outside the scope of the Physical Layer and are sometimes referred to as *Layer 0*.

Layer 2: The Data Link Layer

The second layer of the OSI Reference Model is called the *Data Link Layer*. As is the case with all the layers, the Data Link Layer has two sets of responsibilities: transmitting and receiving. It's responsible for providing end-to-end validity of the data being transmitted.

On the transmit side, the Data Link Layer is responsible for packing instructions, data, and so forth into frames. A *frame* is a structure indigenous to the Data Link Layer that contains enough information to make sure the data can be successfully sent across a local area network to its destination.

Successful delivery entails the frame reaching its intended destination intact. Therefore, the frame must also contain a mechanism to verify the integrity of its contents upon delivery.

Two things must happen for guaranteed delivery to occur:

- The originating node must receive an acknowledgment of each frame received intact by the destination node.

- The destination node, prior to acknowledging receipt of a frame, must verify the integrity of that frame's contents.

Numerous situations can result in transmitted frames either not reaching the destination or becoming damaged and unusable during transit. The Data Link Layer is responsible for detecting and correcting any and all such errors.

The Data Link Layer is also responsible for reassembling any binary streams that are received from the Physical Layer back into frames. Given that both the structure and content of a frame are transmitted, however, the Data Link Layer isn't really rebuilding a frame. Rather, it's buffering the incoming bits until it has a complete frame.

Layers 1 and 2 are required for each and every type of communication, regardless of whether the network is a LAN or WAN.

Layer 3: The Network Layer

The *Network Layer* is responsible for establishing the route to be used between the originating and destination computers. This layer lacks any native transmission error detection/correction mechanisms and, consequently, is forced to rely on the end-to-end reliable transmission service of the Data Link Layer.

The Network Layer is used to establish communications with computer systems that lie beyond the local LAN segment. It can do so because it has its own routing addressing architecture, which is separate and distinct from the Layer 2 machine addressing.

Routable protocols include the following:

- IP
- IPX
- AppleTalk

The use of the Network Layer is optional. It's required only if the computer systems reside on different network segments that are separated by a router.

Layer 4: The Transport Layer

The *Transport Layer* provides a service similar to the Data Link Layer in that it's responsible for the end-to-end integrity of transmissions. Unlike the Data Link Layer, the Transport Layer is capable of providing this function beyond the local LAN segment. It can detect packets that are discarded by routers and automatically generate a retransmit request.

Another significant function of the Transport Layer is the resequencing of packets that may have arrived out of order. This can happen for a variety of reasons. The packets may have taken different paths through the network, for example, or some may have been damaged in transit. In any case, the Transport Layer is capable of identifying the original sequence of packets and must put them back into that sequence before passing their contents up to the Session Layer.

Layer 5: The Session Layer

The fifth layer of the OSI Model is called the *Session Layer*. This layer is relatively unused as a separate layer; many protocols bundle this layer's functionality into their transport layers.

The function of the OSI Session Layer is to manage the flow of communications during a connection between two computer systems. This flow of communications is known as a *session*. It determines whether communications can be uni- or bi-directional. It also ensures that one request is completed before a new one is accepted.

Layer 6: The Presentation Layer

The *Presentation Layer* is responsible for managing the way data is encoded. Not every computer system uses the same data-encoding scheme, and the Presentation Layer is responsible for providing the translation between otherwise incompatible data-encoding schemes, such as *American Standard Code for Information Interchange* (ASCII) and *Extended Binary Coded Decimal Interchange Code* (EBCDIC).

The Presentation Layer can be used to mediate differences in floating-point formats as well as to provide encryption and decryption services.

Layer 7: The Application Layer

The top layer in the OSI Reference Model is called the *Application Layer*. Despite its name, this layer does not include user applications. Rather, it provides the interface between those applications and the network's services.

This layer can be thought of as the reason for initiating the communications session. For example, an email client might generate a request to retrieve new messages from the email server. This client application automatically generates a request to the appropriate Layer 7 protocol(s) and launches a communications session to get the needed files.

The Model's Usage

The vertical orientation of the stack is an acknowledgment of the functional flow of processes and data. Each layer has interfaces to its adjacent layers. In order to communicate, two systems must pass data, instructions, addresses, and so forth between the layers. The differences between the logical flow of communications and the actual flow of the session are illustrated in Figure 1.4.

> **Note:** Although the Reference Model includes seven layers, not all layers are required for any given communications session. For example, communications across a single LAN segment can operate strictly at Layers 1 and 2 of the model, without requiring the other two communications layers.

FIGURE 1.4
Actual versus logical flow of layered communications.

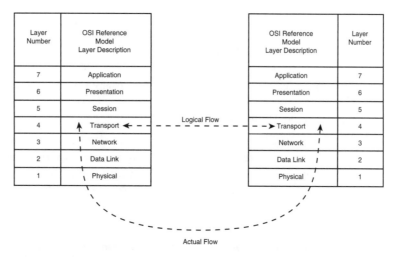

FIGURE 1.5
Use of layered headers to support logical adjacency.

Although communications flow vertically through the stack, each layer perceives itself to be capable of directly communicating with its counterpart layers on remote computers. To create this logical adjacency of layers, each layer of the originating machine's protocol stack adds a header. This header can be recognized and used by only that layer or its counterparts on other machines. The receiving machine's protocol stack removes the headers, one layer at a time, as the data is passed up to its application. This process is illustrated in Figure 1.5.

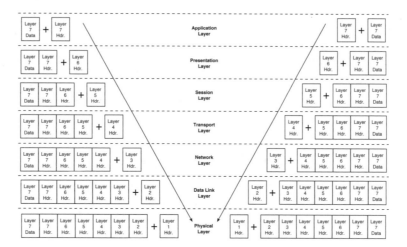

For example, segments of data are packaged by Layer 4 of an origination machine for presentation to Layer 3. Layer 3 bundles data received from Layer 4 into packets (that is, Layer 3 *packetizes* the segments), addresses them, and sends them to the destination machine's Layer 3 protocol by way of its own Layer 2. Layer 2 encases the packets with frames, complete with addressing that's recognized by the LAN. These frames are presented to Layer 1 for conversion into a stream of binary digits (bits) that are transmitted to the destination machine's Layer 1.

The destination machine reverses this flow of handoffs, with each layer stripping off the headers that were added by their counterparts on the origination machine. By the time the data reaches the destination machine's Layer 4, the data is back in the same form into which the originating machine's Layer 4 put it. Consequently, the two Layer 4 protocols appear to be physically adjacent and communicating directly.

Note: Note that most of today's networking protocols use their own layered models. These models vary in the degree to which they adhere to the separation of functions demonstrated by the OSI Reference Model. It's quite common for these models to collapse the seven OSI layers into five or fewer layers. It's also common for higher layers to not correspond perfectly to their OSI-equivalent layers.

In fact, each Layer 3 passes the data down to Layer 2, which, in turn, converts the frames to a bit stream. After the bit stream is received by the destination computer's Layer 1 device, it's passed up to the Data Link Layer for reassembly into a frame. After the frame's receipt is successfully completed, the framing is stripped off and the packet that was embedded in it is passed up to the recipient's Layer 3. It arrives in exactly the same form as that in which it was sent. To the Layer 3's, communications between them were virtually direct.

The fact that communication can appear to occur between adjacent layers (from the perspective of those layers) is a tribute to the success of the model.

Networking Basics

A *network*, at its simplest, is anything that enables two or more computers to communicate with each other and/or other devices. This enables users to use computers and networks to share information, collaborate on a work item, print, and even communicate directly through individually addressed messages.

Networks consist of many components, including both hardware and software. Some components can even be completely intangible.

Before we delve too far into the basic network components, it's important to note that networks have evolved into two distinct categories: *local area networks* (LANs) and *wide area networks* (WANs). The distinction between them is fairly simple. LANs are used to interconnect devices that are in relatively close proximity. WANs are necessary to interconnect LANs across geographic distances.

> **Note:** A third category of network is the *metropolitan area network* (MAN). Although defined through the IEEE's Project 802, the same initiative that standardized LANs, MANs are more closely related to WANs than LANs. They remain relatively obscure and are seldom used.

There are, of course, many exceptions to these two simple definitions. We will use them solely as a starting point, and make their definitions increasingly precise throughout this book.

Hardware Components

The basic hardware components of a network include three types of devices:

- Transmission facilities
- Access devices
- Devices that repeat transmitted signals

These components are basic in that all networks must either contain them or, at a minimum, work around them. We will describe these components as they support LANs and WANs in the remainder of this section. We will continue to describe these details in more depth throughout this entire book.

Transmission Facilities

Transmission facilities are the media used to transport a network's signals to their destination. Media types can include coaxial cables, twisted pair, and even fiber-optic cabling.

LAN media types can also be intangible. They can be light, radio, and even microwave signals transmitted through open air. Although the atmosphere, itself, is the actual media used to support these various forms of transmission, describing it as a media type is rather pointless. It's more useful to describe the mechanisms that generate the transmissions than it is to describe the air that carries the transmissions. We will discuss the more common LAN transmission media in further detail in Chapter 2, "The Physical (and Not So Physical) Layer."

The WAN, too, has its own transmission facilities. Such facilities are often thought of in terms of their clock rates and frame structures rather than simple transmission media (a 1.544Mbps Frame Relay leased line, for example). Their physical media are inconsequential to their actual performance. We will discuss these transmission facilities in more detail in Chapter 11, "Transmission Facilities."

Access Devices

An *access device* is responsible for the following:

- Properly formatting data so that it can be accepted in the network
- Placing that data on the network
- Accepting transmitted data that's addressed to it

In a local area network, the access device is known as a *network interface card* (NIC). The NIC is a circuit board that's installed in a computer and occupies an I/O slot on its motherboard. The network is then cabled to the port provided by this board. The NIC frames data that the computer's applications need to transmit, puts that data onto the network in binary form, and accepts inbound frames that are addressed to that computer. We will discuss the process of framing data and placing it onto the network in Chapter 3, "The Data Link Layer."

In a wide area network, the access device is a router. Routers operate at Layer 3 of the OSI Reference Model and include two types of protocols: routing and routable. Routable protocols, such as IP, are used to transport data beyond the boundary of Layer 2 domains. We will discuss these protocols in much more detail in Chapter 4.

Routing protocols provide all the functions necessary to perform the following tasks:

- Determine optimal paths through a WAN, for any given destination address
- Accept and forward packets through those paths to their destinations

A WAN is used to interconnect two or more LANs. We will cover more information on this topic in Chapter 10, "Wide Area Networking."

Repeaters

A *repeater* is a device that accepts transmitted signals, amplifies them, and puts them back on the network. In a LAN, a repeater—more popularly referred to as a *hub*—enables multiple devices to be networked together by providing multiple ingress points to the network. This function is so critical to today's LANs that its real purpose—signal regeneration—is often forgotten.

The hub's capability to regenerate signals is every bit as crucial to the success of a LAN as its capability to provide ingress points. The inescapable reality is that transmitted signals are affected by the media that transports them. Electronic signals placed on a wire inevitably deteriorate. This deterioration can take one of two possible forms: attenuation or distortion.

Attenuation is a decrease in the strength of the signal. *Distortion* is the unwanted modification of signals in transit. Each of these forms of deterioration must be addressed and rectified separately.

Attenuation can be compensated for by keeping wire lengths short enough to guarantee that the signal is strong enough to reach all destinations on the wire. If the wire must be relatively lengthy, however, a repeater can be installed in the line.

Distortion is a more severe problem for signal transmission. This is different from attenuation. Distorted signals corrupt whatever data is being transported. Repeaters are incapable of differentiating legitimate signals from distorted ones; they repeat signals indiscriminately. There are, however, several other ways to combat distortion:

- Adhere rigidly to any installation guidelines that may have been provided with your transmission media. More information on transmission media is presented in Chapter 2.

- Identify all causes of the distortion. Next, try to route cabling away from those sources. Also, it may be beneficial to use network transmission technologies, such as fiber-optic cabling, that can resist that distortion. We will discuss these technologies throughout this book.

- Use network protocols that are capable of detecting and automatically correcting any transmission errors that may occur. We'll discuss these protocols in Chapter 3 and in Chapter 4.

Software Components

The software components required in a network include the following:

- Protocols that define and regulate the way two or more devices communicate

- Hardware-level software, known as *microcode* or *drivers*, that guide the functionality of individual devices such as network interface cards

- Communications software

Protocols

Providing the physical connectivity for a network is the easy part. The real challenge lies in developing standard ways for computers, and even other network-attached devices, to communicate. These ways are more formally known as *protocols*. The simplest example of a protocol can be found in the way that most people communicate over a telephone. In most of the world, the first thing that is said in any phone conversation is "Hello" (or its regional equivalent).

This simple greeting universally conveys that the calling party has successfully established a communications session with someone else. The next step is for the caller to respond (with their own "Hello") so that the recipient of the phone call can tell that the communications link works in both directions.

If both parties are familiar with each other, this simple two-word exchange is usually sufficient to predicate even the most intimate of conversations. If, however, both parties are unknown to each other, additional protocols are needed to establish each other's identity. After this is established, the conversation can move on to the purpose for the call.

This simple example has become so ingrained that violations of this protocol are often interpreted as a lack of manners or even deliberate rudeness.

Computers are no different. Merely having a network to connect them is only one part of what is needed to support meaningful communications and resource sharing. Direct communications between two computers enables them and their users to share resources. Given that precious few people actually work in isolation, enabling computers to share information and other resources was a revolutionary step toward an information technology infrastructure that more closely approximated the way groups of people actually work.

Protocols for LANs are frequently called LAN *architectures*, as they are embodied in the NIC. They predetermine much of the shape, size, and mechanics of the LAN. We'll discuss these in Part II, "Building Local Area Networks" (Chapters 5 through 9 of this book).

Protocols for WANs usually come in bundles and are responsible for a great variety of services. We'll look more closely at these protocols in Chapter 4.

Device Drivers

A *device driver* is a hardware-level program that controls a specific device. A device driver can best be thought of as a miniature operating system for a single piece of hardware. Each driver contains all the logic and data that's needed to ensure the proper functioning of its particular device. In the case of a NIC, this includes providing an interface for its host's operating system.

The device driver frequently resides in firmware inside the device it operates.

Communications Software

All the previously described hardware and software components of a network stop shy of enabling a user to actually *use* a network. They simply provide the infrastructure and mechanisms that permit its use. The task of actually using the network falls to the specialized application software that controls communications.

The dawn of drag-and-drop computing has made communications software so simple to use that it's not uncommon for a user to be running a communications program and not even know it. Some examples include linking to drives or share areas in Windows NT. Others are a bit more obvious, such as the World Wide Web's (WWW) Hypertext Transport Protocol (HTTP), Telnet, tn3270, file-transfer programs, and even electronic mail.

Regardless of the application's type or sophistication, communications application software is the mechanism that makes the available network bandwidth actually usable.

Making Networks from Components

The hardware and software components—and their functions—still don't make a network. They must be integrated. The following examples of networks demonstrate some of the ways that the hardware components can be integrated to form very simple networks. This should also demonstrate some of the flexibility that you can enjoy when building networks.

Repeaterless LAN

Two stations, equipped with compatible NICs, can communicate directly with each other, without a repeater (also known as a *hub*). This assumes, of course, that the two stations are in close enough proximity. This relationship is illustrated in Figure 1.6.

FIGURE 1.6
Two stations communicating directly without a hub.

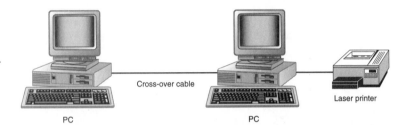

Cross-over cable

Laser printer

PC   PC

Note: The example presented in Figure 1.6 assumes that the wiring provides for the crossover of their transmit and receive paths. This is an issue only with twisted pair wiring. Coaxial cable uses the same physical path for both transmit and receive functions. Twisted pair wiring uses two or more pairs of wire. A two-pair wire scheme would use one pair for transmitting and one pair for receiving. Each pair dedicates one wire for positive and one for negative voltages. Given that such interfaces are standardized, a four-pair twisted pair cable strung between two PCs would result in both PCs attempting to transmit on the same pair of wires. They would also be listening on the same pair of wires for inbound frames. In other words, they would not be able to communicate. A crossover cable inverts the transmit and receive pairs so that the pair on which one device transmits becomes the pair to which the other device listens for inbound transmissions.

Bus-Based LAN

The simplest form of LAN is based on a bus. A *bus* is a network that relies on the interface card to drive communications across the network. Some LAN technologies use a bus topology as a native part of their protocol specification. Alternatively, LAN architectures designed to be used in a hub-based LAN can sometimes be wired together without the hub to form a bus-based LAN.

A bus-based LAN consists of the following components:

- Transmission media (the bus)
- Physical interface, or *transceiver*, for each device to be connected
- Transmission and communications protocols
- Application software that enables the users to communicate and share resources

As evidenced by this list, as well as Figure 1.7, a bus-based LAN doesn't use a signal repeater. This automatically limits both the distances over which the networked devices can communicate and the number of devices that can be networked together.

FIGURE 1.7
Bus-based LAN.

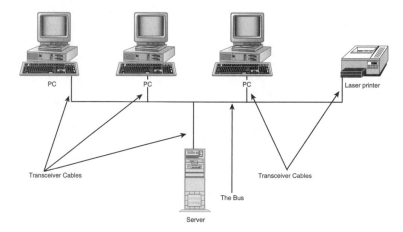

The significant limitations imposed by a bus LAN, in conjunction with the relatively low cost of hubs, makes this an all-but-forgotten network type. Nevertheless, we must acknowledge it as a legitimate network topology. It serves to illustrate the functionality of the basic network components.

Hub-Based LAN

The *hub* is the device that, as its name implies, is the center of the network. A simple, hub-based LAN is illustrated in Figure 1.8. A hub has two advantages over a bus-based LAN. First, the hub repeats signals, thereby enabling the LAN to stretch over greater distances than can be served by a bus. Second, the hub can also connect to one or more other hubs, thereby increasing the number of devices that can be attached to the LAN. Chaining hubs also serves to further increase the distances that can be spanned by the LAN.

FIGURE 1.8
Hub-based LAN.

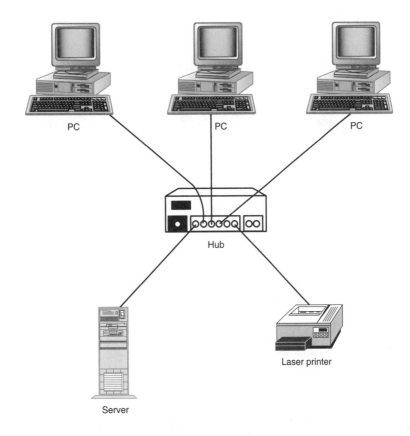

Note: Not all hubs are repeaters. Some hubs are nonrepeating station aggregators. They're used only to provide a star topology to a LAN and to interconnect other hubs. This enables more users to be interconnected to the LAN but does not provide the signal regeneration that would be needed to expand the LAN in terms of its linear dimensions.

Hubs (or repeaters) have been successfully adapted to bus-based LAN architectures to create a new topology: the star bus.

A hub-based LAN requires all the basic components required by the bus-based LAN, in addition to the hub or repeater. These components were listed in the previous section, titled "Bus-Based LAN."

WAN

A wide area network interconnects LANs with a device known as a *router*. This enables each LAN to offer its users access to resources stored on other interconnected LANs without compromising its own identity. In other words, a router interconnects them, without condensing them into just one big LAN. Two LANs are interconnected, using a router, to form a WAN in Figure 1.9.

FIGURE 1.9

A wide area net-work.

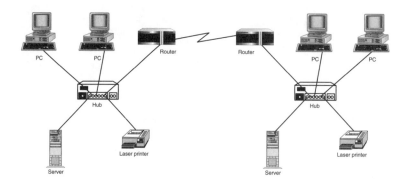

The WAN depicted in Figure 1.9 could span any geographic distance. The LANs could be located in the same building or on different continents. Repeaters, of course, are needed to support the extension of WAN facilities across great geographic distances.

> **Note:** The repeater, a Layer 1 device, takes on different forms for LANs and WANs. LAN repeaters are commonly called *hubs*. WAN repeaters are seldom, if ever, seen by the users and administrators of the WAN. They are, however, integral to the commercial infrastructure that provides the WAN connectivity and remain invisible.

Summary

The basic network components we covered in this chapter, their functions, and even their uses, are just the beginning. They are the proverbial "building blocks" that we will explore in much greater detail throughout the remainder of this book. They have been presented to give you an appreciation for their historical development as well as for some of the fundamental terms and concepts that are indigenous to networking.

These basics are discussed in the context of the various industry standards that dominate networking today. The OSI Reference Model, in particular, is used throughout this book to help you understand the mechanics of these basic networking concepts by presenting a common frame of reference for the different standards.

The Physical (and Not-So-Physical) Layer

The Physical Layer, as defined by the OSI Reference Model, includes all the processes, mechanisms, electronics, and protocols needed for a computing device to transmit and receive binary datastreams. Included in the Physical Layer specification of LAN technologies are the expectations for the performance of the transmission media that interconnects two communicating devices. The model, however, does not extend to the media themselves.

This chapter describes the role and significance of the Physical Layer in LANs and then goes beyond the limitations of that layer in its examination of Physical Layer phenomena. This chapter, in addition to describing the functionality of the Physical Layer, also includes detailed examinations of fiber optics, coaxial cabling, and the myriad grades of twisted pair wiring. Included in this description are the performance characteristics and limitations of each media type.

Local area networks can also be implemented on an intangible Physical Layer. Such networks, known as *wireless LANs*, have been around for quite a few years. Only recently, with the adoption of the Institute of Electrical and Electronics Engineers' (IEEE) 802.11 specification, have any standards existed in this area. Consequently, each manufacturer was previously free to develop highly proprietary and noninteroperable products. The functional disparities between these proprietary products centered around their transmission technologies and techniques. The new IEEE 802.11 standard integrates support for many of these previously proprietary technologies and techniques.

Later in this chapter, we'll examine the various intangible implementations of the Physical Layer, their transmission techniques, and their properties (as dictated by the electromagnetic spectrum), and we'll also look at some of the more salient points of the 802.11 specification.

The Physical Layer

The foundation on which the OSI Reference Model is built is the Physical Layer. It defines everything required to support the transmission and reception of signals. The Physical Layer has four functional areas:

- Mechanical
- Electrical
- Functional
- Procedural

Together, these areas encompass all the mechanisms needed to support the electrical and/or optical transmission of data. Included within these areas are signaling techniques, the voltage of the electrical current used to transport the signal, the media types and their respective impedance characteristics, the electronic components on the network interface card (NIC), and even the physical shape of the connector used to terminate the media.

A very common misperception held about the Physical Layer concerns its scope. It's commonly believed that the OSI Model's Physical Layer includes anything that either generates or carries signals. This is not true. Remember, it's the bottom layer of a protocol stack. The stack must reside on a device. Therefore, the bottom layer is limited to the description and/or specification of the processes and mechanisms needed by that communicating device to support communications with other compatible devices. *The Physical Layer does not include anything that's not contained within the host.* Specific examples of mechanisms that are needed to support data communications but are outside the scope of the Physical Layer include the following:

- Physical media
- Hubs
- Routers
- Switches

These items are necessary to effectively transport signals between the communicating devices but are outside the scope of the Physical Layer.

The lower boundary of this layer is the physical connector port of the communicating device that attaches to the transmission media. Rather than try to define the specifications for the entire network and its subcomponents, the model simply establishes the performance characteristics that it expects of the network and stops there. The model does not include anything else that exists between the physical connectors of the two communicating devices. Consequently, transmission media remain outside the scope of the Physical Layer and are sometimes referred to as *Layer 0*. The confusion over the scope of the Physical Layer seems to stem from the fact that the Physical Layer does provide specifications for the media's performance. In other words, the Physical Layer describes the expected performance of the physical plant but does not define that physical plant.

Physical Layer Functions

The Physical Layer performs the transmission and reception of signals on behalf of the rest of its protocol stack and applications that use that stack. This support requires the Physical Layer to perform several critical functions. For transmission, the Physical Layer must do the following:

- Convert framed data from the Data Link Layer to a binary stream
- Implement the media-access method dictated by the Data Link Layer's media-access method
- Transmit framed data serially (that is, one bit at a time), as a binary stream

For reception, the Physical Layer must perform the following functions:

- Listen for inbound transmissions addressed to its host device
- Accept appropriately addressed streams
- Pass the binary stream up to the Data Link Layer for reassembly into frames

Conspicuously absent from this list is any means of verifying the integrity of received data. This layer transmits and receives only 1's and 0's. It has no mechanism for determining the significance of the bits it transmits or receives. Consequently, it's unable to make an independent determination as to the validity of any given bit or stream of bits. The onus for this is passed on to higher-layer protocols.

Encoding Signals

The Physical Layer is responsible for encoding data into a form that can propagate through transmission media. These forms must, necessarily, vary with the transmission media, because each medium has its own physical characteristics. There are many different techniques for physically encoding data, but all use electromagnetic waves to encode and transport the data.

An *electromagnetic wave* is the physical form of the energy described by the electromagnetic spectrum. This spectrum starts at zero oscillations, rises through the range of frequencies that can be perceived by the human ear (up to 25,000 oscillations per second), through the various forms of light, and finally into the range of ridiculously large numbers inhabited by X-rays and gamma rays.

The electromagnetic wave continuously oscillates in a somewhat symmetrical pattern, from positive to negative, as it travels. The rate at which this oscillation occurs is called *frequency*. It's measured in hertz (Hz). One cycle, or hertz, represents a 360-degree change in one second.

> **Note:** A unit of thousands of hertz per second is abbreviated as *KHz*. Millions of hertz per second is abbreviated *MHz*, and billions of hertz per second is abbreviated as *GHz*.

Another metric used to measure the intensity of electromagnetic energy is a *wavelength*. A wavelength is the distance from the top of one wave's crest to the top of the next wave's crest. Besides this difference in how they are measured, the more important difference between a hertz and a wavelength lies in their application. Hz is used to describe lower-frequency bands, whereas wavelength is reserved for the higher-frequency phenomena, such as light, X-rays, and gamma rays. The length of a wave can be a small as billionths of a meter or as large as several meters. Other than these two differentiating points, you should remember that they're more alike than different. For most purposes (including our look at networking), they can be considered two different views of the same phenomenon. Figure 2.1 illustrates one hertz and one wavelength.

FIGURE 2.1

One hertz versus one wavelength.

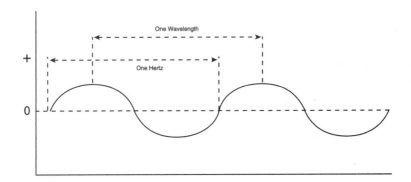

Regardless of whether Hz or wavelengths are used to describe frequency, it's important to note that the physical characteristics of the wave, and its propagation, change with movement along the spectrum. Generally speaking, as frequency increases, the capability to encode data increases. Quite simply, more state changes occur per second at higher frequencies than at lower frequencies. State changes (the change from positive to negative, or vice versa) are used to encode data.

Another important change is the persistence of the signal. Lower frequencies tend to be remarkably durable and can penetrate almost anything without attenuating completely. Toward the portion of the spectrum inhabited by light, however, frequencies and their signals can be completely and instantly attenuated by even the least significant (or dense) of opaque materials. Of course, proceeding into the frequencies beyond light—into the range of X-rays—this statement becomes invalid. For the purposes of encoding and transporting data in LANs, however, this generalization remains valid.

The last change to note is the inverse relationship between wavelengths and frequencies. The longer the wavelength, the lower the frequency. Quite simply, a wavelength of one meter per second oscillates slowly between positive and negative states. In contrast, a wavelength of 850 millionths of a meter (or nanometers, abbreviated as *nm*) has a relatively fast oscillation rate. As indicated previously, the lower the frequency, the lower the potential for carrying data, because there are fewer state changes per unit of time.

Regardless of the wave's intensity, the transmission medium serves two purposes:

- To guide the wavelength's transmission
- To protect the wavelength, to the extent that it's capable, during transmission

Whenever electrical vibrations are used to transport data—whether analog or digital—the series of vibrations is known as a *signal*. Signals can occur at any frequency, although it's generally acknowledged that anything below 300,000Hz does not offer enough bandwidth to be practical for use by electrical devices.

The curvature of the wave presented in Figure 2.2 is distinctly analog in its shape. Digital signals feature flattened plateaus and valleys, with crisp phase changes, as opposed to gradual, organic, changes. The shape of a digital signal, as compared to an analog signal, is presented in Figure 2.2.

FIGURE 2.2
Digital versus ana-log signals.

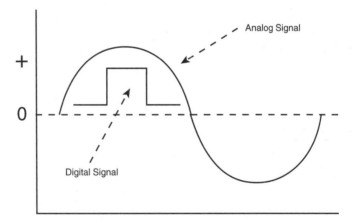

The Physical Layer, as implemented on a network interface card, expects a specific transmission media type. Given this media type, it knows what frequency to use, how to encode data on it, and what bandwidth can be supported over a predetermined maximum cable length.

Bandwidth

Bandwidth is the *width* of a communications channel, measured in Hz. This limits the quantity of data that can be encoded by the Physical Layer electronics, for any given set of frequencies. It's the difference between the upper and lower frequency boundaries of a communications channel. For example, the 902–928MHz band yields 26MHz of bandwidth. This bandwidth provides the basic limiting factor in the signaling and data transmission rates of any data communications technology that would use this band.

Warning: The yield of a band should not be misconstrued as a frequency! In the given example, the band is 26MHz in width. There is also a valid spectral frequency of 26MHz. To get a yield of 26MHz from that frequency would require a band of at least the same width—for example, from 26MHz to 52MHz. Unfortunately, this frequency is so low that it cannot accommodate the inefficiencies of physical signal encoding as well as higher frequency bands. Consequently, you'd be extremely hard-pressed to try and get 26MHz worth of bandwidth from a 26MHz band in that low of a frequency.

To further illustrate this point, the 902–928MHz band was not selected at random. It's the range at which many pagers and other low bandwidth, spread spectrum radio frequency devices operate. The inefficiencies of this band can be demonstrated by examining any of the wireless LAN products (examined later in this chapter) that operate at this range. They're able to eke out only 2Mbps from the 26MHz band.

The overuse, and increasing generalization, of the term *bandwidth* creates the potential for confusion with other concepts, such as *data rate* and even *transmission frequency*. Older concepts, too, such as *baud rate*, add to the complexity of describing the robustness of data transmissions. *Baud* is the number of discrete signaling elements transmitted in one second. Baud is an artifact from the early days of communications, when 300-baud modems were replacing 110-baud acoustic couplers. These modems were capable of transmitting 300bps. At higher signaling speeds, multiple bits can be encoded per baud. Consequently, 2400bps modems actually ran at 1200 baud by placing two bits per baud.

In LAN environments, the actual transmission frequency is all but ignored. The potential bandwidth of a data communications frequency, as well as the physical media that supports its transmission, can be measured more precisely using the number of *bits* per second (bps) that can actually be transmitted, rather than Hz. Hz (the number of cycles per second) is generally used only to describe extremely low frequencies, such as those used for voice communications. At these low frequencies, Hz and bps are usually synonymous.

Note: At the higher frequencies, the relationship between Hz and bits per second becomes obscured. For example, the potential bandwidth of fiber-optic cabling is rated in wavelengths. For instance, 62.5-micron fiber-optic cabling can be rated at 850 nanometers (nm). This reflects the maximum wavelength that can be supported over a specific distance (usually 100 meters).

The communications devices that use the higher frequencies tend to be more sophisticated. Implicit with this increased sophistication are more advanced data encoding techniques. These techniques can support the encoding of more than one bit per Hz or can be used to manipulate one's perception about the robustness of a technology. A good example of an intentional manipulation of perception by misusing communications rate metrics is Gigabit Ethernet. Gigabit Ethernet (which is examined in more detail in Chapter 6, "Ethernet") was cobbled together using the IEEE's 802.3 Data Link Layer and Fibre Channel's Physical Layer. Despite its marketing nomenclature, it uses a maximum signaling speed described as 1,024 megabaud, or 1 gigabaud. The frequencies used vary, based on the selection of physical media.

Gigabit Ethernet uses an encoding scheme known as 4B/5B. Simply put, the Physical Layer of this architecture creates a five-bit pattern for every four-bit string that must be transmitted. This 20 percent overhead at the Physical Layer automatically reduces the maximum bandwidth to 800Mbps. Filtering out the overhead of the Gigabit Ethernet's framing and protocol, the IP packet structure and protocols, and the overhead of any other protocols that exist at Layers 4 through 7 further reduces the effective throughput. Its gross bandwidth is 800Mbps, but actual sustainable, demonstrable data rates are lower. Unfortunately, even ignoring the protocol overhead and calling it "800Mbps Ethernet" lacks the market appeal of "Gigabit Ethernet." Therefore, for the sake of marketing, technical accuracy is compromised.

Given this, it becomes clear that *bandwidth* is the maximum amount of data that can be carried over a specific transmission media.

Distance Implications

The potential bandwidth of any given media type is limited by both the frequency that it can support and the distance over which the media must support it. Distance is a critical factor for several reasons. First, the greater the distance, the longer a signal takes to reach its destination. Also, the greater the distance, the more the signal disperses (radiates). This results in the slow but steady deterioration in the volume of the signal. Ultimately, the signal reaches a minimum threshold, below which it's unintelligible to the recipient. This form of signal degradation is known as *attenuation*.

Long cable distances also directly increase the exposure of the cable and its signals to interference from sources of electromagnetic noise, such as the ballast of fluorescent lamps, AC electrical cables, and so forth. This form of deterioration is known as *distortion*.

Attenuation

Passing an electrical current, which is the form that a transmitted signal takes, results in the slow but steady degradation of the signal's strength. In addition to its continuous radiation of energy, the signal also consumes energy to move along its wire path. Remember, the signal is an electromagnetic wave: Like all electrical currents, it consumes its own energy to overcome the resistance inherent in its conductive media as it moves through it. The result is a continuous decrease in the magnitude of the signal, without altering its shape.

All signals, even optical ones, are inherently electromagnetic. A common misperception is that electrical current is viable for transmission only over conductive materials such as copper. Fiber-optic cabling uses light-based transmissions. Light is still an electromagnetic phenomenon; it just has a much higher frequency than the waves that can pass through metallic conductors. Consequently, even light-based signals are prone to attenuation. The glass media through which light-based transmissions travel tend to have very little electrical resistance. Instead, attenuation of an optical signal is caused by one or both of the following:

- Radial dispersion of signal away from the center axis of the fiber
- Collision with impurities in the fiber

Remember, light is an extremely frangible beam. It attenuates completely whenever it impacts an opaque solid.

The longer a cable is, the more resistance the signal encounters. Left unchecked, normal attenuation can result in a signal deteriorating to the point that its data is no longer discernible by the recipient. Consequently, the Physical Layer dictates a series of specifications to guarantee that this does not happen—at least, not in networks that comply with the specification.

Attenuation can be compensated for by keeping wire lengths short enough to guarantee that the signal is strong enough to reach all destinations on the wire. Alternatively, if the wire must be relatively lengthy, a repeater can be installed in the line. A *repeater* is any device that takes an incoming signal, amplifies its strength, and puts it back on the wire. See Figure 2.3 for a functional depiction of a repeater.

FIGURE 2.3

The regeneration of an attenuating signal using a repeater.

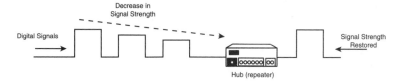

This basic and primary function of a repeater is often lost on the users and administrators of a LAN. To them, the repeater is a hub, and the hub provides only ports for interconnecting multiple devices. For all their successes, repeaters are not without limitations. For example, they are incapable of discerning legitimate data and frame structures from damaged ones. Any errors or distortions received are repeated at a stronger signal level.

Distortion

Distortion is a severe problem for signal transmission. It's the unwanted modification of signals in transit. After data or framing has been distorted, it is useless. The recipient—if it can still determine that it is the intended recipient—passes the binary stream up to its Data Link Layer protocols. These protocols recognize the distortion and notify the frame's originator of the need to retransmit that frame. This is a decidedly reactive approach to combating distortion. Figure 2.4 illustrates a distorted signal.

FIGURE 2.4
A distorted signal.

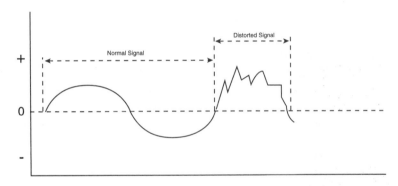

There are, however, several proactive ways to obviate distortion:

- Adhere rigidly to any installation guidelines that may have been provided with your transmission media. Use the correct grade of wire, make sure its installation and terminations are in compliance with manufacturer recommendations, and keep the wire path within acceptable distances. Forcing data to travel over wire paths longer than the recommended maximum is a good way to institutionalize retransmissions.

- Recognize potential causes of distortion and route cabling away from those sources.

- Use network protocols that are capable of detecting and automatically correcting any transmission errors that may occur. These protocols are discussed in Chapter 3, "The Data Link Layer," and in Chapter 4, "The Network and Transport Layers."

> **Warning:** One form of signal distortion is known as crosstalk. Crosstalk is a phe-
> nomenon of twisted pair wiring. Twisted pair uses different wires within the
> same sheath for different functions—for example, one wire for transmitting and
> the other for receiving. *Crosstalk* is the induction of unwanted signals from one
> wire to another within the same sheath. This form of distortion is also some-
> times referenced as *NEXT* (near-end crosstalk). Crosstalk can be avoided by mak-
> ing sure your twisted pair wiring is installed and terminated properly.

You can clean up minor signal distortion through the use of a device that actually regen-
erates the received signal rather than simply amplifying it. For example, in a LAN, a hub
is a simple repeater. It simply amplifies and repeats any distorted signals that it receives.
A *router*, on the other hand, is an intelligent device that can apply logic to its processing
of each packet.

A router receives packets and buffers them while it determines what to do with them. If
the packet's header structure has been damaged in transit, the router is unable to forward
it. For lack of an appropriate route for the damaged packet, the router discards it, leaving
the originating host's transmission control protocol to detect the loss and then retransmit.

Only packets that are received intact and have a destination address that the router recognizes are routed. This process involves looking up the destination address in the routing
table to determine both the next hop and, more importantly, out of which interface the
packet should be sent. Then the packet is sent. Implicit in this description is the fact that
routers regenerate packets; they do not simply amplify them and send them on their way
as repeaters do.

> **Note:** Routers operate at Layer 3 of the OSI Reference Model. As such, they
> receive and transmit packets, not frames. Frames are indigenous to Layer 2 (the
> Data Link Layer).

Physical Transmission Media

In order to reliably and consistently perform its transmit and receive functions, the
Physical Layer must make certain assumptions about the world between the media interfaces of the two communicating devices. For example, the Physical Layer protocols must
assume certain levels of performance for the media types they support. The Physical
Layer expects the actual performance of the media to be in compliance, regardless of
what must be done to maintain that compliance.

Transmission media include any means of actually transporting signals generated by the
OSI's Layer 1 mechanisms. Given this definition, transmission media can be either tangible or intangible. The intangible (wireless) media are described later in this chapter.

Tangible transmission media types include the following:

- Coaxial cable
- Twisted pair wire
- Fiber-optic cabling

Coaxial Cable

Coaxial cable, almost always referred to as *coax*, has two concentric conductors. It is, quite literally, coaxial in that both conductors share a common axis. The most common version of this cable type consists of a single conducting copper wire insulated by dielectric material. This dielectric material is then wrapped in another cylindrical conductor. This cylindrical conductor can be either a solid or braided wire. It is then wrapped in another layer of insulation, and the whole assembly is covered with a protective outer jacket of either polyvinyl chloride (PVC) or Teflon.

A side perspective of coaxial cable is rendered in Figure 2.5, with the layers peeled back to reveal its anatomy. Although coaxial cables may look the same, they have many different grades of impedance. They are rated by a radio grade (RG) scale. For example, the 10Base2 Ethernet variant uses RG-58, which offers a 50-ohm impedance in a wire that's three-eighths of an inch thick. In the 10Base2 Physical Layer specification, this translates into a 10Mbps signaling speed for up to 185 meters.

FIGURE 2.5
Side perspective of coaxial cable.

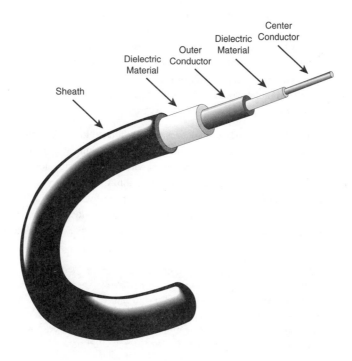

Other, more highly specialized types of coaxial cabling exist, such as fused-disk coaxial cabling, but these are distinctly outside the scope of LANs.

The advantage of coax cable is that it can support high bandwidth communications over relatively long, repeaterless runs. Coax was the original transmission media specified for Ethernet. Since then, it has been almost completely supplanted by the various twisted pair–based Ethernet Physical Layer specifications.

The reasons for this functional obsolescence are simple. Coax is a relatively fragile cable assembly. Coax does not suffer kinks, severe bends, or even crushing pressure gracefully. Any of these can permanently damage the cable structure and directly inhibit signal transmission.

Additional disincentives to use coax are its cost and its size. Coaxial cabling is more expensive than twisted pair, due to its more complex construction. Each cable is also three-eighths of an inch or more in diameter. Therefore, coax consumes a tremendous amount of space in cable ducts, raceways, and so forth. Even a modest concentration of coax devices quickly consumes any available space for cable runs.

Today, coax is generally limited to delivery of broadband Cable Television (CATV) signals to cable subscribers.

Twisted Pair Wire

Twisted pair wiring, long used to support voice communications, has become the *de facto* standard wiring technology for LANs. A twisted pair consists of two relatively thin wires, 18 to 24 American Wire Gauge (AWG), or 0.016 to 0.035 inches in diameter. These wires are coated with a thin layer of polyvinyl chloride (PVC) and spiraled around each other. This twist is highly functional: It helps cancel out any electromagnetic interference (EMI) that would otherwise be inducted into the copper by providing a balanced radiation of energy between the two wires.

The gauge (thickness) of the wire is directly related to its performance capabilities. Thicker wires translate into a wider potential communications band (in other words, greater bandwidth) and longer potential wire runs. Unfortunately, as the bandwidth increases with wire gauge, so does attenuation. Consequently, a balance must be struck between bandwidth and distance for each gauge of wire. Striking this balance is one of the key features of a Physical Layer specification. It does not describe the wire path but does specify gauge, terminator types, maximum distances, and bandwidth.

Warning: Straight, untwisted copper wire of 18–24 AWG is known as an *antenna*! It is more adept at picking up ambient electromagnetic radiation than it is at retaining it. Remember that twisted pair wiring is twisted for a reason; it enables cancellation of signal distortion. Without the twist, this cancellation mechanism is defeated. Remember this the next time you're tempted to install flat wire under your carpets rather than twisted pair.

Twisted pair wiring comes in a wide variety of shapes and sizes that range from a single pair of voice-grade wires all the way up to 600-pair trunk cables. Some of these varieties, such as differing numbers of pairs bundled together, are intended to improve capacity. Others, such as the following techniques, improve throughput.

- Increasing the thickness of the conductor
- Increasing the twist rate
- Using several different twist rates in bundles of multiple pairs
- Shielding the pairs with a metallic barrier

For LANs, four pairs of twisted pair wires are usually bundled together within a common sheathing. The sheathing can be either another layer of PVC or Teflon. Teflon is much more expensive and rigid than PVC, but it does not emit toxic fumes when combusting. Consequently, it must be used for cable runs through any ducts or plenums that supply air to the occupants of a building.

The two main varieties of twisted four-pair are *shielded* and *unshielded*.

Shielded Twisted Pair

Shielded twisted pair (STP) features an extra layer of either foil or braided metallic wire that envelops the twisted pairs. This shielding lies directly below the surface of the jacketing. The intent of its design was to enable the twisted pairs to operate in environments prone to electromagnetic interference (EMI) and/or radio frequency interference (RFI). In practice, it actually impeded the normal functioning of the twisted pairs. Electromagnetic radiation normally emanates from the signals transmitted over a copper wire. This radiation is illustrated in Figure 2.6, and it establishes a point of reference for understanding the implications of using shielded twisted pair.

FIGURE 2.6
Normal electromagnetic radiation.

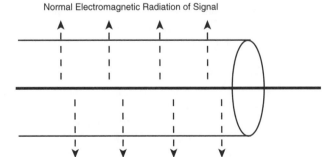

Shielding the wire with a metallic barrier protects the signal from ambient radiation that may be inducted. Induction of external radiation helps attenuate and/or distort the signal. Unfortunately, this shielding also prevents the normal radiation depicted in Figure 2.6

from escaping! Instead, this radiation reflects back into the copper conductor of the wire and can cause a signal to be self-impeding. This situation is illustrated in Figure 2.7.

Figure 2.7
Shielded electro-magnetic radiation.

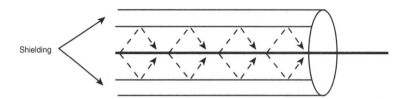

Shielding is critical to the successful transmission over straight, single-conductor wiring (such as coaxial cable), but it's usually more detrimental than beneficial to twisted pair. Twisted pair wiring uses an error-correction mechanism that's capable of canceling out any inducted noise. Coaxial cabling takes the opposite approach. Rather than cancel out inducted noise, it uses shielding to block its entry to the signal path. The layers of dielectric insulation between its two conductors help minimize the radiation of its own signals. Shielded twisted pair successfully prevents extraneous noise from being inducted. Unfortunately, shielding without dielectric insulation results in the self-impedance of signals.

Unshielded Twisted Pair

Twisted pair wiring also comes in an unshielded variety. Unshielded twisted pair, commonly called *UTP*, is available in several different forms, sizes, and grades. As indicated earlier, size refers to the number of pairs bundled together. The standard wiring for LANs is four-pair.

Four-pair UTP features eight wires, separated into groups of two. Each pair consists of a positive and negative wire. Each wire is also called a *lead*. Leads are used in pairs. For example, one pair of leads supports only transmissions, another supports reception. The other wires are not used in most LANs, although LANs that operate at signaling speeds of 100Mbps or higher over UTP typically use all four pairs.

Categories of Performance

Twisted pair wiring is a commodity: Regardless of the manufacturer, you can reasonably expect consistent performance. This is due to the degree of standardization that has occurred in the telecommunications industry. If this sounds a bit vague, it's intentional. No single standards body is responsible for the care and maintenance of standards that define twisted pair. Instead, a loose collaboration of ANSI, the FCC, the EIA, and many other organizations provides the standards for cabling and even cable components, such as terminators.

If this isn't enough of a radical departure from the normal approach to standards setting, consider this: The existing specifications do not define twisted pair! Although some standards do establish guidelines for cabling and/or cable components, twisted pair is defined by *categories of performance*. The categories are defined by their functions, not by any physical standard. In other words, all a given manufacturer has to do to prove compliance is to demonstrate performance, regardless of how the wire was made, how thick it is, from what material it's made, or anything else.

Originally, there were five series of tests to establish benchmark performance categories for twisted pair wiring. These were numbered 1 through 5, and compliant wire was identified as being Category *x*, or Cat-*x*, with *x* being the numeric test series that was achieved. Over time, the market has coalesced into just two viable performance levels: Cat-3 and Cat-5. Categories 1 and 2 were officially made obsolete in 1995 due to inadequate performance vis-à-vis requirements. Cat-4 offers a median level of performance, relative to 3 and 5, but is seldom (if ever) used. Cat-6 and Cat-7 have now been added to the mix, but (at least for now) are very expensive. This should change as more is manufactured and economies of scale go into effect, but for now Cat-3 and Cat-5 are overwhelmingly the best choices.

Category 3 UTP offers 16MHz of bandwidth, which translates into signaling speeds up to 10Mbps at 100 meters. Category 4 can support 20MHz, and Category 5 can support up to 100MHz. This range demonstrates why Cat-4 has failed to gain support in the market. It has not been perceived as providing enough of a performance differential to be worth the bother. Anyone needing more bandwidth than Cat-3 offers can simply install Cat-5. Provided users adhere to the distance limitations of whichever LAN architecture they choose, Cat-5 can provide 100Mbps, 155Mbps, and even 256Mbps. Obviously, as the signaling speed increases, the maximum distance decreases. Nevertheless, the middle ground between Cat-3 and Cat-5 has proved to be uneconomical.

Special Considerations

Twisted pair wiring, regardless of the category or type, uses separate, physical wires for the positive and negative leads of the transmit and receive functions. For two devices to communicate, they must agree on which device (or devices) is to transmit and which is to receive on which wire leads. Consequently, the potential exists for wiring devices together incorrectly.

Under normal circumstances, devices that are to be wired directly together (a PC and a hub, for example) have complementary interfaces that automatically provide the crossover function. Equipment such as the network interface cards (NICs) in PCs and servers is considered Data Terminal Equipment (DTE).

Modems and the ports on a hub, among others, are considered Data Communications Equipment (DCE). The relationship between the lead assignments of DCE and DTE is illustrated in Figure 2.8, using the RJ-45 interface of 10Mbps Ethernet as an example.

FIGURE 2.8
DCE versus DTE.

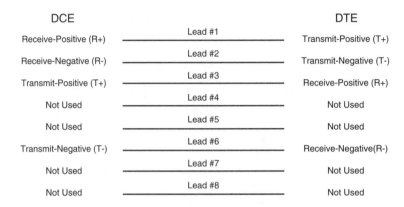

These complementary interfaces enable terminal and communications gear to be directly cabled together without causing conflicts between transmit and receive functions. Under normal operating circumstances, a DCE device always connects to a DTE device, and vice versa, using a four-pair whose leads remain consistent from end to end. Such a cable is called a *straight-through cable*.

The terms *DTE device* and *DCE device* are used on a per-port basis. Therefore, both can apply to any single multiport device. For example, a hub can have both DCE and DTE ports, depending on the nature of the port. Ports that serve as outbound ports to other hubs are set up as DCE. Ports that are used to connect computing equipment (inbound connections) are DTE. Older hubs had a specific port that was reserved for outbound connections. Some were selectable (inbound or outbound).

The current generation of multiarchitecture switching hubs has all but obviated the outbound port. High bandwidth, switched backplanes can be used to create extended LANs. Alternatively, a crossover cable can be used to link two hubs using just inbound ports. The proper uses of straight-through and crossover cables are illustrated in Figure 2.9.

FIGURE 2.9
Crossover wiring for DTE to DTE communications (RJ-45 10BaseT).

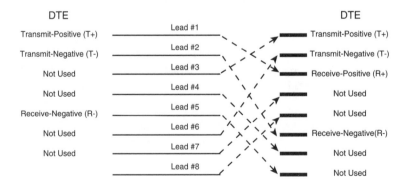

Crossover cables must maintain the polarity of a physical wire. Positive and negative voltages must be kept separate. The only wires that are crossed over are the positive Transmit (T+) to the positive Receive (R+) and the negative Transmit (T-) to the negative Receive (R-).

Fiber-Optic Cable

Fiber-optic cables are capable of carrying the higher frequencies of the electromagnetic spectrum—that is, light. Fiber-optic cables come in a seemingly infinite variety of shapes, sizes, and wavelength ratings. Figure 2.10 demonstrates the side view of a fiber-optic cable. Note that this view is of a typical cable and, consequently, may not exactly depict any particular type.

FIGURE 2.10
Side view of a fiber-optic cable.

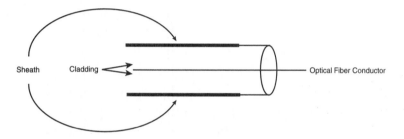

Fiber-optic cabling has only three apparent constants:

- The center axis of the cable is occupied by a high-purity optical media that's capable of reliably carrying light patterns over long distances.

- The lack of either an electrical signal or pliable copper conductor means that fiber-based transmissions are relatively secure. Unlike copper wire, fiber-optic cabling is virtually impossible to tap into. Remember, when stressed sufficiently, glass shatters. That stops the signal.

- The optical media, called the *fiber*, is clad with a concentric, protective layer of plastic.

Aside from these basic truisms, there's a world of variety in fiber optics. For starters, the optical media is almost always glass but can be optical-quality plastic. The diameter varies from 5 microns (millionths of an inch) on up to sizes that are quite a bit easier to see with the naked eye. All types of fiber are usually available in bundles of two or more pairs. Fibers can also come in a variety of frequency ratings; not all are suitable for use in a LAN! The typical LAN-grade fiber-optic cable is the 62.5-micron diameter glass variety. It supports multimode communications driven by a light-emitting diode (LED).

Fibers are usually described with a pair of numbers. For example, an extremely common LAN-grade fiber is known as 62.5/125-micron glass. The first number is the diameter, in microns, of the fiber. The second number, also in microns, measures the diameter of the cladding that protects the fiber.

Fiber-optic cables are used in pairs: one for transmitting and one for receiving. Their use in a LAN is usually limited to either server connections or hub interconnections.

Light can either radiate outward, as in a lantern, or it can be focused directionally, just as a flashlight does. However, even directionally focused light is subject to some measure of dispersion. Anyone who's ever used a flashlight knows that the size of the circle projected by the light's beam increases over distance. This is an important point, because it holds significant ramifications for optical signal transmissions.

Specifically, there are two types of fiber-optic transmissions:

- Multimode
- Single mode

Many differences exist in the way communications are driven in each of these fiber-optic systems. These differences are centered around the transmission techniques.

Multimode

Multimode transmission is driven by a light-emitting diode (LED). An LED that fails, so the old joke goes, becomes a dark-emitting diode (DED).

An LED is not a very concentrated light source; consequently, it requires a fairly wide transmission path. LEDs also have a relatively low frequency (for light, that is), so their bandwidth potential is also fairly limited. The key characteristic of LEDs, however, is their dispersion. LEDs are not capable of tightly concentrating the beam of light. After it's transmitted, the light is subject to dispersion. This rate of dispersion imposes practical maximums on the effective distance of LED-driven fiber-optic cabling.

Figure 2.11 illustrates the normal dispersion of an LED beam within a fiber-optic cable.

FIGURE 2.11
LED dispersion within multimode fiber.

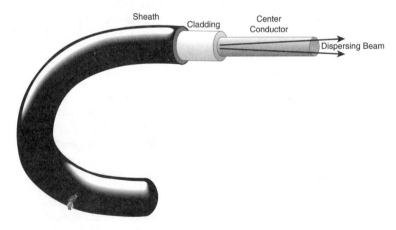

Over enough distance, this dispersion results in some of the LED beam impacting the inside wall of the glass media. When this happens, the impact is at a very shallow angle. Consequently, the light does not escape into the cladding. Rather, it's reflected off the wall at a complementary angle. This reflection puts the dispersed beam(s) onto a collision course with the portion of the beam that remains in an axial transmission path. This is illustrated in Figure 2.12.

FIGURE 2.12

Reflection causes multiple modes.

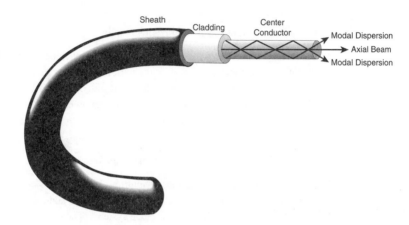

It's important to remember that these reflections still bear the same signal as the beam that remains aligned with the center axis of the glass. But, because they're subjected to a series of ricochets off the walls, they travel farther than the axial beam, whereas the physical media length remains constant. Constant, too, is the speed at which light travels: 186,000 miles per second. Therefore, the axial transmission arrives before the multiple reflections (that is, *modes*) of the same signal.

A more significant implication of this multimodal dispersion is that even photons can have an impact on other photons. The incessant zigzagging of beams means that the multiple modes will inevitably cross the center axis and collide with other signal transmissions. In other words, multimode transmissions are prone to attenuation.

Multiple transmission modes can also be prematurely induced by improper terminations on the fiber-optic cable and/or by connectors that are not securely fastened to the hardware interface. Terminations that are not concentric always increase the modal dispersion of the beam. Similarly, terminations that are not secured tightly to the hardware interface also artificially increase multimodal dispersion. Although multimodal dispersion is normal, and may even be relied upon by the hardware, these two factors exaggerate the multimodal dispersion of the signal. Both cause the beam to enter the fiber at an angle to the center axis. This angled entry has the following results:

- Much steeper angles of reflection than the angles caused by normal radiation of the beam
- Little, if any, of the beam traveling axially

Consequently, little, if any, useable data succeeds in reaching the destination. If the angles of reflection are steep enough, the multimodal paths may be long enough to enable other signals (traveling axially, but transmitted later) to arrive at the destination first! This can confuse the receiving device. If nothing else, it wastes system resources as that recipient tries to decide what to do with these multiple signals.

In short, nothing good can come of these two forms of artificially fostered multimodal dispersion. They should be considered unacceptable.

The myriad performance limitations of multimode fiber optics are balanced against some of their more endearing qualities. Specifically, the cable and hardware that drives it are both inexpensive compared to single-mode systems. The cabling is easier to terminate, because it's several times larger than single-mode fibers.

Single Mode

Single-mode fiber uses an Injection Laser Diode (ILD). Lasers are well known for their highly concentrated beam. This beam still disperses, but almost immeasurably across distances that are practical within the scope of LANs.

In a single-mode fiber-optic system, a laser is used to drive the signal through the glass. Its dispersion characteristics are sufficiently mild so that the beam, even at the outer limits of its practical range, does not disperse enough to begin touching the inside walls of the fiber. Consequently, the stream of data that's transmitted remains aligned with the center axis of the glass along the entire path of the media. It reaches its destination in a single mode (in other words, all at once).

Single-mode fiber optics are usually between 5 and 10 microns, with a 125-micron cladding. The costs of the fiber and the laser hardware, in conjunction with the high available bandwidth, make this more of a commercial-grade infrastructure technology than a LAN technology. Consequently, its greatest use is in the commercial telephone networks.

> **Peter's Principle:** Which Cables Should You Use?
>
> Deciding which cable type is best depends entirely on your particular situation. Many factors need to be considered, including the following:
>
> - Physical premise construction
> - Capability to add new cabling
> - Performance parameters of the various parts of your network
> - Embedded base of wire
> - Fire codes and regulations
> - The Physical Layer specifications supported by the network architecture
>
> It's highly likely that the best cabling scheme for you will be a combination of two, maybe more, types of cable. The *de facto* standard in the marketplace appears to be Category 5 unshielded twisted pair for station connectivity, with 62.5/125-micron fiber optics (rated at 850 nm) used to interconnect hubs as well as to connect hubs to servers.
>
> It's also likely that none of these are well suited to your particular needs. If that's the case, perhaps the "Not-So-Physical" Layer, discussed later in this chapter, is for you.

The Not-So-Physical Layer

Local area networks that use unguided transmissions to transport data and protocols have come to be known as *wireless LANs*. Before exploring the various transmission technologies that are used by wireless LANs, it's necessary to understand the electromagnetic spectrum. The electromagnetic spectrum defines the physical characteristics of transmissions, according to their frequency. Review the sections "Encoding Signals" and "Bandwidth" at the beginning of this chapter to refresh your understanding of frequency and wavelength.

The electromagnetic spectrum starts at zero Hz and reaches in excess of 10 to the 20th power! To put this tremendous range of frequencies into perspective, the human ear is capable of detecting electrical vibrations ranging from 20 up to approximately 16,000–20,000Hz. This varies greatly by age and by person, however. The human ear is adapted to maximize reception of vocal vibrations, and most voice energy falls between 3,000 and 4,000Hz.

The spectrum continues upward, well beyond the range of human hearing, and encompasses frequencies that are categorized by their physical properties. Beyond audible sound are the radio frequencies (which range from 500 kilohertz (Khz) up to 300 gigahertz (GHz) and include microwaves) and the various forms of light, including infrared, the visible spectrum, ultraviolet, X-rays, and gamma rays. The frequencies of light are measured in ridiculously large numbers. Consequently, their wavelengths are used to describe them, instead. Wavelengths, inversely related to frequency, become ridiculously small numbers as you progress through the various forms of light.

The electromagnetic spectrum is illustrated in Figure 2.13, complete with both frequencies and wavelength metrics.

Figure 2.13
The electromagnetic spectrum.

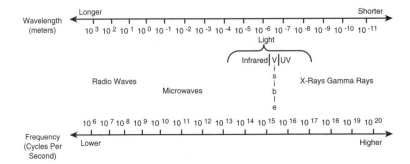

Spectral Characteristics

The characteristics of wave propagation change with the increase of hertz along the spectrum. The three most pertinent characteristics of the wave, at least as far as wireless LANs are concerned, are the following:

- Frangibility
- Directionality
- Bandwidth

The lower frequencies are remarkably durable. They are capable of penetrating opaque solids, with varying degrees of success. Radio waves, for example, can penetrate all but the densest of materials. Therefore, they are not very frangible.

These radio waves also propagate omnidirectionally. That is, they *radiate* (hence, the name *radio*) out uniformly from their transmitter. This is illustrated in Figure 2.14.

The higher frequencies behave more like light. In fact, the higher frequencies *are* light. The visible portion of the spectrum is relatively narrow and is flanked by two other forms of invisible light: infrared and ultraviolet.

Higher frequency signals are very frangible. They become less and less capable of penetrating opaque solids, regardless of their thickness or density, as their frequency increases. They also don't necessarily radiate as illustrated in Figure 2.14. Their propagation can be more directionally oriented. This is illustrated in Figure 2.15.

FIGURE 2.14
*Omnidirectional
radiation of a
signal.*

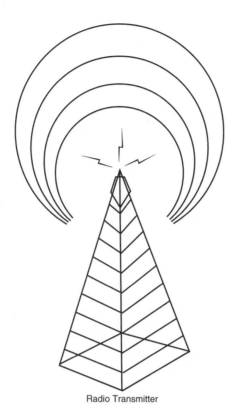

Radio Transmitter

FIGURE 2.15
*Focused
directionality of
light-based
transmission.*

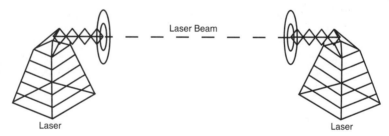

Laser Beam

Laser   Laser

The capability to directionally focus electromagnetic vibrations increases with the hertz rate. The higher the rate, the better the vibrations can be focused. For example, a lamp can radiate light omnidirectionally. However, a flashlight uses a reflective cone to focus radiating light unidirectionally. The focused light continues to radiate and forms a conical shape. This phenomenon is depicted in Figure 2.15. Generally speaking, lower frequencies cannot be focused as effectively as higher frequencies.

Bandwidth is yet another commonly used term that's poorly understood. It is, literally, the *width* of a communications channel, as measured in hertz. The prefix, *band*, was the original term used to describe what's commonly known as a *channel*. A channel is a frequency range, designated for a specific communications purpose.

Bandwidth, then, is the difference between the upper and lower frequency boundaries of a communications channel. For example, the 902–928 megahertz (MHz) band is reserved for unregulated radio communications in support of industrial, scientific, or medical purposes. This portion of the spectrum yields 26MHz of bandwidth.

> **Note:** The Federal Communications Commission (FCC) was established by the Communications Act of 1934. One of the FCC's numerous responsibilities is establishing both the bands and their applications for interstate communications that originate in the United States.

Hertz are typically used only to measure voice or analog communications. Digital communications are more properly measured in *bits per second* (bps). The potential for data rate in fiber-optic systems is usually described in wavelengths, unless a specific fiber-based technology is being described, such as FDDI, in which case *bps* is used.

Hz and bps have a strong, positive correlation—one bit can be transmitted per cycle. Unfortunately, due to the disparities in the modulation techniques required to support digital versus analog transmissions, the potential digital data rate is always less than the Hz rate. Extending this logic, bandwidth is only a valid metric of frequency; it does not directly measure the data rate of a transmission facility. In the real world, bandwidth has been generalized to mean *available bits per second*.

Whenever electrical vibrations are used to transport data, analog or digital, the series of vibrations are known as a *signal*. Signals can occur at any frequency, although it's generally acknowledged that anything below 300,000Hz is not practical for use in electrical devices.

The Relevance of Spectral Characteristics

The point of this exploration of the physical properties of the various portions of the electromagnetic spectrum is to provide the proper context for a meaningful examination of the various approaches to wireless signal transmission in LANs.

Each transmission technology operates in a specific portion of the spectrum. This dictates its physical characteristics. The basic trade-offs between physical characteristics are presented in Table 2.1.

Table 2.1 Spectrally Determined Signal Characteristics

Low Frequency	High Frequency
Broad radiation of	Potential for tightly focused transmitted signal transmitted signal
Persistent signal	Highly frangible signal
Low bandwidth	High bandwidth

The physical characteristics of a transmission technology, in turn, dictate the operational characteristics of the wireless LAN. The characteristics of a wireless LAN that are dictated include the following:

- Maximum effective ranges
- Potential for penetrating Sheetrock walls, cubicle partitions, and other physical obstructions
- Maximum transmission rate

> **Note:** Spectrum selection has an impact on the maximum effective distances of a wireless LAN in more than one way. Effective transmission distances, particularly in the more persistent lower frequencies, are also limited by FCC regulations. These regulations impose maximum limits on the power with which transmissions can be made on any given band. Although artificial, and not an innate characteristic of the electromagnetic spectrum, these limitations are every bit as real and binding.

The transmission technique used determines the wireless LAN's maximum sustainable data rate. Data rates are always less than transmission rates, due to the overhead of the LAN's protocols, inefficiencies in the way that data is placed on the LAN, and numerous other factors.

The issues identified here form the crux of the functional differences between the various wireless transmission technologies. It's essential to recognize their performance impacts and the implications of transmission techniques before selecting a wireless LAN product.

Wireless LANs

The use of either light or radio waves for the unguided transmission of LAN frames and protocols has come to be known as *wireless local area networking*. This name is misleading. The vast majority of the purported wireless LAN products do not eliminate wire as a Physical Layer component. They merely reduce the amount of wire needed to construct a LAN.

At least four different scenarios demonstrate the versatility of wireless transmission technologies within a LAN:

- Wireless station connectivity
- Wireless peer-to-peer connectivity
- Wireless hub interconnect
- Wireless bridges

Each of these scenarios uses wireless transmission technologies in a different way.

Wireless Station Connectivity

Wireless station connectivity enables a mobile user with a laptop to establish a LAN connection without a dedicated, wired connection to a hub. A wire path is still needed to connect individual workstations to a transmitter/receiver. This is illustrated in Figure 2.16. In this diagram, a laptop computer is connected to a portable radio antenna via its PCMCIA slot.

FIGURE 2.16
Wireless station connectivity.

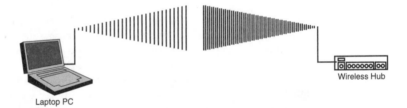

Laptop PC

Wireless Hub

Note: PCMCIA is now widely recognized as the name for a credit card–like device that inserts in a corresponding slot on a laptop computer and provides additional functionality. The abbreviation's expansion, Personal Computer Memory Card International Association, is almost never used.

The laptop's antenna in Figure 2.16 transmits framed data to and receives framed data from the corresponding antenna associated with the so-called *wireless LAN hub*. For the purposes of illustration, it's shown attached, but this antenna is usually a module separate from the hub. This allows the antenna to be mounted much higher than the hub, thereby improving transmission coverage. The two devices must be wired together. The wireless hub is equipped with an uplink wire port that enables it to be physically connected to a more conventional, wire-based LAN backbone. The only thing that's wireless about this example is the connection between the PC and its hub.

This scenario is useful for providing connectivity to a highly mobile workforce.

Wireless Peer-to-Peer Connectivity

A simple (but relatively low throughput) wireless LAN can be established between peers. Each device within the effective transmission range can enjoy resource sharing with peers, provided it has the appropriate permissions.

The relatively informal nature of peer-to-peer networking directly translates into very low performance parameters for wireless peer-to-peer networks.

Wireless Hub Interconnection

Another approach to building wireless LANs is depicted in Figure 2.17. This approach uses only a single pair of transmit/receive antennas for a cluster of workstations. These workstations are cabled to a conventional hub. The uplink port on this hub is wired to the radio gear. This radio is used to communicate with a corresponding radio that's also hard-wired to the LAN's backbone. The only thing that's wireless about this scenario is the hub-to-hub communications. The benefit of this approach is that it obviates the need for wiring from the telephone closets to the user stations. The user stations can be wired relatively easily using preterminated cables.

FIGURE 2.17
Wireless hub interconnectivity.

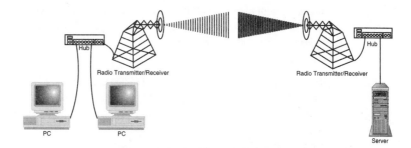

The scenario depicted in Figure 2.17 is extremely useful for providing connectivity in buildings that are difficult and/or expensive to rewire. A building may be resistant to wiring if it's historic and, therefore, protected from further modifications. What's more, a building may have been constructed in such a way as to make additional wire installation prohibitively expensive. Poured concrete floors without raceways for cabling, for example, greatly increase the cost of running cabling to desktops.

Although the example presented in Figure 2.17 uses radio waves, the example would be just as valid using other portions of the electromagnetic spectrum—such as laser or infrared—for its transmission technology.

Wireless Bridges

Wireless technologies can also be applied to other aspects of a LAN. For example, two wire-based LANs can be bridged together using a wireless bridge. This is illustrated in Figure 2.18.

FIGURE 2.18
Wireless bridging of wire-based LANs.

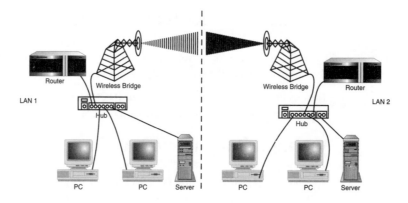

Wireless bridging enables LANs that are in relatively close proximity, but beyond the maximum network diameter supported by their LAN architecture, to be bridged together. This spares the cost of acquiring two routers, as well as the monthly recurring expense of a leased line that would otherwise be required to interconnect the LANs.

Wireless bridges offer approximately 2Mbps of bandwidth across several miles. This is more bandwidth than a 1.544Mbps T-1 leased line can offer, without the monthly recurring expense. The economics of wireless bridging are fairly compelling: For an equivalent startup cost (radio gear versus routers), the wireless bridge offers "free" connectivity for its entire useful life.

These examples are some of the typical implementations of wireless technologies in a LAN. Other implementations are possible, but they tend to be fairly specific to a single transmission technology and are presented within the context of that technology.

Transmission Technologies

The four different transmission technologies each utilize a different section of the electromagnetic spectrum. These four methods are as follows:

- Spread spectrum radio
- Narrowband or single-band radio
- Infrared
- Laser

The first two methods, in keeping with FCC regulations, limit effective transmission ranges by keeping transmission wattage to absolute minimums. The ranges of the last two—laser and infrared—are naturally limited by their inability to penetrate opaque solids of any thickness or density, as well as by FCC regulations. For example, radio waves are quite capable of penetrating all but the very densest of buildings. Typically, several steel-reinforced concrete walls are needed to noticeably attenuate radio waves. Light, like infrared and laser beams, is much more fragile. A piece of paper, or even a puff of smoke or fog, is all that it takes to completely attenuate optically based signals.

> **Note:** The four transmission technologies presented here are solely for your academic enrichment. They may or may not actually be embodied in generally available wireless LAN technologies.

Spread Spectrum Radio Frequency

The FCC, through Part 15.247 of its regulations, has allocated the 902–928MHz and 2.4–2.4835GHz bands of the electromagnetic spectrum for industrial, scientific, and medical (ISM) use. These bands are referred to as the *ISM bands* and have been allocated for spread spectrum radio transmissions within the ISM arena. Additionally, the FCC recently identified the 5.725–5.850GHz band as also being available for spread spectrum radio transmissions.

> **Note:** The 2.4–2.4835GHz band is frequently expressed in the rounded-up form: 2.4–2.484GHz.

Use of these bands is unlicensed in that, beyond establishing guidelines for the electrical and electronic devices that use these bands, the FCC does not actively regulate who uses these bands. This is contrary to the model that the FCC applies to other portions of the spectrum. Typically, an individual or entity is given the exclusive license to operate on a specific band within a specified geographic region. Radio stations are a good example. In return for their guarantee to abide by the guidelines established by the FCC, they are given exclusive, regional licenses to specific bands.

Two primary transmission techniques can be used in conjunction with the previously described spread spectrum transmission technologies. These techniques define the manner in which the "not-so-physical" transmission media are used. These techniques are

- Frequency Hopping
- Direct Sequence

Frequency Hopping

Frequency hopping is a technique that's used only in conjunction with a spread spectrum radio transmission system. *Spread spectrum* provides an unregulated range of radio frequencies. Frequency hopping can be described as a happy medium between baseband and broadband transmissions. An examination of baseband versus broadband helps to make this description clearer.

Baseband transmissions use the entire available bandwidth as a single channel: The same signal is sent across the entire band, completely filling the "pipe" as it transmits. A good example of a baseband transmission mechanism is Ethernet. It uses all available bandwidth, either 10, 100, or more Mbps, as a single transmission vehicle.

Broadband transmissions channelize the available bandwidth into multiple, smaller channels. Each subchannel is used to support a different signal transmission. This is illustrated in Figure 2.19. An example of a broadband transmission vehicle is cable television. A single coaxial cable provides bandwidth that is channelized. Each channel carries different signals, even though it shares a common transmission vehicle with other channels.

FIGURE 2.19
Broadband trans-mission.

Frequency hopping, like broadband, subdivides the bandwidth into multiple subchannels. These channels are used one at a time to support signal transmission. Unlike broadband, a signal hops from channel to channel, at a predetermined rate and according to a predetermined sequence. This is illustrated in Figure 2.20.

FIGURE 2.20
Frequency hop-ping transmission.

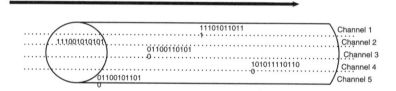

Frequency hopping has several benefits. First, it helps minimize the impact of signal interference. Interference, specifically radio frequency interference (RFI) and electro-magnetic interference (EMI), can distort a signal in transit. Typically, interference from any given source confines itself to a fairly consistent frequency. Therefore, hopping across multiple available frequencies obviates much of the potential harm of RFI and EMI.

Perhaps a more significant benefit of frequency hopping is that it allows multiple access units to be placed within one another's effective transmission zones. Figure 2.21 illustrates the overlap of transmission zones. If the PCs in this figure use a single frequency, baseband transmission, their two transmitters would conflict with each other. The throughputs of both would deteriorate. Using a frequency hopping, spread spectrum transmission system reduces the potential for collisions. Consequently, the user density serviced with this technology can be increased without compromising LAN performance.

FIGURE 2.21
*Overlapping
transmission
zones.*

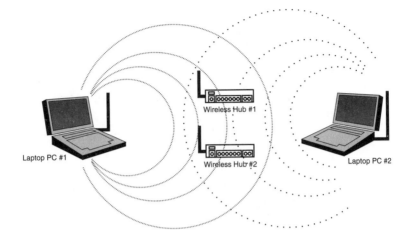

The greatest benefit, by far, is the security of a frequency hopping, spread spectrum transmission system. Spread spectrum transmissions are inherently secure. Anyone attempting to eavesdrop on a transmission must do three things:

- Defeat the physical security established around the limited effective transmission range
- Be able to capture signals transmitted on multiple channels
- Understand the seemingly random sequence of transmissions

Note: Spread spectrum radio transmission was the brainchild of actress Hedy Lamarr. In 1940, she conceived the idea as a means of securing radio transmission. Two years later, she was granted the patent rights to the concept. Unfortunately, decades would pass before the concept would finally be used in a commercial product.

Direct Sequence

Direct sequence, too, is pertinent only to spread spectrum radio frequency transmission systems. Unlike frequency hopping, which hops frequencies in a pseudo-random pattern, direct sequence uses the available subchannels sequentially. Therefore, it's easier to defeat the security of a direct sequence spread spectrum (DSSS) system than that of a frequency hopping system, because the spreading algorithm is much simpler.

Defeating the security of a direct sequence spread spectrum transmission system still requires the defeat of any physical security that may protect the effective transmission range. Additionally, the perpetrator also needs to be able to trap signals on all the subchannels simultaneously.

The IEEE has recently standardized wireless LANs through its 802.11 specification. This specification, described in detail in the section titled "The IEEE 802.11," incorporates support for both frequency hopping and DSSS transmission systems.

The Pros

Spread spectrum is inherently safe from eavesdropping because it "spreads" transmissions one bit at a time into separate frequencies according to a predetermined frequency-hopping algorithm. Defeating the security of this method is almost impossible. It requires gaining physical access to its effective transmission range and knowing the frequency-hopping pattern over which the bits are spread.

The recent allocation of the 2.4–2.4835 and 5.725–5.850GHz bands means that spread spectrum technologies need not be low bandwidth. These higher frequencies contain adequate bandwidth to rival the performance of wire-based LANs.

Spread spectrum systems are also relatively inexpensive because the bands are not licensed. As a result, the manufacturers are able to provide the hardware at a cost much lower than that of comparable dedicated frequency products. More important, you (the customer and user) do not have to apply to the FCC for the rights to use a specific radio band in a specific location. Therefore, you can have a wireless LAN up and running much more quickly and inexpensively than a LAN with a dedicated frequency technology.

The Cons

One of the inherent problems using radio frequency is that radio is not capable of full-duplex communication on a single frequency. Anyone who has used walkie-talkies understands the half-duplex nature of radio communications. Walkie-talkies require a push-to-talk method of transmission. Only one party can talk at a time. All other parties are forced to listen. The radio is either transmitting or receiving, but not both simultaneously.

In Ethernet networks, radio's use of half-duplex mode forces the conversion from the usual Carrier Sense, Multiple Access with Collision Detection (CSMA/CD) protocol to Carrier Sense, Multiple Access with Collision Avoidance (CSMA/CA).

These factors, with the overhead incurred by "spreading," reduce effective throughputs in an Ethernet-compatible network to approximately 2Mbps. Maximum effective throughput in a wire-based Ethernet, after subtracting CSMA/CD overheads, is approximately 5–5.5Mbps. This throughput limitation imposes a bottleneck in the current networking environment and prevents the use of any product embracing this methodology in all but the lowest usage applications.

> **Note:** One solution to the problem imposed by radio's half-duplex nature is to utilize two separate frequencies: one for transmitting and one for receiving. This enables the LAN to be full-duplex. Consequently, network throughput can be kept on par with wire-based Ethernet LANs.

A second concern regarding the use of spread spectrum radio frequency transmission is the lack of FCC licensing that would guarantee the user clear rights to the frequency within a given transmission zone. Given the transient nature of frequency utilization, limiting transmission wattage serves to reduce the possibility of collision. If throughputs are degraded below the existing 2Mbps level by competition with other spread spectrum devices, consumers have no legal recourse and are forced to accept the lower levels of performance. In a LAN environment, typical transmission zones are between 600 and 800 feet. This concentrated transmission range greatly reduces the opportunity for competition with other radio frequency vehicles.

Wireless bridging components, however, are available that have effective ranges of 3 to 5 miles. Pagers and other devices that use the 902–928MHz band are also direct competitors for this bandwidth. The potential for conflict with other radio frequency vehicles across this range, and the subsequent performance impacts, increases with the relative population densities of the transmission zone.

Single-Band Radio Frequency

The opposite of a spread spectrum transmission technique is the single-band transmission. Both are confined to the radio wave portion of the electromagnetic spectrum, but (as its name suggests) single-band uses only a single channel, usually in the microwave band. Microwaves are actually high-frequency radio waves. The lowest frequency microwaves behave very much as radio waves do, whereas the highest-frequency microwaves begin to demonstrate some of the physical properties of light.

The use of a dedicated frequency means that FCC licensing must be obtained before you can legally transmit on that frequency. This technology, as a wireless LAN, was pioneered by Motorola and marketed under the names *Altair* and *Altair II*. Motorola obtained exclusive access to the 18–19GHz band from the FCC for all the major metropolitan markets in the U.S.

Motorola acts as an agent to the FCC on behalf of any customers wanting to utilize their technology. In this fashion, customers are spared the potential agony of obtaining FCC approval for the use of the frequency.

Implementation is facilitated by the retention of existing premise wire-based LAN backbones, hubs, and software drivers. This implementation is illustrated in Figure 2.22.

FIGURE 2.22
A typical, dedicated channel wireless LAN.

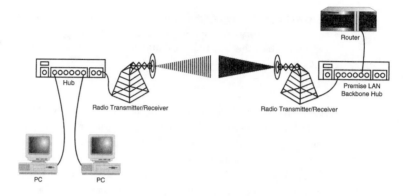

Transmission wattage is approximately 25 milliwatts, which is too low to cause any health concerns that may arise due to the use of microwave transmission in populated areas. This wattage, in combination with the relatively frangible microwave signal, limits the effective range to approximately 140 feet of open air, or 40 feet of obstructed air. Obstructed air assumes three Sheetrock walls as interference.

The gross bandwidth is approximately 15Mbps. Subtracting out standard Ethernet overhead plus the wire-to-wireless-to-wire conversion reduces this to an approximately 5.5Mbps data rate, which is the net equivalent throughput of a wire-based shared Ethernet.

Infrared

The next wireless transmission technology, infrared, operates between the visible part of the electromagnetic spectrum and the shortest microwaves. Although infrared is a form of light, it's not limited to line-of-sight vehicles only. This is because infrared is an invisible light. Even though it cannot penetrate opaque solids, it can reflect off them.

Two methodologies have emerged: diffuse and direct. Direct infrared is analogous to a flashlight's beam, whereas diffuse can best be thought of as a lantern. The flashlight focuses its light in a single direction, whereas the lantern diffuses its light in all directions. A decrease in the intensity of the beam, as in the case of diffusers, results in a commensurate decrease in potential data rates.

Direct infrared technology is used in most, if not all, household consumer electronics with remote control devices. The remote control device must be pointed at the TV, VCR, stereo, and so forth before any commands entered via its keypad can be recognized by the appliance. This same concept applies to a direct infrared LAN.

The diffuse infrared LAN scatters its light omnidirectionally. The intent is to bounce the transmissions off ceilings and walls so that they may contact a transmit/receive device that's not directly in the line of sight.

The Pros

Infrared communications use a nonpersistent signal form: light. They are incapable of penetrating even the least dense of opaque solids. As a result, they do not require FCC licensing to use. Rather, the FCC establishes the guidelines and operating parameters for the physical devices that use the electromagnetic spectrum. These guidelines are adhered to by the wireless LAN manufacturers, thereby guaranteeing the compliance of the user communities. This spares the users any tedious negotiations or complicated paper chases.

The Cons

Line-of-sight communications pose a severe handicap to forms of light-based transmissions. Many office environments are inherently unsuited, as even a single layer of sheet rock completely attenuates the signal.

Diffuse infrared partially overcomes the limitation of line-of-sight transmission by diffusing and using reflectivity to radiate outward in ways not possible with line-of-sight direct transmissions. Unfortunately, given the highly frangible nature of an optical signal, much of the signal is attenuated on impact. Consequently, the effective range of a diffuse infrared system is extremely small (that is, less than 100 feet). The sustainable throughputs of this technology are also extremely modest!

Laser

Laser-based transmissions in a wireless LAN environment can be best thought of as a fiber-optic system without the fiber-optic cabling. This isn't a perfect analogy, because most LANs use fiber-optic systems driven by light-emitted diodes (LEDs). Nevertheless, the analogy conveys the image remarkably well.

The cost of laser precludes its use on a station-by-station basis. Consequently, it's better applied in a virtually identical manner to the direct infrared. That is, multiple stations interconnect to an access unit that transmits and receives laser signals on behalf of a group of stations. Therefore, the cost of the laser is spread across multiple endpoints, thereby improving its cost effectiveness.

When lasers are used in this manner, it's logical to mount the laser devices near the ceiling, as far away from people as possible. This serves two purposes. First, it all but eliminates the possibility of accidental injury to human eyes. Second, it also reduces the possibility that human actions will disrupt the signal.

Alternatively, lasers can be used to bridge together wire-based LANs across parking lots or other modest distances. As was explained in the section titled "Wireless LANs," earlier in this chapter, this application provides more bits per second at less cost than leased lines and routers do.

The Pros

Laser light is extremely concentrated and remains tightly focused. Consequently, it can be used effectively at longer distances than infrared. This enables it to be used as a wireless bridging technology. A laser-based wireless LAN application works on the same principle as a radio wave application, which was illustrated in Figure 2.18, earlier in this chapter.

The Cons

Because both laser and infrared are forms of light, they suffer similar deficiencies. Specifically, their signals are frangible. Unguided lasers and direct infrared are distinguished by two primary differences:

- Unguided lasers and direct infrared use different portions of the spectrum.
- Lasers are actually artificially concentrated light.

These two differences beget other important differences. First, lasers are much more expensive than a comparable infrared system. They require more power to generate and concentrate the signal. They also give off more heat, although probably not enough to overcome a decent climate control system.

Lasers use the visible spectrum of light. As a result, they are a line-of-sight-only device. Their signal can be attenuated easily by smoke, fog, and even raindrops in an outdoor installation.

A greater concern regarding the use of lasers is the potential for permanent injury to the retinal sensors and nerves of the human eye. This requires any installation of a laser transmission system to be carefully planned, especially when it's to be installed in a populated area.

The IEEE 802.11

The IEEE recently completed work on a standard for wireless local area networking (WLAN). Development of this standard lagged behind the market and was greatly complicated by the need to provide for many of the more common transmission technologies and techniques that were already prevalent in the marketplace.

The finished product specified the Media Access Control (MAC) method and numerous physical layers. As with any layered approach, the functionality of any given layer is insulated from the functionality of neighboring layers. In other words, the MAC Layer functions are not dependent on data rates or any other characteristics of the Physical Layer specifications. Given the proliferation of Physical Layer technologies, this layering is essential.

This standard includes several subfunctions, including mechanisms to provide access control (both contention based and noncontention based) to several "not-so-physical" media. Each media type, too, is addressed in a separate Physical Layer specification.

Media Access

The media-access method of 802.11 is a familiar one to long-time Ethernet aficionados: Carrier Sense, Multiple Access with Collision Avoidance (CSMA/CA). This media-access method was used on Ethernet II (or DIX Ethernet).

CSMA/CA strives to avoid collisions by "listening" to the wire before it "talks." In the case of a WLAN, the station that wants to transmit must listen to the channel before transmitting. A clear signal means that it may transmit. If the signal contains framed data, that station must wait.

The CSMA/CA scheme strives to ensure equitable access to the bandwidth while still avoiding collisions. For example, it uses two timing techniques to enforce equitable bandwidth use:

- Minimum time delay
- Random backoff interval

The *minimum time delay* is used to ensure that a single transmitting station does not monopolize the bandwidth. After each successful frame transmission, the transmitter must wait until a minimum time delay elapses before it can transmit another frame.

The *random backoff interval* is used in two different scenarios. First, after enduring the minimum time delay following a successful transmission, the transmitting station must then endure a backoff interval before it can listen to the channel. If the channel is clear, it may then transmit its next frame. If, however, the channel is busy, that station must then endure a second backoff interval. This second use of the backoff interval continues repeatedly until the transmitter senses a clear channel. This arbitration method may, at first, sound unfair. In reality, each backoff is of random duration, and each station contains the same mechanisms for enacting a random duration backoff. Consequently, fairness in media access becomes a pseudo-random phenomenon.

Physical Layers

The three Physical Layer technologies that 802.11 supports include the following ones. Note that DFIR is discussed in the section "Infrared," earlier in this chapter.

- Diffused infrared (DFIR)
- Direct sequence spread spectrum (DSSS)
- Frequency-hopping spread spectrum (FHSS)

Direct Sequence Spread Spectrum

802.11 supports DSSS at 1- or 2Mbps. The different data rates use different modulation techniques. The standard uses a subset of the 2.4–2.4835GHz band and defines four sub-bands:

- .400–2.425GHz
- 2.414–2.440GHz
- 2.429–2.455GHz
- 2.443–2.470GHz

Each subband is 26MHz wide and overlaps its neighboring bands by about 11MHz.

Frequency-Hopping Spread Spectrum

The 802.11 specification also uses the 2.4–2.4835GHz band and supports two different modulation techniques and three hopping patterns. The standards-compliant FHSS WLAN can support data rates of either 1 or 2Mbps, depending on which modulation technique is selected. The hopping patterns are structurally similar and do not affect the sustainable data rate.

Both techniques comply with a single scheme for subbanding. The available bandwidth is split into 79 subbands of 1MHz each. Each subband can support a minimum of 2.5 hops per second (hps) using any of the standardized hopping patterns. The intent of this minimum hps rate is to prevent data frames from being arbitrarily parsed and transmitted on different subbands. Frames that are distorted in transit, either partially or completely, need to be completely retransmitted. This scheme guarantees that packets don't arrive distorted.

Summary

In the Physical Layer of the OSI Reference Model, frames of data are chipped into streams of 1's and 0's (or on and off s) for transmission across the network. Although the Physical Layer does not include the transmission media, it must define its expected performance parameters for anything that lies between the two media interfaces of the devices that are communicating. Therefore, cabling is an extremely important adjunct to the Physical Layer.

Wireless local area networking has been an interesting but somewhat quirky quagmire of noninteroperable products and technologies for the past few years. They've failed to gain any broad acceptance and are limited to market niches. The standardization of a common MAC and Physical Layer by the IEEE promises to overcome many of the previous limitations. The key indicators you should watch for are interoperability and price per desktop. As interoperability increases and price per desktop decreases, WLANs may become more mainstream.

The Data Link Layer

The second layer of the OSI Reference Model, as explained in Chapter 1, "A Networking Primer," is the Data Link Layer. This layer provides the interface between hardware and software.

This chapter closely examines the nature, structure, and function of data frames in a LAN by examining specific—and widely used—LAN architectures. These LAN architectures include Ethernet, Token Ring, and FDDI. The frame structures of these LAN protocols is examined as well as the differences in the ways each one accesses the physical transmission media. The chapter continues with a review of the Data Link Layer technology selection and installation considerations.

Later in this chapter, the various ways these frames are actually placed on the transmission media are discussed. These ways include token passing, contention, demand-priority, and switched. Each has its own unique combinations of features and functional implications, and specific examples of LAN architectures that use each one are presented.

OSI Layer 2

The second layer of the OSI Reference Model is called the *Data Link Layer*. It has two sets of responsibilities: to transmit and receive.

On the transmit side, the Data Link Layer is responsible for packing instructions, data, and so forth into frames. A *frame* is a structure that contains enough information to make sure the data can be sent across a network—either LAN or WAN—to its destination. Successful delivery occurs when the data reaches its intended destination intact. Therefore, the frame also contains a mechanism to verify the integrity of its contents.

The source node (that is, the transmitter) must receive an acknowledgment that the frame was received intact. Frames that either collide or become corrupted in transit must be retransmitted until they arrive safely. Also, any frame whose receipt was not acknowledged by the intended recipient is also retransmitted.

The Data Link Layer is also responsible for reassembling any binary streams received from the Physical Layer back into frames. Before passing the frame up to the next layer, the Data Link Layer performs a mathematical check of the validity of the newly reassembled frame's contents. This is known as a *cyclical redundancy check* (CRC).

Note: CRCs are similar to but more complex than checksums. Checksum values are created by adding the binary value of each alphanumeric character in a block of data. This value is sent with the data to its destination, in a separate field. The recipient recomputes the checksum and compares its value with the value stored in the Checksum field. If the two numbers are different, an error has occurred. If the two numbers are the same, the recipient assumes that no error has occurred. It's feasible that multiple bit errors can occur in transmission that yield the same checksum value.

A cyclical redundancy check is a more robust error-detection algorithm than a checksum. It's also used to determine whether an error has occurred during transmission. However, the CRC's value is derived in a much more rigorous manner than a checksum. The data is read as a binary string: This "number" is divided by another predetermined binary number to form the CRC value. In this manner, it becomes much less likely that multiple transmission errors will yield an unchanged CRC value.

Frames that fail the CRC check are discarded, and the machine identified in that frame's source address is told to retransmit. By virtue of this error-detection mechanism being implemented at Layer 2, Layer 3 protocols can be relieved of the burden of verifying the delivery and integrity of transmitted data. Layer 4 protocols, such as TCP and SPX, may contain and rely on their own error-detection and error-correction mechanisms, regardless of what transpires at Layer 2.

Frames

A *frame* is a structure used to transport a block of data across a network. The size and structure of the frame are determined by the hardware layer protocol that the network uses, such as Ethernet, Token Ring, and so on. A frame is directly analogous to an envelope: Everyone can expect that a #10 envelope is 4 ⅛" × 9 ½". Its payload, however, can vary considerably in size, content, urgency, and so forth.

Knowing the envelope size also does not reveal anything about how it's being shipped to its destination. In a network, the processes used to forward frames are called *protocols*. Protocols also exist at Layer 3 of the OSI Reference Model. These Layer 3 protocols wrap frames in packets and provide for their transport beyond the LAN. These protocols are described in Chapter 4, "The Network and Transport Layers."

Typical Frame Components

The typical frame contains only as many fields, or *substructures*, as is necessary to guarantee safe delivery of the frame to its intended recipient. Commonly encountered fields include the following:

- Start-of-frame delimiter
- Source address

- Destination address

- Data

- Frame check sequence

Frame Definition

Continuing the envelope analogy, after you know the size of the envelopes, you can begin to deploy an infrastructure for processing them in volume. Therefore, standardizing the envelope sizes is crucial to ensure that the forwarding infrastructure can accommodate all envelopes, regardless of who manufactured them.

> **Note:** A Layer 2 data structure that has a regulated, fixed size is called a *cell*. An example of a cell-based Layer 2 protocol is ATM. ATM uses 53-Octet cells: five octets contain all the header information, and the remaining 48 octets carry payload. The payload is always 48 octets, whereas frames can have payloads of differing sizes.

Rather than specifying a single size for all frames, Layer 2 LAN protocols tend to define maximum and minimum sizes for their data frames. Therefore, a frame has a variable length. This allows the protocol to maximize the efficiency of any given transmission by optimizing the overhead-to-payload ratio. This ratio measures the efficacy of a protocol by comparing the amount of framing needed with the payload it can support.

The beginning of each frame is identified by a predetermined pattern of bits. This is known as a *start-of-frame delimiter*. The end of each frame is identified either with an *end-of-frame delimiter* or a *frame check sequence*.

Source and Destination Address Pairs

Just as an envelope traditionally bears enough visible information to identify both its originator and its intended recipient, a frame also contains source and destination addresses. The source address contains the machine address code of its originator. The destination address is the machine address code of its intended recipient.

Placing address information at the beginning of the frame spares potential destination machines the trouble of opening up every frame, examining the contents, and then trying to determine whether that frame is, in fact, addressed to it. That process can be both resource and time intensive, which results in diminished network performance.

Instead, a frame contains two addresses very close to its beginning: a source address and a destination address. Placing these fields as close as possible to the beginning of the frame expedites the frame-forwarding process: examining the first 18 octets of a frame can be done *much* faster than examining 1,500 octets. The information contained in these fields is used either to forward a frame to its intended recipient or to notify the originator that the frame is undeliverable.

The purpose of the various frame header components is to provide the basic information needed to identify the recipient, the originator, and whether the frame needs to be retransmitted. The only other field that's common to all frames is the Data field. This is the field that varies in length; all other frame header components are of fixed length, as determined by the protocol's specifications. This field is also the frame's reason for being. If the data doesn't arrive or is damaged before it arrives at its destination, the entire frame is discarded.

Frame Summary

LANs are, essentially, frame-forwarding mechanisms. To perform this task efficiently, LANs require frames to have a standardized shape and structure. Standardization ensures that different network components made by different manufacturers can interoperate.

These same standards also provide a common basis for the conversion of frame types between dissimilar network types, as in a translation from Ethernet to Token Ring.

Evolution of Proprietary Frame Structures

The world's first LAN was Xerox's PARC Ethernet. This technology originated as an intra-office, baseband transmission technology to interconnect workstations. It was cobbled together by researchers at Xerox's famed Palo Alto Research Center (PARC) for their own use as an expedient alternative to using floppy disks to share information. Therefore, Ethernet was born a fairly crude and simple mechanism, and its simplicity was reflected in its frame structure. This basic technology is the ancestor of today's industry standard frame structures.

Xerox's PARC Ethernet Frame

PARC researchers recognized that their Layer 2 protocol would be transporting higher-level protocols such as the Internet Protocol (IP), Xerox's XNS, and others. These client protocols already had their own limitations on data payloads. Therefore, rather than put too much effort into defining the hardware layer protocol, it was deemed appropriate to simply provide a two-octet Type field that identified the type of higher-level protocol the frame contained. This let the more sophisticated client protocol determine overall frame sizes.

> **Note:** An *octet* consists of eight binary digits (bits), regardless of what those bits signify. Beware the data communications experts who use less accurate terms such as *binary term* and *byte* to describe such structures; they've been spending too much time with programmers. Next, they'll start using even more ambiguous terms such as *records* and *files* to describe quantities of transmitted data!

Xerox's home-grown Ethernet lacked sophistication and relied on client protocols to determine the length of the Data field. As illustrated in Figure 3.1, the PARC Ethernet frame consisted of the following items:

- An 8-Octet preamble
- The intended recipient's 6-Octet MAC address

> **Note:** The Media Access Control (MAC) address is usually the unique *universally administered address*, which is automatically given to Ethernet network interface cards (NICs) at their manufacture. This type of MAC address is represented by six paired hexadecimal numbers, delimited by colons. Here's an example:
>
> 99:02:11:D1:8F:19
>
> The first two numbers are the manufacturer's ID. Each NIC manufacturer must apply to the IEEE for a unique manufacturer's ID and a range of MAC addresses.
>
> Alternatively, these addresses can be customized upon installation. Customized addresses are known as *locally administered addresses*. These addresses can be used to identify the room number, department, owner's voice mail extension, and so on. Using locally administered addresses can provide network administrators with vital information that can expedite trouble resolution. Unfortunately, they can also be extremely difficult and time consuming to maintain.

- The originator's 6-Octet MAC address
- A 2-Octet Type field that identified the client protocol embedded in the Data field
- A Data field of unspecified and variable length

FIGURE 3.1
Xerox's PARC Ethernet frame.

8-Octet Preamble	6-Octet Destination Address	6-Octet Origination Address	2-Octet Type Field	Unspecified Length Data Field

This protocol broadcast packets to all devices connected to the LAN. Consequently, all devices had to compete for available packets. A technique known as *Carrier Sense, Multiple Access* (CSMA) was used to facilitate this competition. Each station would listen to find out whether the network was available for its own use or whether the network was preoccupied with the transmission of another device's frames. If a device could detect the carrier signal, it could begin transmission. This greatly reduced but did not eliminate collisions of frames that were being transmitted by different devices. Recovery from collisions or other events that resulted in undelivered frames was left up to the end devices and not handled by the network protocol.

DIX Ethernet Frame

The commercial potential of Xerox's PARC Ethernet was recognized, and both its frame and protocol were refined to better suit a broader target market. This second-generation LAN, known as *Ethernet II*, was widely used. Ethernet II is also referred to as *DIX Ethernet*, in acknowledgment of its triumvirate of corporate sponsors: Digital, Intel, and Xerox.

Xerox, the owner of the technology and keeper of its proprietary "standards," assigned a two-octet Type code to identify client protocols. Xerox's XNS, Novell's IPX, IP, and DECNet are examples. These are higher-level protocols than Ethernet and have different message size requirements. Unlike its predecessor, Ethernet II couldn't abdicate control over its frame length and still establish the timing needed to support a more sophisticated access method capable of detecting collisions. Therefore, frame size limits were defined.

As illustrated in Figure 3.2, the DIX (or Ethernet II) frame consisted of the following items:

- An 8-Octet preamble
- The intended recipient's 6-Octet MAC address
- The originator's 6-Octet MAC address
- A 2-Octet Type field that identified the higher-level transport protocol being encapsulated
- A Data field of at least 50 octets but not more than 1,486 octets total length
- Zeros (if needed) for padding the frame to a minimum length of 64 octets

FIGURE 3.2

A DIX Ethernet frame.

8-Octet Preamble	6-Octet Destination Address	6-Octet Origination Address	2-Octet Type Field	Data Field > 50 < 1486 Octets	Padding

It's important to note that despite the definition of a minimum frame length, the DIX standard continued to rely on PARC Ethernet's 2-Octet Type field. This field still identified the client protocol which, in turn, was used to define the frame's length. The client-side transport (Layer 3) protocols still had their own packet size requirements, but DIX Ethernet used a more sophisticated access method than its predecessor. The new access method, known as *Carrier Sense, Multiple Access with Collision Detection* (CSMA/CD), imposed fairly specific timing requirements.

Simply stated, this access method required stations to check the wire to determine whether any other station was already sending data. If the LAN seemed idle, the station was free to transmit. Unfortunately, transmission is not instantaneous over copper transmission facilities. Therefore, it was entirely probable that a station would begin to transmit on what appeared to be an idle LAN, only to be hit by an incoming transmission from another station microseconds after initiating its own transmission. This is known as a *collision*.

The addition of collision detection to PARC Ethernet's CSMA enabled the LAN to recover from collisions rather than rely on the end devices. Using CSMA/CD, both stations could detect the collision, back off (or cease) transmitting, and begin anew after a brief delay. The duration of the delay is determined by an algorithm known as the Binary Exponential Back-off algorithm (BEB).

The way DIX Ethernet enabled collision detection was by controlling the time required for the worst-case roundtrip through the LAN. In a 10MHz Ethernet, this round trip is limited to a maximum of 50 microseconds. Therefore, a station has to continue transmitting until after the worst-case roundtrip time has expired. This is enough time to transmit 500 bits. Dividing by 8 bits per octet means that packets have to be a minimum of 62.5 octets in length for collision detection to work. Xerox rounded this up to 64 octets minimum frame size for DIX Ethernet.

Any frame whose payload (which was still dictated by the higher-level transport protocol) resulted in an overall frame size of less than 64 octets was padded with zeros by Ethernet II until the frame reached this minimum size. This solved the timing problem of collision detection but forced each protocol to distinguish data from padding. The DIX frame continued to rely on the Type field to identify the higher-level protocol and, therefore, its Data field length.

Although the Digital/Intel/Xerox version of Ethernet provided additional functionality intended to make Ethernet commercially viable, the only substantive change to the frame was to impose minimum and maximum frame lengths. Xerox, the originator of Ethernet, retained the rights to the technology and, consequently, established and published its standards. This approach to standardization served its purpose: Ethernet became a commercially available product.

Unfortunately, this approach to establishing and maintaining standards for commercial products is not sustainable. A competitive corporation cannot be tasked with maintaining the standards for a commodity product. It will be motivated to act on its own behalf. Therefore, for Ethernet to become a truly successful commercial technology, the responsibility for standardization had to be ceded to a neutral entity.

IEEE Project 802

The standards body that has been responsible for many of the extant standards that support today's high performance networks is the Institute of Electrical and Electronics Engineers (IEEE). This standardization work began in February 1980 (hence, the numeric designation of 802), when the IEEE launched its Local and Metropolitan Area Network Standards Committee, also affectionately referred to as *Project 802*.

This committee is chartered with the creation, maintenance, and encouragement of the use of IEEE/ANSI as well as the equivalent Joint Technical Committee 1 (JTC 1) standards established by the International Standards Committee (ISO). These JTC 1 series of equivalent standards are known as ISO 8802-*nnn*. These standards are basically limited to Layers 1 and 2 of the OSI Reference Model. Layer 1 defines the Physical Layer—for example, the media type and the manner in which data is placed on the media. Layer 2 defines the LAN's frame structure and frame-forwarding mechanisms.

> **Note:** The ISO standards are given three-digit numerical designations under the heading of 8802. Therefore, the *nnn* of ISO 8802-*nnn* is nothing more than a wildcard attribute that references all the substandards in the 8802 family of standards.

The objective also included establishing the rules that enable all types of LANs to easily pass data between themselves and to separate the physical media from the LAN protocols. This permits the implementation of the same LAN on different cable plants, without compromising interoperability.

The committee identified the elements required to support its goals and launched task-specific teams to accomplish them. The accomplishments of these teams included the following:

- 802.1 defined the overview and architecture for interoperability between LANs and MANs. This is the basis for all the 802 initiatives and includes standards for LAN/MAN management and bridging between 802-compliant networks.
- 802.2 defined the Data Link Layer (Layer 2) standard for telecommunications and information exchange between systems, both LAN and MAN based. This specification also provided the backward compatibility required to support a transition from the prestandard versions of Ethernet to the 802.3 standardized version.
- 802.3 established the new standard for a LAN that features Carrier Sense, Multiple Access with Collision Detection. This "new" LAN is properly referred to as *CSMA/CD* but is popularly known as *Ethernet*.
- 802.4 defined a Physical Layer standard for a bus topology LAN with a token-passing media-access method. This LAN is called *Token Bus* and can support 1, 2, 5, or 10Mbps data rates.
- 802.5 established the standards for Token Ring's access methods and physical signaling techniques.

> **Note:** MANs are *metropolitan area networks*. The standards for MANs were also defined by the IEEE's Project 802.

Although not a complete listing of the Project 802 initiatives, these five items convey the intended benefits of the charter for standardizing local and metropolitan area networks. Each specification in this family can interoperate through unsophisticated frame conversions because they all have a common foundation. This charter far exceeded the scope of Xerox's standards and, consequently, made DIX Ethernet obsolete.

IEEE 802.2 Logical Link Control (LLC)

The IEEE Project 802 organized its standards around a three-tiered protocol hierarchy that correlates to the OSI Reference Model's bottommost two layers: the Physical and Data Link Layers. These three tiers are the Physical Layer, Medium Access Control (MAC), and Logical Link Control (LLC). This is valid for all 802-compliant LANs. The MAC Layer addressing specification allows for either a two-octet or six-octet address. The six-octet MAC address is the standard. The two-octet address has been all but relegated to academic discussions.

The IEEE's 802 Reference Model differs from the OSI Reference Model in two significant aspects. First, the 802 Physical Layer is a subset of its OSI counterpart. Second, the OSI's Data Link Layer (Layer 2) is broken into two discrete components: Medium Access Control (MAC) and Logical Link Control (LLC). This correlation is presented in Figure 3.3.

FIGURE 3.3
The IEEE 802 correlation to the OSI Reference Model.

OSI Reference Model Layer Description	OSI Layer Number	IEEE Project 802 Reference Model
Application	7	Service Access Points for Higher Layer Protocols
Presentation	6	
Session	5	
Transport	4	#1 #2 #3
Network	3	Logical Link Control
Data Link	2	Media Access Control
Physical	1	Physical

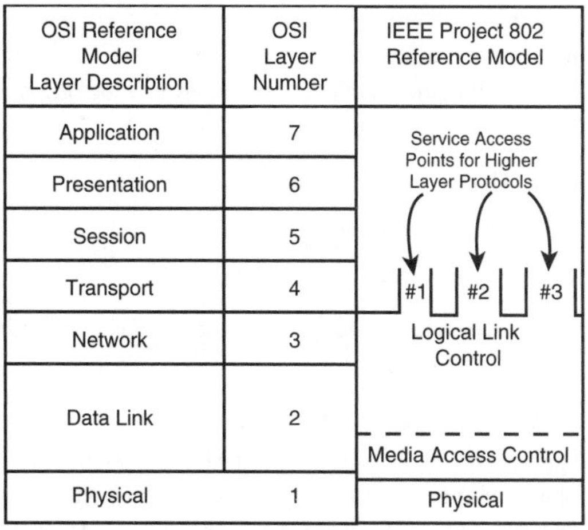

Defining the LLC separately from the media-access control enabled interoperability of 802-compliant networks, despite differences in topologies, transmission media, and, more important, media-access methodologies. The LLC resides above the MAC and

Physical Layers of the 802 Model. In this model, media access, transmission media, and topology are highly interdependent. Therefore, part of the OSI's Physical Layer was defined as the 802's Media Access Layer.

One of the mechanisms that enables LANs of different topologies to interoperate is the *LLC subframe*. This three-field structure is prepended to the Data field of an 802 frame. It's used to identify the destination protocol in multiprotocol machines. This field is necessary due to the limited capability of the 802.3 protocol to identify external protocols. The LLC subframe is illustrated in Figure 3.4 and contains the following structure:

- A 1-Octet Destination Service Address Port (DSAP) field
- A 1-Octet Source Service Address Port (SSAP) field
- A 1-Octet Control field

FIGURE 3.4

The Logical Link Control subframe structure.

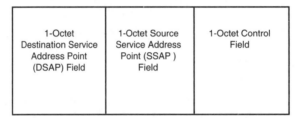

The service access ports indicate for which upper-layer protocol the packet is intended. Protocols are assigned hexadecimal values, which are displayed in the DSAP and SSAP fields of a packet.

The LLC provides addressing and control of the data link. It specifies which mechanisms are to be used for addressing stations over the transmission medium and which are to be used for controlling the data exchanged between the originator and recipient machines. This is done through the use of three LLC services:

- Unacknowledged connectionless service
- Acknowledged connectionless service
- Connection-oriented service

These services are accessed via service access points that are defined between the Network and Data Link Layers.

The first LLC service, *unacknowledged connectionless service*, is a minimal but useful offering. Frequently, Layer 4 protocols such as TCP and SPX are tasked with providing flow control and other reliability functions. Therefore, it makes sense to have a Layer 2 service that doesn't redundantly provide the same functions, albeit at a lower level. This service cuts down on the communications overheads. Some applications, such as time- and latency-sensitive voice and/or video conferencing, may actually suffer performance degradation by having to establish and maintain connections at this layer.

The next LLC service, *acknowledged connectionless service*, provides an acknowledgment of receipt, without having any of the overhead involved in connection management. Less overhead directly translates into faster delivery. Adding guaranteed delivery to this quick delivery service creates a useful service whose applications are almost limitless.

The last LLC service, *connection-oriented service*, provides Data Link Layer mechanisms to establish and maintain connections. This is extremely useful for simple and/or unintelligent devices that might not have Layer 3 or 4 protocols and therefore need to be able to provide these functions at Layer 2. This control function requires the Data Link Layer to maintain a table that tracks active connections.

These services tend to be selected per application and are transparent to application users. Because they are part of the 802.2 foundation specification, they're available to all 802-compliant networks and can be used in internetworking different 802-compliant networks.

IEEE 802.2 Subnetwork Access Protocol (SNAP)

As a means of providing backward compatibility with early, nonstandardized versions of LANs, such as PARC and DIX Ethernet, a subframe structure was developed to provide a mechanism for identifying the upper-layer protocol being transported. The PARC and DIX versions of Ethernet included a Type field in their frame structures. This space was reallocated by the IEEE in its 802.3 standardized version of Ethernet.

The 802.3 Ethernet was a more sophisticated protocol than its predecessors and obviated much of the original need for this field. Some higher-level protocols, however, relied on this Layer 2 function. The need to provide compatibility with existing Layer 3 and 4 protocols necessitated the development of a subframe structure that could identify higher-level protocols. The result was the Subnetwork Access Protocol (SNAP) subframe, which is illustrated in Figure 3.5.

FIGURE 3.5

The 802.2 SNAP subframe structure.

1-Octet Destination Service Address Point (DSAP) Field	1-Octet Source Service Address Point (SSAP) Field	1-Octet Control Field	3-Octet Organizationally Unique Identifier (OUI) Field	2-Octet Protocol Identifier Field

The 802.2 specification also provides a SNAP frame structure. This frame builds on the standard 802.2 frame by adding a 5-Octet field that contains a three-octet Organizationally Unique Identifier (OUI) field and a 2-Octet Protocol Identifier field. The SNAP subframing is an extension of the LLC subframe and must be used with it. It can be used with any 802-compliant LAN.

IEEE 802.3 Ethernet Frame

Project 802 defined a standard basis for all Ethernet frame types. The frames are a minimum of 64 octets and a maximum of 1,500 octets in length, including payload and headers. The headers are used to identify the sender and recipient of each packet. The only limitations on this identification are that each address must be unique and six octets in length.

The first 12 octets of each frame contain the six-octet destination address (the intended recipient's address) and the six-octet source address (the sender's address). These addresses are hardware-level machine address codes, commonly known as *MAC addresses*.

802-compliant frames may contain a destination address of a single machine or refer to a group of workstations with a common, identifying characteristic. Transmission to groups of related machines is known as *multicasting*.

Under normal operating circumstances, Ethernet NICs will receive only frames whose destination addresses match their unique MAC addresses or satisfy their multicast criteria. Most NICs, however, can be set for "promiscuous mode." This results in their reception of all frames on the LAN, regardless of addressing. This can pose a security risk for everyone else on the LAN's broadcast bus as well as a potential performance problem for the user whose machine is operating in that manner, but its required for any station that will be used to capture packets for network management.

Most of the 802.3 standard's changes from the previous versions of Ethernet were changes to the protocol itself. However, there was one other significant change to the 802.3 frame. The 802 committee needed a standard that was complete unto itself and not dependent on the good behavior of other protocols. Therefore, it replaced the 2-Octet Type field of previous Ethernets with a 2-Octet Length field.

Because minimum and maximum field lengths were established based on a worst-case, roundtrip timing window (as previously explained in the section titled "DIX Ethernet Frame," minimum and maximum field lengths were necessary for collision detection purposes), it was no longer necessary to defer the determination of frame size to client protocols. Instead, the 802.3 working group redefined this 2-Octet field to explicitly define the length of a frame's Data field and moved protocol identification to the LLC.

The IEEE's 802.3 basic Ethernet frame replaced the traditional Type field with a Length field. The 802.2 subframe is used, instead, to identify the type of protocol, if this is necessary. Another change in the 802.3 frame from its predecessors was the requirement for the overall frame size to be between 64 and 1,500 octets in length, from the start of the Destination field through the end of the Frame Check Sequence field, as illustrated in Figure 3.6.

The preamble is a 7-Octet string that precedes each frame and enables the synchronization of the transmission. This is followed by the start-of-frame delimiter (SFD). The SFD is fairly self-explanatory: It denotes the start of the frame for all devices in or on the LAN. The SFD is 11 followed by the repeating sequence of 1010101010.

The SFD is sometimes considered an integral part of the preamble and not a part of the frame itself, thus bringing the preamble up to eight octets in length. This represents another subtle distinction between the PARC and DIX Ethernet variants and the 802.3 standard. PARC and DIX Ethernets used a consistent, repeating 10101010 pattern for the entire 8-Octet preamble. This pattern was used for both synchronization and start-of-frame delimiting.

The next mechanism is the frame check sequence (FCS). A mathematically derived value is stored in this field by the frame's originating computer. The destination computer also knows how to calculate this value and does so to verify the integrity of the frame. Frames may be damaged in transit in a variety of ways. Electromagnetic interference (EMI), crosstalk, and so forth can damage a packet without stopping its transmission.

Upon receipt of a frame, the destination computer checks the frame's FCS field for damage through a cyclical redundancy check. The destination computer performs the same calculation as the originating computer did and compares the resulting value to the one stored in the FCS field. If the values are the same, the destination computer knows the data arrived intact. Otherwise, the destination computer requests a retransmission of the frame.

The basic Ethernet frame, illustrated in Figure 3.6, is known as *raw Ethernet*. In reality, raw 802.3 Ethernet is seldom, if ever, used. Instead, it's the basis for extended frames using the 802.2 LLC subframe and/or the SNAP subframe.

> **Note:** Just to confuse you, NetWare uses the terms 802.2 and 802.3, but the definitions differ from the IEEE spec. Novell's 802.3 (the default frame for NetWare 3.11 and earlier) is actually what has been described as "raw" 802.3, whereas Novell's 802.2 (the default for NetWare 3.12 and later) corresponds to the IEEE 802.3 frame.

FIGURE 3.6

The IEEE 802.3 Ethernet basic frame.

7-Octet Preamble	1-Octet Start of Frame Delimiter	6-Octet Destination Address	6-Octet Origination Address	2-Octet Length Field	Variable Length Data Field (> 46 octets < 1482)	4-Octet Frame Check Sequence

Ethernet LLC Frame Structure

The Ethernet LLC frame is a combination of an 802.3 frame and the 802.2 LLC sub-frame. In this implementation, LLC adds three fields to the basic Ethernet frame: Destination Service Access Port (DSAP), Source Service Access Port (SSAP), and Control.

An Ethernet LLC frame is illustrated in Figure 3.7 and has the following structure:

- A 7-Octet preamble that signals the start of a frame
- A 1-Octet start-of-frame delimiter that signals the start of the frame's contents
- The intended recipient's 6-Octet MAC address
- The originator's 6-Octet MAC address
- A 2-Octet Length field that identifies the total length of the Data field, including the LLC and SNAP headers
- A 1-Octet Destination Service Access Point (DSAP) field that identifies, predictably, the LLC's service access point at the destination machine
- A 1-Octet Source Service Access Point (SSAP) field that identifies the originating machine's LLC service access point
- A 1-or 2-Octet Control field that indicates the type of LLC frame being carried
- A Data field that contains either 43 to 1,497 octets or 42 to 1,496 octets of data, depending on the length of the preceding Control field
- A 4-Octet frame check sequence used to check the integrity of the frame

FIGURE 3.7

An IEEE 802.3 Ethernet frame with an 802.2 LLC subframe.

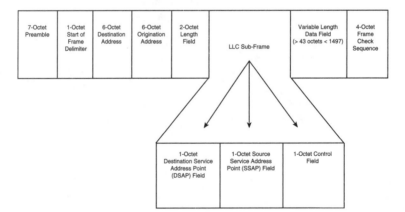

The Ethernet LLC frame integrates the 802.2 subframe structures, or headers, and permits the identification of the higher-level protocol that's the intended recipient of the frame's contents. Having a mechanism to identify higher-layer protocols provides backwards compatibility with earlier versions of Ethernet, whose frames contained discrete mechanisms for protocol identification.

The total length of an Ethernet LLC frame must be at least 64 octets in length (excluding the preamble and start-of-frame delimiter) to permit proper functioning of the CSMA/CD mechanism. Zeros are padded to the end of the Data field to ensure this minimum length. The upper limit is 1,518 octets, including the preamble and start-of-frame delimiter.

Ethernet SNAP Frame Structure

The Ethernet SNAP frame is a combination of an 802.3 frame and the 802.2 Subnetwork Access Protocol's subframe. In this implementation, SNAP adds a 5-Octet Protocol Identification field. This field is inserted in the frame after the LLC header. It consists of a 3-Octet organizationally unique identifier (OUI) and a 2-Octet Type field. These fields identify for which upper-layer protocol the frame is intended.

An Ethernet SNAP frame is illustrated in Figure 3.8 and contains the following fields:

- A 7-Octet preamble that signals the start of a frame
- A 1-Octet start-of-frame delimiter that signals the start of the frame's contents
- The intended recipient's 6-Octet MAC address
- The originator's 6-Octet MAC address
- A 2-Octet Length field that identifies the total length of the Data field, including the LLC and SNAP headers
- A 1-Octet Destination Service Access Point (DSAP) field that identifies, pre-dictably, the LLC's service access point at the destination machine
- A 1-Octet Source Service Access Point (SSAP) field that identifies the originating machine's LLC service access point
- A 1- or 2-Octet Control field that indicates the type of LLC frame being carried
- A 5-Octet SNAP subframe, including a 3-Octet Organizationally Unique Identifier field and a 2-Octet Protocol Type field that identify the upper-level protocol being carried
- A Data field that contains either 38 to 1,492 octets of data or 37 to 1,491 octets of data, depending on the length of the preceding Control field
- A 4-Octet frame check sequence used to check the integrity of the frame

The Ethernet SNAP sub-frame is illustrated in Figure 3.8.

The Ethernet SNAP subframe is designed to enhance the capability of the LLC subframe to provide backward compatibility with earlier versions of Ethernet.

The total length of an Ethernet SNAP frame must be at least 64 octets in length to permit proper functioning of the CSMA/CD mechanism. The upper limit for an Ethernet SNAP frame's size is 1,518 octets, including the preamble and start-of-frame delimiter.

FIGURE 3.8

*An IEEE 802.3
Ethernet frame
with an 802.2
SNAP subframe.*

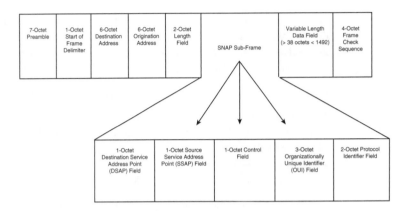

IEEE 802.5 Token Ring

The IEEE also standardized a message format and protocol for a different, more deterministic LAN known as *Token Ring* in its 802.5 standard. Token Ring networks had existed since the mid 1970s and were largely an IBM-specific technology. The 802.5 specification is almost identical to IBM's Token Ring. In fact, the term *Token Ring* is used indiscriminately to describe both IBM's prestandard product and IEEE 802.5-compliant products.

IEEE standardization was pushed by several large companies, including IBM (802.5 Token Ring) and General Motors (802.4 Token Bus). Token Ring offered a more timely and deterministic approach to networking than the 802.3 protocol, albeit at a higher per-port cost. Companies whose applications required timely delivery of data found Token Ring to be the only viable solution for their needs. Although the 802.3 protocol ensures only that the packet has been successfully transmitted, multiple transmission attempts may be required. Therefore, it can't guarantee a timeframe for delivery. On the other hand, the Token Ring topology can, due to its deterministic, ring-shaped topology and orderly access method.

IEEE 802.5 Frame Structure

The 802.5 Token Ring frame structure consists of two parts: the token and the data frame.

The token and data frames are illustrated in Figure 3.9. This figure presents the "raw" Token Ring framing, without the 802.2 LLC or SNAP subframes. Like its 802.3 cousin, Token Ring is seldom used in its raw state. A Token frame contains only the first three fields shown in the figure.

FIGURE 3.9
The IEEE's 802.5 Token Ring data frame.

1-Octet Starting Delimiter	1-Octet Access Control Field	1-Octet Frame Control Field	6-Octet Destination Address	6-Octet Origination Address	Variable Length Data Field (0 to 4099 octets)	1-Octet Ending Delimiter

The token frame consists of three 1-Octet fields:

- The Starting Delimiter
- The Access Control field
- The Ending Delimiter

The Access Control field is the key to making a Token Ring work. It contains eight bits, one of which must be inverted to deactivate the token and convert it into a start-of-frame sequence. The other two fields simply identify the start and end of the frame.

When the token has been converted to a data frame, it consists of several different fields and subfields:

- The Starting Delimiter
- The Access Control field
- The Frame Control field
- The Destination address
- The Origination address
- The Data
- The Ending Delimiter

First is the Starting Delimiter field, which identifies the beginning of the frame. Next is the Access Control field. This field tells 802.5-compliant devices whether they may transmit. This field also contains the bits for Token Ring's priority and reservation system. This is followed by the Frame Control field. This field stores the Type bits that identify the transport protocol. This field is also used to differentiate between data frames and control frames.

The next two fields are the destination and source MAC addresses. Each one is a 6-Octet field. These MAC addresses conform to the previously described Project 802 specification and are identical to those used in Ethernet networks. The Data field for a token-based network varies in size from at least zero octets up to a maximum of 4,099. The last field is the one-octet Ending Delimiter that identifies the end of the frame.

Although not shown, Token Ring also uses LLC and SNAP subframes. This allows them to be bridged with a translating bridge to Ethernet networks without compromising their capability to map received frames to higher-layer destination protocols. The Token Ring LLC and SNAP subframes are only pertinent in environments where Token Ring and Ethernet are bridged together.

FDDI

Officially known as *Fiber Distributed Data Interface*, this American National Standards Institute (ANSI) standard LAN architecture is more commonly identified by its acronym: *FDDI* (pronounced *fiddy*). Although it's widely derided as merely a higher speed Token Ring network, FDDI is fundamentally different in its topology, management, and even token and frame structures.

The raw FDDI data-bearing frame is illustrated in Figure 3.10 and has the following structure:

- An 8-Octet preamble that signals the start of the frame.
- A 1-Octet start-of-frame delimiter that signals the start of the frame's contents.
- A 1-Octet Frame Control field that signals the type of frame (that is, token, MAC or LLC, priority frame, and so forth).
- The intended recipient's 6-Octet MAC address.
- The originator's 6-Octet MAC address.
- A variable-length Data field that contains up to 4,478 octets.
- A 4-Octet frame check sequence used to check the integrity of the frame.
- A Half-Octet (four bits) ending delimiter.
- A 12-bit Frame Status field that contains three Half-Octet subfields: Error, Address-match, and Copied. Each subfield is set to either "S" for *Set* or "R" for *Reset*.

FIGURE 3.10
The FDDI frame.

8-Octet Preamble	1-Octet Starting Delimiter	1-Octet Frame Control Field	6-Octet Destination Address	6-Octet Source Address	Variable Length Data Field, up to 4478 Octets	4-Octet Frame Check Sequence	4-bit Ending Delimiter	12-bit Frame Status

The FDDI frame is a maximum of 4,500 octets in length, including data and all frame components. This is the basic FDDI frame. It's usually implemented in one of two sub-formats: LLC or SNAP. Neither one, excluding the preamble, can be more than 4,500 octets in length.

FDDI LLC Frame Structure

FDDI also supports LLC by building on the IEEE 802.2 LLC layer.

> **Note:** The IEEE 802 family of standards has been adopted by ANSI. Consequently, even though FDDI is not an IEEE standard, it can use IEEE-developed subframe mechanisms. This enhances FDDI's capability to function as a high-bandwidth LAN backbone that interconnects Ethernet LANs.

The LLC frame, illustrated in Figure 3.11, is constructed by adding three fields to the FDDI frame. These fields are the DSAP, SSAP, and Control fields.

FIGURE 3.11
*A FDDI frame
with an 802.2 LLC
subframe.*

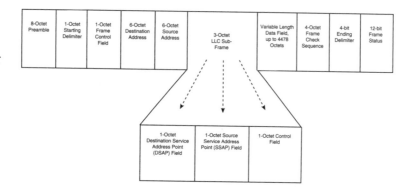

A FDDI LLC frame has the following structure:

- An 8-Octet preamble that signals the start of the frame.
- A 1-Octet start-of-frame delimiter that signals the start of the frame's contents.
- A 1-Octet Frame Control field that signals the type of frame (that is, token, MAC or LLC, priority frame, and so forth).
- The intended recipient's 6-Octet MAC address.
- The originator's 6-Octet MAC address.
- A variable-length Data field that contains up to 4,478 octets.
- A 4-Octet Frame Check Sequence used to check the integrity of the frame.
- A Half-Octet (four bits) ending delimiter.
- A 12-bit Frame Status field that contains three 4-bit subfields: Error, Address-match, and Copied. Each subfield is set to either "S" for *Set* or "R" for *Reset*.

The FDDI frame can be supplemented with the 802.2 LLC subframe structures. This subframe prepends the DSAP, SSAP, and Control fields to the Data field.

FDDI SNAP Frame Structure

FDDI also supports SNAP by building on the 802.2 LLC layer of the FDDI 802.2 frame. The SNAP frame adds a 3-Octet Protocol Identification field and a 3-Octet Type field to the 802.2 LLC subframe structure. This frame is illustrated in Figure 3.12.

FIGURE 3.12

A FDDI frame with an 802.2 SNAP subframe.

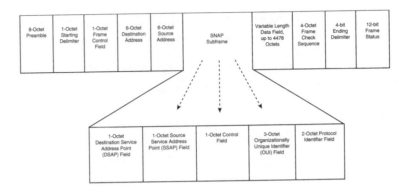

An FDDI SNAP frame contains the following fields:

- An 8-Octet preamble that signals the start of the frame.
- A 1-Octet start-of-frame delimiter that signals the start of the frame's contents.
- A 1-Octet Frame Control field that signals the type of frame (that is, token, MAC or LLC, priority frame, and so forth).
- The intended recipient's 6-Octet MAC address.
- The originator's 6-Octet MAC address.
- A 5-Octet SNAP subframe, including the 3 LLC sub-frame fields described previously, a 3-Octet Organizationally Unique Identifier field and a 2-Octet Protocol Type field that identify the upper-level protocol being carried.
- A variable-length Data field that contains up to 4,473 octets.
- A 4-Octet Frame Check Sequence used to check the integrity of the frame.
- A Half-Octet (four bits) ending delimiter.
- A 12-bit Frame Status field that contains three four-bit subfields: Error, Address-match, and Copied. Each subfield is set to either "S" for *Set* or "R" for *Reset*.

The IEEE's FDDI SNAP frame adds a 3-Octet Organizationally Unique Identifier field and a 2-Octet Type field to the FDDI LLC frame immediately after the LLC header and before the data. These fields are included in the overall length of the Data field.

Selecting a LAN Technology

Each of the LANs in the IEEE 802 family of standards has its own particular framing structure, media-access methodology, and physical transmission media. To select the correct LAN technology, you must understand the benefits and limitations of each frame type, relative to the networking requirements of your users.

The benefits and limitations of each frame type are summarized in this section.

802.3 Ethernet

Ethernet, Fast Ethernet, and Gigabit Ethernet offer you 10Mbps, 100Mbps, and up to 1Gbps transmission rates. Specifications in this family use different physical layers with an almost perfectly interchangeable Media Access Layer. Some minor changes were necessary to the media-access mechanisms to account for differences in the Physical Layer.

Media access for these three specifications is through a chaotic contention method that does not scale very well. Performance may be boosted significantly by implementing these protocols via a switch. Switches decrease the size of the collision domains without affecting the size of the broadcast domain. In a per-port switched 802.3 LAN, the collision domain is reduced to just two devices: the end device and the hub port to which it connects. This greatly relieves the scalability issue that plagues shared versions of these specifications.

802.5 Token Ring

Token Ring offers you 4Mbps and 16Mbps transmission rates with somewhat predictable delays, due to its deterministic access method. Additionally, the token has priority bits that you can set higher to satisfy the more stringent network performance criteria of critical frames.

FDDI

FDDI offers a 100Mbps transmission rate and a self-healing, dual, counter-rotating ring topology. FDDI can be considered a "fast Token Ring" because it conducts token-passing in a deterministic fashion. This, and the 802.1 and 802.2 commonalties, are all that these two networks share.

FDDI's clock rate and timed access methodology distinguish it from Token Ring and position it for different applications within the LAN environment. Its dual counter-rotating rings can automatically and logically wrap together to heal a broken cable. This provides an innate fault tolerance. The drawback to this is a sudden increase in propagation delay in the event of a cable break.

The other major distinction between FDDI and Token Ring is FDDI's loadability. Unlike Token Ring, FDDI can support the transmission of multiple data frames simultaneously. This allows more of its bandwidth to be usable. For more detailed information on FDDI and all of its features, see Chapter 8, "FDDI."

802.12 VG-AnyLAN

VG-AnyLAN provides for the accommodation of both Ethernet and Token Ring frame formats. The proposal appears to be highly media independent because VG-AnyLAN can transmit over four pairs of Category 3 UTP wire, Category 5 UTP or STP, or 62.5 micron fiber-optic cabling.

It also attempts to establish a middle ground between true baseband and true broadband communications by implementing a demand-priority media-access method. Essentially, it establishes a priority architecture that lets time-sensitive packets get needed bandwidth on demand. It lacks a native mechanism to actually reserve bandwidth, however.

VG-AnyLAN has two other potentially significant limitations. First, it requires four pairs of twisted pair wiring. If you use 10BaseT, this may force you to rewire your stations prior to migration. Therefore, even though VG-AnyLAN was intentionally designed for Category 3 wire, you may still find yourself unable to use existing wire if you do not have four pairs of Category 3 wire at each station. The second limitation is that VG-AnyLAN does not interoperate easily with "real Ethernet" because it uses a different media-access method.

Media Access

All networks must have some mechanism for regulating access to the transmission media. This mechanism, known as *media access*, is implemented at Layer 2 of the OSI Reference Model, the Data Link Layer. Although the need for it is universal, there can be quite a bit of variety in the implementation of media-access mechanisms. For example, four distinct approaches to regulating access to the transmission media can be found in local area networks:

- Contention
- Token passing
- Demand-priority
- Switched

Contention-Based Media Access

A LAN that features competition as the basis for arbitrating the right to transmit is more properly described as having a *contention-based media-access method*. The sum total of devices that compete with each other for bandwidth is known as a *collision domain*. This method is embraced by the myriad Ethernet variants that have emerged, including the following:

- Ethernet II or DIX Ethernet
- IEEE 802.3 10Mbps Ethernet (CSMA/CD)
- IEEE 802.3 100Mbps Fast Ethernet
- IEEE 802.3z Gigabit Ethernet

Contention-based access is fairly primitive because it has no centralized regulatory mechanism. Instead, each network-attached device assumes the burden for its own transmissions. Every time a device needs to transmit, it must check the wire to see whether it's available or already in use. If it is in use, the would-be transmitter must back down and wait before trying again. Each device is, in effect, competing for available bandwidth based on the logic and rules established in its Physical Layer. The sum total of the devices that compete with each other for access to the transmission media constitutes the LAN's contention domain.

> **Note:** A contention domain is also sometimes referred to as a *collision domain*. This is logical because collisions can occur only among LAN devices that are in contention for the same bandwidth.

Implicit in this description of contention-based media access is that all network-attached devices transmit and receive on the same frequency band. The transmission media can support only a single signal at a time, and that signal occupies the entire band. In other words, the transmission media supports baseband transmission. This is illustrated in Figure 3.13.

FIGURE 3.13
Baseband transmission.

Baseband transmission technology uses only one channel for all communications. This has two important implications:

- Only one device can transmit at any given time.

- A device can only transmit or receive; it cannot do both simultaneously. This is known as *half-duplex* operation.

Half-Duplex Versus Full-Duplex

A *half-duplex network* permits only one device to transmit at any given time; the others must remain passive and listen for frames that might be addressed to them. This is illustrated in Figure 3.14.

FIGURE 3.14
*Half-duplex,
baseband
transmission.*

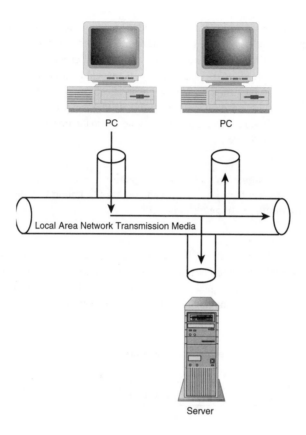

The term *full-duplex network* implies that the available bandwidth is somehow subdivided into discrete channels. Alternatively, physically separate wire paths may be used to create a redundant channel using the same frequency band. The typical full-duplex LAN uses switching technology. In any case, a device may simultaneously transmit and receive. A full-duplex switched connection is illustrated in Figure 3.15

It's important to note that in a full-duplex network that uses a contention-based media-access methodology, only one device per collision domain may transmit at any given time. The key difference is that implementing a full-duplex network requires the use of a switched port for each device connected. Therefore, the number of devices in any given collision domain is just two: the device and the switch port to which it connects.

Timing Is Everything

Regardless of how many devices are in the LAN's various collision domains, or even whether it supports half- or full-duplex transmission modes, some mechanism must exist to regulate the devices' capability to access the transmission medium at any given time. Contention-based media access is one such mechanism. This simple media-access methodology became popular with Ethernet II (or *DIX Ethernet*, as it is sometimes called). It was much more rigorously defined by the IEEE's 802.3 Ethernet specification. Essentially, contention-based media access is a game of timing and mathematics.

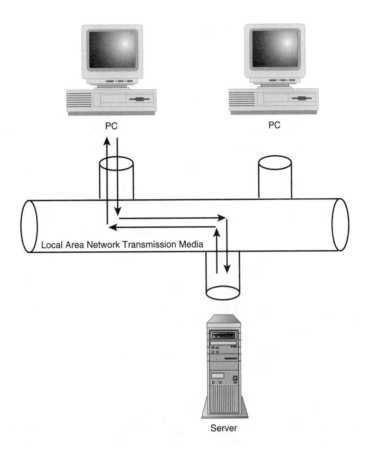

FIGURE 3.15
*Full-duplex,
switched
transmission.*

PC   PC

Local Area Network Transmission Media

Server

For timing to be coordinated across all connected devices, there must be a certain consistency to the Layer 2 (Data Link Layer) frames used across the LAN. By their very nature, however, these frames vary in length. Each one, in theory, can be a different length. Therefore, avoiding collisions becomes a more complicated task.

The way that 802.3 CSMA/CD (today's Ethernet) seeks to avoid collisions is by placing upper and lower limits on the size of a frame. Frames must be at least 64 octets but not more than 1,524 octets in length, including payload and headers. At any given transmission rate, these minimum and maximum frame sizes translate directly into minimum and maximum transmission times for standards-compliant frames.

In a contention-based network, the amount of time necessary for each frame to propagate throughout the entire LAN can be used to detect collisions. Remember, contention-based media access assumes that the architecture uses baseband transmission, so the transmitted frame must be successfully propagated over the entire LAN to ensure that any and all recipients receive it. The frame can be destroyed by a collision anywhere on the LAN. Two factors increase the chance of a collision:

- The number of devices connected to the network
- The physical size of the network

More devices connected to a network means more contention for available bandwidth. The longer the network, the more time the frame must be on the wire. You must carefully regulate both circumstances to ensure acceptable levels of network performance.

The number of devices that can be connected to a LAN has, historically, been reduced through the use of such segmentation mechanisms as bridges, routers, and switches. Although they operate in different ways, each effectively reduces the size of a LAN's contention domain. The network's physical size, however, is dictated by the Physical Layer specifications of the various LAN architectures.

Establishing a precise value for the worst-case roundtrip transmission time was first done in DIX Ethernet. This value was set at 50 microseconds. To ensure that a frame was successfully delivered required the transmitting device to continue transmitting until after this time had expired. This guaranteed that the frame had propagated to the farthest reaches of the network (assuming the LAN was built in compliance with specifications for maximum wire paths and diameters) without a collision. Consequently, operators could be sure that every device on the network could detect the frame on the wire and know not to transmit.

Unfortunately, transmission is not instantaneous over copper transmission facilities. Therefore, it's entirely probable that a station can begin to transmit on what appears to be an idle LAN only to collide with an incoming transmission from another station nanoseconds after initiating its own transmission. Both devices detect this collision, back off from transmitting, and begin anew after a brief delay. This is the essence of collision detection. The potential for collisions is illustrated in Figure 3.16. PC number 1 has already started to transmit, but its transmission has not yet reached PC number 2. This second PC thinks the network is clear and that it may transmit. These transmissions will collide, forcing both PCs to back off, endure a pseudo-random waiting period, and then attempt retransmission.

Fifty microseconds, the worst-case roundtrip time, is enough time to transmit 500 bits at 10Mbps. Dividing 500 by 8 bits per octet yields 62.5. This means that packets have to be a minimum of 62.5 octets in length for collision detection to work. Xerox rounded this up to 64 octets minimum frame size for its DIX Ethernet. This convention was maintained by the 802.3 specification.

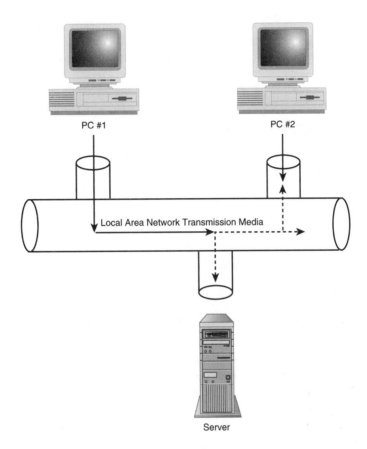

FIGURE 3.16
A collision in the making.

PC #1   PC #2

Local Area Network Transmission Media

Server

Given that the payload of any given frame was still dictated by the higher-level transport protocol, it was quite likely that the occasional frame would be less than 64 octets. Frames that were less than 64 octets long were padded with zeros by Ethernet II until the frame reached this minimum size. Padding solved the timing problem of collision detection but forced each protocol to distinguish data from padding. The DIX frame continued to rely on the Type field to identify the higher-level protocol and, therefore, its Data field length. Although 802.3 doesn't recognize the Type field in this manner, it continues to support the padding of Data fields to enforce the 64-octet minimum frame size.

Tangentially related to CSMA/CD's collision-detection mechanism is the standard interframe gap. The 802.3 variant of Ethernet features a 96-bit gap between frames. All devices know this and expect it. Contrary to many of the rumors that have been generated to explain the presence of this structure, the interframe gap is analogous to a carrier tone in a telephony network. It identifies the transmitter and provides any time that may be needed to continue framing and transmitting data. Therefore, in today's Ethernets, a transmitting device sends a frame followed by a 96-bit gap that's interpreted by other network-attached devices as part of the bit stream from the transmitting device. They may not transmit until this gap has passed and the transmitter relinquishes its control over the communications band.

Collisions

Collisions have a bad reputation among LAN administrators. Even the term *collision* has a negative connotation. Truth be known, collisions are an error condition. However, collisions are part of the normal operation of a contention-based media-access methodology. In networks using this method, collisions do occur. Mechanisms exist to detect and recover from collisions. Consequently, do not pay too much attention to the collision rates, and don't panic whenever the yellow collision light on the hub flashes. Trust the network to operate normally. If you've built it properly, including adhering to all Physical Layer constraints such as maximum distances for each media type, the LAN automatically recovers from collisions.

If network performance degrades noticeably, the best way to reduce collisions is to reduce the number of devices per collision domain. As mentioned earlier, you can use bridges, routers, and switches effectively in this capacity.

It's important to note that the chaotic nature of contention-based media access makes the use of such technologies inappropriate for time-sensitive applications. Time-sensitive applications must have a much more predictable and timely means of accessing LAN bandwidth. Contention-based networks are ideally suited for the more traditional forms of networked computing, such as terminal emulation, file and print sharing, and so forth.

Token-Based Media Access

The next most popular media-access methodology regulates access to the media by passing tokens. Token passing is a phenomenon of LAN architectures that are based on a ring topology. Specific examples are the various implementations of Token Ring and FDDI (Fiber Distributed Data Interface).

A token is a special frame that's passed from device to device in sequence along the ring. It can circulate only when the ring is idle. This frame is only a few octets in length and contains a special bit pattern. This bit pattern can be manipulated to convert it into a *start-of-frame* (SOF) delimiting sequence that informs downstream network-attached devices of the arrival of a data-bearing frame. Immediately following the SOF field are the source and destination address pairs, as identified by the transmitting device.

The token is recognized by all devices as being the arbiter of access to the transmission media. If the token is passed to a device that doesn't need to transmit, the device may hold on to the token for 10 milliseconds (or longer if the default value has been changed). This enables a device to finish framing any data that it may be receiving from higher-layer protocols that link back up to its applications. A device must have this token to place data frames on the network. If it doesn't have the token, it must wait until it gets the token from its downstream neighbor.

If this time expires and the device still doesn't need to transmit, the device relinquishes control of the token and sends it to the next device in the ring. The SOF delimiter of a data frame can be reconverted to a token by only the device that owns it. The token eventually returns to its originator as it travels through the ring. The originator then must reconvert the token to an SOF. Typically, this is done after the intended recipients copy the data off the frame and modify a bit pattern to signify their successful receipt of it. This modified data frame continues its travel around the ring until it returns to its originator. The originator acknowledges successful delivery of its contents and either holds the data frame for the allotted time or uses it for transporting more data. This token-passing scheme is illustrated in Figure 3.17.

FIGURE 3.17
Token passing.

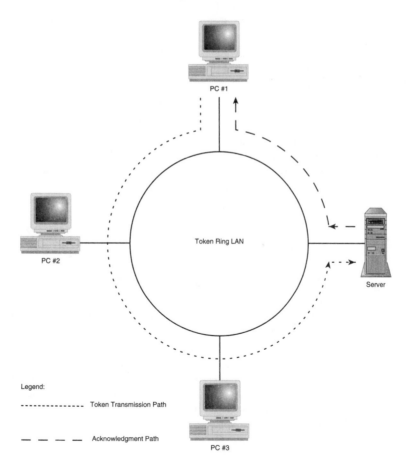

You can calculate the maximum time that can expire before a device is able to transmit. This is done by multiplying the maximum amount of time that any given node can hold a token by the number of devices connected to the ring. To this value add the amount of time required for a token to traverse the ring. Although this doesn't include I/O, processing time, spindle and head movement times of disk drives, or any other processor-based source of time delay, it does provide a reasonable estimation of the maximum network time delay you might experience.

This aggregate time can be manipulated by adding or subtracting nodes from the ring. Consequently, token-passing networks are ideal for any application that requires predictable delays.

FDDI Token-Based Media Access

FDDI uses a modified form of the token-passing scheme described in the previous section. This modification is subtle, but significant. Rather than keeping all stations idling until the originator receives the acknowledgment of delivery, FDDI uses a quick release mechanism to allow other devices to transmit, even while the original frame is in transit. The quick release mechanism is actually quite simple. Immediately after transmitting a frame (which contains a token modified into an SOF), the transmitter then transmits another token. Therefore, downstream stations do not have to wait for the original data frame to return to its originator before they can transmit. Control over the transmission media is relinquished much more quickly in FDDI's version of token-based media access. This is illustrated in Figure 3.18.

The benefits of a quick release of transmission control are obvious. The next device downstream enjoys the opportunity to transmit much sooner. This device can begin to pull the new token off the ring and convert it to a SOF delimiter even before the first data frame is received by its intended recipient.

The second benefit of this scheme is that it makes the network much more efficient. Consequently, the maximum sustainable throughput of a network equipped with a fast release can approach the theoretical maximum throughput.

Demand-Priority Media Access

The *demand-priority access method* (DPAM) is used by the IEEE 802.12 100Mbps VG-AnyLAN specification. DPAM is a round-robin arbitration method in which a central repeater (the hub) regularly polls ports connected to it. This polling is performed in port order and is conducted to identify ports that have transmission requests. After the need to transmit is established, the repeater determines whether the priority is high or normal. These priorities are designed to service time-sensitive requests before servicing normal-priority requests for bandwidth. An idle signal is automatically generated by any port that's not transmitting data. This can include any devices that either are idle or have a pending transmission request.

FIGURE 3.18
*Token passing
with a quick
release.*

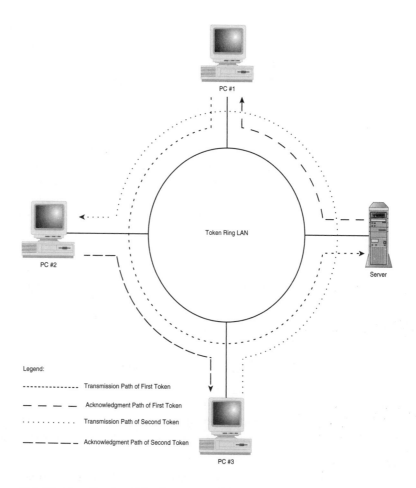

This idle signal is cleared by the repeater if that station is selected as the next in the priority sequence to transmit. In other words, the repeater identifies the next station in its priority sequence and then instructs it to halt transmission of its idle signal. When the port on that device senses its own "silence" (in other words, the idle signal ceases), it begins to transmit.

When this happens, the repeater alerts the other stations that they may receive an incoming message. The repeater then reads the incoming packet's destination address, looks in its link configuration table, and switches the packet to that destination address as well as to any promiscuous ports.

The central, or *root*, repeater controls the operation of the priority domain. The priority domain can include up to three levels of cascaded hubs. This enables interconnected repeaters to function as a single large repeater. The central repeater sends all traffic to each lower-level repeater. Each lower-level repeater, in turn, polls its active ports for requests after packet transmission.

No station is permitted to transmit twice in a row if other stations have same-priority requests pending. The central repeater does not allow a high-priority request to interrupt a normal-priority request if that request is already in progress. In a lower-level repeater, the normal-priority request is preempted so that the high-priority request can be accommodated. To ensure that a request isn't completely ignored, any normal-priority requests that have been waiting longer than 250 milliseconds are automatically elevated to high-priority status.

This access method is used only by the IEEE 802.12 specification for a 100Mbps network that uses either an Ethernet or Token Ring frame format (but not both simultaneously) and a star topology. Known as VG-AnyLAN, which stands for *voice grade wiring, any LAN architecture*, it can operate over four pairs of Category 3 UTP, STP, Category 5, and fiber. There can be up to three levels of cascaded repeaters with up to 100 meters between the repeaters and the stations. The network may be up to 4,000 feet in diameter.

VG-AnyLAN has almost completely failed in the marketplace. Although DPAM is technically superior to CSMA/CD as a LAN media-access method, it's quickly being relegated to the role of an interesting footnote in the history of local area networking. The higher-speed CSMA/CD LANs, such as Fast Ethernet and Gigabit Ethernet, offer much simpler migration paths from 10Mbps CSMA/CD Ethernets than VG-AnyLAN does.

Switched LAN Media Access

In addition to the three basic types of media access, a fourth methodology exists. Although this isn't a clearly defined access methodology, it is being used increasingly in lieu of the other methodologies to bolster the efficiency and performance of LANs. Switching is rewriting the conventional rules about LAN topologies and access methodologies.

As explained in Chapter 5, "LAN Types and Topologies," a *switch* is a multiport, Data Link Layer (OSI Reference Model Layer 2) device. A switch "learns" MAC addresses and stores them in an internal lookup table. Temporary switched paths are created between the frame's originator and its intended recipient, and the frames are forwarded along that temporary path.

Switching can either be used to interconnect shared hubs or used to interconnect individual devices. Segmenting shared hubs with a switching hub is known as *segment switching*. This is illustrated in Figure 3.19.

In a port-switched LAN, each port on the switching hub is connected to a single device. The devices can be workstations, servers, or even printers. This is illustrated in Figure 3.20.

FIGURE 3.19
Segment
switching.

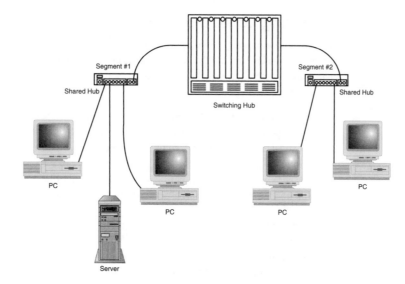

FIGURE 3.20
Port switching.

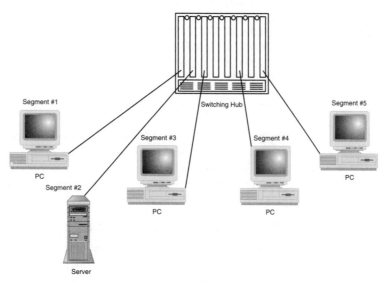

Each device connected to a switched port enjoys its own Layer 2 domain, shared only with that switched port. Switching can be used to improve the performance of both contention-based and token-passing LAN architectures.

Switching Contention-Based Networks

In a contention-based protocol, port switching effectively reduces the collision domain to just the switch port and the device it connects to the network. Depending on the hardware at both ends, switched CSMA/CD can support either full- or half-duplex connections.

A switched full-duplex connection represents the maximum performance that this protocol can support at any given transmission rate. Each device in the two-device collision domain (device and port) enjoys its own separate network paths, with their own separate bandwidth, for transmitting and receiving. For example, in a 10Mbps Ethernet that uses twisted pair wiring, one pair of wire supports the transmit function, and another pair supports the receive function for each port-switched device.

Peter's Principle: Two Times One Is Not Necessarily Two

You might think that a full-duplex, switched network connection yields twice the bandwidth of one that's half-duplex. It certainly seems logical, and manufacturers' advertising will draw you to that conclusion. Don't be fooled. This technique does, in fact, improve performance, but it does not necessarily double throughputs. Since both the transmit and receive functions are serviced by the same network interface card (NIC)—and must compete for CPU cycles through a common bus port on the motherboard—it's illogical to expect that performance will double. Rather, the performance bottleneck simply moves elsewhere in the LAN.

Separating the transmit and receive functions obviates any competition that may have existed. In a full-duplex implementation, the pair of wire used for the switch's transmissions becomes the pair of wire that the connected device uses to receive (and vice versa for the switch's receive wire path). There can be no collisions in this scenario. This was depicted in Figure 3.17, earlier in the chapter.

Switching Token-Passing Networks

Port-switching can improve token-passing LANs in much the same way it can improve contention-based LANs. The number of devices that pass tokens is reduced to an absolute minimum number of two: the switch port and the device connected to it. The only difference is that these devices pass tokens rather than compete for available bandwidth.

Unlike a contention-based LAN, a token-passing LAN requires the transmitted frame to return to its originator for reconversion to a token before any other devices can communicate. This remains true in a switched environment. Consequently, token-passing networks don't experience the same performance benefit as a contention-based network from full-duplex operations.

Summary

The Data Link Layer defines local area networking. Its two primary components are framing and media-access control. Each LAN architecture has its own unique combination of supported physical transmission media, framing conventions, and media-access control methodologies. When selecting a network architecture, such as Ethernet, Token Ring, FDDI, and so forth, you must give careful consideration to each of these criteria. They must be considered individually and in combination to determine whether they're capable of delivering the required LAN performance.

4

The Network and Transport Layers

The term *network protocols* specifically refers to those protocols that reside at Layer 3 of the OSI Reference Model. These protocols provide addressing that enables data to be delivered across unspecified distances, beyond the domain of the sender's LAN. Typically, Layer 3 protocols use a structure known as *packets* for transporting data.

Although Layer 3 protocols provide the networking mechanisms for forwarding packets, they lack the sophistication to make sure the packets are actually received, and received in the right order. These tasks are left to Layer 4 transport protocols. Transport protocols accept data from higher layers, embed them into segments, and pass the segments to Layer 3.

This chapter describes the functions and interactions of Layers 3 and 4 of protocol stacks before examining the intricacies of some of the more common networking protocols.

Protocol Stacks

A *protocol stack* is a suite of related communications protocols that offer users the mechanisms and services required to communicate with other network-connected machines. From the user's perspective, the protocol stack is what makes a network usable.

Previous chapters examined the first and second layers of a protocol stack—in particular, Chapter 2, "The Physical (and Not So Physical) Layer," and Chapter 3, "The Data Link Layer." These layers are tightly integrated and interrelated. The Physical Layer is dictated by your selection of a Data Link Layer architecture, such as Ethernet, Token Ring, and so forth.

In this age of open networking and computing, selection of a LAN architecture does not limit the choice of higher-level protocols. Instead, a protocol stack should offer mechanisms that interface with existing, standardized network access vehicles for Data Link Layer protocols.

In much the same way that the first and second layers are interrelated, the third layer of the OSI Reference Model is tightly interrelated with the fourth layer. Layer 3 is the Network Layer, and Layer 4 is the Transport Layer. They are illustrated in Figure 4.1. Together, they provide the mechanisms that enable the transfer of information between source and destination machines across a communications network that spans beyond a Layer 2 domain, as well as other functions, such as resequencing packets received out of order and retransmitting packets not received or received damaged.

FIGURE 4.1
Network and Transport Layers of the OSI Reference Model.

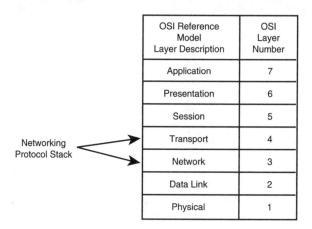

OSI Reference Model Layer Description	OSI Layer Number
Application	7
Presentation	6
Session	5
Transport	4
Network	3
Data Link	2
Physical	1

Networking Protocol Stack

Given that these protocols must rely on a Layer 2 and Layer 1 LAN architecture to actually deliver the data, they must have some means of communicating with these layers. The technique they use is called *"wrapping."* The Layer 4 protocol packages its data, received from higher-layer protocols, into segments. These segments are handed off to their Layer 3 counterpart. The Layer 3 protocol promptly wraps a packet structure, complete with source and destination addressing, around the segment and hands it off to the Layer 2 protocol. Layer 2 then wraps a frame and addressing around the Layer 3 data packets. These packets contain addressing that's recognizable by Layer 3 devices such as routers and IP switches. Wrapping a Layer 3 (IP) packet in a Layer 2 frame (Ethernet) is illustrated in Figure 4.2. The packet structure counts as part of the frame's data field, even though it isn't really data—just a different layer's structure.

FIGURE 4.2
Wrapping an IP packet with an Ethernet frame. See Chapter 6, "Ethernet," for an explanation of the structure.

7-Octet Preamble	1-Octet Start of Frame Delimiter	6-Octet Destination Address	6-Octet Origination Address	2-Octet Length Field	20 + Octet IPX Header	20 + Octet TCP Header	Variable length Data Field (>46 octets < 1482)	4-Octet Frame Check Sequence

The frames are used to transport the data and to address the data to the Layer 3 internet-working vehicle at the edge of their Layer 2 domain. This device, typically a router, accepts the framed packet, strips off the frame, and reads the Layer 3 addressing information. It uses this information to determine the next hop in the route to the packet's destination. The packet is then routed to its destination. The last router in the path to the packet's destination must rewrap the packet in a Layer 2 framing structure that's consistent with the LAN architecture in use at that remote destination.

Layer 3 only provides internetwork data transfers. Layer 4, the Transport Layer, provides the Layer 3 network mechanisms with end-to-end reliability and integrity. The Transport Layer may be required to guarantee error-free delivery of packets and sequencing of delivered packets as well as to provide quality-of-service guarantees. An example of a Layer 4 protocol is the Transmission Control Protocol (TCP). TCP is almost always referenced in combination with its Layer 3 counterpart, the Internet Protocol (IP), as *TCP/IP*.

The use of Layers 3 and 4 by applications to pass data to other computers/applications implies that the source and destination computers are not connected to the same LAN, regardless of how close or distant they are. The two different networks must be internetworked to support the requested transmission. Consequently, the communications mechanisms of Layer 2 are inadequate and must be augmented with Layer 3 addressing.

Although Layers 3 and 4 exist specifically for this purpose, applications can pass data to each other using protocols at these layers, even though they're connected to the same LAN and subnet. For example, if both the source and destination computers are connected to the same LAN, they may communicate satisfactorily using only Layer 2 network frames and protocols, or the applications that are passing data might require any of the higher-layer protocols' features to support their communications.

Two types of networking protocols operate at Layer 3: routed protocols and routing protocols. Routed protocols are those that encapsulate user information and data into packets and are responsible for transporting the packets to their destinations. Routing protocols are used between routers to determine available routes, communicate what is known about available routes, and forward routed protocol packets along those routes. Routing protocols are further examined in Chapter 10, "Wide Area Networking." This chapter focuses on the most common routed protocols.

The Internet Protocol, Version 4 (IPv4)

The Internet Protocol (IP) was developed approximately 20 years ago for the Department of Defense (DoD). The DoD needed a way to interconnect the various brands of proprietary computers, and their equally proprietary support networks, across a common internetwork. This was achieved by way of a layered protocol that insulated applications from networking hardware. This protocol uses a model that's slightly different from the OSI Reference Model. It's known as the *TCP/IP Model*.

Unlike the OSI Reference Model, the TCP/IP Model focuses more on delivering inter-connectivity than on rigidly adhering to functional layers. It does this by acknowledging the importance of a hierarchical arrangement of functions but still leaving protocol designers ample flexibility for implementation. Consequently, the OSI Reference Model is significantly better at explaining the mechanics of intercomputer communications, but TCP/IP has become the internetworking protocol of choice in the marketplace.

The flexibility of the TCP/IP Model, in comparison with the OSI Reference Model, is shown in Figure 4.3.

FIGURE 4.3

A comparison of the OSI Reference Model and the TCP/IP Model.

OSI Reference Model Layer Description	OSI Layer Number	TCP/IP Equivalent Layer Description
Application	7	Process/ Application
Presentation	6	
Session	5	Host-to-Host
Transport	4	
Network	3	Internet
Data Link	2	Network Access
Physical	1	

The TCP/IP Model, developed long after the protocol it explains, offers significantly more flexibility than its OSI counterpart because it emphasizes the hierarchical arrangement of functions rather than strict functional layering.

Dissecting TCP/IP

The TCP/IP model includes four functional layers: Network Access, Internet, Host-to-Host, and Process/Application. These four layers loosely correlate to the seven layers of the OSI Reference Model without compromising functionality.

The Process/Application Layer

The Process/Application Layer provides protocols for remote access and resource sharing. Familiar applications and protocols such as Telnet, FTP, SMTP, HTTP, and many others all reside and operate in this layer and depend on the functionality of the underlying layers.

The Host-to-Host Layer

The IP Host-to-Host Layer correlates loosely to the OSI Reference Model's Session and Transport Layers. It consists of two protocol entities: Transmission Control Protocol

(TCP) and User Datagram Protocol (UDP). A third entity is being defined to accommodate the increasingly transaction-oriented nature of the Internet. This protocol entity is tentatively called *Transaction Transmission Control Protocol* (T/TCP).

TCP provides a connection-oriented data transmission between two or more hosts, can support multiple data streams, and allows for flow and error control and even the reordering of packets that may have been received out of order.

The TCP protocol header is a minimum of 20 octets and contains the following fields:

- *TCP Source Port (16 bits)*. This field contains the number of the port that initiates the communications session. The source port and source IP address function as the packet's return address.

- *TCP Destination Port (16 bits)*. This field is the address of the port for which the transmission is destined. This port contains the interface address of the application on the recipient's computer to which the packet's data is passed.

- *TCP Sequence Number (32 bits)*. This sequence number is used by the receiving computer to reconstruct the fragmented data back into its original form. In a dynamically routed network, it's quite possible for some of the packets to take different routes and, consequently, arrive out of order. This sequencing field compensates for this inconsistency of delivery.

- *TCP Acknowledgment Number (32 bits)*. TCP uses a 32-bit acknowledgment (ACK) of the first octet of data contained in the next expected segment. TCP is able to calculate this number by incrementing the number of the last octet received by the number of octets in each TCP segment. The number used to identify each ACK is the sequence number of the packet being acknowledged.

- *Data Offset (4 bits)*. This field contains the size of the TCP header, measured in a 32-bit data structure known as a *word*.

- *Reserved (6 bits)*. This field is always set to zero. It's reserved for an as-yet unspecified future use.

- *Flags (6 bits)*. This field contains six 1-bit flags that enable the control functions of urgent field, acknowledgment of significant field, push, reset connection, synchronize sequence numbers, and finishing sending data.

- *Window Size (16 bits)*. This field is used by the destination machine to tell the source host how much data it's willing to accept per TCP segment.

- *Checksum (16 bits)*. The TCP header also contains an error-checking field known as a *Checksum*. The source host calculates a mathematical value based on the segment's contents. The destination host performs the same calculation. If the contents remained intact, the result of the two calculations is identical, thereby proving the validity of the data.

- *Padding*. Extra zeros are added to this field to ensure the TCP header is always a multiple of 32 bits.

The User Datagram Protocol (UDP) is IP's other Host-to-Host Layer protocol (which corresponds to the Transport Layer of the OSI Reference Model). UDP provides basic and low-overhead data transmissions known as *datagrams*. The simplicity of datagrams makes UDP inappropriate for some applications but perfect for more sophisticated applications that can provide their own connection-oriented functionality.

Alternatively, UDP can be used for exchanges of such data as broadcasted NetBIOS names, system messages, and so forth, because these exchanges do not require flow control, acknowledgments, reordering, or any of the functionality that TCP provides.

The UDP protocol header has the following structure:

- *UDP Source Port Number (16 bits)*. This field is the connection number on the source computer. The source port and source IP address function as the packet's return address.

- *UDP Destination Port Number (16 bits)*. This field is the connection number on the destination computer. The UDP destination port is used to forward a packet to the correct application, after the packet arrives at the intended destination machine.

- *UDP Checksum (16 bits)*. This field is an error-checking field that's calculated based on the contents of the segment. The destination computer performs the same mathematical function as the originating host. A discrepancy in the two calculated values indicates an error has occurred during the transmission of the packet.

- *UDP Message Length (16 bits)*. This field informs the destination computer of the size of the message. This provides another mechanism for the destination computer to use in determining the message's validity.

The major functional difference between TCP and UDP is reliability. TCP is highly reliable, whereas UDP is a simple "best effort" datagram-delivery mechanism. This fundamental difference results in vastly different uses of the two Host-to-Host Layer protocols.

The Internet Layer

The Internet Layer of IPv4 consists of all the protocols and procedures necessary to enable data communications between hosts to traverse multiple networks. The data-bearing packets must be routable. The Internet Protocol is responsible for making data packets routable.

The IP header has the following size and structure:

- *Version (4 bits)*. The first four bits of the IP header identify the operating version of IP (for example, version 4).

- *Internet Header Length (4 bits)*. The next four bits of the header contain the length of the header, expressed in multiples of 32.

- *Type of Service (8 bits)*. This field contains 1-bit flags that can be used to specify precedence, delay, throughput, and reliability parameters for the packet of data.

- *Total Length (16 bits)*. This field contains the total length of the IP datagram measured in octets. Valid values can range from 576 to 65,536 octets.

- *Identifier (16 bits)*. Each IP packet is given a unique identifier.

- *Flags (3 bits)*. The next field contains three 1-bit flags that indicate whether fragmentation of the packet is permitted and whether it's used.

- *Fragment Offset (8 bits)*. This field measures the offset of the fragmented contents relative to the beginning of the entire datagram. This value is measured in 64-bit increments.

- *Time to Live (TTL) (8 bits)*. The IP packet cannot be permitted to roam the WAN in perpetuity. It must be limited to a finite number of hops (see the following note). The TTL field is incremented by one for each hop the packet makes. After reaching its maximum limit, the packet is destroyed.

> **Note:** IP packets are forwarded across different networks by devices known as *routers*. Each router that a packet passes through is considered a hop. Establishing a maximum hop count ensures that packets do not loop continuously in a dynamically routed network.

- *Protocol (8 bits)*. This field identifies the protocol that follows the IP header, such as VINES, TCP, UDP, and so forth.

- *Checksum (16 bits)*. This is an error-checking field. The destination computer or any gateway nodes in the network may recompute the mathematical calculation on the packet's contents as the source computer did. If the data survived the trip intact, the results of these two calculations are identical. This field also informs the destination host of the amount of incoming data.

- *Source IP Address (32 bits)*. The *source address* is the IP address of the source computer.

- *Destination IP Address (32 bits)*. The *destination address* is the IP address of the destination computer.

- *Padding*. Extra zeros are added to this field to ensure the IP header is always a multiple of 32 bits.

These header fields reveal that IPv4's Internet Layer is inherently connectionless: The packet-forwarding devices in the network are free to determine the ideal path for each packet to take through the network. This layer also doesn't provide any of the acknowledgments, flow control, and sequencing functions of higher-level protocols such as TCP. It leaves such functions to those higher-level protocols.

The Internet Layer must also support other route-management functions beyond just IP's packet formatting. It must provide mechanisms for resolving Layer 2 addresses into Layer 3 addresses, and vice versa. These route-management functions are provided by peer protocols to IP. These routing protocols are described in Chapter 1, "A Networking Primer," and include Interior Gateway Protocol (IGP), Exterior Gateway Protocol (EGP), Address Resolution Protocol (ARP), Reverse Address Resolution Protocol (RARP), and Internet Control Message Protocol (ICMP).

Typical IPv4 Operation

The Application Layer places a header onto the data packet, identifying the destination host and port. The Host-to-Host Layer protocol (either TCP or UDP, depending on the application) breaks that block of data into smaller, more manageable pieces. Each piece has a TCP header prepended to it. This structure is known as a *TCP segment*.

The segment's header fields are populated appropriately, and the segment is passed to the Internet Layer. The Internet Layer adds the addressing, protocol type (TCP or UDP), and checksum information. If the segment was fragmented, the Internet Layer populates that field as well.

The destination machine performs the reverse of the operation just described. It receives the packets and passes them to its Host-to-Host Layer protocol for reassembly. If necessary, the packets are reordered into data segments that are passed up to the appropriate application.

IP Addressing Scheme

IPv4 uses a 32-bit binary addressing scheme to identify networks, network devices, and network-connected machines. These addresses, known as *IP addresses*, are strictly regulated by the Internet Network Information Center (InterNIC). Although it's entirely possible for a network administrator to arbitrarily select unregistered IP addresses, this practice should not be condoned. Computers having such spurious IP addresses can only function properly within the confines of their domain. Attempts to access the Internet are sure to demonstrate the ramifications of this short-sighted act. Results can be highly variable, depending on a wide variety of factors, but are sure to be unfavorable.

The five classes of IP addresses are each identified by an alphabetic character: Class A, B, C, D, and E. Each address consists of two parts: a network address and a host address. The five classes represent different compromises between the number of supportable networks and hosts. Although these addresses are binary, they're normally identified with a dotted decimal–style format (for example, 135.65.121.6) to facilitate human usage. The dots are used to separate the address's four octets.

> **Note:** *Dotted decimal notation* refers to the conversion of the binary address to the decimal (Base 10) number system. A dot (.) is used to separate the node and network numbers. For example, 100.99 refers to device 99 on network 100.

The five classes divide host and network addresses as follows:

- *Class A IP address*. The first bit of a Class A address is always 0. The next seven bits identify the network number. The last 24 bits (for example, three dotted decimal numbers) of a Class A address represent possible host addresses. The possible Class A addresses range from 1.0.0.0 to 126.0.0.0. Each Class A address can support 16,774,214 unique host addresses.

- *Class B IP address*. The first two bits of a Class B address are 10. The next 16 bits identify the network number, and the last 16 bits identify potential host addresses. The possible Class B addresses range from 128.1.0.0 to 191.254.0.0. Each Class B address can support 65,534 unique host addresses.

- *Class C IP address*. The first three bits of a Class C address are 110. The next 21 bits identify the network's number. The last octet is used for host addressing. The possible Class C addresses range from 192.0.1.0 to 223.255.254.0. Each Class C address can support 254 unique host addresses.

- *Class D IP address*. The first four bits of a Class D address are 1110. These addresses are used for multicasting but have seen only limited usage. A *multicast address* is a unique network address that directs packets with that destination address to predefined groups of IP addresses. Class D addresses range from 224.0.0.0 to 239.255.255.254.

Warning: The obscurity of the Class D IP address creates a potential disparity between reality and common perception. Although the IETF (Internet Engineering Task Force) has defined Classes C and D as separate and distinct in terms of their numeric ranges and their intended functionality, it's not uncommon to find the Class D address range lumped in with the Class C range. This is incorrect but apparently is being reinforced through certain networking certification curricula.

- *Class E IP address*. A Class E address has been defined but is reserved by the InterNIC for its own research. Therefore, no Class E addresses have been released for use on the Internet.

The large gaps between these address classes waste a considerable amount of potential addresses. Consider, for example, a medium-sized company that requires 300 IP addresses. A Class C address (254 addresses) is inadequate. Using two Class C addresses provides more than enough addresses but results in two separate domains within the company. Alternatively, stepping up to a Class B address provides all the needed addresses within a single domain, but wastes 65,234 addresses.

Fortunately, this is no longer the case. A new interdomain routing protocol known as *Classless Interdomain Routing* (CIDR) has been developed to enable multiple smaller address classes to function as a single routing domain.

IP addressing requires each machine to have its own unique address. Subnet masks can compensate for the tremendous gaps between address classes by customizing the length of the host and/or network addresses. These two numbers are used to route any given IP datagram to its destination.

Because TCP/IP is capable of supporting multiple sessions from a single host, it must then provide a way of addressing specific communications programs that may operate on each host. TCP/IP does so with port numbers. The IETF has assigned some of the more common applications their own well-known port numbers. These numbers are reliably constant, per application, from host to host. Other applications are simply assigned an available port number.

IPv4 Conclusion

IPv4 is almost 20 years old. Since its inception, the Internet has experienced several significant changes that have diminished IP's effectiveness as a universal interconnectivity protocol. Perhaps the most significant of these changes has been the commercialization of the Internet. This has brought with it an unprecedented growth in the Internet's user population and a shift in its demographics. This, in turn, has created the tandem need for more addresses and Internet Layer support for new types of services. IPv4's limitations have been driving the development of a completely new version of the protocol. This new version is called *Internet Protocol, version 6* (IPv6) but is also commonly referred to as the *next generation of Internet Protocol* (IPng).

The Internet Protocol, Version 6 (IPv6)

IPv6 is designed to be a simple, forward-compatible upgrade to the existing version of IP. This upgrade is also intended to resolve all the weaknesses that IPv4 is currently manifesting, including the shortage of available IP addresses, the inability to accommodate time-sensitive traffic, and the lack of Network Layer security.

> **Note:** IPv6 was originally referred to as IP: The Next Generation (or IPng). The name was probably inspired by science fiction. As the specification was being developed, its name was changed to IP, version 6 (IPv6). This name change may or may not be reflected on certification examinations.

In addition to these issues, routing is also driving the development and deployment of the new IP protocol. IPv4 is hampered by its 32-bit address architecture, its two-level addressing hierarchy, and its address classes. This two-level addressing hierarchy (host and domain name) simply does not allow construction of efficient address hierarchies that can be aggregated by routers on the scale that today's global Internet requires.

The next generation of IP—commonly known as IPng but more correctly identified as IPv6—resolves all these issues. It offers a vastly expanded addressing scheme to support the continued expansion of the Internet and an improved capability to aggregate routes on a large scale.

IPv6 also supports numerous other features, such as real-time audio and/or video transmissions, host mobility, end-to-end security through Internet Layer encryption and authentication, as well as auto-configuration and auto-reconfiguration. It's expected that these services will provide ample incentive for migration as soon as IPv6-capable products become available. Many of these features still require additional standardization, so it would be premature to expound on them at any great length.

The one aspect of IPv6 that can, and should, be expounded upon is its addressing. IPv4's 32-bit address length gave the protocol a theoretical capability to address about 4 billion devices (2 to the 32nd power). Inefficient subnet masking techniques, among other wasteful practices, have squandered this resource.

IPv6 uses a 128-bit address and is theoretically capable of 2 to the 96th power times the size of the IPv4 address space. This results in 340,282,366,920,938,463,463,374,607,431,768,211,456 mathematically possible addresses. Only about 15 percent of this potential address space is currently allocated. The remainder is reserved for unspecified future use.

In reality, the assignment and routing of addresses requires the creation of hierarchies. Hierarchies can reduce the number of potential addresses but increase the efficiency of IPv6-capable routing protocols. One practical implication of the IPv6 address length is that Domain Name Service (DNS) becomes an absolute necessity, and not the luxury it had been in the IPv4 network environment.

Note: *Domain Name Service* is the network utility that's responsible for translating mnemonic host names (such as www.microsoft.com) into numeric IP addresses.

As significant as the increased potential address space is, even greater flexibility is afforded with IPv6's new address structures. IPv6 dispenses with the previous class-based addressing. Instead, it recognizes three kinds of unicast addresses, replaces the former Class D address with a new multicast address format, and introduces a new address type. You must understand these new addressing structures prior to undertaking an IPv6 migration.

IPv6 Unicast Address Structures

Unicast addressing provides connectivity from one endpoint to another endpoint. IPv6 supports several forms of unicast addresses. They're described in the following sections.

Internet Service Provider (ISP) Unicast Address

Whereas IPv4 presumed clusters of users requiring connectivity, IPv6 provides a unicast address format designed specifically for use by Internet Service Providers (ISPs) to connect individual users to the Internet. These provider-based unicast addresses offer unique addresses for individuals or small groups that access the Internet through a provider. The architecture of the address provides for efficient aggregation of routes in an environment characterized by individual users, as opposed to large concentrations of users.

The ISP unicast address format is as follows:

- A three-bit ISP unicast address flag that's always set to 010
- A Registry ID field that's n bits in length
- A Provider ID field that's m bits in length
- A Subscriber ID field that's o bits in length
- A Subnet ID field that's p bits in length
- An Interface ID field that's 125 $(n + m + o + p)$ bits in length

The alphabetic characters n, m, o, and p denote variable-length fields. The length of the interface ID is 125 bits (the maximum length of an IPv6 address is 128 bits, minus the 3-bit flag) minus the sum of these variable fields.

An example of this type of address is 010:0:0:0:0:x, where x can be any number. Given that much of the new address space has yet to be allocated, these addresses will contain lots of zeros. Therefore, groups of zeros may be shortened with a double colon (::). This shorthand notation is 010::x.

The other unicast address types are designed for local use. Local use addresses can be assigned to networked devices within a standalone intranet or to devices on an intranet that needs to have access to the Internet.

Link-Local Use

The link-local address is for use on a single link for purposes such as auto-address configuration, neighbor discovery, and when no routers are present. Link-local addresses have the following format:

- A 10-bit Local Use flag that's always set to 1111111011
- A reserved, unnamed field that's n bits in length but defaulted to a value of 0
- An Interface ID field that's (118 minus n) bits in length

The interface ID can be the MAC address of an Ethernet network interface card. MAC addresses, being theoretically unique addresses, can be concatenated with standard IP address prefixes to form unique addresses for mobile or transitory users. An example of a Link-Local Use address with a MAC address is 1111111011:0:*mac_address*.

Site-Local Use Unicast Address

Site-local addresses are designed for use in a single site. They may be used for sites or organizations that are not connected to the global Internet. They do not need to request or "steal" an address prefix from the global Internet address space. IPv6 site-local addresses can be used instead. When the organization connects to the global Internet, it can then form unique global addresses by replacing the site-local prefix with a subscriber prefix that contains registry, provider, and subscriber identification.

Site-local addresses have the following format:

- A 10-bit Local Use flag that's always set to 1111111011
- A reserved, unnamed field that's *n* bits in length but defaulted to a value of 0
- A Subnet ID field that's *m* bits in length
- An Interface ID field that's 118 ($n + m$) bits in length

An example of a site-local address is 1111111011:0:*subnet*:*interface*.

IPv6 Transitional Unicast Address Structures

Two special IPv6 unicast addresses have been defined as transition mechanisms to enable hosts and routers to dynamically route IPv6 packets over IPv4 network infrastructures, and vice versa.

IPv4-Compatible IPv6 Unicast Address

The first unicast address type is called an *IPv4-compatible IPv6 address*. This transitional unicast address can be assigned to IPv6 nodes and contain an IPv4 address in the last 32 bits. These addresses have the following format:

80 Bits	*16 Bits*	*32 Bits*
000...0000	00...00	IPv4 address

IPv4-Mapped IPv6 Unicast Address

A second, similar type of IPv6 address that also contains an IPv4 address in its last 32 bits is known as an *IPv4-mapped IPv6 address*. This address is constructed by a dual protocol router and enables IPv4-only nodes to tunnel through IPv6 network infrastructures. The only difference between IPv4-mapped IPv6 addresses and IPv4-compatible IPv6 addresses is that IPv4-mapped addresses are constructs only. They're built automatically by dual-protocol routers and cannot be assigned to any nodes. This address is formatted as follows:

80 Bits	*16 Bits*	*32 Bits*
000...0000	FF...FF	IPv4 address

Both the IPv4-mapped and the IPv4-compatible unicast addresses are essential to tunneling. *Tunneling* enables the transport of packets through an otherwise incompatible network region by wrapping those packets in an externally acceptable framework.

IPv6 Anycast Address Structures

The *anycast address*, introduced in IPv6, is a single value assigned to more than one interface. Typically, these interfaces belong to different devices. A packet sent to an anycast address is routed to only one device. It's sent to the nearest interface having that address, as defined by the routing protocols' measure of distance. For example, a World Wide Web (WWW) site may be mirrored on several servers. By assigning an anycast address to these servers, requests for connectivity to that WWW site are automatically routed to only one server: the server nearest the user.

> **Note:** In a routed environment, the "nearest" interface might not be the one that's closest. Routers use a surprisingly wide array of metrics to calculate routes. Identifying the nearest one depends on the actual routing protocol used as well as that protocol's metrics.

Anycast addresses are formed from the unicast address space and may take the form of any unicast address type. Anycast addresses are formed simply by assigning the same unicast address to more than one interface.

IPv6 Multicast Address Structures

Multicasting was supported in IPv4 but required the use of obscure Class D addressing. IPv6 eliminates Class D addresses in favor of a new address format that permits trillions of possible multicast group codes. Each group code identifies two or more packet recipients. The scope of a particular multicast address is flexible. Each address can be confined to a single system, restricted within a specific site, associated with a particular network link, or distributed globally.

It should be noted that IP broadcasts, too, have been eliminated in favor of the new multicasting address format.

IPv6 Conclusion

Despite the potential benefits of IPv6, the migration from IPv4 is not risk free. The extension of the address length from 32 to 128 bits automatically limits interoperability between IPv4 and IPv6. IPv4-only nodes cannot interoperate with IPv6-only nodes because the address architectures are not forward compatible. This business risk, in combination with the ongoing evolution of IPv4, will likely forestall the acceptance of IPv6 in the marketplace.

Novell's IPX/SPX

The Novell protocol suite is named after its two primary protocols: Internet Packet Exchange (IPX) and Sequenced Packet Exchange (SPX). This proprietary protocol stack is based on Xerox's Network Systems (XNS) protocol used with first generation Ethernets. IPX/SPX became prominent during the early 1980's as an integral part of Novell's NetWare network operating system (NOS). NetWare became the *de facto* standard NOS of first generation LANs.

IPX is much like IP. It's a connectionless datagram protocol that does not require or provide an acknowledgment for each packet transmitted. IPX also relies on SPX in the same way that IP relies on TCP for sequencing and other Layer 4 connection-oriented services. The IPX/SPX protocol stack is compared to the OSI Reference Model in Figure 4.4, and explained in the next section "Dissecting IPX/SPX."

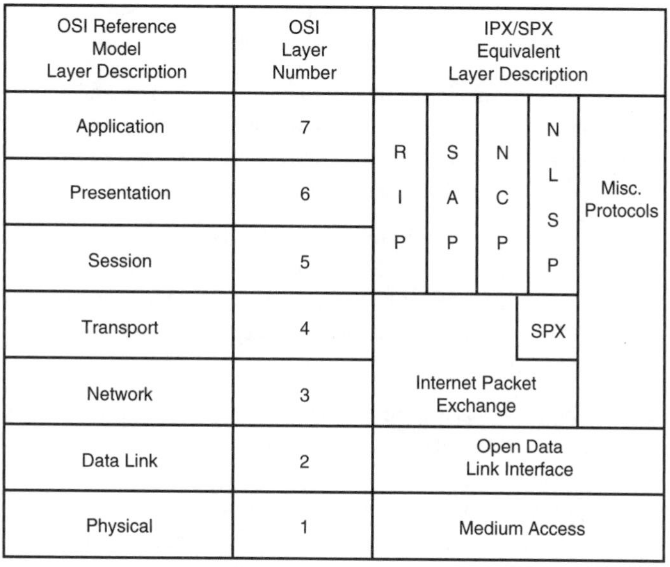

FIGURE 4.4

A comparison of the OSI Reference Model and IPX/SPX.

OSI Reference Model Layer Description	OSI Layer Number	IPX/SPX Equivalent Layer Description				
Application	7	R	S	N	N	Misc. Protocols
Presentation	6	I	A	C	L	
Session	5	P	P	P	S	
					S	
					P	
Transport	4				SPX	
Network	3	Internet Packet Exchange				
Data Link	2	Open Data Link Interface				
Physical	1	Medium Access				

Novell's IPX and SPX protocols provide functionality equivalent to OSI Layers 3 and 4, respectively. The full suite of IPX/SPX protocols provide the functionality of the other OSI layers in four layers.

Dissecting IPX/SPX

The IPX/SPX protocol stack includes four functional layers: Application, Internet, Data Link, and Medium Access. These four layers loosely correlate to the seven layers of the OSI Reference Model without compromising functionality.

Application Layer

Novell's Application Layer encompasses the Application, Presentation, and Session Layers of the OSI Model, although some of its application protocols extend as far down the stack as the OSI Network Layer. The primary Application Layer protocol in this stack is the NetWare Core Protocol (NCP). NCP can interface directly with both SPX and IPX. NCP is used for printing, file sharing, email, and directory access.

Other Application Layer protocols include the Routing Information Protocol (RIP), the proprietary Service Advertising Protocol (SAP), and the NetWare Link services Protocol (NLSP), among others.

RIP is the default routing protocol for NetWare. It's a distance-vector routing protocol that uses only two metrics: ticks and hops. A *tick* is a measure of time, and a *hop count*, as explained earlier in this chapter, is the running tally of routers that have handled the routed packet. These two metrics are the basis for IPX routing path decisions. Ticks are the primary metric for determining paths. Hops are only used as a tie breaker in the event of two or more paths having the same tick value.

RIP is a very simple and mature routing protocol. In addition to its limited number of distance-vector metrics, it suffers from a high level of network overhead. This overhead is incurred because RIP routing table updates are broadcast every 60 seconds. This rate of update can have adverse affects on large or very busy networks.

SAP is a unique, proprietary protocol that Novell has successfully used to enhance the client/server relationship. Servers use SAP to automatically broadcast their available services throughout the network immediately after becoming active on the network. They periodically make SAP broadcasts to keep clients and other servers informed of their status and services.

SAP broadcasts generated by a server advertise that server's status and services. These broadcasts include the server's name and type, its operational status, as well as its network, node, and socket numbers. Routers can store information from a SAP broadcast and propagate it to other network segments. Clients can also initiate a SAP request when they need a specific service. Their request is broadcast throughout the network segment. Hosts can then respond and provide the client with enough SAP information to determine whether the service is available within a reasonable distance.

Unfortunately, SAP is a mature protocol that's becoming increasingly ill-suited to functioning in contemporary networks. As with RIP, service advertisements occur every 60 seconds. On today's large, flat, switched LANs, this degree of broadcasting can be problematic.

The newest Application Layer protocol is NetWare Link Services Protocol (NLSP). NLSP is a link-state routing protocol that Novell intends to use as a replacement for the aging RIP and SAP protocols. NLSP only updates routes when changes have been made.

Internet Layer Protocols

The Internet Layer of IPX/SPX correlates loosely to both the Network and Transport Layers of the OSI Reference Model. IPX is predominantly a Layer 3 (Network Layer) protocol, although it's capable of directly interfacing with the Application Layer. SPX is distinctly a Layer 4 (Transport Layer) protocol and cannot directly interface with the Data Link Layer's ODI (Open Datalink Interface). It must pass data through IPX and let IPX interface with the ODI. IPX and SPX function as sublayer protocols within a common Internet Layer.

SPX is connection oriented and can be used to transmit data between a client and server, two servers, or even two clients. As with TCP, SPX provides reliability to IPX transmissions by managing the connection and providing flow control, error checking, and packet sequencing.

The SPX header has the following size and structure:

- *Connection Control (8 bits)*. The first octet of the SPX header provides four two-bit flags that control the bidirectional flow of data across an SPX connection.
- *Datastream Type (8 bits)*. The next field of the header define the type of datastream.
- *Source Connection Identification (16 bits)*. This field identifies the process responsible for initiating the connection.
- *Destination Connection Identification (16 bits)*. This field is used to identify the process that accepted the inbound SPX connection request.
- *Sequence Number (16 bits)*. This field provides the destination host's SPX protocol with a count of packets transmitted. This sequential numbering can be used to reorder the received packets if they arrive out of sequence.
- *Acknowledgment Number (16 bits)*. This field indicates the next expected segment.
- *Allocation Number (16 bits)*. This field is used to track the number of packets sent, but not acknowledged, by the intended recipient.
- *Data*. The last field in the SPX header contains the data. Up to 534 octets of data may be transmitted per SPX packet.

Novell's Network Layer protocol is IPX. IPX provides a connectionless "best effort" datagram-delivery service. It prepares SPX (or other protocols') packets for delivery across multiple networks by prepending an IPX header to them. This new structure is called an *IPX datagram*. This datagram's header contains all the information necessary to route the packets to their destinations, regardless of where that might be.

The IPX header is 11 octets long and has the following structure:

- *Checksum (16 bits)*. The IPX header begins with a legacy field that exists solely to provide backward compatibility with its ancestral XNS protocol. XNS used this field for error checking, but IPX defaults this field to FFFFH and trusts higher-level protocols to detect (and correct) any transmission errors.

- *Packet Length (16 bits)*. This field defines the length of the IPX datagram, including the header and data. Packet length is checked to verify packet integrity.

- *Transport Control (8 bits)*. This field is used by routers during the forwarding of the datagram. IPX sets it to 0 prior to transmission. Each router that receives and forwards the datagram increments this field by one.

- *Packet Type (8 bits)*. This field identifies the type of packet that's embedded in the IPX datagram. This field enables the destination host to pass the contents to the next appropriate protocol layer. Types can include RIP, NCP, SPX, error, and so forth.

- *Destination Network Number (32 bits)*. This field identifies the network number of the destination node.

- *Destination Node (48 bits)*. This field contains the node number of the destination machine.

- *Destination Socket Number (16 bits)*. Because IPX allows for multiple simultaneous connections to one system, it's essential to identify the socket number of the process or program receiving the packets. This field provides this information.

- *Source Network Number (32 bits)*. This field identifies the network number of the source node.

- *Source Node Address (48 bits)*. This field contains the node number of the source machine.

- *Source Socket Number (16 bits)*. This field identifies the socket number of the process or program sending the packets.

Typical IPX/SPX Operation

SPX creates and maintains a connection-oriented bit stream between two networked devices. The protocol accepts large blocks of data from higher-level protocols and breaks them into more manageable pieces that are up to 534 octets long. The SPX header is prepended to the data to create SPX data segments. These segments are passed to the Internet Layer protocol, IPX. IPX stuffs these segments into the data field of its packets and populates all the fields in the IPX header.

These header fields include the network addressing, length, checksum, and other header information, before the packet is passed on to the Data Link Layer.

Figure 4.5 shows the positioning of the IPX and SPX headers within an 802.3 Ethernet frame. This is the structure used to pass data between the two sublayers of Novell's Internet Layer.

FIGURE 4.5

The structure of an 802.3 Ethernet frame encapsulating an IPX/SPX payload. See Chapter 6, "Ethernet," for an explanation of an Ethernet packet's structure.

7-Octet Preamble	1-Octet Start of Frame Delimiter	6-Octet Destination Address	6-Octet Origination Address	2-Octet Length Field	30-Octet IPX Header	Variable Length IPX Header	Variable Length Data Field (>46 octets < 1482)	4-Octet Frame Check Sequence

The destination machine performs the reverse of the operation just described. It receives the packets and passes them to its SPX protocol for reassembly. If necessary, the packets are reordered into data segments that are passed up to the appropriate application.

Data Link and Medium Access Layers

NetWare's equivalents of the OSI Physical and Data Link Layers are the Medium Access and Data Link Layers. The Data Link Layer is directly compatible with the Open Data-Link Interface (ODI) standard. Similarly, the Medium Access Layer is directly compatible with all common, standardized media-access protocols.

This low-level adherence to open industry standards enables NetWare and the IPX/SPX protocol stack to be implemented almost universally.

IPX Addressing

IPX addresses are 10 octets (80 bits) long. This is significantly larger than IPv4's 32-bit address but less than IPv6's 128-bit address. Each address is comprised of two components: a network number up to 32 bits in length and a 48-bit node number. These numbers are expressed in dotted hexadecimal notation. For example, 1a2b.0000.3c4d.5e6d could be a valid IPX address, where the 1a2b represents the network number and 0000.3c4d.5e6d is the node number.

IPX addresses, too, can be fabricated by a network administrator. However, fabricated numbers run the risk of having address conflicts when they're taken into an internetwork. Invention of network numbers places the burden of maintaining and managing all such fabricated numbers on the network administrator. The better approach is to obtain registered IPX network numbers from Novell.

The universally assigned address (MAC address) on the network interface card (NIC) is usually used as the IPX host number. Given that these addresses are unique (at least in theory and to the extent of the manufacturer's quality assurance), this provides a convenient, unique host numbering.

As with IP, IPX is capable of supporting multiple simultaneous sessions. This creates the need for identifying the specific process or program that's communicating on any given session. This identification is achieved through the use of a 16-bit "socket" number in the IPX header. This socket number is analogous to TCP/IP's port number.

IPX/SPX Conclusion

Novell has watched the market share of its proprietary IPX/SPX protocol stack plummet under competitive pressure. As open protocol stacks such as OSI, IP, and others became available, IPX/SPX suffered. Commercially available office automation software bundles also cut into Novell's sales. Although responsible for its initial success, Novell's proprietary, tightly coupled series of products has become a liability in a marketplace that values openness and interoperability.

Novell has demonstrated its commitment to regaining its lost prominence by making IPv6 its default protocol for future versions of NetWare beginning with NetWare 5. To successfully implement this change of strategy, Novell must ensure the compatibility of IPv6 and IPX/SPX. To achieve this goal, Novell has worked closely with the Internet Engineering Task Force (IETF) during the design of IPv6. This has resulted in numerous IPX services becoming integral to IPv6.

Having "set the stage" for its future, Novell now must ensure a seamless migration of its current protocol stack and application suite to this new environment. More important, it needs to provide value-adding products and services using an open network platform. Novell's vision for the future is to provide Network Directory Services (NDS) and related products for two customer bases: the Internet community and corporate intranet communities.

NDS provides a single, global, logical view of all network services and resources. This enables you to access network services and resources with a single login, regardless of your location or the location of the resources. More about NDS and other Directory Services can be found in Chapter 18, "Directory Services."

Apple Corporation's AppleTalk Protocol Suite

As Apple computers increased in popularity, and their users became increasingly sophisticated in their use, the need to network them together became inescapable. It's no surprise that the network Apple developed is as user friendly as its computers. AppleTalk, the name for Apple's networking protocol stack, and its necessary hardware are included with every computer Apple sells.

Connecting to the network can be as simple as plugging in the network connection and powering up the Apple computer. The AppleTalk network is a peer-to-peer network that provides basic functionality such as file and printer sharing. Unlike client/server networks, there are no hardened definitions constraining the functionality of a peer-to-peer network. Each machine can act simultaneously as both a client and a server.

AppleTalk has also been embraced by many other operating system (OS) manufacturers. It's not uncommon to find support for the AppleTalk protocol stack available on non-Apple computers. This enables customers to use AppleTalk and Apple computers to create or join existing non-Apple client/server networks.

Dissecting AppleTalk

The AppleTalk protocol stack contains five functional layers: Application, Zone Information, Network, Datagram Delivery, and Network Access. Apple's AppleTalk protocol stack closely follows the functionality of the OSI Reference Model on its Network Transport and Session Layers. The Physical and Data Link Layers are collapsed into numerous, frame-specific, individual layers. Similarly, AppleTalk integrates the Application and Presentation Layers into a singular Application Layer. Figure 4.6 illustrates this functional relationship.

FIGURE 4.6
A comparison of the OSI Reference Model and AppleTalk.

OSI Reference Model Layer Description	OSI Layer Number	AppleTalk Equivalent Layer Description
Application	7	Application
Presentation	6	Application
Session	5	Session
Transport	4	Transport
Network	3	Datagram Delivery
Data Link	2	Network Access
Physical	1	Network Access

Apple's AppleTalk protocol stack closely follows the functionality of the OSI Reference Model on its Network, Transport, and Session Layers, but collapses the other four layers into just two.

The AppleTalk Application Layer

AppleTalk combines the functionality of the OSI Reference Model's Application and Presentation layers into a single Application Layer. Because AppleTalk is a fairly simple protocol stack, there is only a single protocol occupying this layer. It is the AppleTalk Filing Protocol (AFP). AFP provides network file services to applications that exist separate from the protocol stack, such as electronic mail, print queuing, and so forth. Any application running on an Apple computer must pass through AFP if it needs to send or receive information across the network.

The AppleTalk Session Layer

AppleTalk's version of the OSI Session Layer contains five primary protocols that provide such services as full-duplex transmission, logical name-to-address resolution, printer access, packet sequencing, and others.

The first Session Layer protocol is the AppleTalk Data Stream Protocol (ADSP). ADSP provides full-duplex connection-oriented services in a highly reliable manner by establishing a logical connection (session) between the two communicating processes on client machines. ADSP also manages this connection by providing flow control services, sequence management, and acknowledgment of transmitted packets. ADSP uses socket addresses to establish this process-to-process logical connection. After the connection is established, the two systems can exchange data.

Another AppleTalk Session Layer protocol is AppleTalk Session Protocol (ASP). This protocol provides reliable data delivery using sequence-oriented session management and the transport services of AppleTalk Transport Protocol (ATP), a Transport Layer protocol.

The AppleTalk Update-Based Routing Protocol (AURP) is used in larger AppleTalk networks. AURP is used primarily for route management and information exchange between routing devices, particularly exterior gateway routers.

AppleTalk's Session Layer also includes the Printer Access Protocol (PAP). Although PAP was originally developed for managing access to networked printers, it can be used for a variety of data exchanges. It provides a bidirectional session between two devices, complete with flow control and sequence management.

The last of the AppleTalk Session Layer protocols is the Zone Information Protocol (ZIP). ZIP provides a mechanism for logically grouping individual networked devices using user-friendly names. These logical groups are called *zones*. In an extended network, computers can span multiple networks but still be logically grouped into a zone. However, in small, nonextended networks, only one zone can be defined.

ZIP uses the Name Binding Protocol (NBP), a Transport Layer protocol, to translate these names into network and node numbers. It also uses the ATP protocol for delivery of zone information updates.

These five Session Layer protocols provide AppleTalk clients with logical connections and data transfers between computers, regardless of how near or far apart they are.

The AppleTalk Transport Layer

The AppleTalk Transport Layer offers transport services to the layers above it. There are four distinct protocols in this layer. The most frequently used protocol in this layer is the AppleTalk Transport Protocol (ATP).

ATP provides a reliable, loss-free mechanism for packet delivery between two computers. ATP uses the sequence and acknowledgment fields in the packet header to ensure packets are not lost en route to their destinations.

Another significant AppleTalk Transport Layer protocol is the Name Binding Protocol (NBP). As previously indicated, NBP enables ZIP to translate user-friendly names into actual addresses. NBP performs the actual translation of zone names into network and node addresses. NBP contains four basic functions: registration, lookup, confirmation, and deletion of names:

- *Name registration*. Name registration registers a unique logical name in an NBP registry database.

- *Name lookup*. Name lookup is provided to a computer that requests another computer's address. This request is made and resolved transparently. If the request is made using an object name, NBP converts that name to a numeric address. NBP always attempts to resolve such requests by looking at local node numbers. If no match is found, it broadcasts a request to other internetworked AppleTalk networks. If a match still cannot be found, the request times out and the requestor receives an error message.

- *Name confirmation*. Confirmation requests are used to verify object-address relationships.

- *Name deletion*. Devices on any network are periodically shut down or removed. When this happens, a name deletion request is sent, and object name-to-addressing tables are automatically updated.

AppleTalk Echo Protocol (AEP) is another Transport Layer protocol. It's used to determine the accessibility of a system and for computing the Round Trip Transmit (RTT) time.

The last Transport Layer protocol is AppleTalk's Routing Table Maintenance Protocol (RTMP). Because AppleTalk uses routed protocols in its Network Layer, it must provide for management of routing tables. RTMP provides routers with content for their routing tables.

The AppleTalk Datagram Delivery Layer

AppleTalk's Datagram Delivery Layer, directly analogous to OSI's Layer 3 (Network Layer), provides connectionless, packetized datagram delivery. This is the basis for establishing communications and delivering data over an AppleTalk network. This layer is also responsible for providing the dynamic addressing of networked nodes as well as MAC address resolution for IEEE 802 networks.

The primary protocol in this layer is the Datagram Delivery Protocol (DDP). DDP provides best-effort data transmission in a connectionless fashion across multiple networks. It adapts its header types, depending upon the intended destination. The basic components remain constant; additional fields are added, as needed.

Datagrams that are to be delivered locally (in other words, on the same subnetwork) use the "short header" format. Datagrams that require routing to other subnetworks use the "extended header" format. The extended format contains network addresses and a hop counter field.

The DDP header contains the following fields:

- *Hop Count.* This field contains a counter that's incremented by one for each router device the packet travels across. Hop count is only used in the extended header.

- *Datagram Length.* This field contains the length of the datagram and can be used to determine whether it was damaged in transit.

- *DDP Checksum.* This is an optional field. When used, it provides a more robust form of error detection than simply checking the length of a datagram does. Checksum verification detects whether the contents were changed even slightly, regardless of whether the length of the datagram was changed.

- *Source Socket Number.* This field identifies the communicating process of the machine that initiated the connection.

- *Destination Socket Number.* This field identifies the communicating process of the machine that responded to the connection request.

- *Source Address.* This field contains the network and node numbers of the originating computer. This field is only used in the extended header format, and it enables routers to forward datagrams across multiple subnetworks.

- *Destination Address.* This field contains the network and node numbers of the destination computer. This field is only used in the extended header format and enables routers to forward datagrams across multiple subnetworks.

- *DDP Type.* This field identifies the upper-layer protocol that's encapsulated in the datagram. It's used by the destination computer's Transport Layer to identify the appropriate protocol to which it should pass the contents.

- *Data.* This field contains the data being transmitted. It can vary in size from 0 to 586 octets.

The Datagram Delivery Layer also contains a protocol that's used to resolve node addresses into MAC addresses for machines connected to IEEE 802 networks. This protocol is the AppleTalk Address Resolution Protocol (AARP). AARP can also be used to determine the node address for any given station. AARP stores its information in the Address Mapping Table (AMT). Due to the dynamic assignment of node numbers, the table used by AARP is constantly and automatically being updated.

The AppleTalk Network Access Layer

AppleTalk's Network Access Layer provides the functionality of the OSI Reference Model's Physical and Data Link Layers. This functionality is integrated into frame-specific sublayers. For example, EtherTalk is a Network Access Layer protocol that provides all the OSI Physical and Data Link Layer functionality into a single sublayer. This sublayer enables AppleTalk to be encapsulated in an 802.3-compliant Ethernet framing structure.

There are similar AppleTalk sublayers for Token Ring (known as *TokenTalk*) and for FDDI (known as *FDDITalk*). These protocols are called *Access Protocols* because of the physical network access services they offer.

EtherTalk uses a line-access protocol known as *EtherTalk Link Access Protocol* (ELAP) to package data and place the 802.3-compliant frames onto the physical medium. This line-access protocol naming convention and functionality holds true for the remainder of the access protocols. For example, TokenTalk relies on the TokenTalk Link Access Protocol (TLAP).

In addition to access protocols that conform to industry standards, Apple offers a proprietary local area network protocol in its Network Access Layer. This protocol is known as LocalTalk. LocalTalk operates at 230Kbps over twisted pair wiring. It uses, predictably, the LocalTalk Link Access Protocols (LLAP) to assemble frames and place them onto the network. LLAP also includes mechanisms for medium access management, data link–level addressing, data encapsulation, and bit representation for frame transmission.

The AppleTalk Addressing Scheme

The AppleTalk addressing scheme consists of two parts: the network number and the node number.

Network numbers are usually 16 bits long, although unary numbering may be used for nonextended or very small extended networks. These numbers must be defined by the network administrator and used by AppleTalk to route packets between the different networks. The network number 0 is reserved by the protocol for use in connecting new network nodes for the first time. The network number must have a value between 00000001 and FFFFFFFF.

Node numbers are eight-bit addresses consisting of four hexadecimal numbers. The valid range of addresses for hosts, printers, routers, and other devices is from 1 to 253. Node numbers 0, 254, and 255, although mathematically possible within an 8-bit binary address, are reserved by AppleTalk for use on extended networks. All node numbering is done dynamically by AppleTalk's Data Link Layer.

AppleTalk addresses are expressed in dotted decimal notation. As explained previously in this chapter, the binary address is converted to the decimal (Base 10) number system, and a dot (.) is used to separate the node and network numbers. For example, 100.99 refers to device 99 on network 100. The leading zeroes are suppressed.

AppleTalk Conclusion

AppleTalk is a proprietary protocol stack designed expressly for networking Apple's Personal Computers. Its future is directly tied to the fortunes of Apple Corporation and the trajectories of its technologies. As with Novell's proprietary stack, the Physical and Data Link Layers are used to provide compatibility with networking technologies based on established standards. One exception to this is a proprietary LocalTalk Physical Layer that can interconnect Apple computers using twisted pair wiring at up to 230Kbps.

NetBEUI

One last protocol that's worth examining is NetBEUI. This unwieldy name is part abbreviation and part acronym. It stands for NetBIOS (which is an abbreviation for *Network Basic Input/Output System*) Extended User Interface. NetBEUI was developed by IBM and introduced to the marketplace in 1985. It's a relatively small but efficient LAN communications protocol.

IBM's vision for distributed computing at that time predicted the segmentation of LANs based on the need to share work. The individual segments would service a community related by its work processes. Any data that needed to be accessed, but was outside this segment, could be retrieved using some type of application gateway. Given this origin, it's not surprising to find that NetBEUI is at its best in small LANs. This vision also explains why NetBEUI is not routable.

This protocol spans Layers 3 and 4 of the OSI Reference Model. Figure 4.7 presents this comparison.

FIGURE 4.7

A comparison of the OSI Reference Model and NetBEUI.

OSI Reference Model Layer Description	OSI Layer Number	
Application	7	
Presentation	6	
Session	5	
Transport	4	NetBEUI
Network	3	NetBEUI
Data Link	2	
Physical	1	

As evident from Figure 4.7, NetBEUI establishes communications between two computers and provides the mechanisms to ensure reliable delivery and sequencing of data.

Microsoft recently released NetBEUI 3.0. This release is significant for several reasons. First, NetBEUI 3.0 is more tolerant of slower transmission facilities than previous versions. This version is also completely self-tuning. The most significant change made to NetBEUI in release 3.0 is the elimination of NetBEUI. Yes, you read that right. The name was kept so as not to confuse users.

NetBEUI was replaced with the NetBIOS Frame (NBF) protocol in Microsoft's network operating systems. Both NetBEUI and NBF are closely related with NetBIOS. Consequently, NetBEUI 3.0 (NBF) remains completely compatible and interoperable with Microsoft's earlier versions of NetBEUI.

> **Warning:** NetBEUI, regardless of which version, is integral to Microsoft's network operating systems. If you attempt to run Windows NT 3.x (or higher), Windows for Workgroups 3.11, or even LAN Manager 2.x without NetBEUI installed, your computer cannot communicate.

NetBEUI Conclusion

NetBEUI is a Microsoft-specific LAN transport protocol only. It's not routable. Consequently, its implementations are limited to Layer 2 domains that are homogeneously populated with computers that use Microsoft operating systems. Although this is becoming less and less of a handicap, it does effectively limit computing architectures and technology applications.

The advantages of using NetBEUI are as follows:

- Computers using Microsoft networking software or operating systems can actually communicate.
- NetBEUI is completely self-tuning and runs best in small LAN segments.
- NetBEUI enjoys minimal memory requirements.
- NetBEUI provides excellent protection against and recovery from transmission errors.

NetBEUI's limitations are that it cannot be routed and does not perform well over WANs.

Peter's Principle: Protocol Protocol, or What You Need to Know

Although it's very important that you understand the workings of NetBEUI, AppleTalk, and IPX/SPX, you should note that both Microsoft and Novell have moved to IP as the default protocol in their latest network operating systems (Windows 2000 and NetWare 5), while retaining the possibility of using the older protocols for both backward compatibility and the use of older, no longer supported clients. Knowing IP will prepare you for the future's networks, but knowing the relationship between IP and these older protocols will help you move today's networks into the future.

Summary

Network protocols reside above the Data Link Layer. When they're properly designed and developed, they're decoupled from LAN architectures (described in Part II, "Building Local Area Networks") and provide end-to-end management of transmissions across LAN domains.

This chapter has presented a low-level look at each of today's common network protocols (IP, IPX/SPX, Appletalk and NerBEUI) showing their differences and similarities through comparison with the OSI Reference model.

PART II

Building Local Area Networks

LAN Types and Topologies

Local area networks (LANs) have become ubiquitous in today's business environment. Despite their familiarity, they remain little more than a mystery to most people. It's easy to point to the hubs or switches (or both) and declare them to be "the network." However, they're just pieces of one type of network.

As was explained in Chapter 1, "A Networking Primer," LANs are easiest to understand when they're dissected into their physical components. Often, these components are stratified into layers, as defined by the Open Systems Interconnect (OSI) Reference Model. This model was presented in detail in Chapter 1. Within this model, each layer supports a distinct functionality set.

A necessary prerequisite to this layered dissection of a LAN is an exploration of two other attributes: resource access methodology and topology. A LAN's *resource access methodology* describes the manner in which network-attached resources are shared. Frequently, this aspect of a network is referred to as its *type*. The two prevailing types are peer-to-peer and client/server.

A LAN's *topology* refers to its physical arrangement of hubs and wiring. The basic topologies include bus, star, ring, and switched.

Together, these attributes help form the context for your detailed exploration of a LAN's functional layers. This chapter explores all the possible permutations of both LAN types and topologies. Their benefits, limitations, and possible uses are also presented.

LAN-Attached Devices

Before we delve into LAN types and topologies, it's beneficial to first examine some of the basic resources that can be found on a LAN. The three most common primary devices are clients, servers, and printers. A *primary device* is one that can either directly access other devices or be accessed by other devices.

A server is any LAN-attached computer that hosts resources shared by other LAN-attached devices. A *client* is any computer that accesses resources stored on servers, via the LAN. Printers, of course, are output devices that produce hard copies of files. Numerous other devices, such as CD-ROM drives and tape archives, can also be accessed via a LAN, but they tend to be secondary resources. That is, they're connected to a primary device. Subordination of a device to another device, such as a CD-ROM drive to a server, is known as *slaving*. Printers, too, can be slaved off a primary device, or they can be primary devices directly connected to the network. Figure 5.1 illustrates the primary resources found in a LAN as well as the relationship of primary to secondary resources.

FIGURE 5.1
Primary and secondary LAN resources.

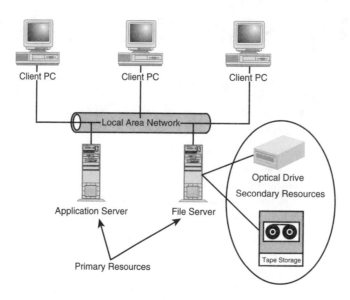

Types of Servers

Server is a word frequently used generically to describe all multiuser computers. It's important to note, however, that servers are a rather heterogeneous group. They're frequently specialized by function and described with an adjective. For example, there are file servers, print servers, and application servers.

File Servers

One of the most basic and familiar of the specialized servers is the *file server*. The file server is a centralized storage mechanism for files needed by a group of users. Placing these files in one centralized location, rather than scattered across numerous client-level machines, imparts several benefits. These benefits include the following:

- *Centralized location*. All users enjoy a single, constant repository for shared files. This provides a dual benefit. Users don't have to search multiple potential storage locations to find a file; instead, files are stored in one place. Users also are relieved of the burden of maintaining separate logon credentials to multiple machines. One logon provides them with access to all the files they require.

- *Electric power conditioning*. The use of a centralized server for file storage also enables the introduction of many techniques that can provide protection for data from inconsistencies in electric power. Fluctuations in the frequency of electricity, or even the sudden loss of power, can damage both a computer's data and hardware. Power filtration and battery backup through an uninterruptible power supply (UPS) is cost effective on a single server. Similar protection in a peer-to-peer network might be cost prohibitive because of the numbers of computers that would need protection.

- *Consistent data archiving*. Storing all shared files in a common, centralized location greatly facilitates backups, because only a single output device and routine are required. Decentralized storage of data (at every desktop, for example) means that every desktop's data must be backed up separately. Backups are an essential protection against lost or damaged files. Suitable devices for backups include tape drives, writable optical drives, and even hard drives. Multiple hard drives can also be used in a technique known as *striping*. Striping involves multiple, simultaneous writes to different hard drives. Although this is primarily done to provide faster reading of data, it can also be used to create redundancy with every write operation.

- *Speed*. The typical server is a more robust and fully configured platform than the typical client computer. This directly translates into a demonstrable performance gain relative to retrieving files in a peer-to-peer network.

The use of a file server does not always yield an increase in speed. You can usually access files stored locally more quickly than files stored on a remote computer and retrieved over a LAN. The speed increase discussed here is relative to the speed with which files can be retrieved from other client-level machines in a peer-to-peer network, not the speed with which files can be retrieved from a local hard drive.

Print Servers

Servers can also be used to share printers among the users of a LAN. Although the costs of printers, especially laser printers, have decreased considerably since their introduction, most organizations would be hard pressed to justify one for every desktop. Instead, servers are used to share one or more printers among the user population. This doesn't mean that a PC used as a print server cannot also be used as a desktop machine. Both NetWare and Windows NT allow workstations to share the use of a printer attached to it.

Alternatively, the print server software can run on the file server and share printers attached to it. The third possibility is a dedicated print server device, usually a very small "black box" with an Ethernet port and one or more parallel ports.

The alternative to using a print server is to directly attach the printer to the LAN. Many printers can be configured with a network interface card (NIC), which enables them to be directly attached to the LAN. This enables the printers to become print queue servers. Connecting printers directly to the LAN works well for all but the most print-intensive operations.

A print server's only function is to accept print requests from all networked devices, put them in a queue, and *spool* (send) them to the appropriate printer. This arrangement is illustrated in Figure 5.2.

FIGURE 5.2
A simple print server arrangement.

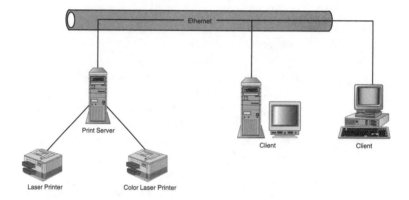

Note: Although the term *spool* has become synonymous with *printing*, it's actually an acronym. SPOOL originally meant *Simultaneous Peripheral Operations On Line*. It's the temporary storage of programs and/or data in the form of output streams on magnetic media for later output or execution.

Each printer connected to a print server has its own queue (or waiting list). These queues represent the pecking order of all requests that are temporarily stored and waiting their turns to print. Requests are generally processed in the order they were received, although some network operating systems do allow for print jobs to be prioritized in other ways (so you could ensure that your boss's jobs went immediately to the top of the queue!).

Application Servers

Servers are also frequently used to run application software. Application servers, although superficially similar to file servers, are unique creatures. An application server hosts executable application software. To run that application software, a client must establish a connection across a network to the server. The application runs on that server. Servers that enable clients to download copies of an application for execution on their desktop computers are file servers. Their files are actually application software files, but they're functioning as file servers. The distinction isn't where the file is stored, but where the application executes.

Application servers can enable an organization to reduce its overall cost of application software. Purchase prices and maintenance of a single, multiuser copy of an application are usually much less than the costs of acquiring and maintaining separate copies for each desktop.

> **Warning:** Installing a commercially purchased single-user application software package on an application or file server might violate the terms and conditions set forth in its license agreement. In much the same way that an individual user might pass around the original install media of an application, a server makes a single copy of a program available to any and all network users. Always ensure that any software package you install on a server has been purchased through some form of multiuser agreement.

Although it's usually desirable to separate application software from its data files by using separate servers (for example, an application server and a file server), there's one important exception to this rule. Because some applications build and maintain large relational databases, these applications and their databases should reside together on the application server.

The reason for this is simple: The mechanics of retrieving data from a database is very different from simply pulling down a Word or Excel file. The relational database application releases only the data requested and keeps everything else in its database. Office automation applications, such as Word and Excel, store information in standalone files that, typically, are not interdependent with other data in a complex structure. The relational database application is directly responsible for the integrity of the database and its indices. Managing the database across a network increases the risk of corrupting the indices and disabling the application.

Network Type

The network's *type* describes the manner in which attached resources can be accessed. Resources can be clients, servers, or any devices, files, and so on that reside on a client or server. These resources can be accessed in one of two ways: via peer-to-peer networks or server-based networks.

Peer-to-Peer Networks

A *peer-to-peer network* supports unstructured access to network-attached resources. Each device in a peer-to-peer network can be a client and a server simultaneously. All devices in the network are capable of accessing data, software, and other network resources directly. In other words, each networked computer is a peer of every other networked computer; there is no hierarchy.

Figure 5.3 illustrates a peer-to-peer network.

Figure 5.3
A peer-to-peer network.

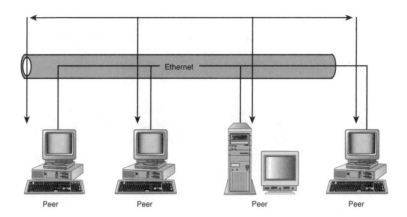

Benefits

There are four main benefits to having a peer-to-peer network:

- Peer-to-peer networks are relatively easy to implement and operate. They're little more than a collection of client computers that have a network operating system that permits peer-to-peer resource sharing. Therefore, establishing a peer-to-peer network requires only the procurement and installation of network cards, hubs, computers, wiring, and an operating system that permits this resource-access methodology.

- Peer-to-peer networks are also inexpensive to operate. They lack expensive, sophisticated, dedicated servers that require special administrative care and climate conditioning. The lack of dedicated servers also eliminates the attendant expenses of staffing and training as well as the additional real estate costs for developing a climate-controlled room just for the servers. Each machine resides, at least in theory, on a desktop and is cared for by its primary user.

- A peer-to-peer network can be established with familiar operating systems such as Windows 95/98, Windows NT/2000, and Windows for Workgroups.

- Their lack of a hierarchical dependence makes peer-to-peer networks much more fault tolerant than server-based networks. In theory, a server in a client/server network is a single point of failure. Single points of failure are a vulnerability that can impact the entire network. In a peer-to-peer network, the failure of any given machine results in the unavailability of only a subset of the network's attached resources.

Limitations

Peer-to-peer networking is not without its risks and faults. Some of the more serious of these limitations are in the areas of security, performance, and administration.

The peer-to-peer network suffers from numerous security weaknesses:

- Users must maintain multiple passwords, typically one for each machine they need to access. Users tend to devise very creative means of coping with an excess of passwords. Most of these ways directly compromise the security of every machine in the peer-to-peer network.

- The lack of a central repository for shared resources imposes the burden of finding information squarely on each user. This difficulty can be overcome with methods and procedures, provided each member of the workgroup complies.

- Like the network-attached resources, security is distributed evenly throughout the peer-to-peer network. Security in this form of network usually consists of user authentication via an ID and password, coupled with specific access permissions for specific resources. It's up to the "administrator" of each networked computer to define these permission structures for all other users in the network.

  Although each machine's user can be considered that machine's administrator, it's rare for these users to have the knowledge and skill sets to be proficient at their administrative duties. It's even rarer for the administrative skill levels to be consistent across even a small workgroup. This is one of the pitfalls of peer-to-peer networking.

- Unfortunately, technical proficiency is usually not homogeneously distributed. Consequently, the security of the entire network is predicated upon the skills and abilities of the least technically proficient member! One of the better metaphors used to describe this scenario is that of a chain, which is only as strong as its weakest link. Security in a peer-to-peer network is only as strong as its weakest peer.

Although the administrative burden is less in a peer-to-peer network than in a client/ server network, this burden is spread across users. This creates some logistical issues. Here are two of the gravest:

- Uncoordinated, and probably highly inconsistent, backups of data and software. Each user is responsible for his own machine, so it's possible, and even likely, that each is going to perform backups at his own leisure.

- Decentralized responsibility for enforcing filenaming conventions and storage locations. Given that there's no central repository for stored information or any other logic by which LAN-attached resources are organized, keeping current with what information is stored where can be quite challenging. As with everything else in a peer-to-peer network, the effectiveness of the whole is directly dependent upon the degree to which methods and procedures are adhered to by all participants.

Lastly, performance also suffers. An integral aspect of a peer-to-peer network is that each machine is a multiuser machine. The typical machine is better suited for use as a single-user client-only computer than it is for multiuser support. Consequently, the performance of any given machine suffers noticeably, as perceived by its primary user, whenever remote users log on and share its resources.

The availability of files and any other resources that a given peer may host are only as available as that host. In other words, if a machine's primary user is out of the office and left it powered down, its resources are unavailable to the rest of the networked computers. This can be circumvented by leaving all machines powered on all the time, but doing so raises questions about other issues, such as security.

Another, more subtle aspect of performance is *scalability*. The peer-to-peer methodology is inherently nonscalable. The more peers are networked together, the more unmanageable the network becomes.

Uses

Peer-to-peer networking has two primary uses. First, it's ideally suited for small organizations with a limited budget for information technologies and limited need for information sharing. Alternatively, workgroups within larger organizations can also use this methodology for a tighter sharing of information within a particular group.

Server-Based Networks

Server-based networks introduce a hierarchy designed to improve the manageability of a network's various supported functions as the size of the network scales upward. Often, server-based networks are referred to as *client/server networks*. Figure 5.4 illustrates this hierarchy of clients and servers.

FIGURE 5.4
A client/server network.

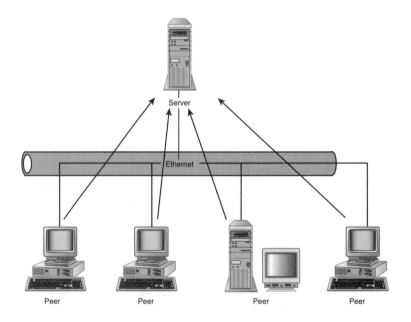

In a server-based network, frequently shared resources are consolidated onto a separate tier of computers, known as *servers*. Servers, typically, do not have a primary user. Rather, they're multiuser machines that regulate the sharing of their resources across the base of clients. In this type of network, clients are relieved of the burden of functioning as servers to other clients.

Benefits

There are many benefits inherent in the server-based approach to accessing network resources. These benefits directly correspond to the limitations of a peer-to-peer network. The areas of benefit are security, performance, and administration.

Server-based networks can be made, and kept, much more secure than peer-to-peer networks. Multiple factors contribute to this. First, security is managed centrally. Networked resources are no longer subjected to the "weakest link in the chain" theory that's an integral part of a peer-to-peer network.

Instead, all user accounts (also known as *IDs*) and passwords are centrally managed and verified before any user is granted access to requested resources. Coincidentally, this also makes the lives of the users better, by diminishing the need for multiple passwords.

Another benefit of this centralization of resources is that administrative tasks, such as backups, can be done consistently and reliably.

Server-based networks offer improved performance for networked computers in several ways. First, each client is relieved of the burden of processing requests from other clients for its stores. Each client in a server-based network need only keep up with the requests generated by its primary or only user.

More significantly, this processing is offloaded onto a server whose configuration is optimized for that service. Typically, a server contains more processing power, more memory, and larger, faster disk drives than those found in a client computer. The net effect is that users' client computers are able to better satisfy their own requests, and requests for resources centralized on a server are fulfilled much more effectively. Users, too, are spared the effort that would otherwise be required to learn which resources are stored where in a network. In a server-based network, the possible "hiding places" are reduced to just the number of servers on the network. In a server environment, server-based resources can be linked to as a logical drive. After the network drive linkage is established, remote resources stored on the server can be accessed as easily as any that are locally resident on a user's PC.

A server-based network is also very scalable. Regardless of how many clients are connected to the network, the resources are always centrally located. In addition, these resources are always centrally managed and secured. Consequently, the performance of the aggregate network isn't compromised by increases in scale.

Limitations

The server-based network has one limitation: It costs much more to implement and operate than a peer-to-peer network. There are many facets of this significant cost difference.

First, the hardware and software costs are significantly increased because of the need for a separate, networked computer that services the clients. Servers can be fairly sophisticated—which translates into *expensive*—machines.

The costs of operating a server-based network are also much higher. This is due to the need to have a trained professional administer the network and its servers. In a peer-to-peer network, each user is responsible for the maintenance of his own machine; no individual needs to be dedicated to this function.

The last aspect is the potential cost of downtime. In a peer-to-peer network, the loss of any given peer translates into only a modest decrement in the available resources on the LAN. In a server-based LAN, the loss of a server can directly, and significantly, impact virtually all the users of the network. This increases the potential business risks of a server-based network. Numerous approaches, including clustering servers for redundancy, can be used to combat this risk. Unfortunately, every one of these approaches only serves to further drive up the cost of a server-based network.

Uses

Server-based networks are extremely useful in large organizations. They can also be useful in any circumstances that warrant tighter security or more consistent management of network-attached resources. The added cost of server-based networks, however, might place them beyond the reach of very small organizations.

Combination Networks

The distinctions between peer-to-peer and server-based networking aren't quite so clear as the preceding sections might suggest. They were presented as distinct types intentionally, as well as for academic purposes. In reality, the distinctions between them have been blurred through the capabilities of numerous operating systems, such as Microsoft's Windows for Workgroups, Windows 95/98, and Windows NT/2000.

The norm today is a combination of peer-to-peer and server-based resource access in a single network. An example of this is a network with a server-based architecture that centralizes resources that are universally needed. Within this context, local workgroups can optionally provide peer-based access among themselves.

Peter's Principle: One Size Does NOT Fit All

Just as there's no single "best" network operating system, there's also no best type or best topology. Every enterprise, network, or administrator is different. Each has strengths and weaknesses, and each has unique needs. Thorough planning for your network and an understanding of your enterprise's needs are at least as important as, if not more than, being able to enumerate all the varieties of types and topologies. Remember, too, that no one has a better understanding of these needs than the people who use the network daily, so listen to your users at least as much as you listen to vendors.

LAN Topologies

Local area network topologies can be described using either a physical or a logical perspective. A *physical topology* describes the geometric arrangement of components that make up the LAN. The topology is not a map of the network. It's a theoretical construct that graphically conveys the shape and structure of the LAN.

A *logical topology* describes the possible connections between pairs of networked endpoints that can communicate. This is useful in describing which endpoints can communicate with which other endpoints and whether those pairs capable of communicating have a direct physical connection to each other. This chapter focuses only on physical topological descriptions.

Until recently, there have been three basic physical topologies: bus, ring, and star. Each basic topology is dictated by the physical LAN technology selected. For example, Token Ring networks, by definition, have historically used ring topologies. However, MSAUs (Token Ring's hubs, known more properly as *Multistation Access Units*), blurred the distinction between a ring and star topology for Token Ring networks. The result is known as a *star ring*. Similarly, the introduction of LAN switching is, again, changing the perception of topology. Switched LANs, regardless of frame type or access method, are topologically similar. The ring that used to exist at the electronics level within Token Ring's MSAUs no longer interconnects all the devices connected to that hub. Instead, each enjoys its own mini ring that's populated with just two devices: the station device and the switch port. Consequently, *switched* should now be added to the long-standing triad of basic LAN topologies as a distinct fourth topology.

Tip: Switches implement a star topology, without regard for the Data Link Layer protocol for which they're designed. Given that the word *switch* has become readily understood (thanks to the tireless marketing campaigns of switch manufacturers!), it has become more descriptive and readily understood than *star bus* or *star ring*. Consequently, switching can be regarded as a topology unto itself. For the purposes of any MCSE/CNE exam that might be lurking in your not-too-distant future, however, you might want to remember the terms *star bus* and *star ring*.

Switching has decoupled this historic coupling of topology and LAN technology: Literally all LAN technologies can be purchased in a switched implementation. This has significant ramifications for network access and, consequently, overall network performance. These ramifications are explored in more detail in the section titled "Switched Topology."

> **Note:** Even though switches can be purchased to support any LAN type, including Ethernet, Token Ring, FDDI, and so forth, they're not translating bridges. That is, they're incapable of switching frames between dissimilar LAN architectures.

Bus Topology

A bus topology features all networked nodes interconnected, peer to peer, using a single, open-ended cable. This cable can support only a single channel. The cable is called the *bus*. Some bus-based technologies use more than a single cable. Consequently, they can support more than one channel, although each cable remains limited to just one transmission channel.

Both ends of the bus must be terminated with a resistive load, known as a *terminating resistor*. These resistors serve to prevent signal bounce. Whenever a station transmits, the signal that it puts on the wire automatically propagates in both directions. If a terminating resistor is not encountered, the signal reaches the end of the bus and reverses direction. Consequently, a single transmission can completely usurp all available bandwidth and prevent any other stations from transmitting. An example of bus topology is illustrated in Figure 5.5.

FIGURE 5.5
A typical bus topology.

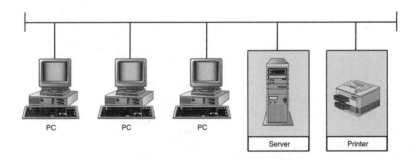

The typical bus topology features a single cable, supported by no external electronics, that interconnects all networked nodes in a peer-to-peer fashion. All connected devices listen to the bussed transmissions and accept those packets addressed to them. The lack of any external electronics, such as repeaters, makes bus LANs simple and inexpensive. The downside is that it also imposes severe limitations on distances, functionality, and scalability.

This topology is impractical for all but the smallest of LANs. Consequently, today's commercially available LAN products that use a bus topology are inexpensive peer-to-peer networks that provide basic connectivity. These products are targeted at home and small office environments.

One exception to this was the IEEE's 802.4 Token Bus LAN specification. This technology is fairly robust, deterministic, and bears many similarities to a Token Ring LAN. Deterministic LANs offer the administrator a high degree of control in determining the maximum amount of time a frame of data can be in transmission. The primary difference, obviously, was that Token Bus was implemented on a bus topology.

Token Bus found extremely limited market support. Its implementation tended to be limited to factory production lines. Bus topologies, in general, prospered in myriad other forms. Two early forms of Ethernet, 10Base2 and 10Base5, used a bus topology and coaxial cabling. Buses also became a critical technology for interconnecting system-level components and peripheral devices within the internal architectures of computers.

Ring Topology

The ring topology started out as a simple peer-to-peer LAN topology. Each networked workstation had two connections: one to each of its nearest neighbors (see Figure 5.6). The interconnection had to form a physical loop, or *ring*. Data was transmitted unidirectionally around the ring. Each workstation acted as a repeater, accepting and responding to packets addressed to it and forwarding the other packets onto the next workstation on the ring.

The original LAN ring topology featured peer-to-peer connections between workstations. These connections had to be closed; that is, they had to form a ring. The benefit of such LANs was that response time was fairly predictable. The more devices there were in the ring, the longer the network delays. The drawback was that early ring networks could be completely disabled if one of the workstations failed.

These primitive rings were made obsolete by IBM's Token Ring, which was later standardized by the IEEE's 802.5 specification. Token Ring departed from the peer-to-peer interconnection in favor of a repeating hub. This eliminated ring networks' vulnerability to workstation failure by eliminating the peer-to-peer ring construction. Token Ring networks, despite the name, are implemented with a star topology and a circular access method, as shown in Figure 5.7.

LANs can be implemented in a star topology, yet can retain a circular access method. The Token Ring network illustrated in Figure 5.7 demonstrates the virtual ring formed by the round-robin access method. The solid lines represent physical connections, and the dashed line represents the logical flow of regulated media access.

Figure 5.6
A peer-to-peer ring topology.

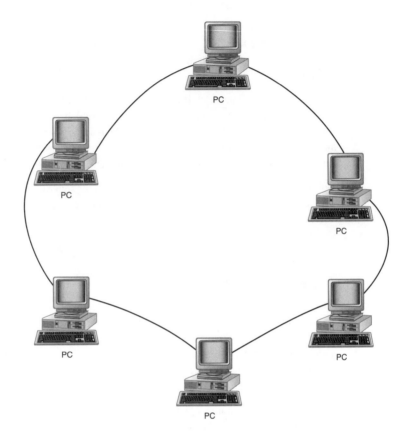

Figure 5.7
A star-shaped ring topology.

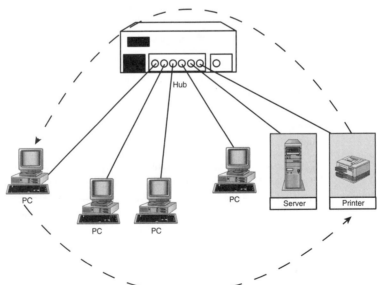

Functionally, the access token passes in a circular sequence, round-robin fashion, among the networked endpoints, even though they're all interconnected to a common hub. Therefore, many people succumb to the temptation of describing Token Ring networks as having a "logical" ring topology, even though they're shaped like a star. Evidence of this is found in Microsoft's Networking Essentials course and exam, which regard Token Ring as having a ring, not a star topology. In fact, the Token Ring hub, known properly as a Multistation Access Unit (MSAU), provides a physical ring internally, at the electronics level.

Star Topology

Star topology LANs have connections to networked devices that "radiate" out from a common point (that is, the hub, as shown in Figure 5.8). Unlike ring topologies—physical or virtual—each networked device in a star topology can access the media independently. These devices have to share the hub's available bandwidth. An example of a LAN with a star topology is 10BaseT Ethernet.

FIGURE 5.8

A star topology.

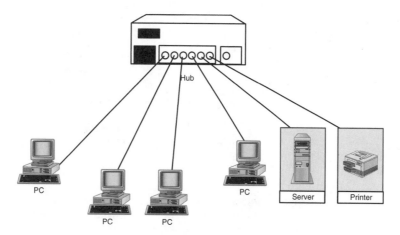

A small LAN with a star topology features connections that radiate out from a common point. Each connected device can initiate media access independent of the other connected devices.

Star topologies have become the dominant topology type in contemporary LANs. They're flexible, scalable, and relatively inexpensive compared to more sophisticated LANs with strictly regulated access methods. Stars have all but made buses and rings obsolete in LAN topologies and have formed the basis for the final LAN topology: switched.

Switched Topology

A *switch* is a multiport, Data Link Layer (OSI Reference Model Layer 2) device. A switch "learns" Media Access Control (MAC) addresses and stores them in an internal lookup table. Temporary, switched paths are created between the frame's originator and its intended recipient, and the frames are forwarded along that temporary path.

The typical LAN with a switched topology is illustrated in Figure 5.9. It features multiple connections to a switching hub. Each port, and the device to which it connects, has its own dedicated bandwidth. Although originally switches forwarded frames based on the frames' MAC addresses, technological advances are rapidly changing all that. Switches are available (called "Layer 3" switches) that can process cells, frames, and even packets that use a Layer 3 address like IP.

FIGURE 5.9
A switched topology.

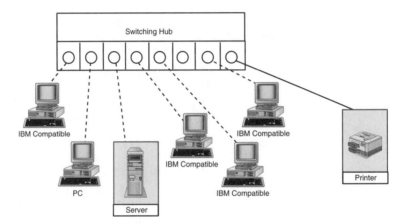

Note: A *frame* is a variable-length structure that contains data, source, and destination addresses as well as other data fields required for its carriage and forwarding in Layer 2 of the OSI Reference Model. Cells are very similar to frames, except they feature a *fixed*, not variable, length. Packets are a construct of protocols that operate at Layer 3 of the OSI Reference Model. IP and IPX are two examples of Layer 3 protocols that use packets to encapsulate data for transport to foreign domains.

Switches can improve the performance of a LAN in two important ways. First, they increase the aggregate bandwidth available throughout the network. For example, a switched Ethernet hub with eight ports contains eight separate collision domains of 10Mbps each, for an aggregate of 80Mbps of bandwidth.

The second way that switches improve LAN performance is by reducing the number of devices forced to share each segment of bandwidth. Each switch-delineated collision domain is inhabited by only two devices: the networked device and the port on the switching hub to which it connects. These are the only two devices that can compete for the 10Mbps of bandwidth on the segment. In networks that do not utilize a media access method that's based on competition for bandwidth—such as Token Ring and FDDI—the tokens circulate among a much smaller number of networked machines than are typically supported in competition-based networks.

One area for concern with large switched implementations is that switches do not isolate broadcasts. They bolster performance solely by segmenting collision, not broadcast, domains. Excessive broadcast traffic can significantly and adversely impact LAN performance.

Complex Topologies

Complex topologies are extensions and/or combinations of basic physical topologies. Basic topologies, by themselves, are adequate for only very small LANs. The scalability of the basic topologies is extremely limited. Complex topologies are formed from these building blocks to achieve a custom-fitted, scalable topology.

Daisy Chains

The simplest of the complex topologies is developed by serially interconnecting all the hubs of a network, as shown in Figure 5.10. This is known as *daisy-chaining*. This simple approach uses ports on existing hubs for interconnecting the hubs. Therefore, no incremental cost is incurred during the development of such a backbone.

FIGURE 5.10
Daisy-chaining hubs.

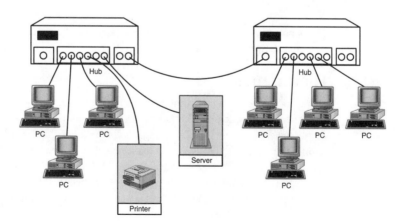

Small LANs can be scaled upward by daisy-chaining hubs together. Daisy chains are easily built and don't require any special administrative skills. Daisy chains were, historically, the interconnection method of choice for emerging, first-generation LANs.

The limits of daisy-chaining can be discovered in a number of ways. LAN technology specifications, such as 802.3 Ethernet, dictate the maximum size of the LAN in terms of the number of hubs and/or repeaters that may be strung together in sequence. The distance limitations imposed by the Physical Layer, multiplied by the number of devices, dictate the maximum size of a LAN. This size is referred to as a *maximum network diameter*. Scaling beyond this diameter adversely affects the normal functioning of that LAN. Maximum network diameters frequently limit the number of hubs that can be interconnected in this fashion. This is particularly true of contemporary high-performance LANs, such as Fast Ethernet, that place strict limitations on the network diameter and the number of repeaters that can be strung together.

> **Note:** A *repeater* is a device that accepts an incoming signal, amplifies it back to its original volume, and places it back on the network. Typically, signal amplification and repetition functions are incorporated into hubs. Consequently, the two terms (*repeaters* and *hubs*) can be used synonymously.

Daisy-chaining networks that use a contention-based media access method can become problematic long before network diameter is compromised, however. Daisy-chaining increases the number of connections—and therefore the number of devices—on a LAN. It does not increase aggregate bandwidth or segment collision domains. Daisy-chaining simply increases the number of machines sharing the network's available bandwidth. Too many devices competing for the same amount of bandwidth can create collisions and quickly incapacitate a LAN.

This topology is best left to LANs with less than a handful of hubs and little, if any, wide area networking.

Hierarchies

Hierarchical topologies consist of more than one layer of hubs. Each layer serves a different network function. The bottom tier is reserved for user station and server connectivity. Higher-level tiers provide aggregation of the user-level tier. In much simpler terms, many user-level hubs are interconnected via a lesser number of higher-level hubs. The hubs themselves can be identical devices; their only distinction lies in their application. A hierarchical arrangement is best suited for medium- to large-sized LANs that must be concerned with scalability of the network and with traffic aggregation.

Hierarchical Rings

Ring networks can be scaled up by interconnecting multiple rings in a hierarchical fashion, as shown in Figure 5.11. User station and server connectivity can be provided by as many limited size rings as are necessary to provide the required level of performance. A second-tier ring, either Token Ring or FDDI, can be used to interconnect all the user-level rings and to provide aggregated access to the wide area network (WAN).

FIGURE 5.11

A hierarchical ring topology.

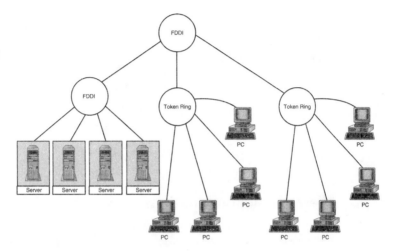

Small ring LANs can be scaled by interconnecting multiple rings hierarchically. In Figure 5.11, two distinct 16Mbps Token Rings, shown logically as loops, are used to interconnect the user stations, and separate FDDI loops are used for the servers and backbone tier.

Hierarchical Stars

Star topologies, too, can be implemented in hierarchical arrangements of multiple stars, as shown in Figure 5.12. Hierarchical stars can be implemented as a single collision domain or segmented into multiple collision domains using switches, routers, or bridges.

> **Note:** A *collision domain* consists of all the devices that compete for the right to transmit on a shared media. Switches, bridges, and routers all segment the collision domain (that is, they create multiple, smaller collision domains).

A hierarchical star topology uses one tier for user and server connectivity and the second tier as a backbone.

FIGURE 5.12
A hierarchical star topology.

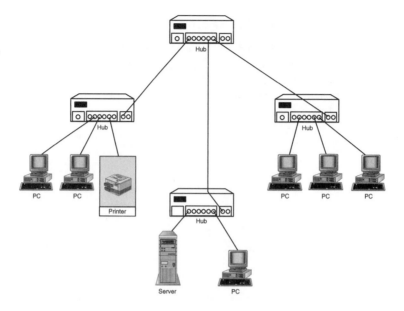

Hierarchical Combinations

Overall network performance can be enhanced by not force-fitting all the functional requirements of the LAN into a single solution. Today's high-end switching hubs enable you to mix multiple technologies. New topologies can be introduced by simply inserting the appropriate circuit board into the multislot chassis of the switching hub. A hierarchical topology lends itself to combinations of topologies, as shown in Figure 5.13.

FIGURE 5.13
A hierarchical combination topology.

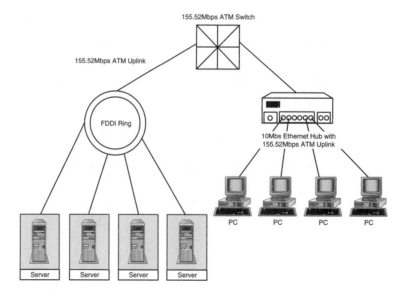

In this example of a hierarchical combination topology, an Asynchronous Transfer Mode (ATM) backbone is used to interconnect the user-level hubs. FDDI interconnects the server *farm* (that is, a group of servers isolated on their own segment); Ethernet interconnects the user stations. This approach differentiates the LAN into functional components (station-connect, server-connect, and backbone) and enables the ideal technology for each function to be used. These functional areas are addressed further in the next section, "LAN Functional Areas."

LAN Functional Areas

Topological variation can be an important way to optimize network performance for each of the various functional areas of a LAN. LANs contain four distinct functional areas: station connectivity, server connectivity, WAN connectivity, and backbone. Each may be best served by a different basic or complex topology.

Station Connectivity

The primary function of most LANs is station connectivity. *Station connectivity*, as its name implies, is the portion of the LAN used to connect the user stations to the network. This functional area tends to have the least stringent performance requirements of the LAN's functional areas. There are obvious exceptions to this, such as CAD/CAM workstations, desktop videoconferencing, and so on. In general, though, compromises in the cost and performance of this part of a LAN's technology and topology are less likely to adversely affect the network's performance.

Providing connectivity to machines that have divergent network performance requirements may require the use of multiple LAN technologies, as shown in Figure 5.14. Fortunately, many of today's hub manufacturers can support multiple technologies from the same hub chassis.

LANs provide basic connectivity to user stations and the peripherals that inhabit them. Differences in the network performance requirements of user station equipment can necessitate a mixed topology/technology solution.

Server Connectivity

Servers tend to be much more robust than user workstations. Servers tend to be a point of traffic aggregation and must serve many clients and/or other servers. In the case of high-volume servers, this aggregation must be designed into a LAN's topology; otherwise, clients and servers suffer degraded network performance. Network connectivity to servers, typically, should also be more robust than station connectivity in terms of the available bandwidth and the robustness of the access method.

FIGURE 5.14
*A station
connectivity LAN.*

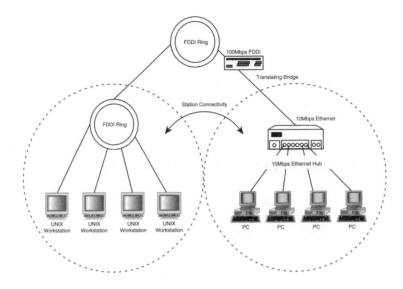

LAN topologies can also be manipulated to accommodate the robust network performance requirements of servers and server clusters. In Figure 5.15, for example, a hierarchical combination topology is employed. The server farm is interconnected with a small
FDDI loop; the less robust user stations are interconnected with Ethernet.

FIGURE 5.15
*A server connec-
tivity LAN.*

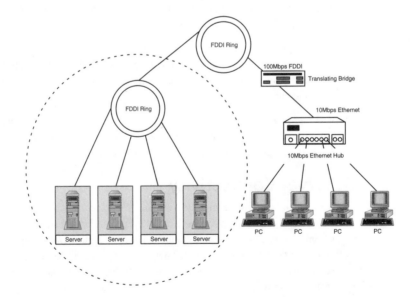

WAN Connectivity

A frequently overlooked aspect of a LAN's topology is its connection to the wide area network (WAN). In many cases, WAN connectivity is provided by a single connection from the backbone to a router, as shown in Figure 5.16.

FIGURE 5.16

*A WAN connectiv-
ity LAN.*

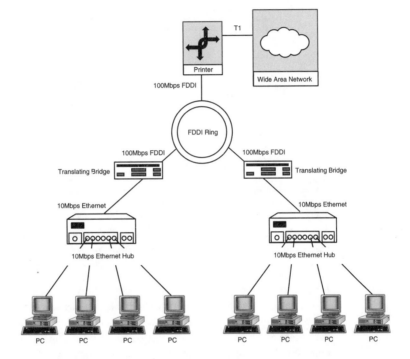

The LAN's connection to the router that provides WAN connectivity is a crucial link in a building's overall LAN topology. Improper technology selection at this critical point can result in unacceptably deteriorated levels of performance for all traffic entering or exiting the building's LAN. LAN technologies that use a contention-based access method are highly inappropriate for this function.

Networks that support a large quantity of WAN-to-LAN and LAN-to-WAN traffic benefit greatly from having the most robust connection possible in this aspect of their overall topology. The technology selected should be robust in terms of its nominal transmission rate and its access method. Contention-based technologies should be avoided at all costs. The use of a contention-based media, even on a dedicated switched port, may become problematic in high-usage networks. This is the bottleneck for all traffic coming into and trying to get out of the building's LAN.

Backbone Connectivity

A LAN's *backbone* is the portion of its facilities used to interconnect all the hubs. A backbone can be implemented in several topologies and with several different network components, as shown in Figure 5.17.

FIGURE 5.17
A LAN backbone.

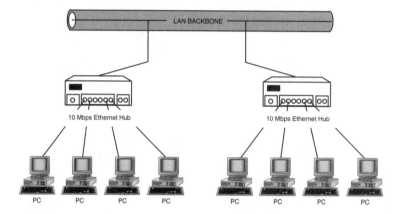

The LAN's backbone provides a critical function: It interconnects all the locally net-worked resources and, if applicable, the WAN. The logical depiction of a backbone, as shown in Figure 5.17, can be implemented in a wide variety of ways.

Determining which backbone topology is correct for your LAN is not easy. Some options are easier to implement, very affordable, and easy to manage. Others can be more costly to acquire and operate. Another important difference lies in the scalability of the various backbone topologies. Some are easy to scale, up to a point, and then require reinvestment to maintain acceptable levels of performance. Each option must be examined individually, relative to your particular situation and requirements.

Serial Backbone

A *serial backbone*, shown in Figure 5.18, is nothing more than a series of hubs daisy-chained together. As described in the preceding section, this topology is inappropriate for all but the smallest of networks.

Distributed Backbone

A *distributed backbone* is a form of hierarchical topology that can be built by installing a backbone hub in a central location. A building's PBX room (the telephone closet) usually serves as the center of its wiring topology. Consequently, it's the ideal location for a distributed backbone hub. Connections from this hub are distributed to other hubs throughout the building, as shown in Figure 5.19.

FIGURE 5.18

*A serial backbone,
also known as a
daisy chain.*

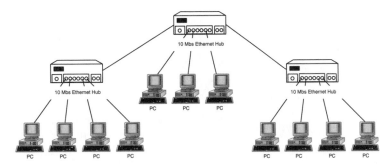

FIGURE 5.19

*A distributed
backbone.*

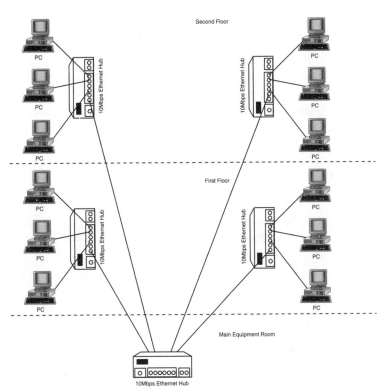

A distributed backbone can be developed by centrally locating the backbone hub.
Connections are distributed from this hub to other hubs throughout the building. Unlike
the serial backbone, this topology enables LANs to span large buildings without compromising maximum network diameters.

If you consider a distributed backbone, make sure you understand the building's wire topology and the distance limitations of the various LAN media choices. In medium-to-large locations, the only viable option for implementing a distributed backbone is probably fiber-optic cabling.

Collapsed Backbone

A *collapsed backbone* topology features a centralized router that interconnects all the LAN segments in a given building. The router effectively creates multiple collision and broadcast domains, thereby increasing the performance of each of the LAN segments.

Routers operate at Layer 3 of the OSI Reference Model. They are incapable of operating as quickly as hubs. Consequently, they can limit effective throughputs for any LAN traffic that originates on one LAN segment but terminates on another.

Collapsed backbones, like the one shown in Figure 5.20, also introduce a single point of failure in the LAN. This is not a fatal flaw. In fact, many of the other topologies also introduce a single point of failure in the LAN. Nevertheless, that weakness must be considered when planning a network topology.

FIGURE 5.20
A collapsed backbone.

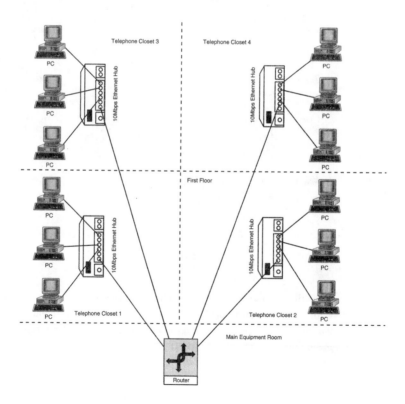

An important consideration in collapsed backbone topologies is that user communities are seldom conveniently distributed throughout a building. Instead, users are scattered far and wide. This means that there's a good chance they will be found on both sides of the LAN's collapsed backbone router. Subsequently, simple network tasks among the members of a workgroup are likely to traverse the router. Care should be taken when designing collapsed backbone LANs to absolutely minimize the amount of traffic that must cross the router. Use it as a traffic aggregator for LAN-level resources, such as WAN facilities, and not indiscriminately as a bridge.

Parallel Backbone

In some of the cases where collapsed backbones are an untenable solution, a modified version may prove ideal. This modification is known as the *parallel backbone*. The reasons for installing a parallel backbone are many. Here are some examples:

- User communities may be widely dispersed throughout a building.
- Some groups and/or applications may have stringent network security requirements.
- High network availability may be required.

Regardless of the reason, running parallel connections from a building's collapsed backbone router to the same telephone closet enables supporting multiple segments to be run from each closet, as shown in Figure 5.21.

FIGURE 5.21
A parallel backbone topology.

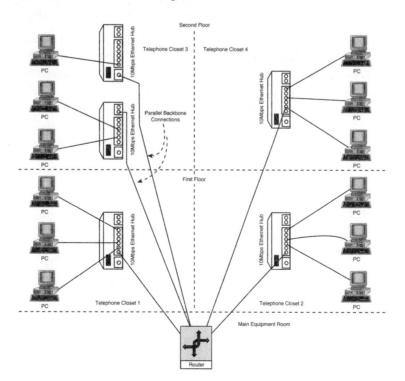

The parallel backbone topology is a modification of the collapsed backbone. Multiple segments can be supported in the same telephone closet or equipment room. This marginally increases the cost of the network, but can increase the performance of each segment and satisfy additional network criteria, such as security.

A careful understanding of the performance requirements imposed by customers, stratified by LAN functional areas, is the key to developing the ideal topology for any set of user requirements. The potential combinations are limited only by your imagination. Continued technological innovation will only serve to increase the topological variety available to network designers.

> **Note:** Many of the complex topologies presented in this chapter are for your edification only. They are of more practical use on the job than they are during certification exams. In fact, vendors frequently refer to many of these complex topologies by different names. Rather than get caught up in names, try to grasp their concepts, strengths, and weaknesses.

Summary

An important aspect of a LAN is the manner in which it supports resource access. Although this is more a function of the network operating systems than it is LAN hardware, it directly impacts the traffic flow and performance of the LAN.

LAN topology, too, is directly related to the efficacy of your LAN. The four basic topologies (bus, star, ring, and switched) can be mixed and matched, stacked or linked, in an almost infinite variety. Understanding the benefits and limitations of the basic topologies, as well as using them wisely, is critical to the selection of one that best satisfies the expected demands.

The topics presented in this chapter should reinforce the fact that there's more to networks than just their hardware and wiring. The way the physical components are arranged and the manner in which attached resources are accessed are equally important in technology selection.

Ethernet

Ethernet, born a quick-and-dirty mechanism to enhance researchers' capabilities to develop new technologies, has proven itself one of the most valuable and persistent of all information technologies. It has entered its third decade of life, experiencing significant evolution along the way. Some of these evolutionary changes, however, have made it virtually impossible to develop a concise definition of Ethernet.

The ubiquitous Ethernet has been so successful at satisfying network requirements that it has been treated to constant refreshes and updates by the Institute of Electrical and Electronic Engineers (IEEE), its caretaker. The two most significant updates involve increased signaling speed.

The first of these faster Ethernets accelerated the original 10Mbps Ethernet to 100Mbps. This necessitated the development of a completely new Physical Layer and, consequently, modest alterations to the Data Link Layer to accommodate the new Physical Layer. This new standard, dubbed *Fast Ethernet*, appears to have beaten Asynchronous Transfer Mode (ATM) in the high-speed LAN market.

The second of these updates is a bit more radical. Most of Ethernet's Layer 2 specifications were grafted on to a completely different Physical Layer—one borrowed from the 1gigabit per second (Gbps) Fibre Channel. This change, still being hammered out by the IEEE's 802.3z working committee, will change CSMA/CD (Carrier Sense, Multiple Access with Collision Detection) Ethernet in many ways. One of the most interesting of the changes posited by 802.3z is the elimination of the familiar CSMA/CD media-access method.

This chapter examines the various potential meanings of "Ethernet" and identifies the myriad Physical Layer implementations of today's 10Mbps Ethernets. Also covered are some of their performance limitations, including both specified and practical limits. We'll then go on to explore the differences between Fast Ethernet, Gigabit Ethernet, and the traditional 10Mbps, half-duplex, CSMA/CD Ethernet that spawned these variants.

History of Ethernets

Ethernet originally referred to the proprietary LAN cobbled together by research scientists at Xerox's Palo Alto Research Center (PARC). Rather than being a bold new technology developed for its vast market potential, Ethernet was a simple tool that enabled the researchers to easily share data as they tried to develop real technologies.

This crude network lacked sophistication. It was half-duplex and used thick coaxial cabling for interconnecting devices. Its signaling speed was 10Mbps. This original Ethernet is now known as PARC Ethernet, or even Ethernet I (*I* being the Roman numeral for the number 1). Obviously, both of these names were applied after the emergence of other forms of Ethernet. Today, this original form of Ethernet is obsolete and is referenced here for historical and contextual purposes only.

Xerox, recognizing the potential value of this technology, recruited two partners to help bring it to market: Intel and the Digital Equipment Corporation (DEC). Together, they instituted a series of improvements to PARC Ethernet and made it a somewhat open standard. This new Ethernet was called *Ethernet II*.

Note: Ethernet II, also known as DIX Ethernet for its triumvirate of creators (Digital, Intel, and Xerox), could not be considered a truly open standard because it was controlled by the three primary manufacturers of its components.

One of the first steps was to legitimize Ethernet as a standalone networking protocol. This meant it could no longer rely upon Network and Transport Layer protocols to define its frame sizes.

As important as this development was, it paled in comparison to the refinement of Ethernet's media-access methodology. The original Ethernet used a very primitive "listen before talking" scheme that was called *Carrier Sense, Multiple Access* (CSMA). In essence, any station that wanted to transmit first had to listen to the wire to see whether it was available. The improvement that was made was the addition of collision-detection capabilities. Ethernet II's new media-access methodology was called *Carrier Sense, Multiple Access with Collision Detection* (CSMA/CD). For more information on the mechanics of CSMA/CD, refer to Chapter 3, "The Data Link Layer."

In February of 1980, the IEEE assumed the responsibility for turning the budding Ethernet into a truly open standard. Its goal was not simply to standardize Ethernet but to create standardization and interoperability across multiple networking technologies. It launched Project 802, with numerous subcommittees and technical working groups, to hammer out standards for local area networks (LANs) and metropolitan area networks (MANs).

Project 802 decomposed the typical network into its functional components and layered them in a logical sequence. Open standards were developed for hardware-level addressing, network management, and network monitoring. These standards formed the basis for numerous local area network architectures such as Ethernet, Token Ring, Token Bus, and other even more obscure architectures.

The fact that these architectures enjoyed a common basis for hardware-level addressing, management, and monitoring meant that mixed topology networks could be built without compromising interoperability across otherwise dissimilar network platforms. More importantly, the disparate platforms could be managed and monitored with a common set of standards-compliant tools.

The IEEE's version of Ethernet was formally named 802.3 CSMA/CD. This unwieldy name is almost always forsaken in favor of *Ethernet*. The CSMA/CD media-access methodology was retained, as was the original coaxial-based transmission media and half-duplex transmission mode. Another specification for thin coaxial cabling was added and, over time, other Physical Layer specifications for twisted-pair wiring and fiber-optic cabling were also developed.

Fundamentals of Ethernet

Today, it's becoming more correct to identify Ethernet with adjectives other than CSMA/CD. Within the past two years, the original 802.3 specification was extended to include a 100Mbps version of Ethernet. This necessitated the development of new Physical Layer specifications, as well as some minor modifications to the media-access mechanisms. More important, support for full-duplex transmission was added. Full-duplex Ethernet enables a device to communicate over one physical transmission path, ostensibly one pair of twisted-pair wiring in a four-pair bundle, while simultaneously receiving data over another pair. Implemented in a port-switched configuration, full-duplex Ethernet effectively obviates contention-based access to the transmission media. The transmitting device can place frames on the LAN at near wire speeds. Consequently, the use of CSMA/CD to describe the IEEE's 802.3 Ethernet variant is no longer accurate.

> **Note:** *Wire speed* is the rate at which electrons flow through copper media. This rate is the theoretical maximum rate that data (which is ultimately converted to a flow of electrons) can travel through the media.

As if this weren't confusing enough, there are even specifications for a broadband, not baseband, 10Mbps Ethernet. One such example is the 10Broad36 specification. Fortunately for you, broadband Ethernets are well out of the mainstream and only superficially resemble the more familiar Ethernets. Consequently, this chapter focuses on just the baseband variants.

To avoid confusion, this book uses the term *Ethernet family of standards* to describe the 802.3 series of standards as a generic, cumulative technology set. The term *Ethernet* is used to describe just the 802.3 series of standards that signal at 10Mbps. The term *Fast Ethernet* is used to describe the 802.3 series of standards that signal at 100Mbps. Similarly, *Gigabit Ethernet* describes the series of emerging standards that signal at 1,024Mbps. This book also refers to specific, individual Ethernet technologies by describing the Physical Layer's Medium Dependent Interface (MDI) specification (for example, 10BaseT). This specificity is necessary because Ethernet now encompasses quite a vast and diverse array of standards and emerging standards.

Supported Hardware

Before we delve too far into the intricacies of Ethernet, it's necessary to first examine the various hardware components used to build an Ethernet network. These components are independent of media types and are referred to throughout the remainder of this chapter, so it's essential to provide the proper context for an examination of their implications in the network.

The hardware that may be used in support of an Ethernet network includes network interface cards (NICs), repeating hubs, nonrepeating hubs, bridges, routers, and switches.

Network Interface Cards

A *network interface card* (NIC) is a printed circuit board that's installed in a computer's I/O bus. The back of the card contains a physical interface for a specific connector type. Each connector type is designed for a specific transmission media. This card provides the connectivity between a computer's internal system resources and the external resources connected to the network. It embodies the logic of the LAN's Data Link and Physical Layers.

Repeaters

A *repeater* is a relatively simple device that takes an incoming signal, amplifies it without modifying its shape, and puts the signal back on the media. This device operates strictly at Layer 1 of the OSI Reference Model.

The functions of signal amplification and repetition have been bundled into multiport devices that are used to interconnect multiple devices across the LAN. These devices are commonly known as *hubs*, although they really are just multiport repeaters.

Non-Repeating Hubs

A *nonrepeating hub* is very similar to a repeating hub. The sole difference is that it does not repeat, or *amplify*, the signals. These hubs do little more than provide a star topology by aggregating multiple station connections onto a single network device.

Bridges

A *bridge* is a Layer 2 mechanism that enables two segments of a LAN to be linked together. Because bridges operate at Layer 2, they do not recognize the higher-layer protocols that are embedded in the frames they forward. They forward these frames based on a MAC address. For example, the bridge "learns" which MAC addresses are connected to the networks on its various ports. Whenever a bridge receives a frame with a MAC address that does not reside on the LAN segment on which it was generated, the bridge looks up that address in its bridging table (a compilation of MAC addresses, by port number) and forwards the frame to the correct LAN segment for delivery.

Stringing several bridges together, or even just using them in an environment that's characterized by MAC broadcasts, is a good way to find the limitations of these devices. They have, for the most part, failed to keep up with the increasing demands placed on network devices and have become little more than an obsolete curiosity.

Routers

A *router* is not a Layer 2 Ethernet device. Rather, it's a Layer 3 packet-forwarding mechanism. Nevertheless, routers do support interfaces for all standard LAN technologies. The primary use of a router is to connect the LAN with the networks beyond the LAN's domain. This has three important implications for network design.

First, the wide area network (WAN) is clearly beyond the LAN's domain. Routers remain the technology that must be used to interconnect LANs that are dispersed across large enough geographic regions as to warrant using long-haul transmission technologies. Such technologies include dedicated leased lines and switched circuits.

Second, multiple LAN domains may coexist in relatively close proximity. In fact, a single office premise may contain numerous LANs that are dedicated to individual workgroups. Concerns over security may warrant some degree of separation yet not preclude interconnection. In such cases, bridging the LANs together would be undesirable. Routers provide a little more security, through mechanisms such as Access Control Lists, and can effectively internetwork LANs while preserving the integrity of their Layer 2 collision and broadcast domains.

The third implication is borne of performance requirements. Ethernets can become large enough to start collapsing under their own mass. For example, a building may contain an Ethernet that's approaching 1,024 devices in size. If the applications supported by this LAN use Layer 2 broadcasts (don't ask why, this is a hypothetical scenario presented for academic value!), it's quite possible that segmenting the LAN with bridges or switches won't improve performance. In effect, the LAN will have had its collision domain segmented but not its broadcast domain. In this situation, a router may be your only viable option.

Switches

Switching is a term that's used in today's industry for any high-speed data-forwarding technology—from ATM to bridging to routing to telephone circuits. Even a term seemingly as specific as *Ethernet switch* is used to cover a number of different products. When employing a LAN switch, make sure you're aware of not only what type of switching your switch is doing but what other forms of switching are possible. Is it Layer 2 (bridging) or Layer 3 (routing)? Or is it something else? Layer 2 switches forward packets only by MAC address and ignore all higher-layer aspects of a packet. Layer 3 switches forward packets based on Layer 3 protocols, such as an IP subnetwork or an IPX network address. (Note that some LAN switches perform both Layer 2 and 3 switching.) Even more sophisticated switches that offer Layer 4 switching are becoming commonplace. Some vendors are planning switching at higher layers. We'll have to wait to determine just how useful upper-layer switching will become. Switching at the various layers of the protocol stack should be an architectural issue. For example, workgroups would use Layer 2, whereas points of aggregation (such as backbones) would use Layer 3 switching. However, the massive increase in performance for Layer 2 and Layer 3 switching, as well as an increase in the number of services a LAN switch can offer (for instance, priority and security), has muddied the water.

Some vendors call the hybrid Layer 2/Layer 3 forwarding used to improve performance *Layer 3 switching* when it's actually *Layer 2 routing assist*, which is used to reduce load on a router. Layer 2 routing assist forwards Layer 3 packets that would typically be routed as if they were Layer 2. If you have, say, an enterprise router such as a Cisco 7500 with a single Fast Ethernet link to three or four high-density switches that are aggregating your workgroups, Layer 2 routing assist would monitor and learn traffic flows routed between subnetworks by the Cisco device. A switch can (if connected to both subnets) bypass the router and forward the packets directly without the router even seeing them. Therefore, the router does all the brain work, and the switches do the grunt work. This scenario also applies if you're using a routing function that's internal to the switch.

There are several pros to Layer 2 routing assist. First, the router can cool off and not route every single packet that must be routed. Performance is exponentially improved because the switches can do this "pseudo routing" at all ports (for example, 50 ports at 100Mbps have a potential of 500Mbps of throughput). The router may have only one or two physical connections to the switch; if the router had to do all the routing, the maximum possible throughput would be maybe 100Mbps. Latency is reduced because the packet need only hit the switch and can avoid traversing the router. However, there are also some cons to this method. Pseudo routing is not real routing. Also, the packet is forwarded at Layer 2, which means that little or no Layer 3 information is processed. Checksums are not checked, so bad packets can propagate the network. Also, IP time-to-live fields (and similar fields in other protocols) are not assessed, so the possibility exists that a packet that has reached its hop limit will not be "killed." In addition, there can be no Layer 3–based security, and other sophisticated routing functions would not be implemented. However, most of the drawbacks won't have much of an impact on a well-designed network. Considering the performance gains, most of us can live with the loss of Layer 3 field checking (some of which is done upon session initiation before the Layer 2 switches can learn the flow and take over).

Layered Functions

The members of the IEEE began their standardization efforts by separating the necessary functions of local and metropolitan area networking into modules, or *layers*, based on the sequence of events that occur during a normal communications session. Like many other standards organizations, the IEEE created its own protocol stack rather than adhere strictly to the OSI Reference Model. Figure 6.1 illustrates the IEEE's model, complete with the separation of functions into layers, sublayers, and even different modules within the various layers.

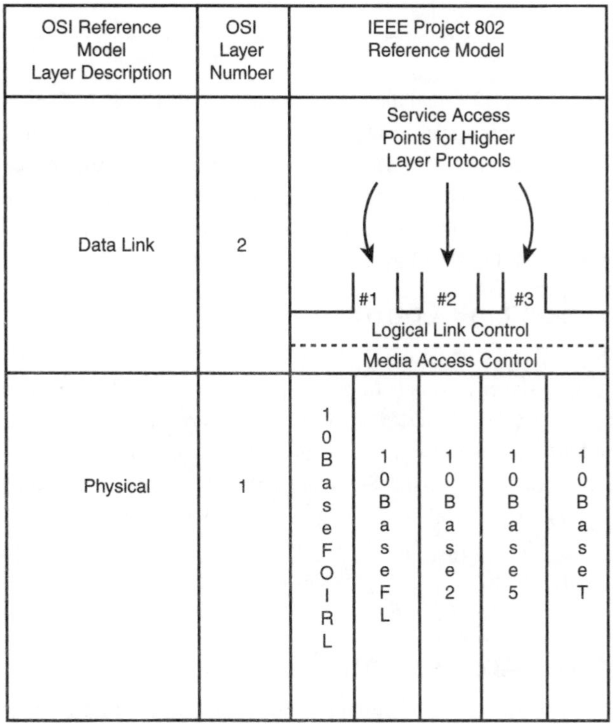

FIGURE 6.1

A block diagram of the IEEE's 10Mbps Ethernet versus the OSI Reference Model.

OSI Reference Model Layer Description	OSI Layer Number	IEEE Project 802 Reference Model			
		Service Access Points for Higher Layer Protocols			
		#1	#2	#3	
Data Link	2	Logical Link Control			
		Media Access Control			
Physical	1	10BaseFOIRL	10BaseFL	10Base2	10Base5	10BaseT

Data Link Layer Functions

The IEEE's 802 specification series breaks the OSI Reference Model's Data Link Layer (Layer 2) into two discrete components—Logical Link Control (LLC) and Media Access Control (MAC). Their relationship is illustrated in Figure 6.2.

FIGURE 6.2
The IEEE's Data Link Layer components.

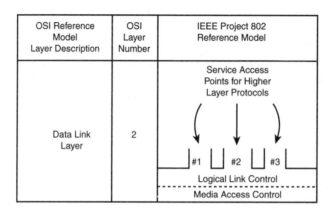

OSI Reference Model Layer Description	OSI Layer Number	IEEE Project 802 Reference Model
Data Link Layer	2	Service Access Points for Higher Layer Protocols #1 #2 #3 Logical Link Control Media Access Control

Together, the LLC and the MAC are the heart of Ethernet. They provide the framing and addressing that encapsulate the data and enable it to be transmitted to its destination. They also contain error-detection mechanisms and are responsible for initiating the retransmission of any damaged or lost frames. In short, they control the transmission and reception of data frames, although they do not perform the actual transmission. This is ceded to the Physical Layer.

Logical Link Control

The LLC is the uppermost "part" of the two Data Link Layer components. It insulates the upper-layer protocols from the specific access methodology and transmission media. Remember, the 802 series of specifications provides for interoperability between different LAN architectures. The LLC is the mechanism that separates Network and Transport Layer protocols from the vicissitudes of LAN architecture. These higher-layer protocols need not know whether they're going to be transported across an Ethernet, Token Ring, or even a Token Bus. Nor do they need to know which Physical Layer specification they'll be using. The LLC provides a common interface for all 802-compliant LAN architectures and variants.

Media Access Control

The MAC Layer is the bottom most of the Data Link Layer's components in the IEEE architecture. It's responsible for interfacing with the Physical Layer and ensuring that successful transmissions and receptions occur. This entails a tandem set of functions: transmit and receive.

The MAC Layer is responsible for encapsulating all data received from the LLC into a frame. This frame contains all the addressing and structure needed to transport the data to its destination(s). The MAC Layer is also responsible for implementing the data integrity test that's used to verify that the contents of a frame were not damaged or altered during transmission.

The MAC Layer must also determine, via the Physical Layer mechanisms, whether the communications band is available for transmission. If it's available, the framed data is handed off to the Physical Layer for transmission. Otherwise, the MAC Layer enacts its *binary exponential back-off algorithm*. This awkward name describes an algorithm that generates a pseudo-random waiting period that must be endured before another attempt at retransmission can be made.

The last significant MAC Layer function is monitoring the status of transmitted frames for any signs of a collision. Whenever it detects a collision of one of its own frames, the MAC Layer identifies the data that must be retransmitted, enacts its back-off algorithm, and then reattempts transmission. It continues to enact its back-off algorithm until the frame is transmitted successfully. This is simultaneously a strength and a weakness of Ethernet. It guarantees higher-layer protocols that their data will be delivered. Unfortunately, the chaotic nature of the contention-based media-access mechanism can make this an arduous and time-consuming task.

Physical Layer Functions

As with its implementation of the Data Link Layer, the IEEE's implementation of the Physical Layer is broken down into discrete components. The modularity of these components provides flexibility in the adoption of new technologies. If this were not the case, every time a new transmission media needed to be supported, an entire Layer 1 stack would have to be developed. Using the modular approach, only the mechanism that's responsible for interfacing with the new physical transmission media needs to be developed; the remainder of the Physical Layer functions can be used, ideally, without alteration. The IEEE's Physical Layer components are illustrated in Figure 6.3 and explained in the remainder of this section.

The four components of the Physical Layer are the Physical Signaling Sublayer (PLS— yes, that's correct, PLS!), the Attachment Unit Interface (AUI), the Physical Medium Attachment (PMA), and the Medium Dependent Interface (MDI).

Together, these components provide the entire definition of how transmission occurs between any two devices on a network. This includes the cable types (including minimum levels of expected performance), cable connector types, pin assignments of the cable (for twisted-pair media only), voltage levels (for electrical signal transmission) or optical wavelength levels (for transmission over fiber-optic cables), timing, and even the physical network interface (that is, *transceiver*) that performs the transmission and reception.

FIGURE 6.3
The IEEE's
Physical Layer
components.

OSI Reference Model Layer Description	OSI Layer Number	IEEE Project 802 Reference Model
Physical	1	Physical Signaling Sublayer
		Attachment Unit Interface
		Physical Medium Attachment
		Medium Dependent Interface

The Physical Signaling Sublayer (PLS) mechanism is indigenous to data terminal equipment (DTE) devices that use 10BaseT. It defines the signaling scheme as well as the interface to the transceiver cable that's used.

The Attachment Unit Interface (AUI) provides the definition of the transmission media specifications. The Physical Medium Attachment (PMA) defines the operational processes and specifications of the transceiver.

The Medium Dependent Interface (MDI) is the most visible aspect of the 802.3 Physical Layer. There are multiple supported MDIs, each one describing the mechanisms needed to support transmission via a different transmission media. The AUI, PMA, and MDI are often embodied in a single device known as a *Medium Attachment Unit* (MAU). This is the term that the IEEE uses rather than *NIC*.

Note: The MDI does *not* define the transmission media! Rather, it defines all the mechanisms and processes required to support transmission over a given media type. Its definitions assume a specific, minimum level of performance to be provided by the media, as well as the physical connector type to be used to connect to that media. This is, however, not a definition of the media itself.

The Physical Layer's Medium Dependent Interfaces

Five distinct MDIs for 10Mbps baseband Ethernet are defined by the IEEE. These MDIs are bundled into modules that define every aspect of the Physical Layer for the different transmission media. Of these five MDIs, two are based on coaxial cable, two on fiber-optic cable, and one on twisted pairs of copper wire. Some basic specification limitations apply to all the MDIs.

For example, all media types must comply with a maximum signal path. The maximum allowable signal path is four repeaters. This enables five cable segments to be interconnected, provided that at least two of those segments are inter-repeater links only! This limit is frequently referred to as the 5-4-3 rule, because of the five segments, four repeaters, and maximum of three populated segments.

This numeric limitation can easily be translated into maximum network diameters for each of the physical media by multiplying the number of links by the maximum allowable transmission distance for each media and then adding all the products together.

Although it would be a bit tougher to come up with a cute, if not mnemonic, moniker for it, 802.3 also imposes a limit of seven bridges for a LAN segment. This applies to all media types.

Another limitation is imposed on the number of devices that a segment may contain. Each segment, regardless of media type, may contain a maximum of 1,024 devices. Networks that need to support more than this number must use either a switch or router to create multiple segments.

The two coaxial cables allow for some topological variety not supported by the other MDIs, because coaxial cable can be tapped. *Tapping* is a process whereby the two conductors of the cable are pierced, but not broken, with a device known as a *tap*. The tap provides for continuity along the original cable path while simultaneously enabling a new cable path to be branched off of it. This new cable can be used to connect to other network devices, including repeaters, servers, printers, and client machines. 802.3-compliant, coaxial-cabled Ethernets can support up to 64 devices off each tap. Each tap must be at least 2.5 meters away from any other tap.

Twisted-pair and fiber-optic cables are point-to-point transmission media and cannot be tapped. Radial expansion of a network using either of these media must be accomplished using a hub.

10Base2

10Base2, like most of the other Ethernet MDIs, derives its name from the following convention: the signaling speed (in Mbps) plus the transmission method (baseband, in this case) plus the maximum number of meters that the cable can be, rounded to the nearest 100, divided by 100.

If this sounds complicated, consider 10Base2. This specification describes a 10Mbps baseband network protocol. It uses a 50ohm coaxial cable that can be a maximum length of 185 meters in length. Rounding 185 up yields 200. Dividing 200 by 100 yields 2, the last digit of the MDI's name.

10Base2 networks can be extended beyond 185 meters by using repeaters, bridges, or routers. Using a router to segment an Ethernet actually creates 10Base2 segments that can be tapped up to 30 times, with each tap supporting a maximum of 64 devices.

10Base5

As its name implies, the maximum length for 10Base5 coaxial cable is 500 meters. This MDI uses a much thicker coaxial cable than 10Base2. Transmission efficacy, in copper media, is a function of the conductor's thickness. The greater the conductor's diameter, the more bandwidth that can be achieved. Consequently, 10Base5 can be tapped up to 100 times, with a maximum of 64 devices per tap.

Mathematically, one could argue that this means a 10Base5 segment could be built that contains 6,400 devices. Unfortunately, an overarching device number limitation of 1,024 is applied to all 802.3 specifications.

10BaseT

If 10BaseT had adhered to the naming conventions applied to the coaxial specifications, its name would have been 10Base1, because it's limited to a 100-meter segment length. For whatever reasons it may have had, the IEEE broke from convention and designated this MDI with a *T* to symbolize its physical media: twisted pair.

10BaseT, contrary to popular belief, does not specify a cable type but rather a signaling technique that works on four wires that equal or surpass the Category of Performance #3 (CAT 3) unshielded twisted pair. The four wires are named for their function and polarity. One pair of wires is used to support the positive and negative poles of the transmit circuit, whereas the second pair supports the positive and negative poles of the receive circuit. The four wires are named: T+ (for the positive transmit wire), T- (for the negative transmit wire), R+ (for the positive receive wire), and R- (for the negative receive wire).

The 10BaseT specification calls for these four wires to be wired to specific pin assignments in the twisted-pair cable. 10BaseT repeaters/hubs use pin assignments that enable NIC ports to be cabled to them. For Ethernet repeaters and other data communications equipment (DCE), these assignments are provided in Table 6.1.

Table 6.1   DCE Pin Numbers and Functions

DCE Pin Assignment	Function
1	R+
2	R-
3	T+
4	Not used
5	Not used
6	T-
7	Not used
8	Not used

For Ethernet NICs and other data terminal equipment (DTE), these assignments are listed in Table 6.2.

Table 6.2 DTE Pin Numbers and Functions

DTE Pin Assignment	Function
1	T+
2	T-
3	R+
4	Not used
5	Not used
6	R-
7	Not used
8	Not used

Under normal operating circumstances, a DTE device always connects to a DCE device. These complementary interfaces enable terminal and communications gear to be directly cabled together without causing conflicts between transmits and receives. Under normal operating circumstances, a DCE device always connects to a DTE device, using a four-pair cable whose leads remain consistent from end to end. Such a cable is called a *straight-through cable*. There are, however, certain exceptions to this simple DCE-to-DTE connectivity scheme.

Interconnecting the current generation of hubs results in a DCE-to-DCE connection. This is the first exception. Hubs used to have separate "out" ports that were configured as DTE. The sole purpose of these out ports was to interconnect with the "in" ports of another hub, bridge, and so forth. Many of today's hubs, however, have eschewed this feature in favor of high bandwidth, fully meshed switched backplanes in robust, multislot chassis. The manufacturers reason that the backplane can interconnect any LAN hubs that are inserted. Consequently, all ports are configured as "out" ports (that is, they have a DCE pin configuration).

Interconnecting two hubs that have only DCE ports presents a problem. They both transmit on the same pair of wire and listen on the other pair. The end result is that every packet sent across this link either experiences a collision or is not acknowledged by the recipient. (Not a good thing.) The answer is to use a crossover cable that simulates a DCE-to-DTE interface, given a DCE-to-DCE scenario.

The second scenario that can result in something other than a DCE-to-DTE interface is the direct interconnection of two devices equipped with NICs, without having a repeater/hub in between them. This results in a DTE-to-DTE connection, the opposite of the first scenario. Regardless, the net effect remains the same. Communications do not work.

Clearly, this is a highly unusual situation. In fact, outside of testing, there aren't many reasons to interconnect two machines in this manner. This may, however, be changing. The emergence of clustering technologies for low-end computing architectures creates a need for a robust connection to internetwork two devices that are in very close proximity. Given that most early clusters will be limited to two computers, there's little reason to install a repeating hub between them. In fact, the use of a hub in this manner only introduces unnecessary propagation delays. The cluster operates more efficiently without it! The computers' NICs can be cabled directly together using a crossover cable.

Crossover cables must maintain the polarity of a physical wire. Positive and negative voltages must be kept separate, because they're directly tied to the signaling scheme used by Ethernet. The only wires that are crossed over are the positive transmit (T+) to the positive receive (R+) and the negative transmit (T-) to the negative receive (R-).

Differential Signaling

The use of positive and negative leads, or *wires*, for each function enables the use of a signaling technique known as *differential signaling*. Differential signaling is designed to cancel out the effects of electromagnetic noise on the data. Noise is relatively easily inducted into the wires, and it constitutes one of the graver concerns of transmitting on unshielded twisted pair.

The transmitting device using differential signaling places the opposite forms of the same signal on both transmit leads, T+ and T-. T- receives the inverse of the signal placed on T+. At the other end of the wire, the T- signal is inverted again. T- and T+ should then, theoretically, be equals. Any noise that's inducted is inducted equally across both pairs, at least in theory. Therefore, what appears to be a spike on the T+ lead appears as an equal, yet opposite, valley on the T- lead. Adding the two signals together at the terminus of the wire results in the restoration of the original signal. The spike and the valley literally cancel each other out.

10BaseFL

The 10BaseFL specification provides for the baseband transmission of 10Mbps Ethernet over multimode 62.5/125–micron fiber-optic cable. The maximum distance for a cable run is 2,000 meters. Like twisted pair, fiber-optic cabling cannot be tapped: It's strictly a point-to-point medium.

10BaseFL can be used to interconnect repeaters, or even to connect servers to a repeater. Such connections tend to be slightly more expensive than comparable 10BaseT connections, but they can be extended over much greater distances.

10BaseFOIRL

A relatively recent addition to the 802.3 series is 10BaseFOIRL, 10Mbps baseband transmission over fiber-optic inter-repeater links. Implicit in this definition is that this technology is strictly limited to the interconnection of repeaters. In other words, it's for hub-to-hub connectivity over fiber-optic cabling. There can be no other devices attached.

10BaseFOIRL uses an 8.3-micron diameter fiber-optic cable that must be driven by an injection laser diode (ILD). This hardware/media combination provides effective transmission of 10Mbps baseband signals for up to 5,000 meters. Unfortunately, both ILDs and single-mode fiber tend to be fairly expensive, which has limited their adoption in the marketplace.

> **Note:** It's quite common for fiber-optic cables to be described as 9 microns in diameter. This is the 8.3-micron diameter fiber-optic cable rounded up to the next whole number. Curiously, multimode fiber, which is 62.5 microns in diameter, is always referred to as 62.5 microns!

Media Type Mixing

The different Physical Layer specifications and their transmission media should not be considered mutually exclusive. In fact, the very point of having an 802 family of LAN/MAN standards was to facilitate interoperability across different LAN architectures and manufacturers. Therefore, it would be rather silly if the specifications did not provide for topologies constructed from a mixture of supported transmission media.

It's quite common for the media type to be matched to the requirements of the LAN's functional areas. Historically, there have been three functional areas: station connectivity, server connectivity, and repeater connectivity.

Each of the three functional areas also presents a different set of performance expectations. For example, station connectivity, assuming your work environment has a structured cable plant, typically involves very short runs of copper-based wiring. Good choices are either 10Base2 or 10BaseT, although 10BaseT is vastly preferable. Even the relatively thin wiring of 10Base2 can quickly clog cable ducts and raceways.

Server connectivity is much like station connectivity, except that it functions as a traffic aggregation point. Consequently, it's difficult to apply too much bandwidth to this LAN functional area. Good choices are either 10BaseT or, preferably, 10BaseFL.

Repeater interconnectivity is a long-winded way of saying LAN backbone. The links between repeaters can be lengthy. Additionally, LAN backbones are also a natural traffic aggregation point in the network (that's their primary function!). Consequently, media that can span long distances and still support adequate bandwidth are essential. Logical choices are either of the fiber specifications, although 10BaseT can work (provided, of course, you adhere to its distance limitations). Also, if you insist on a coaxial cable plant, 10Base5 is well suited to LAN backbones.

Fast Ethernet

During the early 1990s, trade publications were filled with glowing reviews of a revolutionary new LAN protocol: Asynchronous Transfer Mode (ATM). Originally a telecommunications protocol intended to service central office–to–central office traffic, ATM was envisioned as a grand unifier. It could integrate LANs and WANs so completely as to make their differences academic.

> **Note:** *Central offices* (COs) are the physical premises where the copper telephone wiring from residences and business locations aggregate and terminate in a large telecommunications switch. Each CO is trunked to one or more COs. Together, the overall network forms the commercial switching fabric for telephony.

This vision was derailed by numerous pedestrian factors, not the least of which were the slow pace with which ATM LAN standards (and products) were being developed and Ethernet's refusal to die. Ethernet, waited quietly in the wings until the industry consortium of competitors bogged down under their own mass. An equally daunting challenge facing the ATM Forum was the difficulty of providing robust backward compatibility with existing, but highly dissimilar, LAN infrastructures. LAN manufacturers began talking about a 100Mbps Ethernet as a stop-gap alternative to ATM LANs.

A stop-gap solution was necessary because existing LANs were showing their age, relative to the processors and application types that they were supporting. ATM was still viewed as the ultimate solution, but politics within the Forum, as well as the practical limitations of manufacturing sciences, were slowing its progress. Meanwhile, customers were clamoring for a higher-performance LAN technology.

While the world was waiting for ATM, Ethernet, it was reasoned, could be given a quick makeover. The Data Link Layer protocols could be retained and its signaling speed increased by an order of magnitude. The only thing that really needed any work was the Physical Layer—a series of new physical interfaces would have to be developed to accommodate the faster clock rate. It seemed easy enough. The new Ethernet would give LAN managers an option in their migration to ATM.

A myriad of proposals, which came to be known generically as *Fast Ethernet*, finally coalesced into two competing proposals, both sanctioned by the IEEE under its 802 family of standards. One proposal, which is known today as *Fast Ethernet*, is literally just the traditional 802.3 CSMA/CD protocol with a signaling speed one order of magnitude faster. Fast Ethernet was standardized as an extension of the existing 802.3 standard.

The other proposal became known as *VG-AnyLAN* and was standardized under 802.12. This technology, although technically superior with respect to its capability to accommodate isochronous traffic (as well as its removal of collisions entirely), posed a slightly less gracious migration from 10Mbps Ethernet. For this and many other reasons, including the lack of any must-have isochronous applications, VG-AnyLAN failed to garner any market share.

Fast Ethernet's Media Choices

The 100Mbps extensions to 802.3 comprise three different media-dependent interfaces:

- 100BaseTX defines the original 100BaseX specification for Category 5 unshielded twisted pair (UTP) and for Type 1 shielded twisted pair (STP).
- 100BaseFX defines 100Mbps Ethernet over fiber-optic cabling.
- 100BaseT4 defines 100Mbps Ethernet over Categories 3, 4, and 5 UTP.

The term *100BaseX* is used to refer to both 100BaseTX and 100BaseFX. Similarly, the two twisted-pair interfaces, 100BaseTX and 100BaseT4, are sometimes described as *100BaseT*. It's important to note that 100BaseX and 100BaseT are *not* physical interfaces! They are generic descriptions of a group of similar interfaces.

Further confusion is caused by the unfortunate naming convention selected by the 802.3 working committee for the two signaling schemes that are used by the Fast Ethernet interfaces. These signaling schemes are 100Base4T+ and 100BaseX. Yes, that's correct: 100BaseX. The same term is used to describe a signaling scheme as well as two physical interfaces.

To avoid confusion, the specific interfaces are referred to by their full names throughout this chapter. The terms *100BaseT* and *100BaseX* are reserved for use only when referring to both physical variants encompassed by those names. Additionally, whenever the term *100BaseX* is used in the context of a signaling scheme, it's identified as such.

100BaseTX

The first classification is called 100BaseTX. This encompasses shielded twisted pair (STP) Category 1 wire and unshielded twisted pair (UTP) Category 5 wire. Changes have been made to the Media Access Controller (MAC) Layer to enable that layer's mechanisms, which had originally been designed for a 10Mbps network, to operate at 100Mbps.

Because this standard is an extension to the IEEE 802.3 specification for Ethernet, great pains were taken to ensure that this Fast Ethernet product would bear a very strong resemblance to 10BaseT. For example, 10BaseT can run on two pair of Category 3 (Cat 3) unshielded twisted pair (UTP) wire. Therefore, it became important for Fast Ethernet to use two-pair wire so that migration would not require users to rewire stations. Indeed, Fast Ethernet can run on just two pairs, but those pairs must be Category 5 wire, not Category 3. This tends to obviate the intended benefit of this feature, because not every station wired with Category 3 UTP was given a full four pairs in its original installation. Consequently, many LAN administrators find themselves faced with the need to rewire, despite the availability of a 100Mbps LAN technology that supports Cat 3 transmissions.

Note: It's important to note that although the IEEE's 802.3 specification defines numerous physical interfaces for 10Mbps Ethernet, Fast Ethernet most closely resembles 10BaseT.

100BaseFX

100BaseFX is the fiber-optic equivalent of 100BaseTX. They share a common signaling scheme and data-encoding technique but use different physical media. 100BaseFX can support the 100Mbps data rate up to 400 meters over two strands of 62.5/125–micron fiber-optic cable. This greatly expands the reach of Fast Ethernet and, as a result, is best used for inter-repeater links.

100BaseT4

100BaseT4 is designed to allow transmission of 100Mbps over four pairs of voice-grade wiring for distances up to 100 meters. Voice-grade wiring is defined to be a minimum of Category 3 UTP. It's also capable of transmission using Categories 4 and 5 UTP.

Note: 4T+ does not support 25-pair bundles of Category 3 horizontal wiring. This type of wire was used fairly extensively in the wire distribution systems of many older commercial buildings.

One important functional difference between 100BaseT4 and its siblings is that this specification does not support continuous signaling between frames. This continuous signaling is known as the *interframe gap*. Typically, continuous signaling is used by the transmitting device to maintain its hold on the right to transmit. Other devices interpret the meaningless string of 96 bits as a busy line. If they need to transmit, but see this string, they implement their binary exponential back-off algorithms and wait. Therefore, a specification that does not support this type of signaling has reduced power requirements. This consideration is important for laptop computers and in any other circumstances where power consumption is a critical factor.

Signaling Schemes

Fast Ethernet uses two different signaling schemes for its twisted pair interfaces. These schemes, confusingly named *100BaseX* and *100Base4T+*, both support a data rate of 100Mbps. This rate can be supported for a maximum of 100 meters from the hub to the workstation, and a distance of 10 meters from hub to hub, albeit over different physical media. Fiber can be used to transcend the hub-to-hub distance limitation.

> **Note:** The term *data rate* should not be confused with *signaling speed*. Fast
> Ethernet, widely understood to support 100Mbps, actually signals at 125Mbps.
> Subtracting the Physical Layer overheads, including the encoding technique,
> results in a 100Mbps data rate. This is true of 10Mbps Ethernet as well: It signals
> at 12.5Mbps, but offers a net data rate of 10Mbps.

100Base4T+

The 100Base4T+ signaling scheme enables the 100BaseT physical interfaces to run over
most existing Category 3 wiring. The qualification "most existing Category 3 wiring" is
necessary because this signaling scheme requires four pairs. This signaling technique
uses three pairs to carry data bi-directionally in half-duplex mode, whereas the fourth
pair is used in receive-only mode for collision detection.

If this fourth pair detects a signal at the far end of the wire, it informs the Physical Layer
protocols that now is not a good time to transmit. The remaining three pairs are used to
transmit and receive data, but not both simultaneously.

Each of these pairs can support a data rate of 33.33Mbps. Together, they yield 100Mbps
of usable bandwidth. (Let's not hear any complaints from the mathematicians: 3×33.33
is close enough to 100 to warrant the claim.)

Three wire paths are necessary because of the 8B6T encoding scheme used in
100Base4T+. In essence, the MAC Sublayer passes down octets of binary data to the
Physical Layer. The Physical Layer converts each octet, or eight bits (this is the *8B* part
of the 8B6T name), to six ternary symbols. Each group of six ternary symbols is known
as a *6T group*. These 6T groups are then split across the three available serial channels—
that is, the three pairs of wire available for transmission and reception of data.

> **Note:** For readers infatuated with techno-trivia, each ternary symbol (six are
> created from each octet of data) takes approximately 40 nanoseconds to trans-
> mit at a signaling speed of 125Mbps.

100BaseX

100BaseX was adapted from the full-duplex signaling mechanism of FDDI (Fiber
Distributed Data Interface—see Chapter 8) to work with the Ethernet's CSMA/CD. The
FDDI signaling mechanism supports two physical interfaces: Category 5 UTP and
62.5/125-micron multimode fiber-optic cabling. Consequently, 100BaseX supports the
same cable types and distance limitations as FDDI for these two physical media.

FDDI's interface is called the *Twisted Pair Physical Medium Dependent* (TP-PMD) interface. It uses two pairs of Category 5 UTP to support 100Mbps, full-duplex communications up to 100 meters. If four-pair wiring is used, the remaining two pairs can, theoretically, carry voice-grade communications but not another high-speed LAN.

100BaseX also supports the FDDI Fiber Physical Medium Dependent (F-PMD) interface, which calls for 62.5/125–micron multimode fiber. This interface provides a 100Mbps full-duplex data rate for up to 400 meters.

The 100BaseX signaling scheme uses a 4B/5B encoding scheme. This scheme accepts *nibbles* (four bits, or a half octet) of data from the MAC Sublayer and encodes them into 5-bit symbols for transmission. These 5-bit symbols are known as *code groups*. These code groups are indigenous to the 100BaseX mechanisms only and are meaningless outside of that context.

A 5-bit binary field has 32 possible codes. These codes are used to represent the 16 code groups of the hexadecimal character set (0 through F). Additionally, four code groups are used as transmission-control mechanisms. The remaining 12 possible codes are used as interstream filler or remain undefined.

Maximum Network Diameter

Interoperability at the hub is achieved via a repeater. The specifications for 100BaseT include a universal repeater that supports both physical layers. Up to two universal repeaters, located a maximum of 10 meters apart, can be used in a 100BaseT network.

Segmentation with routers can also increase the network's potential diameter beyond this two-repeater limit.

Gigabit Ethernet

A new proposal to increase the signaling speed of Ethernet is called *Gigabit Ethernet*. The standard for Gigabit Ethernet was developed by the IEEE under the auspices of the 802.3z task force and accepted as a standard in September, 1998.

Due to its inclusion within the 802.3 umbrella of specifications, every effort was made to make Gigabit Ethernet as compatible as possible with its lower-speed siblings. For example, Gigabit Ethernet continues to use the same CSMA/CD protocol, frame format, and frame size as the other Ethernets. These features make backward and forward compatibility with 10Mbps and 100Mbps Ethernets possible.

Gigabit Ethernet is initially intended to serve as a backbone that interconnects 10/100BaseT switches. Not far behind are proposals that will make it viable for connecting high-performance servers to the LAN. Gigabit Ethernet is even envisioned as eventually stretching up to 100 meters over Category 5 UTP to desktop processors.

Physical Interfaces

To jumpstart the standards work, the 802.3z team elected to use many elements of the ANSI Fibre Channel's Physical Layer. Fibre Channel, originally developed as a next-generation mainframe channel technology, has been standardized and converted into a LAN technology. To date, there has been little market response to Fibre Channel LANs, although they're being used widely in the emerging storage area network (SAN) implementations.

Despite its lack of market success for LANs, Fibre Channel offered a proven and viable Physical Layer for the 802.3z team to start from. Given that the intent of the IEEE is to acquire the broadest possible support for its standards, all IEEE standards are presented to ANSI for consideration as a national (versus industrial) standard. Therefore, it makes sense to embrace elements of a Physical Layer that has already been ratified by ANSI.

One of the minor problems encountered has been the signaling speed. Fibre Channel signals at 1.063Gbps using an encoding scheme that generates an extra two bits for every octet transmitted. This scheme (known as *8B/10B*), as well as its close relative, 4B/5B, results in less than 1Gbps of usable bandwidth. The actual amount is more like 800Mbps. This is still a significant increase over most of the extant LAN technologies, but it lacks the psychological impact of breaking the gigabit barrier. In time, it's expected that the signaling technologies can be bolstered to run at 1.25Gbps. This will yield a net of 1Gbps of bandwidth, assuming the continued use of an 8B/10B encoding scheme.

Gigabit Ethernet offers these choices of transmission media, each with its own physical interface specification:

- Copper coaxial cabling
- Multimode fiber-optic cabling (both 62.5 micron and 50 micron)
- 8.3/125–micron single-mode fiber-optic cabling

These interfaces are described in the next three sections. The maximum link distances specified in each medium-dependent interface were intended to provide adequate performance for most existing cable plants, assuming a worst-case implementation.

1000BaseSX

1000BaseSX is the IEEE 802.3z proposed specification for multimode transmission using short wavelength lasers. *Short wavelength lasers* are defined as those lasers that produce light in the 850-nanometer range.

This proposal actually recognizes two different media: 50-micron and 62.5-micron diameter fiber-optic cabling. The 50-micron variant can support the full gigabit signaling rate for a maximum of 550 meters. The 62.5-micron diameter variant is limited to a maximum of 260 meters per cable segment.

1000BaseLX

1000BaseLX is the proposed specification for long wavelength laser transmissions. Laser transmissions that are 1,300 nanometers in length are considered to have long wavelengths.

This proposal includes both 62.5-micron and 50-micron multimode fiber-optic cabling as well as 8.3-micron single-mode fiber-optic cabling.

In its current form, the 62.5-micron multimode fiber can extend to a maximum of 440 meters. The 50-micron multimode fiber can be extended up to 550 meters in length. The 8.3-micron single-mode fiber specification, ostensibly the most expensive to manufacture and install, can support gigabit signaling for up to three kilometers.

1000BaseCX

1000BaseCX defines the 802.3 proposed specification for transmission over high-quality shielded twisted pair or coaxial cabling. The maximum distance for transmission over either media is limited to just 25 meters.

The very short transmission distance limits this physical interface significantly. One of the proposed uses is to interconnect gigabit switches using a low-cost copper alternative to fiber optics.

Left unspoken by the contributors to the Gigabit Ethernet standards work is that signaling at such a high rate over copper is problematic. Copper transmission facilities can do wonders, provided enough electricity is supplied: the more electrical power is pumped through it, the higher the bandwidth. Unfortunately, copper makes a wonderful electromagnetic radiator. Higher transmission power and frequency result in higher levels of electromagnetic radiation (EMI). EMI emission is carefully regulated by the Federal Communications Commission (FCC) because it uses frequency bands that the FCC regulates.

The net effect is that gigabit signaling can be supported for only very modest distances over copper transmission facilities using today's signaling schemes.

1000BaseT

A separate task force worked on the standard for 1000BaseT, gigabit Ethernet over unshielded twisted pair. This team and its standard are called *802.3ab*, just approved by IEEE in the spring of 1999. The goal was to match the performance of Fast Ethernet over four pairs of Category 5 unshielded twisted pair, albeit at a signaling speed of 1,024Mbps. This effort was split from the remainder of the 802.3z Gigabit Ethernet work simply because of the amount of work that needed to be done. Remember, the bulk of Gigabit Ethernet was created by mixing and matching the existing Data Link Layer and Physical Layer specifications of different networking technologies. This limited the predominant development efforts to reconciliation of minor disparities.

The 802.3ab work is viewed as critical if Gigabit Ethernet is to ever prove itself cost effective as a station-connect technology. The vast majority of installed cable plants utilize twisted pair as the station-connect wiring. Much of this is only Category 3. However, as user groups move, change their station environments, and engage in numerous other activities, the installed base of Cat 3 UTP continues to suffer attrition. Their work presupposes that all new wiring that's installed to support these activities is Cat 5 UTP. As Cat 5 UTP proliferates, the costs of migrating to Gigabit Ethernet (using the 1000BaseT interface) automatically decrease.

IEEE 802.3 Ethernet Frame

Project 802 defined a standard basis for all Ethernet frame types. The frames are a minimum of 64 octets and a maximum of 1,518 octets in length, including payload and all headers (except the preamble and start-of-frame delimiter). The headers are used to identify the sender and recipient of each packet. The only limitation on this identification is that each address must be unique and six octets in length.

The first 12 octets of each frame contain the 6-Octet destination address (the intended recipient's address) and a 6-Octet source address (the sender's address). These addresses are hardware-level machine address codes, commonly known as *MAC addresses*. They can either be the unique *universally administered address* that's automatically given to each Ethernet network interface card (NIC) at its manufacture or customized upon installation. Customized addresses are known as *locally administered addresses*. Although potentially valuable, they are extremely difficult to maintain. Consequently, they have fallen into disuse.

The 802.3 Technical Working Group needed a standard that was complete unto itself, not dependent upon the good behavior of other protocols. Therefore, it replaced the 2-Octet Type field of previous Ethernets with a 2-Octet Length field. This 2-Octet field defines the length of the frame's data field. The basic IEEE 802.3 Ethernet frame is depicted in Figure 6.4.

FIGURE 6.4

The basic, or "raw," IEEE 802.3 Ethernet frame.

7-Octet Preamble	1-Octet Start of Frame Delimiter	6-Octet Destination Address	6-Octet Origination Address	2-Octet Length Field	Variable Length Data Field (> 48 Octets < 1500)	4-Octet Frame Check Sequence

Note: The basic IEEE 802.3 frame is often called a *raw Ethernet frame*, because it's seldom actually used in that form. Instead, the basic frame serves as a foundation for supporting subheaders that facilitate protocol identification for higher-layer protocols at the destination machine.

The IEEE's 802.3 basic Ethernet Frame replaced the traditional Type field with a Length field. The 802.2 subframe is used, instead of that Type field, to identify the type of protocol, if this is necessary. Another change in the 802.3 frame from its predecessors was the requirement for the overall frame size to be between 64 and 1,518 octets in length, from the start of the Destination field through the end of the Frame Check Sequence field.

Some confusion persists about the exact length of an Ethernet frame. This confusion is caused by three factors:

- The variety of Ethernet frame types
- The flexible-sized payload
- The inconsistency with which the preamble and start-of-frame delimiter are referenced

As demonstrated in Chapter 3, "The Data Link Layer," there are five different types of Ethernet frames: PARC Ethernet, DIX Ethernet, Basic 802.3, 802.3 with LLC subframe, and 802.3 with SNAP subframe. These five varieties represent three different sets of minimum and maximum frame sizes.

Peter's Principle: You Should Consider the Category of Performance Rating of Wire Before Purchasing.

It has been said that the great thing about standards is that there are so many to choose from! Two sets of standards can get you into trouble when dealing with Ethernet: cable standards and framing standards.

The standards for twisted-pair wiring are based on levels of performance rather than on physical attributes. Pay careful attention to the Category of Performance rating of any twisted-pair wiring *before* you purchase it. Ratings numbering 1 through 5 are established and are referenced with the abbreviation *Cat #*. Today, only Cat 3 and Cat 5 remain viable choices for LAN wiring. Choose one or the other, but don't mix them in a LAN!

Ethernet frame types each have a useful purpose, but that purpose isn't to interoperate. Whenever possible, choose one frame type and stick to it throughout your network.

If you're ever called on to troubleshoot communications problems—two devices on a network that can't "see" each other—its always wise to first verify that the cable and frame used are consistent from one end of the network to the other.

Notice the intentional avoidance of specific frame sizes. With flexible payloads, the best you can do is identify the minimum and maximum allowable frame sizes. Understand and expect that actual frames may be any size in between these values.

The last point of confusion involves the preamble and start-of-frame delimiter (SFD). The preamble is a seven-octet string that precedes each frame and allows the synchronization of the transmission. It's a necessary part of the frame, but it's seldom considered part of the frame itself.

The preamble is immediately followed by the one-octet SFD. The SFD is sometimes considered an integral part of the preamble, and not a part of the frame itself. Alternatively, you need not look very long or hard to find references that identify the SFD as the official start of the frame.

To avoid confusion, whenever frame sizes are referenced in this chapter, they're specifically identified and qualified with a description of their starting and ending field names.

Ethernet LLC Frame Structure

The Ethernet LLC frame is a combination of an 802.3 frame and the 802.2 LLC subframe. In this implementation, LLC adds three fields to the basic Ethernet frame: Destination Service Access Port, Source Service Access Port, and Control.

Because the 802.3 frame abandoned its predecessors' Type field in favor of a Length field, it was unable to determine which protocol was embedded in the payload. Consequently, a frame received by a computer that supported multiple communications protocols might not be routed to the correct protocol! In other words, the 802.3 frame was adequate to ensure the forwarding of the frame to its destination, but it fell short of being able to guarantee delivery to higher-layer protocols within that destination machine.

Consequently, the IEEE developed an 802.2 subframe structure and standard to rectify this issue. This new subframe is referred to as either an 802.2 subframe or an LLC frame (see Figure 6.5).

FIGURE 6.5
The Ethernet LLC frame.

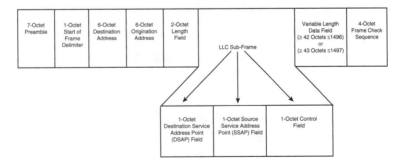

When embedded in an 802.3 Ethernet frame, the new frame has the following structure:

- A 7-Octet preamble that signals the start of a frame
- A 1-Octet start-of-frame delimiter that signals the start of the frame's contents

- The intended recipient's 6-Octet MAC address
- The originator's 6-Octet MAC address
- A 2-Octet Length field that identifies the total length of the Data field, including the LLC and SNAP headers
- A 1-Octet Destination Service Access Point (DSAP) field that identifies, predictably, the LLC's service access point at the destination machine
- A 1-Octet Source Service Access Point (SSAP) field that identifies the originating machine's LLC service access point
- A 1- or 2-Octet Control field that indicates the type of LLC frame being carried
- A data field that contains either 42 to 1,496 or 43 to 1,497 octets of data, depending upon the length of the preceding Control field
- A four-octet Frame Check Sequence that's used to check the integrity of the frame

The total length of an Ethernet LLC frame must be at least 64 octets (excluding the preamble and start-of-frame delimiter) to permit proper functioning of the CSMA/CD mechanism. Zeroes are padded to the end of the Data field to ensure this minimum length. The upper limit is 1,518 octets, excluding the preamble and start-of-frame delimiter.

Ethernet SNAP Frame Structure

After the LLC subframe was developed, concerns arose over the adequacy of that structure. Specifically, it was felt that it could not be used to identify all the higher-layer protocols that would eventually need to be identified.

The IEEE went back to work and developed the Subnetwork Access Protocol (SNAP) subframe. SNAP adds a five-octet Protocol Identification field. This field is inserted in the frame after the LLC header. It consists of a 3-Octet organizationally unique identifier (OUI) and a 2-Octet Type field. These fields identify which upper-layer protocol the frame is intended for on the receiving end.

An Ethernet SNAP frame is illustrated in Figure 6.6. It contains the following fields:

- A 7-Octet preamble that signals the start of a frame
- A 1-Octet start-of-frame delimiter that signals the start of the frame's contents
- The intended recipient's 6-Octet MAC address
- The originator's 6-Octet MAC address
- A 2-Octet Length field that identifies the total length of the Data field, including the LLC and SNAP headers
- A 1-Octet Destination Service Access Point (DSAP) field that identifies, predictably, the LLC's service access point at the destination machine
- A 1-Octet Source Service Access Point (SSAP) field that identifies the originating machine's LLC service access point

- A 1- or 2-Octet Control field that indicates the type of LLC frame being carried
- A 5-Octet SNAP subframe, including a three-octet organizationally unique identifier field and a two-octet protocol type field that identify the upper-level protocol being carried
- A data field that contains either 37 to 1,491 octets or 38 to 1,492 octets of data, depending on the length of the preceding Control field
- A 4-Octet Frame Check Sequence that's used to check the integrity of the frame

FIGURE 6.6
The Ethernet SNAP frame.

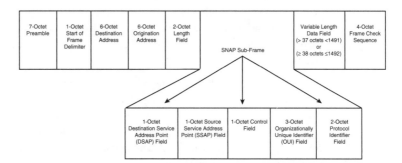

The Ethernet SNAP frame integrates the 802.2 subframe structures, or headers, and permits the identification of higher-level protocols that are the intended recipients of the frame's contents. This provides backward compatibility with earlier versions of Ethernet whose frames contain discrete mechanisms for protocol identification.

The total length of an Ethernet SNAP frame must be at least 64 octets to permit proper functioning of the CSMA/CD mechanism. The upper limit for an Ethernet SNAP frame's size is 1,518 octets, including the preamble and start-of-frame delimiter.

For more information on the various Ethernet frame structures, see Chapter 3.

Changes for Gigabit Ethernet

A fair question to ask is, "Besides the need for completely new Physical Layer media interfaces, what else is new?" The answer, so far, is not much. Great pains have been taken to preserve as much of the content of the various existing 802.3 specifications as possible. This was done to ensure continued interoperability within the 802 and 802.3 families of specifications. The two areas that have undergone notable change (other than the signaling speed, data rate, and physical interfaces!) are the protocol's interframe gap and the contention-based media-access method.

Interframe Gap

The size of the interframe gap is one significant change to the 802.3 protocol that was made necessary by Gigabit Ethernet. The 802.3 CSMA/CD protocol provides for a gap between frames of 96 bits. This gap is actually just a random string of binary characters. Its only purpose (contrary to any rumors that you may encounter on newsgroups!) is to keep the line busy. In other words, it's a stall tactic embedded in the protocol to enable a transmitting station to hold the line while it prepares another data frame for transmission.

With Gigabit Ethernet, 96 bits fly by so quickly that the electronic components on the NIC lose that legitimate stall tactic. More importantly, at the gigabit signaling speed, the minimum frame size of 64 octets is too small to ensure detection of a collision over the network. Remember, the minimum frame size was selected based on the amount of time it would take, at 10Mbps, for a frame to reach all stations on the LAN. Adjusting this to gigabit speeds means a significant increase in the minimum frame size. This compromises interoperability with the other, slower 802.3 Ethernets. This was deemed unacceptable.

The answer to both quandaries was to increase the size of the interframe gap. The gap, in Gigabit Ethernet, is now 512 octets long. One could argue the inefficiencies of using a 512-Octet interframe gap for frames that can be as small as 64 octets, but efficiency was not the goal. Interoperability was. To placate the complaint artists, a new feature was incorporated into the 802.3z protocol. This feature, known as *frame bursting*, enables the transmitting station to transmit up to 8,192 octets every time it successfully competes for bandwidth.

Contention-Based Media Access

Although not necessarily new—in the sense that it preexisted the 802.3z initiative—Ethernet's contention-based media-access method has been rendered moot. As the IEEE was developing the Fast Ethernet variants described earlier, provisions were made for full-duplex operation.

Full-duplex transmission means that a device can transmit and receive simultaneously, although over separate paths. In essence, the transmitter of one device (for example, the switch port) has a dedicated path to the receiver of another device (for example, a NIC in a computer), and vice versa. This eliminates the competition for the same bandwidth (between transmit and receive functions) that every Ethernet device previously suffered.

In a switched environment, the collision domain is reduced to just two devices: the switch port and the device to which it connects. Implementing full-duplex transmissions over a switched connection literally makes competing for available bandwidth unnecessary. Each device can obtain permission to transmit, as well as place frames on the media, at near wire speeds. CSMA/CD becomes superfluous—a relic of Ethernet's past.

Gigabit Ethernet builds on this success of Fast Ethernet. In fact, many manufacturers are designing their products to be full-duplex only. This is a testament to the success of full-duplex, switched networking.

Delay Budgets

Ethernet's CSMA/CD protocol allows for a maximum of 51.2 microseconds for a roundtrip transmission at 10Mbps signaling speed. Each component in the network, including each of the transmission media types and the physical devices, has its own propagation delay characteristics. Consequently, it's a good idea to calculate out the total delay of any given Ethernet *before* you actually build it.

Estimates of Propagation Delays

The following tables provide estimates of the propagation delays that can be expected with each of the listed devices and media. Table 6.3 provides a breakdown of estimated delay, by device type.

Table 6.3   Estimated Delay (by Device Type)

Device	Estimated Delay (in Microseconds)
Fiber-optic repeater	1.55
Multi-port Repeater	0.1
Fiber-optic transceiver	0.20
Twisted pair transceiver	0.27

Note: The values listed for propagation delay are to be considered estimates only! Numerous factors, including temperature, humidity, and even the age and/or manufacturer of an electronic device, can all affect its performance. Your mileage may vary!

Table 6.4 provides a breakdown of estimated delay, per meter, of the common transmission media types.

Table 6.4   Estimated Delay (by Media Type)

Media Type	Delay (Microseconds per Meter)
10Base2	0.00514
10Base5	0.00433
Unshielded twisted pair (UTP)	0.0057
Shielded twisted pair (STP)	0.0057
Fiber optic	0.005

Delay Budget Calculations

Calculating the estimated delay budget of your LAN is a fairly simple process. First, map out the arrangement of network devices, including the length of the links between devices and the type of media used for each link. Next, count how many of each device type is going to exist in the network and multiply that number by the delay budgeted for its type. Repeat this process for each of the devices and total up the products of each device type's delay. This is the total hardware delay budget for your network.

This figure must be augmented with the total cable delay budget. Calculating this is equally easy. For each link, multiply the length, in meters, by the number of microseconds delay that can be expected for the media type used. Repeat this process for each of the links and total up the products. This is the total cable delay budget for your network. Adding the total hardware delay budget and total cable delay budget yields the total network delay budget. In order for CSMA/CD to work properly, this value must be less than 51.2 microseconds. If it's greater than or equal to this value, you're likely to experience some operational difficulties. If the total network delay budget is close to 51.2, but still less, you may experience operational difficulties as your network's infrastructure ages.

> **Warning:** Avoid the temptation to find the edges of your network's operational abilities. It's a game not worth playing, especially when you consider that the network exists to support users and business processes, not your heuristic indulgences.

Summary

Ethernet is a rich and diverse collection of technologies. Ethernets can be baseband or broadband, full- or half-duplex, use any one of five different physical media (more, if you're brave enough to venture outside the sanctity of standards!), and support signaling speeds that range from 10Mbps up to 1Gbps.

This chapter provided an overview of the more salient Ethernet specifications. This included the various framing conventions, typical hardware components, media types, limitations of the protocol, how to calculate delay budgets, and even the differential signaling scheme used for transmitting over unshielded twisted pair.

Token Ring

Token Ring is another IEEE standardized LAN architecture. It shares many common attributes with Ethernet and the other LAN architectures contained within the IEEE 802 family of network standards. As a result, it can interoperate with them through the use of a translating bridge.

Token Ring has also received its fair share of updates since its inception. Originally a 4Mbps technology, it was later updated to 16Mbps. Today, proposals exist that will increase the signaling speed of Token Ring even further, to 100 or even 128Mbps, and eventually 1Gbps.

This chapter provides a description of the mechanics of Token Ring. This includes its myriad frame structures, its physical media specifications, its operational mechanics, and a glimpse of its future.

Fundamentals of Token Ring

In its standardized form, Token Ring is a highly deterministic and robust LAN architecture. It owes its name to its round-robin scheme for media access. Unlike Ethernet, with its multiple-access methodology, Token Ring permits only a single device to transmit at any time. There can be no collisions.

Media access is arbitrated by passing a token in an orderly fashion. There can be only one token, and it's modified by a transmitting device to form the header of a data frame. Without this token, the data frame's header cannot be constructed, and there can be no transmission. The data in the frame is copied off by the recipient device, with some of the bits in the frame's header inverted to signal receipt. The frame itself is left to continue traversing the ring. When it returns to its originator, that device takes the frame off the network and strips the addressing and data out. If that device needs to send more data, it may do so. Otherwise, the header is reconverted back into a token and placed on the transmission media, where it travels to the next device downstream.

Passing the token in a round-robin fashion, as illustrated in Figure 7.1, provides each device an opportunity to transmit. To ensure that no single station hogs the bandwidth, a mechanism known as the *Token Holding Timer* is used to track and regulate the maximum amount of time that any given station can monopolize transmission rights. This timing mechanism is also useful in restoring normal operation of the network in the event that a station holding the token ceases to function. Another beneficial side effect of this token-passing media-access technique is that Token Ring networks scale up in size and transmission volumes much more gracefully than do contention-based networks.

FIGURE 7.1
Tokens passed sequentially, in a round-robin pattern.

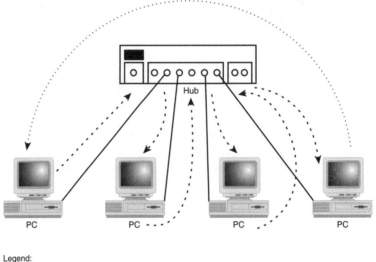

Legend:
——————— Physical Wiring
- - - - - Flow of Tokens and Frames

Standardization of Token Ring

Token Ring, by information technology standards, is ancient. It was originally conceived by IBM as a data center technology for networking mainframe computers. It was first proposed to the IEEE for standardization in 1969. After personal computers (PCs) were developed, it became apparent that Token Ring could serve to interconnect them as well. This was the impetus behind its inclusion in the IEEE's Project 802.

Standardization under the 802 umbrella necessitated making some changes to its Data Link Layer so that it would support hardware-level addressing and bridging with other 802 LAN architectures.

The IEEE designated Token Ring its 802.5 specification. This specification is almost identical to IBM's Token Ring. In addition to the aforementioned hardware-level changes, the IEEE also standardized the message format and Layer 2 protocols. IBM, incidentally, was a major proponent of the IEEE standardization efforts.

Token Ring offered a more robust, timely, and deterministic approach to networking than the 802.3 Ethernet protocol, albeit at a higher per-port cost. Companies whose applications required timely delivery of data found Token Ring to be the only viable solution for their needs. Although the 802.3 protocol ensures the packet will be successfully transmitted, it may require multiple transmission attempts. Therefore, it can't guarantee a time frame for delivery. The Token Ring topology can, due to its deterministic, ring-shaped topology and orderly access method.

Token Ring Frame Structures

By now, it should be fairly clear that Token Ring devices cannot transmit anything without a token. The basic token serves two purposes:

- It's used to arbitrate transmission privileges.
- The basic token frame gets converted to the header of the various specialized frames.

In fact, any function (including data transmission) requires the use of a specific frame structure.

Token Ring supports the following frame types:

- Token frame
- Data frame
- LLC data frame
- MAC management frames
- Abort frame

The Token Frame

The IEEE's 802.5 Token Ring uses a special bit sequence construct, known as a *token*, to control access to the transmission media. A token contains Starting Delimiter, Access Control, and Ending Delimiter fields. Each field is one octet (eight bits) in length. The token frame is illustrated in Figure 7.2.

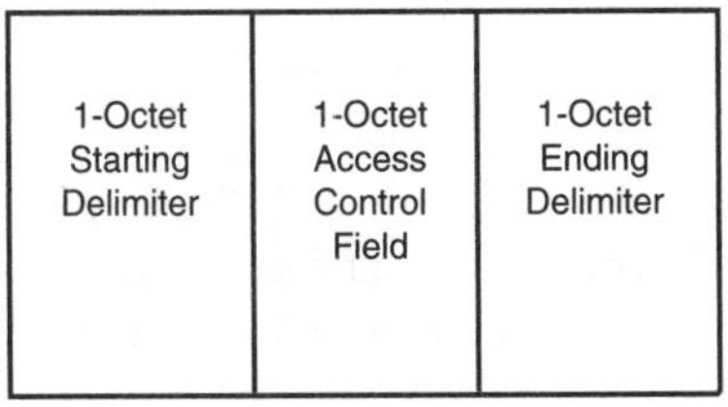

FIGURE 7.2
The IEEE 802.5 token frame.

1-Octet Starting Delimiter	1-Octet Access Control Field	1-Octet Ending Delimiter

This frame is passed from device to device and arbitrates transmission rights among the devices on the ring. Given that there's only one token frame, only one station can transmit, or attempt to transmit, at any point in time.

Access Control Field

The Access Control field is the key to the token. Each of its eight bits is significant. As illustrated in Figure 7.3, the Access Control field of the token frame contains the following fields:

- A 3-bit Priority field
- A 1-bit Token field
- A 1-bit Monitor field
- A 3-bit Request Priority field

FIGURE 7.3

*The Access
Control field.*

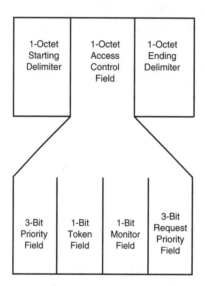

The Priority bit field is used to indicate the priority of the token itself. This value can range from 000 to 111 and is set by the transmitting station. It cannot be modified by other stations. Only stations that have a priority equal to or greater than this field's value may use it.

The Token bit is alluded to earlier in this chapter as the bit that must be manipulated to convert a token into a start-of-frame sequence. Actually, the Token bit is set to 1 to tell other stations that the token is now a part of a frame (that is, it's in use). Tokens, as illustrated previously in Figure 7.2, have this bit set to 0 as they circulate the ring, polling stations.

The Monitor bit is initially set to 1 by the Active Monitor when it generates a frame. It's reset to zero by a lobe when it grabs the frame. A newly generated token can be recognized by having the token bit set to 0 and the monitor bit set to 1.

The Request Priority field permits stations to request higher priority service. Such stations have high priority data and need to transmit as quickly as possible. Stations can communicate their priority needs by setting the Request Priority bits according to the priority of their data (valid ranges are from 000 to 111). This informs the token's issuer of their needs. Ostensibly, the issuer sets its next Priority bit field according to the Request Priority value just received. In this manner, the station with a high priority can secure the next token, regardless of how many stations lie between it and the issuer on the ring.

> **Note:** The priority bits range in significance from left to right. The leftmost bit is the most significant. That is, it carries a higher priority than the middle or rightmost bits. Consequently 010 is a higher priority than 001.

The Data Frame

The minimum length of a Token Ring data frame is 21 octets. The maximum data frame size is determined by the ring's signaling speed. The time that's required to transmit a frame must be less than the Token Holding Time that has been established. This time is 10 milliseconds by default. In a 4Mbps Token Ring, this works out to a 4,500-octet maximum data frame size. In a 16Mbps Token Ring, data frames can be up to 18,000 octets long.

The 802.5 Token Ring data frame structure consists of two parts: the token and the data frame. When a device seizes this token and inverts the Token bit value in its frame, it has taken the first steps towards creating a *data frame*. The next step is to insert and populate the other fields required in the protocol's data frame structure. The complete data frame is depicted in Figure 7.4.

FIGURE 7.4
The IEEE 802.5 data frame.

1-Octet Starting Delimiter	1-Octet Access Control Field	1-Octet Frame Control Field	6-Octet Destination Address	6-Octet Origination Address	Variable Length Data Field (0 to 4332 octets for 4Mbps LANs, or 0 to 17,832 for 16Mbps LANs)	3-Octet Frame Check Sequence	3-Octet Ending Delimiter	1-Octet Frame Status

As evidenced in Figure 7.4, the three 1-octet fields of the token frame are retained in the data frame. To this basic structure, six other fields and subfields are added.

The first field is the Starting Delimiter, which identifies the beginning of the frame. Next is the Access Control field (which was described in the section titled "Access Control Field") and the 8-bit Frame Control field. This field stores the "type" bits that identify the transport protocol. This field is also used to differentiate between data frames and control frames.

The first two bits identify the type of frame: data or MAC management. The next six bits are used to inform the recipient of the priority of the data Protocol Data Unit (PDU) and/or MAC PDU. If this is a MAC frame, this field also identifies which specific MAC management frame type this is. The Frame Control field is depicted in Figure 7.5.

FIGURE 7.5

The Frame Control field.

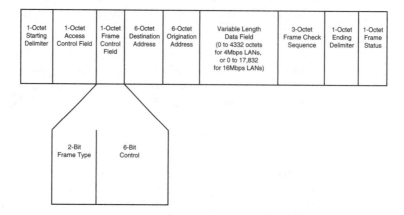

The next two fields are the destination and source MAC addresses. Each one is a 6-octet field. These MAC (Media Access Control) addresses conform to the previously described Project 802 specification and are identical to those used in Ethernet networks.

The data field for a token-based network varies in size, based on the signaling speed of the ring. 4Mbps Token Rings can support data fields that range from at least zero octets up to a maximum of 4,332. 16Mbps Token Rings can support data fields that are between 0 and 17,832 octets long. These values represent the maximum size of a frame, assuming a 10-millisecond Token Holding Time, minus the 168 octets of the basic frame structure.

The last three fields in the data frame are the 32-bit Frame Check Sequence (FCS), the 8-bit Ending Delimiter, and the 8-bit Frame Status. The Frame Check Sequence contains a mathematically derived value, a checksum that's calculated based on the length and content of the frame. The recipient and transmitter each apply the same algorithm to the frame. If the recipient computes the same checksum value stored in the FCS field (which was calculated by the transmitter), it can reasonably assume that the contents were not compromised during transmission.

The last two octets, which encompass the Ending Delimiter and Frame Status fields, are considered the end-of-frame sequence.

LLC Data Frame

The previous section defined the basic, or *raw*, form of the Token Ring data frame. In practice, it's used in conjunction with the Logical Link Control mechanisms of the

IEEE's 802.2 specification. This specification calls for an additional subframe structure to be prepended to the data frame for the purposes of identifying the higher-layer protocol for which the frame's contents are intended. This is essential in today's environment of multiprotocol computing and communications. The Token Ring data frame with an 802.2 subframe is known as a *Token Ring LLC data frame*. For more information on the 802.2 subframe structure, refer to Chapter 6, "Ethernet."

The MAC Management Frames

The IEEE 802.5 Token Ring protocol establishes four Network Management Agents (NMAs). These agents reside at each Token Ring station device and are used in the normal management operation of the ring

- Active Monitor (AM) or Standby Monitor (SM)
- Ring Error Monitor (REM)
- Configuration Report Server (CRS)
- Ring Parameter Server (RPS)

Given that the only way to transmit on the ring is to use a token-based frame, it shouldn't be a tremendous surprise that each of these agents can generate several different, highly specialized MAC management frame types. In fact, in an IEEE Token Ring, these four agents have the capability to generate and use 25 different MAC frames! If you feel the need for even more control, the IBM extensions to the IEEE MAC frame structures add another 17 MAC frames, for a total of 42 different MAC frames.

Each MAC frame performs a specific network management function. Some of these functions include the following:

- Lobe test
- Initialize ring
- Ring purge
- Claim token
- Several Active Monitor functions

The relatively large number of frames makes it pointless to examine them individually. Suffice it to say that these MAC frames are used to collect network performance metrics that can be fed to standards-compliant network-management products. Many are described in their operational context throughout the remainder of this chapter.

The Abort Frame

The Abort frame consists of just Start and End Frame delimiter fields. Although such a frame structure may seem pointless due to its lack of content and addressing, the Abort frame is used to immediately terminate transmissions.

The structure of the Abort frame is illustrated in Figure 7.6.

Figure 7.6
The IEEE's 802.5 Abort frame.

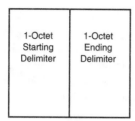

| 1-Octet Starting Delimiter | 1-Octet Ending Delimiter |

The Fill Sequence

The one transmission vehicle used by Token Ring that's not frame-based is the *fill sequence*. This sequence does not have a starting or ending delimiter. It's comprised of virtually any sequence of 1's and 0's.

The fill sequence is generated by the transmitting station. Remember, there's only one token, so only one station can transmit at any given time.

The fill sequence is used in conjunction with the various frame types in the previous list to avoid quiet time on the ring. *Quiet time* occurs whenever no token or frame is traversing the ring. Quiet time is interpreted by the Active Monitor and each station as a broken ring. Consequently, they initiate their auto-recovery mechanisms to isolate the extent of the break and identify any unreachable stations. This can be counterproductive if the ring hasn't been compromised. For example, if the ring goes quiet because a station has received the token and is holding it while framing data being received from higher-layer protocols, there is no traffic on the ring. Other stations can interpret this lack of activity as an error condition.

To combat an erroneous reaction to quiet time, the transmitting station generates a random sequence of 1's and 0's while it's preparing to send a real frame or token. This Fill Sequence is transmitted before and after a frame or token is transmitted. Fill Sequences can also be used by a transmitting station to stall for time. That is, by transmitting a random pattern of bits in lieu of a real frame or token, the transmitting station can stop the clock on its Token Holding Timer. This enables it to hold the token for longer than it would otherwise be entitled.

Token Ring Mechanics

The review of Token Ring's various frame structures should demonstrate that it's a fairly complex and very robust LAN architecture. A quick synopsis of its operational mechanics should provide ample context for a more detailed examination of its physical and logical components.

Token Ring uses a token to arbitrate access to the transmission media. Tokens are recognized, and supported, by all stations on the network. There can be only one token, and only the holder of that token may transmit.

This token is passed from station to station in a sequential manner and in one direction only. Because a ring has no clearly defined beginning or end, the token simply passes around the ring continuously. This is known as a *round-robin polling technique*. Each station that receives the token may convert its bit structure into a start-of-frame (SOF) sequence if it needs to transmit. The token is used to build the data frame. The transmitting station modifies the SOF sequence, adds the necessary data, addresses it, and places it back on the network.

Alternatively, that station may simply put the token back on the network for the next station if it doesn't need to transmit. When the frame arrives at its intended destination, the receiving device does not pull the frame off the network. Instead, it simply copies the frame into a buffer for further internal processing. One bit in the original frame's Access Control field is modified to inform the originating device that the frame has been received. The frame then continues on its journey through the ring until it returns to its originating device. Reception by the originating device constitutes a successful transmission of the frame's contents; the frame's contents are deleted, and the frame is reconverted into a token.

This is the essence of a Token Ring network's mechanics. Of course, it's highly simplified and does not describe any of the details of the various steps and processes. The rules that govern this basic functional behavior of the devices on a Token Ring network are governed by one station on the ring. This station is known as the *Active Monitor* (AM). The AM is reviewed in further detail in this chapter, under the section titled "The Active Monitor."

Given this description of the mechanics of token passing, it's obvious that an 802.5-compliant device is inherently half-duplex. That is, it operates in only one of two modes: transmit or listen. A device that's listening simply forwards the token to the next device in the ring. If the token has been converted to an SOF sequence, a listening device checks to see whether it is the destination of that frame. If it is, it buffers the data and passes the still-modified token back to the originator of the frame that it received. The originator then has to acknowledge that the frame was sent successfully, convert the SOF frame back to a token, and put the token on the network.

In transmit mode, as previously described, the device alters the token's bit structure to make the SOF sequence. Once this is done, the device then appends the necessary data and headers. This methodology, contrary to that of Ethernet, runs more efficiently under heavy traffic loads. It does so because transmission permissions are not chaotic (as Ethernet's are), and the frame is not limited to a maximum number of octets.

Token Ring Hardware

Token Ring uses a basic set of hardware components that can be used to construct a myriad of topologies in support of token-passing media access. In addition to the requisite network interface cards (NICs), these hardware components include the following:

- Trunk cable
- Lobe cable
- Multi-Station Access Units
- Trunk Coupling Unit

Each component is described in the following sections.

Trunk Cable

The *trunk cable* is the backbone of the Token Ring network. It's the cable that interconnects each of the hubs (or *Multi-Station Access Units*, in Token Ring-ese).

Trunk cables can be either fiber-optic cabling or shielded or unshielded twisted pair. Twisted pair offers an extra benefit when used as trunk cabling: It provides a redundant transmission path. The connection is achieved with a single pair; the other pairs of wires in a two-pair or four-pair UTP cable are not used. If a break occurs (assuming that it affects only one pair of wires), the second pair can be used to wrap the ring back around the damaged section.

Lobe Cable

Lobe cables are used to attach individual stations to a port on the Token Ring hub. As with trunk cables, either fiber-optic or shielded or unshielded twisted pair cabling can be used.

It's important to note that, in most twisted pair wire distribution systems installed in commercial facilities, the lobe cable is not a single cable. Rather, it's a series of cables patched together to form a continuous path.

Multistation Access Units

A device that serves as both a repeater and point of access for multiple stations (in other words, a *hub*) is known as a Multistation Access Unit (MSAU). MSAUs, like many hubs, can be strung together to form larger networks.

As with Ethernet hubs, care must be taken to not interconnect two DCE (data communications equipment) ports. MSAUs come with ports that are designated as either Ring In (RI) or Ring Out (RO). It should be obvious that the RI ports are used for inbound connections: They are DCE. The RO ports are used to connect to the RI ports of other hubs: They are DTE (Data Transmission Equipment). Attempts to interconnect two MSAUs with a pair of either RI or RO ports does not work, unless you use a crossover cable.

The typical MSAU has between 8 and 24 RI and/or RO ports. These ports are known more formally as *Trunk Coupling Units* (TCUs).

Trunk Coupling Units

Trunk Coupling Units (TCUs) on an MSAU are the physical ports, and the electronics and logic that support those individual ports provide connectivity for stations and other hubs. Inherent in the TCU is the intelligence and electronics to add and remove stations to/from the ring. This TCU capability enables the ring's membership to be dynamically and automatically managed.

> **Note:** Stations that are inactive, for whatever reason, are not really removed from a Token Ring. Instead, the TCU recognizes the station's inactive state and bypasses it electrically when passing tokens and frames around the ring.

Topology

The physical components just examined are the proverbial building blocks of Token Ring. They can be arranged in a wide variety of shapes, known as *topologies*. The basic topology is a ring: a unidirectional transmission vehicle without a clearly defined beginning or end. In Token Ring, the ring itself can be either physical or logical.

Early implementations of Token Ring were based on lobe cables tapped into a trunk cable. The entire ring consisted of nothing more than lobe cabling strung between peers. In this topology, illustrated in Figure 7.7, the ring is physical.

The use of repeaters, also known as *hubs* or *MSAUs*, to build a ring results in a physical star topology that serves as the basis for a logical ring. This topology was illustrated earlier in Figure 7.1.

In a basic star topology Token Ring, the MSAU serves as the backbone: There is no trunk cabling. Each station connects to the MSAU's TCUs using lobe cables.

This topology can be expanded by adding MSAUs and trunk cabling. Expanding a Token Ring can be a complicated undertaking. Its performance parameters are much more constricting than those of Ethernet. The number of stations per token-passing domain is limited to only 260 devices. This and the time that may be required to service that number of devices with a single token may make seemingly easy expansions much more complex.

Figure 7.7
Physical ring topology.

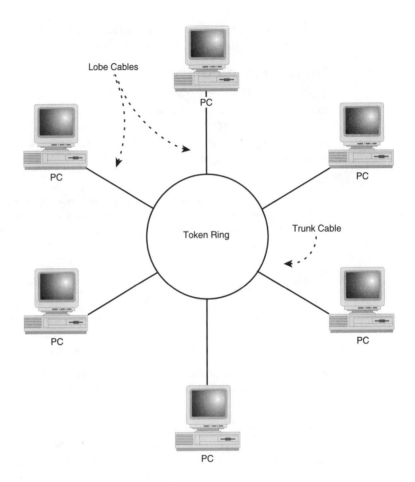

Lobe Cables

PC

PC

PC

Token Ring

Trunk Cable

PC

PC

PC

Dynamic Ring Membership

An important part of a Token Ring network's normal operation is its capability to support dynamic changes in its membership. Membership changes can occur in two ways:

- Normal station insertions and deletions
- Network failures

Understanding the mechanics of this important aspect of Token Ring requires an examination of its membership-change processes.

Adding Stations

The simple act of powering a station up does not automatically result in its addition to the ring. It must first pass a series of insertion tests before it's accepted. Insertion tests automatically occur whenever the Token Ring network interface card (NIC) is initialized.

The first of the insertion tests is known as the Lobe Test. The Lobe Test requires the station to transmit a series of Lobe Media MAC frames. This tests the physical continuity of the transmission media between the station and its MSAU.

If this test is successful, the station must next attempt to physically insert itself into the ring. The station must send a low-voltage DC signal, known as a *phantom current*, to the MSAU. This signal is low enough in voltage that it does not have any effect on any data signals that may be traversing the lobe cable. Hence, the source of its name: phantom current.

The MSAU contains relay circuitry that prevents polling of unused ports. Unfortunately, the distinction between an unused port and a used port connected to an inactive device is nonexistent at the Physical Layer. Consequently, the Token Ring uses the phantom current to notify the MSAU that an inactive device is becoming active. The MSAU responds by enabling the station to physically insert itself into the ring's electronics through the previously dormant port. This physical insertion must occur within five milliseconds, which is the maximum time that the ring may be broken without generating fault-recovery processes.

This physical insertion process enables the joining station to identify the ring's signaling speed and determine whether an Activity Monitor (AM) already exists on the LAN. If no active AM is present, that station becomes the AM upon completing its insertion. The station gleans this knowledge through listening for the presence of one of the following MAC management frames:

- The Active Monitor Present (AMP) frame
- The Purge Ring (PRG) frame

If it detects either of these frames, it knows that an AM is alive and well on the ring. If it fails to detect these frames, it transmits a *claim token* and initiates arbitration for AM responsibilities.

The station's next step in joining a ring is to verify that no other stations already have its address active on the ring. This is done via yet another MAC management frame known as the *Duplicate Address Test* (DAT) frame. This simple frame is self-addressed. If the frame returns to the originator as acknowledged by another recipient, that originating station removes itself from the ring by deactivating its network connection and protocols.

If, however, the frame successfully navigates the entire ring and returns to the originating station, it can be assured that no other stations on the ring have its address. However, the station is not yet a member of the ring! It must next identify its nearest active upstream neighbor (NAUN) and nearest active downstream neighbor (NADN).

These discovery processes help the station define its place within the ring by giving it relatively fixed points of reference. Rather than this being indigenous to the ring insertion process, the mechanism that facilitates neighbor discovery is one of the Active

Monitor's ongoing responsibilities. It regularly broadcasts Active Monitor Present MAC management frames. These are sent to its downstream neighbor. This neighboring station accepts the frame and sets the Address Recognized and Frame Copied bits of its header. It also stores the address of the AM and then sends a Standby Monitor Present (SMP) frame to its downstream neighbor. The downstream neighbor repeats this process. The net effect is that all stations are continuously made aware of any membership changes.

The very last rite of passage that a station must pass before becoming an active station on a ring is the Request Initialization process. In this process, the joining station requests the ring's various operational parameters by transmitting a Request Parameters MAC frame. This frame is addressed to a special server, known as a *Parameter Server*. If no Parameter Server exists or is available, the joining station uses its default parameters. After this is accomplished, the station has successfully been inserted into the ring.

Deleting Stations

After having endured the arduous series of tasks required to insert a station, you can rest easy. The deinsertion process is much simpler! If, for any reason, a station is disconnected from the ring, the MSAU's port recognizes the loss of the phantom current and automatically opens its relays for that port. The port, and anything that might be connected to it, are electrically isolated from the ring. This simple process can occur without compromising the functionality of the ring.

Failures

If a station detects a failure in the ring, it responds by beaconing. A *beacon* is a special frame that's transmitted by the station to inform the other stations of the failure. The originating station knows its relative position in the ring and uses the acknowledged beacons to identify the extent of the failure. Stations that fail to respond are assumed to be cut off by the failure. In this manner, the Token Ring protocol allows for some automatic detection and recovery from network-level failures.

The Active Monitor

Token Ring's many rules are enforced by a single station. This station, known as the *Active Monitor* (AM), can be any station in the ring. Usually, it's the first station to become active; however, after more stations activate, the responsibility can be contested and passed to another station. The AM monitors all traffic, ensures that the ring's protocol rules are adhered to, and is responsible for initiating any actions that might be necessary to overcome protocol violations or failures.

All the Token Ring station devices have the capability to be the AM, but only one can be the AM at any point in time. The other stations are known as Standby Monitors (SMs).

The AM's duties include the following:

- Initializing the ring by issuing a Ring Purge MAC frame upon startup
- Creating tokens
- Providing timing for the network
- Ensuring that tokens and frames do not traverse the ring more than once by inverting the Monitor bit of the Access Control field of the token/frame

The Active Monitor is also responsible for providing many other ring-management functions, including latency buffering. Token Ring's protocol requires the LAN to be large enough to hold an entire token. Some smaller networks might not be large enough to do this, given their transmission speed. Latency buffering is the use of a memory buffer to simulate a larger network than actually exists.

A latency buffer equivalent to a minimum of 24 bit times must be provided. A *bit time* is the amount of time it takes to transmit one bit of information. This AM-provided buffer is known as the *Assured Minimum Latency Buffer*. This buffer is required by the IEEE 802.5 protocol to guarantee that the LAN's ring is at least big enough to accommodate one token. Given that the token is 24 bits long and the signaling speed is either 4 or 16Mbps, the ring must be large enough to support a roundtrip time of either 250 nanoseconds or 62.5 nanoseconds. This shouldn't be a problem, but, as a precaution against unpredictable performance in extremely small rings, the AM is responsible for providing any needed buffering to meet this latency requirement.

Selecting a New AM

The monitor contention process uses the Claim Token MAC frame to arbitrate AM. responsibilities. This process is initiated by any of the SMs whenever they detect a possible failure of the AM. Numerous possible symptoms can trigger this process:

- Failure of the AM to transmit a good token frame at least once every 2.6 seconds.
- Failure of the AM to transmit an Active Monitor Present MAC frame at least once every 15 seconds.
- Unsuccessful ring purge attempts.
- Inconsistencies with the clock.
- Absence of Active Monitor Present or Standby Monitor Present MAC frames after a station insertion. Such frames are normally transmitted within 18 seconds of a successful station insertion.

Other factors can also result in the arbitration of a new AM, but these examples should adequately demonstrate the various ways that SMs continuously monitor the AM's performance. Failure to perform its duties can be caused by numerous factors, including the AM losing power, experiencing a hardware or software failure, and simply being physically disconnected from the LAN.

Regardless of the actual cause, if an SM detects a violation of the AM's responsibilities, it immediately generates a Claim Token MAC frame. After this frame is generated, all stations enter into the contention process.

The AM arbitration process requires each SM to transmit a Claim Token MAC frame to every other station on the ring. The source addresses of these claim tokens are compared numerically to their own MAC addresses to determine which station has the lowest numeric address value. If a station's address is less than the address of a received claim token, it repeats the higher value token frame and abandons its own. If, however, its address is greater than the received claim token's address, it discards that token and transmits its own. In this fashion, a new AM is selected based upon a consensus of the stations' numeric addresses.

Token Ring's Future

Token Ring, overshadowed in recent years by newer and/or faster and better publicized LAN architectures, is beginning to emerge from the doldrums. This rebirth is facilitated by the use of switching technologies to forward frames, as well as numerous attempts to further accelerate Token Ring's signaling speed.

Switching and Dedicated Token Ring

The first major development is the use of port-level switching. A switch is used (instead of a repeating hub) to interconnect the ring's devices. Each port enjoys its own dedicated bandwidth. Competitors for tokens are reduced to just two devices: the station device and the switched hub port to which it connects. Using the correct physical media enables this dedicated connection to support full-duplex transmission. In other words, the station device and the switched port to which it connects can both transmit and receive simultaneously over separate wire paths.

The use of full-duplex port-switching technologies provides the foundation for Dedicated Token Ring (DTR). DTR puts the onus on the switch to develop tables that track MAC addresses and correlates them with switched port numbers. Each frame that's received by the switch triggers a table lookup to determine the appropriate path through which to switch it. This is a vast improvement over the traditional half-duplex transmission mode of shared Token Ring.

> **Note:** In this context, DTR signifies *Dedicated Token Ring*. However, anyone who's ever used a modem and bothered to look at the pretty lights on its face will recognize DTR from its more commonly accepted usage: Data Terminal Ready.

Faster Transmission Speed

Several different attempts have been made to accelerate Token Ring's transmission speed from 16Mbps to 100Mbps, and even higher. One proposal calls for a new signaling speed of 128Mbps. Others have embraced 100Mbps, with a Physical Layer that could also stretch up to 1Gbps!

The responsibility for hammering out a High-Speed Token Ring standard ultimately lies with the IEEE's 802.5 committee. This committee will separate the task into three components, which will be rolled out in stages as they are ready.

100Mbps over Copper

The first component will define the 100Mbps standard for Token Ring over copper transmission media. The plan of action is to leverage existing work in order to bring High-Speed Token Ring products to fruition as quickly as possible. Therefore, 100Mbps Token Ring will use 100BaseTX as a Physical Layer foundation. The 802.5 Data Link Layer will be grafted onto the 100BaseTX MDI of the 802.3 Physical Layer to create the first High-Speed Token Ring.

At first glance, this sort of hybridization may appear heretical, especially to long-time devotees of either Token Ring or Ethernet. Remember, the modularity of the IEEE standards was intentional; there are no interdependencies. Even though 100BaseTX was designed to support an Ethernet Data Link Layer, it was not so tightly coupled as to preclude its use with other Data Link Layer specifications.

As was explained in Chapter 6, "Ethernet," 100BaseTX can support transmission at a signaling speed of 100Mbps over Category 5 unshielded twisted pair (CAT 5 UTP) for a maximum of 100 meters. An automatic speed negotiation mechanism is included that will control throttling back to a subrate if, for any reason, the maximum signaling rate cannot be sustained over any particular connection.

> **Note:** The 100BaseTX and 100BaseFX specifications were created during the extension of the 802.3 CSMA/CD to 100Mbps signaling speed. This extension is better known as *Fast Ethernet*. For more information on Fast Ethernet, 100BaseTX, or 100BaseFX, refer to Chapter 6.

100Mbps over Glass

The second specification will be a 100Mbps Token Ring that uses fiber-optic transmission media. Much like its copper-based sibling, this Token Ring specification will be based on 100BaseFX.

1Gbps

Lastly, the 802.5 committee will be focusing on a 1Gbps version of Token Ring. It's likely that this effort, too, will borrow heavily from work either done or in progress on accelerating Ethernet's signaling speeds. It's expected that a 1Gbps Token Ring will be supported over a fiber-optic transmission media, but a copper version won't be far behind.

The 1Gbps version of Token Ring, as with the similar acceleration of Ethernet, promises to be more involved than the leap from 16 to 100Mbps. The extent to which its Data Link Layer will need revision is not yet clear. It does appear unlikely that a 4/16/100/1Gbps auto-sensing network interface card will be a practical reality any time in the near future. The differences in both the Physical Layer and the Media Access Control portion of the Data Link Layer that are necessary to support 1Gbps appear too great to be supported on the same printed circuit board (PCB) as its slower-speed sib-lings.

Will It Work?

Although the application of switching technologies and faster signaling speeds sounds extremely promising, there remains the nagging question, "Will it work?"

Port-switching, although it's being used to support Dedicated Token Ring, may actually render a High-Speed Token Ring moot. The original benefit of a Token Ring network over an Ethernet network was its use of an orderly and deterministic media-access methodology. Token Ring could always use more of its available bandwidth than an Ethernet could. As was explained in Chapter 6, "Ethernet," the emergence of full-duplex, port-switched Ethernet products changes this. In a full-duplex, port-switched Ethernet connection, there is no competition for bandwidth. The transmitting device is able to put frames on the wire at wire speed. Today, it's possible to drive Ethernets at 98+ percent of their signaling speed. Consequently, the differences between a 100Mbps Ethernet and a 100Mbps Token Ring become much more subtle and even subjective.

Similarly, the basic strategy of developing a multirate product has also been demonstrat-ed with 802.3 products. The intent of manufacturers is to produce 4/16/100Mbps Token Ring products that are capable of automatically negotiating the highest possible signaling speed that any given wire or fiber path can support. The trick will be extending this to 1Gbps.

Other problems, too, threaten High-Speed Token Ring's market acceptance. The two most significant are FDDI (Fiber Distributed Data Interface) and port switching. FDDI is already a 100Mbps deterministic ring-based LAN architecture. It will always outperform a 100Mbps Token Ring due to its Fast Release feature. Fast Release, as is explained in Chapter 8, "FDDI," permits the transmitting station to relinquish control over the trans-mission media by immediately generating a new token after transmitting a data frame. Therefore, the very next downstream device can accept the token and begin transmitting its own data, even before the first data frame is off the network.

> **Peter's Principle:** But Will They Buy It?
>
> Many LAN manufacturers are hoping that the effort to create High-Speed Token Ring will stem the tide of customers who are migrating to Ethernet because of Token Ring's perceived lack of a future. Providing a future at this late stage may do little more than simply reduce the rate of defection to Ethernet.
>
> The bottom line is that, technically, there's little doubt that a High-Speed Token Ring will work. Whether it will be practical, cost effective, and (most important of all) accepted by the market is not clear.

Benefits of Token Ring

Shared Token Ring has numerous advantages relative to other LAN architectures. For example, by not using contention as the basis for its access method, shared Token Ring can offer highly deterministic performance. A maximum time can be calculated between the time that a station needs to transmit and when it receives the token that enables it to transmit. This access time can be reduced in predictable increments by decreasing the number of devices on the ring.

This orderly access methodology also imparts other benefits. Unlike shared Ethernet, which can collapse under the weight of its own collisions with as little as 20 percent utilization, shared Token Ring becomes more efficient under loads. If the load approaches the maximum that can be supported, performance does degrade, but in a predictable and controlled manner that's graceful by comparison to Ethernet.

Token Ring also excels at network performance monitoring. Its Physical Layer specification provides several important mechanisms. These include the Station Management (SMT) agents for data collection and reporting. It also has mechanisms for automatically detecting and advertising hardware failures to other stations on the ring. The Physical Layer also contains some mechanisms for tuning the performance of the ring (if you know how to use them!).

Lastly, Token Ring can support frame sizes up to 18KB. For networks whose applications are characterized by large file transfers, this represents an extremely low overhead-to-payload ratio.

Limitations of Token Ring

Token Ring is not without its disadvantages. As hinted at in the section on its benefits, performance tuning on a Token Ring requires an in-depth understanding of the protocol. Given that its performance-tuning capabilities exceed those of other protocols, the limitations of this are somewhat blunted.

A greater disadvantage is the low population density supported by Token Ring. Whereas Ethernet can support up to 1,024 devices per segment, Token Ring is limited to only 260.

Summary

Token Ring has long been regarded as a technically superior and more robust LAN architecture than Ethernet. Recently, however, it has not been treated to the same rate of renovation that its 802.3 sibling has received. Its market share has suffered as a result of this. Recent attempts to shore up this aging architecture appear promising, but only time will tell whether they are too little, too late to save Token Ring.

Some of Token Ring's endearing qualities remain, albeit somewhat muted by technological advances. It still offers a stronger access prioritization mechanism than Ethernet, better MAC-level error detection and correction, as well as a better ratio of payload-to-frame overhead. Whether these mechanisms are enough to validate its continued development and existence can be fodder for highly emotional debate.

Despite these uncertainties about its future, Token Ring does exhibit numerous benefits and limitations in its present form.

FDDI

One of the older, and more robust, of the LAN technologies is the Fiber Distributed Data Interface (FDDI). FDDI was standardized via the ANSI X3T9.5 specification during the mid 1980s. At that time, high performance UNIX workstations were beginning to appear. These workstations needed a higher performance network than was available. This provided the impetus for ANSI to develop the specification for a suitable LAN.

As local area networking matured, different functional areas began to emerge from what used to be a homogeneous network. Each functional area supported a specific task: server connectivity, desktop connectivity, hub interconnectivity, and so forth. Each of these areas has also experienced an increase in the demand for bandwidth. FDDI, with its high data rate and potential for reliability, became a natural choice for connecting servers as well as for interconnecting hubs in the LAN's backbone.

This chapter examines FDDI, its physical media and distance limitations, its frame structures, its mechanics, and some of its benefits. These provide the context for defining FDDI's role in contemporary and future networking.

Fundamentals of FDDI

FDDI is an acronym for *Fiber Distributed Data Interface*, but nobody uses that mouthful of a name. In fact, most people don't even spell out F-D-D-I; they slur the letters together and pronounce it *fiddy*. FDDI is a robust and reliable LAN technology that dates back to the mid 1980s. FDDI features a 100Mbps data rate and dual counter-rotating rings. These rings can span up to 200 kilometers using fiber-optic cables. Access to this transmission media is regulated through a token-passing scheme that's similar to Token Ring. The token can pass in only one direction.

In the event of a network failure, the repeaters and/or stations are capable of sensing the loss, determining the extent of the network that has lost connectivity, and automatically (but logically) splicing the two rings together. This is known as *wraparound* or *wrapping*; this restores connectivity to as much of the network as possible.

FDDI's self-healing capabilities, plus its high data rate, made it the only viable LAN technology for applications with either high bandwidth and/or high reliability requirements. This remained the case for over a decade. Any LAN that needed to support data rates in excess of 16Mbps had to use FDDI. Similarly, any LAN that couldn't afford downtime found FDDI its only viable option. Unfortunately, because it used a fiber-optic transmission media, FDDI was also the most expensive option. This tended to limit its implementation to those highly specialized environments that required either its throughputs or its reliability.

Eventually, other LAN technologies were developed that also reached 100Mbps and beyond. The competition, ATM and Fast Ethernet, were able to meet or exceed FDDI's data rate. This forced FDDI's prices down considerably. Today, FDDI is no longer the elite technology it once was. It remains fairly specialized and is most commonly found in mixed topology LANs. Its two primary uses are to connect servers to multiprotocol switching hubs and even to interconnect switching hubs into a LAN backbone.

Functional Components

FDDI is comprised of four distinct functional components. Each component is defined through its own series of specifications:

- Media Access Control (MAC)
- Physical Layer Protocol (PHY)
- Physical Layer Medium (PMD)
- Station Management (SMT)

These components and their correlation to the OSI Reference Model are presented in Figure 8.1.

FIGURE 8.1

The FDDI protocol stack versus the OSI Reference Model.

OSI Reference Model Layer Description	OSI Layer Number	FDDI	
Application	7	No Specifications Defined	
Presentation	6		
Session	5		
Transport	4		
Network	3		
Data Link	2	MAC	S M T
Physical	1	PHY	
		PMD	

Media Access Control

As depicted in Figure 8.1, the top layer of FDDI is Media Access Control (MAC). This layer is equivalent to the Data Link Layer of the OSI Reference Model. The MAC sublayer is responsible for defining the media-access methodology and the myriad frame formats. Additionally, the MAC sublayer is also responsible for token and frame generation/management, MAC addressing, and even performing error detection and correction upon receipt of data frames.

Physical Layer Protocol

FDDI's Physical Layer Protocol (PHY) correlates to the upper sublayer functions of the OSI Reference Model's Physical Layer. It's responsible for accepting a data bit stream and converting it to a more suitable format for transmission. This is known as *encoding*. The actual encoding scheme used is a four-bit/five-bit encoding scheme. This scheme accepts four-bit nibbles (half-octets) from the MAC Layer and encodes each one as a five-bit symbol. This five-bit symbol is what actually gets transmitted. It's important to note that because the MAC Layer is responsible for generating the frames and for framing the data, every piece of the frame is encoded into five-bit symbols.

The PHY is also responsible for setting the clocking for the LAN. FDDI actually runs on a 125MHz transmission clock. The PHY is responsible for generating this transmission clock and synchronizing it across the other stations on the network.

Physical Layer Medium

The Physical Layer Medium (PMD, really!) specifies all the attributes that are expected of the transmission medium:

- Medium type
- Transmission signal strength
- Acceptable error rates
- Physical connector types

FDDI originally was limited to a single Physical Layer Medium (PMD): 62.5/125–micron diameter multimode fiber-optic cabling. It remained a glass-only technology until the 1990s. Then, the high cost of fiber-optic cable started cutting into its market share. The answer seemed obvious: develop a copper-based PMD that could support the FDDI protocols.

In June of 1990, ANSI formed a working committee to build the specification for a twisted pair PMD (TP-PMD). The TP-PMD was, originally, a proprietary product that grafted the FDDI Layer 2 onto a Category 5 unshielded twisted pair (UTP) Physical Layer. The end result was marketed as CDDI, for *Copper Distributed Data Interface*. This specification became an ANSI standard in 1994.

A single-mode fiber-optic version (SMF-PMD) has also been developed. Based on 8.3-micron diameter fiber-optic cabling and driven by a laser rather than a light-emitting diode (LED), this PMD is more expensive than its multimode counterpart. In its favor is the fact that it can maintain the integrity of the signal for much greater distances: up to 60 kilometers (versus the paltry 2 kilometers of the multimode fiber).

> **Note:** Although the term *laser* has come into common usage as a noun, it's actually an acronym. It describes the physical process by which the concentrated energy associated with lasers is created. The acronym stands for *Light Amplification through Stimulated Emission of Radiation. Laser*, however, is much simpler.

Station Management (SMT)

Station Management (SMT, really!) is a separate module that spans the full stack of FDDI protocols. It communicates directly with the MAC, PHY, and PMD layers to monitor and manage the ongoing operation of the station and the ring. The three areas of SMT functionality, as defined in the ANSI X3T9.5 specification, are

- SMT Frame Services
- Connection Management
- Ring Management

Together, these three functional areas encompass many different services. They are essential to the normal operation of the station and the FDDI ring. Although there are many others, some of the services provided include the following:

- Station insertion
- Station removal
- Statistics gathering
- Fault identification
- Fault recovery

Although any given station may have multiple instances of the MAC, PHY, and PMD (as is normal with dual-attached stations), there can be only one SMT.

Building FDDI Networks

FDDI has been stereotyped as having a dual, counter-rotating, ring topology. The truth is, there are several different ways to construct a FDDI network. The dual ring is just one of its many forms. To build more effective FDDI networks, you must understand the various port types and the ways that stations can attach to the network.

Port Types and Attachment Methods

FDDI recognizes four different port types:

- Port A: Primary In, Secondary Out
- Port B: Primary Out, Secondary In
- Port M: Master Concentrator Port
- Port S: Slave Port for single-attach devices

These port types can be interconnected in a variety of ways. Before you examine them, however, you should understand the different connection types that are supported. The two basic attachment methods that can be used to connect FDDI devices to the network are

- Dual-attached
- Single-attached

These attachment methods can be used either with or without repeaters. Attachments can be made between a variety of port configurations. This adds further variety and functionality to the ways that FDDI LANs can be built and used.

Dual-Attached Stations

Dual-attached stations (DASs) feature two sets of media interfaces. This enables a DAS device to have a physical connection to each of FDDI's two rings. Figure 8.2 illustrates the way that a dual-attached station connects to the LAN. Each DAS device has two sets of media interface ports, each containing both A and B ports. Each port contains physical connections for two physical media. Therefore, a DAS device actually has four fibers connected to it.

FIGURE 8.2
A dual-attached station.

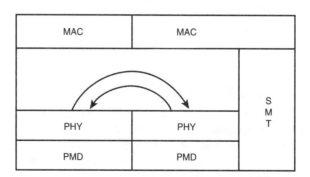

Note: A concentrator is a device that aggregates multiple LAN connections onto a common electrical backplane. The most common type of LAN concentrator is known as a *hub*. Concentrators, too, can be dual-attached. Consequently, it would be correct to reference both concentrators and stations with the phrase *dual-attached* (DA) without specifically identifying the devices.

As shown in Figure 8.2, the physical device actually becomes an integral part of the two rings, because the network interface card (NIC) provides physical continuity for the two rings between the A and B ports. DAS connections can form a repeaterless, peer-to-peer LAN. This is accomplished by connecting the A port of one device's interface to the B port of another device, and vice versa. The drawback to this is that each DAS device must be powered on and functioning for the rings to be complete. FDDI is capable of wrapping around a break in the ring, but this directly impacts the performance of the entire ring. More significantly, if multiple stations are simultaneously powered down or otherwise out of service, the net result might be two or more smaller ring pairs.

Single-Attached Stations

Single-attached stations (SASs) eliminate the potential performance problems inherent in DAS by getting rid of the wraparound feature. Each SAS device has just a single communications interface, S, with two media ports. The separate fibers are used to transmit and receive. Both fibers terminate at the concentrator, which provides the connectivity to both rings. A single-attached station and its concentrator are illustrated in Figure 8.3.

FIGURE 8.3
A single-attached station.

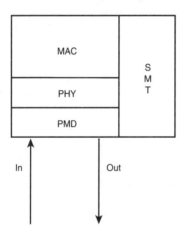

Valid Connections

Given this background on port types and attachment methods, a quick survey of the valid types of port connections should complete your understanding of the various connections that can be made with FDDI. Table 8.1 presents all the valid port connection combinations. (See the section "Port Types and Attachment Methods" earlier in this chapter if you can't remember what the letters stand for.)

Table 8.1 Valid Port Combinations

Port Connection Combination	Use
A and B	Connection of DAS devices in a repeaterless dual ring
A and M	Connection of a DAS device to a concentrator in a dual-attached configuration
B and M	Connection of a DAS device to a concentrator in a dual-attached configuration
M and S	Connection of an SAS device to a concentrator
S and S	Peer-to-peer connection of SAS devices

Note: The inverse of the port connection combinations presented in Tables 8.1 and 8.2 are also true. Therefore, B and A is a valid port connection combination that's functionally indistinguishable from the A and B combination listed in Table 8.1.

Table 8.2 presents those port connection combinations that are deemed undesirable. They still function but are not optimal.

Table 8.2 Undesirable Port Combinations

Port Connection Combination	Consequences
A and A	Can establish a peer-to-peer connection but results in confusing, tangled rings.
B and B	Can establish a peer-to-peer connection but results in confusing, tangled rings.
A and S	This is a wrapped ring. It can be built manually but should be left to FDDI's protocols to logically splice together.
B and S	This is a wrapped ring. It can be built manually but should be left to FDDI's protocols to logically splice together.

Note: For more information on wrapped rings, see the next section, "Topologies and Implementations."

The only port connection combination that's considered illegal and invalid is M and M. This creates a "ring of trees," which is not very useful. This term is explained in the next section.

Topologies and Implementations

The previously described port types and attachment methods lend themselves to topological and implementation-level variety. Contrary to the persistent myth, FDDI is not just dual, counter-rotating rings. This is, arguably, its most important topology, but there are many other useful topologies and implementations. Some of the more common variations that FDDI networks can use include the following:

- Dual ring
- Dual ring with trees
- Single tree
- Dual home
- Wraparound

Each of the first four topologies offers a different combination of performance features and limitations. The fifth one, wraparound, is actually seen only during a network failure.

Dual Ring

The basic dual ring topology, sometimes referred to as a *dual ring without trees*, is built from dual-attached stations interconnecting directly with each other. This forms a pair of peer-to-peer rings. This is illustrated in Figure 8.4.

The disadvantages of relying on each member in the ring for the entire ring's functionality should be obvious. The rings depend equally upon each of the member devices. If any machine is powered down or out of service for any reason, the physical rings are compromised. FDDI detects and automatically limits the extent of the damage, but the point is that risks are inherent in this topology. It should be limited to small, highly specialized environments.

Dual Ring with Trees

The dual ring with trees topology is an enhancement to the dual ring topology. This one features tree-like appendages that grow out of FDDI's dual rings. Developing this topology requires the use of dual-attachment concentrators, single-attachment concentrators, and single-attachment stations. Figure 8.5 illustrates a dual ring with trees topology.

The key difference between this topology and the basic dual ring topology is that devices need not connect directly to the rings. Instead, SAS devices connect to single-attached concentrators. These concentrators, in turn, connect to the DAS concentrators that comprise the backbone of the tandem rings.

FIGURE 8.4
A dual ring topology.

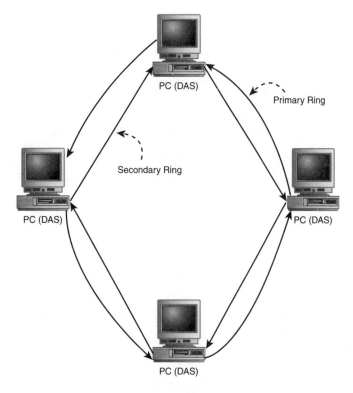

FIGURE 8.5
A dual ring with trees.

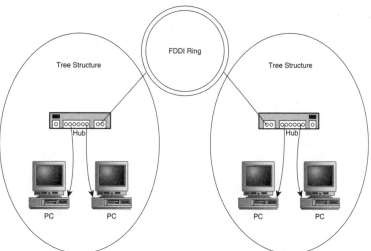

This topology combines the reliability of dual rings, which automatically wrap around in the event of a failure, with lower costs. SAS components, including concentrators and network interface cards (NICs), are substantially less expensive than their DAS counterparts.

Single Tree

The single tree topology, as its name implies, consists of only a single tree-like grouping of devices. There is no dual ring, nor are there any DAS components. Given that FDDI uses a round-robin token-passing media-access methodology, this tree should be regarded as a logical ring. Tokens still pass in a circular pattern across the network, but the topology is based on a concentrator and, therefore, is star-shaped.

The obvious drawback to this is that there is no redundant path. This directly reduces the reliability of the network. The benefits, however, are many. First, the cost of building a single tree FDDI network is much lower than that of other topologies due to two main factors:

- All the devices (concentrators and stations) are the relatively low-cost single-attach variety.
- The cost of wiring the LAN's backbone is halved due to the use of only two fibers rather than four.

The other main benefit is reliability. Although this may sound contradictory, given the lack of a second ring, the use of only single-attached devices holds an important implication for the overall reliability of the LAN. The impact of the failure of any given single-attached device is much lower than the failure of an equivalent dual-attached device. If an SAS station fails, the remainder of the network is not affected at all. Similarly, if an SAS concentrator fails, the worst that can happen is that the devices connected to it are isolated from the rest of the network. It doesn't trigger a wraparound. Wraparounds, although touted as a reliability feature, directly impact performance by almost doubling the cable length of the network. Depending on the specific situation, one could make a credible case that auto-recovery via a wraparound is less desirable than simply isolating a few workstations in the event of a concentrator failure.

Figure 8.6 shows a single tree topology.

FIGURE 8.6

A single tree topology.

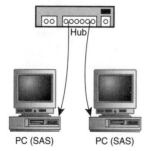

Dual Home

Dual homing is a specialized use of a dual attachment that provides redundant physical paths for critical networked resources. Such resources may include file and/or application servers, bridges, or even your boss's workstation! Note, however, that dual homing does not necessarily have to include every device on the LAN; therefore, it's not truly a topology. Instead, it's an optional means of implementing LAN connectivity. It can be used very specifically for individual devices rather than broadly for all devices.

This implementation can be used only on a *dual ring with trees topology*. Each device to be dual homed, by definition, must be DAS capable. Lastly, it must connect to the network via a dual-attached concentrator. Dual homing enables a critical device to have a primary and a less-desirable (from the FDDI protocol's perspective) alternate connection to the LAN.

The Station Management protocols of the dual-homed device activate the primary connection and leave the alternate connection in a standby mode. Each connection terminates at a different dual-attached concentrator. The Station Management protocols can detect this difference in the two connections via their neighbor-discovery mechanisms. Station Management then activates the A-port connection as the primary path and idles the B-port connection. If the A-port connection is lost, for any reason, Station Management attempts to activate the standby connection.

Figure 8.7 illustrates a server configured for dual homing within a dual ring with trees topology.

FIGURE 8.7
Dual homing.

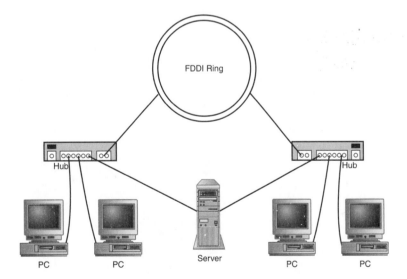

Wraparound

A wraparound isn't really a discrete topology that you would build. Rather, it's automatically constructed by FDDI's station-management mechanisms in the event of either a station failure or a wire path failure. The failure is isolated by logically splicing the primary and alternate rings immediately upstream and downstream from the failure. Implicit in this definition is the fact that only topologies based on a dual ring can wrap around.

Although the mechanics of recovering from either one are similar, there's one fundamental difference between them. Wire path failures can enable all stations to remain active on the wraparound ring network. A failed station, on the other hand, decreases the population of active devices on the network by one.

In Figure 8.8, a wire failure has afflicted Station 2. Its neighboring stations, 1 and 3, wrap their transmissions around this failure onto the secondary ring to preserve the integrity of the loop. The new ring has a total physical media length almost double the size of the original ring. For this reason, the practical maximum media length in a double ring topology should always be half the maximum supportable length for any given media type.

FIGURE 8.8
*Wraparound ring
(wire failure).*

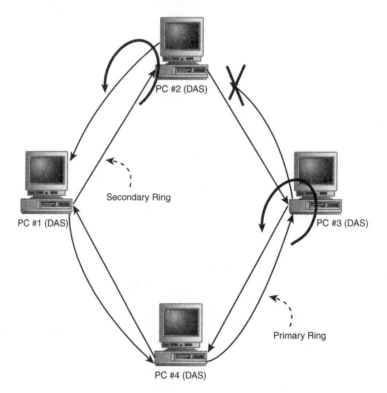

Although Figure 8.8 depicts a wire failure in the primary path of a station, similar failures can occur in the LAN's backbone. Dual-attached concentrators, too, can use the alternate ring to wrap their transmissions around wire failures.

If Station 2 in Figure 8.8 had failed completely, the wraparound would have looked slightly different. The ring would no longer extend to that device. Instead, it would be wrapped around at Stations 1 and 3. This is illustrated in Figure 8.9.

FIGURE 8.9
Wraparound ring (station failure).

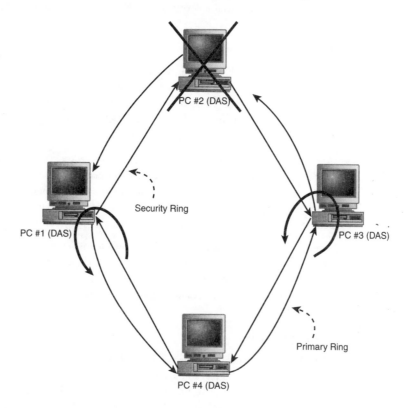

PC #2 (DAS)

Security Ring

PC #1 (DAS)

PC #3 (DAS)

Primary Ring

PC #4 (DAS)

Devices known as *optical bypass switches* can be used to prevent station failures from forcing a wraparound. These devices are installed in between the station and the concentrator. In the event of a station failure, these bypass switches maintain the continuity of the wire path without the station.

Network Size

FDDI was designed to be a robust network, capable of supporting high-performance workstations. To maintain high performance for all attached devices, FDDI must impose strict limits on the size of the network. The size of the network can be measured in terms of the following items:

- The number of attached devices
- The physical size of the ring
- The physical distances between devices

All are equally important in developing LANs that can deliver the potential performance of FDDI.

Maximum Devices

The maximum number of devices that any FDDI ring can support is 500. This limitation is actually a function of the maximum allowable propagation delay that FDDI's protocols can endure without compromising its functionality. Each connection adds a measurable amount of propagation delay. The cumulative delays of more than 1,000 physical connections exceed FDDI's delay budget.

Although it may seem simple enough to count 500 devices, the challenge lies in being able to precisely identify a device. In a dual-attached configuration, each device requires two physical connections and, consequently, counts as two connections. Each device in which those connections terminate counts as an additional connection. Therefore, a concentrator port and the device to which it connects actually constitute two devices.

A dual-attached backbone concentrator, one that has no station connections, is counted as two connections. Its ports count as a device only when they are used. A dual-attached station, regardless of whether the two attachments home into the same concentrator or two different concentrators, counts as two devices. Single-attached stations count as only one device.

Ring Length

The ANSI X3T9.5 standard does not explicitly state a maximum ring length. Given that the Physical Layer (contrary to popular belief) does not extend to the media itself, this shouldn't be surprising. In keeping with the intent of the Physical Layer, as defined by the OSI Reference Model, the ANSI standard does establish performance parameters that, given any physical media type, impose maximum distances.

In a multimode fiber-optic ring, the total fiber path must be less than 200 kilometers. Unless your FDDI is to span across a large geographic area, like a metropolitan area network (MAN), this limitation shouldn't be much of a constraining factor in your design. What is important to note, however, is the phrase *total fiber path*.

Two important implications lurk in those key words. First, building a large ring that measures 190 kilometers works until a failure forces a wraparound. Then, the wrapped ring measures something closer to 380 kilometers, and the entire network fails. Therefore, the maximum ring length must always be cut in half when you're designing the LAN.

Second, *total fiber path* means just that: All the fiber lengths must be added together to determine the total ring length. This includes the main ring and all the branch cables that connect to stations.

Drive Distance

The drive distance is the maximum distance between any two devices. Attenuation is a factor, regardless of which PMD is used. Therefore, the distance between devices must be short enough to guarantee the integrity of the signal upon arrival.

For multimode fiber-optic cabling, the maximum drive distance is 2 kilometers. With single-mode fiber, this increases to 60 kilometers. However, the copper-based PMDs are much more limited. Shielded twisted pair (STP) and Category 5 unshielded twisted pair (UTP) must be kept to less than 100 meters.

FDDI Frames

FDDI is much like Token Ring: All media-based functions must be enveloped in a frame. Consequently, FDDI has numerous frame types that are used in its normal operation and maintenance:

- Basic data frame
- LLC data frame
- LLC SNAP data frame
- Token frame
- An assortment of Station Management frames

Basic Data Frame

The most familiar of the frame types is the raw data frame. This is illustrated in Figure 8.10.

FIGURE 8.10
The FDDI data frame.

8-Octet Preamble	1-Octet Starting Delimiter	1-Octet Frame Control Field	6-Octet Destination Address	6-Octet Source Address	Variable Length Data Field, up to 4478 Octets	4-Octet Frame Check Sequence	1-Octet Ending Delimiter	3-Octet Frame Status

The FDDI frame is a maximum of 9,000 symbols in length, including data and all frame components. This is the basic FDDI frame. It's usually implemented in one of two sub-formats: LLC and SNAP. Neither one, excluding the preamble, can be more than 4,500 octets in length.

> **Peter's Principle:** Be Sure You Don't Mistake FDDI Field and Frame Lengths as Interchangeable.
>
> FDDI's field and frame lengths are frequently cited in references using symbols, octets, or bytes. These terms are not completely interchangeable. Understanding the mechanics of FDDI's encoding scheme can clarify the differences. Unfortunately, very few people care to explore FDDI in this level of detail.
>
> The Physical Layer FDDI protocols encode each data nibble (a half-octet or four bits) into a five-bit pattern, or *symbol*, for transmission. Therefore, each eight-bit byte (to use the programmer's term) of data passed down from the Application Layer becomes 10 bits, or 1.25 octets. For this reason, the terms *bytes* and *octets* are not interchangeable!
>
> The frame and its structural components can be measured in either octets or symbols. This should not be misconstrued as meaning that octets and symbols are synonymous. For example, the MAC Layer generates frames that are a maximum of 4,500 octets long. These octets, both data and framing, are transmitted in five-bit symbols. At the physical level, these octets are cut into halves, and each four-bit half is translated into a five-bit binary symbol. As transmitted, the frame is a maximum of 9,000 five-bit symbols in length. Each maximally sized MAC frame becomes 5,625 octets long when transmitted.

The basic frame contains the following fields:

- An eight-octet preamble that signals the start of the frame.
- A one-octet start-of-frame delimiter that signals the start of the frame's contents.
- A one-octet Frame Control field that signals the type of frame, such as token, MAC or LLC, priority frame, and so forth.
- The intended recipient's six-octet MAC address.
- The originator's six-octet MAC address.
- A variable-length data field that contains up to 4,478 octets.
- A four-octet Frame Check Sequence that's used to check the integrity of the frame.
- A half-octet (four bits) Ending Delimiter padded with four 0 bits so that a full-octet is used.
- A three-octet Frame Status field that contains three one-octet subfields: Error, Address-match, and Copied. Each subfield is set to either S for *Set* or R for *Reset*.

LLC Data Frame

The basic FDDI data frame can also be used to support the functionality specified in the IEEE 802.2 specification for Logical Link Control (LLC). The LLC frame, illustrated in

Figure 8.11, is constructed by adding a three-field LLC subframe to the FDDI frame. These three fields are the Destination Service Access Point (DSAP, called the *destination address* in the diagram), Source Service Access Point (SSAP, called the *source address* in the diagram), and Control fields. They are appended to the beginning of the data field and count as part of its payload.

FIGURE 8.11

FDDI frame with an 802.2 LLC subframe.

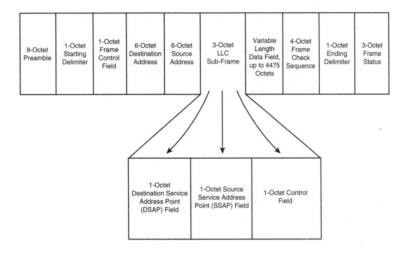

An FDDI LLC data frame has the following structure:

- An eight-octet preamble that signals the start of the frame.
- A one-octet start-of-frame delimiter that signals the start of the frame's contents.
- A one-octet Frame Control field that signals the type of frame, such as token, MAC or LLC, priority frame, and so forth.
- The intended recipient's six-octet MAC address.
- The originator's six-octet MAC address.
- The three-octet LLC subframe, which includes the one-octet DSAP, SSAP, and Control fields.
- A variable-length data field that contains up to 4,475 octets.
- A four-octet Frame Check Sequence that's used to check the integrity of the frame.
- A half-octet (four bits) Ending Delimiter padded with four zero bits so that a full-octet is used.
- A three-octet Frame Status field that contains three one-octet subfields: Error, Address-match, and Copied. Each subfield is set to either S for *Set* or R for *Reset*.

The LLC structure was originally intended to augment Ethernet's capability to route received frames to the appropriate protocol/application upon arrival at its destination. This was crucial in multiprotocol machines, because the original Ethernet specification was designed at a time when there were only a few communications protocols. FDDI doesn't, necessarily, suffer from the original Ethernet's limitations. However, by supporting the LLC subframe, it can interoperate with Ethernet clients through a MAC Layer translating bridge without compromising end-to-end functionality.

LLC SNAP Data Frame

Similarly, FDDI supports the LLC SNAP subframe. The FDDI frame, with the IEEE's SNAP subframe, adds a three-octet organizationally unique identifier and a two-octet Type field (called the *Protocol Identifier*)to the FDDI LLC frame immediately after the LLC header and before the data. These fields are included in the overall length of the data field. This frame is illustrated in Figure 8.12.

FIGURE 8.12

FDDI frame with an 802.2 SNAP subframe.

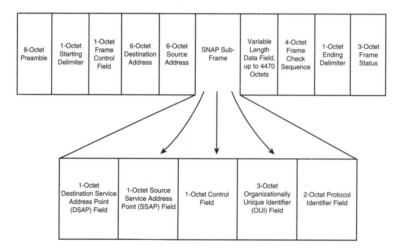

As shown in Figure 8.12, the FDDI SNAP frame contains the following fields:

- An eight-octet preamble that signals the start of the frame.
- A one-octet start-of-frame delimiter that signals the start of the frame's contents.
- A one-octet Frame Control field that signals the type of frame, such as token, MAC or LLC, priority frame, and so forth.
- The intended recipient's six-octet MAC address.
- The originator's six-octet MAC address.
- The three-octet LLC subframe, which includes the one-octet DSAP, SSAP, and Control fields.

- A five-octet SNAP subframe, including a three-octet Organizationally Unique Identifier field and a two-octet Protocol Type (Protocol Identifier) field that identify the upper-level protocol being carried.

- A variable-length data field that contains up to 4,470 octets.

- A four-octet Frame Check Sequence that's used to check the integrity of the frame.

- A half-octet (four bits) Ending Delimiter padded with four zero bits so that a full-octet is used.

- A three-octet Frame Status field that contains three one-octet subfields: Error, Address-match, and Copied. Each subfield is set to either S for *Set* or R for *Reset*.

FDDI supports the LLC and SNAP subframe structures solely to provide bridging capability with Ethernet. This is necessary only when bridging Ethernet to FDDI, using either Novell's IPX/SPX protocols or AppleTalk. Nevertheless, this functionality reinforces FDDI's capabilities as the backbone in a multitopology LAN.

Token Frame

The FDDI Token Frame consists of four fields:

- An eight-octet preamble that signals the start of the frame.

- A one-octet start-of-frame delimiter that signals the start of the frame's contents.

- A one-octet Frame Control field that signals the type of frame, such as token, MAC or LLC, priority frame, and so forth.

- A half-octet (four bits) Ending Delimiter padded with four zero bits so that a full-octet is used.

The FDDI token frame is illustrated in Figure 8.13.

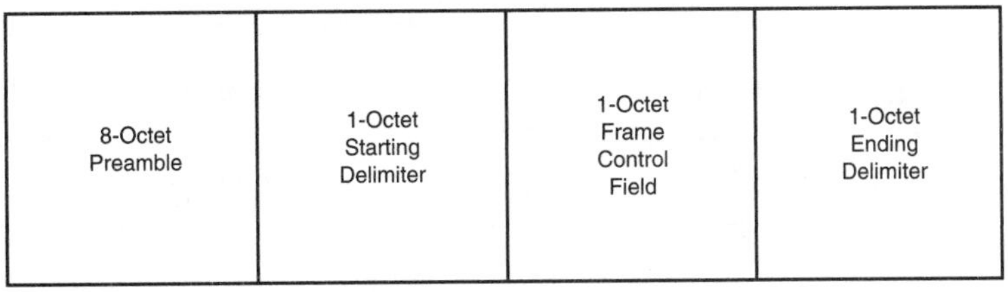

FIGURE 8.13
FDDI token frame.

8-Octet Preamble	1-Octet Starting Delimiter	1-Octet Frame Control Field	1-Octet Ending Delimiter

The token is passed along the ring, in one direction only. The station that has the token may use it to gain access to the transmission media. This is done by inverting a sequence of bits in the Frame Control field to change its state from token to data frame.

Unlike Token Ring, FDDI uses a quick-release mechanism. Immediately after converting the token to a data frame and transmitting data, that transmitting device generates a new token. This token is sent to the nearest downstream neighbor. The neighboring device may use it to transmit or simply pass it on. Either way, the original transmitting device quickly relinquishes control over the transmission media. The data frame does not need to return to its originator before another station may transmit.

The quick-release mechanism is one of FDDI's better performance-enhancing attributes. It will continue to provide FDDI with an advantage over Token Ring after that framing protocol is given faster signaling and data rates.

SMT Frames

FDDI, like Token Ring, uses frames to conduct its Station Management (SMT) functions. The basic SMT functions include the following:

- Claim frames (CF) for bidding purposes
- Echo frames (ECF) for echo testing
- Neighbor information frames (NIF) for obtaining neighbor information
- Status information frames (SIF) for obtaining status information
- Status reporting frames (SRF) for providing status information
- Request denied frames (RDF) for denying invalid requests
- Parameter management frames (RMF) for providing remote access to other stations

Together, these frames enable the myriad SMT management protocols to support the normal operation of an FDDI network. The actual mechanics of ring operation are explained in the following section.

The Mechanics of FDDI

By now, the frame-passing mechanics of FDDI should be well understood. Like Token Ring, everything is done through the use of frames.

The basic mechanics of FDDI are best understood by examining the protocols by which a station becomes active and is inserted into the ring. Other protocols are adjunct to this, including ring initialization and station deinsertion. These processes demonstrate the role the various FDDI components—SMT, MAC, PMD, and PHY—play in the operation of the network.

Station Initialization

A logical starting point is the processes by which a station initializes itself prior to joining the ring. This initialization is a series of tests that verify the physical integrity of the media link to the ring (or tree) and the readiness of the ring and its attached stations. The station initialization routine is a function of the Physical Connection Management (PCM) protocol. PCM is one of the components of Station Management (SMT).

The PCM initiates a series of tests that ends with the successful insertion of the station into the ring. These tests begin with the detection of a viable connection to the network. Station initiation begins with the transmission of Quiet symbols to the PHY of the nearest downstream station. The recipient station halts any transmissions of its own and enters the Break state. This state is so named because, as a station enters it, it must break any existing transmissions and accept the inbound Quiet symbols.

> **Note:** Symbols are the five-bit binary structures that are used to encode data. Given that there are more possible unique structures (32) than there are hexadecimal characters (16), it stands to reason that some symbols cannot be used to encode data. These symbols are reserved for network-level functions. The Quiet symbol and the Halt symbol are examples of these reserved symbols.

The Break state is merely a transitional state that lasts only long enough for the recipient to halt its own transmissions. After this is accomplished, that station enters the *Quiet Line state*. The quiet line state is characterized by both the newly active station and its nearest active downstream neighbor simultaneously sending Quiet symbols to each other. This allows both to know that they're in synchronized states.

After this synchronization occurs, both stations begin repetitively transmitting a different symbol: the Halt symbol. Halt symbols are used to synchronize the transmission clocks of the two stations. After the transmission clocks are synchronized, the stations exit the Halt state and enter, curiously enough, the Next state.

During the Next state, the two stations exchange information about each other's ports. Up to this point, each station knows only that the other exists and that both their transmission clocks are synchronized. They do not have any information about what each other looks like. By exchanging port information—such as A, B, M, or S ports (see the section "Port Types and Attachment Methods" earlier in this chapter)—they have a better understanding of each other. This information is also used to identify the port connection combination that's in effect between them. These data are necessary for later station initialization tests.

After these data have been developed, the two stations enter Signal state. A brief transitional state, known as the *Idle Line state*, separates the Next and Signal states. During this transition, both stations transmit a series of Idle symbols. These symbols tell both stations that the transmitters are ready to accept incoming signals.

Next comes the Link Confidence Test. This protocol requires each station to see whether the other has a MAC Layer. If so, the two stations engage in MAC frame transmission and token-passing tests. Otherwise, they simply exchange another series of Idle symbols. If these tests are completed successfully, the stations may progress to the Join state. The Join state's sole purpose is to ensure that both stations activate simultaneously.

After this exchange is successfully completed, both stations' PCMs enter the Active state. This state change completes the station initialization process and signals the station's management function that it's ready to join the ring.

Ring Initialization

After the station initialization process is complete, the ring must be initialized. This entails determining which station is to generate the first token and establishing the Operational Token Rotation Time (T_OPR). Stations must bid for the right to issue this token. Bidding is done by assessing each station's default timing requirements. These requirements, stored in a value known as the Token Rotation Timer (TRT), identify how frequently the token must reach that station. The bidding begins with the first active station generating a Claim frame.

The Claim frame contains the transmitting station's address and TRT value. This frame is sent downstream, where it's received and compared to the TRT value of the next station. If the recipient's TRT is lower, it discards the received Claim frame and issues its own. Otherwise, that recipient repeats the original Claim frame for the next downstream station. This process continues until one of the stations receives its own Claim frame. It can then be assured that it has the lowest TRT value on the ring and may issue the first token. Its TRT becomes the Operational Token Rotation Time for the entire ring.

This is the essence of the deterministic nature of FDDI: Each station has the opportunity to determine the maximum amount of time that may elapse between token visits. The performance of the entire ring may be improved by decreasing the size of the ring (as measured by the number of stations connected to it) or by using the TRT to improve token-rotation times.

Summary

For years, FDDI was the only stable, mature, and well-behaved high-speed LAN technology available. Its price, however, tended to limit its implementation to small market niches that demanded high performance. In recent years, FDDI has seen its place in the market challenged by newcomers. Initially, FDDI proponents could confidently assert that theirs was the only stable high-speed LAN. Over time, the competitors became standardized and stable, thereby legitimizing their competitiveness.

Today, FDDI's remaining differentiating points are its reliability and its highly deterministic nature. This combination makes FDDI well suited for use as a LAN backbone and for connecting servers to the LAN.

ATM

Asynchronous Transfer Mode, better known in the data communications world as *ATM*, was originally conceived as an asynchronous transfer mechanism for Broadband Integrated Services Digital Network (B-ISDN) by the Comite Consultatif Internationale de Telegraphique et Telephonique (CCITT). As such, its use would have been limited to central office–to–central office (CO-to-CO) transmissions. During the early 1990s, its combination of high throughput and low latency was perceived as being ideal for a next-generation local area network. It could, in theory, support the high-bandwidth, low-latency requirements of desktop videoconferencing as easily as it could support traditional interactive applications. Even better, having ATM at the LAN and at the WAN could seamlessly integrate the two.

Note: CCITT, loosely translated into English, is the International Consulting Committee for Telephone and Telegraph. The CCITT has since been renamed the *International Telecommunications Union*, or ITU.

This grand vision of network unification launched an unprecedented amount of activity, both marketing and developmental. The ATM Forum emerged as an industry consortium that fed proposed standards to the CCITT. So compelling was the promise of this technology that the ATM Forum's membership soon numbered in the hundreds. The political machinations that inevitably accompany such a large consortium quickly paralyzed the Forum's standards work. It began to seem that ATM was destined to remain that which it was originally conceived to be: a CO-to-CO technology.

Today, after much opportunity has been lost to accelerated and switched versions of Ethernet, FDDI, and Token Ring, the ATM Forum appears to be regaining its lost momentum. It may, once again, become the next-generation LAN. This chapter describes ATM's cell structure, basic services, and operational mechanics, including Local Area Network Emulation (LANE) and switching IP packets over ATM.

Fundamentals of ATM

ATM inverts the traditional networking paradigm. Traditional networking features connectionless packets that are launched by their transmitting stations with just enough information to identify their origin and intended destination. Therefore, the stations can be relatively unsophisticated. The network, however, is given the onerous task of figuring out exactly how to get that packet to its destination.

ATM is the exact opposite of this. The onus is on the end stations to establish a virtual path between themselves. The switches that comprise that path are given a relatively simple role: relaying cells along a virtual channel through the switched network based on their header information. This is a deceptively simple explanation of an ATM network. To further your command of ATM, it's necessary to understand the nature of its logical connections as well as some of the more basic aspects of an ATM network, such as its transmission rates and supported media, topology, and interfaces. These topics are examined in this section, which provides the context for a more meaningful exploration of the operational mechanics of ATM that concludes this chapter.

Virtual Connections

Two types of virtual connections can be established across an ATM network:

- A virtual circuit
- A virtual path

A virtual circuit is a logical connection between two end devices through a switched network. These devices communicate by passing cells of data back and forth through the logical circuit. A virtual path is a logical grouping of these logical circuits. Recognizing such groupings enables ATM switches to perform operations in the aggregate, rather than having to manage each individual virtual circuit.

Each ATM cell contains both virtual path information (VPI) and virtual circuit information (VCI). The ATM switch uses these to relay received cells to the appropriate next device. To do this, the ATM switch must build and maintain switching tables. Much like the old bridge tables, the switch table is nothing more than a list that correlates VPI and VCI information with the physical interfaces of that switch.

If you remember nothing else about ATM, remember that it's connection oriented. It can be used to support connectionless protocols, such as TCP/IP and IPX/SPX, but it does so within the context of a logical connection.

Connection Types

ATM is a connection-oriented protocol that can support two types of connections:

- Point-to-point connections
- Point-to-multipoint connections

Point-to-point connections bind two devices together in a virtual connection through ATM's switching fabric. Such connections can be used for uni-directional or bi-directional transfers of data. This type of connection is illustrated in Figure 9.1.

The second type of connection, point-to-multipoint, is a bit more complicated. This can be used to support only uni-directional transmissions from the single point of origin to the multiple identified recipients. This is illustrated in Figure 9.2.

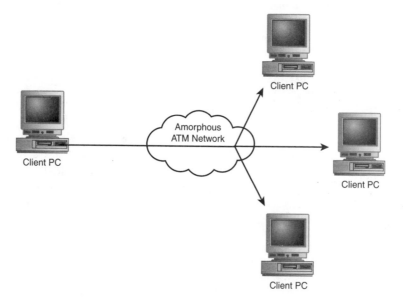

Unfortunately, ATM's protocols are not well suited to provide bi-directional point-to-multipoint communications. Nor can they support multipoint-to-multipoint communications of any kind. Both of these forms of communications would be relatively easy to implement in shared-media Layer 2 protocols because such protocols would have complex Media Access Control mechanisms that could accommodate multiple simultaneous recipients.

Both point-to-point and point-to-multipoint connections can be established in one of two ways: switched or permanent virtual circuitry. The original focus of the ATM Forum was on permanent virtual circuits (PVCs). In much the same way as in Frame Relay, connections through a (pardon the term) "cloud" of switches can be software defined. These connections always remain active in normal operation, regardless of their traffic volumes.

It remains a bit trickier to develop protocols for switched virtual circuits (SVCs). SVCs are created on demand between two or more endpoints. Cells are then forwarded through this logical channel. After the communications cease, the channel is disassembled and the network can reuse its bandwidth.

Transmission Rates

ATM can operate at many different transmission rates. These rates were, originally, to be based on the Optical Carrier (OC) line specifications. This was consistent with ATM's original mission as B-ISDN's asynchronous transport protocol. Therefore, the basic rate of ATM transmission was set to the OC-3 standard of 155.52Mbps. Provisions were made to support the OC-1 rate of 51.84Mbps as well as to scale upward to the 2.488Gbps of the OC-48 specification. This ensured that ATM would scale well within the well-accepted architecture of the public switched networks.

> **Note:** There's even work in progress to scale ATM up to a 10Gbps rate, although this is not intended for use in a LAN.

Adapting ATM to the LAN environment created the need for some variation from its original set of capabilities. Specifically, support needed to be developed for copper-based transmission media that would be consistent with the optically based specifications. Additionally, it was strongly felt that a rate less than the 51.84Mbps of OC-1 would have to be developed for ATM. Two competing proposals were developed: 25.6Mbps and 25.9Mbps. The 25.9Mbps proposal was more logical, because it could be evenly scaled upward into the OC architecture.

The 25.6Mbps specification was cobbled together from IBM's Token Ring chip set. It was believed that such a basis would make 25.6Mbps ATM more reliable than any proposal that lacked a similar, well-engineered heritage. Its heritage, however, resulted in an odd (but relatively functional) data rate. This specification can provide connectivity over Category 3 UTP for up to 100 meters. Ultimately, the 25.6Mbps proposal was adopted by the ATM Forum.

The copper-based variant of OC-1 was designed to provide 51.84Mbps over a maximum of 100 meters of Category 5 UTP. Unfortunately, this specification was based on a new modulation technology known as *Carrierless Amplitude Phase Modulation* (CAP or CAP-M). Although proven successful in laboratory environments, this technology proved virtually impossible to manufacture on any large scale.

ATM's full rate of 155.52Mbps was also treated to a pair of new physical media interfaces for the LAN environment. The first was Category 5 UTP, which can be up to 100 meters long. The other was 62.5-micron, multimode fiber-optic cabling. This media can stretch for up to 2 kilometers.

Peter's Principle: A Pig in a Poke?

At one time, there was a decided push by networking gear vendors to port 25Mbps ATM to the desktop. Switches and network cards were developed and a full marketing blitz was started, but the market failed to materialize. The high cost of the hardware as well as the high cost of supporting what was seen as a non-LAN technology led most companies to steer clear of ATM to the desktop. Unfortunately, quite a bit of hardware was manufactured that may still be available on the market at very low "clear-it-out" prices. Don't be tempted! Look into high-speed Ethernet or Token Ring (at 100Mbps or higher) for fast desktop connections.

Topology

Unlike many of today's Layer 2 networking protocols that are being implemented on switches, ATM was designed to be switched. Therefore, it features a star topology. Each device connects directly to the ATM switch (it's not a hub or repeater) and enjoys its own dedicated bandwidth to that switch.

This raises an interesting issue: If each station has its own dedicated bandwidth to its switch, does the dedicated bandwidth stop there? Clearly, some multiplexing must be used somewhere in the network, particularly as one exits the LAN and enters the WAN. It's a rare organization that can afford to provide 155.52Mbps of dedicated bandwidth to all its members. Switches that can support simultaneous, full-rate transmissions to all connected devices are called *nonblocking*. Nonblocking switches require a backplane whose throughput must be at least as great as the aggregate bandwidth it supports to stations. That is, the backplane must operate at a minimum of 155.52 times the number of ports on the switch to qualify as nonblocking. For example, an ATM switch with eight ports must have a backplane speed of 8×155.52, or 1.244Gbps, to qualify as nonblocking. Any switches with eight ports at 155.52Mbps with an available backplane bandwidth of fewer than 1.244Gbps would have to block some of the transmissions if all eight stations attempted to send simultaneously.

ATM Interfaces

There are many types of highly specialized ATM interfaces. Many are closely related, with only slight and subtle differences made necessary by the arcane legislation that continues to haunt the U.S. telecommunications industry. A closer look at just two of ATM's interfaces should provide the necessary context for understanding ATM's architecture. Here are the two most familiar interfaces:

- User-to-Network Interface (UNI)
- Network-to-Network Interface (NNI)

These names are fairly self-explanatory. UNIs are used to connect user equipment to the ATM network, whereas NNIs are needed to interconnect the ATM switches that comprise the network. These two interfaces are illustrated in Figure 9.3.

FIGURE 9.3
ATM's user-to-network and network-to-network interface signaling.

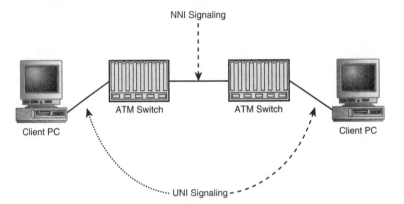

Note: Due to its origins as a broadband ISDN technology, ATM's UNI was developed to describe Customer Premise Equipment. Therefore, a UNI interface can be used by a privately owned ATM switch that connects to a telecommunications carrier's public ATM network.

The ATM Forum is also nearing completion of a Private Network-to-Network Interface (P-NNI). The protocols in this interface will allow dynamic routing in private ATM networks with multiple switches.

ATM Reference Model

What protocol would be complete without its very own reference model? ATM is no exception. The ATM Protocol Reference Model, however, puts an innovative spin on the familiar layered model: It uses planes. Planes, unlike layers, are three dimensional. Without getting hung up on the technicalities of geometry, suffice it to say that each plane represents a separate protocol suite. Together, they comprise the ATM protocol suite. The ATM Protocol Reference Model is illustrated in Figure 9.4, as it compares to the OSI Reference Model.

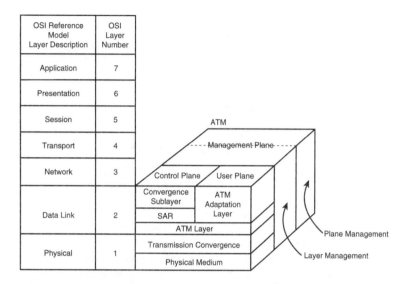

FIGURE 9.4
ATM Reference Model versus OSI Reference Model.

Note: Although Figure 9.4 depicts the Convergence Sublayer as a fixed part of the ATM Reference Model, it's needed by only a subset of its Adaptation Layers. Consequently, certain classes of service may be provided without using the Convergence Sublayer. This point is further expanded later in this section.

As is evident in Figure 9.4, ATM is limited to Layers 1 and 2 of the OSI Reference Model. Above this would be the traditional transport network protocols and applications. Upper-layer mechanisms include provisions for end-to-end data transfer and signaling. These are referred to as the *User* and *Control* planes, respectively.

Physical Layer

The ATM's version of the OSI Physical Layer consists of two sublayers:

- Transmission Convergence (TC)
- Physical Medium (PM)

ATM's Physical Layer has twin responsibilities for data transmission and reception. For data transmissions, the Transmission Convergence mechanism accepts cells from the ATM Layer, generates a checksum value that can be used for some limited degree of forward error detection, and then transmits the cell's header and payload one bit at a time over the media.

For data reception, the Physical Medium accepts inbound cells, verifies the checksum value to determine whether the header was damaged in transit, and then forwards the bits up to the ATM Layer for reconstruction into cells.

Transmission Convergence Sublayer

The Transmission Convergence (TC) Sublayer is the uppermost of ATM's Physical Layer components. It's responsible for numerous functions, including the following:

- Cell delineation
- Generation of the Hardware Error Control (HEC) sequence
- Cell-rate decoupling
- Transmission frame adaptation, generation, and recovery functions

Cell delineation is a fancy term for preserving the integrity of cell boundaries upon receipt. This function is critical to the successful extraction of cells from the received bit stream.

Hardware Error Control (HEC) is nothing more than a checksum value. Transmitting stations must generate and check this value, based on the header contents of the cell. Recipients must recalculate this value to determine the likelihood of the contents having been damaged in transit. Unfortunately, this checksum is computed only on the five-octet header, not the entire 53-octet cell. This adds support to the old argument that ATM doesn't really provide forward error detection, despite having a mechanism for it. Many of the Data Link Layer components, though, do provide forward error correction, which pretty much renders this argument moot. (See Chapter 3, "The Data Link Layer," for details.)

Cell-rate decoupling is a mechanism that's used to match the cell rate of the ATM Layer with the cell rate of the media interface. For example, if the ATM Layer operates at the full rate of 155.52Mbps, but the media interface is limited to 25.6Mbps, the Transmission Convergence Sublayer is responsible for throttling back transmissions. Preferably, this is done by suppressing any unassigned cells. Similarly, this sublayer can also insert blank cells to accelerate the ATM Layer's cell stream, if it's slower than the media's cell rate.

The last bundle of functions for which the TC is responsible may seem a bit counterintuitive. These functions involve transmission framing. Transmission frame adaptation is the process by which the TC packages cells into frames that are acceptable to the specific physical media that they're to traverse. Similarly, frame generation and recovery are ancillary functions that create and maintain the appropriate Physical Layer frame structure.

> **Note:** The protocol data units (PDUs) created and used by ATM's various Data Link Layer mechanisms are also called *frames*. PDUs are examined in much more detail in the section "ATM Adaptation Layer."

Physical Medium Sublayer

The Physical Medium Sublayer encompasses all the functions that are medium dependent. This includes synchronizing the timing of transmissions across a virtual circuit and transmitting/receiving bits, as needed. It's important to note that because the Physical Medium Sublayer is medium dependent, a separate PM specification exists for each of the supported physical media.

ATM Adaptation Layer

As was presented in Figure 9.4, ATM's version of the OSI's Data Link Layer is comprised of two sublayers: the ATM Layer and the ATM Adaptation Layer (AAL). The AAL is a protocol suite that occupies the upper reaches of ATM's Data Link Layer. Although it's named the *AAL Layer*, there are actually three mechanisms contained in this Layer. The AAL is the most obvious, but there are also the CS (Convergence Sublayer) and SAR (Segmentation and Reassembly).

The Convergence Sublayer provides the funnel through which data intended for transmission is received from Layer 3 protocols and through which any received data is passed back to those protocols. The CS is responsible for properly mapping higher-layer protocol requests for AAL, SAR, and ATM services on both outbound and incoming data. This service is needed only for mapping other protocols such as TCP/IP and IPX/SPX as well as other Layer 2 protocols such as Frame Relay.

The SAR is the mechanism that actually chunks data structures received from higher-layer protocols into the 48-octet structures that neatly fill ATM's payload fields. These data structures are passed to the ATM Layer where they become the payloads of cells.

Five different AALs, numbered 1 through 5, were planned. Each one was designed to support one of ATM's four different classes of service: These are known as Classes A, B, C, and D. Each class supports transmissions in different ways and, consequently, requires a separate set of protocols at the end stations. Each AAL places the data it receives from the SAR into a precellular structure known as a *Segmentation and Reassembly Protocol Data Unit* (SAR-PDU). SAR-PDUs are passed to the ATM Layer, where five-octet headers are grafted onto them to form the familiar 53-octet ATM cells.

> **Note:** Although five AALs were planned, only three remain. AAL 2 was never completed, and 3 and 4 have been combined into a single AAL named "3/4." Therefore, the surviving AALs are 1, 3/4, and 5.

Class A Service

Class A service uses the AAL 1. It features Constant Bit Rate (CBR), connection-oriented synchronous traffic. These transmission characteristics are necessary to support isochronous communications such as voice traffic and even high-quality video transmissions. Additionally, AAL 1 can be used to emulate DS-1 links of T-carrier circuits. It's important to note that data is fed into AAL 1 at a constant bit rate; the AAL cannot make consistency out of chaos! The bit rate constancy must be driven by the application. If the application cannot maintain the data rate at a uniform pace from beginning to end, there's very little that the ATM protocols can do to create a constant bit rate.

> **Note:** For more information on DS-1 links and the T-Carrier system, refer to Chapter 11, "Transmission Facilities."

SAR-PDUs created via AAL 1 have two four-bit fields prepended to their payload. These fields are Sequence Number (SN) and Sequence Number Protection (SNP). The Sequence Number is a four-bit counter that's reset to 0 for each data unit segmented by the SAR. The SNP is a four-bit Cyclical Redundancy Check (CRC) number, calculated using only the four bits of the sequence number. This reduces the payload field of an AAL 1 cell to 47 octets.

An example of an AAL 1 SAR-PDU is illustrated in Figure 9.5.

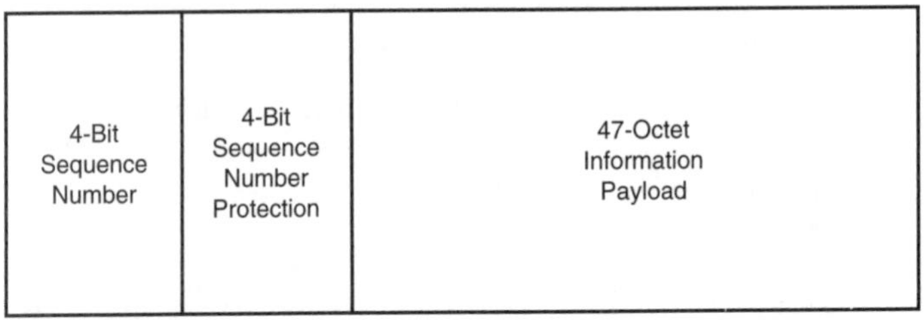

FIGURE 9.5
AAL 1 SAR-PDU.

4-Bit Sequence Number	4-Bit Sequence Number Protection	47-Octet Information Payload

Class B Service

Class B traffic is like Class A traffic. They are both connection oriented and synchronous. The only difference is that Class B doesn't require a Constant Bit Rate. Instead, it uses a Variable Bit Rate (VBR). In other words, the application has a high time value, and its transmissions must be carefully synchronized, but they come at irregular intervals. This subtle distinction is enough to warrant a separate adaptation layer: AAL 2.

Some video applications, particularly those that feature algorithms that refresh only the changed pixels, are ideal for Class B. Unfortunately, the specification for AAL 2 has never been completed by the ATM Forum. Therefore, many information sources identify only AALs 1, 3, 4, and 5, although 3 and 4 are lumped together and designated "3/4." Without a specification defining its structure, any attempt at illustrating an AAL 2 SAR-PDU is purely speculative. Consequently, none is provided.

Class C Service

Class C traffic is connection oriented and uses a Variable Bit Rate (VBR). More importantly, there are no timing requirements to be satisfied between the endpoints; Class C is asynchronous. Originally, Class C traffic was to be satisfied via AAL 3. However, sometime during its development, a decision was made to combine AAL 3 and AAL 4 into a single AAL that could service both Class C and Class D.

> **Note:** The combined AAL was rather uncreatively named "3/4," which is pronounced *three-four* rather than expressed as the fractional *three-fourths*. In retrospect, given that a subset of Class C traffic was treated to yet another AAL (#5), perhaps the fractional pronunciation is more appropriate!

Many protocols, including Layer 2 protocols such as Frame Relay and X.25 as well as higher-layer protocol suites such as TCP/IP and IPX/SPX, represent Class C traffic. Although these protocols are inherently connectionless, ATM requires that a connection first be established before any cells can be relayed between any two stations. After the virtual connection is established, no restrictions limit what the payloads of those cells may contain. A connection-oriented protocol is capable of encapsulating and relaying packetized data from connectionless protocols.

This creates the need for careful convergence of the higher-layer protocols' functions into the mechanics of the ATM Layer. This is where the Convergence Sublayer is useful. The CS creates a CS-PDU for AAL 3/4. This CS-PDU is illustrated in Figure 9.6.

FIGURE 9.6
AAL 3/4 CS-PDU.

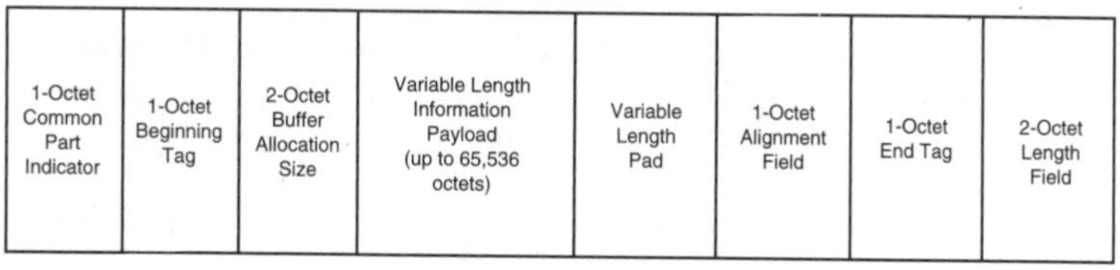

1-Octet Common Part Indicator	1-Octet Beginning Tag	2-Octet Buffer Allocation Size	Variable Length Information Payload (up to 65,536 octets)	Variable Length Pad	1-Octet Alignment Field	1-Octet End Tag	2-Octet Length Field

As illustrated in Figure 9.6, the AAL 3/4 CS-PDU has the following structure:

- A 1-Octet Common Part Indicator field (CPI).
- A 1-Octet Beginning Tag field (BTag).
- A 2-Octet Buffer Allocation Size Indicator field (BASize).
- A variable-length Information Payload field. (Someone wisely avoided using the already widely used acronym *IP* for this field!)
- A variable-length Padding field (PAD).
- A 1-Octet Alignment field (AL).
- A 1-Octet End Tag field (ETag).
- A 2-Octet Length field.

Each of these fields is significant to the functioning of the AAL. The CPI indicates the usage of the other CS-PDU fields. This usage can vary by operation. The BTag contains a numeric value. The same value is placed in the ending tag (ETag). Together, they identify the beginning and end of each CS-PDU. This is necessary because downstream operations are likely to result in each CS-PDU being further segmented into an as-yet-undetermined number of SAR-PDUs.

The buffer allocation size indicator is used to warn the recipient AAL of the size of buffer it needs to successfully reassemble this incoming CS-PDU. The information payload is limited to the maximum size identifiable by the previous field. Given that BASize is a binary structure that's two octets long, its maximum value is 2 to the 16th power, which is 65,536. This is the maximum size of the information payload. Obviously, this is much larger than the size of an ATM cell's payload, so further segmentation is necessary.

Note: The buffer allocation size indicator is sometimes not used to describe the actual length of the payload. Rather, it's automatically set to a large (if not maximum) value. This is useful in streaming applications where the AAL might not know the exact size of the PDU.

The PAD field is used in those cases where the information payload does not equal a multiple of 32. As padding, it's used only to maintain consistent length, and its contents are set to zeros.

The next field is the Alignment field. This one-octet field is used solely to increase the CS-PDU's trailer to four octets. It's set to zero and functions as structural padding.

The last two fields are ETag (end tag) and Length. The ETag field, as previously explained, mirrors the value in the BTag field. The Length field is set to the actual length of the Information Payload field.

The CS-PDU is then passed to the SAR, where it's segmented into as many SAR-PDUs as are needed. This SAR-PDU has the following structure:

- A 2-bit Segment Type field (ST)
- A 4-bit Sequence Number field (SN)
- A 10-bit Multiplexing Identification field (MID)
- A 44-Octet Information Payload field
- A 6-bit Length Indicator field (LI)
- A 10-bit Cyclic Redundancy Check field (CRC)

This SAR-PDU, if you've been counting, is exactly 48 octets in length—the exact length of the ATM cell payload. All that remains is to graft on the appropriate five-octet header, and you've created a cell. This SAR-PDU is illustrated in Figure 9.7.

2-Bit Segment Type	4-Bit Sequence Number	10-Bit Multiplexing Identifier	44-Octet Information Payload	6-Bit Length Indicator	10-Bit CRC

Given that many of the fields contained in this SAR-PDU are already familiar, it should suffice to describe the functionality of only the ones not yet presented. The only field not yet discussed is the Multiplexing Identification (MID) field. This field is used to identify all the cells that are created from any given CS-PDU. These structures can range up to 65,536 octets in length, so they can be chipped into 1,365 cells! This field ensures that the cells are uniquely identifiable as belonging to the same CS-PDU by the recipient. The recipient, in theory, may be receiving multiple streams of cells from different sources simultaneously—hence, the reason for this field's existence.

At the risk of understating the painfully obvious, AAL 3/4 is quite complex and awkward to use. As testimony to this awkwardness, AAL 5 was developed to satisfy a subset of Class C traffic only. AAL 5 is the one adaptation layer that will be used the most. This statement is predicated on the rather dangerous double assumption that, first, ATM will actually be used, and, second, that the majority of applications supported will continue to rely on the traditional connectionless communications protocols.

AAL 5 was designed to be a simple and efficient AAL, targeted at the most used portions of AAL 3/4. This AAL also produces a CS-PDU, albeit a much more streamlined one than the one just examined.

The first field in the AAL 5 CS-PDU is the Information Payload field. This field can be anywhere from 0 to 65,536 octets long, although a zero-octet payload would be rather pointless. This is followed by the PAD field. Padding is used to ensure that the payload is a multiple of 48, which facilitates cell creation in the ATM Layer. Next is a one-octet Control field, which hasn't yet been given any usefulness and is therefore defaulted to zeros. The last two fields are the Length and CRC fields. Again, the Length field is two octets long, which yields the maximum value of the Information Payload field. The CRC field is four octets long and calculated using the entire contents of the CS-PDU (from the start of the Information Payload field to the end of the Length field).

This CS-PDU is illustrated in Figure 9.8.

Variable Length Information Payload (0 to 65,536 octets)	Variable Length Pad	1-Octet Control Field	2-Octet Length Indicator	4-Octet CRC

The AAL 5 CS-PDU is then passed to the SAR for conversion to a SAR-PDU. The AAL 5 SAR-PDU is a rather unspectacular structure that contains only 48 octets of payload, with no SAR-specific headers or trailers. The simplicity of this AAL makes it relatively inexpensive and easy to implement. The fact that AAL 5 is tailored to what is likely to be the bulk of ATM's traffic also positions AAL 5 as the workhorse of the adaptation layers.

Class D Service

Class D service features a connectionless, asynchronous data transfer. This is useful for relaying LAN or SMDS traffic over an ATM backbone. AAL 3/4 is the combined adaptation layer that services both Class C and D traffic. This almost makes sense when one considers that the only distinction between Classes C and D is that one is connection oriented and the other is connectionless.

ATM Layer

The ATM Layer and the ATM Adaptation Layers correspond to the Data Link Layer of the OSI Reference Model. Of these, the ATM Layer is the lower of the two and is responsible for establishing virtual connections and for passing cells received from the AAL through those connections. Much of the ATM Layer's functionality depends on whether that layer resides in an end station or a switching device. Consequently, it makes sense to examine the two alternatives independently.

End Station

The ATM Layer of an end station needs to be able to signal other stations that it has data to send them and negotiate the construction of a switched virtual circuit with those stations. Although this may sound simple, entire books can be written about the signaling techniques used to support circuit construction.

The logical circuit must be constructed before the ATM Layer can accept data from the AAL. Data from the AAL is received in the form of a Protocol Data Unit, which must be converted into a cell. This is easily accomplished via the addition and population of the header fields.

Switch

The functionality of a switch's ATM Layer is much simpler than its station-based counterpart. Upon receipt of a cell from any of its ports, the switch is only required to look at the VPI/VCI (Virtual Path Identifier/Virtual Channel Identifier, discussed in the following section) values contained in that cell's header and compare them to its table of VPI/VCI assignments. This table lookup accomplishes two important tasks. First, it determines what the new VPI/VCI assignments should be. Second, it identifies the port to which that cell must be relayed.

These are the primary functions of a switch's ATM Layer. Additional functions may include setting the Payload Type Indicator (PTI) field (if the network is congested) and implementing any traffic policies that may be in effect. This layer must also provide any buffering and reordering of cells made necessary by competition between multiple input ports for the same output port.

> **Note:** "Passing a cell out of a port" implies that the ATM Layer hands off the cell to that port's Physical Layer components. The Physical Layer recomputes the HEC value and then both creates and transmits the bit stream. In effect, the relayed cell is a very different cell than it was when it was received. Its header has been modified extensively.

Cell Structure

Once you've seen how the AALs create the basic Protocol Data Units (PDUs), exploring the structure of the actual ATM cells is almost anticlimactic. Nevertheless, the cell is ATM's basic data transport structure. Unlike most other LANs, this Layer 2 structure is of fixed length. ATM's cell is always 53 octets in length. This may sound like an unusual length, especially to anyone who's accustomed to Base 2 and/or Base 16 number systems, and for good reason! The cell length was derived through the time-honored convention of compromise rather than mathematics. The North American contributors to the CCITT's ATM standards body were in favor of a 64-octet payload, whereas the European and Asian representatives felt that a 32-octet payload would be more appropriate. CCITT split the difference and standardized a 48-octet payload with a five-octet header—hence, the less-than-intuitive length.

There are actually two different cell structures: one for UNI and one for NNI. The differences are all accounted for in the format of the five-octet header.

UNI Cell Structure

The UNI cell has the following structure:

- A 4-bit Generic Flow Control field (GFC)
- An 8-bit Virtual Path Identifier field (VPI)
- A 16-bit Virtual Channel Identifier field (VCI)
- A 3-bit Payload Type Indicator field (PTI)
- A 1-bit Cell Loss Priority field (CLP)
- An 8-bit Header Error Control field (HEC)
- A 48-Octet payload

This cell is illustrated in Figure 9.9.

Figure 9.9
The UNI cell structure.

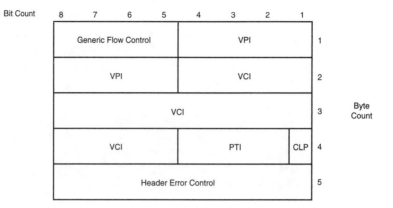

The Generic Flow Control field was envisioned as a mechanism to regulate the flow of data (cells) across UNIs only. Establishing the need for this mechanism and the length of its field were easy tasks. Specifying the actual method and processes by which the flow of data between the two end stations in a connection could be regulated proved much more daunting. Of all the higher-level services that needed to be defined to extend ATM to the LAN environment, flow control proved to be one of the more divisive and intractable. Today, the GFC is deemed to have local value only. That is, its contents are not carried across an entire virtual circuit.

The VPI field of the UNI cell is eight bits long. It's used to identify virtual paths, although this is more of an NNI function. Consequently, the UNI VPI field is defaulted to all zeros and can be set to other values to facilitate network management functions. As the cell travels into NNI regions of the network, the VPI field may be used by those NNI switches. Remember, switches aren't simple repeaters: They process the cell and rewrite its header before relaying it.

Virtual Channel Identifier is a 16-bit field that uniquely identifies the virtual connection established during the signaling process. The ATM switch uses the VPI, in conjunction with the VCI, to relay received cells to the appropriate physical port.

Payload Type Indicator is a three-bit field, and each bit is significant:

- The first bit indicates whether the cell's payload originated from within the user or control planes.
- The second bit indicates whether that cell has encountered congestion in the network.
- The third bit is used to flag the last of a series of cells that are made from a single AAL 5 PDU.

The Cell Loss Priority field is just one bit long. It indicates whether the cell should be discarded if it encounters heavy congestion during its passage through the network.

Traditional application types require guaranteed integrity upon delivery and rely on Layer 4 protocols to reorder any packets delivered out of sequence. It's more important for these packets to arrive intact than it is for them to arrive on time and in order.

This is in stark contrast to the next-generation, latency-sensitive applications such as voice and/or video conferencing. These applications require that the data arrive on time. Period. If the packets are late or damaged in transit, they are simply discarded by the recipient application. Time value is the highest priority. Therefore, the Cell Loss Priority bit provides a mechanism for the network to discriminate between high and low time-value cells. High time-value cells that are going to be discarded by their application aren't worth carrying all the way to that application, so the network can simply discard them.

The last field of the UNI cell is Header Error Control. This is an eight-bit field that contains the output of a checksum algorithm calculated using the contents of the cell's header fields, excluding the HEC.

NNI Cell Structure

The NNI cell was designed for ATM's original role as a CO-to-CO transport for broadband-ISDN. Its structure reflects that role. The NNI cell contains the following fields:

- A 12-bit Virtual Path Identifier field (VPI)
- A 16-bit Virtual Channel Identifier field (VCI)
- A 3-bit Payload Type Indicator field (PTI)
- A 1-bit Cell Loss Priority field (CLP)
- An 8-bit Header Error Control field (HEC)
- A 48-octet payload

This cell is illustrated in Figure 9.10.

FIGURE 9.10
The NNI cell structure.

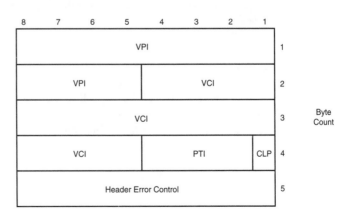

Given that each of the NNI cell's fields is also included in the UNI cell, it hardly seems worth the effort to revisit these fields. The key differences between the fields in the UNI and NNI cells are the lack of a four-bit flow control field and the expansion of the VPI to 12 bits. Expanding the VPI field is essential in network backbones. The primary role of a backbone is the aggregation of traffic. Therefore, it's possible to have many virtual paths aggregated from the countless virtual circuits that are extended through the network.

Local Area Network Emulation (LANE)

It has long been recognized that one of the greatest barriers to ATM's acceptance as a LAN technology was the tremendous installed base of applications designed for existing LAN technologies. This was particularly true of the IEEE's 802.3 (Ethernet) and 802.5 (Token Ring) specifications. ATM LANs differ in three distinct ways from these IEEE LANs:

- ATM LANs are connection oriented, whereas the other LANs encourage applications to use connectionless messaging.
- Ethernet and Token Ring can perform broadcasting and multicasting readily via their shared media.
- The IEEE MAC addresses are based on manufacturers' serial numbers, not LAN topology.

The ATM Forum met these three challenges to the acceptance of ATM LANs by developing a new ATM service that emulated the IEEE LAN environments. This service is called *Local Area Network Emulation* (LANE).

> **Note:** Networks that are built using the LANE protocol suite are known as *emulated local area networks* (ELANs). ELANS can emulate either 802.3 Ethernet or 802.5 Token Ring, but not both simultaneously because no translation bridging mechanism has been defined.

LANE works by enabling end systems—which can be any device connected to the periphery of a network—to connect directly to the ATM LAN. Their software applications still function as though they were directly connected to either an Ethernet or Token Ring LAN. This capability will be critical to any organizations that attempt a graceful, phased-in migration to ATM from either of these other LAN types.

LANE enables ATM LAN clients to access and use existing LAN applications through a software layer added to the emulating devices. This software layer becomes an integral part of that device's ATM protocol stack. The resulting stack is illustrated in Figure 9.11.

FIGURE 9.11
The LANE protocol stack.

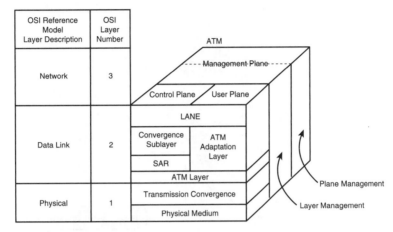

The emulating device uses a new interface: the LUNI (LANE User-to-Network Interface). This term is just the tip of the acronym iceberg. For example, the emulated LAN is called an *ELAN*. Each client in the ELAN is a LAN Emulation client, or *LEC*. The individual LECs are addressed via their MAC address.

Each ELAN must have a single LAN Emulation Service (LES). The LES may be contained within a switch or an end-station computer. Regardless, the LES consists of a LAN Emulation Configuration Server (LECS) as well as a Broadcast and Unknown Server (BUS).

As if this weren't enough, there's even a new acronym for the type of logical connection that's established between LECs and the LES in an ELAN: VCC. The VCC is a virtual channel connection, and separate ones are required for ATM's control and user planes.

To visualize this as something other than alphabet soup, refer to Figure 9.12.

In Figure 9.12, there are two LECs and one LES (resident on a server). The LES server functions as the gateway to the IEEE LAN. The clients may access resources out on that LAN via the LES. This service employs MAC emulation.

FIGURE 9.12
Typical LANE configuration.

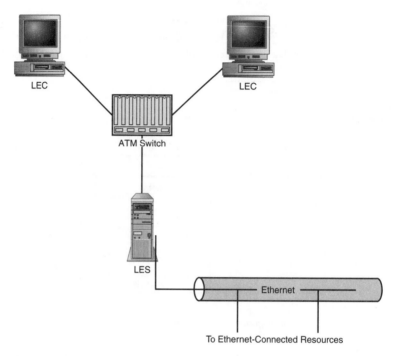

LEC

LEC

ATM Switch

LES

Ethernet

To Ethernet-Connected Resources

Summary

The original vision of ATM remains compelling: a single technology for both local and wide area networking that's equally capable of transporting high-bandwidth, low-latency isochronous traffic as well as the more traditional interactive and bulk data communications. The challenges facing ATM and the ATM Forum have remained somewhat constant:

- Complete the specifications through an open standards process dominated by corporate politics.
- Develop a cost-effective ATM solution set that will entice customers to migrate from embedded platforms.

For many years, it was difficult to determine which of these was the greatest obstacle. Today, it appears that the ATM Forum has regained its lost momentum and is moving quickly toward completion of the suite of open ATM specifications. That's the good news.

The bad news is that the remainder of ATM's competitive environment has not stagnated. Over the past few years, many other communications technologies have been treated to life-extending refreshes and updates. Therefore, they are more formidable competition, in terms of both their technical capabilities and their price/performance ratio, than ever before. Therefore, as ATM appears to be overcoming the first of its two obstacles, the second is becoming even more formidable. Only time will tell whether the ATM Forum ever succeeds in achieving its vision for ATM.

PART III

Building Wide Area Networks

Wide Area Networking

Wide area networks (WANs) are comprised of routers, routing protocols, and transmission facilities. Properly constructed, WANs enable LANs to be networked together, regardless of how much geographic distance separates them. The key words here are *properly constructed*. Designing, building, and administering WANs requires a very different set of skills than does client/server or LAN administration. This chapter examines the various components that make up a WAN as well as the relative costs and benefits of each.

Understanding WAN Technologies

Wide area networks (WANs) and their component technologies continue to increase in importance. Not very many years ago, about the only need most companies had for WANs was to internetwork two or more work locations. This is still a valuable and important use of WAN technologies, but other possible uses are rapidly appearing. For example, a company with only a single work location might need a robust connection to the Internet to support marketing, customer care, and many other functions. Alternatively, outsourcing certain operations or functions, as well as collaborative efforts with other companies, can necessitate the internetworking of privately owned LANs.

Unfortunately, WANs are very different from LANs. Most LAN technologies adhere tightly to industry standards. WANs are composite structures built from many different technologies—some standard, some highly proprietary. Many of the competing technologies also differ radically in features, performance, and cost. The most difficult part of building a WAN is matching the appropriate technologies in such a way as to satisfy the underlying business requirements. This requires a deep understanding of each aspect of every WAN component.

The wide area network's technology base includes the following:

- Transmission facilities
- Communications hardware, including CSUs/DSUs (Channel Service Unit/Data Service Unit—the digital equivalent of a modem) and premises edge vehicles (routers and switches)
- Internetwork addressing
- Routing protocols

Each of these technology categories expands into a surprisingly wide array of choices of individual technologies. Within each technology category lies additional variation in terms of manufacturers, models, and configurations. Before selecting vendors and specific products, you should examine each technology for potential performance capabilities relative to your expected WAN traffic load and performance requirements. Although an exhaustive review of each manufacturer's product line is outside the scope of this book, a survey of each technology can provide a solid foundation for your own evaluation of actual products.

Using Transmission Facilities

Transmission facilities used to construct the WAN present the richest array of options for the network planner. These facilities cover a wide range of sizes, varieties, and costs. For example, transmission facilities can range in size (bandwidth) from 9.6Kbps to 44.736Mbps, and beyond. These transmission facilities support a digital stream of data at a fixed and predetermined transmission rate. They can be implemented over a variety of physical media, including twisted pair or fiber-optic cabling, and can also support numerous framing formats.

Note: The DS-3 specification (see Chapter 11, "Transmission Facilities") offers 44.736Mbps of bandwidth. When discussed, this bandwidth is frequently referred to simply as *45Mbps*.

These facilities also vary greatly in the manner in which they provide connections. There are two primary types of facilities: circuit switched and packet switched. These two types encompass all versions of facilities, although technological innovation may be blurring their boundaries somewhat. Some would also include a third type of facility, called *cell switched*, but this is so closely akin to packet switched that there's little difference between them. These technologies are briefly described in this chapter to provide a context for selecting the correct WAN. More detailed information on leased line transmission facilities is available in Chapter 11.

Circuit-Switched Facilities

Circuit switching is a communications method that creates a switched, dedicated path between two end stations. A good example of a circuit-switched network is the telephone system. A telephone is hard-wired to a central office telecommunications switch that is owned and operated by the local exchange carrier (LEC). There are many LECs and even more telecommunications switches in the world, yet any telephone can establish a connection to any other telephone through a series of intermediary central office switches. That connection is a physical circuit and is dedicated to that session for the duration of the communications session. After the telephones terminate their sessions, the physical circuit through the switched telecommunications infrastructure is torn down. The resources are then freed up for the next call.

The creation of a dedicated physical circuit through switches is the essence of circuit switching. Every unit of transmission, regardless of whether it's a cell, a frame, or anything else that may be constructed, takes the same physical path through the network infrastructure. This concept may be applied in several different formats. Three examples of circuit-switched transmission facilities include leased lines, ISDN, and Switched 56, all discussed in the sections that follow.

Leased Lines

The leased line is the most robust and flexible of the circuit-switched transmission facilities. These circuits are called *leased lines* because they're leased from telecommunications carriers for a monthly fee.

In North America, the dominant system for providing digital leased line service is known as the *T-Carrier system*. The T-Carrier enables 1.544Mbps of bandwidth to be channelized into 24 separate transmission facilities over two pairs of wire. Each channel is 64Kbps wide and can be further channelized into even smaller facilities, such as 9.6Kbps. The 1.544Mbps facility is known as the T-1. A higher capacity facility also exists within the T-Carrier system. This is the 44.736Mbps T-3 facility.

> **Note:** Leased lines are frequently called *dedicated* or *private* lines because their bandwidth is reserved for only the company that's leasing them.

For more information on leased lines and the T-Carrier system, refer to Chapter 11, "Transmission Facilities."

Integrated Services Digital Network (ISDN)

ISDN is a "dial-on-demand" form of digital circuit-switched technology that can transport voice and data simultaneously over the same physical connection. ISDN can be ordered in either Basic Rate (BRI) or Primary Rate (PRI) Interfaces.

The BRI offers 144Kbps in a format known as *2B+D*. The *2B* refers to two 64Kbps B channels that can be bonded together to form one logical connection at 128Kbps. The D channel is a 16Kbps control channel used for call setup, takedown, and other control functions.

The PRI is, typically, delivered over a T-1 facility at a gross transmission rate of 1.544Mbps. This is usually channelized into 23 64Kbps B channels and one 64Kbps D channel. Higher-rate H channels of either 384, 1536, or 1920Kbps can be used instead of, or in combination with, the B and D channels.

> **Note:** The 1920Kbps H3 channel is usable only in Europe where the standard transmission rate is 2.048Mbps, rather than the 1.544Mbps rate standard in the U.S., Canada, and Japan. Attempts to use an H3 channel over a 1.544Mbps transmission facility result in unusable channels.

Although ISDN is technically a circuit-switched facility, it can support circuit-switched, packet-switched, and even semipermanent connections.

Switched 56

Another dial-on-demand circuit-switched variant is Switched 56. Switched 56 offers 56Kbps of bandwidth between any two points that subscribe to this service. As with any dial-on-demand service, no circuit exists until a call is placed. Then the circuit is constructed between the origination and requested destination points. The actual path taken through the switched communications infrastructure is invisible, and immaterial, to the end users. This circuit is torn down when the session is terminated.

The nondedicated nature of Switched 56 makes it an affordable alternative to leased lines. You pay based on usage rather than for the luxury of having bandwidth reserved for you, regardless of whether it's being used. Balanced against affordability is performance. Switched 56 circuits must set up calls to requested destinations. This takes time. Therefore, establishing a communications session can be done much more quickly over a 56Kbps leased line than it can over a Switched 56. After the call is established, performance should be comparable.

Switched 56 is a mature and declining technology. It once offered a combination of lower cost than leased lines but much higher performance than modems and POTS lines. Today, advances in signaling techniques have enabled modems to close the performance gap. Switched 56 still offers a slight improvement over the so-called 56Kbps modems (despite what their name says, they cannot provide and sustain that transmission rate), but not much. Today, Switched 56 is probably best suited as an emergency contingency to leased lines.

Packet-Switched Facilities

Packet-switching facilities feature an internal packet format that's used to encapsulate data to be transported. Unlike circuit-switched facilities, packet-switched facilities do not provide a dedicated connection between two locations. Instead, the premises access facility interconnects with the telecommunications carrier's switched infrastructure. Packets are forwarded in a connectionless manner through this commercial packet-switched network (PSN). The lack of an easily defined path between any two locations has led to the overuse of the cloud symbol as the ubiquitous, but amorphous, network. Two examples of packet-switched networks are the old but familiar X.25 and its more up-to-date cousin, Frame Relay, both discussed in the following sections.

X.25

X.25 is a very old WAN communications protocol developed by the CCITT (now known as the *International Telecommunications Union*, or ITU). It was first offered as a commercial service by telecommunications carriers in the early 1970s.

> **Note:** The ITU's specifications are sometimes identified with the prefix *ITU-T*. The *T* suffix identifies the specification as part of the ITU's telecommunications standards.

X.25 supports the use of both switched and permanent virtual circuits. Switched virtual circuits (SVCs) are established as needed and are dismantled as soon as the communications session ends. Permanent virtual circuits (PVCs) are predefined, logical connections through a switched network between two points. The advantages of SVCs are that they're flexible and can be used to connect any two points within the X.25 network on demand. Their limitation lies in the call setup time that must be endured prior to exchanging information with another device on the network.

PVCs aren't flexible and must be defined in advance. Their primary benefit lies in the elimination of a call setup period. Therefore, PVCs are typically used to support communications between devices that need to communicate on a routine and ongoing basis. SVCs are used for *ad hoc* communications.

X.25 contains a robust suite of error-detection and error-correction mechanisms that enable it to be a highly reliable protocol, having to traverse a noisy electromechanical switching equipment infrastructure. X.25 sacrificed throughput for reliability. Today, in the era of digital and optical communications, the error-detection/correction mechanisms of X.25 are unnecessary overhead. These functions are now more appropriately contained at the communicating devices rather than embedded in every network device. Applications that still require the use of the X.25 protocol may find better performance in emulating that protocol over a different transmission facility.

Frame Relay

Frame Relay is a faster version of X.25 packet switching that features smaller packet sizes and fewer error-checking mechanisms. Frame Relay currently supports transfer of packets through only permanent virtual circuits (PVCs) between the network's endpoint routers. Eventually, SVCs will be supported in this protocol, although no timelines for its deployment have been proffered by any of the commercial service providers.

The PVC's endpoints are defined by Data Link Connection Identifiers (DLCIs) and are given a committed information rate (CIR) through the Frame Relay network. DLCI pairs are also given a minimum available quantity of bandwidth, with the option to temporarily burst beyond that limit under certain circumstances. The use of DLCIs in Frame Relay networks is illustrated in Figure 10.1.

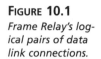

FIGURE 10.1

Frame Relay's logical pairs of data link connections.

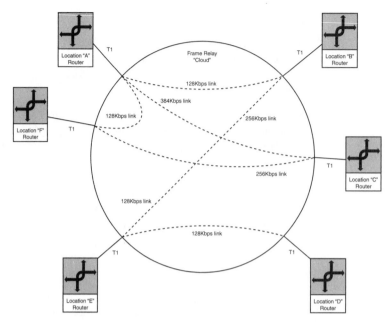

Frame Relay WANs are built by provisioning a point-to-point private line from the work location to the nearest central office that provides this service. At the central office, this private line terminates in a Frame Relay switch that's either fully or partially meshed with the other Frame Relay switches that compose the carrier's Frame Relay commercial infrastructure. Much like the central office voice switches that compose the Public Switched Telephone Network (PSTN), the Frame Relay switches remain invisible to the user community and its applications.

Frame Relay's primary benefit is that it can reduce the cost of networking locations that are geographically dispersed by minimizing the length of premises access facilities. These circuits are commercially available at 1.544Mbps, with CIRs used to create logical subrate connections to multiple locations.

Balanced against this minimization of access facilities cost for point-to-point leased lines is a reduction in performance. Frame Relay introduces a significant amount of overhead in terms of framing and protocol, which is added to the overheads of the point-to-point leased line. The rule of thumb that guides engineering the DLCI and CIRs on a Frame Relay connection is to subscribe a maximum of 1.024Mbps of the 1.544Mbps of available bandwidth. This guarantees that each DLCI receives its committed information rate and that a margin of extra bandwidth is available for temporarily bursting beyond this rate.

Warning: Bandwidth subscription is the allocation of bandwidth to channels carved from a larger transmission facility. In Frame Relay, each DLCI must have a rate subscription associated with it. This subscription is the committed information rate (CIR).

It's possible to define a series of DLCIs with a cumulative CIR that's greater than the bandwidth available on the transmission facility. Continuing the example of T-1–based Frame Relay, one could configure 2.048Mbps worth of CIRs over the 1.544Mbps facility. This is known as *oversubscription*. Oversubscription is a bad practice. It assumes that not all the DLCIs will be active and therefore not consuming their entire CIR at any given time. This is not an unreasonable assumption, but oversubscription results in the sporadic degradation of service during peak usage periods. If at all possible, avoid using telecommunications carriers that habitually oversubscribe their circuits.

Cell-Switched Facilities

A close relative to packet switching is *cell switching*. The difference between a packet and a cell is the length of the structure. A *packet* is a variable-length data structure, whereas a *cell* is a fixed-length data structure. The most familiar cell-switched technology is Asynchronous Transfer Mode (ATM). Although, technically speaking, ATM is currently a circuit-switched technology, it's best categorized independently.

ATM was designed to take advantage of the higher-speed transmission facilities such as T-3 and the SONET architectures.

Asynchronous Transfer Mode (ATM)

ATM was originally designed as an asynchronous transport mechanism for broadband ISDN. ATM's low latency and high bit rate, it was speculated, would make it equally ideal for use in local area networks. The subsequent market hype has almost completely cemented its reputation as a LAN technology, to the exclusion of its capabilities as a WAN technology.

As a cell-switched WAN technology, ATM is commercially available at 1.544Mbps (DS-1) or 44.736Mbps (DS-3), although this availability varies geographically. Initially, wide area ATM was available using only permanent virtual circuits, much like the DLCIs of Frame Relay. Ultimately, however, wide area ATM will be a switched technology that's capable of forwarding individual cells without requiring the overhead of establishing a permanent virtual circuit or reserving bandwidth.

Choosing Communications Hardware

The communications hardware needed to build a WAN includes three basic categories: customer-provided telephony equipment (CPE), premises edge vehicles, and data communications equipment (DCE). In this context, DCE refers to the telecommunications carriers' gear. As such, there's very little you can do to actually select DCE; therefore, it's not discussed in this section.

CPE refers to the physical telephony mechanisms that are used to tie premises communications equipment, including routers, LANs, switches, and so forth, to the commercial telephony network of the communications carrier.

Premises edge vehicles are those mechanisms that connect the LAN to the CPE. They generally operate at Layers 2 and 3 of the OSI Reference Model and are responsible for forwarding and receiving packets, based on internetwork addresses. Edge vehicles are the mechanisms that separate LAN from WAN, in the context of telecommunications. Both CPE and edge vehicles are customer provided.

Telecommunications carriers, of course, deploy a considerable amount of hardware to support the transmission facilities they provide to customers. Such hardware typically remains invisible to the users and LAN administrators. As such, it remains outside the scope of this book.

Note: CPE is also widely interpreted as *customer premises equipment*. Both interpretations of this acronym are acceptable and convey the same meaning.

Customer-Provided Equipment (CPE)

CPE is the Physical Layer telephony hardware that encodes signals and places them on the transmission facility. This hardware is almost always provided by the customers and is installed in their physical premises, on their side of the demarcation point. The demarcation point, referred to as the *demarc*, is the official boundary between the physical plant of the telecommunications carrier and the customer's physical plant that's connected to the carrier's telephony infrastructure.

The demarc is usually just a modular jack box that's labeled with the circuit identification numbers. The telecommunications carrier owns this box, as well as everything that's hard-wired to it. The customer is responsible for all equipment that connects to the modular jack receptacle. This customer-provided equipment is the CPE.

The types of CPE varies by transmission technology. The two most common forms of CPE are the CSU/DSU and the PAD. Both of these are further examined in the following sections.

Channel Service Unit/Digital Service Unit (CSU/DSU)

The typical WAN is constructed with leased line, circuit-switched transmission facilities. Therefore, the typical CPE is known as a CSU/DSU (Channel Service Unit/Digital Service Unit). The CSU/DSU assumes that the transmission facility is a leased line and that no dial-up connections are possible.

CSU/DSUs are data communications equipment that terminate channelized and digital transmission facilities. This termination typically takes the form of a modular jack. The CSU/DSU also features a serial connection to the router at the customer's premises edge, as illustrated in Figure 10.2.

FIGURE 10.2
The CSU/DSU interconnecting the router with the transmission facility.

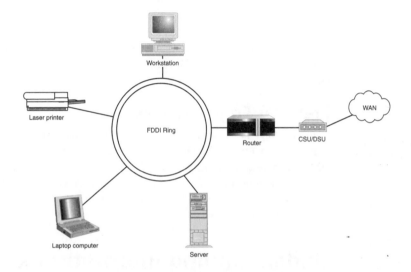

> **Note:** It's not uncommon to find people who also categorize routers as *customer-provided equipment*. This miscategorization is based on the compound assumption that the router is an essential part of extending connectivity beyond the local premises and that it must be provided by the customer. These assumptions are generally true, but the router is not considered a telecommunications device and therefore cannot be CPE—it's a premises edge vehicle.

The CSU/DSU provides more functionality than simply transmitting and receiving the physical signals. Depending on the brand and model, CSU/DSUs can also perform line conditioning and respond to diagnostic queries from the central office. These units are essential in any leased circuit that supports transmission rates of 56Kbps or greater.

Packet Assembler/Disassembler (PAD)

Transmission facilities that use packet switching may require a different device to create and dismantle the packets. This device is known as a *PAD*. PAD is actually an acronym for *Packet Assembler/Disassembler*. A good example of a network technology that uses PADs is the X.25 network. X.25 typically used a 9.6Kbps transmission facility to interconnect a user's premises to the telecommunications carrier's switched network infrastructure. The terminating device on these relatively low-speed facilities was the PAD.

Today's packet-switching technologies tend to use circuit-switched transmission facilities. For example, Frame Relay has clearly evolved from X.25, yet it doesn't use a PAD. Instead, LANs can be interconnected via Frame Relay using logical subchannels carved out of a T-1 facility. Given that the T-1 provides 1.544Mbps of bandwidth, it must terminate in a CSU/DSU at the customer's premises, regardless of which transmission technology it supports. Therefore, a WAN built using Frame Relay features routers and CSU/DSUs at each site. The CSU/DSU at each site connects to a T-1 transmission facility that interconnects them via the Frame Relay network.

Premises Edge Vehicles

A *premises edge vehicle* is the equipment that interconnects a customer's local area network with the CPE. In the typical LAN environment, this is a router. Routers function as the boundary between the LAN and the WAN. As such, their primary responsibility is keeping track of the routes to known internetwork addresses. These addresses are stored in routing tables that correlate the address with the physical interface on the router that must be used to get to that address.

Understanding Internetwork Addressing

Wide area networking invariably creates the need for addressing devices that reside beyond one's local LAN. Internetworking addresses are constructs of Layer 3, the Network Layer of the OSI Reference Model. These addresses are used to access and exchange data with hosts on other subnetworks within the WAN.

The address architecture is determined by the routable protocol that's used within the WAN. Some of the possibilities include IPv4, IPv6, IPX, and AppleTalk. Each has its own unique addressing scheme. Therefore, the choice of protocol determines the possible address hierarchies that can be implemented.

Ensuring Unique Addressing

The single most important aspect of internetwork addressing is *uniqueness*! With the solitary exception of IPv6, any network protocol you select requires that at any given point in time, there's only one endpoint with any given address. Redundant internetwork addresses create routing errors and compromise the consistency of your user's network-based operations.

ARCHITECTURE

> **Architecture:** IPv6 contains a new address architecture known as *anycast*. Anycast addresses are easily (even unintentionally) created by giving the same IP address to more than one device. When the network receives packets addressed to an anycast address, it simply routes those packets to the nearest device with that address. This does mean that anycast devices must be completely interchangeable from both an operational and functional perspective, but it can save time and trouble in locating what are essentially network appliances, such as fax or print servers.

Theoretically, if your WAN is not going to be directly interconnected with the Internet, or to any other network, internetwork addresses can be arbitrarily selected. Generally speaking, arbitrarily selecting internetwork addresses is short-sighted and a gross dereliction of duties. That being said, Request for Comment (RFC) #1597 was released in May, 1993 and posited a plan to the contrary. Three ranges of addresses that could be used for internal networking purposes only were identified and reserved. These ranges include one each of IPv4's Class A, B, and C addresses. They are as follows:

- 10.0.0.0 to 10.255.255.255
- 172.16.0.0 to 172.31.255.255
- 192.168.0.0 to 192.168.255.255

These ranges are reserved by the Internet Assigned Numbers Authority (IANA) for use in private networks. One stipulation of RFC #1597 is that these addresses can't be used when directly accessing the Internet. Companies that use these addresses, and subsequently find the need to access the Internet, can use a proxy server (a server which forwards requests on behalf of another) with a unique and registered IP address as an intermediary. Alternatively, Network Address Translation (NAT) can be used.

> **Note:** If you implement RFC #1597's reserved addresses, you must still guarantee the uniqueness of each device's address within your private network domain. The addresses may not be unique globally, but they must be unique locally.

Internetworking with Different Protocols

Not every WAN has the luxury of using a single routed protocol. Multiprotocol networks present some basic challenges that must be overcome. The problem is providing connectivity across dissimilar protocols. Two approaches can be used: tunnels and gateways.

Tunnels

Tunnels are a relatively simple construct that can be used to pass data through an otherwise incompatible network region. Data packets are encapsulated with framing that's recognized by the network that transports it. The original framing and formatting is retained but treated as "data."

Upon reaching its destination, the recipient host unwraps the packet and discards the "wrapper." This results in the packet being restored to its original format, complete with its original internetwork addressing. Figure 10.3 illustrates the tunneling of IPv4 packets through an IPv6 network region. Because of the inherent difference in the length of these two protocols' addresses, they're not directly compatible. To overcome this incompatibility, IPv4 packets are wrapped in IPv6 by Router A for transmission through an IPv6 WAN. Router B removes the IPv6 wrapper and presents the restored IPv4 packet to the destination host in a form it can recognize.

FIGURE 10.3

Tunneling IPv4 packets through an IPv6 region.

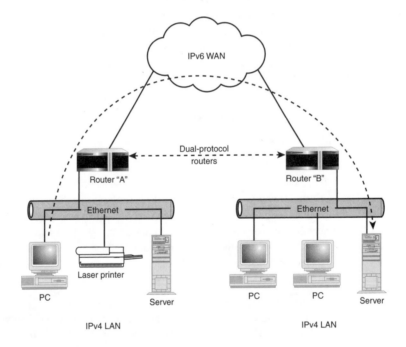

For more information on the Internet addressing of routable protocols, refer to Chapter 4, "The Network and Transport Layers."

Gateways

If your WAN requires the interconnection of subnetworks with dissimilar routed protocols, you need a gateway at the border of the dissimilar regions. A gateway is any device that can translate between the address architectures of the two protocols. Gateways can be routers or hosts. The only criterion is that the device must be capable of translating between the two protocols' address architectures.

Routers have two ways of performing such an address translation. First, they can use two different routing protocols. This requires the router to calculate routes, forward route information, and forward packets in both protocols. Routers were designed to operate in multiprotocol environments, so this should not represent any operational difficulties.

Alternatively, a router may have an integrated protocol that is simultaneously capable of routing two different protocols and addresses. Examples of this form of routing protocol are the emerging series of "ng" protocols that are designed to facilitate the migration between IPv4 and IPv6. Specific examples are OSPFng and RIPng.

Using Routing Protocols

Dynamic routing protocols are used by routers to perform three basic functions:

- Discover new routes
- Communicate the discovered route information to other routers
- Forward packets using those routes

Dynamic routing protocols fall into three broad categories: distance-vector, link-state, and hybrids. Each are discussed in the sections that follow. Their primary differences are in the way they perform the first two of the three aforementioned functions. The only alternative to dynamic routing is *static routing*, which is described in the section titled "Static Routing."

Distance-Vector Routing

Routing can be based on distance-vector algorithms (also sometimes called *Bellman-Ford algorithms*), which require that routers periodically pass copies of the routing tables to their immediate network neighbors. Each recipient adds a distance vector (its own distance "value") to the table and forwards it to its immediate neighbors. This process occurs omnidirectionally between immediately neighboring routers.

This step-by-step process results in each router's learning about other routers and developing a cumulative perspective of network "distances." For example, an early distance-vector routing protocol is *Routing Information Protocol*, or *RIP*. RIP uses two distance metrics for determining the best next path to take for any given packet. These distance metrics are time sensitive, as measured by "ticks" and hop count.

> **Note:** Routers can use a surprising variety of metrics to determine optimal routes between any given source and destination pair. These metrics are euphemistically referred to as *distances*. Distances may actually be time, number of router hops, and so forth, and they're not limited to physical distances.

The cumulative table is then used to update each router's routing tables. When completed, each router has learned vague information about the distances to networked resources. It does not learn anything specific about other routers or learn the network's actual topology.

This approach can, under certain circumstances, actually create routing problems for distance-vector protocols. For example, a failure in the network requires some time for the routers to converge on a new understanding of the network's topology. During the convergence process, the network may be vulnerable to inconsistent routing and even infinite loops.

Certain safeguards may mitigate many of these risks, but the fact remains that the network's performance is at risk during the convergence process. Therefore, older protocols that are slow to converge may not be appropriate for large, complex WANs.

Link-State Routing

Link-state routing algorithms, known cumulatively as *shortest path first* (SPF) protocols, maintain a complex database of the network's topology. Unlike distance-vector protocols, link-state protocols develop and maintain a full understanding of the network's routers, as well as of how they interconnect.

This understanding is achieved via the exchange of link-state packets (LSPs) with other directly connected routers. Each router that has exchanged LSPs then constructs a topological database using all received LSPs. A "shortest path first" algorithm is then used to compute reachability to networked destinations. This information is used to update the routing table. This process is capable of discovering changes in the network topology that may have been caused by component failure or network growth. In fact, the LSP exchange is triggered by an event in the network rather than running periodically.

Link-state routing has two potential areas for concern. First, during the initial discovery process, link-state routing can flood the network's transmission facilities, thereby significantly decreasing the network's capability to transport data. This performance degradation is temporary but very noticeable.

The second area for concern is that link-state routing is memory and processor intensive. Routers configured for link-state routing tend to be more expensive because of this problem.

Hybridized Routing

The last form of the dynamic routing discipline is *hybridization*. Although "open" balanced hybrid protocols exist, this form is almost exclusively associated with the proprietary creation of a single company, Cisco Systems, Inc. This protocol, Enhanced Interior Gateway Routing Protocol (EIGRP), was designed to combine the best aspects of distance-vector and link-state routing protocols, without incurring any of their performance limitations or penalties.

The balanced hybrid routing protocols use distance-vector metrics but emphasize more accurate metrics than conventional distance-vector protocols. They also converge more rapidly than distance-vector protocols but avoid the overheads of link-state updates. Balanced hybrids are event driven rather than periodic, thereby conserving bandwidth for real applications.

Static Routing

A router that's programmed for static routing forwards packets out of predetermined ports. After static routes are configured, routers no longer have any need to attempt route discovery or even communicate information about routes. Their role is reduced to simply forwarding packets.

Static routing is good for only very small networks that have only a single path to any given destination. In such cases, static routing can be the most efficient routing mechanism because it doesn't consume bandwidth trying to discover routes or communicate with other routers.

As networks grow larger and add redundant paths to destinations, static routing becomes a labor-intensive liability. Any changes in the availability of routers or transmission facilities in the WAN must be manually discovered and programmed. WANs that feature more complex topologies that offer multiple potential paths absolutely require dynamic routing. Attempts to use static routing in complex, multipath WANs defeat the purpose of having that route redundancy.

Protocol Selection

Selection of a routing protocol should be done carefully and with an appreciation for the long-term implications of your selection. Your selection of any given protocol directly affects the selection of a router vendor as well as the operational efficiency of the WAN. The preceding sections on the different classes of routing protocols, as well as the section on static routing, should have amply demonstrated the operational implications of each category of routing protocol. These implications should help you narrow down your options to a single category or class of protocols.

The next step is to determine whether you're going to use one or more router vendors in your WAN. If at all possible, try to select a single manufacturer's products. The reason for this is simple: Open routing protocols enable each manufacturer some latitude for variation. Therefore, one manufacturer's version of an open routing protocol is likely to be less than 100 percent interoperable with another manufacturer's version. Perhaps the best example of this is the well-documented differences between Bay Networks' and Cisco System's versions of the Open Shortest Path First (OSPF) protocol.

If you select a router manufacturer before you select a routing protocol, understand how doing so can limit your selection of protocols. Some routing protocols are proprietary and, consequently, available from only a single vendor.

Understanding WAN Topologies

The topology of a WAN describes the way the transmission facilities are arranged relative to the locations that they interconnect. Numerous topologies are possible, each one offering a different mix of cost, performance, and scalability. More subtly, some functional specialization may be introduced by a topology that has a direct bearing on the transmission facilities. The more common WAN topologies include the following:

- Peer-to-peer WANs
- Ring WANs
- Star WANs
- Full-mesh WANs
- Partial-mesh WANs
- Multitiered, including two-tiered and three-tiered WANs
- Hybrids

Although some of these may sound more like LAN topologies than WAN topologies, they are quite applicable in both arenas. Each of these is described and illustrated throughout the rest of this section. Their relative cost, performance, scalability, and technology implications are also examined.

Peer-to-Peer Topology

A peer-to-peer WAN can be developed using leased private lines or any other transmission facility. This WAN topology is a relatively simple way of interconnecting a small number of sites. WANs that consist of just two locations can be interconnected in this manner only. A small peer-to-peer WAN is depicted in Figure 10.4.

FIGURE 10.4

A peer-to-peer WAN constructed with leased lines.

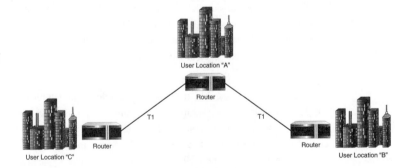

This topology represents the least-cost solution for WANs that contain a small number of internetworked locations. Because each location contains, at most, one or two links to the rest of the network, static routing can be used. Static routing can be time intensive to establish but avoids the network overheads of dynamic routing protocols. Given that there are no redundant routes to be had in this simple topology, the benefits of dynamic routing are limited.

> **Note:** In a routed WAN, the number of routers between you and your destination is directly related to the amount of time a transmitted packet is en route to its destination. Therefore, a metric has been developed to track the number of routers in a given network path. This metric is called a *hop count*. Each router counts as one hop.

Unfortunately, peer-to-peer WANs suffer from two basic limitations. First, they do not scale very well. As additional locations are introduced to the WAN, the number of hops between any given pair of locations remains highly inconsistent and has an upward trend. This results in varied levels of performance in communications between any given pair of locations. The actual degree to which performance varies depends greatly on many factors, including the following:

- Geographic distances between locations
- The type and capacity of transmission facility
- The degree to which the transmission facility is being utilized.

The second limitation of this approach is its inherent vulnerability to component failure. Only a single path exists between any given pair of locations. Consequently, an equipment or facility failure anywhere in a peer-to-peer WAN can split the WAN. Depending on the actual traffic flows and the type of routing implemented, this can severely disrupt communications in the entire WAN.

Another significant implication of the peer-to-peer topology's lack of route redundancy is that using a dynamic routing protocol to calculate routes and forward packets is a waste of time and CPU cycles. The route calculated between any two points can never change! Therefore, statically defining the routes may result in a better performing network.

Ring Topology

A ring topology can be developed fairly easily from a peer-to-peer network by adding one transmission facility and an extra port on two routers. This minor increment in cost provides route redundancy that can afford small networks the opportunity to implement dynamic routing protocols. Given that the cost of most transmission facilities is mileage sensitive, it would be wise to design the ring so as to minimize the overall distances of those facilities. This WAN topology is illustrated in Figure 10.5.

FIGURE 10.5
A ring-shaped WAN.

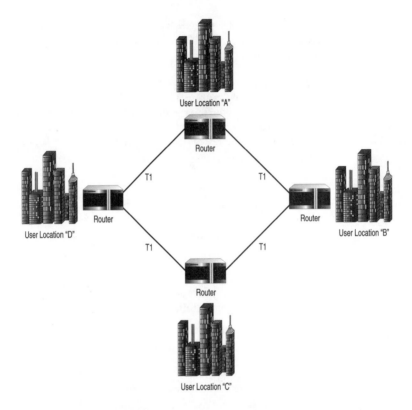

A ring-shaped WAN constructed with point-to-point transmission facilities can be used to interconnect a small number of sites and provide route redundancy at a potentially minimal incremental cost. The existence of redundant routes through the network means that the use of a dynamic routing protocol affords flexibility not available with static routing. Dynamic routing protocols can automatically detect and recover from adverse changes in the WAN's operating condition by routing around the impacted links.

Rings, too, have some basic limitations. Depending on the geographic dispersion of the locations, adding an extra transmission facility to complete the ring may be cost prohibitive. In such cases, Frame Relay may be a viable alternative to dedicated leased lines, provided that its performance limitations are acceptable relative to the projected traffic loads.

A second limitation of rings is that they're not very scalable. Adding new locations to the WAN directly increases the number of hops required to access other locations in the ring. This additive process may also result in having to order new circuits. For example, as shown previously in Figure 10.5, adding a new location, X, that's in geographic proximity to Sites C and D, requires that the circuit from location C to D be terminated. Two new circuits have to be ordered to preserve the integrity of the ring—one running from C to X and the other running from D to X.

The ring topology, given its limitations, is likely to be of value in interconnecting only very small numbers of locations. It's preferable to the peer-to-peer interconnection of locations only because of its capability to provide a redundant path to the locations within the ring.

Star Network Topology

A variant of the peer-to-peer topology is the *star topology*, so named for its shape. A star is constructed by homing all locations into a common location. One could argue that this, in essence, creates a two-tiered topology. The distinction between a star and a two-tiered topology is that the center router in a star topology may also be used to interconnect the LANs installed at that location with each other as well as the WAN.

In a two-tiered topology, as discussed later in this chapter, the second-tier router should be dedicated exclusively to interconnecting the transmission facilities of the other locations. More importantly, a two-tiered topology provides route redundancy by supporting the development of networks with multiple concentration points.

The star topology can be constructed using almost any dedicated transmission facility, including Frame Relay and point-to-point private lines. A star-shaped WAN is shown in Figure 10.6.

FIGURE 10.6
A star-shaped WAN.

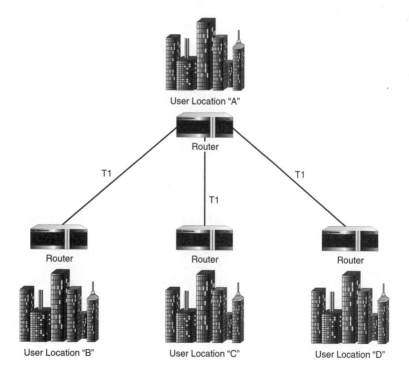

A star topology WAN with point-to-point transmission facilities is much more scalable than a peer-to-peer or ring network. Adding locations to the star does not require the reengineering of existing transmission facilities. All that's required is to provision a new facility between the concentration router and the router at the new location.

The star topology rectifies the scalability problems of peer-to-peer networks by using a router to interconnect, or *concentrate*, all the other networked routers. This scalability is afforded at a modest increase in the number of routers, router ports, and transmission facilities compared to a comparably sized peer-to-peer topology. Star topologies may actually be developed with fewer facilities than ring topologies, as Figures 10.7 and 10.8, later in the chapter, demonstrate.

The scalability of the star topology is limited by the number of ports that the router at the center of the star can support. Expansion beyond its capacity requires either a reengineering of the topology into a two-tiered topology or the replacement of the existing router with a much larger unit.

Another benefit of a star topology is improved network performance. Overall network performance in a star topology is, in theory, always better than in either a ring or peer-to-peer network. This is because all network-connected devices are just three hops away from each other. These three hops include the router at the user's location, the concentrator router, and the router at the destination. This degree of consistency is unique to the star topology. However, there are two drawbacks to this approach:

- It creates a single point of failure. The existence of a single point of failure means that all WAN communications can be disrupted if the concentrator router experiences a failure.
- There is no route redundancy. The lack of route redundancy means that if the concentrator router fails, you're out of service until the failure is rectified. Dynamic routing protocols are not able to calculate new paths through the network because there are none!

Full-Mesh Topology

At the extreme high end of the reliability spectrum is the *full-mesh topology*. This topology features the ultimate reliability and fault tolerance. Every networked node is directly connected to every other networked node. Therefore, redundant routes to each location are plentiful. Implicit in this statement is that static routing is utterly impractical. You're virtually forced into selecting one of the dynamic routing protocols to calculate routes and forward packets in this type of network. A fully meshed WAN is illustrated in Figure 10.7.

This approach minimizes the number of hops between any two network-connected machines. Another benefit is that it can be built with virtually any transmission technology.

FIGURE 10.7
*A fully meshed
WAN.*

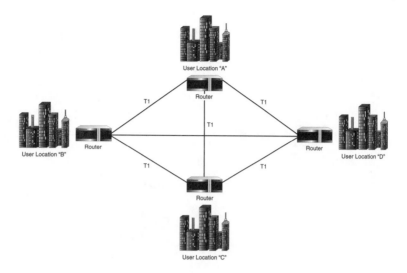

Some practical limitations are inherent, however, in a fully meshed topology. For example, these WANs can be fairly expensive to build. Each router has to be large enough to have a port and transmission facility for every other router in the WAN. This tends to make both startup and monthly recurring operational costs expensive. It also places a finite (although substantial) limit on the scalability of the network. Routers do have a limit on the number of ports they can support. Therefore, full-mesh topologies are more of a Utopian ideal with limited practical application.

One application would be to provide interconnectivity for a limited number of routers that require high network availability. Another potential application is to fully mesh just parts of the WAN, such as the backbone of a multitiered WAN or tightly coupled work centers. This option is described in more detail in the section titled "Hybrid Topologies."

Partial-Mesh Topology

A WAN can also be developed with a *partial-mesh topology*. Partial meshes are highly flexible topologies that can take a variety of very different configurations. The best way to describe a partial-mesh topology is that the routers are much more tightly coupled than any of the basic topologies but are not fully interconnected, as would be the case in a fully meshed network. This topology is illustrated in Figure 10.8.

A partially meshed WAN topology is readily identified by the almost complete interconnection of every node with every other node in the network. Partial meshes offer the capability to minimize hops for the bulk of the WAN's users. Unlike fully meshed networks, a partial mesh can reduce the startup and operational expenses by not interconnecting low-traffic segments of the WAN. This enables the partial mesh network to be somewhat more scalable—and therefore affordable—than a full-mesh topology.

FIGURE **10.8**
*A partial-mesh
topology.*

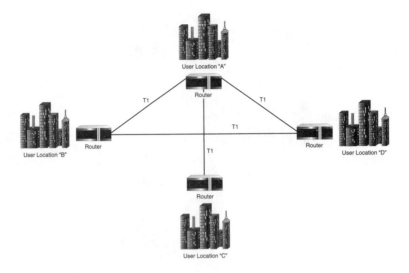

Two-Tiered Topology

A *two-tiered topology* is a modified version of the basic star topology. Rather than single concentrator routers, two or more routers are used. This rectifies the basic vulnerability of the star topology without compromising its efficiency or scalability.

Figure 10.9 presents a WAN with a typical two-tiered topology. The worst-case hop count does increase by one, as a result of the extra concentrator (the backbone) router. However, unlike the peer-to-peer network presented earlier in Figure 10.4, the hop count is not adversely affected every time a new location is added to the WAN.

FIGURE **10.9**
*A two-tiered
WAN.*

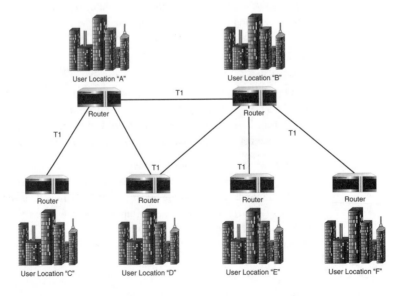

A two-tiered WAN constructed with dedicated facilities offers improved fault tolerance over the simple star topology without compromising scalability. This topology can be implemented in a number of minor variations, primarily by manipulating the number of concentrator routers and the manner with which they're interconnected. Having three or more concentrator routers requires the network designer to select a subtopology for the concentrator tier. These routers can be either fully or partially meshed, or they can be strung together from peer to peer.

Regardless of the subtopology selected, hierarchical, multitiered topologies function best when some basic implementation principles are adhered to:

- The concentration layer of routers should be dedicated to their tasks. That is, they're not used to directly connect user communities.
- The user premises routers should internetwork with only concentrator nodes and not with each other in a peer-to-peer fashion.
- The interconnection of user premises routers to concentrator routers should not be done randomly. Some logic should be applied in determining their placement. Depending on the geographic distribution of the users and the transmission facilities used, it may be prudent to place the concentrator nodes so as to minimize the distances from the user premises.

Given that one or more routers are dedicated to route aggregation, this topology can be an expensive undertaking. This tends to limit the use of these topologies to larger companies.

Three-Tiered Topology

WANs that need to interconnect a very large number of sites, or are built using smaller routers that can support only a few serial connections, may find the two-tiered architecture insufficiently scalable. Therefore, adding a third tier may well provide the additional scalability they require. This topology is illustrated in Figure 10.10.

A three-tiered WAN constructed with dedicated facilities offers even greater fault tolerance and scalability than the two-tiered topology. Three-tiered networks are expensive to build, operate, and maintain. They should be used for interconnecting only very large numbers of locations. Given this, it seems foolish to develop a WAN of this magnitude and not fully mesh the uppermost (or backbone) tier of routers.

FIGURE 10.10
*The three-tiered
WAN topology.*

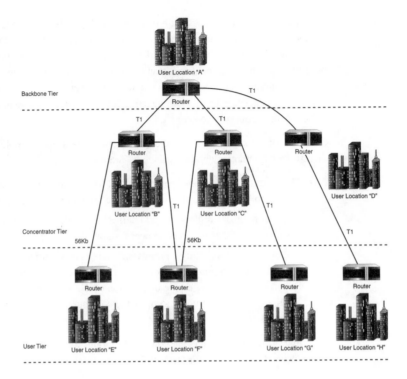

Hybrid Topologies

Hybridization of multiple topologies is useful in larger, more complex networks. It enables administrators to tailor the WAN to actual traffic patterns, rather than try to force-fit those patterns into a rigid topological model. In other words, the basic topologies presented in this section are little more than academic constructs intended to stimulate creative thought. There are no limits on the topological variety that can be introduced to a WAN. The effectiveness of each topology, and the subsequent combination of WAN technologies, depends directly on your particular situation and performance requirements.

Multitiered networks, in particular, lend themselves to hybridization. As previously discussed, a multitiered WAN can be hybridized by fully or partially meshing the backbone tier of routers. Although there's no right or wrong way to build a hybrid topology, one example of this WAN is illustrated in Figure 10.11. Due to space considerations, the building icons have been omitted from the backbone tier in this illustration.

An effective hybrid topology may be developed in a multitiered WAN by using a fully meshed topology for the backbone nodes only. This affords a fault tolerance to the network's backbone and can provide some of the hop minimization of a full mesh network without experiencing all its costs or incurring its limitations on scalability.

FIGURE 10.11

A hybrid topology.

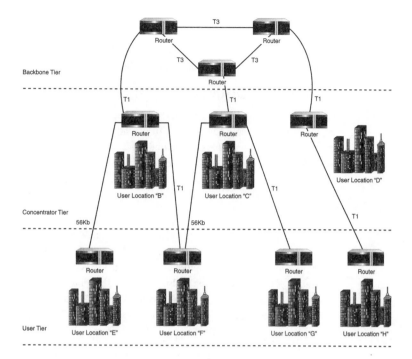

Fully meshing the backbone of a multitiered WAN is just one form of hybridized topology. Other hybrids can also be highly effective. The key is to look for topologies and subtopologies that can be used in combination to satisfy your particular networking requirements.

Designing Your WAN

Designing a WAN requires the successful integration of all the technical components described in this chapter. Successful integration means that the performance of the finished network meets, or exceeds, performance requirements and user expectations. Therefore, it's imperative that you identify and quantify (to the extent that users cooperate) these performance criteria before you begin the design.

WAN Performance Criteria

Many different criteria, or *metrics*, can be applied to measure the success of a WAN. Many of these are fairly objective and can be automatically extracted from the network-monitoring protocols native to virtually every network device. Others are subjective and can be next to impossible to determine in advance. Some of the more common metrics include the following:

- Component uptime
- Traffic volumes

- Delays and latency
- Resource utilization rates

Each of these metrics is discussed in more detail in the following sections.

Component Uptime

Each physical component of the WAN can be monitored and measured for its availability using *uptime*. Uptime is the opposite of downtime: It's the amount of time that the device is functional and in service, relative to the users' requirements for its availability. It's quite common for uptime to be statistically overstated by measuring it on a 7 × 24 basis, even though the users' requirements may be for only 5 × 12. Remember to tailor this, and every other metric, as closely as possible to your users' stated requirements for network performance.

All electronic devices—even the most highly reliable—eventually fail. Most manufacturers provide a Mean Time Between Failure (MTBF) rating for their equipment as a reassurance of how reliable their products are. Typically, MTBF ratings are in the tens of thousands of hours. Conceivably, this could translate into years of trouble-free service. Unfortunately, these ratings are statistically derived. The actual time between failures of any given device depends greatly on a number of factors. These factors include the following:

- Ambient temperature ranges of its operating environment
- The cleanliness of its commercial electric power
- How well it's handled before and during operation

In other words, your actual mileage will vary! Monitoring and tracking uptime of individual components enable you to demonstrate to your user community how well you are satisfying their requirements for the network's availability.

Trends in component uptime data can also be followed over time to identify potentially problematic components in your network infrastructure. Such trends can provide information about the general reliability of a given type or brand of hardware, which then can be used to identify individual components that may be at risk of failure.

Note: The term *availability* is sometimes used to generically describe aggregate network uptime. It is not, however, a good metric. In theory, network availability provides a quantified synopsis of the network's readiness. In practice, *availability* is so nebulous as to be almost meaningless. To illustrate this point, if a router at a premises location fails, the entire network is unavailable to the users at that location. The network, however, is available to users at every other location. They are not able to access hosts at the impacted location but are not impeded from accessing every other host in the network. The extent to which the network is available varies greatly by location and by usage requirements. Therefore, quantifying network availability can be more onerous than it is valuable.

Traffic Volumes

One of the more important metrics for any WAN is the volume of traffic it is expected to support. Volume is almost always volatile; it varies with time, business cycles, seasons, and so on. In other words, you can count on traffic volumes' being anything but constant. Given this volatility, it's important to measure volumes using maximum volumes and average volumes:

- The maximum volume you expect the network to support is known as the *peak volume*. As its name implies, this is the greatest amount of traffic you expect the network to have to support.

- Average volumes are the normalized traffic loads that you can reasonably expect during the course of a business day from any given work location. That is, the base traffic on an average day, not a numerical average of all your traffic!

Establishing these two traffic volumes is critical to the sizing of the WAN's transmission facilities as well as its routers. For example, if you expect any given location to generate a traffic load of 100Kbps during the course of a business day, it's clear that a 56Kbps transmission facility is inadequate.

Note: If you use one of the more complex topologies described earlier in this chapter, you need to identify the aggregate traffic patterns and volumes that are going to be placed across your network's backbone routers and transmission facilities.

Delay

Delay is one of the more common metrics that can be used to measure network performance. Delay is the time that elapses between two events. In data communications, these two events are typically the transmission and reception of data. Therefore, delay is the total amount of time required by the network to transport a packet from its point of origin to its destination. Given this definition, delay is an aggregate phenomenon, with many potential causes. Three of the more common causes include the following:

- *Propagation delays.* This term refers to the cumulative amount of time that's required to transmit, or *propagate*, the data across each transmission facility in the network path that it must take. The size and quantity of each transmission facility in the network path directly contribute to the aggregate forwarding delay of any given transmission. An additional contributor to propagation delay is *traffic volume*. The more traffic that's flowing across a given facility, the less bandwidth that's available for new transmissions. Propagation delays are indigenous to terrestrial circuits, regardless of whether they traverse glass or copper media.

- *Satellite uplink/downlink delays.* Some transmission facilities are satellite based. They require the signal to be transmitted up to the satellite and back down from the satellite. Due to the potentially great distances between the terrestrial transmission facilities and the satellite, these delays can be quite noticeable.

- *Forwarding delays.* The forwarding delay in a network is the cumulative amount of time that each physical device needs to receive, buffer, process, and forward data. The actual forwarding delay of any given device may vary over time. Individual devices that are operating at or near capacity ordinarily experience a greater forwarding delay than comparable devices that are lightly utilized. Additionally, forwarding delays can be exacerbated by heavy traffic or error conditions in the network. Forwarding delays are frequently identified as latency in individual components.

Resource Utilization

The degree to which the various physical resources of the WAN are being used is a good indicator of how well or how poorly the WAN is performing relative to the performance requirements. Two main categories of resource utilization rates should be monitored carefully:

- Router CPU and memory utilization rates
- Transmission facility utilization rates

Router Resources

Routers are among the most vital components of any WAN. Unlike the transmission facilities, they are outside the purview of the telecommunications carrier. Therefore, they're distinctly the responsibility of the customer. Fortunately, a router is an intelligent device that contains its own CPU and memory. These physical resources are indispensable in the calculation of WAN routes and the forwarding of packets. They can also be used to monitor the performance of the router.

If either CPU or memory utilization rates approach 100 percent, performance suffers. Numerous conditions can result in either utilization rate temporarily spiking upward, with consequential performance degradation. One example might be a sudden increase in transmissions from the LAN to the WAN. LANs can operate at speeds up to 1Gbps but usually only at 10, 16, or 100Mbps. Any of these speeds is a gross mismatch with the typical WAN transmission facility, which offers a paltry 1.544Mbps of bandwidth. This mismatch in bandwidth must be buffered by the router's memory. It doesn't take long for a router to become resource constricted, given a sustained period of heavy LAN transmissions.

If such situations are rarely experienced, they should be considered aberrations. Aberrations should be monitored, but they shouldn't drive physical upgrades. However, if these resource constrictions recur or constitute a trend, something needs to be done.

Usually, this requires an upgrade to the next larger router or an expansion of memory. If a router is chronically at or near 100 percent of capacity with its memory, it's time to purchase additional memory.

Responding to chronically high CPU utilization rates might not be as simple as a memory upgrade. There are really only two options for improving high CPU utilization rates:

- Upgrade to a more powerful router
- Investigate the WAN's traffic patterns to see whether the load on the problematic router can be reduced

Manipulating traffic patterns is really a viable option only in larger WANs with complex topologies that afford route redundancy. Even so, if the router in question is a premises edge vehicle (as opposed to a backbone router), your only option is likely to be the fork-lift upgrade.

Transmission Facility Rates

Transmission facilities, too, can be monitored for utilization. Typically, this utilization rate is expressed in terms of the percentage of consumed bandwidth. For example, if you're using a T-1, a given sample might indicate that 30 percent of its 1.544Mbps of available bandwidth is currently being utilized.

These rates can be tricky to analyze and may be misleading. For example, it's not uncommon for network-management software packages to capture utilization data in time intervals. These can be one hour, five minutes, or just about any other interval. The sampling frequency, if set too coarsely, can miss short-duration fluctuations in bandwidth consumption. If the sampling is too frequent, you could find yourself mired in a meaningless morass of data points. The trick is finding the correct frequency that provides meaningful data about how the network is performing relative to the users' expectations.

Beyond merely selecting the sampling rate lies the issue of sampling windows. A *sampling window* is the timeframe within which samples are to be taken. Establishing a sampling window consists of establishing the frequency and duration of the sampling. The sampling window should be determined by the users' requirements for WAN availability. If the utilization samples are spread over a 24-hour day and a 7-day week, but the users work only 10 hours per day, 5 days per week, the statistical data will not be indicative of how well the users' requirements are being met.

Utilization rates are a wonderful statistical tool for monitoring and measuring the status of transmission facilities. They are not, however, the only metric for assessing a network's performance. The network is successful only if it satisfies the users' requirements. Therefore, a combination of performance metrics that provides a multifaceted, composite perspective is likely to provide a better assessment of the network's successfulness.

Peter's Principle: Buyer Beware!

Before spending a lot of money on possibly unneeded hardware and transmission facilities, consider the possibility of lowering WAN traffic volume by duplicating applications and data at both local and remote sites. Additional software licenses are a lot less expensive than routers and T-1 lines. Data that does not have to be synchronized up to the minute can be duplicated at the remote site and then updated during off hours when there's little other WAN traffic.

Costs of the WAN

Tempering any evaluation of these performance criteria is cost. The costs of owning and operating a WAN include the initial startup costs as well as the monthly, recurring expenses. Not surprisingly, the larger and more powerful network components are much more expensive than smaller, less robust components. Therefore, designing a WAN becomes an economic exercise in which a careful balance of performance and cost is achieved.

Achieving this balance can be painful. No one wants to design a WAN that will disappoint the users with its performance, but no one wants to design a WAN that blows the budget, either! Fortunately, a few truisms can help guide administrators as they choose the design of a WAN that satisfies existing requirements, provides flexibility for future growth, and doesn't exceed the budget:

- The capital investments in routers and other network hardware become a fixed part of the network. After they're placed into operation, the logistics of replacing them become quite complicated. Plus, depending upon your depreciation schedule for capital equipment, you might find yourself obligated to use them for five or more years! It might behoove you to purchase a larger but relatively unpopulated router. You can add hardware (memory, CPUs, and interfaces) in the future, as the need for them arises. This makes future expansion possible at modest incremental costs and little (if any) operational downtime.

- The transmission facilities are relatively easy to replace with other transmission facilities. They're expense items, not a capital investment, so there's no depreciation expense to retire. They can be replaced with other facilities as often as your lease agreement with the carrier permits. Therefore, you might want to explore your options for meeting performance requirements with the various available transmission facilities and technologies.

Applying the wisdom behind these truisms can help you meet your users' present and future expected requirements—all within the constraints of your budget.

Summary

Wide area networks are complex structures that don't necessarily adhere to any published or open standard. Designing, building, and operating a WAN that consistently satisfies your users' requirements can be a Herculean task. Success lies in understanding the capabilities, limitations, and costs of the various WAN component technologies. This understanding forms the context for their integration. The objective is to build a network in which each component technology is well matched with the performance capabilities of each other component and balanced against any budgetary constraints.

Transmission Facilities

WANs have traditionally been constructed from digital telecommunications facilities that are leased from a telecommunications carrier. These facilities offer customers dedicated bandwidth that can span up to almost 45Mbps. Such transmission facilities are known as *leased lines*. They are an integral part of most WANs, yet they remain poorly understood. Their modular connectors hide a vast, complex telecommunications infrastructure as well as a series of standards.

In the past few years, however, new facilities have emerged to challenge leased lines for the WAN backbone niche. In particular, circuit-switched networks (for example, ATM) and packet-switched networks (for example, X.25) are garnering more and more of the private WAN connection market.

This chapter examines the standards that support leased line, circuit-switched, and packet-switched WANs as well as some of their fundamental mechanics, demystifying them and enabling you to better design, operate, and troubleshoot WANs.

Peter's Principle: Jargon alert!

Telecommunications and wide area connectivity have their own set of terms, acronyms, and jargon that can be just as confusing to the seasoned network administrator as data networking terms are to the average computer user. Rather than make very expensive mistakes, study this chapter in detail—or engage the services of a telecomm consultant—before attempting to set up a wide area network using telecomm transmission facilities.

Leased Lines

Leased lines were originally designed as digital voice communications facilities (now largely superceded by circuit-switched facilities, covered later in this chapter). Conversion of voice signals to digital format offered numerous advantages, including enhanced regeneration of attenuated signals and more efficient aggregation of multiple streams of data onto a common transmission media. This aggregation is known as *multiplexing*.

Three factors combined to force a radical shift in the way that digital leased lines were used: the increased base of digital telecommunications equipment in the carriers' infrastructure, development of the support mechanisms for digital telephony, and the emergence of a customer need for high-capacity data communications.

Carriers reluctantly began leasing these lines to their customers for concentrated voice communications requirements such as call centers and large office buildings with their own private branch exchange (PBX). As distributed networking technologies matured, leased lines began to prove their worth as data transmission facilities. The leap from digitized voice to digitized data was natural; binary digits are binary digits, regardless of what they represent. Leased lines have proven so successful as data communications vehicles that their original purpose has been all but lost to historical trivia.

Multiplexing Techniques

Leased lines were originally designed to aggregate multiple voice channels onto a single higher-capacity transmission facility. This function required the development of a mechanism that takes multiple incoming communications streams, regulates their transmission over a common transmission facility, and deaggregates them back into their individual components for subsequent delivery to their individual destinations. Multiplexing enabled a more efficient intermediary switching of calls. Multiplexing is primarily done in one of two ways: by dividing the available bandwidth into timed sections (called *time division multiplexing*) or by dividing the available bandwidth into subfrequency bands (called *frequency division multiplexing*).

Time Division Multiplexing

Time division multiplexing (TDM) features the division of the available bandwidth into time slices. A communicating device can monopolize the entire bandwidth for the duration of a time slice. These slices are then shared according to a predetermined algorithm. To give you an appreciation for the complexity of a TDM system, the time slice on a T-1 (a 1.544Mbps leased line) is 125 microseconds.

TDM is inherently efficient because a transmitting station is permitted the use of the entire band. If a station doesn't need to transmit, its time slice is allocated to another station that does. In this manner, the use of the transmission facility's available bandwidth is maximized.

TDM does, however, introduce overhead to maintain synchronization. If synchronization is lost, the transmitted data becomes corrupted. Synchronization can be maintained by either adding bits or adding channels. Both methods are valid and deployed in today's leased lines. The European digital signaling standard has implemented the channel-adding technique, whereas North America uses added bits.

Frequency Division Multiplexing

The alternative to TDM is frequency division multiplexing (FDM). FDM is a technique that subdivides the available bandwidth into bands of subfrequencies. Each of these subfrequency bands is dedicated to a specific user or device. Each remains permanently dedicated and, consequently, unavailable for use by other devices even when it's idle! This inherent inefficiency has resulted in the widespread preference for TDM over FDM in telecommunications carriers' systems.

Benefits and Drawbacks of Leased Lines

One of the more prevalent—but misleading—monikers of leased lines is *point-to-point private line*. From a strictly functional perspective, leased lines offer a dedicated connection between two locations, with minimal communications overhead or framing. However, they do not form a direct connection between two points.

As illustrated in Figure 11.1, this type of dedicated line can take a circuitous path through telecommunications carriers' switching centers. The terrestrial circuit mileage is always greater than the geographic mileage separating the two ends of the circuit because the circuit must traverse the telecommunications carrier's transmission infrastructure.

FIGURE 11.1
Leased lines are not direct lines.

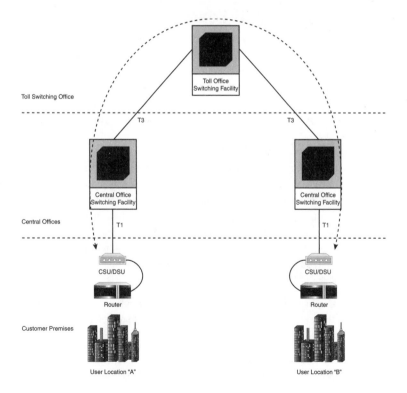

One could argue that this is much less efficient than running direct connections between pairs of customer locations. The inefficiencies, however, are more than offset by the extensibility of this method of service provisioning. Point-to-point runs of a transmission media become worthless as soon as the two locations at either end of that point-to-point run no longer need to communicate with each other.

Connecting all customer locations back to the telecommunications carrier's nearest switching center results in a reusable infrastructure. Regardless of changes in communications requirements or aggregate traffic patterns, the connection between the central office and the customer's location remains essential.

An additional benefit of interconnecting locations via central offices is the enabling of remote diagnostics. If a telecommunications carrier were to string cabling directly between two customer locations, it would have to dispatch a technician to perform even rudimentary trouble analysis when the service failed. By having the carrier's switching center in the middle of a leased line, the telecommunications carrier can perform loop-back and other diagnostic tests across the entire circuit from the comfort of the switching center. This remote diagnostic capability saves time and money in the isolation of a failure in the network.

Topology of Leased Lines

The actual topology of a leased line can be surprisingly convoluted. Figure 11.1 presented an intentionally simplified perspective of a leased line. In reality, virtually all but the shortest of leased lines require the building of a circuit through two or more switching centers. The exact shape of the leased line is directly dependent on both geography and the number of carriers that must be involved. Fortunately, the exact topology of a leased line is seldom of any consequence outside the carriers' domain.

Switching Centers

Many data communications concepts and terms become muddled over time and through misuse and incomplete understanding. The term *central office* (CO) is no exception. It has become overused and now generically describes telecommunications carriers' switching facilities. In reality, a central office (also known as an *end office*) is the bottom layer in a multitiered switching topology that constitutes the commercial telephony infrastructure. It's through this bottom layer that the customer premises equipment (CPE) is physically interconnected to the switched telecommunications infrastructure of the carriers.

As such, it's the layer most visible to consumers and data communications personnel employed outside the telecommunications industry. Therefore, it's not surprising to find the term *central office* applied generically to all telecommunications switching centers.

The other four layers provide route redundancy in a very large and complex hybrid topology. These layers are the regional switching center, the sectional switching center, the primary switching center, and the toll switching center.

These are numbered according to their class. Before the divestiture of the Bell System on January 1, 1984, telephone communications were provided by the Class 5 switching centers—the central offices. Such calls were essentially toll free because the Bell System subsidized the costs of local calls with the revenue generated by long distance calls. Today, this hierarchical model is more of a theoretical target than a rigidly adhered-to service architecture.

The toll switching centers were responsible for interconnecting the central offices that were in close geographic proximity to each other. Therefore, local calls could be made despite the origination and destination points being connected to different central offices. The toll switching centers also provided connectivity to the toll-based, or *long-distance*, portion of the telecommunications infrastructure.

The top three layers represented different levels of geographic aggregation for toll calls. The regional switching centers were the backbone of the entire network; there was one in each region of the country, and they were all interconnected. The sectional and primary switching centers were lower levels of geographic aggregation. This complex architecture was designed to provide the most efficient path through the network for any given pair of endpoints. Its size and complexity also provided route redundancy that could mitigate the impacts of congestion or a failure somewhere in the network.

These five basic classes of switching centers were designed to satisfy the needs for call aggregation, simplification of billing data, and route redundancy in the pre-divestiture days of telecommunications in North America. Although the architecture proved highly successful in these respects, divestiture forced dramatic changes.

Post-Divestiture Telephony Infrastructure

Divestiture is the name given to the complex legal processes that broke up the Bell System into fully separate entities. Severe restrictions are now placed on each entity for the sake of stimulating competition and technological innovation, including the following:

- Restrictions on the geographic areas in which each entity can operate
- Restrictions on the types of service that each new entity can provide

Together, these two sets of restrictions have effectively compartmentalized the telecommunications infrastructure and created some new terms and concepts. The most obvious compartmentalization is between local and long distance communications. Carriers that provided local connectivity have become known as *local exchange carriers* (LECs). LECs are barred from providing long-distance communications. Their domains are known as *local access and transport areas* (LATAs).

Carriers such as AT&T that were limited to long-distance communications became known as *interexchange carriers* (IXCs). This name is derived from the pre-divestiture term *exchange*, which refers to a toll-free area. In the post-divestiture environment, all traffic between exchanges, or LATAs, must be carried by an IXC.

LECs are required by law to provide all IXCs with equal access to their customer bases. This concept, known as *equal access*, has necessitated the development of *points of presence* (POPs). A POP is some form of IXC presence within an LEC-owned switching center. POPs ensure that all inter-LATA traffic is carried by an IXC. Any communications traffic that's addressed to an endpoint in a different LATA must be routed to an IXC's POP, even if both the origination and destination endpoints reside within LATAs operated by a single LEC. In this manner, the local and long-distance communications networks remain completely separated, with POPs serving as the boundary between them. The POP itself can be as simple as a wire or fiber-optic patch panel that connects the LEC's switching facilities to the IXC's switching facilities, or it can be a telecommunications switch.

The net result of divestiture is that the same five classes of switching remain, but they're now a patchwork of privately owned networks operated by the various local and interexchange carriers. This patchwork is simultaneously collaborative and competitive in nature. This telephony infrastructure is used to support all types of telephonic connections in the United States, including leased lines.

Recently, changes to this alignment of LECs and IXCs have been promulgated by the FCC and the courts. The result of the changes should be that LECs can offer long-distance services and IXCs can offer local services, provided that each does not erect barriers to the other. What this will mean in practice is yet to be seen.

Digital Signal Standards

Much as any other standard networking technology, leased lines feature standardized transmission schemes. Such schemes define transmission rates and media types as well as framing formats and multiplexing methodologies.

There are many such schemes, and they vary by geography and technology. Some of the more commonly encountered standards include the following:

- ANSI's Digital Signaling Hierarchy
- ITU's Digital Signaling Hierarchy
- SONET's Optical Carrier System
- SONET's Synchronous Transport Signal system

ANSI's Digital Signal Hierarchy

The *American National Standards Institute* (ANSI) set the standards for digital signal transmission during the early 1980s. This family of standards became known as the *Digital Signal Hierarchy* (DSH). This hierarchy consists of five specifications, numbered DS-0 through DS-4. These specifications, their corresponding bandwidths, and the number of supported voice channels are presented in Table 11.1.

Table 11.1 ANSI's Digital Signal Standards

Digital Signal Standard	Bandwidth	Number of Voice Channels
DS-0	64Kbps	1
DS-1	1.544Mbps	24
DS-1C	3.152Mbps	48
DS-2	6.312Mbps	96
DS-3	44.736Mbps	672
DS-4	274.176Mbps	4032

Note: DS-0 defines the minimum amount of bandwidth required to transport digitized voice. Given that voice communication typically occurs using an 8KHz circuit, and digitizing it requires an eight-fold increase in bandwidth, the DS-0 band was defined at 64Kbps. It is not, however, the basic building block of leased lines. That honor goes to the DS-1 specification. DS-0 describes the voice channels that are carved from the other digital signaling specifications.

ANSI's DS standards have been implemented in a telephony carrier system that's called the *T-Carrier system*. There's a direct, one-to-one correlation between T-Carrier circuits and their DS namesakes. For example, the DS-1 standard is embodied in the T-1 transmission facility, and T-3 is the physical implementation of the DS-3. For more information on the T-Carrier system, refer to the section titled "The T-Carrier System," later in this chapter.

After even a cursory glance through Table 11.1, you can probably recognize at least one of the standards. The T-1 has become so prevalent in networking that almost every network-aware technical person recognizes the 1.544Mbps bandwidth and associates it with that transmission facility. Some people might even recognize the 44.736Mbps of the T-3. The other standards, however, might not be as readily recognized.

The DS-1C, from a functional perspective, is two DS-1s integrated into a common transmission facility. The DS-2 and DS-4 standards have never achieved widespread utilization. This is primarily due to their cost versus performance ratios. DS-3 service is also expensive but offers a better combination of price and bandwidth than its alternatives.

Today, virtually every situation that requires bandwidth in excess of the DS-3 is satisfied with SONET technology (covered in a following section). Therefore, the T-Carrier system is used only for T-1, fractional T-1, and T-3 services. The remaining T-*n* specifications have fallen into disuse.

ITU's Digital Signal Hierarchy

In Europe, the International Telecommunications Union (ITU—formerly CCITT) created its own family of standards for digital signaling. These standards were named after the committee that recommended them to the ITU: the Conference of European Posts and Telecommunications Administration (CEPT). These CEPT standards are listed in Table 11.2.

Table 11.2   ITU's Digital Signal Standards

Digital Signal Standard	Bandwidth	Number of Voice Channels
CEPT-1	2.048Mbps	30
CEPT-2	8.448Mbps	120
CEPT-3	34.368Mbps	480
CEPT-4	139.264Mbps	1920
CEPT-5	565.148Mbps	7680

Although the ITU standards use the same basic channel as the 64Kbps DS-0, their aggregations are very different. Thus, the European version of a T-1 is known as the *E-1*, and it supports 2.048Mbps, compared to the T-1s 1.544Mbps. Internetworking between Europe and North America presents the challenge of mismatched standards and usually results in unusable channels.

> **Note:** If you perform the mathematics, you can see that the CEPT-1 standard (implemented in the European E-1 transmission facility) actually contains enough bandwidth for 32 channels of 64Kbps each. The CEPT-1, and consequently the E-1 circuit, can support a maximum of 30 usable channels. The remaining two are reserved for synchronization and signaling. This differs from ANSI's approach in its DS specifications. ANSI imposes framing and timing within each channel, thereby reducing available bandwidth from the stated transmission rate.

SONET's Carrier Systems

SONET is an acronym for *Synchronous Optical Network*. It's basically a series of optically based transmission systems. It's a highly specialized technology set that was designed expressly for use by telecommunications carriers. It was intended to provide interoperability between switching systems made by different manufacturers as well as to buffer the disparities in capacity and transmission rates of those myriad systems.

To fulfill this role, physical interfaces, framing conventions, and two families of signaling standards were developed. These two families range from 51.84Mbps to 2.48Gbps.

Note: SONET is an ANSI standard that has been embraced but not wholly adopted by the ITU. The ITU's version varies subtly, but in significant ways. It's known as the *Synchronous Digital Hierarchy* (SDH). The basic rate of transmission in SDH is 155.52Mbps, unlike the 51.84Mbps basic rate of SONET.

Another fairly minor difference is that SDH's copper-based transmission standards are known as synchronous transport *modules* (STMs) instead of synchronous transport *signals* (STSs).

SONET supports two transmission systems: the Optical Carrier (OC) system for fiber and the Synchronous Transport Signal (STS) system for copper wire.

Optical Carrier System

Table 11.3 presents the OC standards, their bandwidth, and the number of DS-0 and DS-1 channels that each supports.

Table 11.3   Optical Carrier Bandwidths

Optical Carrier Line	Bandwidth	DS0 Channels	DS1 Channels
OC-1	51.84Mbps	672	28
OC-3	155.52Mbps	2016	84
OC-9	466.56Mbps	6048	252
OC-12	622.08Mbps	8064	336
OC-18	933.12Mbps	12096	504
OC-24	1.244Gbps	16128	672
OC-36	1.866Gbps	24192	1008
OC-48	2.488Gbps	32256	1344

This table, in theory, can be expanded nearly infinitely by continuing to multiply the basic OC-1. As optical signaling technology continues to improve, it's reasonable to expect greater multiples of the OC-1 rate to become standardized. In fact, the technology exists to transmit at an OC-192 rate! It's also likely that these larger multiples will be retrofitted into the SONET and/or SDH standards.

Synchronous Transport Signal System

SONET's OC rates can also be implemented over an electrical signaling system using copper wiring. These electrical rates are indicated with an STS designation (Synchronous Transport Signal) rather than the familiar OC designation. Aside from this physical difference, there's a one-to-one correlation between the two standards. In other words, STS-1 is directly equivalent to OC-1, STS-3 equals the OC-3 rate of 155.52Mbps, and so forth.

It's important to note that the STS-n standards span up to STS-48, which yields 2.488Gbps of bandwidth. Providing this bandwidth to electrical signals over copper presents some significant technical challenges. For that matter, driving a copper wire at rates in excess of 155.52Mbps becomes problematic over distances greater than 100 meters. Consequently, only STS-1 and STS-3 are actually defined and usable. The remainder are little more than theoretical constructs.

The T-Carrier System

The digital signaling standards listed in Table 11.1 are implemented through a physical carrier system. The most prevalent carrier system in North America is the T-Carrier system. The leased lines delivered by this carrier system are prefaced with the letter *T*. For example, a leased line delivered by T-Carrier that conforms to the DS-1 standard is known as a T-1. This important distinction is frequently lost on even the most technical people! Consequently, the terms *DS*-n and *T*-n (where *n* identifies a specific number) are often incorrectly used interchangeably. They are *not* interchangeable. DS-n identifies a standard, whereas T-n identifies a standards-compliant circuit.

The T-Carrier system was originally designed to provide multiplexed voice communications over a single transmission facility. These facilities were used to transport calls between the various switching centers. Twenty-four calls could be carried on a single T-1 circuit. Because the calls were in digital form, they could be amplified and regenerated en route to their destination. Therefore, digitized voice signals were inherently more clear than analog voice communications, which couldn't be regenerated.

T-Carrier Services

As described earlier in this chapter, in the section titled "ANSI's Digital Signal Hierarchy," only two of the DS standards are available as commercial services. These are the T-3 and the T-1. A third service is also available: *Fractional T-1*. Fractional T-1, however, is a subrated variant of the DS-1 specification and not a productized form of the DS-0 specification.

The T-3 transmission facility provides 44.736Mbps of bandwidth. This bandwidth can be channelized into 672 separate channels of 64Kbps each or 28 T-1 equivalent channels. T-3s tend to be very expensive, especially as geographic distances increase, but for any networking application that requires more bandwidth than a couple T-1s can provide, a T-3 may actually prove to be the more economical solution.

The T-1 transmission facility is the foundation of the T-Carrier system. This basic service provides customers with 1.544Mbps of gross bandwidth. This can be channelized into as many as 24 channels of 64Kbps each, or it can be left whole for high-bandwidth networking applications.

Networks that either can't afford the cost of a full T-1 or don't need its bandwidth may find the Fractional T-1 service more attractive. Fractional T-1 is actually constructed from a T-1 circuit. Bandwidth on that circuit is fractionalized using a device known as a *channel bank*. The subcircuit is usually a 56Kbps circuit, but it can be as small as 9.6Kbps. These subrate channels can then be delivered to different customers.

Subrating a T-1 creates the need for maintaining timing across each subchannel. One technique is *bit robbing*. Bit robbing maintains the synchronicity of a channel by appropriating the least significant bit of every eighth frame in the stream for use as a pulse. Robbing these bits, in effect, makes the entire frame that was robbed unusable. Therefore, every eighth eight-bit frame is unusable. This effectively reduces the bandwidth available on a 64Kbps DS-0 channel to only 56Kbps. Clear-channel 64Kbps facilities may be ordered from your carrier. These facilities are nothing more than a DS-0 channel from a T-1, without its own timing mechanism.

> **Note:** Frames, in this context, differ substantially from the highly developed and feature-rich frames used in LANs. DS frames are minimalist structures. Their functionality is limited to the synchronization of the transmission, and in some instances, error detection and network monitoring. As such, a digital signal frame is usually nothing more than a single bit inserted at fixed intervals in a bit stream.

Line Encoding

Being the first digital system, the T-Carrier system needed a completely new line-encoding technique. One of the challenges in developing this encoding technique was maintaining the synchronization of the line with an absolute minimum amount of overhead.

Unipolar Binary Encoding

The simplest form of binary encoding is *unipolar*. In other words, the signal is either on (a positive electrical charge) or off (no charge). Although it's simple, the fatal disadvantage is that a series of either consecutive ones or consecutive zeros appears as a flat line.

Given the normal attenuation of a signal over distance, it would be relatively easy for the timing, or bit count, to become corrupt. This would adversely affect the data that was encoded. Therefore, unipolar encoding was not well suited for long-distance transmissions.

Bipolar Binary Encoding

The alternative to unipolar encoding is *bipolar encoding*. Bipolar encoding, as its name implies, features the use of both poles of the electric signal. By using both positive and negative polarity, a transition through zero (no voltage) is necessary between digits. This transition, generically speaking, is known as a *return to zero*. It provides an innate boundary between the transmitted bits.

The T-Carrier system uses a variety of bipolar encoding called *alternate mark inversion* (AMI). AMI uses both poles to represent a binary one, and no voltage to represent a zero. Consecutive ones are represented by alternating poles, and zeros are always represented by no voltage.

Although this solved the boundary issue between consecutive ones, it left the T-Carrier system vulnerable to loss of timing due to a consecutive string of zeros. To counter this, the T-Carrier system implemented a protocol known as the *Ones Density Rule*. This rule limits the number of consecutively transmitted zeros to 15. To enforce this rule, a technique was developed that substituted eight consecutive zeros with a predetermined pattern. This pattern is called a *word*. This technique was saddled with the rather ungainly name of *Bipolar Eight Zero Substitution*, or B8ZS.

Of course, reserving any random string of eight bits for use as a zero substitution string creates the potential for that string to occur randomly as part of the bit stream, which would inadvertently result in the translation of eight legitimate bits of data into zeros. Therefore, to differentiate between the fictional word for the eight zeros and legitimate strings of data, the bipolar variation of transmitted ones has to be violated. To signal the start of the fictional word for eight zeros, two positive-voltage ones are transmitted.

B8ZS is the timing method used on T-1s. It's implemented by the CSU/DSUs at each end of the leased line.

Framing Formats

The T-Carrier system recognizes three distinct forms of framing: D-4 format, extended superframe (ESF) format, and M1-3 format.

D-4 Format

The most common frame for T-1 circuits is the D-4, named for the D-4 channel banks that implemented it. This technique places a timing bit before each 24 octets of data. If 24 seems a familiar number, it is—that's the number of eight-bit channels supported by a T-1. One D-4 frame consists of the following:

- A 12-bit frame alignment signal
- A 1-bit timing signal
- A 192-bit data field

The 192-bit data field is constructed of one octet from each of the T-1's channels. If you do the math, you can see that the D-4 frame adds up to 205 bits. The D-4 frame, however, is universally accepted as being only 193 bits long. The discrepancy arises from the fact that the alignment signal, much like Ethernet's preamble, is not considered a part of the frame.

Extended Superframe Format

AT&T, developer of many of North America's telephony technologies and standards, developed the extended superframe (ESF) in the early 1980s. The ESF was implemented in the D-5 channel banks, successor to the time-honored D-4.

The ESF was designed to further improve the operational efficiency of T-1 transmission facilities. The essence of this technique is a reduction in the number of framing bits used by the D-4 method. Whereas D-4 requires 24 timing bits for 24 D-4 frames, the ESF needs only six. Every fourth 193-bit frame has a timing bit. Six of the other bits are used for error correction, and the remaining 12 are used for nonintrusive monitoring of the network. This monitoring is nonintrusive in that it does not add any overhead to the bit stream.

M1-3 Format

T-3s use a completely different framing technique called *M1-3 framing*. This naming convention is derived from its functionality: It multiplexes DS-1 channels onto a DS-3. Mathematically, 28 DS-1 channels equal 43.232Mbps of aggregate bandwidth. This fits nicely onto the 44.736Mbps available with DS-3, plus a surplus for use in frame alignment, error detection, and timing.

> **Note:** M1-3 is actually just one of a family of three multiplexed interface standards that are known collectively as *MX-3*. The other two are the MC-3 and the M2-3.
>
> The MC-3 multiplexes 14 DS-1C's onto one DS-3. The M2-3, as its name implies, multiplexes seven DS-2s to one DS-3. Given that the DS-1C and the DS-2 are functionally obsolete, their multiplexed interfaces have suffered a similar fate.

M1-3 features a 4,760-bit frame, of which 4,704 bits are dedicated to carrying data. The remaining 56 bits are used for error correction and timing.

Circuit Switched Transmission Facilities

Almost everyone in the United States works with circuit switched transmission facilities every day. Yet, most people are not aware of their presence. By their very nature, circuit switched networks transmit data reliably and consistently. This high level of reliability has caused the circuit switched network to be used by popular technologies such as Frame Relay and ATM.

The most widely used network in the world, the Public Switched Telephone Network (PSTN), is based on the idea that conversations across a network should have reserved bandwidth and must follow the same path until the connection is broken. Although this may not be the best method to use for all types of data, it's extremely well suited to the multimedia, real-time requirements of voice, video, and electronic conferencing. As these technologies become more popular in modern networks, so will circuit switched networking.

Switched 56

Switched 56 is generally the least expensive wide area network digital service. It operates at 56Kbps. Switched 56 is provided via standard twisted pair wiring. Similar to the PSTN, connections are made by specifying a seven-digit telephone number and connecting to another switched 56 circuit or ISDN (Integrated Services Digital Network) line.

A major advantage of Switched 56 is that connections are active only when needed, and billing is based on usage. In fact, it's common practice for providers to charge the same price for a Switched 56 circuit as for a standard voice circuit. Therefore, if local voice calls are free in your service area, Switched 56 connections may also be free.

The downside of Switched 56 is that it's not easily upgraded; if you need to move to a faster connection, you have to upgrade to a different technology. Another disadvantage of the Switched 56 technology is the lack of availability. Today, most parts of the country cannot find a provider for Switched 56 service.

Switched 56 Technologies

Different technologies are used for Switched 56 connections. These technologies are defined in EIA/TIA-596. Only one is really popular.

This technology, named *switched 56 Service Type III*, was developed by Northern Telecom and works on standard telephone wire. This is a great benefit, because those deploying the technology may make use of an existing cable plant, thus significantly reducing the installation costs.

Data is transmitted across the wire at 64Kbps. This may come as a surprise, because the "56" in the name of the technology refers to the transmission speed. The remaining 8Kbps are used for call setup and signaling.

Frame Relay

Frame Relay is a packet switched network commonly used as a WAN link to connect remote offices. Although it's packet switched, it emulates a circuit switched network through the use of permanent virtual circuits (PVCs), which map a path through many switches.

Frame Relay exists solely at the lowest two layers of the OSI Model. Routers are used at each end of the link to connect the individual networks to the Frame Relay network. Distant offices pay for only a leased line to their provider and trust the provider to carry the traffic between offices. Redundancy is provided for within the network, further reducing costs and administrative overhead for companies that purchase public Frame Relay services. The companies that purchase Frame Relay carrier services substantially reduce WAN overhead costs. Further, Frame Relay's reliability reduces costs associated with downtime.

Frame Relay is commonly used as an upgrade to the outdated X.25. Frame Relay was designed for a new era of networking based on digital transmissions and fiber media, sacrificing unnecessary error-checking overhead in favor of speed.

Another advantage of Frame Relay is that it combines many connections, or *virtual circuits*, over a single link such as a leased line.

In recent years, Frame Relay has been used more and more as a transport for legacy traffic, combining several separate leased lines into a single Frame Relay circuit. Even traditionally analog data such as voice is being carried, thus providing remote offices with a more economical alternative to long-distance charges.

Frame Relay Versus Leased Lines

Frame Relay is commonly seen as a competitor of the more traditional leased line. Perhaps the largest factor driving the growth of Frame Relay is its rapid adoption in place of leased lines from a telephone company.

Frame Relay is generally a less-expensive alternative to building a wide area network. An organization that chooses leased lines is responsible for the high cost of each connection, one or many of which may span a very large distance. An organization that chooses to implement WAN networking over Frame Relay implements connections across the Frame Relay network and is responsible for only a leased line from the organization to the cloud itself.

> **Note:** The term *cloud* is to wide area communications what *black box* is to local area networks. It represents something that provides connectivity or service, but whose inner workings are beyond your scope or control. Mathematicians use *X*, old time cartographers wrote "Here be dragons," and WAN architects use the cloud symbol.

This is an especially attractive option to organizations that are connecting over great distances, because Frame Relay does not charge based on the distance between endpoints. Typically, the breakeven point in leased line versus Frame Relay pricing happens at between 10 and 20 miles. At less than 10 miles, it's usually less expensive to get a single leased line. At greater than 20 miles, Frame Relay is the more financially attractive option.

By connecting to a Frame Relay cloud, a physical organization can connect to several different partners with a single connection into the cloud. A value-added benefit to this type of architecture is the Internet gateway, a service offered within public Frame Relay clouds that lets customers with existing connections access the Internet, often with the added security of managed firewalls.

Connecting to anyone within a Frame Relay network requires only configuring another SVC or PVC, thereby avoiding the cost and complication of bringing another leased line into a building, configuring a separate router, and maintaining the connection.

Leased lines in themselves have no redundancy; a leased line is simply a single connection between any two points. If a line is damaged by construction, all connectivity through that link may be lost. To make matters worse, telephone companies often make mistakes or have equipment failures that bring circuits down for no good reason. Frame Relay does not suffer from this weakness because it's a switched network; if a link between two parts of the network is lost, traffic is simply rerouted with a short delay. If a switch within the cloud stops functioning properly, the other switches detect the problem and begin routing frames through an alternate path. The inherent redundancy of a Frame Relay cloud makes it a more reliable service than leased lines.

Leased lines have guaranteed bandwidth through time-division multiplexing. This is an advantage because it simplifies planning, but it's a disadvantage because the bandwidth is always committed, regardless of whether it's used. Furthermore, it does not have the capacity to grow as more bandwidth is required or at times of peak demand. Billing is less than efficient because an organization is charged for the entire bandwidth of the circuit, regardless of how much is used or needed.

Frame Relay overcomes these limitations by using *statistical multiplexing*. This enables Frame Relay to not commit all required bandwidth at the beginning of the connection. Although it does offer a CIR (Committed Information Rate) property (guaranteeing companies a particular amount of capacity), it also allows for increased bandwidth at times of higher utilization while not charging for this increased bandwidth when it's not in use. Billing is based on traffic, so companies that use less pay less, and those that need more have the option to use it.

Leased lines must be designed around peak traffic needs, which are difficult to anticipate and often change dramatically as a company grows. Frame Relay networks, because of CIR and burst capabilities, are designed to meet average traffic needs. These needs are more predictable, and because of the burst capability, less rigid.

Finally, the Frame Relay cloud is more efficient for the provider to offer to customers because it permits shared bandwidth. The provider needs to guarantee that it has enough bandwidth to enable each customer to utilize the full CIR, but bandwidth above that can be shared by many customers. In contrast, leased line providers (generally telephone companies) must have all the bandwidth each customer may ever use provisioned at all times. This gives leased line providers a much lower bandwidth utilization than Frame Relay providers.

Extended Frame Relay

DLCIs (Data Link Connection Identifiers) only identify a connection between a router and the Frame Relay network; to identify a final destination, these DLCIs must be statically mapped to destinations within the Frame Relay cloud. There is no provision for an address-resolution protocol to dynamically map DLCIs to Frame Relay destinations.

LMI (Local Management Interface) extensions make Frame Relay more robust and provide for many advanced features, not the least of which is *global addressing*. Global addressing makes DLCIs unique within a cloud, assigning a specific DLCI to a specific router. This makes the Frame Relay cloud more compatible with common higher-level protocols such as TCP/IP, which assign distinct IDs to each node.

Another useful LMI extension is *multicasting*. DLCIs in the range 1019 to 1022 are reserved as multicast addresses, known to the cloud as signifying multiple endpoints.

Permanent Virtual Circuits Versus Switched Virtual Circuits

Frame Relay provides for two types of virtual circuits: permanent virtual circuits (PVCs) and switched virtual circuits (SVCs). A PVC is statically defined at the time of configuration and ensures the data between two points always follows the same path, making data transfer properties more consistent. SVCs calculate the path each time the connection is established, enabling the circuit to bypass failures within the network. Because a different path is used each time the connection is established, performance characteristics such as jitter and delay may vary. Figure 11.2 details the differences between SVCs and PVCs.

Frame Relay is flexible and can be used on links ranging from 56K to T-3 (45Mbps) speeds. Furthermore, public Frame Relay clouds generally charge based on traffic, avoiding unnecessary charges for less frequently used links.

FIGURE 11.2

A line-by-line comparison of PVCs and SVCs.

Permanent Virtual Circuits	Switched Virtual Circuits
Connection established only once	Connection established on a call-by-call basis
Frames always follow the same path	Frames may follow a different path for each call
Consistent and reliable	Less consistent and less reliable
Connection is always configured, whether or not it is in use	Connection is released when there is no more information to send
Permanent and guaranteed connections, but poor utilization	Better utilization of frame relay cloud
Difficult to manage	Easier to maintain
Requires a rigid network architecture and more connections for high levels of redundancy	Allows a flexible network architecture requiring fewer connections for highly-meshed networks
Pay a predictable, monthly charge	Pay based on usage: Bandwidth, call length, and number of frames sent.

Basic Frame Relay Format

The term *frame* refers to the groups of data that are switched within the network because Frame Relay exists at only the first two levels of the OSI Model and not at the Network Layer, where groups of data are called *packets*.

Packets are passed from individual LANs into the Frame Relay network; Frame Relay, however, makes no distinction between different Network Layer protocols. Frame Relay handles these protocols transparently by encapsulating them within Frame Relay headers and footers. To be efficient, this encapsulation adds a total of only six bytes.

Ten bits of the first two bytes are dedicated to the Data Link Layer address, which is equivalent to a MAC address on an Ethernet network. This data link address is called the *Data Link Connection Identifier*, or *DLCI* for short. Rather than simply identifying a destination, the routers use the DLCI to identify a circuit at each end of the network. It's important to note that either side of a PVC does not necessarily use the same DLCI number; DLCIs are significant only to a particular DTE/DCE (data terminal equipment/data communications equipment) pair. In this way, DLCIs are different from MAC addresses, which are unique universally. DLCIs have too small a range to be universally unique.

Of the remaining six bits in the address, three bits are used for flags that provide for congestion notification: One bit enables frames to be set to a lower priority; the remaining two are reserved for future use.

Frame Relay Networks Design

One of the advantages of Frame Relay networking is the adjustable, scalable bandwidth. When Frame Relay services are purchased, the provider specifies a Committed Information Rate (CIR). The CIR defines the guaranteed bandwidth between any two locations.

UNI Versus NNI

Two parts of the Frame Relay specification define protocols for User-to-Network Interface (UNI) connections and Network-to-Network Interface (NNI) connections. UNI was developed by ANSI and the International Telecommunications Union Telecommunication Standardization Sector (ITU-T) and provides specifications for a DTE to speak to a DCE. The UNI specifications are not unlike the United States Postal Service's specifications for addressing a letter: they describe a specific format for the end user to provide but do not detail how the letter gets there after it's dropped in a mailbox. Instead, the postal service provides certain guarantees as to service, such as delivery time and reliability, and the person mailing the letter is left to trust the postal service to follow through.

Frame Relay works the same way: The network and the end user communicate through UNI standards. The network defines certain quality-of-service guarantees such as Committed Information Rate (CIR), Committed Burst Size (Bc), and Excess Burst Size (Be). Exactly how the network delivers on its promise is up to the provider's discretion.

NNI, developed by the Frame Relay Forum, enables two networks to exchange data without either one having to understand the structure within the individual networks. By using NNIs, Frame Relay providers can expand the usefulness of their networks by providing gateways into other providers' networks, thus enabling organizations to partner without choosing the same provider.

Going Above the CIR

The strength of Frame Relay depends on two parameters called *Committed Burst Rate* (Bc) and *Excess Burst Rate* (Be), both of which are specified at the time a PVC is provisioned. Bc is the amount of traffic a Frame Relay carrier can transport above and beyond the CIR for a limited amount of time if and only if the traffic pattern averages out to the CIR over a given period of time. The Be is the maximum amount of traffic the provider can accept. Traffic that arrives at a rate between the Bc and the Be is not guaranteed. The relationship between the three properties must be specified at the time of provisioning.

The Frame Relay switch that receives the data calculates the average rate to exceed the CIR and can react in a couple different ways. The nicest thing it can do is pass all data on to the central office but mark the Discard Eligible (DE) bit in each frame header. The DE bit is used to mark data as low priority: If congestion occurs somewhere else in the network, low-priority data may be dropped in favor of higher-priority frames. Another possibility is that the switch may simply drop packets that exceed the CIR. This is normally done in periods of congestion.

Flow Control in the Frame Relay Network

Two fields in the frame header allow for flow control. These fields are called Forward and Backward Explicit Congestion Notification (FECN and BECN), and they enable switches to ask the end nodes to reduce their bandwidth usage before frames need to be dropped. In this way, the network can slow the rate of traffic from the source instead becoming overcrowded.

A Frame Relay switch marks the FECN bit in a frame when it experiences congestion and wants to notify the receiving node. It's then the responsibility of the receiving partner to throttle back the network usage. Alternatively, a switch may mark the BECN bit on traffic returning to the node that's sending too much data. Using the BECN bit is more efficient than using the FECN bit because the host is notified directly.

Only recently has DTE equipment begun to listen and respond to the FECN and BECN bits. If the customer equipment does not act on the requests, these bits are not useful.

Voiceover Frame Relay (VoFR)

A new feature of Frame Relay is the capability to multiplex various kinds of data onto a single physical circuit. Cost factors are driving the adoption of voiceover Frame Relay, thus enabling remote offices to exchange telephone calls without using the PSTN or leased lines. Organizations that have chosen to use Frame Relay for their data communications and have already made the investment in Frame Relay equipment have an easy migration path to voiceover Frame Relay.

Voiceover Frame Relay presents an interesting challenge because packet switched networks rely on statistical multiplexing, which works well for data but can degrade real-time applications such as voice if congestion occurs. In order to reduce the amount of bandwidth required by each voice circuit and to improve overall utilization of the links, voice streams are compressed by removing pauses and redundant information. Typically, only about 22 percent of typical voice connection bandwidth is required for high-quality service.

To transmit this data over the Frame Relay network, the information is compressed as described previously and encapsulated within a data frame. A Frame Relay multiplexer then places these frames onto the same outgoing connection as other network data that may be traveling over the same physical circuit. By combining voice and data onto the same circuits, organizations reduce costs substantially over what they incur in maintaining separate network equipment and links.

Along with the benefits of compression and multiplexing come several drawbacks. Compression, particularly on congested networks, can be *lossy*, a term that describes compression in which quality is sacrificed for efficiency. Although a voice conversation may continue despite the lossy compression, the quality is less than that which most people are accustomed to on toll networks such as the PSTN. Another disadvantage is the lack of accounting standards for voiceover Frame Relay; existing systems that track and bill for calls may need to be replaced when upgrading to Frame Relay. Packet switched networks such as Frame Relay also suffer from delay and jitter, which further degrade quality. ATM was designed specifically to better support real-time applications such as voice, and it's a better, though more costly, alternative.

Internetworking Frame Relay with ATM

ATM (Asynchronous Transfer Mode—see the next section of this chapter) is a rapidly emerging technology for many of Frame Relay's current uses. To ease the transition, most public Frame Relay providers are offering or planning to offer transparent internetworking with ATM. Using a gateway, an organization can upgrade parts of its Frame Relay network while maintaining full interoperability with remote offices still using existing Frame Relay networks. This also enables a company to migrate to ATM within its own backbone and keep Frame Relay connections with other partners.

Many new networks are still being implemented based on Frame Relay rather than ATM. Internetworking with ATM through a gateway gradually eases a company into the world of high-speed networking and provides experience to network personnel. By choosing to first develop a backbone based on the well-established Frame Relay technology, an organization avoids the high startup costs associated with a complete switchover to ATM.

ATM

Asynchronous Transfer Mode (ATM) was developed as a broadband alternative to the ISDN network. Operating at speeds from 1.54Mbps to 622Mbps, ATM is well suited to handle varying types of traffic such as data, voice, and video. One of ATM's primary advantages is that it adapts well to new technologies, offering features such as Quality of Service. A further advantage is that the network may be able to take advantage of higher bandwidths during periods of bursting, thus utilizing unused time on the wire.

ATM does not switch packets as does a conventional network; instead, it switches *cells*. A cell is different from a packet because a cell has a fixed length. In ATM, this length is 53 bytes (48 bytes of data and five bytes of header). This fixed length enables the switching hardware to operate at much faster speeds than conventional variable-length switches can handle because only the header needs to be processed. Conventional variable-length packet switches must read and process every bit that comes across the wire to be able to determine the beginning and end of any particular packet.

For more about ATM and its development, see Chapter 9, "ATM."

ATM Layers

To allow for greater flexibility, the ATM specifications are divided into multiple layers. Although not designed to correspond to the OSI Model, the primary ATM layers are roughly analogous to the lowest two layers: the Physical and Data Link Layers.

Physical Layer

The ATM Physical Layer is directly analogous to the Physical Layer described in the OSI Model; it's media dependent and is responsible for actually transmitting the bits. This layer is subdivided into the Physical Medium Sublayer and the Transmission Convergence Sublayer. The lower half, the Physical Medium Sublayer, is responsible for placing bits onto the network medium (usually fiber) and providing timing.

The Transmission Convergence Sublayer is responsible for maintaining cell boundaries, providing for header error control checking, and maintaining the media-dependent frame structure.

ATM Layer and ATM Adaptation Layer (Data Link Layer)

The ATM Layer is responsible for establishing connections across the ATM network by mapping the Network Layer addresses to Data Link Layer addresses. Four addressing schemes have been developed; the public format is shared by Narrowband ISDN networks.

The ATM Adaptation Layer (AAL) provides the translation functionality between the upper-layer protocols and the actual ATM cells. For example, the AAL splits apart TCP/IP packets into 48-byte segments and encapsulates them in the ATM header. To support different types of data, different AAL specifications have been provided.

AAL1 was designed to carry analog traffic that would normally be carried by dedicated circuits. It requires a lower-layer media that supports timing control, such as SONET. It provides for guaranteed end-to-end bandwidth.

AAL3/4 is intended to transmit Switched Multimegabit Data Service (SMDS) packets over an ATM network.

AAL 5 is the most commonly used ATM Adaptation Layer for connection-oriented network data. It's used for classical IP over ATM and LAN emulation.

ATM Cell Format

The ATM cell is 53 bytes long, with a five-byte header.

Two distinct header formats are used. The User-to-Network Interface (UNI) header type is used for all cells sent between end-users and the ATM network.

The header is composed of six fields:

- *Reserved (one bit)*. The first bit of the ATM cell is set aside for future use. Although a single bit is little to work with, in the future, it may be used to change the meaning of the rest of the header.

- *Header Error Control (HEC; eight bits)*. To detect errors within its own header, ATM includes a single byte of parity called the Header Error Control (HEC). This enables switches to detect whether a single bit has been modified from what was originally sent and to actually correct the error.

- *Generic Flow Control (zero or four bits)*. Intended to be used to establish switched virtual circuits, this functionality has not yet been implemented in the ATM standards.

- *Maintenance Payload Type (two bits)*. These bits indicate to a switch whether a cell is being used for network maintenance or normal traffic. In this way, cells can be used in the same way that ICMP and NSMP packets are used on a TCP/IP network: to test functionality and measure performance.

- *Priority Type Identifier (PTI; one bit)*. This bit is used to enable the ATM network to distinguish between cells with different Quality of Service requirements. The particular meaning of the bit can be defined per cell, channel, or path.

- *Virtual Path/Circuit Identifier (VPI/VCI; 8 or 12 bits)*. The VPI/VCI field stores the path and channel of the cell destination. This information is unique within an ATM network. The Virtual Path Identifier describes an entire route, endpoint to endpoint. The Virtual Circuit Identifier is a connection between two directly connected switches. Each time a switch receives a cell, it may change both values before passing the cell on to the next switch on its way to the destination. A simple lookup of the VPI and VCI gives the switch the information it needs to know the destination port and the next-hop VPI/VCI.

The Network-Node Interface (NNI) header type is similar but does not contain the Generic Flow Control field. Instead, it uses its bits for an expanded Virtual Path Identifier, which is renamed the *Virtual Channel identifier*.

ATM Connections

ATM provides for two types of connections: permanent virtual connections (PVC) and switched virtual connections (SVC). PVCs are maintained by the ATM service provider and operate in much the same way as Frame Relay connections. A PVC requires careful network design and uses the topologies as leased lines.

When a PVC is provisioned, several properties must be specified to the provider. Each PVC is assigned a Class of Service (COS). The COS specifications include choosing between a variable bit rate and a constant bit rate type of service. COS is defined each time an SVC is created, allowing for greater flexibility because multiple SVCs can be created between organizations, each with a different COS.

Another property that must be specified is the Peak Cell Rate (PCR). ATM cells are a fixed size; because of that, the Peak Cell Rate specifies the bandwidth allocated to a particular circuit. Furthermore, the PCR can be different for each direction on a circuit, making it asymmetric. PCR is similar to the Committed Information Rate (CIR) defined for Frame Relay circuits.

> **Note:** Asymmetric traffic patterns occur for many types of client-server relationships. An excellent example is the common Web server: a client issues a simple GET / request to the Web server, and the Web server responds with a lengthy front page. If this is a typical use for a circuit, the PCR could be much smaller for the client than the server.

SVCs are still very much under development. They will enable end stations to dynamically create connections and will reduce the need for a rigid, preplanned topology.

Quality of Service

Quality of Service (QOS) is an important concept for ATM networks. QOS describes the traffic properties, such as peak and sustained bandwidth, guaranteed to any given connection. Data that exceeds these specific requirements may or may not be dropped, depending on the configuration of the individual ATM switches.

To avoid losing data, ATM switches use *traffic shaping* to force data into predefined constraints. For example, if an end node sends a greater amount of data than a given connection can support, the receiving ATM switch queues as much of the data as it can and transmits it evenly within the bandwidth constraints.

An alternative to shaping the data is *traffic policing*. With this policy, incoming data that does not conform to the constraints is dropped or marked as low priority. Cells with a low priority may be dropped farther along in the connection should congestion occur.

Signaling

Virtual connections within a PVC are established on ATM networks using *signaling*. In order to establish a connection, a router sends a signaling cell that contains special information—such as QOS parameters—to the destination router.

Every switch along the path examines the signaling cell and determines whether it has the capacity to support the connection. If it does, the switch passes the cell on to the next hop toward the destination. If it does not, the switch returns a notification message to the source and the connection is refused.

If everything goes well, the signaling request reaches the destination. Assuming the destination can also support the QOS parameters specified, it returns an acceptance message to the requester. On the message's return path, each switch notices the acceptance and makes note of the connection, dedicating whatever resources are necessary. After the message reaches the requester, the VPI and VCI are stored for later uses and the connection is established.

Interoperating with LANE

In Chapter 9, "ATM," you learned about ATM LAN Emulation, or *LANE*. LANE provides high-speed networking to the local area network by providing functionality that's inherently missing from ATM: broadcasts, name resolution, and more. By combining an ATM backbone with LANE, features such as videoconferencing and high bandwidth–utilizing applications are brought directly to the desktop. Neither the backbone nor the LAN topology becomes a bottleneck, and Quality of Service can be guaranteed end to end.

Packet Switched Transmission Facilities

Packet switched transmissions differ from the circuit switched transmissions described earlier in this chapter. Packet switched networks route each packet through a network individually, rather than through a preset path of switches as with circuit switched networks. This offers the advantage of greater flexibility, because packets can be routed around failed equipment. However, because the route must be computed for each packet, switching in packet switched networks is substantially slower than switching in circuit switched networks.

X.25

The X.25 protocol defines the interface between a network node such as a router (the data terminal equipment, or DTE) and a packet switched network (the data communications equipment, or DCE). The network is responsible for carrying the traffic to the remote partner, which has a similar configuration. However, the way the network carries that traffic is not part of the X.25 standard!

Each provider determines the most efficient method of carrying traffic between customers. Therefore, the term *X.25 network* is really an oxymoron; a more correct term would be *X.25 connection*. The term was adopted for the entire network because X.25 is the most well-known standard.

The communication begins when one customer of an X.25 packet switched network wants to connect to another. A call is placed, similar to the way calls are placed on standard telephones. If the called system accepts the connection, the two systems begin to transfer data back and forth. After the desired information has been transferred, either party can end the connection in the same way a party on the telephone hangs up the receiver.

History of X.25

X.25 was originally designed by telephone companies and other network providers in 1976 as a reliable method of transporting digital data over analog lines. Because it was designed by several different telephone companies, the specification works well regardless of the type of network that carries the traffic. Since then, it has been constantly evolving, with revisions done every four years.

Pros and Cons of X.25

X.25 is an old standard, and that is both its greatest advantage and disadvantage. On the downside, the maximum speed X.25 supports is 56Kbps. This is rarely sufficient to support modern networking, but the high level of compatibility keeps many customers connected into X.25 clouds. It's also the most global standard; most places in the world have a provider offering a connection. In fact, it's administered by an agency of the United Nations, the ITU-T (International Telecommunications Union).

X.25 is usually far less expensive overall than its most similar peers—Frame Relay and ATM.

Common Uses

X.25 is still used extensively for applications such as automatic credit card systems, teller machines, loan application processing, medical records databases, and inventory monitoring. Recently, X.25 has become adept at carrying IP traffic, using encapsulation in much the same way as ATM and Frame Relay do.

Originally, the most common node attached to an X.25 cloud was a simple text-based terminal. Terminals attach to the network via a translating service called a Packet Assembler/Disassembler (PAD). The PAD provides a connection to the network and translates the text to and from the terminal into packets that the X.25 network's DCE can accept.

Comparison to the OSI Reference Model

The X.25 protocol corresponds to the lowest three layers of the OSI Model: the Physical, Data Link, and Network Layers. Nothing in the standard specifies any higher layers, such as X.25-specific applications.

The Physical Layer

A variety of protocols provide for physical connections between DTEs and DCEs. Some of these protocols are X.21, X.21bis/RS232C, RS449/422 and V.35.

The X.25 Link Layer at the OSI's Data Link Layer

A separate protocol describes X.25's corollary to the Data Link Layer: LAPB. LAPB (Link Access Protocol Balanced) is a reliable, error-checking protocol for transferring frames between the DTE and DCE. The LAPB protocol is responsible for initializing the link between the DTE and DCE as well as for framing the packets before handing them off to the Physical Layer.

The LAPB standard includes special fields for synchronizing the beginning and end of frames. These flags contain a special bit sequence, 01111110 (or 126 in decimal format). The DCEs at each end of the virtual circuit understand that this particular bit sequence never, ever occurs on the incoming line unless it marks the beginning or end of a frame. It's certainly possible that someone might try to transmit this special byte across an X.25 network; when this happens, it's replaced by yet another special character.

The second byte in the frame header is the address, which directs the frame between the DCE and DTE.

The third byte, Control, is used to identify the frame format, whether it's an Information, Supervisory, or Unnumbered frame. It also carries the send/receive sequence numbers.

The byte after the frame's data is the Frame Check Sequence (FCS), a CRC checksum. When a host receives a frame, it first verifies that the checksum is consistent with the data carried within the frame. If the frame fails this test, the receiver transmits a Reject (REJ) packet back to the sender to ask that the frame be retransmitted. If the checksum is validated, a Receiver Ready (RR) or Receiver Not Ready (RNR) is sent, indicating whether more data can be accepted.

This checksum is key to the reliability and inefficiency of X.25. Unlike most protocols, if a packet needs to be retransmitted, it's the responsibility of the *network*. In this way, an X.25 network guarantees 100-percent reliable transfer of data between end nodes. This reflects a very different philosophy from most modern protocols, which instead pass the reject notification directly to the host that originally transmitted the data, making the *host* responsible for resending it. This is a substantial commitment because all data that's sent across the network must be cached by the network hardware until receipt has been confirmed.

LAPB has three separate tasks to perform. The first of these tasks is link setup—initiating a connection across a virtual circuit. The second responsibility is information transfer—the actual sending and receiving of information useful to the end users. After a connection is no longer needed, LAPB performs the disconnection.

The LAPB standard specifies three distinct frame formats, designated by the value in the Control field. Each frame type is useful for carrying a distinct type of data. Information frames carry data that's sequenced and capable of full-duplex transmission. To perform these tasks, it uses a send sequence number and receive sequence number frame. Supervisor frames provide control information, including flow control and acknowledging information frames. Unnumbered frames do not carry sequence information and are used for control purposes, such as starting and stopping a connection.

The Packet Level at the OSI's Network Layer (X.25)

The X.25 packet level actually exists only at the Network Layer, but the name is used to refer to the entire suite of protocols. This layer establishes a connection and provides for call establishment, data transfer, flow control, error recovery, and call clearing. Each packet can be a maximum of 128 data bytes long.

The Network Layer is responsible for managing each virtual circuit and is capable of maintaining as many as 128 simultaneous connections. The fields that make up the Network Layer header are illustrated in Figure 11.3.

FIGURE 11.3
The X.25 packet structure.

1	1	1	1	4	8	3	1	3	1	Variable
Q	D	0	1	Group	Channel	Rec #	M	Send #	0	Data

The first bit, Q, signals qualified data and is intended to be used by the encapsulated protocol to separate control packets from data packets. The second bit, D, is used to flag whether the packet is of local significance and traveling between two DCEs (a value of 0) or of end-to-end significance and traveling between two DTEs (a value of 1). The third and fourth bits are always set to 0 and 1, respectively. Together, these four bits make up the General Format Identifier (GFI) field.

The next two fields are Logical Channel Group Number (LGN) and Logical Channel Number (LCN). Often, these 12 consecutive bits are treated as a single field and referred to as the Logical Channel Identifier (LCI). The LCI identifies a specific connection to the packet switched network. The final byte of the packet header is split into Receive Number and Send Number subfields, which are used for tracking sequence.

One bit of this byte is the M bit, which is used to group blocks of related information that are too large to be placed into a single packet. The M stands for *More*, specifying that the data is split between multiple packets with a value of 1. This bit takes on a 0 value when the packet is the last of a group. You may recognize this process from other networks; it's very similar to packet fragmentation in IP networks.

CCITT Recommendation X.121 defines the exact format of the Network Layer addresses, or International Data Numbers (IDNs). These addresses identify a unique destination on the X.25 network. The first four digits of the IDN are the Data Network Identification Code (DNIC). The first three digits of the DNIC are country specific, and the last digit identifies a specific public switched network. The rest of the address is used to identify a specific node within the network and is called the *National Terminal Number* (NTN).

After the connection has been established, the X.121 address is no longer necessary. Instead, the Logical Channel Identifier (LCI) is used to identify the connection. The LCI is similar to the DLCI in a Frame Relay network because it has only a local significance. X.121 addresses are not needed at all for virtual circuits that have been configured manually; LCIs are used instead to identify a specific circuit.

The Network Layer protocol is responsible for setting up network connections across the X.25 cloud, between remote DTEs. This is in contrast to the Link Layer addressing, which connects a DTE to a DCE.

The X.25 Network Layer connects DTEs end to end; the Link Layer connects DTEs to DCEs.

The individual routers use the services of the X.25 protocol to establish a connection to the remote DTE. The connection is initiated by the transmitting DTE sending a call request packet, which contains the destination DTE's X.121 address, to its DCE. The DCE is responsible for transporting that packet across the X.25 cloud. After the packet reaches the destination, the receiving DCE forwards it to the receiving DTE, which verifies that it's the proper destination and decides whether to participate in a conversation. Assuming it accepts the call, it responds with a call-accept packet and the connection is established.

After the connection is complete, the two participants are ready to send data in either direction. From this point forward, the X.121 address is no longer used. The connection is simply identified to the DCE using the LCN.

Different Types of Networks

In the many years X.25 has been in service, it has been ported to several different network platforms. Each of these different platforms requires a separate Network Layer protocol.

Different networks cannot be mixed on the same physical interface, although many providers support point-to-point connectivity over a Public Data Network.

Public Data Network (PDN)

Defined by RFC 1356, X.25 PDN services provide data connections between customers. These connections are commonly used to transport IP and OSI traffic using protocol encapsulation. In this way, X.25 networks have become useful as WAN links between distant networks rather than just as a simple transport for data terminal traffic.

When a provider carries IP traffic to the Internet, it becomes an Internet service provider (ISP). The available bandwidth on this type of network is too low for heavy-duty file transfers to and from the Internet, but it does allow convenient access to those corporations with an existing X.25 link.

Defense Data Network (DDN)

The DDN is a component of the Defense Communications System and is primarily used for switching government data and connecting distant military locations. MILNET, parts of the Internet, and highly restricted classified government networks make up the collective Defense Data Network. This network is managed by the Defense Information Systems Agency.

Point-to-Point

A point-to-point X.25 connection is essentially a private X.25 network running between two systems. These systems may be connected by anything ranging from a serial cable to a 56K leased line. It may seem odd that someone would choose a packet-switching protocol for a point-to-point connection, but it provides a simple and inexpensive way to expand on existing networks.

X.25 Specifications (RFC 1356)

The actual specifications on which X.25 is based are difficult to read through. To make it even more complicated, the term *X.25*, as it is commonly used, is actually a suite of standards. Fortunately, most network managers rarely have to refer to the actual specifications to connect to X.25 networks. Only hardware manufacturers designing network equipment and software developers creating X.25-compatible software need the level of detail these documents provide.

ITU-T (Formerly CCITT)

The International Telecommunications Union provided the specifications (or *recommendations*, as they call them) for the X.25 protocol suite. They can be found online at http://www.itu.int. Although the full text of recommendations must be purchased, you can still find some useful information. Recommendations of particular interest are Rec.X.25 Version 10/1996 and Rec.X.121 Version 10/1996.

IETF

The Internet Engineering Task Force has released several standards of interest to the X.25 community. Among these are RFC 1356, "Multiprotocol Interconnect on X.25 and ISDN in the Packet Mode," RFC 877, "Transmission of IP Datagrams over Public Data Network," and RFC 1236, "IP to X.121 Address Mapping for DDN." The full texts of RFCs are readily available on the Internet.

Summary

Leased lines are a vital component of today's WANs but are complex and poorly understood. As with any network technology, they have their own Physical Layer technologies and their own Data Link Layer protocols and framing structures. By understanding these aspects of leased lines and their equally complex topologies, one can become more adept at designing, building, operating, and troubleshooting WANs.

Frame Relay and ATM have become two of the most common methods of connecting remote networks. By providing interconnectivity with each other, X.25 networks, and the Internet, these networks allow a great deal of flexibility with each physical connection. Both types of networks allow digital and analog traffic, but ATM was designed specifically for real-time applications such as voice and video.

X.25 is an international standard for low-speed data communications. Although many in the industry consider it an aging, outdated standard, it's still widely used and very popular. It provides reliable, sequenced data transmission to anywhere in the world over standard copper wiring.

Modems and Dial-Up Technologies

This chapter examines the capability of modems to extend the reach of a network. The cables and topologies examined in earlier chapters show you how to connect a network within limited distances. To communicate over longer distances, additional options need to be considered. This chapter examines one of the possible options.

How Modems Work

The word *modem* is a telecommunications term applied to devices that adapt an electronic signal from a business machine into a tone signal that can be transmitted over a communications link. The word itself is a contraction of the words *modulator* and *demodulator*. To *modulate* a signal is to convert it from one state to another. Therefore, the modulator/demodulator device, or *modem*, is a signal converter.

The word *modem* is actually a relatively new word to telecommunications. Originally the devices were known as *data sets*. Before 1977, companies that needed to connect a device to a telephone line had to use equipment provided by the then-monopoly phone companies. Following a ruling from the Federal Communications Commission in 1977, individuals and corporations were permitted to provide their own equipment to connect to telephone lines. To this day, all modems must still comply with this FCC ruling known as Part 68.

A computer cannot simply connect to a telephone line and send signals over it—a computer speaks a digital language consisting of electronic signals or states, whereas a regular telephone line can transmit only analog pulses or sound. The PC itself, being a digital device, talks in a language known as *binary*, which codes information using either an "off" state, represented by a zero, or an "on" state, represented by a one. Digital transmission is always in an exact form of either off or on; there are no in-between states. On the other hand, analog transmission is constantly varying in amplitude (signal strength) and frequency (changes per cycle). See Figure 12.1 for an example of digital and analog signals.

FIGURE 12.1
Digital and analog signals.

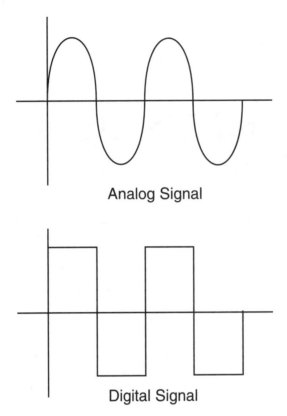

Analog Signal

Digital Signal

For shorter distances, regular network cables are sufficient. However, when a computer needs to speak to another computer over longer distances, some other form of communication media must be used. The most logical and available choice is the standard telephone line. Unfortunately, as was just pointed out, you cannot take a computer that speaks a digital language and have it communicate with another computer at the other end if the communications media being used supports only analog transmission. For the two machines to communicate over telephone lines, a modem must be placed at both ends of the transmission. The computer sending the transmission must have a modem to convert the digital signals it creates into an analog format to be sent over the telephone line. Additionally, the computer on the receiving end of the transmission must have a modem to receive the analog transmission and convert it back into a digital signal that the computer can comprehend. Figure 12.2 illustrates the transmission between two computers using a telephone line.

FIGURE 12.2
Communication over a telephone line.

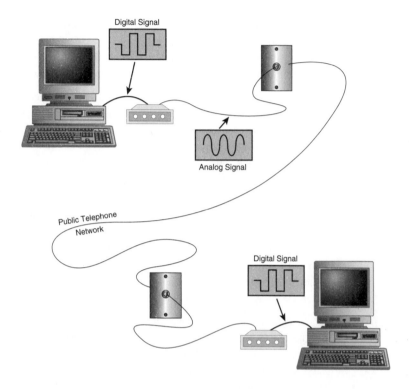

Data communication usually takes place between two devices known as the *DCE* (data communications equipment) and the *DTE* (data terminal equipment). A modem is an example of a DCE. It, in turn, connects to the PC, which is the DTE. The wide variety of equipment available and the diversity of applications on both sides of the DTE/DCE interface dramatize the need for standardizing its mechanical, electrical, and functional characteristics. Some of those standards are examined later in this chapter.

Bits and Bauds

In order for the modem to modulate the digital signal from the computer to one that consists of analog tones to send over the phone line, it has to have some method for varying the amplitude, frequency, and phase of the tones that it sends. The number of times one of these line conditions changes during one second is referred to as the *baud rate*.

The term *baud* is used to represent the unique line conditions that can exist. Each unique line condition is also referred to as a *symbol* in most modern documentation. Each of these symbols is capable of representing a specific bit pattern of information. The bit pattern being represented is commonly referred to as a *token*. The term *baud rate*, itself, was actually coined in honor of the French inventor Emile Baudot, who, in 1875, created a five-bit code to represent the alphabet. Each five-bit pattern is a token representing a particular letter of the alphabet.

Unfortunately, because the public telephone network was designed for voice signals and not data, it has certain limitations that have to be accommodated. Because the majority of the energy created by the human voice falls between 300 and 3,300 hertz (Hz), communications circuits were designed to carry frequencies between 0 and 4,000Hz (or 4KHz).

In the early days of modem transmission, the terms *bits per second* and *baud rate* were thought by most people to be synonymous. However, that was true only because of the way the signal was being sent. When each baud (or change in line condition) in a message represents one bit of information to be sent, then the baud rate equals the bits per second. For example, imagine a message transmitted at 300 baud (300 line condition changes per second). If each change in line condition represents one bit, the message is transmitted at 300 bits per second (bps).

In order to send more than one bit of information per baud, modulation schemes have been developed that allow for higher bps rates. To send data over the telephone circuit, modem designs typically use a carrier frequency somewhere in the middle of the voice band and superimpose the data on that frequency by modulating it appropriately. The output of the modulation process needs to have a spectrum resembling the truncated portion of the entire voice spectrum that fits within the telephone bandwidth.

For example, imagine that you want to send 2,400 symbols per second. To do so, you must be able to create 2,400 cycles per second (Hz). To use 2,400Hz to send the transmission, you must select 1,800Hz as the carrier frequency and modulate it up or down by 1,200Hz to create a range of 2,400Hz. This puts the total bandwidth between 600Hz and 3,000Hz, which fits inside the range of available bandwidth on a typical phone line (0 to 4000Hz). This range is illustrated in Figure 12.3. Interestingly, this is the form of modulation that's used by the V.32 standard discussed later in this chapter in the section "ITU-T (CCITT) Modem Standards."

FIGURE 12.3
A 2,400Hz bandwidth modulated on a 1,200Hz carrier.

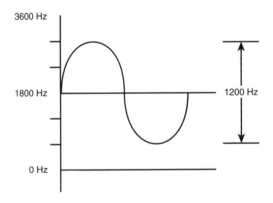

Over time, the quality of the phone network has improved, which has led to more usable bandwidth on a typical phone line. As an additional example, the V.34 standard—discussed later in this chapter in the section "ITU-T (CCITT) Modem Standards"—uses a carrier frequency of 1,959Hz and modulates 3,429 symbols per second, using a total bandwidth from 244Hz to 3674Hz.

For a voice circuit to carry data efficiently, the modulation technique should be designed to tailor the waveform to the characteristics of the channel. This tailoring process gives rise to much ingenuity. The modulation technique must be devised to maximize the quantity of data transmitted and minimize the effects of noise and distortion. A number of internationally recognized methods and transmission rates have established today's data communication standards.

Different modulation schemes enable line conditions to represent different pairings of binary digits. Using a modulation scheme that enables four different frequencies to represent the binary pairings of 00, 01, 10, and 11 actually enables 1,200 bits to be delivered per second, even though the baud rate is only 600. Faster transmission speeds can be achieved by enabling more line conditions (or *symbols*) to represent more bit combinations.

Modem Modulation Types

The process of using a carrier—in this case, the phone line—to carry information between two points is referred to as *modulation*. The analog sound of a human voice constantly varies in frequency and amplitude. If one looks at it on an oscilloscope, the human voice resembles a series of sine waves. Any series of pulses, sounds, waves, or voltages can be represented using a sine wave. The definition of a particular sine wave is characterized by its amplitude, frequency, and phase.

The amplitude of a sine wave is its height relative to a value on the y-axis. The frequency of a sine wave is the position on the x-axis (time) where the wave begins to repeat. The phase of a sine wave is relevant to this discussion only when comparing it with another sine wave of the same frequency and amplitude. A change in the phase of a sine wave occurs when the wave is time-shifted to cross the x-axis at a point that's directly opposed to its normal pattern. Figure 12.4 shows the characteristics of a sine wave.

FIGURE 12.4
Characteristics of a sine wave.

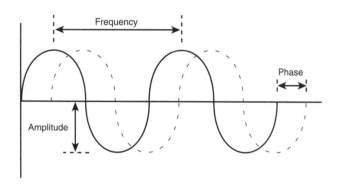

Changing one of the defining characteristics of the sine wave by modulating the carrier is how modems transmit information. Analog modulation can occur in three ways: amplitude modulation, frequency modulation, and phase modulation. Figure 12.5 gives an illustration.

FIGURE 12.5

The three types of analog modulation techniques.

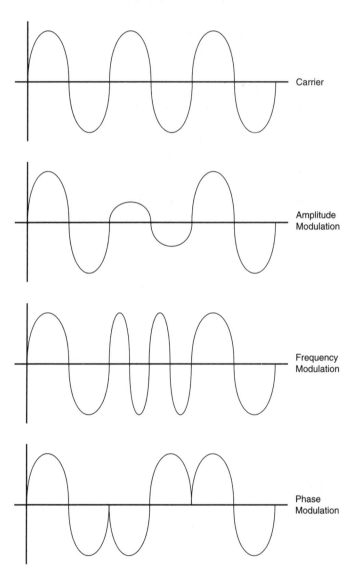

As you can see from Figure 12.5, the first type of analog modulation is *amplitude modulation*. Amplitude modulation varies the strength of the signal to determine whether a zero or a one bit is being transmitted. In Figure 12.5, a signal with a low amplitude represents a zero (or *space*), and a signal that has a high amplitude represents a one (or *mark*).

The second type of analog modulation is *frequency modulation*. Frequency modulation uses a change in the number of times per second the sine wave repeats to indicate a zero or a one. Figure 12.5 shows a sine wave that has a particular frequency being used to represent the zero (space) and a frequency that is twice the original to represent the one (mark).

The last type, *phase modulation*, uses a change in the phase of the wave to indicate a zero or a one. The phase of a sine wave is its position relative to the x-axis. Figure 12.5 shows a sine wave being used to create the zero and a phase shift being used to indicate a one.

Combinations of these three forms of modulation can be used to create more symbol possibilities and, therefore, higher throughput rates. Quadrature Amplitude Modulation (QAM) is just one example of this. In QAM, a combination of phase shifts and amplitude shifts are used to create 16 different states that allow for four bits per baud. If you have a baud rate of 2400, you could effectively send 9,600bps (2400 changes per second X 4 bits per change = 9,600bps).

Another modulation technique is Pulse Amplitude Modulation (PAM). PAM is the method used in the downstream connection for the new 56K modems that don't need an initial analog-to-digital conversion performed on their data streams. These modems still use QAM to send their data back at speeds of up to 33,600bps. For more information on 56K technology, see the standards at the end of this chapter in the section "ITU-T (CCITT) Modem Standards."

Asynchronous and Synchronous

When two devices attempt to communicate with one another, they have to have some way to control the flow of data so that they understand where the characters being sent begin and end. The data stream that's actually sent through the modem to the other end of the connection can be sent using one of two forms of coordination. One way to control the timing of the signals being sent and received at either end is by sending the data *asynchronously*.

Asynchronous communication is the most widespread form used by conventional modems. In asynchronous communication, the information (character, letter, number, or symbol) that's sent from one device to the other is represented as a string of bits. Each string of bits is separated from the other bit strings by a start bit and a stop bit. By using a start bit and a stop bit for each character transmitted, each device knows when it's sending or receiving a character, and no external timing signals have to be present to control the flow of data.

One of the complaints about asynchronous communication is that approximately 20 to 25 percent of the data being sent is used for control information to "synchronize" the conversation between the devices. The alternative to asynchronous communication is *synchronous communication.*

In synchronous communication, a timing signal must be present to control the transmission of blocks of characters, called *frames.* No start and stop bits are used in the transmission. Synchronization characters are used to begin a transmission and to check the accuracy of the transmission. Figure 12.6 offers a comparison of asynchronous and synchronous communication.

FIGURE 12.6

Comparing asynchronous and synchronous communication.

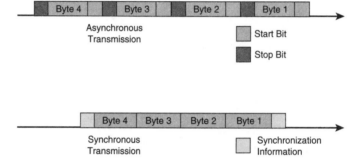

Protocols used in synchronous transmissions perform functions that are not performed by asynchronous protocols. Here are some examples:

- Checking the information sent for accuracy
- Formatting the data into frames
- Adding control information

Synchronous protocols are used in digital environments. The analog world typically uses asynchronous communications. Most network communications are performed synchronously as well. Some common synchronous protocols are Binary Synchronous Communication Protocol (bisynch), Synchronous Data Link Control (SDLC), and High-Level Data Link Control (HDLC).

Standard Modem Interfaces

Although there are numerous "recommended standards," by far the most important one to the world of modem technology is the RS-232 interface. There are several versions of the RS-232 interface, and each one is distinguished by a letter that follows the RS-232 designation. The most common implementation of the RS-232 interface standard is the RS-232C version.

The RS-232 specification is a standard of the EIA (Electronic Industries Association). It's virtually similar to the V.24 standard issued by the ITU-T (International Telecommunication Union–Telecommunications Standardization Sector) formerly known as the CCITT. The RS-232 standard covers four basic areas of information:

- The mechanical characteristics of the interface
- The electrical signals used in the interface
- The function of each signal
- Divisions of the signals for specialized applications

RS-232 and its counterparts provide for serial transmission of data across the interface. In a serial interface, the bits composing the data are transmitted across the interface bit by bit, either synchronously or asynchronously.

Even though the DB-25 connector is commonly associated with the RS-232C interface, it was not defined as part of revision C. The DB-25 connector was actually defined in the D revision of the RS-232 specifications. Each of the pins in the connector has an assigned responsibility, as shown in the following list:

- Pin 1: Protective Ground (Frame Ground)
- Pin 2: Transmit Data
- Pin 3: Receive Data
- Pin 4: Request to Send
- Pin 5: Clear to Send
- Pin 6: Data Set Ready
- Pin 7: Signal Ground
- Pin 8: Data Carrier Detect
- Pin 9: Reserved
- Pin 10: Reserved
- Pin 11: Unassigned
- Pin 12: Secondary Data Carrier Detect
- Pin 13: Secondary Clear to Send
- Pin 14: Secondary Transmit Data
- Pin 15: Transmit Clock
- Pin 16: Secondary Receive Data
- Pin 17: Receive Clock
- Pin 18: Unassigned
- Pin 19: Secondary Request to Send
- Pin 20: Data Terminal Ready

- Pin 21: Signal Quality Detector
- Pin 22: Ring Indicator
- Pin 23: Data Rate Select
- Pin 24: External Clock
- Pin 25: Unassigned

For the transmission of data to take place, the following steps must occur:

- The communications software in the PC places a voltage on pin 20 (DTR) to indicate that the PC is ready to transmit data. At the same time, the modem places a voltage on pin 6 (DSR) to let the PC know that the modem is ready to receive data or instructions.
- The PC sends a command to the modem via pin 2 (TD) to let the modem know to go off hook and dial a specified number. The modem responds to the PC with an acknowledgment on pin 3 (RD).
- After a connection has been established between two modems, the modem sends a signal to the PC on pin 8 (DCD) to let the PC know that a communication path exists and that data transfer can begin.
- When the PC is ready to transmit data, it sends a signal to the modem on pin 4 (RTS), called a *request to send*. Unless the modem is busy, it responds to the PC with a signal on pin 5 (CTS) to let the PC know that it may begin transmission of data on pin 2 (TD).

The principal drawback to the RS-232 interface is the distance limitation of 50 feet. This is typically not a problem for a connection between a PC and a modem, but it can be a concern if the modem has to be placed some distance away from the PC. However, because the normal throughput limitation of an RS-232 interface is considered to be 19,200bps, a shorter cable must be used if you want to achieve the higher throughput rates available with today's modems. Most modem manufacturers recommend an RS-232 cable of 12 feet or less, and a 6-foot cable is very common.

Although RS-232 is the most commonly used choice for a modem connection, a few others bear mentioning here. They are RS-422, RS-423, RS-449, and RS-530.

RS-422 and its counterpart, X.27 (V.11), cover the electrical characteristics of balanced (or differential) circuits (those in which the positive and negative signal lines are isolated from ground). The balanced circuit is less susceptible to noise and offers higher data rates and longer cable runs.

RS-422 is designed for applications that use twisted pair wire at distances up to 4,000 feet and data rates to 100,000bps. A data rate of 10,000,000bps is available at a distance of 40 feet or less. These characteristics make it possible to interconnect equipment within a facility without expensive data sets.

RS-423 and its counterpart, X.26 (V.10), define unbalanced electrical characteristics similar to those of the RS-232 interface. The new standard, however, permits data rates ranging from 100,000bps over 40 feet to 10,000bps over 200 feet of cable. The present unbalanced standard is roughly limited to 20,000bps and 50 feet.

RS-422 and RS-423 define only the electrical characteristics of the interface; a companion standard, RS-449, defines the functional and mechanical requirements for implementation. Although these new standards were intended to replace RS-232, they have not yet done so.

RS-449 and its companion standards differ significantly from the older RS-232 standard. At the interface control level, 10 new functions provide capabilities for testing, speed selection, and standby operation. Perhaps the most significant new functions are the local and remote loopback signals. These permit, to a degree, the diagnosis of equipment and circuit faults by allowing a loop back to the DTE, to the analog side of the local DCE, or to the digital side of the remote DTE.

RS-530 was introduced as a standard to operate at data rates from 20,000bps to 2,000,000bps using the same 25-pin DB-25 connector that RS-232 uses. The major improvement in RS-530 is that it's not an electrical specification but rather refers to two other standards, RS-422 and RS-423. These new standards take advantage of the improved performance now possible with integrated circuit technology.

ITU-T (CCITT) Modem Standards

One of the most basic rules about communication is that in order for communication to take place effectively and efficiently, there must be rules that are adhered to so that the communicating devices understand all the components of the communication process. These rules of order are referred to in the data communications world as *protocols* and *standards*.

There are many different standards in the modem environment, most of which have been standardized by the ITU-T (International Telecommunication Union– Telecommunications Sector). These standards are commonly known as the *V-Series Recommendations*. Here are just a few of the more important V-Series Recommendations:

- *V.22.* The V.22 standard outlines a 1,200bps duplex modem designed for use in the public switched telephone network and on leased line circuits. It's structurally similar to the Bell System 212A standard but is not backward compatible to the 212A's 300bps speed. Also, the 212A uses Frequency Shift Keyed (FSK) modulation at its lower speed of 300bps, and the V.22 uses Phase Shift Keyed (PSK) modulation at its low speed of 600bps.

- *V.22 bis.* The V.22 bis (bis means *second*) standard describes a duplex modem operating at 2,400bps using a frequency division technique standardized for use on the public switched telephone network. It can also be used on a point-to-point two-wire leased line circuit.

- *V.26*. The V.26 standard specifies a 2400bps modem for use on a leased line circuit. It's a full-duplex 1,200 baud modem that uses Dibit Phase Shift Keyed (DSPK) modulation.

- *V.26 bis*. The V.26 bis standard specifies either a 2400bps or a 1200bps modem for use on a nonleased facility.

- *V.26 terbo*. The V.26 terbo (terbo means *third*) standard essentially added an echo cancellation technique to the previous versions of the standard.

- *V.27*. The V.27 standard outlines a 4,800bps modem that uses differential phase shift keying and can operate in half-duplex or full-duplex mode. It also has a manual equalizer adjustment. The modulation technique used identifies eight different phases. It's intended for use on dedicated or leased facilities. The terbo version of V.27 allows for a connection to a nondedicated facility.

- *V.29*. The V.29 standard describes a full-duplex, four-wire, 9600bps modem used on a leased facility. The carrier frequency for a V.29 modem is 1,700Hz, and it has a baud rate of 2,400.

- *V.32*. The V.32 standard outlines a family of two-wire duplex modems that operate at speeds of up to 9,600bps. These modems can also be used on the public switched telephone network as well as on leased line circuits. These modems use QAM (Quadrature Amplitude Modulation) and achieve full-duplex operation due to the echo cancellation technique that's used.

- *V.32 bis*. The V.32 bis standard is very similar to the V.32 standard mentioned previously. The only major difference is in the speed. These modems can communicate at speeds of up to 14,400bps. This is achieved by using six bits per the 2,400 baud rate.

- *V.32 terbo*. The V.32 terbo specification is actually not a standard but something that was proposed and used by AT&T. It allows communication speeds of up to 19,200bps and works between two modems that support it.

- *V.33*. Although the V.33 standard is very similar to the V.32 standard for switched services, V.33 is intended for use on dedicated facilities. The other major difference between V.32 and V.33 is that the V.33 has a multiplexing option that enables it to combine several data sources into a total data stream of 14,400bps.

- *V.34*. The V.34 standard was originally written to specify data signaling rates of up to 28,800bps, but it has been modified since the original standard to include data signaling rates of up to 33,600bps. One of the newer characteristics implemented with the V.34 class is the capability of the modem to continuously monitor the communication channel and raise or lower the negotiated data signaling rate as line conditions change. V.34 is also compatible with the V.42 compression standard, thus allowing for faster throughput on the connection. It's also backward compatible with previous modem standards so that it can negotiate a connection with older, slower modems. V.34 is, like the previous standards, capable of working with a public switched network connection as well as a leased line configuration.

- *V.42*. The V.42 standard is used to define error detection and correction procedures for DCE devices. It actually defines two types of error detection and correction: LAPB and MNP Class 4. Link Access Protocol Balanced (LAPB) is the method used by the Network Layer (Layer 3 of the OSI Model) protocol known as HDLC (High Level Data Link Control). LAPB is the preferred method of error detection and correction under the V.42 standard. MNP Class 4 is actually a secondary method that's available as an alternative.

- *V.42 bis*. The V.42 bis standard is an enhancement to the error detection and correction capabilities of the V.42 standard. V.42 bis provides for data compression by the DCE using the error correction procedures outlined in V.42.

- *V.90 (56K)*. Two competing technologies that enable the user to obtain a 53,000bps downstream transmission and a 33,600bps upstream transmission were merged into the V.90 standard in 1998. Most 56K modems purchased before the V.90 standard was adopted can be upgraded through a software patch to meet the new standard. Even though the technology theoretically allows for a speed of up to 56,000bps downstream, the FCC currently limits that transmission to 53Kbps. The idea behind this new technology is that some of the noise involved in performing an analog-to-digital conversion (called *quantization noise*) can be eliminated in the downstream line if the connection from the upstream modem back to the network is an entirely digital connection. The V.90 standard, then, eliminates the need to perform an analog-to-digital conversion downstream, thus eliminating quantization noise and improving the throughput possibility.

Peter's Principle: Buy Only What You Need

It's very easy to become confused by all of the "V dots" (V.90, V.32, and so on) listed on the modem box. For now, V.90 is what you should look for because it will interoperate with almost all modems sold in the past few years. More important, you should look at the services provided. If you only need to send data back and forth, fax and/or voice support isn't necessary. Therefore, if you don't need them, don't pay for them. The higher price tags (and better markup) on data/fax/voice modems mean that these are the featured items. Dig in your heels and hold out for data only. Why pay for something you won't use?

Modems and Microsoft Networking

Modems can be used in the Microsoft networking environment to extend a network's reach. In order to use a modem to establish a remote network connection, you must first set up the modem. In both Windows 95 and Windows 98, as well as Windows NT 4.0 (and, most likely, Windows 2000), the modem is set up through the Modem applet that's available from the Control Panel. After the modem has been installed and configured appropriately, you can set up the remote network connection properties.

With Windows 95/98, you have to use the Dial-Up Networking applet to connect to a remote network or device. Each connection that's set up under Dial-Up Networking can be configured by modifying the connections' properties. Figure 12.7 shows the Server Types properties for a dial-up networking connection. The dial-up networking connection has several properties that configure the way the connection performs. Each connection may have different requirements for each property tab. In Figure 12.7, the properties have been set to establish a connection with an ISP (Internet service provider). This particular ISP uses a PPP (Point-to-Point Protocol) connection, which works best if none of the advanced options are chosen. Other ISPs require different advanced options to establish a connection. The lower part of the Server Types tab in Figure 12.7 shows the allowed network protocols. Most connections use TCP/IP (Transmission Control Protocol/Internet Protocol) as the only protocol used for a connection. Although a connection may be set up to use any or all of the allowed protocols, choosing only the protocol(s) needed simplifies the connection and any troubleshooting, and it also allows for improved performance.

FIGURE 12.7

Properties for a Windows dial-up server networking connection.

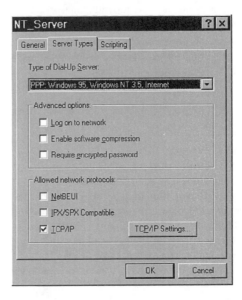

With Windows NT 4.0, you must also configure the Dial-Up Networking applet to connect to a remote system. If the NT system is to be used as a server to which clients connect, the Remote Access Service must be installed and running. Administration of the Remote Access Service (RAS) is handled by the Remote Access Admin tool that's available as one of the Administrative Tools when RAS is installed. With Windows NT Workstation, only one remote user can connect at a time. However, Windows NT Server supports up to 256 simultaneous remote connections. After a user makes a remote connection, the telephone line becomes transparent and users can access all network resources as though they were connected locally to the network.

The Remote Access Service is installed in Windows NT 4.0 by using the Add button on the Services tab in the Network properties window. To add the Remote Access Service to the list of installed services, you need to have a modem installed and configured, and you have to select some setup options, such as the protocols you want to allow dial-in and dial-out callers to use. If you haven't run the Windows NT modem installation, the RAS setup prompts you to do that when the service is installed.

Other options available with RAS include the capability to select whether ports (COM1, COM2, and so forth) are available for use as dial-out ports, dial-in ports, or both. In addition, each protocol that's chosen as an allowed dial-in protocol has a configure option that allows for other configuration changes. Each protocol has a different list of settings, with TCP/IP having the most extensive set of additional options. One other option available with RAS is the capability to require encrypted authentication. If you select to require Microsoft encrypted authentication, you can also use data encryption.

Summary

As modem technology improves, so does the capability to extend the reach of modern networks as well as the speed at which they operate. Already available for the home market, technologies such as cable modems, ADSL (Asymmetric Digital Subscriber Line), and wireless connections will offer new and exciting possibilities for extending networks and connecting with others. To make these new technologies both successful and available, newer and better standards and protocols will need to enforce the regulation of the communication process.

Remote Access Services (RAS)

Time was that the only users you needed to worry about were those physically connected to your network. Then came portable/laptop/notebook/hand-held computers, and the age of mobile computing packed with road warriors and telecommuters was born. This was followed by the success of the World Wide Web on the Internet, which created the need for an internal Web-like presence, called an *intranet*. What's more, clients, customers, suppliers, and vendors needed access to your files and documents. Adding them created what's now called an *extranet*. We're going to lump all these topics together as *Remote Access Services*, because most of this access—whether by employees, vendors, or clients—is remote from your location.

Users today expect to be able to use the same applications and services no matter where they're located at any given time. Business partners also want access to your data because they need it to supply your company, buy from it, or cooperate on projects. Anyone not directly connected to your corporate network is using RAS in one form or another, whether that's a dial-up connection via modem or a secured Internet connection, also called an *extranet* or a *virtual private network* (VPN). This demand for connectivity has placed a tremendous burden on Information Technology (IT) departments. In order to understand why there's such a need for reliable RAS service, this chapter begins by examining the chain of events leading up to modern RAS. It then goes on to examine intranets, extranets, and VPNs, with specific emphasis placed on their functional distinctions, their operational implications and uses, as well as some of their key component technologies.

History of Remote Access Networking

In the late 1950s, computer data centers were mystical places filled with people in white lab coats. These data centers made computer services accessible for the masses, but users of these early data centers were forced to deal with the many rules and requirements put forth by the data center personnel. Many times, these rules would place serious constraints on the users. Inconvenient hours, formatting requirements, and any of a myriad of requirements made all users feel subservient to the data center. Consequently, managers began looking for ways to gain access to the mainframe systems without having to go through the actual data center.

In larger corporations where mainframes were responsible for tracking budgets and inventories, management began to realize the importance of decentralizing this information.

If the executives and middle managers were forced to access this data with large, cumbersome weekly printouts, the data they were using was only as good as the last printout. In many cases, a seven-day lag in information was unacceptable. This led to more printouts, and many managers felt that using these reports on a daily or weekly basis was a waste of time. Something had to happen. Access to the data in these mainframes needed to reach the user level, and it had to reach it fast.

Something monumental did happen: Line drivers and line conditioners became available. These devices allowed the data center to remotely connect terminals to the mainframe computer. The first candidates for these terminals were the managers of the data center themselves. Following that, terminals began to appear all over the workplace. Soon, the information that had been available in only one location within the organization was being put into the hands of the people *needing* the information. Imagine that!

The 1970s

In the early days of "number crunching," it was very rare to find an organization dispersed over a geographical area. For that reason, there was little interest in networking large mainframes together. Corporations, universities, and government agencies were the only major users of mainframe systems, and of the three, the government was the only entity interested in connecting computers that were separated geographically. However, as the U.S. Defense Advanced Research Projects Agency (DARPA) began to perfect the idea of computers communicating with other nonsimilar computers, the private sector began to take notice.

The modem became an extremely important device at this time, and the first modems were really nothing more than acoustic coupling devices that enabled a telephone to interface with a port on a computer system. A user connected to one data center could now gain access to information in other data centers via the network connections that existed between the centers. The modern data network was born.

Computer professionals then began to connect smarter terminal equipment to their mainframe systems. At the same time, terminals started to have built-in memory capabilities. This enabled them to store setup information. That way, when a terminal was used to establish a connection or session with a computer, the common setup commands could be automatically sent between the computer system and the terminal.

This convenience served only to whet the appetite of many mainframe users. The small computer system had arrived on the scene.

Users of data services began to experiment with connecting small computers via modems to their larger cousin—the mainframe. Although the original users of remote access connections were computer scientists and technicians, the concept was proven sound. Now it was possible to pass data back and forth between small computers and large mainframe systems.

The 1980s

The IBM personal computer (PC) was introduced in 1981. Soon, several local area network (LAN) operating systems became available. As small computer LANs became a standard in the workplace, the desire to remotely access these LANs from anywhere via a dial-up connection grew. Modems became cheap and available, and users began to demand quality dial-up connections for their PCs.

Novell, IBM, and Microsoft began to introduce various software packages embedded in their operating systems. These packages were designed to accommodate dial-up service. With emulation programs such as ProComm, PC users could dial in to large computer systems or networks configured with standalone modems or modem pools.

The Advanced Research Projects Agency Network (ARPANET) became the Internet in 1969. Universities and private corporations were soon exploiting it, and in 1984 there were 1,000 mainframe computers connected to each other via the Internet. Between 1987 and 1994, the Internet grew from 10,000 connected hosts to two million connected hosts. Users began to demand Internet access from their homes, and Novell and Microsoft were happy to accommodate them. Remote access in the 1990s has been able to closely duplicate and emulate the LAN services that users have come to depend upon.

The Craze of the 90s

Today, it's not uncommon to see the acronym *RAS* used as frequently as the acronym *PC*. Users are demanding that RAS networking be able to provide the same power of a LAN connection when dialing into servers and network systems. Microsoft has built RAS into its 32-bit operating systems (Windows 95/Windows 98 and Windows NT/Windows 2000), and many third-party software packages now exist. RAS has become one of the most important technologies in the world of computing.

For these reasons, any potentially successful IT professional needs a full understanding of RAS. Many corporations are geographically dispersed, and RAS is the best way employees can maintain constant ties to corporate computing resources. Email, work sharing, and many other applications are RAS-capable these days. RAS has earned its rightful place in the IT community. The next sections discuss what RAS does and the features it provides.

Remote Connection Setup

In order to accommodate a dial-up connection, protocols must be used to standardize the way each end of the connection negotiates the data flowing between the host and the user.

> **Note:** For the purposes of this chapter, the term *host* refers to the server, computer system, or network that the RAS user connects to. The term *user* refers to the computer that the RAS user connects from.

In the early days of dial-up connections, the PCs doing the dialing were meant to emulate directly connected terminal equipment. These dial-up connections were used to enable the PC to look and act the same as a terminal directly connected to the host. As a result, the only software needed in the user's PC was dialing software and a program that simulated the same character signals (that is, ASCII or EBCDIC codes) that a terminal produced.

> **Note:** *ASCII* refers to the American Standard Code for Information Interchange; it's a seven-bit character code. *EBCDIC* refers to Extended Binary Coded Decimal Interchange Code, an 8-bit character code invented by IBM.

These first dial-up systems were effective, but they were also slow. Modem connect speeds were generally less than 1,200bps (bits per second). Some of the earlier connections were acoustic coupling devices in which the telephone receiver was connected to an acoustic coupler resembling two Mickey Mouse ears.

Early Protocol Standards

The only protocols that came into play during these early, point-to-point, user-to-host remote connections were the protocols defining the electromechanical standards between the modems and the telephone lines themselves. In the United States, the Bell Telephone Company established standards defining modem-to-modem connections. Early standards were the Bell 103 and Bell 212A. Later, these were adopted internationally, and the CCITT developed standards V.21 and V.22. These standards define the transmission between two connected modems.

> **Note:** *CCITT* is an acronym for the French title of the International Telecommunications Consultative Committee. The "V" and "X" standards apply to data communications connections. Typically, the V standards are for data connections and modem use over voice and dial-up circuits. The X standards refer to digital/data standards. These standards are occasionally updated or deleted. The CCITT defines standards recommended for use by the entire world. Recently reorganized, the CCITT is now called the *International Telecommunications Union* (ITU).

The AT Command Set

Hayes, Inc. came out with the Hayes Smartmodem and standardized the AT (attention) command set for use with PCs and dial-up modems. This AT command set is still used. Today, the AT command set is incorporated into most terminal-emulation software for the PC. It's this command set that enables a PC to force a modem off hook, to dial, and so on. Remember, though, in the early days users had to manually enter AT commands to force the modem to do something.

This connection limited users to performing only those functions the host system could perform. If the direct-connection terminals in the data centers did not have access to network resources, then typically the dial-up users didn't have access either.

Perhaps the best example of terminal remote access service is the type of networking that was used on computer systems for banks during this period. Banks would network smaller host systems in branch offices with larger mainframe hosts in the parent office. The smaller branch systems were set up to update the larger, central hosts.

Many times, these banks would set up the branch systems to perform an "upward" passage of data to the central host on a real-time basis. This was done on dedicated telephone lines and modems. However, the "downward" flow of data from the central host to the branch systems was done only once a day. Figure 13.1 shows an example. Branches A and B are indeed connected to the central system. However, they're not connected to each other. Data flowing from the branch systems to the central system is constant, but data flowing from the central system to the branches is on a once-a-day basis. Therefore, the data in the branch systems is always from the previous business day.

FIGURE 13.1

A central system with branch connections.

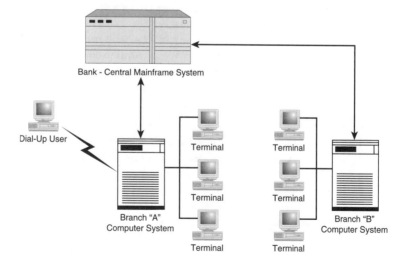

Bank - Central Mainframe System

Dial-Up User

Terminal

Terminal

Terminal

Terminal

Terminal

Terminal

Branch "A" Computer System

Branch "B" Computer System

Basically, all dial-up access came through a branch office. Dial-up access in those days tried to mimic what the terminals connected to the mainframe by direct wiring were capable of doing. The next section examines the upper-level processes that take place when users initiate remote access sessions with host systems.

RAS Connection Protocols

To examine the upper-level processes of remote connections, you need to explore the two most prevalent connection protocols in use today on remote access connections. As an introduction to the discussion of these protocols, a quick summary of the process that occurs when a user-to-host remote access session is established is in order.

Establishing a Session

To initiate a remote connection, one end (usually the user) dials out to the other end (usually the host). Today, the user's PC running some sort of dialing program accomplishes this. Windows 95/98 and NT/2000 have a built-in dial-up networking function. After the modems have negotiated a connection with each other via the telephone line and the carrier is stable between them, digital signals on the output port of the modem pass this information back to the user's PC.

> **Note:** *Carrier* refers to the *pilot* (or main analog signal) that a modem transmits to another modem over a communications link when a data communications connection is established between the two devices.

Second, the user invokes the software program he is using to communicate with the host system. This may be some terminal emulation package such as ProComm, or it may be a built-in dialing program. Again, Win32 has built-in negotiation software in its dial-up networking function. Whatever the user needs to do in order to negotiate upper-level processes in the host is done at this time. For example, perhaps the user invokes some unique program written exclusively for a particular corporation.

TCP/IP Access Protocols

Most people who are involved with remote access connections are connecting to the Internet or a company intranet. For this reason, Transport Control Protocol/Internet Protocol (TCP/IP) is the protocol suite used to pass data back and forth over the connection. Today, when TCP/IP is being used as the main transport protocol suite, either SLIP or PPP (see the next two sections) will be used as the main access protocol for dial-up sessions between a PC and a RAS server.

SLIP

The main carrying mechanism that moves data in the TCP/IP world is the *IP packet*. Without going into a lengthy discussion of IP and IP addressing, you should note that IP is the connectionless Internet protocol that moves TCP and User Datagram Protocol (UDP) packets from one place to another. TCP and UDP packets carry the data the user has sent. In other words, consider IP as the carrier and the TCP or UDP packet as the item being carried.

Any dial-up connection that could carry IP packets needed to be configured to transmit all the characters in the IP packet. Therefore, 3COM developed a new protocol called the *Serial Line Internet Protocol* (SLIP). SLIP has never become a standard Internet protocol. All SLIP does is "frame" an IP packet and send it through from one end to the other. This protocol provides no addressing, packet type identification, error control, or compression. However, this lack of capabilities also means SLIP is very easy to implement.

Rick Adams implemented SLIP for Berkeley UNIX in 1984, and released it into the public domain. Remote access for Internet services became commonplace.

To this day, many PC connection programs designed for Internet connectivity have a SLIP option. The fact that there's no standard SLIP specification means there's no maximum defined packet size. Many forms of SLIP came into being in the late 1980s, but SLIP provides only a frame for carrying IP packets over serial lines. Remember, the user's PC still has to communicate with its modem using AT commands. The modem still has to dial out and establish a connection with the host computer's modem. Today, ITU standards are responsible for maintaining modem-to-modem connectivity.

SLIP comes into play only after a stable connection has been made between the modems, and the user and host system have established connectivity. After this occurs, the SLIP protocol enables the passage of IP packets over this serial user-to-host connection. Remember this: SLIP passes no address information. This means that each computer (host and user) must know the other's address in order for packets to pass back and forth effectively. This is always a function of whatever type of SLIP software/dialer you're using in the user PC and the SLIP software in the host system.

SLIP has many limitations, and users demand error-free connections when dialing into host systems. The fact that SLIP could not perform any compression, addressing, or error checking made users demand a better connection protocol. This gave way to the birth of PPP.

PPP

The Point-to-Point Protocol (PPP) is another design that grew out of user demand. This protocol is designed primarily to provide a link between two peers on serial ports. Typically, the use of PPP is limited to dial-up user-to-host connections. However, some people use PPP in host-to-host or host-to-router connections. This chapter examines PPP as it's used in remote access, dial-up connections.

PPP has been standardized as a true Internet protocol. SLIP never earned that distinction. Many users still swear by SLIP, but the error rate can be astronomical at times. If you want a remote access connection that operates properly when passing IP packets, PPP is the protocol of choice.

Like SLIP, PPP also packages the IP packets within its frame, but other actions are occurring in addition to framing the data. PPP also sets up a session of link control between the user and host, and this session is controlled by the Link Control Protocol (LCP). LCP then sets up the link between the user and the host on a PPP session.

This is actually the first thing that happens when a PPP session begins. LCP packets are transmitted between the user and the host. These packets actually configure and test the link that's established. Issues such as link quality and link echo are tested to ensure the link is stable. Here are the three classes of LCP packets:

- *Link Establishment packets.* Used to establish and configure a link
- *Link Termination packets.* Used to terminate a link
- *Link Maintenance packets.* Used to manage and debug a link

LCP ensures that the link is running and stable and then passes this information to the main PPP protocol to declare the link up. After this has happened, PPP sends out what is called a *Network Control Protocol packet* (or *NCP packet*). The NCP packet is specific to the type of data to be passed over the PPP link.

An NCP packet is sent by the originator of the PPP connection (in most cases, the user who dialed the host). This NCP packet tells the host what type of traffic is to be passed over the PPP link. The name of the PPP Network Control Protocol (NCP) for IP datagrams is called *IP Control Protocol* (IPCP) and is responsible for configuring, enabling, and disabling IP functionality at both ends of the link. IPCP packets may not be sent until LCP has finished the configuration negotiation phase. After that phase is complete, the IPCP protocol will signal that it's ready to begin forwarding IP packets and datagrams.

After this happens, the user and the host are capable of transmitting and receiving IP datagrams and packets. As discussed previously, IP is the mainstay of the Internet today in terms of the carrying mechanism. For that reason, it makes no sense to discuss other NCPs that PPP may use to transfer data. However, many other NCP protocols are incorporated into some versions of PPP.

Current Trends

SLIP and PPP are definitely the workhorses of remote access sessions these days. It's rare to see users of remote access services using anything other than these two protocols when passing data between themselves and a host system. For setting up RAS servers in Windows NT, the PPP protocol is used in 99 percent of the implementations today. However, you also need to understand the services RAS servers are required to provide after a PPP connection has been established.

Remote Access Transport Services

In the world of RAS, users are interested in being able to connect to a host system, using that host system for whatever purpose they need, and then disconnecting the RAS connection. It would be impossible in a chapter this size to go into all the different services a user may use on a remote connection. Instead, this chapter reviews today's most-used services.

How RAS Users Are Currently Connecting

Most large organizations, many mid-sized ones, and quite a few small businesses have established corporate intranets. Users of a corporate intranet are generally using PCs located in their work areas. However, if they're active telecommuters, on-the-road workers, or work-at-home types, they may take a laptop PC from place to place.

In order for these people to be productive when using remote access connections, these connections must provide identical services to the users' PCs in all locations. Whether he's sitting at the desk in his corporate office using a direct LAN connection or dialing in from a hotel, what a user sees on the PC screen must be the same at all times. After allowing for exceptions, this should be the goal of any RAS arrangements being implemented on a corporate intranet.

Some users may be used to dialing into a computer at their central headquarters on a regular basis. If so, dialing in from home or a place of employment should be the same. Many corporations have one central dial-up host that serves the entire corporation. Other users are many times dialing into an Internet Service Provider (ISP) and simply using the ISP's email capabilities to pass mail to people in other organizations.

Given any situation, you can make several assumptions about most RAS connections:

- Most RAS connections are established for users to gain access to a LAN, a corporate intranet, or the Internet.
- After the connection is made, PPP is the protocol most often used to handle the passage of data through the connection.
- The main data transport service that will be used on this connection is TCP/IP in most cases.

Every rule has exceptions, and these statements can be challenged. However, in most cases, these statements hold true. The next section discusses what TCP/IP can do for its remote users.

TCP/IP: The RAS Workhorse

No discussion of RAS would be complete without a discussion of TCP/IP. TCP/IP is one of the most misused terms in the world of computing and telecommunications. TCP/IP is actually two things. First, it's a combination protocol. This combination protocol was formed when the Transport Control Protocol (TCP) was combined with the Internet Protocol (IP). Second, TCP/IP forms the basis of a suite of other protocols used on the Internet and in corporate intranets.

A discussion of these other protocols is not within the scope of this chapter (see Chapter 4, "The Network and Transport Layers," for an in-depth discussion); however, the more common protocols, such as Telnet, File Transfer Protocol (FTP), and Simple Mail Transfer Protocol (SMTP), are all part of this TCP/IP suite. The Internet was the proving ground for these protocols, and long before the Open Systems Interconnect (OSI) Reference Model was put together, TCP/IP was an entirely open system (see Chapter 1, "A Networking Primer"). *Open* simply means that any system claiming to be TCP/IP compliant can communicate with any other system claiming to be fully TCP/IP compliant.

When TCP/IP is fully implemented in RAS user-to-host connections, all the wonderful "toys" users are addicted to on their office LANs can also be used on their remote PCs. Web browsers such as Netscape and Internet Explorer, email programs such as Eudora, FTP programs such as WS-FTP, and others can all be implemented in the remote users' PCs.

TCP/IP has limitations, but it's still the number-one protocol used today to move data around. The future may change the way an IP packet looks, as the entire networking industry is looking to implement IPv6 addressing on all the Internet hosts, using a 128-bit versus 32-bit addressing scheme (see Chapter 4, "The Network and Transport Layers").

As far as RAS is concerned, TCP/IP is currently the number-one workhorse, being implemented in all RAS connections. After the RAS connection has been established, TCP/IP is then implemented and activated by peer processes in the user and host computer systems. For this reason, the user system is assigned an IP address. This IP address is what's used to properly address and control the flow of data from user to host and from host to user.

Assigning IP Addresses

Any corporate LAN or intranet using TCP/IP as its means to address systems on the network also assigns IP addresses to RAS users and RAS connections. These IP addresses are either *static* (that is, never changing) or *dynamic,* which means that the network assigns a different IP address every time the RAS connection is made. Typically, this is done by the host system using a protocol known as *Dynamic Host Configuration Protocol* (DHCP). This protocol is implemented in a DHCP server (host system), and it assigns and keeps track of the IP addresses that are handed out on RAS connections. DHCP can also be used on LANs to hand out IP addresses when LAN users log on to their PCs.

After the RAS Connection Is Established

To establish a RAS connection, the user's PC (using a modem) dials the host system. The host system answers the call, establishes the connection, and upper processes in the host cooperate with upper processes in the user system to get the transport system running. With TCP/IP, the host either reads the IP address of the user system (if it's static) or assigns an IP address (in other words, dynamic IP is being used). Either one of these actions gets TCP/IP up and running.

After this has happened (that is, true TCP/IP connectivity is established between the user and the host), the user is now free to start the applications to be used over the RAS connection. These applications can now be used to give the user full access to the same services on the office PC.

Most users and hosts initiate TCP/IP as the main transport service on a connection. However, many people out there in smaller enterprises are still using the NetBEUI protocol as well as IPX/SPX. These purely local area networking protocols are discussed in depth in Chapter 4, "The Network and Transport Layers," but we'll briefly look at why neither is today's protocol of choice for remote access.

NetBEUI is not the protocol of choice for several reasons:

- NetBEUI is not a routable protocol like TCP/IP. NetBEUI signals have no real means to travel outside the confines of a LAN. In some cases, Token Ring source routing has been used to route NetBEUI from a Token Ring LAN, but this method is neither efficient nor effective. NetBEUI is optimized for the LAN environment only.

- NetBEUI does not support the routing of messages to other networks, and its interface must be adapted to other protocols such as IPX and TCP/IP. If you feel you *must* use NetBEUI, the best method is to install both NetBEUI and TCP/IP in each PC on the LAN. Then you can set the server up to use NetBEUI for communication within the LAN and TCP/IP for communication beyond the LAN. This provides the best way to ensure that NetBEUI causes minimal problems. On a large LAN, TCP/IP is all you need; NetBEUI just slows things down.

- NetBEUI is a very chatty protocol. A lot of information is passed back and forth on computers that use NetBEUI as a data-transfer mechanism. This continual passing of information causes NetBEUI to hog a lot of space on the LAN when it's being used. The originating system sends out a broadcast packet to determine where the other computer is. Each computer on the LAN must examine this packet. On a large LAN, this amounts to constant packet examination by all the PCs on the LAN.

Some LANs still use NetBEUI. RAS users dialing into these LANs need to use a program in their PCs that's capable of performing NetBEUI connectivity over the dial-up connection. Win32 systems provide this capability in its dial-up networking program. However, the bottom line is that you don't really want to use NetBEUI unless you have to.

One thing makes Novell's IPX/SPX combination a winner: It can be routed. It also performs error checking and allows internetworking of LANs. Because IPX is always dynamically routed and the routing architecture works by learning network addressing automatically, nothing special needs to be done in the setup of an IPX network to get routing to function. IPX/SPX networking has several drawbacks, however:

- It's more limited in terms of how many addresses are available. It consists of a four-byte network number, a six-byte node number, and a two-byte socket number. The node number is the hardware address of the actual user's PC network interface card (NIC). This number must be unique inside the particular IPX network. The network number must be the same for all nodes on a physical network segment. Socket numbers correspond to the particular service being accessed.

- IPX/SPX connections require the capability to broadcast to other NetWare servers and IPX routers on the network. That's how they can all find one another on Novell networks. Because there's no effective way to broadcast using IP, all the servers and routers on the network need to maintain a list of the IP addresses of the other IPX servers and routers on the network, which can be a limiting factor.

Today, RAS users of Novell networks (up through version 4.x) are able to utilize certain TCP/IP transport mechanisms by *tunneling* IPX over TCP/IP. Tunneling is done by using UDP, another member of the TCP/IP suite. Novell networks can be set up to take IPX packets and place them inside UDP packets. These UDP packets are then packaged inside an IP packet the very same way TCP packets are packaged in a larger IP packet. After this has occurred, the IPX data is transmitted over the network in these IP packets. With NetWare 5, Novell has implemented full IP connectivity as a replacement for IPX/SPX.

In summation, RAS users are generally on TCP/IP connections when dialing into the host; however, there may be times when NetBEUI or IPX/SPX can be used. Therefore, it behooves you to know and understand these other two transport protocols.

PPTP

The Point-to-Point Tunneling Protocol (PPTP) is gaining a lot of attention lately because it enables RAS users to connect to a host system that may be far away on the other end of a TCP/IP network. In other words, a RAS user can dial into one host system, and this host system can then transfer the RAS user's data to another host system very far away on the same TCP/IP. Now you're probably wondering why this seems different from a RAS user simply dialing into a host that's connected to the Internet. After all, after he has done this, that connection provides access to all the resources on the Internet. However, when a corporation wants to maintain a private network and it's not large enough to financially afford the costs of a large intranet, PPTP can help build an "intranet on the Internet."

That's the real utility of PPTP. It enables corporations to set up *virtual private networks* (VPNs) via the Internet. PPTP comes prepackaged with Windows NT/2000, and can be added onto Windows 95/98. RAS users can use the PPTP protocol to securely connect to a private network as a remote access client via the Internet. In other words, PPTP enables users to set up and take down on-demand, virtual private networks over the Internet.

PPTP has been successful because a PPTP forum was developed. The companies of the PPTP forum, which include Microsoft, Ascend Communications, 3Com/Primary Access, ECI Telematics, and US Robotics, are all working together to ensure the future of PPTP. Figure 13.2 shows how PPTP sets up these VPNs over the Internet.

FIGURE 13.2
PPTP and VPN networks.

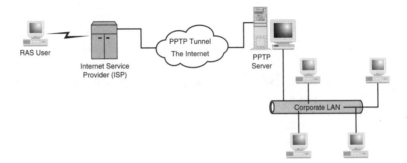

The process starts when the RAS user connects to a local ISP with a modem. This connection uses the PPP protocol to establish the connection and encrypt data packets. After a connection to the Internet established by the PPP protocol has been established, the PPTP protocol steps in and creates a control connection from the RAS user to the distant PPTP server on the Internet. This is a TCP/IP connection over the Internet, but because it was established by PPTP, it's called the PPTP *tunnel*.

Finally, the PPTP protocol creates IP datagrams containing encrypted PPP packets that are then sent through the PPTP tunnel to the PPTP server. The PPTP server disassembles the IP datagrams, decrypts the PPP packets, and then routes the decrypted packets to the VPN, which is typically a LAN on the other side of the PPTP server. In this way, PPTP creates a private network connection over the Internet. It's gaining a lot of attention these days, and ISPs are anxious to work with their clients to provide dial-up PPTP for travelling, hotel-bound, or telecommuting workers.

This means that small companies can have an intranet-like private network that runs over the Internet. In this situation, the costs to establish a wide area network (WAN) using PPTP can be a lot cheaper than having to actually purchase and install dial-up host systems all over the country. The dial-up access is provided by an ISP. When you look at the cost of leased lines to connect hosts together, the amount can be staggering. However, the cheap, flat-rate pricing that most ISPs can offer makes it a common-sense choice to use PPTP to create a private network.

Network Operating Systems and RAS Capabilities

All three major local area networking operating systems—NetWare, Windows NT/Windows 2000, and Banyan Vines—support RAS in very similar ways. Although the discussion that follows focuses on Windows NT/2000 (which we'll call "NT" for simplicity's sake) , the same scenarios will work for all three networking systems.

To begin, we'll examine the two most common implementations of Windows NT RAS:

- As an Internet gateway/router for a LAN
- As an Internet access provider for dial-in users

Using RAS As an Internet Gateway/Router for a LAN

In order to act as a router or a gateway, an NT server must have two separate networks connected to it.

An NT server can sit between two separate networks, such as a LAN and the Internet. Within the NT server are two separate network interfaces. For this discussion, assume one of these interfaces is a modem. In almost all cases in which NT is configured to perform Internet gateway routing via RAS, the other network interface is a standard Token Ring or Ethernet network interface card (NIC). Figure 13.3 illustrates this point.

In Figure 13.3, Network A is an Ethernet LAN connected to the NT server's NIC card, and Network B is simply a modem for connectivity to the Internet. This arrangement enables the users connected to the LAN to have access to the Internet through the NT RAS server. NT basically routes information between these two separate networks based on the IP address and subnet mask information.

As an example, assume that the IP address assigned to the Ethernet NIC in Figure 13.3 (Network A) is 234.56.78.90, with a subnet mask of 255.255.255.0. This means the NT server will assume any IP address between 234.56.78.1 and 234.56.78.254 resides on Network A. Any other IP address the NT server encounters is assumed to be out on the Internet (Network B) side of the server.

On the other side of the NT server, a modem connects to the Internet (Network B). The NT server has an account on an ISP, and the ISP assigns the block of IP addresses from 234.56.78.1 through 234.56.78.254 to this NT server.

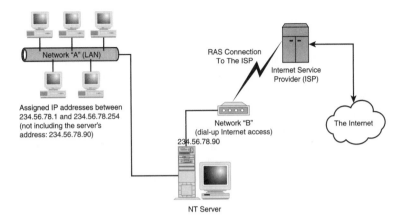

FIGURE 13.3

RAS as a gateway/router for a LAN.

If a user on the Internet sends data destined for IP address 234.56.78.50, this information is routed to the ISP via the Internet. After the ISP gets the data, it initiates a call by dialing the telephone number of the modem on the NT server. The server's modem answers the ISP's modem and establishes a PPP connection. Now the data destined to the NT server passes through the PPP connection to the NT server. The NT server, in turn, looks at the IP address being sent to it.

Because that address is one of the addresses the server knows is on the Ethernet LAN attached to its NIC card, it sends this data destined for 234.56.78.50 out on the LAN. This data then flows to a PC assigned this address. That's how Internet data reaches the user on the LAN via the RAS gateway. Now consider the way information from the LAN destined for the Internet gets through the NT RAS server and out to the Internet.

Whenever users on the LAN send information to each other via TCP/IP, they, of course, use their assigned addresses. Because all the addresses assigned in the example are between 234.56.78.1 and 234.56.78.254, you can have 254 users on the LAN constantly sending information to each other. This includes the NT server, because it has address 234.56.78.90 in this example.

You may be wondering how the NT server knows LAN traffic is passed among users on the LAN and does not need to pass through the server and go out to the Internet. If you recall, the subnet mask programmed into the NT RAS server for Network A is 255.255.255.0. This is the magic that's making the gateway function work. Because it has a subnet of 255.255.255.0, the server looks at each IP packet transmitted on Network A, the LAN segment. As long as the first three octets of a packet begin with 234.56.78, the server assumes this data belongs on the LAN and not the Internet. The subnet mask tells the story.

This is how subnet masking works. A mask of 255.255.255.0 is telling the server to review the first three octets. If the subnet mask is 255.255.0.0, the server reviews the first two octets, and if the subnet mask is 255.0.0.0, the server reviews the first IP address octet only.

When the appropriate number of subnet bits match the same number of the IP address physically assigned to the server, the server reviews the remaining bits and ensures it's not 90. If it is 90, the server assumes the data in this IP packet is addressed to itself, and in this example, it is.

Now, imagine that one of the users on the LAN sends out IP packets destined for IP address 236.45.11.2 and the data is destined for the Internet. The NT server looks at the address. Because the first three octets are not 234.56.78, the server knows this data is destined for a system out on the Internet. It passes that data out through the RAS setup, the modem dials the ISP's modem, and this establishes a PPP connection to send the data along its way.

We've just perfected an Internet/LAN gateway in both directions! This is probably the most common RAS setup utilized in NT servers hosting small LANs of between 5 and 75 users who want Internet access at an affordable rate. Most ISPs happily assist their users in setting this up. Your ISP can assign the IP addresses and subnet mask for your LAN based on your needs, your number of users, and the addresses it has available.

Using RAS to Provide Internet Access for Dial-in Users

If you want to look at the other side of the RAS coin, you need to understand how RAS implemented on an NT server can provide Internet access for a corporation's employees, as shown in Figure 13.4.

FIGURE 13.4
Using RAS to provide Internet access.

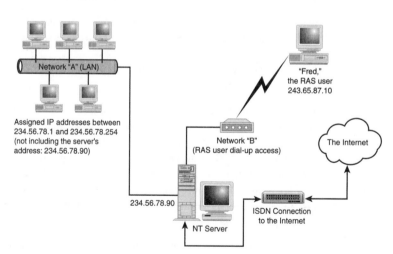

In Figure 13.4, Network A is a NIC connection, as in the previous example. However, in this example, the NT RAS server is also tied to the Internet via an Integrated Services Digital Network (ISDN) connection.

Network B has the same setup as before. However, this NT RAS server is now a dial-in Internet access point for RAS users as well as an Internet gateway for the LAN users in Network A. The sequence of events that provide Internet access for a LAN user is pretty much the same as it was before, except this time, the RAS setup in the NT server is enabled for dial-in access only. Because this is the case, any IP packets addressed to an address other than one on the LAN are sent via the ISDN connection to the Internet.

If a dial-in user wants Internet access, the sequence of events is as follows. First, a user (Fred, in this example) dials into the modem (Network B). When a PPP connection is set up between Fred's PC and the NT RAS server, TCP/IP begins to flow across this PPP connection. Fred then sends out data destined for the Internet.

Assume for the purposes of this discussion that the IP addresses are the same as those used before. If you recall, the NIC in the server was assigned IP address 234.56.78.90, and the subnet mask being used on the LAN segment (Network A) was 255.255.255.0. Assume also that all the remote dial-in RAS users are assigned static IP addresses. (A static IP address is an address permanently assigned to a user.)

In this example, you can use the address 243.65.87.10 to dial up Fred. Now, when Fred gets the TCP/IP flowing between his PC and the NT server, the NT server recognizes that Fred's address does not belong on the LAN. After all, it's not between 234.56.78.1 and 234.56.78.254, and it doesn't match up with anything else on the server. The server knows 243.65.87.10 is assigned to Fred. Anything Fred sends out not addressed to himself that does not fit between 234.56.78.1 and 234.56.78.254 is sent out to the Internet via the ISDN connection.

As mentioned earlier, the RAS is set up for dial-in access only, which is easily accomplished in NT RAS setup options. However, this does not mean that bidirectional IP traffic doesn't flow over the PPP link. It simply means the NT server knows incoming requests are to be handled by the RAS modem only, and this also means that Internet traffic coming to and from the LAN traverses the Internet ISDN link.

Likewise, after a remote RAS user has dialed into the server and established a TCP/IP connection, any Internet traffic coming to and from the RAS user traverses the Internet ISDN link. If Fred starts transmitting data destined for 166.34.27.128, the NT server knows that address is not on the LAN (Network A). The server also recognizes it as not being destined for the server's NIC card or for Fred. Consequently, data goes out the ISDN connection to the Internet.

In summation, two major RAS setups are being used today:

- NT RAS can provide routing/gateway service to the Internet for a small, connected LAN.
- NT RAS can provide an excellent gateway to the Internet for dial-in RAS users while still providing the same gateway services for a connected LAN.

RAS Security Issues

Security is always a concern on any network, and RAS setups are just as susceptible to security problems. However, the security issues for RAS are really no different than they are for any other network configuration, with a few exceptions. For a complete discussion of security, see Chapter 17, "Protecting the Network," where we'll talk about some precautions administrators should take with RAS specifically in mind.

Because Windows NT is the main operating system being used for RAS access, we'll discuss security issues in NT terms, but the principles apply to all operating systems.

No system is ever secure, and as soon as you place a modem on your network, you always open a door to would-be bad guys (sometimes wrongly called *hackers*). For example, recall the previous discussion about banks. They used to pass data from their central computers to their branch computers once a day. This practice was an early form of security. Any infiltrator who could get into a branch computer system could not use that access to get to the central computer in terms of adding money to an account. It also eliminated pulling money down to the branch office.

Three forms of security are used on RAS connections:

- Passwords
- Dialers
- Callback systems

Passwords

Anyone setting up a RAS system should set up user login IDs and passwords for the users who connect to the server. In NT, Novell NetWare Connect, Banyan Intranet Connect, and any other remote package, passwords are a standard option.

You must educate users not to use their names, Social Security numbers, and so on as their passwords, because these are easily detectable. They're the first passwords an infiltrator tries to use. Password use and administration are common sense. Passwords are the first line of defense on most RAS servers.

Dialers

Dialers provide another wall of defense following passwords. Most dialers function by requiring a secret code number to be transmitted to the server by the user of the RAS services. When the user dials into the RAS server, it's configured to ask for a certain code number. This code number may be randomly generated by the dialer or put into the dialer each time the user uses the system to make a RAS connection.

Dialers, code dialers, and code-generating dialers are very popular with large corporations. If a corporation has a large, almost unmanageable amount of people using its RAS services, a dialer can provide an excellent way to ensure that security is maintained. Weekly code updates can be distributed only to valid employees. In this manner, a former employee or infiltrator is thwarted when trying to log onto the network.

Callback Systems

These systems date back to the 1960s. In those days, infiltrators weren't as computer savvy. Therefore, security consisted of adding a simple callback system. When an authorized user entered his login ID and password, the system would hang up and dial a predetermined number to call this user back, thereby ensuring that he was at the appropriate physical station. This worked fairly well until criminals learned how to tap the lines coming out of the computer system. By doing this, they could answer the callback.

Today, callback is used very rarely in private industry, but when used, it's usually combined with some sort of code-generating software. This ensures that the person being called back is not an infiltrator who tapped into the computer system's telephone lines. This type of security is not a standard part of NT's RAS software, and any callback service implemented has to be done with a callback software application. However, if done correctly, callback can be one of the strongest ways to keep bad guys out of your system. For that reason, the U.S. government and many security agencies have implemented personalized callback systems that are virtually foolproof in most cases. Many private industry organizations are actually reconsidering the virtues of callback systems, because they can be made almost airtight when combined with code-generation software.

Intranets and the Internet

Initially, intranets weren't really intranets. They were amalgamations of leased lines and routers that companies used to forward packets of data for their users and traditional business application types. The predominant internetworking protocol used in these private leased-line networks was the Internet Protocol (IP). The commercialization of the Internet and the proliferation of hypertext led to the evolution of private IP networks into intranets. Many companies unwittingly began this evolution when they interconnected their private IP wide area networks (WANs) to the Internet. Ostensibly, this was done to provide access to the rich and vast data stores of the Internet, but this was just the first step in a fundamental change in the way they would use IP WANs in the future.

After the interconnection with the Internet was established, the evolution from IP WAN to intranet became inevitable. Companies immediately began to look for ways to turn the cost of the interconnection into a source of revenue, rather than strictly an added expense. This meant exploring the technologies needed to build, maintain, and support a presence on the Internet.

Users, too, began exploring the new world. Browsers were free (if you didn't mind downloading a new evaluation copy every 30 days!), and the Net beckoned. These adventurous users quickly tired of surfing. They began experimenting with creating their own individual and/or organizational home pages. The net effect was a somewhat *ad hoc* acceptance of the tools and technologies that would transform internal IP WANs into intranets. The actual transformation would have to wait until companies figured out what they could do (besides play) with these new technologies.

What's So Special About the Web?

The key enabling technology that made the Internet's content available to the masses, both individuals and companies, was the hyperconnectivity of the World Wide Web (WWW or Web). The Web is, arguably, the first successful *universal* middleware. Its combination of protocols, programming language, and universal client-presentation mechanism enables its executable programs, known as *content*, to run on almost any physical platform. This is possible because Web programs use a software-based runtime environment: the browser.

> **Note:** *Middleware* is any software that performs a translation, conversion, or other intermediary function. As such, the term can be applied to an incredibly wide variety of software products. The benefit of having an intermediary is that it provides a consistent application programming interface (API), independent of physical platforms.

The Hypertext Transfer Protocol (visible as the browser's HTTP command) was developed by CERN, a Swiss particle physics laboratory, to facilitate research on the Internet. This protocol put the Internet's content a mouse-click away. Hiding content location behind a point-and-click graphical user interface (GUI) made obsolete much of the older, more painful means of finding and retrieving Internet files, such as the File Transfer Protocol (FTP) of the IP protocol suite. FTP is still useful, and very much needed; it just isn't used as a primary Internet information-retrieval mechanism.

What About Intranets?

The success of the Internet and its World Wide Web accelerated the evolution of IP WANs to intranets. This was facilitated by the continuous development of Web-based software tools that were expressly designed for corporate environments. Software manufacturers realized that the real money to be made in Internet and Web technologies would come from companies, not individual users. Consequently, they targeted this market aggressively and developed everything from graphical user interface tools for the creation and management of sites and their content to new programming languages specifically designed for private, corporate Web environments.

Database companies, too, provided APIs for their products, as well as middleware that would enable users to extract data from their databases using a browser. The result of these investments in intranet technologies was the rapid success of almost anything Web related. Internal IP WANs became intranets when they embraced the WWW middleware and began using it broadly in support of their business processes. To be sure, early adopters limited their efforts to posting pictures of their families, pets, houses, cars, and so forth on the Web, but these insipid efforts were a necessary part of learning the capabilities of the new Web technologies.

Today, the browser is well on its way to becoming the universal presentation layer for all interactive applications. Even traditional, interactive applications are poised to become enveloped by intranets. Some of the more obvious examples include the replacement of conversant telephony systems and paper forms with Web-based systems. The possible uses for an intranet are limited only by one's imagination and budget.

The Key Differences Between the Internet and Intranets

Although they may appear technologically and functionally similar, intranets and the Internet must remain quite separate and distinct. The Internet is intentionally not secured. It's designed to be accessible by the general public, as well as by members of companies, educational facilities, government and/or research organizations, and so forth.

Intranets cannot afford such unrestricted accessibility. Access to networked resources must be parsed out on a need-to-have basis, even among the employees of the company. If such restrictions are essential to maintaining the integrity of the data, the implications of using IP to interconnect that carefully controlled network environment to the wild and (relatively) unregulated Internet are staggering.

The information assets of private IP WANs that are interconnected to the Internet must be protected from access by the general public. Typically, mechanisms such as firewalls (see the section "Firewalls Are No Panaceas," later in this chapter), access lists, host and application layer security, and so forth are used to limit access to the intranet resources from the Internet. Given that the networked computing resources of an intranet are blocked from general access, the intranet (and its content) can't really be considered part of the Internet. Therefore, its inward-focused mimicry of the Internet has resulted in its name: *intranet*.

Extranets

As information technology architects have become increasingly familiar with the usage and capabilities of intranets, the need for selectively extending intranets beyond their traditional borders has become apparent. Specifically, any scenarios that feature tightly coupled or interlocking business processes between two or more companies are logical candidates for an extranet. An *extranet* is a selective integration of two or more intranets for the purposes of facilitating specific business processes.

Developing the extranet requires the interconnection of the participants' networks or intranets. Providing any connectivity at all using IP, or any other open internetworking protocol, results in the exposure of the entire contents of both intranets to accessibility from the other. Any security lapses on one side of the extranet automatically become security lapses for both intranets. The net effect of interconnecting two intranets is the creation of one large but semiprivate network. Ostensibly, some measure of trust and mutual dependence or interdependence must first exist on the business level before an extranet can be considered. Similarly, the benefits of an extranet must also be quantifiable and desirable to both parties; otherwise, they would not knowingly undertake such a risky venture.

The key to successful extranetting is to manage the risks down to an acceptable level. This requires understanding the risks inherent in the internetworking technologies.

The Trouble with Open Protocols

Open protocols, by their very nature, are insecure. Their specifications are well known and agreed upon throughout the industry. This shouldn't be misconstrued as advocacy of security through obscurity; it's simply an acknowledgment of the increased risk factors of open protocols. It's a fact that the more well-known a protocol is, the more well-known its fundamental weaknesses are. These weaknesses can be exploited to gain illicit access to otherwise forbidden networked computing resources.

Open protocols also increase risk by virtue of their enjoying broad support. The more manufacturers support the protocol, the easier it is to develop distributed computing networks with hardware and software from different vendors. Unfortunately, open protocols are not necessarily consistent in their implementation from vendor to vendor. Open standards are developed via a consensual process. The proposed standard is published in a

Request for Comment (RFC). The RFC identifies the basic structure, logic, and functionality of the proposal. These are given different levels of priority:

- Must have
- Should have
- May have

Over time, and through consensus, the proposal becomes an accepted industry standard. The finished product retains these three levels of priority for its features. Therefore, it's sometimes trivially easy to find and exploit potential holes between vendor platforms with an open protocol, based on the disparities between the various vendors' implementations of it.

The other danger of an open protocol is that the more hosts and devices on a network that support it, the more opportunities there are to infiltrate the network. The larger a network grows, the more difficult it becomes to keep access privileges and other security mechanisms up-to-date and synchronized with each other.

The Trouble with Connectionless Protocols

A connectionless protocol is one that does not, in and of itself, establish a consistent path for its data transmission. IP is a connectionless Layer 3 protocol. It simply provides enough information in the header fields of its packet structure to identify the originator and the intended recipient. These packets are launched, and the network is entrusted to forward them appropriately. It's neither necessary nor probable that two sequential packets will travel the same path between source and destination in a very large and busy network. In other words, IP works in a connectionless manner. It does not require that a physical path, or bandwidth, be reserved at the time the communications session is first set up. Each packet is launched independent of the others.

When connectionless protocol is used, it's quite feasible for packets to be received out of sequence. Remember, this is a feature, not a flaw! IP relies on higher-level protocols such as TCP (Layer 4) to make sure that all received packets are resegmented properly before being passed up to higher-layer protocols and/or applications.

> **Note:** Although IP is inherently connectionless, it can function in a connection-oriented mode through the use of a Layer 4 protocol such as TCP. Not all Layer 4 protocols are connection oriented! UDP, for example, is also commonly used with IP, but it is connectionless. Remember this for any certification exams you may take.

The key to the successful operation of a network that uses a connectionless Layer 3 protocol is the routers that compose the network. More specifically, the key to success is the way the routers are programmed as well as how they calculate routes and forward packets.

Routers accept incoming LAN data frames, strip off the framing to reveal the Layer 3 packetized data, and then forward the packet. In doing so, they discard the MAC address pairs. This breaks the audit trail that otherwise would exist between a source and destination machine pair.

This discontinuity at the MAC Layer, although not necessarily significant, demonstrates some of the disconnects that can exist between the protocols that operate at different layers of the stack. This discarding of MAC addresses prevents the use of end-to-end security based on MAC addresses across a router. This creates an opportunity for the unscrupulous.

Even greater opportunity for security compromise lies in the forwarding of open, connectionless protocols between routers. Remember, a connectionless protocol has no clearly defined path between source and destination. Therefore, the routers are trusted to calculate the optimal path between the communicating nodes and to forward packets accordingly. *Calculating the optimal path* is a euphemistic phrase that masks the complexity of routing connectionless protocols and the various metrics that routers might use to assess path efficiencies in a dynamic network. It also can be misleading.

In theory, a router is capable of discriminating among multiple possible paths to reach a given destination and selecting the "lowest-cost path." The cost can be measured in time, distance, and so forth. After the lowest-cost path is identified, the packet is forwarded out the port interface that connects to the next hop in that path. The downstream routers perform similar table lookups and calculations; they're not obligated to deliver the packet along the actual path calculated by any previous routers. Each router is concerned only with forwarding the packet to the next hop. The remainder of the network beyond that port is inconsequential. In other words, the protocol is connectionless. A connection-oriented protocol requires the identification and maintenance of a fixed path through the network of routers. This lack of continuity represents an inherent vulnerability in connectionless protocols.

A more troubling vulnerability is the inability of a router to differentiate between legitimate and fraudulent addresses. They trust that the source and destination address pairs identified in the packet header are both legitimate and correct. Their routing tables correlate the destination address with a port number. They forward the packet out that port's interface. Any security mechanisms based solely on the access rights of the source IP address contained in a packet are easily defeated.

Therefore, the stage is set for numerous ways to exploit network-based vulnerabilities. These include hijacking a host address, spoofing a client address, and denial of service.

Hijacking a Host Address

It's quite possible to hijack the IP address of a destination and intercept packets intended for it. In a large, complex network, there may well be multiple paths to get to any given destination. Depending on how the network addressing scheme is defined, a router may actually be fooled into believing that there are two paths to the same host when, in fact, there are really two hosts: one legitimate and one counterfeit.

Obviously, this is an oversimplification that does not get into the minutiae of how to defeat the other layers of security that may exist at either the network or application layer. Defeating them can be a monumental task, if not a logistical impossibility. Nevertheless, this example demonstrates that routers can be duped quite easily. The point in hijacking a host's address is to intercept streams of data, including valid ID and password pairs, that would be routed to it. There are, however, other ways to abuse an ill-gotten IP address.

Spoofing an Address

The other danger with the relative unintelligent forwarding of packets is that it's possible to pretend to be another device, for the purposes of "borrowing" that device's access permissions. Rather than actually steal an address, all that spoofing requires is to somehow manage to generate a stream of packets with the source address of another machine. This is a useful way to defeat simple address-filtering mechanisms, such as those used in router access lists.

Denial of Service

Breaches of security are not necessarily done to gain anything for the perpetrator. The preceding two examples demonstrate such circumstances, but an equally serious threat is known as a *denial-of-service attack*. The perpetrator gains access to a network, host, or application and proceeds to do anything possible to make that resource unavailable to its legitimate users.

Mixing Open Protocols and Extranets

At this point, it should be fairly obvious that building an extranet based on open, connectionless protocols is a risky proposition, even under the best of circumstances. These risks should not be taken lightly. It's already well established that the borders of any IP network must be protected and guarded vigilantly. Failing to do so places all the networked assets at risk. Given this, extending intranets beyond the perimeter of established defenses seems ludicrous. Nevertheless, there are significant potential business benefits that warrant this risk. There are also numerous ways to identify and minimize the risks.

Assessing the Risks

Identifying the risks goes far beyond merely identifying the assets that can be jeopardized by the extranet, either directly or indirectly. Remember, you're assessing risks, not compromising your assets. There is a difference!

Assessing the risks of extranetting must begin with identifying the tangible assets that can be compromised through illicit access. These include the following:

- Data
- Application source code
- Application executables
- Network components
- Network-attached hosts

As important as these items are, they're just the tangible assets. They're the business data, logic, and technical infrastructure that support the business. They are not, however, the business. Including the business functions and processes that rely on these tangible items rounds out one's estimate of the magnitude of risk inherent in extranetting. As companies become increasingly dependent on their intranets to support their business processes, the risks must include the integrity of those processes and the capability to perform them. Therefore, the capability of a company to function is directly exposed to risk via extranetting.

Clearly, the business risks of unrestricted access over an extranet outweigh any potential business benefits. Consequently, access across an extranet must be carefully controlled and maintained. Access must be limited to just what is absolutely necessary to support the interlocking business processes.

The next issue is how to secure data in transit as it passes across the extranet. Many business managers would have you believe that a properly written partnership agreement affords you all the protection you need. This train of thought is ill-conceived and wrongheaded. All it accomplishes is blame attribution *after* a compromise occurs.

A better approach is to carefully plan every aspect of the extranet's security mechanisms *before* implementation. Equal diligence is due daily to the maintenance of the security mechanisms. Day-to-day moves, changes, installs, and other rearrangements of the network components can quickly erode the validity of any logic or filters that may be used to enforce security across the extranet. Security technologies, such as authentication and even encryption, are quickly emerging as indigenous extensions of network protocols. Carefully applied, they can almost completely protect the sanctity of data in transit over unsecured transmission facilities.

Rules for Securing an Extranet

Securing an extranet should begin with the identification of a set of rules that describes the desired functionality of the extranet. These rules are the nucleus of the business logic to be enforced via router access control lists, firewalls, host and application layer permissions, and any other security mechanisms that might be deemed necessary.

The single most important step is to first identify just those resources that must be made accessible across the extranet. *Access to everything should be explicitly denied throughout the entire intranet!* This should always be your first rule: **Deny access to everything automatically and then explicitly define those permissions that are required.**

Permissive rules can be fairly specific. For example, the allowable access of the client with IP address number 128.*xx*.*xxx*.*x* can be limited to the host at 135.*xx*.*xxx*.*x*. Alternately, rules can be more generic and apply to ranges of IP addresses. Just be careful! Security rules are a double-edged sword. The more stringent and effective they are, the more onerous they are to maintain. Do not succumb to the temptation of establishing rules based solely on their ease of maintenance. If you, or your company, employs a designated data communications/networking service provider, do not let that provider talk you into lax security rules. Providers are motivated to minimize their own administrative burden rather than maximize the security of your networked resources.

> **Note:** As a rule set for a firewall or router becomes more complex, more CPU cycles are required to apply it. Consequently, the processing delays increase directly with the effectiveness of the security. In circumstances where end-to-end delays must be minimized, it may be necessary to substitute fewer, broader (and Draconian) rules, for many individual ones.

Firewalls Are Not Panaceas

If it's deemed necessary to have a firewall installed between the two intranets, it should be acknowledged that firewalls are not panaceas. Firewalls are only as good as their rules. Incomplete sets of rules, rules that are poorly defined, and even rules that are not well maintained can all undermine the effectiveness of a firewall. Firewalls may be a critical component in securing your extranet, but they're only as good as the people who program and maintain them.

Other firewall-related issues include the number of firewalls needed and the distribution of administrative responsibilities. Technically, all you really need is one firewall. Properly programmed, it can provide bidirectional protection for both extranet partners. A single-firewall solution is illustrated in Figure 13.5.

Note: The extranets illustrated in Figures 13.5 and 13.6 may both appear to be just a single, physical connection between two routers. However, this is not quite the case. The connection represents the point at which two intranets develop a commonality. This commonality is known as the *extranet* and extends to all the network-attached resources made accessible across the physical connection between the two intranets.

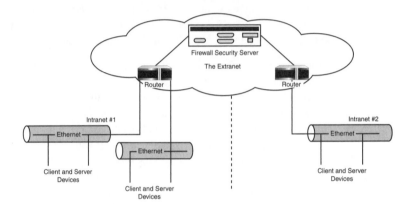

From many perspectives, the single-firewall solution is nearly ideal. It keeps the processing overhead and delays to an absolute minimum. Likewise, costs are also kept to a minimum. Unfortunately, this solution suffers one devastating drawback. Remember, this is the device that separates your intranet from another company's intranet. Do you trust the other company to administer this firewall? Can you logically expect this other company to trust you to do it? The answer to both questions is "probably not."

The solution is to have redundant firewalls back to back. This is illustrated in Figure 13.6.

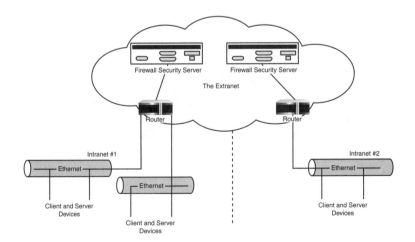

Redundant firewalls double the cost, operational effort, and processing delays. From these perspectives, the use of redundant firewalls is hardly an ideal solution. Despite this, if mutual peace of mind is essential for both extranet partners, this solution may be the only viable one.

Peter's Principle: More than Just a Name Change

The success of the Internet has permanently changed the way businesses build and use IP-based wide area networks. These networks have evolved into intranets, extranets, and even virtual private networks. The significance of these networks transcends their mere name change. They enable business processes to evolve. A company that can manage the successful evolution of its business processes has the potential for substantial improvements in its competitive posture. The key to this success is understanding the capabilities and limitations of each technology. This knowledge should provide the context for the application of each network technology. Ideally, the networking technologies can be used to create new opportunities without exposing the company to unnecessary risks.

Am I Wasting My Time?

The point of this rather exhaustive exploration of the fundamental traps of extranetting with IP is to elevate your awareness of those traps. This awareness will help you develop more comprehensive and effective security defenses. The point is not to scare you away from extranetting. On the contrary, extranets are likely to increase in their significance in the future.

Over time, extranets will emerge as the preferred interconnectivity vehicle between business partners. In the longer term, the distinctions between the Internet, intranets, and extranets will likely be almost completely erased by technological advances. Improvements in Network Layer authentication, certification, and (to a lesser extent) encryption will likely afford companies the capability to tear down their firewalls and other physical perimeter defenses around their WANs. In their place will be logically defined intranets and extranets. When this happens, we'll have come full circle. The various networks will have reintegrated into a single, ubiquitous network with logical—not physical—subdivisions. These logical structures are known as *virtual private networks* (VPNs).

Virtual Private Networks

One approach to using the Internet as a secured alternative to an expensive, dedicated, private communications network involves virtual private networks. VPNs are actually a new twist on an old concept. X.25 packet-switched networks have for decades provided companies with a software-defined, secure network within a larger, public switched network. The public switched network was owned and operated by the telecommunications provider, and access facilities were extended to each of the customers' premises. Each customer could use the network as if it were his own private network and never see the traffic put on the network by other customers. The X.25 network provided the functionality of a private network, without the cost of building and running a private network.

VPNs are a new implementation of this old X.25 approach to networking. The key difference is that they use more robust transmission facilities and networking protocols. More significantly, they're being used in different ways to support the needs of the business. VPNs are ideal for any situation where it's not cost effective to deploy a privately owned network. Here are some examples:

- A company with a highly mobile work force
- Smaller companies that cannot justify the cost of their own private communications network

VPNs can be bought from a telecommunications carrier, much like the old X.25 service. Alternatively, they can be created using an existing network infrastructure, such as the Internet or the public switched telephone network, by using tunneling software.

Carrier-provided VPNs

Carrier-provided virtual private networks are logical, private networks constructed within the carrier's public network. The telecommunications industry enjoys tremendous economies of scale. The huge amounts of capital required to build, operate, and maintain public networks must be spread across a very large population of users in order for the service to be affordable. The same concept applies, albeit on a smaller scale, to the private communications networks of companies.

A VPN is a concept, not a product. VPNs have been used extensively for years in both voice and data networks, and they continue to enjoy success in both arenas. The reason for this is simple: Many companies find it cost-prohibitive to build and operate private communications networks. Rather than build such networks or deny themselves that functionality, they seek a provider that can sell them that service.

The recent interest in VPNs is being generated by the Internet. Many companies, especially the Internet Service Providers (ISPs) and backbone carriers of the Internet, are anxious to increase demand for Internet connectivity and usage. Curious as this may sound, the explosive demand for Internet connectivity has actually leveled off. Consequently, the ISPs find themselves locked in competition for a market that views their service as a commodity.

One of the tactics to increase demand is to find new ways to use the Internet. Remembering that the real money lies within the coffers of corporations (not individual consumers), their quest is to find more ways to drive up corporate demand for Internet connectivity. Using the Internet as a virtual private network is just one solution.

The Internet can be used as a VPN in one of two ways. First, remote workers can access corporate intranet resources by dialing into their local ISP and riding through the Internet to their intranet. This relieves the corporation of having to support dial-in modem pools, but it comes at the cost of increased security concerns.

The second approach is to eliminate the intranet almost entirely in favor of a virtual private network within the Internet. This approach, to date, remains more of a theoretical solution than a practical one.

The benefit of either approach is the reduction in the costs of owning, operating, and maintaining communications networks.

Tunneling

Tunneling is a process by which communications occur within the confines of a logical structure established by another communications protocol. This can solve several different network problems that range from the need to secure data in transit to overcoming incompatibilities with either external protocols or addressing schemes.

Regardless of which protocols are used or what the intent of the tunnel is, the basic technique remains relatively consistent. Typically, one protocol is used to establish connectivity to a remote destination, and another is used to encapsulate data and instructions for transmission through the tunnel.

An example of using a tunnel to overcome incompatibilities in both protocols and addressing is found in the Simple Internet Transition (SIT) suite of tools that accompanies the upcoming release of IPv6. One tool provided by the Internet Engineering Task Force (IETF) to facilitate the migration from version 4 of the Internet Protocol (IPv4) to version 6 (IPv6) is a tunneling technique. These two versions are dissimilar enough as to preclude direct interoperability. Interoperability is simulated by tunneling IPv4 through IPv6, and vice versa.

Tunneling also secures data as it traverses otherwise unsecured domains by providing a protective shell or wrapper. One tunneling protocol that's designed exclusively for this purpose is the Point-to-Point Tunneling Protocol, discussed earlier in this chapter.

Summary

In this chapter, you read about where Remote Access Service (RAS) came from and where it's most likely going. You also read about the way modem connections are made, and learned about the SLIP and PPP protocols. These protocols set up the upper-level peer process connection. You read about how TCP/IP rides on top of SLIP or PPP, and you learned that PPP is used more often than SLIP.

You also looked at the PPTP protocol and how private networks can be "built" on the Internet with this protocol. You then explored the two main ways RAS is being utilized today: first, as a gateway from a LAN to the Internet via RAS-enabled Internet connections and, second, as an Internet access provider to remote RAS dial-in users.

You also read about the ways security can be implemented on RAS servers and connections. RAS is no doubt here to stay. The developments most apparent in the future are faster modems, better telephone lines, and improved user applications. These three things will combine to make RAS even better than it is today. As long as there are telecommuters, traveling employees, and people who like to work at home, RAS will stay around.

PART IV

Operating Networks

Network Operating Systems (NOS)

The world of networking has gone through many phases in the last 40 years. Starting with the connection of so-called "dumb terminals" to mainframe systems, there has always been a desire to access information and share that information among many users. To that end, a number of different software vendors have developed what are called *network operating systems*—first to simply bring about the sharing users wanted and then to add additional services for both end users and administrators. By the early 1990s, three companies stood out as NOS vendors: Banyan, Novell, and Microsoft. This chapter examines these three companies and their network software offerings.

History of Network Operating Systems

Following the introduction of IBM's personal computer (PC) in 1981, many users were happy to simply use these devices as IBM had intended: as replacements for dumb terminals. However, many users wanted to connect these intelligent machines together. With this in mind, this chapter takes a short look at the development of general NOS systems before discussing the various systems in the NOS world.

Only two short years after IBM's introduction of the PC, Novell came along with its first NetWare product. This was the first truly configurable NOS. At the same time, IBM was busy inventing its early PC networking capabilities. In order to connect its PCs, IBM created NetBIOS (Network Basic Input/Output System), later extending it to be called NetBEUI (NetBIOS Extended User Interface).

Novell Dominates the Market

NetBIOS/NetBEUI enables applications on different computers to communicate within a LAN. IBM's NetBEUI enables PCs to send data to other PCs without requiring more than one return acknowledgment to show that the data has reached its destination. Microsoft obtained permission from IBM to use NetBEUI in its Microsoft products, but neither IBM nor Microsoft was able to parlay the use of NetBEUI into anything even closely resembling NetWare.

Novell was on top of the world in those days. At one point in 1986, it was claimed that Novell controlled nearly 85 percent of the PC network business, and it may have had closer to 95 percent. Everywhere you looked, Novell LANs were chugging away. Microsoft didn't see Novell as a threat; Microsoft was busy trying to establish a graphical interface for PC users.

The two main protocols invented by Novell that enabled NetWare to be so successful are IPX and SPX. IPX stands for *Internetwork Packet Exchange.* It's a connectionless protocol designed to carry data from one place to another. SPX (Sequenced Packet Exchange) is a connection-oriented complement to IPX (see Chapter 4, "The Network and Transport Layers," for a full discussion of protocols, both connection oriented and connectionless).

IPX/SPX was, and is, a force to be reckoned with. This combination of two protocols is what gave Novell its competitive edge. Microsoft's MSNet product, and its successors, LAN Manager and Windows NT Advanced Server, used the NetBEUI protocol as the main protocol. Because NetBEUI is not a routable protocol (IPX/SPX is), the Microsoft networking products languished in small, departmental LANs while Novell moved on to larger and larger installations.

New Players Emerge

It was not until Microsoft came out with Windows for Workgroups (WFWG) that any of Microsoft's corporate strides were considered important to the world of NOS development. In the meantime, Novell continued to improve NetWare's capabilities while capturing the market. Another player emerged in the 1980s as well, Banyan Systems, Inc.; the product it created was called VINES.

The VINES system has always been considered the most enterprise ready of the major LAN systems, but add-ons and configuration changes were very expensive, so Banyan's marketing attempts have become textbook cases in how *not* to advertise and sell a product.

By 1990, Microsoft had started to realize the importance of PC networks and, more importantly, peer-to-peer networking, where end users decide what to share with whom. NetBEUI was added to the very successful Windows 3 desktop operating system to create Windows for Workgroups. This enabled users with very small network needs, perhaps 1 to 100 users, to get a network up and running very quickly.

Microsoft Takes Hold

Microsoft began to see the light in the late 1980s. When users began to believe that a graphical user interface was a great idea, Microsoft reacted with the development of Windows 3.0. This was the first practical graphical user interface Microsoft developed. Novell designed its system to enable DOS and Windows users to network their PCs quite easily. You would think this was a marriage made in heaven, but apparently, Microsoft felt as though networking services should be incorporated into its Windows system.

Novell had done what it set out to do. It had created a seamless network interface capable of passing data on large, interconnected PC networks. Also, because Novell client stations ran DOS, Windows, and other operating systems, users of Novell could use applications with which they were already familiar. Novell simply gave them the capability to share files and other resources, such as printers and tape drives.

Microsoft decided to change its strategy at this point. When it became apparent that its networking capabilities were far behind those of Novell and Banyan, Microsoft decided to incorporate networking services within the Windows operating system. With that in mind, Microsoft developed the Windows NT system.

Traditional Services of a NOS

Throughout the development of network operating systems, users have traditionally required three major services in a NOS: file and resource sharing, configurability and usability, and support after sale.

File and Resource Sharing

There has always been demand for file sharing. This was probably the most fundamental requirement users stressed when demanding network services. Following that, there has always been a marked demand for resource sharing—in other words, sharing printers, tape drives, and myriad other expensive resources. These are the two basic tenets for a NOS to be considered usable.

Configurability and Usability

The next area of concern is configurability and usability. Novell NetWare administrators all swear by NetWare, and Windows NT administrators tell you that not until the graphic environment of NT came along was there ever a good NOS. Still others, such as users of VINES or other lesser-known systems, tell you that their NOS is, without a doubt, the best. However, there's no doubt that Windows NT provides the easiest interface by far. That ease, however, comes at a price. Although a graphical user interface (GUI) may seem easier to use, many times it does not provide informative explanations as to why something is not working correctly. Microsoft's interface is wonderful as long as everything is working correctly. However, when something goes wrong, many times the user is presented with a graphic message that says something to the effect of "Kernel Error 322," with an OK button beneath the message. Clicking the button may make the user feel he is accomplishing something, but in reality, he is not. Obviously, the error is not OK, so unless someone can get to the root of the problem, the interface offers no clues. Microsoft's documentation has historically been less than complete, and many times administrators do not know what they're doing when they simply click a certain icon or area on the screen. Organizations are therefore forced to expend a great deal of money to train people to use NT properly.

Novell may not have had a graphical interface in the beginning, but it had something no other NOS vendor had: the best documentation on the market. Those bright red NetWare books were absolutely splendid. Novell continues to provide the best documentation of all NOS vendors, although today it's in an electronic format. Microsoft is getting better, but Novell's documentation continues to make the setup, configuration, and administration of NetWare an easy task. Banyan's interface is easy to use, and it's quite easy to set up a Banyan network. However, the documentation leaves much to be desired. It's not nearly as clear as Novell's, and the first-time user of the product is usually quite perplexed as to how to get the network up and running.

When Windows for Workgroups (WFWG) came along, things got slightly easier. Recall that Windows for Workgroups was preloaded with NetBEUI only, so if you wanted to use WFWG on a LAN, you needed to load an additional protocol into the system. This was done via the graphical interface, and it generally worked well enough. However, there were times when Microsoft's interface was at best cryptic, when providing status or error messages.

Again, Microsoft had missed the boat as far as ease of use was concerned. Not until Windows NT Server did Microsoft finally come up with an easy-to-use interface. As mentioned earlier, this was (and is) a double-edged sword. Furthermore, Microsoft's documentation on early versions of NT was worthless.

Support After Sale

If you wanted to get any kind of useful information, it was necessary to seek it from someone who had learned how to do it on his own. Microsoft's support structure was often described as "disastrous" in those days. Hours on the telephone listening to music were what usually ensued whenever someone called Microsoft. Microsoft was so inundated with calls after the release of Windows 3.0—most of which it could not address in a timely manner—that its reputation was nearly ruined. Microsoft's support structure, at this time, was not adequate for the number of calls it was receiving. Many people became very discouraged with the waiting associated with each call.

Novell, on the other hand, has always provided excellent support and service to its customers. It is prompt, usually courteous, and helpful. Banyan is a mixed bag. Sometimes it's excellent; other times, it's not. Configurability, usability, and support are always important to users of NOS software and systems.

Let's continue by looking at the three major vendors and their NOSs in detail.

Banyan Network Systems

Banyan has tried to assert itself as a leader in enterprise-wide network solutions with its NOS software called VINES. Banyan has always made claims that its networks are transparent to the user. By making all the resources on a distributed network seem as if they're compiled into one seamless network, Banyan claims VINES to be the choice for PC-based network solutions. The following sections review VINES' applications and services.

Services and Applications of VINES

The key to making VINES work over distributed network systems is the Enterprise Network Services (ENS) portion of VINES. ENS includes the following services and applications:

- Directory Services (StreetTalk)
- Network Management Services
- Intelligent Messaging Services
- Security Services

All four services work with each other across an entire wide area network (WAN) or distributed network. The next sections briefly review each of these services.

Directory Services (StreetTalk)

Directory and file services are the real "meat" of any NOS, and Banyan has an excellent package to perform these services. The software that enables VINES to provide across-the-board services to all users of the network is called *StreetTalk*. Banyan developed StreetTalk to standardize file and directory services. This product basically lets you share file and directory resources on a Banyan LAN with other types of file services such as NFS (UNIX), NTFS (Windows NT File System), and the old DOS-style FAT (File Allocation Table) systems. The product works well. StreetTalk automatically integrates newly added network locations into the existing network. This makes it very easy to set up and use.

> **Note:** If you are unfamiliar with the term "Directory Services," you should jump ahead to Chapter 18, "Directory Services" for a full explanation.

Another important feature of StreetTalk is that it exists on each VINES server in the network. When one server running StreetTalk fails, the entire network directory/file sharing capabilities do not fail, as you might expect. Each server maintains a part of the "puzzle" and, together, the StreetTalk information on all the servers combines to form the entire picture. When one server fails, the other servers are still able to locate the users and resources they support.

StreetTalk is fully integrated into every other part of VINES. Mail, print, and file services all use StreetTalk in order to locate a user or resource on the network. StreetTalk enables users to log in from anywhere on the VINES network; interfaces look the same whether users are on the road or in the office. When new devices, users, and resources are added to the network, StreetTalk assigns each of them a name. This is how StreetTalk is able to keep track of everything.

An excellent feature of StreetTalk is its capability to keep users "straight" when they move to a new location on the network. Network changes are a fact of everyday life. StreetTalk enables administrators to leave a user's workstation exactly as it is when the user moves to a new location. StreetTalk determines the new location as soon as the user logs in for the first time. This is a real timesaver for network administration personnel.

Finally, the StreetTalk Directory Assistance (STDA) service enables users and administrators to look up items, in much the same way they would view the Yellow Pages. All resources can be listed in alphabetical order using STDA. This makes it very easy to find users, resources, and servers on large VINES networks.

Network Management Services

VINES includes what Banyan calls *Network Management Services* (NMS). VINES NMS has an easy-to-use interface that provides reliable information to administrators. Items such as user activities, network changes and deletions, security, applications, and performance are all manageable with VINES NMS.

Coupled with this is the VINES Assistant. This service provides useful utilities designed to maximize network performance and the control of resources for administrators. VINES also includes password-control utilities, network-optimization utilities, and many others. It's a menu-driven system that steps you through each operation.

Intelligent Messaging Services

VINES messaging sets itself up automatically and works well with any third-party email program. It's fully integrated with StreetTalk, so users need to be registered in the StreetTalk database on only one server. Users are then free to "wander" around the network, use their email login to receive mail at any workstation, and view address information pertaining to users on the network no matter where they're located. This is made possible due to the fact that user address information is maintained in StreetTalk only. Therefore, users may choose any email client program to use, and it will correctly communicate with VINES messaging services. Further, these messaging services are tied into the NMS system as well, so administrators can monitor all email if need be.

Security Services

VINES security services are transparent to users of the network, but they are very effective. VINES security services can secure files, printers, gateways, applications, and all other resources. Control of resources is at the source, so even if a hacker is physically connected to a server, he's not going to gain access to a resource unless he's in the Access Rights List (ARL) for that server. The ARL keeps track of who is authorized to use what on the network. Using the ARL is a very easy way to manage the security of resources on a VINES network.

VINES-Supported Standards

VINES can support a variety of standards and protocols on its communication links as well as on several client operating systems. Here are the major standards supported by VINES:

- *Communications standards.* LAN, dial-up, X.25, SNA, TCP/IP, and IBM 3270 Gateway connections are all supported when interconnecting geographically separated VINES networks into one single system.

- *Operating system clients.* DOS, Windows, OS/2, and Macintosh can be used as the client operating system. VINES provides network resources through the native interfaces of these operating systems. Therefore, users don't need to learn a "special" network interface in order to access network resources on their client workstations running these operating systems.

Strengths and Weaknesses of VINES

Banyan does not want you to know that VINES has its roots in UNIX. In fact, UNIX is the underlying operating system that makes VINES operate. UNIX is sometimes frowned upon by supporters of current technology. Although UNIX has been around for a long time, it's still an excellent operating system. However, the age of UNIX tends to scare some people. The real strength of VINES lies in its StreetTalk Directory Service. This hierarchical naming of people and resources for enterprisewide directory services is actually the first of its kind. It's very reliable and configurable. Another strength of VINES is that it supports multiple platforms via ENS: NetWare, UNIX (AIX, SCO, and Solaris), and NT versions. This enables all these other LAN systems to be included in the StreetTalk directory services.

Despite its compelling strengths, the weaknesses of VINES are many. Hardware device support is extremely limited. (Windows NT can detect and set up most hardware devices in seconds.) The fact that VINES is built on an old UNIX platform means that detection is not viable. Furthermore, VINES can support only a limited number of devices. This fact, coupled with the dismal technical support available for VINES, makes it a poor choice for a new network starting up. Banyan does not appear to be committed to continued research and development of the VINES product. Unfortunately, the future does not look good for Banyan VINES.

Novell NetWare

Novell set the standard when it came to the rapid growth of LANs in the world. Banyan, on the other hand, may have beat Novell to the punch in creating directory services. After all, Banyan's StreetTalk was really the first LAN directory service. Novell, however, didn't wait long to play catch-up. In fact, after Novell poised itself to take on networking and LANs, it did so with a mighty force.

There were no other corporations around that took networks and LANs as seriously as Novell did in the early 1980s. For that reason, Novell is still the top player in the NOS business. According to International Data Corporation (IDC), in 1996, worldwide shipments of server operating systems totaled 2.4 million units. Of this total, IDC attributed a 41 percent share to Novell. Between 1996 and 2000, IDC has projected Novell's share of the network operating systems market to grow at a compound rate of 8 percent.

Recall that Novell was the first NOS to support multiple platforms. It was also the first NOS to support multiple and varying topologies and routes between these differing topologies. The real boost for Novell is that it was the first NOS to support all DOS-version networks. Novell also gave Apple a fair deal—NetWare was the first NOS that could provide TCP/IP services to Apple systems. That was a big plus in the heyday of AppleTalk and other Apple systems. The next section discusses the primary features of NetWare. These features make Novell NetWare the powerhouse that it is.

Features of NetWare

The main reason Novell NetWare servers typically outperform other network servers is that NetWare is, by design, a network operating system. Recall that Banyan has its roots in UNIX. Microsoft NT is also an operating system, but it wasn't designed strictly for network performance and service, as NetWare was. A NetWare server is optimized for network activity. This gives it a great edge over other NOS servers. The following sections review NetWare's main features:

- Novell Directory Services (NDS)
- Security services
- Database services
- Messaging services
- Print services
- NetWare Loadable Modules (NLMs)

Of these six main features, the NDS offering is what makes Novell a strong competitor of Windows NT. Following Banyan's creation of StreetTalk, Novell fought back with NDS. The next sections discuss NDS as well as the five other features of NetWare.

Novell Directory Services (NDS)

Novell decided to adhere to the CCITT (the International Consulting Committee for Telephone and Telegraph, abbreviated from the French) X.500 standard when setting up its NDS system. In fact, Novell has been fairly good about following open standards when defining its network products. By adhering to the X.500 hierarchical namespace structure, NDS prevents the creation of duplicate objects. Each object must have a *distinguished name* (DN). For example, if you have an employee named Bill in the sales department, the DN for the user object BILL in the sales department, which is part of the 2345 organization, would be BILL.SALES.2345. The username BILL (without SALES.2345) is called an RDN, which stands for *relative distinguished name*.

In Novell NDS, you must uniquely identify every object in the directory tree. This is accomplished by defining its location in the tree. For that reason, you can use the same RDN in more than one container. In Novell NDS, a container is like a repository of information pertaining to a group or cluster of people that exists on certain servers. For example, you can use the RDN of BILL in both the SALES.2345 container and the HR.2345 container. This is a very powerful feature of the NDS system. To further break things down, NDS includes intermediate objects, which Novell calls *container objects*. These are Organization (O), Organizational Unit (OU), Country (C), and [Root].

Containers are repositories of other components and resources. These are called *leaves* or *leaf objects* by Novell. Usually these leaf objects are users, printers, servers, directory maps, and so on. Novell's use of the term *leaf object* can be confusing, but it makes sense if you think about it. In traditional tree discussions, a leaf is an object at the end of a branch—an object that doesn't contain any objects. Likewise, Novell uses the term to refer to a noncontainer object—an object that can't contain any objects. Therefore, if something is a "leaf object," it's at the "end" of the directory tree. It's usually a printer or a user, in most cases.

It's possible to create an unlimited number of container and leaf objects in NDS. NDS ships prepackaged with 37 types of container and leaf objects. These types enable you to manage all your network resources. If new resources are connected to the network, you can define new types of objects and then add them to the NDS namespace structure.

Because NDS is displayed in a neat, graphically arranged order, objects such as users, printers, workstations, and application servers are shown in an organized structure to the system ADMIN user. You can log in as the ADMIN user from any workstation. This enables you to manage the entire directory tree. You can add and remove users, servers, and other network resources. Users need to log in only once in order to gain access to all network resources. NDS is probably the best directory service in the business. See Chapter 18, "Directory Services," for a comprehensive discussion of this important network service.

Security Services

Security is another area in which NetWare shines. As the inventor, in 1983, of usernames, passwords, and user profiles (as far as LANs are concerned), Novell set the standard for security services. The user profile information is stored on the NetWare network disk in an encrypted format. The wonderful thing about this is the fact that even at the physical server level, a user running DOS, UNIX, OS/2, or Windows cannot access these network files.

In fact, all password information flows back and forth from the NetWare server to the client workstation in an encrypted format. Even the administrator cannot look at a user's password on the server. The administrator can remove and add user permissions, but only the users know their own passwords. The administrator can define how often a user must change his password and can even change a user's password, but once a password is changed by the user, no one else can read it.

Even if users get to the physical NetWare server, they have no greater access to resources than they would have on their own workstations, because NetWare security is built into the NetWare system at the lowest possible level. All attempts to access information or resources on the network go through the NetWare security services system. Novell NDS is closely tied to NetWare security as well. The security service ensures that users can access those services only in the NDS database that their passwords and privileges enable them to access. NetWare security has very few holes compared to UNIX- and Windows NT–based networks.

Database Services

Novell also made a splash early on by offering LAN database services in a client/server environment. These services make life much easier for those who are developing applications to run on Novell NetWare LANs. Because these database services provide a central repository for information on the server, users had yet another reason to make Novell the leader in LAN network operating systems for many years. Three major database management systems (DBMSs) are available on NetWare: NetWare C, NetWare SQL, and the Oracle DBMS. Here are details of each:

- Btrieve is actually a database record management system, indexed with a database key, designed for easy development of vertical applications. Many corporations use the Btrieve system to store records of data on a NetWare server. Users on the client stations are then able to access these records in a speedy fashion. Btrieve has shipped with every version of NetWare since release 2.

- NetWare SQL was developed in an attempt to adhere to industry standards. SQL stands for *structured query language*—the standard used for accessing records stored in a relational database system. SQL has many versions, but Novell tried hard to stick with the SQL standard when developing its LAN version. NetWare SQL takes record management a bit further than Btrieve—it provides the capability to access Btrieve records from multiple platforms and applications.

- Oracle is the world leader in database management systems. Its SQL-based system is used by many business-critical applications in many different lines of business. All NetWare 4 and 5 servers ship with a five-user version of the Oracle DBMS.

Messaging Services

In the past few years, there have been many developments in the area of messaging services. Novell is not alone in the area of messaging services development.

From NetWare 2 through NetWare 4.1, Novell provided a messaging service called *NetWare Message Handling Service* (MHS). This service provided for ease of message transmission between many front-end applications. These applications can share data over LANs and Novell WANs. The MHS service could be set up on a standalone PC on the network. It could be configured to transmit message data when the user specifies. For that reason, it could take advantage of transmitting when rates on the network are cheaper or traffic volume is lower.

When Novell acquired, then sold, the WordPerfect corporation to Corel, it kept the messaging component of WordPerfect Office and renamed it *GroupWise*. GroupWise has replaced MHS as Novell's messaging solution and is available as an add-on to NetWare systems, but it's also bundled with Novell's Small Business Server Suite.

Print Services

Print services in NetWare are native to the NetWare operating system environment. The basic services enable users to share up to 16 printers per print server on the network. NetWare networks are capable of having multiple print servers on the network, and the real flexibility of printing in NetWare is the fact that printers need not be attached to the actual print server in order to operate properly.

Indeed, a printer can be attached to the server, but it may also be attached to a user's workstation somewhere on the network. Although the print server still manages the printers not physically attached to it, you don't need to install print server software on workstations that are hosting network printers. All that's needed is a small Terminate and Stay Resident (TSR) program on the workstation that hosts the printer. Therefore, many combinations of printers and print servers may be configured on Novell networks.

NetWare Loadable Modules (NLMs)

NLMs are very important to the functionality of NetWare software. Starting with NetWare 3, NLMs became a mainstay of Novell network operations. These are not applications running on top of the NOS, but, when loaded, they become an integral part of the operating system. This provides the power needed to support heavily used network services in the server. NLMs have the same access to the NetWare security services, making them safe to control and administer.

NLMs can be loaded and unloaded as needed. You can even set up batch files to load and unload NLMs when appropriate. Many toolkits are offered by Novell to aid developers designing applications to run as NLMs.

NetWare-Supported Standards

NetWare can support a variety of standards and protocols on its communication links as well as several client operating systems. Here are the major standards supported by NetWare:

- *Communications standards.* LAN, dial-up, X.25, SNA, SDLC, ISDN, T-1, TCP/IP, and IBM 3270 Gateway connections are all supported by NetWare. In addition, Novell has its own product line of NetWare-friendly routers and bridges. The NetWare Link/64 is a device that enables NetWare users to connect geographically separated workstations at speeds between 9.6bps and 64Kbps. The NetWare Link/T-1 does the same thing, except at speeds up to 2.084Mbps. The NetWare Multiprotocol Router supports IPX, IP, and AppleTalk protocols. It enables users to connect Ethernet, Token Ring, LocalTalk, and ARCnet networks in any desired combination. It also provides for a transparent use of all network resources across each individual network so that users can access all the resources on the connected networks.

- *Operating system clients.* DOS, Windows (both 16-bit and 32-bit systems), OS/2, UNIX, and Macintosh can all be used as the client operating systems on NetWare client workstations.

Strengths and Weaknesses of NetWare

The major strength of Novell's NetWare product lies in its established history and position as the most-used LAN NOS in existence. Although Microsoft has recently stolen some of Novell's thunder, these strengths are still worth noting. First, NetWare has the best print and file server software in the business, and it's the sharing of files and printers that makes a network important and useful.

NetWare boasts the best enterprisewide directory services in the business. The NDS system discussed previously is by far the best of all LAN NOS directory services. When you follow that up with the fact that strong utilities for NetWare are available from hundreds of companies, you can see why NetWare is still a logical choice when you want to establish an enterprise network. Microsoft is very weak on the enterprise level.

Novell can use improvement in some areas. First, NetWare lags as an application server. NetWare is an excellent provider of basic file and print sharing, but when it comes to being a distributed client/server application provider, it falls flat on its face. This is an area in which Windows NT has NetWare beaten hands down.

NetWare is also poor at providing useful data for monitoring network status and overall network management. Although NetWare does have some built-in network management tools, these tools are not very powerful. Many NetWare administrators feel they're unsure as to the status of their networks—whether they are running efficiently or not.

Peter's Principle: Don't put the cart before the horse!

It may come as a surprise that selecting a network operating system is one of the last things you should do when designing a network. Choosing the NOS first can lock you into choices farther down the road that are not in the best interest of your network or business. Instead, start by identifying the network users and their needs and then pick the applications that best meet those needs. Think about the connectivity issues you'll face (remote connectivity, Internet connectivity, and so on) and the amount and level of security required. Create a checklist of all the requirements you've identified and then (and only then) compare the various network operating systems to see which one best satisfies those requirements.

Microsoft Windows NT

Windows NT was the follow-on product to Microsoft's LAN Manager system, incorporating backward links to LAN Manager as well as new capabilities and features that were the result of the cooperative effort with IBM to develop OS/2. "Windows NT 3.5, Advanced Server" was quite a mouthful to say and quite a departure from the traditional Microsoft peer-to-peer networking paradigm because it was a true network server operating system.

More important, Microsoft realized that server-based applications were the coming trend in network servers and designed Windows NT as, first and foremost, an application server that also handles the more traditional file and print services.

Microsoft then further developed the NT platform, giving it the same basic graphical interface as Windows 95, thus easing the transition from Windows 95's peer-to-peer LAN to Windows NT's client/server LAN.

Windows NT Server, version 3.5 had numerous problems and anomalies that seemed to present themselves almost daily, but the next release—3.51—was (at least for a Microsoft operating system) "rock solid"—so much so, that today, years after the release of Windows NT 4 and with Windows 2000 (previously known as Windows NT 5) ready to go, many enterprises continue to run version 3.51.

Microsoft has taken pieces of network services, combined them in Windows NT, and very effectively married these services with the applications running on the clients and servers. The network versions of Microsoft Office (Office 2000), for example, and the thousands of other applications that Windows NT is capable of supporting have provided Microsoft an extremely comfortable edge over Novell's NetWare in the number of new servers installed.

Today, anyone who wants to make it in the development of applications had better be developing for the Windows NT system. Whether one agrees with it or not, Windows is a dominant force. The next section discusses the main features of Windows NT.

Features of Windows NT

Windows NT has so many features that it's not feasible to list them all in a chapter of this size. For this reason, you should visit Microsoft's NT Web site: `http://www.microsoft.com/ntserver`. You'll find some white papers there about most of NT's features. Here's a list of the major features and a description of what they do:

- **NT interface**—The Microsoft Windows 95 operating system user interface has been integrated into Windows NT, making the server interface easier to use and consistent with Windows 95.

- **Administrative wizards**—These little helpers place common server tools in a single area and walk you through the steps for completing tasks such as adding user accounts, determining file and folder access, and so on. These wizards walk you through the steps involved with relative ease.

- **Network Monitor**—Network Monitor enables you to examine network traffic to and from the server at the packet level. You can also capture traffic for later analysis. This is a nice feature for troubleshooting possible problem areas on your network. This tool shows you where the weak parts of your network are by assessing the flow of traffic. By doing this, Network Monitor can pinpoint congestion sources, and it will tell you specifically where the problem traffic is being generated.

- **Policy Editor and Profiles**—This feature gives you the right to manage and maintain the user work environment and actions. This makes it possible for users to have the same interface no matter where they log on.

- **Task Manager**—Task Manager is used for monitoring applications and tasks. It provides information on each application and process running on a workstation as well as memory and CPU usage. It can be handy, but to many administrators, it's a superfluous function.

- **Internet Information Server (IIS)**—Microsoft has captured a niche with this feature. This service enables you to set up a World Wide Web (WWW) server with great ease. It's tightly integrated with the Windows NT NOS. It provides an easy way to set up Web services on the LAN server. Basically, any files that exist on a server can be advertised on the Web by using this utility. In the past, setting up Web servers was generally done on older UNIX boxes. Microsoft has come up with a graphically driven method to do what used to take hours. Before there were HTML editors, many people were forced to write HTML code using text editors. After the code was written, it would have to be transferred to the Web server either by copying it directly or by using the File Transfer Protocol (FTP). This took a lot of time. IIS allows you to do all these tasks by pointing and clicking your way through some setup sequences. This is a strong product, and Microsoft was wise to introduce IIS when it did. Note, though, that IIS is a favorite target of crackers. Visit the IIS web site (`http://www.microsoft.com/ntserver/web/`) and especially the Microsoft security site (`http://www.microsoft.com/security/`) frequently if your Windows NT IIS is connected to the Internet.

- **Microsoft Index Server**—This service automatically indexes the full text and properties of all files on a Windows NT server. This comes in handy when you're searching for something particular on a Windows NT system. If you need to find a specific part of a specific file out on the network, this service enables you to do so. Also, you can search using keywords within a file. This utility ensures that all instances of the word you're searching for are found.

- **Point-to-Point Tunneling Protocol (PPTP)**—This protocol provides a way to use the Internet to create a virtual private network (VPN). This VPN can then be used to hook up client PCs with servers. PPTP can support multiple protocols via TCP/IP connections over these VPNs.

- **File and printer sharing**—Microsoft's Domain Service uses a flat namespace structure to define logical network names for users, printers, and other resources in a Windows NT environment. A flat namespace structure is acceptable for simple networks in single geographic locations; however, it has significant limitations in environments that are more complex. In fact, all your users and network resources are organized in one list. You can see why organizing users and network resources in one list is time consuming when you don't use hierarchical file systems. This is why Novell is still considered a better choice in this area of functionality.

- **Microsoft Cluster Server (MSCS)**—MSCS provides automatic recovery from server and application failures by providing "clustered" offerings of important applications. MSCS lets you perform rolling upgrades on your NT servers. This means you can perform network maintenance without taking important data and applications offline. As long as one of the servers in the cluster is up, the applications remain intact.

- **Microsoft Message Queue Server (MSQS)**—MSQS provides reliable delivery of messages and data across a Windows NT network. Even if the network and servers are unavailable or unreliable, MSQS uses store-and-forward techniques to ensure that the messages eventually get to where they need to go. This works by keeping a copy of the messages or data in a file queue until the destination is available to accept delivery. This is especially useful during times when the network is busy or when a specific destination workstation has failed or is offline.

- **SMP Server—Windows NT** allows the use of Server Multiprocessor (SMP) systems. These are very reliable, fast servers in which more than one CPU can be installed. Windows NT scales smoothly from a single CPU all the way up to an eight-way SMP server.

Windows NT–Supported Standards

Windows NT can support a variety of standards and protocols on its communication links. The major communications standards supported by Windows NT are LAN, dial-up, X.25, SNA, SDLC, ISDN, T-1, TCP/IP, and IBM mainframe connectivity. Microsoft is to be commended for ensuring that any communications link you can dream up is supported by Windows NT. If you happen to find something Windows NT has a problem with, a third-party company is always out there willing to develop a fix for your problem.

Windows NT Security

When Windows NT was introduced, it was the first time in Microsoft's history that it presented an operating system with security. Windows 3.x and Windows for Workgroups provided no password capabilities other than network login security. Any files or directories on PCs using these operating systems could be easily viewed, changed, or deleted. Windows 95/98 asks for a Windows password, but it seems to do absolutely nothing after you enter it. The Windows NT password is real—it works, and it cannot be breached easily. Security is very serious in Windows NT. From the administrator's point of view, security is highly configurable. Using what Microsoft calls *User Manager for Domains*, you can assign any level of security to any user for virtually anything. The sharing properties of Windows NT mean that files, directories, and entire hard drives can be set up to allow read, read/write, delete, or ownership access to only those users with legitimate needs. Windows NT uses the Windows NT File System (NTFS) when writing its files to a drive partition. NTFS provides the owners of files, directories, and hard drives with the ability to totally control what other users on the network may see, use, copy, delete, or write, as far as these owners' files and directories are concerned. This can all be done by users with the proper privileges. This takes a lot of the load off you as the administrator because you don't have to monitor and control the security of all the files and directories. As for passwords, you can make users change them at fixed intervals. There's also a feature that ensures certain users have access to the network only during certain times of the day or night. Overall, Windows NT security is excellent.

With Windows 2000, Microsoft has introduced the Active Directory Service (ADS), a full-blown directory service to rival Novell's NDS. Chapter 18, "Directory Services," includes a more detailed look at ADS.

Strengths and Weaknesses of Windows NT

When looking at the strengths of Windows NT, you must look again at the fact that it has multiple-platform support that far surpasses the other NOS systems. Windows NT supports Intel, MIPS, PowerPC, and DEC Alpha platforms with ease. This means anyone starting a new LAN can possibly take advantage of the speed and efficiency of a DEC Alpha server as the LAN's main server. At the same time, the client workstations can be cheap, Intel-based 80486 or Pentium systems.

The next area in which Microsoft has won out over Novell is *application support*. Windows NT is without a doubt the best of the best when it comes to being an application server. The user never sees any differences between standalone and network versions of applications running on Windows NT networks. It's seamless and invisible to the client workstations when network resources are used for certain applications.

A third strength lies in the fact that a strong financial base is being applied toward research and development of Windows NT, Windows NT server applications, and Windows NT capabilities. Furthermore, almost 80 percent of the application development taking place in this country is geared toward Windows NT development in general. That fact, coupled with the fact that Microsoft has pledged "undying" technical support to any of these development efforts, means Windows NT can only get bigger, better, and more reliable as time goes on. What that means for users will no doubt be better graphical interfaces, better applications, easy-to-use Internet tools, and many other possibilities.

The weaknesses of Windows NT are in those areas that NetWare is strongest—security, scalability, administration and directory services.

Sometimes it seems that not a week goes by without one group or another announcing a newfound security vulnerability in Windows NT. While Microsoft is quick to fix these vulnerabilities, it does require that you visit the Microsoft security Web site frequently: (http://www.microsoft.com/security/).

NT's scalability and directory services problems (and a large part of the administrative problems) are a direct result of the domain system used to administer versions 3.5x and 4.0. Chapter 18, "Directory Services" goes into more detail about this weakness, as well as about Windows 2000's Active Directory, which alleviates some of these problems, but is still a domain system "under the covers."

Administratively, Windows NT has been called a network manager's nightmare. Over 20 different applications must be used to administer users and servers on an NT 4.0 network. In Windows 2000, Microsoft has enabled the Microsoft Management Console (MMC) to act as a repository for many of these management functions, similar to NetWare's "ConsoleOne" and "Network Administrator" applications.

Summary

This chapter examined network operating systems (NOSs) in a general manner, covering the most important features any NOS must provide: file sharing and resource sharing, configurability and usability, and support after sale.

Of the bunch, Microsoft's Windows NT product is by far the easiest to use. Although Banyan's VINES operating system is dying out, it was the first LAN system to develop network-wide directory services. Novell followed suit with its NDS service, which is considered the best in the business to this day.

Although Microsoft has configured its networking capabilities in a piecemeal fashion, it has been successful. This is due to Microsoft's strategy of application development and support winning out over Novell's strategy of providing the best network platform services.

Network Administration

So far, this book has discussed the basic elements of a network, such as cabling, computers, network adapter cards, and so forth. But these elements alone do not enable you to be productive. Good administrative habits are essential. This chapter discusses the elements necessary for administering a network: planning, performance monitoring, and troubleshooting.

What Is Network Administration?

Network administration should be proactive rather than reactive. It consists of planning, configuring, and managing all the elements of the network. Some of these elements are local and remote resources, user accounts, and connectivity devices. The goal of network administration is to increase productivity by providing access to necessary resources.

Network administration begins when someone decides that a network is needed. The first item of business is to define what you, as a network administrator, want your network to do for you. The answer to this question determines the network's design and the path to take from now until everyone is using the network.

The most important part of your role as a network administrator is documenting your network's lifecycle, starting with the planning stage and continuing throughout the life of your network. This is also the most commonly neglected component. Think of this as fault tolerance for the network administrator.

The purpose of documentation is to provide for continuation of your network. When creating your documentation, ask yourself what a new administrator would need to know if you were suddenly and completely unavailable. In this vein, administrative passwords should be written down, placed in an envelope, and secured under lock and key. Other key personnel should know where these passwords are located.

The documentation should start with your current configuration and include answers to the following questions:

- What hardware and software—and which versions—are you presently using?
- Are these (the hardware and software) adequate for your needs?
- What do you see in the way of growth over the foreseeable future?

You should include a diagram of all your wiring, including routers, bridges, and so forth, as well as the configuration of each. Be sure to designate a central location for all hardware and software manuals with a tracking system in case materials are loaned out. Last, but not least, you should include a chronological narrative of each change or addition you make, including hardware and software changes. Keeping a copy of this documentation offsite allows for faster recovery in the case of a disaster.

Peter's Principle: Plan, then Plan Again

Nothing is more important to your network than proper planning. Carpenters have a slogan: "Measure twice, cut once." This could be adapted to networks as "Plan twice, install once." A poorly designed network, once installed, is almost impossible to correct by making the limited amount of changes and "tweaks" a running network allows. Taking the extra time necessary to properly plan may seem like a waste of time now, but it will actually save valuable time in the long run.

Managing Network Accounts

Before you have your network up and running, you need to decide how to manage access. You want to establish a consistent approach to managing the users' network access. Access includes not only logging on to a particular workstation but also accessing to resources. Before making this decision, you must define the method you're going to use to assign usernames and your password requirements. The two main types of network accounts that allow you to manage your users are user accounts and group accounts.

User Accounts

Several global elements may be used to manage user accounts and make administrative tasks easier, such as how you name your users and groups. These names should enable you to easily identify the location or job function of the user as well as the purpose of each group. An additional tactic that makes your job easier involves the rules you apply to passwords. One of these rules sets forth whether you want accounts to be locked out after unsuccessful logon attempts and, if so, how long they should remain disabled.

Tip: If you suspect your network has become the object of a break-in attempt, you can verify this by requiring manual reactivation of accounts that are disabled after three unsuccessful logon attempts. In this way, a user must notify you if he is unable to log on. If the user is not the one responsible for the lockout, you know that an unauthorized individual has been trying to gain access to your network.

One of the most important aspects of network security is passwords. If the passwords are unique and hard to guess, your system is more secure. When planning how to manage passwords, you might want to consider doing some or all of the following:

- Instruct users not to use dictionary words.

- Remind users not to use birth dates; names of spouses children, or pets; or other personal information.

- Have a minimum password length.

- Keep a password history.

- Require periodic password changes.

Passwords should be easy to remember so that users do not have to refer to written notes. However, they should be hard to crack. One of the most basic methods of breaking into a system is by using a list of dictionary words and trying each one as the password in an effort to gain access. Using names of family members, dates of birth, pets names—in short, anything which could be considered public information associated with the user—should be definitely discouraged. It's too easy for a determined cracker to discover this information.

> **Tip:** Users often look to the system administrator for assistance in choosing an adequate password. One easy method is for the user to pick two short words, such as *dog* and *walk*, and separate them by a nonalphanumeric character such as a percent sign (%). This results in the password "dog%walk," one that cannot be cracked by a dictionary-based password-cracking program but is still easy to remember.

Long passwords enhance your network's security by being hard to crack. This is especially true when alphabetic and numeric characters are mixed. Keeping a password history also reduces unauthorized access to your network. A password history prevents users from reusing two or three passwords, only cycling through them when they make changes. Then, if a password should become compromised, it does not become valid every other cycle. In other words, if a disgruntled ex-employee knows Lisa's password, Lisa is not able to reuse that password the next time she has to change it.

The security of your network is further enhanced by requiring that passwords be changed periodically. If a user's password to an account is learned by an outsider, access is blocked when the password is changed. This limits the time your network is exposed.

Creating User Accounts

In a peer-to-peer network, anyone who sits down at a computer can access that machine and all its resources. Access to shared resources from other computers might not require that you know a password. This model works well in the small network (usually fewer than 10 users), where security is not an issue.

In a larger server-based network, access is given to each user through an individual account. It's through the creation of user accounts and the attributes applied to these accounts that you manage access to resources.

Before you create the first user account (and even before you install the network operating system), a naming convention must be established.

> **Note:** Although it's perhaps more fun to enable each user to designate an individual, creative name, such as Bugsy, HighRoller, and so forth, this leads to administrative difficulties in identifying a particular user. In addition, this method of user identification also causes confusion when users try to send messages to other users or identify from whom a particular message was sent.

The most workable system for creating usernames is one that enables easy identification of users yet is flexible enough to allow unique naming. A naming system that consists of either the first initial and last name or the first name and last initial are two that are workable and limit user confusion.

NetBIOS Naming Conventions

NetBIOS names (used in most Microsoft network operations) are used to identify a specific computer or group of computers, not a particular user. These names must be unique and are 16 characters in length. Microsoft, however, reserves the sixteenth character for use as a suffix to define different services or functions on the registered device.

Originally, both NetBIOS and TCP/IP utilized a flat namespace. This meant that each name had to be unique. As networks became more complex, the available names were exhausted. As a result, a hierarchical naming system was developed. With TCP/IP, this two-part naming convention became *host* and *domain* (for example, www.microsoft.com *contains the host "www" and the domain "microsoft.com")*; with NetBIOS, it consists of NetBIOS name and NetBIOS scope. Windows NT combines the NetBIOS name with the domain name to create the fully qualified domain name (FQDN) for compatibility.

The first implementation of this hierarchical naming scheme relied on flat files for maintenance—the HOST file for address resolution using TCP/IP and the LMHOSTS file for NetBIOS name resolution. The implementation of Domain Name Servers and Windows Internet Naming Servers alleviated the need to maintain these flat files.

After a naming convention has been determined, you can begin creating the necessary user accounts. This is usually done through a utility provided by the network operating system. In Windows NT or Windows 2000, User Manager or User Manager for Domains is used. The equivalent utility for NetWare is Syscon for NetWare, version 3.x, or NWAdmin for versions 4.x and 5.x. Although some UNIX operating systems also provide such a utility, the user accounts are usually created at the user prompt. These user-management utilities can be used to designate options such as password requirements and group memberships. Figure 15.1 shows the screen for creating a new user account.

FIGURE 15.1
New User window in User Manager.

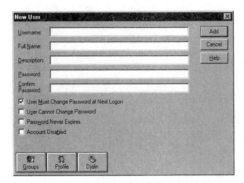

A user policy that you may wish to implement is the application of an expiration date for an account. This is a failsafe measure for when you're managing users who require only temporary access to your network, such as student employees. You may also designate what hours the user can log on to the network and even limit which workstations the user can use to log on.

Using Templates to Create User Accounts

Most network operating systems create both an administrator account and a guest account during installation. However, the administrator must then create accounts for all the network's users. Adding a large number of users at one sitting can be a time-consuming process. Not only does each user account need to be created, but each user's group memberships and access rights need to be assigned.

One way around this is to use a template for the creation of users. First, create a dummy user account with the necessary access rights and group memberships, making sure that the account is disabled. When a new user's account needs to be created, simply copy the template and make necessary changes, such as username and password. This method significantly speeds up the process of adding several users at a time.

> **Tip:** In Windows NT, you may add users from the command line by using the cacls.exe utility. This can be used along with a text file containing all the users' information if you must add a large number of users at one time. NetWare 3.x provides the same service with the makeuser utility, whereas NetWare 4 and 5 use one called uimport.

Disabling/Deleting User Accounts

After creating all the user accounts, you can now sit back and think about other things besides user administration. *Wrong!* Users come and go as well as change jobs internally, all of which cause additional work for the administrator. It's important that users who have left the company do not continue to have access to confidential information. It's your responsibility to ensure that a system is in place to notify you as soon as a user no longer needs an account or when a user's access needs have changed. No one is more irate than a user who cannot access the applications and data necessary for performing his job.

> **Tip:** When an employee leaves your company, disable her account rather than delete it. Not only does this make your life easier if she returns, but when a new employee is hired to do the same job, you can just rename the account and change the password for the new employee. This way, all the necessary permissions and group memberships are already assigned for that individual to accomplish her job. Just be sure to create a reminder to delete that account after an appropriate amount of time has passed.

Group Accounts

Groups are used to organize users into logical collections based on how users need to access your network. Users are granted the necessary resource permissions based on their group rather than on an individual basis. Each user who is a member of a group has the same access permissions as the group. Not only does this make your job easier to manage when permissions need to be altered later, but this practice also decreases the possibility of forgetting to give the boss his needed access. Using Directory Services, such as NetWare's NDS and Windows 2000's ADS, introduces the use of *containers*, which can alleviate the need for groups. See Chapter 18, "Directory Services," for more information.

Local Versus Global

In NetWare, all groups are global in scope. That is, they exist throughout the network. Windows NT and Windows 2000 complicate this a bit. In these systems, a group is part of either the individual machine's security database or the security database for the entire network. As such, groups are referred to as either local or global. *Local groups* are stored on the individual workstation or server and are used to access resources on that computer. *Global groups* are stored on the PDC (Primary Domain Controller) and are available throughout the domain.

A resource is controlled by a particular computer, either a server or a workstation. The resource may be a file, a folder, a printer, or any other object that might be shared. The local security database controls access to that resource. To grant access to your users, use a group that belongs to the same security database. Therefore, when you're providing access to a printer, that access should be granted to a local group on the print server. Global groups or users may be added to the local group to provide user access.

> **Tip:** One easy way to remember how to use local versus global groups is to think of resources as "living" on a particular computer rather than belonging to the entire network. Therefore, it becomes logical to use a local group to control access to the resource living on that computer.

Global groups are used to organize users at the network level, whereas local groups are used on individual computers. Each user may be a member of several different groups. Groups may be organized by function, administrative division, geographic location, or any other logical sorting you might imagine.

For example, if all users in the Accounting department need to have access to files in a directory or folder on server S1, a global group can be created, perhaps named *Accounting*, and this group can be added to a local group on S1, perhaps named *S1Accounting*. Then on server S1, permission to access the directory Accounting Docs is given to the group named S1Accounting.

Another use for global groups is to provide access to resources across trusts. A *trust* is a special relationship created to allow users from one domain to access resources in another domain (again, this is only in Windows NT/Windows 2000 systems). Trusts are used to provide for wider access to resources. Local groups cannot cross from one domain to another. By placing users from the trusted domain in a global group, that global group may then be added to a local group on the trusting domain. This enables users from the trusted domain to access needed resources located in the trusting domain.

> **Tip:** When creating a new group using the User Manager in Windows NT, select the users you want to add as members of that group while holding down the Ctrl key. After selecting all the users you want to include, create the group. The users you've selected are then made members of that group.

Built-In Groups

Network operating systems provide built-in groups with the predefined rights and privileges that are necessary for accomplishing certain routine tasks. These groups are capable of performing certain administrative tasks, such as creating accounts and performing backups. This provides a relatively easy format that enables the administrator to delegate certain tasks without granting administrative privileges to others.

See Table 15.1 for global groups that are built into Windows NT and Table 15.2 for local groups that are built in to Windows NT. Not all these groups have default members; however, they can be populated to reduce your workload.

NetWare provides only one built-in group, called *Everyone*. As you might guess, all users are, by default, members of this group.

Table 15.1 Built-In Global Groups

Group	Managed By	Contains
Domain Admins	Administrators	Administrator
Domain Users	Administrators and Account Operators	Administrators and New Users
Domain Guests	Administrators and Account Operators	Guest

Table 15.2 Built-In Local Groups

Group	Managed By	Auto Contents	Permissions
Administrators	Administrators	Domain Admins and Administrator (user)	Can do anything except auto access files on NTFS.
Backup Operators	Administrators	None	Backup and restore, log in locally, and shut down system.
Server Operators	Administrators	None	Share/unshare resources, format server disks, back up and restore, log in locally, and shut down servers.
Account Operators	Administrators	None	Manage user and group accounts. Cannot assign user rights or modify local built-in groups.
Print Operators	Administrators	None	Manage printers, log in locally, and shut down.

Group	Managed By	Auto Contents	Permissions
Power Users	Administrators	Power Users	Set up users, create and modify user accounts, add users to Users, Guests, and Power Users groups, and start and stop sharing of local resources.
Users	Administrators Account Operators and Administrator (user)	Domain Users	Cannot log on locally to DC. Access resources via the network only.
Guests	Administrators and Account Operators	Domain Guests	Utilize domain resources via the network.
Replicator	Administrators	None	Manage replication of files.

Multiple Logins

It may be important for security reasons that users log in at only one computer at a time. If a user logs on to one machine and then walks off, the network can be accessed by anyone who walks up to that machine. If you prevent multiple simultaneous logons, a user who tries to log on to another machine is reminded that he is already logged on at another station. This feature may be implemented through the operating system or via a third-party product.

Managing Resources

A network exists to provide for the efficient use of resources, whether a resource is a database of customer information or the color laser printer. Administering resource access is one of the most time-consuming tasks for any administrator.

Resource management begins with determining a method of naming servers, hosts, printers, and other devices on your network. As when naming user accounts, stick to descriptive names rather than imaginative ones. A good naming plan identifies the location or purpose of each device.

After the resource has been installed, you must provide access to those users who will use it. When assigning access to resources such as printers, make your groups as all-inclusive as possible while still taking into consideration each group's unique needs.

Hardware Resources

Hardware resources are the most costly and most visible of network resources. They include printers, scanners, modems, cameras, slide makers, and so on. You have to apply appropriate permissions to give needed access as well as instruct users in how to access the resources.

When one of these resources is not available to a user, either through equipment failure or denied access, you'll face the user's displeasure. A proactive plan or regular servicing and auditing can help prevent the unexpected loss of use of these resources.

Disk Quota

Throughout the ages, it has been shown that any stored object grows in size until it completely fills its container. The same axiom applies to files, whether stored on the server or the user's personal computer. If no policy is implemented that restricts the amount of space a user can use, you'll soon find that all the disk space is completely filled up—often with documents, programs, and other minutiae whose purpose or origin has been forgotten. Certain networking operating systems have the built-in capability to limit the amount of disk space each user can use. The capability to set the point at which the shrinking percentage of free space triggers an alert is also often available. In addition, many third-party vendors offer products to fill this need. This capability does not presently exist in Windows NT but is offered in a basic form in Windows 2000.

Files and Directories

Files, and the directories containing them, are generally not thought of as network resources, yet they're accessed by users all day long. All users want to be able to access their own files when desired and want to know that others cannot see them. Windows NT, Windows 2000, and NetWare all provide the capability to control access on the directory and file level. These permissions are more efficiently managed by assigning users with like needs to appropriate groups. These groups are then assigned the necessary access permissions. Windows 95/98 allows for a limited amount of access control for remote users (but anyone using the PC can access anything stored on it.)

Software Installation/Upgrades

An important consideration when you're selecting the software packages to be installed is the selection of a virus-checking program. This program should be relatively maintenance free and provide for scanning of workstations as well as servers. It should also provide you with methods for logging significant events and generating reports.

When planning your network, you need to decide what you want your network to do for you. Many classifications of software packages, such as groupware applications, may be added to your network to increase productivity. Important features include document sharing, group scheduling, and communication (via email, for example).

After a particular software package is implemented, you must plan how and when software upgrades are to be done. The cost of installation on your client base becomes significant as your user base increases. This makes planning your upgrades very important.

Remote installation can significantly reduce the cost of your network. This may be accomplished either through *push technology*, where the server sends instructions to the workstation to install a program, or *pull technology*, where the workstation asks the server to send the program. Microsoft provides the System Management Server, which has the capability to inventory client machines as well as automate software installation or upgrades. NetWare 4 and 5 use the Novell application Z.E.N.Works for this purpose.

Email Applications

Email provides for fast, reliable communication within your organization as well as worldwide. In its most basic form, an email system is a store-and-forward application that consists of a post office, where mail is stored, and individual mailboxes for each user. You are responsible for creating and deleting users and groups and managing the email directory. If your local system is attached to another system or the Internet, you must also oversee the communication with these other systems.

Network Printing

Probably the most common reason for networking, especially in smaller organizations, is to allow for the sharing of printers. Sharing printers often justifies the purchase of more expensive printers, because fewer are needed. Be aware, though, that when printers do not work, users cannot be productive. As the size of a network grows, the diversity of printers grows.

Each brand of printer and each operating system provides administrative challenges. Various tools are available to allow for easier administration. The difficulty with these tools is that they tend to be proprietary and provide information for only a particular type of printer. One of the newest types provides the capability to manage printers via a Web browser.

Important administrative tasks include replenishing of printer supplies and attending to regular servicing. The most effective administrative tools are those that encourage proactive administration by providing easy access to data such as the total number of pages printed and the levels of remaining supplies such as paper or toner. Another useful feature is the generation of an alert when supplies are low or the time for routine servicing is near.

Many of the newer printers come with installed hardware or software that functions as a print server, thereby eliminating the need for the printer to be attached to a computer functioning as a print server. You must then decide whether a single, dedicated print server should be used to manage all printers.

When a file and print server are used to provide access to your printers, utilization of computer resources becomes an issue. The computer may experience degradation of its performance if it must manage several printers and support a large number of users. On the other hand, if a dedicated print server is used—even if it's no more than a board installed on the printer itself—it becomes another server that you have to manage.

When printing to a network printer, the job is sent first to the print server by the computer's redirector. The print server then "spools" the print job. The purpose of the spooler is to store print jobs until the print device is available. Spooling is useful when several jobs are sent at the same time or if a slow printer cannot keep up with the rapidity of jobs being sent.

The spooler may reside on the print device, in volatile memory on the print server, or on the hard drive of the print server. After the appropriate print device becomes available, the job is forwarded.

After a printer is attached to the network, access must be granted if users are to be able to print to it. First, the virtual printer or queue must be created and named, including loading the correct print driver. Any special printer features must also be configured, such as multiple paper types and duplexing. Once the printer has been created and configured, you need to provide for user access. In Windows NT, the Print Manager is used to accomplish this task. Figure 15.2 shows a printer being set up for sharing.

FIGURE 15.2
Printer properties.

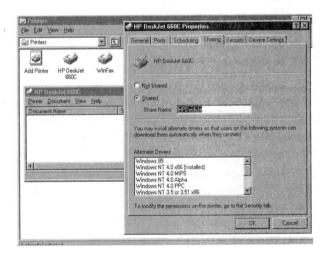

Each client must then be configured to connect to the printer. The names of the print server and the printer are used to create this connection.

Management Tools

A wide variety of tools and utilities are available to assist you in managing the network. The larger the network, the more complex administration becomes and the more vital it is that you have the right tools.

Microsoft Management Tools

Microsoft provides a variety of management tools to help you in the day-to-day management of a Windows NT network. The most frequently used tools are the User Manager for Domains, the Server Manager, the Event Viewer, and the Network Client Administrator.

User Manager for Domains

Windows NT's User Manager for Domains enables you to perform the following tasks:

- Select the domain or computer you want to manage
- Manage the auditing policy
- Set the security policies for your domain or computer
- Create, delete, and change user and group accounts

The User Manager for Domains is used to create user and group accounts, but it's also used to set global account policies, such as password length and expiration, password history, and the number of failed logon attempts that trigger an account lockout. You can also set a policy to forcibly disconnect a user after expiration of the allowed logon hours. Figure 15.3 illustrates the various global account options available to you.

FIGURE 15.3
Account policies available under User Manager for Domains.

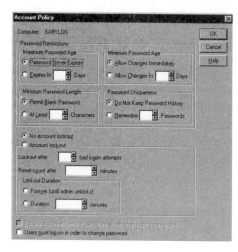

The User Manager for Domains is used to grant rights to users and groups. *User rights* are rules governing what actions a user can perform. These rights are computer specific and differ from permissions that apply to objects. It's generally a better practice to add users to groups that have the needed rights rather than grant rights to individual users.

User Manager for Domains enables auditing. With Windows NT, you can audit both system-wide events and specific actions of a particular user. To track events such as file access and unsuccessful login attempts, you must first enable auditing, as shown in Figure 15.4. You may then use the appropriate tool (for example, Windows Explorer) to indicate which events you want to track. Although auditing provides valuable information for the administrator, it does increase the workload of the computer that's being audited.

FIGURE 15.4
Enabling auditing.

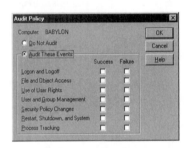

Server Manager

The Server Manager is used to manage both local and remote computers in your workgroup or domain. When administering a single computer, you may perform the following tasks:

- View connected users, disconnect users, and send messages to connected users
- View shared resources and directories
- Manage services and directory replication

Domain-related tasks accomplished through the Server Manager include the following:

- Adding computers to your domain
- Promotion and demotion of Primary Domain Controllers (PDCs) and Backup Domain Controllers (BDCs)
- Synchronization of the security database from the PDC to the BDC

Figure 15.5 shows the Server Manager.

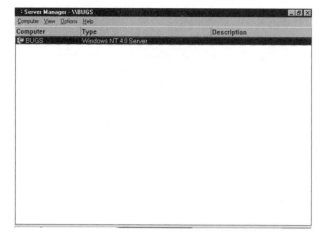

FIGURE 15.5
Server Manager.

Event Viewer

The Event Viewer is the first place to look if you suspect a problem with your computer. It displays the Security, System, and Application logs. The System log monitors events such as the failure of a driver or service to start. The Security log helps identify any possible breaches to your system's security, and the Application log shows events generated by various applications. You may select to view the logs of the local or remote computers.

Network Client Administrator

Microsoft's Network Client Administrator enables you to create startup disks that can start a client, connect to installation files on the network, and install the operating system. You can also create client installation disk sets that contain the files needed to install the network client software. The Network Client Administrator also copies the client-based network administration tools to be used on either Windows NT Workstation or Windows 95/98 clients. The last feature of the Network Client Administrator is the capability it gives you to view information on Remoteboot Clients. NetWare provides similar services through the ACU (Automatic Client Update) utility.

Zero Administration

Microsoft's concept of *zero administration* refers to the effort to simplify administrative tasks. It combines various administrative tools and guidelines to implement centralized management. User access is managed through the use of system policies and user profiles. The goal of zero administration is to reduce the total cost of ownership by reducing helpdesk calls and still provide user access to needed applications and data. Novell provides this as part of its Z.E.N.Works package.

Management Console

NetWare 4 and 5 are normally administered through the NWADMIN interface, but Novell has recently introduced ConsoleOne—a Java-based console—to host all administrative functions. Microsoft, meanwhile, has introduced the Microsoft Management Console (MMC) to answer the commonly voiced complaints from system administrators about the plethora of tools used to administer the network. Microsoft presently employs separate utilities, each of which provides the capability to accomplish one task. The MMC is not a new management tool but rather provides a single interface where other tools may be plugged in. This provides a one-stop place where administrators can find the tools used to administer the network rather than having to open and close multiple programs. Not only does this interface make your life easier, it also reduces the load placed on the network.

Summary

Network management begins with planning the network, from cabling and connectivity to the network operating system and software packages. It continues with day-to-day activities of user, group, and resource administration. But just as important, network management involves the long-term planning of the future course of the network. This involves evaluation of how the network presently functions   and what growth is projected. This chapter has discussed some of the tools and techniques you, the network administrator, can utilize to achieve these goals.

Managing Network Performance

Networks, as you've seen throughout this book, are amazing things, made up of myriad pieces from different vendors and manufacturers that blend together to form a working whole. The fact that you can, with relative ease, put together a network that enables computers to communicate at such amazing speeds, using parts designed and manufactured by so many different sources, is mind-boggling to ponder at times.

It's reasonable to expect something so complex to suffer from problems caused by that complexity, and with networks, that expectation is often well founded. Careful planning, design, and implementation can significantly reduce the amount of time you, as a network administrator, spend troubleshooting network performance issues. No matter how well designed and well laid out your network may be, however, it's essential that you have an understanding of the problems you can run into as well as the tools available to help you solve them.

This chapter discusses a number of the most common issues that can impact network performance. In addition, it examines some of the more common tools and techniques used to isolate those issues.

Potential Network Performance Problems

This section looks at some of the issues that can cause problems with your network's performance. Some of these problems are more common than others, but knowing about all of them can help you resolve problems with your network, ranging from the simple to the frustrating.

Physical Layer Issues

During the life of a network, the Physical Layer receives most of its attention from network administrators at the very beginning, when the network is first being designed and installed. From that point onward, many administrators forget the Physical Layer, expecting it to cause little or no future problems.

Although the Physical Layer is, indeed, often quite robust and reliable, it can still be the source of many performance problems. These problems include exceeding media limitations, interference, and wear and tear.

Exceeding Media Limitations

All types of physical media, whether twisted pair wiring, fiber-optic cabling, or infrared wireless, have performance limitations, based primarily on distance. Exceeding these limits, even by a small amount, can cause performance problems as data degrades to garbage by the time it arrives —or simply isn't received at all. Problems resulting from exceeded media limitations are difficult to diagnose; problems such as running a cable beyond the recommended length, stringing repeating devices beyond recommended specifications, or improperly terminating bus-based media rarely cause a network to simply cease functioning. Instead, intermittent speed and reliability problems plague the network, producing symptoms that can be extremely difficult to track down. The best way to avoid these problems is to familiarize yourself with the recommended limits for length, segment extension, and other such attributes and take care during design and installation to never exceed those limits.

> **Note:** Check Chapter 2, "The Physical (and Not So Physical) Layer," for information on the limitations that apply to various physical-level media types.

Interference

Most types of network media are susceptible to at least one form of interference. The same electromagnetic wavelengths used to transmit data are often generated by environmental, mechanical, or electronic phenomena, causing noise and interference that can wreak havoc on network communications. Such mistakes as running twisted pair wiring near fluorescent lighting can result in severely degraded network performance from noise. Wireless networks are even more susceptible to interference because they lack even the rudimentary shielding provided by twisted pair wiring. Problems generated by interference can be extremely difficult to isolate. In addition, it can be difficult and expensive to implement fixes to interference problems. As with media limitations, the best strategy for dealing with interference is to avoid problems during the network's installation. Be careful to consider any potential sources of interference and either carefully deal with them during installation or use a media type that's not susceptible to the interference.

Wear and Tear

Although generally not an issue with wireless networks, wear and tear on network cabling can take its toll on network performance. Whether caused by physical trauma or degradation over time in low-quality components, damaged network media can cause a range of problems, from intermittent connectivity drops in shared media, such as coaxial wiring, to more elusive performance issues, such as increased vulnerability to interference in a wire with frayed shielding. Wear-and-tear issues are less significant in modern networks; in particular, the replacement of coax wiring with twisted pair in many Ethernet networks has nearly eliminated many of the issues revolving around the rather vulnerable, fragile, and exposed wiring and connectors used by that media. The careful planning and installation of wiring in protective conduits, as well as the use of customized data jacks, can prevent most problems with network wear and tear.

Tip: Are you still using 10Base2 coax wiring? Sick and tired of dropped networks due to broken cable? You can reduce the number of bus breaks caused by simple human error with a simple step at each workstation installation and configuration stop. When (and if) your support staff needs to touch a user's workstation, take a minute to show that machine's user(s) how to properly disconnect the workstation from the network and explain the importance of cable integrity. Although this doesn't eliminate breaks caused by improper cable disconnection, it does sharply reduce their frequency. In addition, you may receive a more subtle payoff when users check the integrity of the wiring in their offices or cubicles before calling the help desk whenever there's a network outage.

Tip: When verifying the physical integrity of your network cabling, don't rely on sight alone, particularly when dealing with bus-based media. Physically check the integrity of each connection. A loose soldering joint or crimp may not be visible at first glance but can still expose the conductors whenever stress or tension is applied to the cable, thus increasing the bus's vulnerability to interference and possibly even disconnecting the wire.

Network Traffic Issues

At the same time networks have transformed the way users do their jobs, the utilization of networks has increased greatly. Whether generated by increased reliance on network services, the use of bandwidth-intensive applications, hardware problems, or sheer numbers of users, network traffic increases are a fact of life on modern networks. Most networks are designed with high levels of traffic in mind; however, as traffic increases, performance can degrade, and often in ways not normally expected. A variety of issues related to network traffic can degrade the performance of networks; these issues are discussed in the following sections.

Network Collisions

Ethernet networking is the most common form of local area network used. As you probably know by now, Ethernet's CSMA/CD method of bus contention generates a jamming signal, known as a *collision*, whenever more than one NIC (network interface card) attempts to send a packet over the network. (For more information on Ethernet and CSMA/CD, see Chapter 6, "Ethernet.")

As more and more workstations attempt to transmit over the network, the number of collisions inevitably rises. Because each collision causes every transmitting workstation to pause briefly, having a huge collision count is definitely a bad thing. In fact, on an Ethernet network, it's possible (although highly unlikely) that the collision load may get so high that a workstation may never get a chance to send its packets.

If you're detecting a huge number of network collisions (see the section titled "Tools and Techniques," later in this chapter), your network is probably overloaded. You can try moving to a more efficient media type or one with higher bandwidth; you can also try splitting up your network into multiple collision domains (segments on which workstation traffic can collide), either by using more segments or by implementing switching.

> **Note:** CSMA/CD networks aren't the only types of networks susceptible to this type of bandwidth clogging. In a Token Ring network, for instance, even though each workstation always gets an opportunity to receive a token and send data over the wire, high levels of traffic can cause extremely long delays between passes of the token.

Inefficient Network Protocols

Different network protocols implement their communication and address-resolution processes in different ways, some of which are less efficient than others. Many protocols that provide easier setup and administration via dynamic name resolution, in particular, pay for that ease by hogging the network with name resolution broadcasts. AppleTalk, the peer-to-peer networking protocol used by Macintosh, is notorious for this behavior. NetWare devices using IPX/SPX are also very chatty, sending out SAP (Service Advertisement Protocol) broadcasts on a very frequent basis. NetBIOS browsing, as implemented by LAN Manager and NT-based networks, can also be rather chatty, whether implemented over TCP/IP, IPX/SPX, or NetBEUI.

In a network severely hampered by excessive broadcasts, a number of potential resolution techniques are available, ranging from configuring workstations to eliminate or reduce broadcasts as much as possible, to filtering broadcasts at the router level, to actually switching to a different communication protocol.

Hardware Overload

As network traffic increases, so does the load on the hardware handling that traffic. Intelligent devices such as routers, which must check the headers on a large percentage of packets to determine routing paths, are most affected by traffic. As network traffic increases, the amount of load on these devices increases as well, until the device cannot keep up with the traffic. In some devices, high levels of network traffic can even cause the device to begin generating garbage of its own.

Hardware overload solutions can be dealt with in a number of ways. Using dedicated routing devices rather than multihomed workstations is a way to increase routing efficiency. In addition, adding routers and splitting your network into smaller networks helps distribute the processing load across multiple devices; however, it also makes the process of routing data more complex.

Poorly Implemented Network Stacks

As networks have become more and more mature, so have the techniques used to develop network stacks and NIC driver software. Many intelligent NICs, for instance, carefully examine each Ethernet broadcast and interrupt the CPU only if the data being broadcast requires actual system processing time. However, many older NICs and drivers are not so intelligent and can actually slow down workstations as network traffic increases. Purchasing modern, high-quality NIC devices can help you avoid this problem.

Some network stacks either do not properly implement certain types of network services or do not implement them at all. This problem is seen most often with older TCP/IP stacks, which don't implement more modern services used over TCP/IP, such as multicasting. When a multicast occurs, for instance, some older TCP/IP stacks do not know how to handle the data being sent and can generate confusing error messages, or even crash, thus adversely affecting the reliability of the system. These problems can be difficult to detect and diagnose; many times, these problems are assumed to be an "inexplicable crash" and show up only in long-term, detailed logs generated by network analysis software. (See the section titled "Tools and Techniques," later in this chapter, for more information on network analyzers.)

Garbage

Some traffic situations can actually be caused by faulty hardware. It's not uncommon, for example, to see a dying or faulty Ethernet card generate huge numbers of spurious garbage packets, flooding the network with garbage data and collisions.

Garbage can also be generated by electromagnetic interference. In addition, some overloaded hubs, repeaters, routers, and gateways are sometimes observed to generate garbage packets at extreme traffic load levels.

Denial-of-Service Attacks

As the Internet has grown, and more and more enterprises have connected their LANs and WANs to it, attacks against those networks over the Internet have become more and more frequent. One major type of attack is the denial-of-service attack, which takes advantage of bugs in TCP/IP implementations or problems inherent in the design of TCP/IP to "flood" a system, causing it to waste huge amounts of processor and network bandwidth responding to false or garbage requests. Some denial-of-service attacks can even cause a system to crash.

Denial-of-service attacks can be countered by keeping up with the latest patches and updates to your operating system and by making careful use of error logging and network analysis.

Address Resolution Problems

Even if a network has low traffic and high bandwidth, and every workstation can send data without apparent limitation, it's all for naught if your network stack can't resolve the address of the destination of your data. Resolution failures, whether caused by the failure of a centralized service (such as Domain Name Service or Windows Internet Name Service) or misconfiguration, can wreak havoc on a working network and often confuse users and novice support providers. Address resolution problems can be detected and resolved using some of the techniques listed in the "Tools and Techniques" section of this chapter.

Internetworking Issues

Many of the problems already discussed in this chapter can also affect you remotely, even if you're not experiencing those particular problems on your own network. An overloaded router upstream in your connection to the Internet, for instance, can severely limit or even eliminate your Internet connectivity, as can a misconfigured or downed router or gateway. Major failures on large networks such as the Internet can cause a domino effect, as *failover traffic* (the traffic from the failed links that now has to be carried on redundant links) overloads redundant links, causing connection after connection to drop or slow down. The next section, "Tools and Techniques," describes some methods useful for detecting remote internetworking problems.

Tools and Techniques

Now that many of the potential issues that can affect performance on your network have been introduced, it's time to discuss some of the tools and strategies you can use to isolate and correct those performance problems.

Ping

Ping is probably the first and most important diagnostic tool for a network using TCP/IP. Ping is a tool that sends out an "Are you there?" request to a specified host; if that host is alive, it responds with a "Yes, I am" reply to the originator. The Ping software counts the time elapsed between the origination of the ping request and the receipt of the reply, and it lists the elapsed time. Ping not only tells you whether a particular machine is up and responding, but it can also show you whether there are long delays in communication between the two; this is invaluable for isolating both outages and performance problems. Figure 16.1 illustrates a typical Ping session.

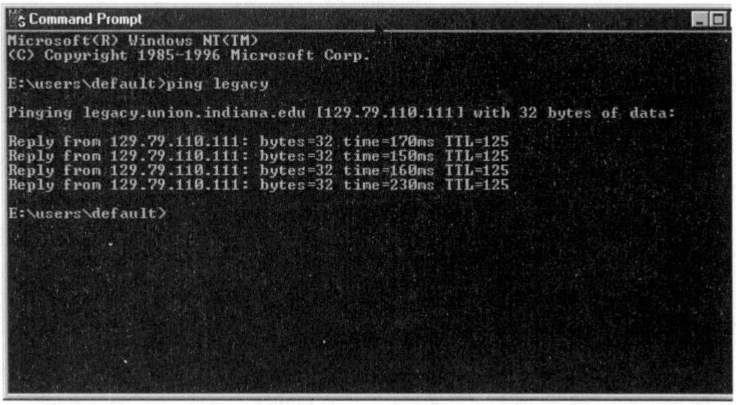

FIGURE 16.1
Windows NT Ping utility.

This example shows a call to Ping with a host name ("Legacy") and no command-line switches. By default, Ping sends out four sequential ping requests, and lists whether a reply was received and the response time for each ping. Ping has a number of tweaks that can be performed, including changing the number of ping requests, altering the size of the ping packets, adjusting the TTL (time to live) for the ping packets, and other configuration options. Most of these are not needed for standard diagnostics. For more information on those switches, type **PING /?** at the command prompt.

> **Warning:** Be careful adjusting the size of your ping packets! Many TCP/IP stacks have recently proved to be vulnerable to denial-of-service attacks using the Ping utility. If, when you run Ping, you specify an extremely large ping packet (normally around 64KB) rather than rely on the default packet size, the host TCP/IP stack receiving the ping packet locks up, dropping network connectivity and possibly even crashing the host system. Most affected operating systems have patches available to fix this problem, but not all administrators have applied those patches. Because there's really no good reason to use such a large ping packet size, you're best off playing it safe and avoiding excessively large ping packets.

When you're experiencing a network outage or performance problem, use Ping in the following order to help you determine exactly where the problem lies:

1. Ping a host on your TCP/IP subnet by host name. If the ping fails, ping that host by IP address. If the ping still fails, you know that TCP/IP connectivity is down, at least for your workstation; if it fails on the host name attempt but works by IP address, you know that name resolution isn't functioning properly.

2. If the host responded properly when pinged by host name, ping the gateway address. If it replies, you know your gateway is alive; if not, you may have any of a number of problems communicating with your gateway device, including incorrect subnet mask and/or gateway address configuration, a polluted ARP (Address Resolution Protocol) cache, or a gateway that's simply down.

3. If your gateway responds, ping a host on another local subnet, if available. If that host replies, you know your intranet is functioning; if not, you may have connectivity problems between gateways or between ports on the same gateway.

4. Ping your intranet's gateway to the Internet. If it responds, your Internet gateway is alive; if not, you have probably isolated your problem.

5. Ping various hosts on the Internet. This enables you to determine how localized your connectivity failure is. (This step assumes, of course, that you're not running a firewall or other security system that prevents you from successfully pinging hosts on the other side of that system.)

If, rather than an outage, you're experiencing slow performance, the same steps can help you determine where the slowdown is taking place—if you pay attention to the response times listed in each ping request.

Tip: Does your network use other protocols in addition to TCP/IP? TCP/IP diagnostic tools such as Ping are useful for more than just testing your IP connectivity; because the same gateway devices are normally used to route both TCP/IP and other protocols, and because most hosts on your network use those same additional protocols, Ping enables you to determine whether those hosts are alive at all. You can also use Ping in combination with other protocols' diagnostic tools (such as SLIST on a NetWare network) to determine whether the outage or performance issue applies to only one protocol or affects all your network connectivity.

Traceroute

As you may have noticed, using Ping to comprehensively diagnose the location of an outage or slowdown can be rather tedious. Fortunately, there's a tool that can ease some of that tedium: Traceroute (or TRACERT, as the tool is named under Windows NT).

You initiate a traceroute by running the program and passing it the name of the destination host. Every TCP/IP connection between yourself and that host is tested to ascertain both network connectivity and response time. The Traceroute utility sends a special traceroute packet to the first upstream host (normally your TCP/IP gateway), listing the destination of the traceroute. That first upstream host, if alive, responds to the originator by sending the equivalent of a ping response, with a confirmation of receipt, and forwards the traceroute packet on to the next upstream host. This process continues until the destination is reached or the TTL for the traceroute packet is exceeded. Figure 16.2 shows a typical Traceroute session under Windows NT.

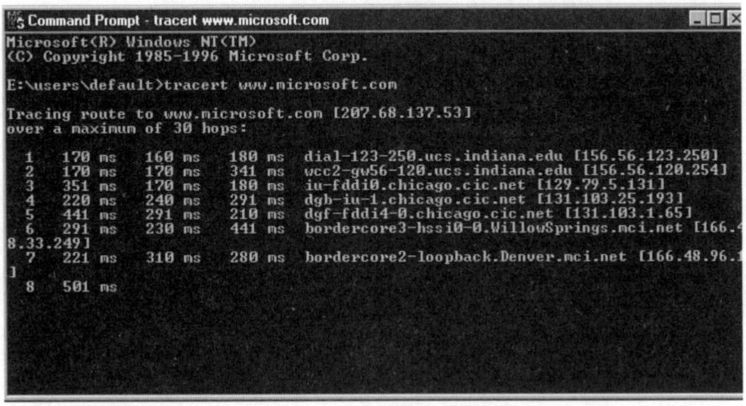

FIGURE 16.2

Windows NT TRACERT utility.

```
 Command Prompt - tracert www.microsoft.com                          _ □ x
Microsoft(R) Windows NT(TM)
(C) Copyright 1985-1996 Microsoft Corp.

E:\users\default>tracert www.microsoft.com

Tracing route to www.microsoft.com [207.68.137.53]
over a maximum of 30 hops:

  1    170 ms    160 ms    180 ms  dial-123-250.ucs.indiana.edu [156.56.123.250]
  2    170 ms    170 ms    341 ms  wcc2-gw56-120.ucs.indiana.edu [156.56.120.254]
  3    351 ms    170 ms    180 ms  iu-fddi0.chicago.cic.net [129.79.5.131]
  4    220 ms    240 ms    291 ms  dgb-iu-1.chicago.cic.net [131.103.25.193]
  5    441 ms    291 ms    210 ms  dgf-fddi4-0.chicago.cic.net [131.103.1.65]
  6    291 ms    230 ms    441 ms  bordercore3-hssi0-0.WillowSprings.mci.net [166.4
8.33.249]
  7    221 ms    310 ms    280 ms  bordercore2-loopback.Denver.mci.net [166.48.96.1
]
  8    501 ms
```

Like Ping, the Traceroute utility has a number of configuration options. For more information on options under the TRACERT utility on Windows NT, type **TRACERT /?** at the NT command prompt.

Traceroute is extremely useful for isolating the point of a network failure, because it can show which gateway device is not responding and even reveal whether one port on a gateway device is dead. Traceroute can also show you, with the response time statistic for each response, where network slowdowns are taking place. When used in combination, Traceroute and Ping are, perhaps, the most valuable software tools available to the administrator of a TCP/IP network.

Note: Don't like the command-line Ping and Traceroute utilities included with Windows NT? For Windows 95/98 and Windows NT/2000, the free NetLab utilities application provides a graphical Ping and Traceroute along with other useful TCP/IP troubleshooting tools. Its available from the PCWin Resource Center at http://www.pcwin.com/.

Windows NT Performance Monitor

Windows NT/2000 includes a powerful tool for diagnosing bottlenecks of various types, including network performance problems: the Performance Monitor.

The Performance Monitor (located in the Administrative Tools program folder under the Start menu) is a flexible, powerful tool for monitoring system and network activity. See Figure 16.3 for a picture of the Performance Monitor in action.

FIGURE 16.3

Windows NT Performance Monitor charting an RAS session.

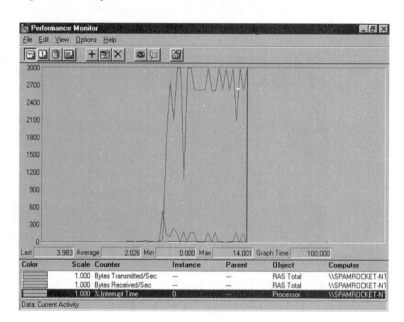

The Performance Monitor enables you to watch statistics for various network services, including raw TCP/IP statistics as well as statistics for the various network services, such as Server and Workstation. Watching how these statistics adjust under various types of loads enables you to determine whether your performance bottleneck is, in fact, your network bandwidth or is based on another problem entirely, such as an overloaded disk I/O subsystem, a pegged processor, or some other such issue. The Performance Monitor gives you flexibility in how you gather data, as well: You can interactively watch statistics in the Chart screen, generate logs of performance over time with the Log function, view raw numerical data in the Report screen, or set threshold alerts in the Alert screen. The NT Performance Monitor can be overwhelming at first, but it provides a variety of powerful features for identifying system-specific performance problems.

Network Analyzers

Network analyzers (or *packet sniffers*, as they're more commonly known) are designed to watch the flow of data across a network. They enable network administrators to watch the type and order of packets sent over a wire and to actually open up packets and see what data is contained in them. Network analyzers, although complex and sometimes difficult to use, provide network administrators the capability to watch how their networks interact with performance problems that are difficult to diagnose or reproduce. If you've set up your network as instructed, but the behavior isn't what you expected, you can watch how the network behaves on a packet-by-packet basis to best determine how to reconfigure your network. Network analyzers are often useful with problems that aren't even seen as network issues; for example, if several machines seem to inexplicably freeze at the same time, you can use a network analyzer to capture logs and see exactly what's happening on the wire at the time of the freeze and determine whether the network, itself, is the cause.

There is a variety of network analyzers, ranging from expensive, dedicated hardware devices to software utilities. Windows NT/2000 Server includes a network analyzer called Network Monitor, which can analyze either the wire to which the server is directly connected or the wire of another NT Server or Workstation on the network (using the Network Monitor Agent service, running remotely on another system). LANalyzer by Novell is another popular network-analysis tool, designed to run under DOS and Windows.

> **Note:** Network analyzers, with their capability to pull open each and every packet on the network, pose a potential security risk. Because many networks and applications (such as AppleTalk and even Telnet and FTP) use clear-text passwords passed over the wire, anyone with a packet sniffer can determine the passwords people are using. If at all possible, limit the people who have access to packet-sniffing systems to a trusted few. If you cannot do this, make certain that any passwords sent as clear text over the network are not duplicated by your users on other, more secure machines.

Hardware Troubleshooting

One of the most commonly ignored places to check for network performance problems is at the hardware level. (Ever found yourself spending hours diagnosing a communications outage, only to find that the Ethernet cable wasn't plugged into your NIC?) It's critically important for you to examine the actual hardware your system is using, particularly if you're finding a performance problem you can't duplicate.

When diagnosing network hardware, you need to consider the various potential points of failure and diagnose each one systematically until you discover which is causing the problem. Figure 16.4 illustrates several points of vulnerability, each of which can cause a network outage or performance problem.

FIGURE 16.4
*Potential points
of network hard-
ware failure.*

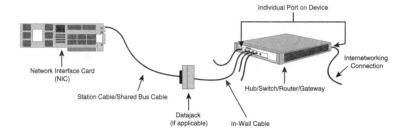

In order to detect the hardware problem, trace your way back from the most likely to the least likely cause. Network interface cards, for instance, fail far more often than expensive leased T1 lines.

To examine this step-by-step technique, consider an example based on a real-life network outage. Sarah, a network administrator for a company on the West Coast, has a new workstation that doesn't appear to see anything on the network, whether on her corporate intranet or out on the Internet itself. Sarah's first step to determine what's going wrong is to go to another workstation on the same network and check that machine's connectivity. A machine in the office next door is working just fine; this fact lets her eliminate upstream hardware or configuration problems. Depending on how her network is laid out, this revelation might enable her to eliminate differing amounts of hardware; in this case, Sarah is using switched 100BaseT, with in-wall data jacks connected to the actual switch ports and individual station cables then plugged into those data jacks. Therefore, Sarah has just eliminated the possibility of failure of the switch itself (although one port in the switch may still be dead) or in its connection to the rest of the network and Internet (see Figure 16.5).

FIGURE 16.5
*The first step in
eliminating hard-
ware failure
points: fewer
potential points
of failure.*

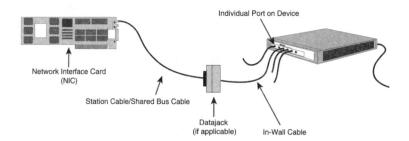

Now, Sarah's going to begin by looking at the most likely points of failure: the NIC itself and its connection to the wall jack. First, she checks to see whether any of the card's lights are active. Most network interface cards have at least one light that flashes to indicate network activity (with Ethernet, normally whenever a collision is detected). Better cards also have another light, to indicate when the card is properly connected to the network and to indicate whether the cable being used is of the proper polarity.

> **Peter's Principle: You Often Get What You Pay For**
>
> There's a wide range of networking hardware available at different price points, each providing different levels of features and reliability. The temptation is often strong to simply buy the cheapest NIC, hub, or router available to save some money.
>
> If you're tempted to do this, allow me to plead with you: Don't do it! The money you save on cheap, no-name devices with lousy drivers, no diagnostic lights, and difficult hardware configuration options is later spent many times over on the additional time supporting it. My mantra on the subject is this: The little bit of extra money spent on better hardware always pays for itself in reduced support costs.

In this case, Sarah isn't seeing any lights on the card. This doesn't eliminate any points of failure; at this point, however, many would assume that the Ethernet card is simply dead, particularly if the workstation worked fine before. However, a few more steps are necessary to more precisely isolate the problem. Sarah checks the station cable, looking for damage and making sure the cable is plugged firmly into the NIC and into the data jack. Because the cable seems fine, she grabs a cable that she knows is good (possibly from a machine that's working fine), and swaps it with the station cable on the machine she's diagnosing. Still no lights, and no connectivity. She knows she's eliminated another point of failure: the station cable (see Figure 16.6).

FIGURE 16.6

The second step in eliminating hardware failure points: fewer potential points of failure.

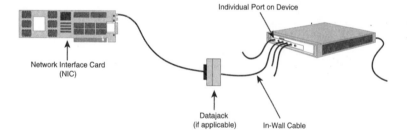

Now, Sarah examines the Ethernet card, checking to make sure it's properly configured and seated in its slot on the workstation's motherboard. All seems to be well, and she needs to try to isolate the problem further. To do so, she connects another workstation and cable that are working fine to the data jack—no connectivity. To double-check, she plugs the machine she's diagnosing into another data jack, and suddenly it has connectivity. Now, she's eliminated the workstation's Ethernet card; the problem has to be either defective wiring between the data jack and the switch or a dead port on the switch (see Figure 16.7).

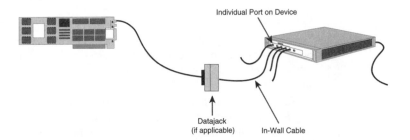

Individual Port on Device

Datajack
(if applicable)

In-Wall Cable

Sarah now checks the connection at the data jack, itself, and determines that the in-wall wiring has a broken connection at the data jack. She quickly repairs the broken connection, and the data jack begins providing connectivity. By systematically isolating potential points of failure, Sarah has avoided stabbing in the dark and has fixed the problem in far less time than if she had made a rash decision as to where the failure occurred.

Summary

The process of managing your network's performance can be more complicated than the actual design and installation of the network itself. Understanding the troubleshooting process, the available tools and strategies for diagnosing and repairing your network, and the details of your network's layout is your most powerful weapon as a network administrator. With that knowledge, you can turn the immensely complex task of diagnosing network problems into a far less daunting process.

Protecting the Network

Protecting the network involves far more than simply security considerations, although these are important. In this chapter, we'll look at data security—keeping the bad guys away from your sensitive information. We'll begin, though, with the thoughtful, practical steps you, as a network administrator, can take to reduce the chance of major system failure and to reduce your vulnerability to such failure as much as possible. We'll also examine ways to protect the data and make sure it arrives unharmed by discussing a number of different methods and techniques that can prevent, to the greatest degree possible, the loss of your users' critical data (and the placement of your head on the chopping block).

Ensuring Data Integrity

It's easy to overlook data integrity concerns, particularly in the modern age of highly reliable hardware and advanced network operating systems. However, a number of ugly—but important—facts still apply to every network server, and they eventually come around to bite you if you don't pay attention to them:

- Every disk drive will fail.

  Disk drives are highly complex mechanical devices, built to exacting tolerances. The reliability and life span of disk drives have increased significantly over the past decade, but disk drives still can and will fail; it's just a matter of when. In addition, drives are highly sensitive to their environment; many large, high-speed drives can be induced to fail if relatively strict temperature tolerances are exceeded (for example, if the air conditioning fails). Trusting your data to the reliability of a magnetic disk drive is a bold but incautious act.

- Mechanical devices have a limited life span.

  This is an extended version of the first fact. Every mechanical or electrical device will someday fail, whether you're talking about cooling fans, power supplies, or motherboards.

- Electricity is fickle.

  The power provided to most residences and businesses and used by most computer systems is filthy, subject to unpredictable brownouts, surges, and spikes, which can fry your system or simply destroy the power supply. In addition, an act of God or bad weather can cause a power failure at any time. Perhaps you're one of those lucky people who has a machine room with filtered power. Even so, is there anything to stop a fellow administrator from accidentally kicking your power cord out of its jack?

- Murphy wasn't kidding.

  Whatever can go wrong, will go wrong. For instance, most CPUs last far longer than their useful life span; that does not, however, mean you should rely on your CPUs to never fail. Does your integrity plan include contingency plans for tragic circumstances, such as a fire or a structural failure in your building? Could your business recover from a major environmental or natural disaster?

This part of the chapter discusses the various strategies and techniques you can implement to protect yourself and your customers from system failure. Some techniques may be unnecessary for many enterprises or outside their means; many strategies in this chapter, however, apply to every site, no matter how big or small. Although many details focus on Windows NT Server (including NT 3.51, NT 4, and Windows 2000), most techniques in this chapter can be applied to any network operating system.

Protecting the Operating System

Windows NT, like most modern network operating systems, is a remarkably reliable operating system. However, as previously discussed, bad things can and do happen, and eventually your server may crash and damage essential files in the process, thus preventing itself from rebooting. As anyone who has experienced this can tell you, the process of repairing a dead Windows NT server (or any network server, for that matter) can be a nerve-wracking experience, particularly because many of the techniques involved are counterintuitive to some.

However, you can greatly reduce your vulnerability by planning ahead and taking a number of simple steps that can make those painful hours spent after a major system failure far less stressful and that can significantly reduce your chances of losing data.

Installation Procedures

You can use a number of different strategies during installation to greatly reduce the chance of having to struggle to bring your server back online in the event of an emergency as well as to reduce your chance of losing data after a crash.

File Systems

Windows NT Server can use a number of different file systems; most people simply use NTFS (NT File System) for their entire server, which, at first glance, appears to be the obvious choice. NTFS was specifically designed for the high-performance network operating system environment in which Windows NT exists; in the process, the designers of Windows NT improved upon FAT (the File Allocation Table file system used for MS-DOS), eliminating many of its flaws. For example, FAT, being originally designed for small hard drives, could originally access only very small partitions; in order to provide support for larger partitions while still maintaining backward compatibility, newer versions of FAT use highly inefficient clustering schemes on larger drives, thus wasting large amounts of disk space for small files. NTFS uses much more intelligent clustering, greatly reducing the amount of wasted disk space. NTFS also provides support for features that FAT simply cannot, such as file- and directory-level security, customizable streams for serving different file system types to other operating systems, and transaction logging, which enables Windows NT to easily recover from file system corruption caused by inadvertent system halts. All these excellent features make NTFS a shoo-in for the file system used on most NT servers, as well they should; for the actual data on your server, NTFS is normally the best and, in fact, the only choice. However, you may want to consider maintaining a small FAT partition on your server's boot disk.

> **Note:** Many of the problems and advantages of NTFS also apply to NetWare's NSS (Novell Storage System) file system, introduced with NetWare 5. For this reason, it's recommended that a NetWare server's SYS volume (the one it boots from) be installed with the older NetWare File System and that you reserve NSS for other volumes.

After reading all the advantages of NTFS over FAT, it may seem patently insane to suggest maintaining a FAT partition on your boot drive. However, the value of having a small FAT partition on your boot disk can often outweigh the potential drawbacks. FAT can be accessed by nearly any operating system, including (obviously) MS-DOS. If your server should crash, you can easily boot to a copy of MS-DOS on the FAT partition (or even boot from a DOS floppy) and attempt to repair the essential system files, run the Repair process from the Windows NT installation program, or even reinstall Windows NT from that partition.

It's recommended that you keep a healthy FAT partition (from 300 to 500MB) on the boot disk, with a copy of the NT Server installation files, as well as backup copies of the machine's essential startup files (NTLDR, NTDETECT.COM, BOOT.INI), copies of the system boot sector and master boot record (made with DISKSAVE.EXE, from the Windows NT 4.0 Server Resource Kit), a full bootable copy of MS-DOS, and enough free disk space to accommodate the temporary space needs of the Windows NT Server installation program, should you need to run it.

These procedures provide a number of advantages: First, you can install Windows NT from the hard drive rather than from a CD, which makes the install run much faster. Second, if the server crashes, you can always reboot into MS-DOS and begin repair efforts from there. Should you need to simply replace an essential startup file, you can do it quickly and easily. You can also run basic DOS diagnostic tools on the system's hardware to determine its functionality, or you can use a simple DOS network client to grab needed files from other servers during the repair process.

The primary downside to this strategy is security; someone who can boot the machine into MS-DOS can also wreak havoc on the server. However, no security plan is valid without formidable physical security measures. Even an NTFS machine can be booted with a DOS floppy. What's more, the hard drive can be wiped and NTFS files can be modified (using the freeware NTFSDOS utility) if someone can gain access to the console.

Windows 2000 does change some of this information. The new Distributed File System (DFS), for example, only works with NTFS partitions. Also, on many newer computers a parameter can be changed so that the machine can boot directly from the Windows 2000 CD, obviating the need for a FAT boot partition to simplify installation. Nevertheless, and particularly if you use any 16-bit applications for network maintenance, a small FAT partition is still recommended.

Keep Backup Copies of Your OS Directory

Another technique useful for server installations is to make a backup copy of the default operating system installation directory (which, for NT 4.0, is \WINNT). It's simple: After you've completed the installation of the operating system and everything seems to be running well, copy the directory to another directory (for example, \WINNTBKP). Then modify your BOOT.INI file to give you the option to boot into that second directory. Should later changes or problems cause the system to be unable to load, you can always boot into your backup copy and retain the same hardware and driver settings and the same SAM (Security Accounts Manager) database. It gives you instant "rollback" capability—you can return to a functional operating system immediately rather than stay down until you can repair the damage just done.

> **Tip:** If you use this technique, it's important to remember to update your backup copy whenever you're confident you've reached a new, stable point in the server's life or just before you're about to make a major change to the server. For example, it's wise to make a fresh backup copy immediately before installing a new Service Pack.

Using Domain Redundancy Features

Planning on using a Windows NT domain? If so, you should always have at least one Backup Domain Controller (BDC) in a production environment, if at all feasible. If you're strapped for resources, use a lower-end machine for your BDC; the only capability it needs is to receive updates to the Domain SAM database. If, for whatever reason, your Primary Domain Controller (PDC) goes down, it's nice to be able to maintain standard production login and logout services until your PDC can come back online. If disaster strikes and your PDC must be reinstalled, you still have a copy of your critical Domain SAM. Making certain that you cannot lose your Domain SAM is invaluable, particularly in large, multidepartmental production environments with complex structures of user rights and trust relationships that can come crashing to a halt, thus requiring a great deal of reconfiguration if you're forced to re-create your domain.

> **Tip:** Do you work in a multilocation, wide area network (WAN) environment? If so, consider keeping one of your BDCs offsite; that way, if something catastrophic happens to your normal work site, you're all the more able to maintain production services.

> **Note:** Redundancy also applies to NetWare's NDS (Novell Directory Services), where multiple replicas of the tree partitions should be stored at different places in the network.

Maintenance Techniques

Now that you've reduced your vulnerability to data loss as much as possible during the installation process, it's time to focus on the preventative maintenance measures you can take during the life of the server to minimize downtime.

The Three Boot Disks

The three boot disks are the first three disks of the Windows NT installation disk set. These three disks enable you to boot your system and initiate the repair process or begin reinstallation, even if you're running NTFS and/or using SCSI controllers. Keep these three disks handy!

If you can't locate the three floppies, you can make them from the Windows NT installation CD. Just pop in the CD (or find your copy of the installation media on disk or over the network), switch to the appropriate directory for your hardware (for example, \I386 for Intel platforms), and run the following command from a DOS prompt:

```
WINNT /OX
```

You'll need three blank floppy disks.

NT Boot Floppy

Old DOS wizards are used to being able to boot their machines from a floppy disk, in case of emergency, to access the data on the hard drive. Unfortunately, there's no obvious way to do this under Windows NT; it can, however, be done.

First, format a floppy disk under Windows NT. Note that in order for this disk to function as a Windows NT boot disk, you must format it under Windows NT. Formatting this disk under Windows NT ensures that the boot sector of the disk attempts to execute the NT Boot Loader (or NTLDR). If, for example, you attempt to boot your system with this floppy in the A: drive, you receive the following message:

```
Cannot load NTLDR
```

Obviously, then, the process is not quite done. To complete the process, copy the following files (from the root directory of your server's boot partition) to the floppy disk:

```
NTLDR
NTDETECT.COM
BOOT.INI
```

This disk enables your system to begin the boot process, perform essential hardware detection, and locate the Windows NT system files on your hard drive. This is no guarantee that you can then boot the system; if the kernel is corrupted, for instance, or the Registry cannot initialize, the boot process still fails. However, if your problem is simply a corrupt or missing boot file, this disk enables you to restart the server and replace the damaged files.

Tip: Make sure you create an updated version of this disk after a successful Service Pack installation, in case any changes have been made to these files.

Emergency Repair Disks

One of the most neglected, yet most handy, techniques to keep yourself and your data out of trouble is to religiously maintain and update your Emergency Repair Disk. The Emergency Repair Disk contains a number of different files and Registry hives that are critical to the startup and functionality of a Windows NT system. If your system becomes corrupt or unable to boot, you can run a repair process to replace your damaged files and/or Registry hives with the hives from the Emergency Repair Disk or, alternatively, from a repair directory on your hard disk.

An out-of-date Emergency Repair Disk can be as bad as not having an Emergency Repair Disk at all. If you've significantly modified your hardware settings, applied Service Packs, or added large numbers of users and groups since the last time you generated an Emergency Repair Disk, an unpleasant surprise awaits you when you use it to "repair" your system. Your Windows NT machine will suddenly regress in time to an older, less functional version of itself, thus losing any new users, groups, and hardware or software customizations. The machine may not even be able to start at all.

You update your Emergency Repair Disk with the Repair Disk utility, or RDISK. To start the Repair Disk utility, run the program RDISK.EXE from a command prompt or from the Start menu. The Repair Disk utility is simple and easy to use; see Figure 17.1 for an illustration.

FIGURE 17.1

The Repair Disk Utility in Windows NT 4.0.

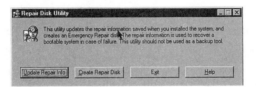

As you can see, you have only two options (other than to pull up the Help utility or to quit the application): Update Repair Info and Create Repair Disk. The first option makes a copy of the latest versions of all the pertinent files into the %SYSTEMROOT%\REPAIR directory on your hard disk; when the copying process is over, you're asked whether you want to make an Emergency Repair Disk with those new files (you need a blank disk if you want to create the Emergency Repair Disk). The second option creates an Emergency Repair Disk with the files already in %SYSTEMROOT%\REPAIR.

The Emergency Repair Disk (and the %SYSTEMROOT%\REPAIR directory) contains the following files, by default:

- AUTOEXEC.NT and CONFIG.NT. These files are used by the 16-bit MS-DOS subsystem to initialize environmental settings for MS-DOS and Windows 3.*x* applications running under Windows NT.

- DEFAULT._. This file contains a copy of the Registry hive HKEY_USERS\.Default, which contains system environmental settings for all users.

- SAM._. This file contains the default SAM (Security Account Manager) database created during initial operating system installation; this SAM contains only the default groups included with Windows NT and the administrator username and password you selected during installation.

- SECURITY._. This file contains the default security information for the SAM database created during initial operating system installation; see the preceding discussion on SAM._ for more details.

- SETUP.LOG. This file contains the locations of essential system and application files to be replaced during the installation process, as well as cyclical redundancy check (CRC) information used to verify the repair files themselves.

- SOFTWARE._. This file contains a copy of the Registry hive HKEY_LOCAL_MACHINE\SOFTWARE, which contains initialization and customization information for the software installed on the Windows NT system. This key contains much of the information traditionally stored in INI files in 16-bit Windows.
- SYSTEM._. This file contains a copy of the Registry hive HKEY_LOCAL_MACHINE\SYSTEM, which contains operating system, driver, and hardware settings.

Initiate the repair process by starting the Windows NT installation program using either the Windows NT CD in a bootable CD-ROM drive, the first three floppies of the Windows NT setup disk set, or the copy of Windows NT's installation media you've stashed on your FAT partition (see how handy that's become?). Then select "R" for Repair a Previous Installation. You can select which areas you want Setup to examine for possible repair. Here are your options:

- Inspect Registry Files
- Inspect Startup Environment
- Verify Windows NT System Files
- Inspect Boot Sector

Eventually, you're asked for your Emergency Repair Disk; if you don't have it, Setup attempts to read the necessary information from the %SYSTEMROOT%\REPAIR directory, if it can find this information.

You are asked whether you want to restore Registry files; you can select which ones, if any, to restore from the copies on your Emergency Repair Disk.

Tip: If you choose to replace the SECURITY and SAM data, your current list of users, groups, and security policies is replaced with the default ones created when Windows NT was first installed. On many systems, particularly domain controllers, this is a bad thing.

You can, however, use the latest version of your SAM database and security policies in your repair information, in place of the original data. You do this by specifying a command-line switch (either "/s" or "/s-") to the RDISK command.

You can use two different switches. The first, /s, skips the dialog box and immediately begins updating the repair information in %SYSTEMROOT\REPAIR. You're then asked whether you want to save that information to a new Emergency Repair Disk.

The second switch, /s-, behaves like /s, but it does not prompt you to create an Emergency Repair Disk; it simply exits immediately after updating your repair information.

continues

It's important to note that your SAM and SECURITY files can grow to exceed the size of one floppy disk, depending on how many users and groups you have in your database; this can cause the repair disk generated to be flawed and can corrupt the repair data on your hard drive. For this reason, it's always wise to make a backup copy of %SYSTEMROOT%\REPAIR before attempting to use either of these command-line switches to ensure that you can still make an Emergency Repair Disk if the process fails.

As the repair process continues, Setup prompts you when it finds a version problem with a file. You can choose to not repair the file (in case you have manually installed drivers or updated files since the system was installed), to go ahead and repair the file, or to repair all problem files automatically. It's probably best to let Setup prompt you for each file so you can verify that it's not replacing drivers or other files you've manually installed.

Note: It's important to update your Emergency Repair Disk whenever you update your system with a new Service Pack so that a repair process won't roll you back to a pre–Service Pack state or break any software that requires a certain Service Pack level. Check the README file included with your most recent Service Pack for more detailed information on keeping your Emergency Repair Disks current to that Service Pack level.

When the repair process is complete, you're prompted to remove the disk from your floppy drive and restart. If all goes well, your system then boots and functions normally.

Keep in mind that the Emergency Repair Disk is no substitute for a sound backup strategy; you still need to perform regular system backups to keep complete backups of the Registry, as well as nonsystem data, on the machine.

Also, it's probably a good idea to keep multiple copies of your Emergency Repair Disk. Label each one with the date, time, and status of your system at generation time. Then set the write-protect tab on each disk, make backup copies of them (with a program such as DISKCOPY, included with Windows NT, or the shareware package WINIMAGE), and store them somewhere safe. Don't keep updating the same floppy, in case you ever have to fall back to a previous configuration.

Disk Administrator Configuration Disk

There's another disk that's just as important to maintain as your Emergency Repair Disk, but even fewer administrators use it (or even know that it exists, for that matter). This disk, which can be generated by the Disk Administrator application (located in the Administrative Tools common program folder), contains the following information:

- Disk partition configuration
- Drive letter assignments
- Fault-tolerant sets (such as RAID arrays and volume sets)

It's critical to maintain a reliable Disk Administrator configuration backup disk, particularly if you're using any type of fault-tolerant disk set; if you don't, repairing or reinstalling your operating system could result in permanent data loss, which can really ruin your day. You should create a new configuration backup disk whenever you update disk partition or fault-tolerant set information.

To create a backup disk, you need a formatted floppy disk. Start up Disk Administrator (located in the Administrative Tools program folder), go to the Partition menu, select Configuration, and then select the Save option from the submenu. You're prompted to insert a formatted floppy disk; do so and click OK.

To restore your configuration from that disk, run Disk Administrator and then select Restore from the Configuration submenu in the Partition menu. You're asked whether you're sure you want to restore your configuration information; click Yes to continue.

Just as with an Emergency Repair Disk, it's a good idea to keep all your Disk Administrator backup disks and to keep backup copies of each one.

Service Packs and Hotfixes

Another important part of keeping your server (both Windows NT and NetWare) as reliable as possible is keeping up-to-date on the latest Service Packs available from the vendor. Service Packs contain regression-tested updates to the operating system that fix known bugs and security problems, ranging from minor annoyances to severe reliability concerns. Running the latest Service Pack level on your system helps you make sure your system is as reliable and secure as possible. Service Packs are cumulative releases; you need apply only the latest Service Pack to receive all fixes and updates made available with previous packs.

Occasionally, a problem with Windows NT crops up that's too severe to allow Microsoft to wait for the next Service Pack to provide a fix to its customers. For this reason, Microsoft has recently begun the process of making *hotfixes* available. Hotfixes contain emergency patches to security or reliability problems. Hotfixes generally require you to be running a certain Service Pack level in order to use them. Keep in mind that Microsoft does not regression-test hotfixes before releasing them and that they can cause problems in certain environments; for this reason, Microsoft recommends that you apply hotfixes only if you're experiencing trouble with the specific problem the hotfix addresses. However, in a real-world environment, administrators often find themselves applying hotfixes as soon as they come out, as a preventative measure, particularly with the rash of TCP/IP security hotfixes recently made available.

> **Note:** The installation of a Service Pack or hotfix replaces Windows NT default installation files and drivers with modified versions that contain updated code. When you change hardware settings or add drivers, Windows NT often copies default system installation files during the configuration process; these default files overwrite the Service Pack or hotfix files, thus eliminating the benefits of that patch. For this reason, you should try to avoid using Service Packs or hotfixes until your system's configuration is as static as possible; if you make changes, you must reapply the latest Service Pack and any hotfixes you're using.

Before applying a Service Pack or hotfix, make sure you have all the following:

- A recent, reliable backup of your system
- A fresh Emergency Repair Disk
- A fresh Disk Administrator backup disk
- Copies of all custom hardware drivers on disk
- A Windows NT boot disk

More recent Service Packs give you the option to keep an `Uninstall` directory so you can roll back to a pre–Service Pack state in case of problems; hotfixes, however, do not provide this option. In both cases, it's wise to have all the resources necessary to enable you to fall back to your previous configuration, in case the Service Pack or hotfix breaks your system in any way.

After you test your system following the update, create a new Emergency Repair Disk and back up your system again. Check the `README` file included with your update for any specific procedures for making sure your backup contains the updated system files.

Protecting Your Hardware

So far, this chapter has introduced ways to keep your operating system as reliable as possible and to quickly repair it if disaster should strike. However, even the most reliable, best-cared-for operating system is only as good as the hardware on which it runs; if your hardware continually suffers failures—whether from reliability issues or outside influences—you're bound to suffer downtime. Luckily, such hardware-related downtime can be reduced or even prevented in a number of ways.

Uninterruptible Power Supplies

Computer systems, of course, use electricity. The sheer complexity and compact size of the electronics in your system make them quite sensitive to problems with power. In an ideal world, the electricity used by your system would always operate at the same frequency, with no fluctuations or terminations in service. Unfortunately, in the real world, electricity is delivered to you across a vast grid of conductors, where it's also being tapped by thousands of other devices. The electrical grids in use today were never originally designed for the exacting tolerances of computing devices; therefore, problems ranging from constant fluctuations in the power to complete power failures are ubiquitous.

Everyone has, at one time or another, lost work due to a power failure; it's the ironclad lesson on the importance of saving work often. Fortunately, such occurrences on a PC normally affect only one user's work. Ponder for a moment, however, the detrimental effect a power-induced downtime can have on a network server used by many, many people. In addition, power problems can cause data loss; if a system crashes or loses power in the midst of a critical operation, data can be rendered useless, operating systems can be prevented from booting, or the actual hardware itself can even be damaged.

Four major power-induced problems need to be addressed:

- *Power failures*. This first problem is the most obvious. If you lose power, your computer shuts down immediately, often in the midst of a critical operation, causing untold damage.

- *Electrical noise*. Electromagnetic radiation caused by improperly shielded electronic devices, or even environmental phenomena, can pollute the power supply with electrical noise that can wreak havoc on sensitive electronic devices.

- *Power surges*. Ever had a TV or telephone destroyed by a lightning strike? That was a dramatic (and rare) version of a power surge, in which the power supply suddenly delivers electricity that spikes to a level far higher than needed—high enough to actually destroy the equipment drawing that current. Most power surges aren't nearly that dramatic; but small surges are far more common, and even a slight surge can damage some equipment.

- *Brownouts*. Brownouts are the negative twin of power surges; they occur when the electrical supply is strained beyond its capacity to deliver the needed current, so the supply delivers less power instead. Lights suddenly dim, and electronic devices may flicker on and off from the lack of power or even be damaged.

The most common power protection device used by computer owners is the surge suppresser; this device is designed to provide protection against sudden spikes in the electrical supply by clamping down on the current, thus preventing the excess power from leaking through. Many of these devices also provide filtration for excess noise.
Unfortunately, the vast majority of these devices on the market aren't capable of protecting against truly massive surges, and their protection may also be weakened or eliminated by a surge. In addition, they provide no protection against voltage sags or complete power failures.

However, there is a better solution: the uninterruptible power supply (or *UPS*, for short). UPSs were designed originally for one purpose, as implied by their name: to give a reliable power supply to computers. Every UPS uses a battery that charges during power service; if power fails, the device switches over to battery power, giving users enough runtime to save their work and gracefully shut down their system, or, on some very large units, to continue with their work. As UPSs have evolved, even more services have been added to some. These services include surge suppression, power filtration, and remote shutdown capabilities.

Many UPSs are equipped with advanced circuitry, designed to enable them to communicate with the operating system on the machine they're protecting. The UPS can log data such as system temperature, humidity, and power quality on the host system. In addition, when power fails, the UPS can log the event and track the remaining runtime on its battery; if power isn't restored within a certain period of time, these UPSs can even gracefully shut down the system they're protecting and then power off!

Modern UPSs equipped with such services are ideal for a modern networking environment; a properly configured UPS can protect a system without any human intervention, and some models can even page an administrator in case of an emergency.

Due to their great expense, UPS devices were once a luxury; now, however, even superb devices with high-quality software are reasonably priced, and the protection they provide to your hardware is absolutely invaluable in a production environment.

It's important to consider a number of factors when searching for a UPS, including type, load capacity, signaling capability, battery replacement, and other features.

UPS Type

There are two different types of UPS—offline and online.

An *offline UPS* is the simplest and the least costly. An offline UPS uses the AC (alternating current) power delivered from the wall outlet both to provide electricity to its loads and to charge its battery. When a power failure is detected, the UPS rapidly switches its loads over to the battery. When main power is restored, the UPS then switches back to that current. Although they're cheaper to produce, offline UPSs have a number of problems. First, the amount of time necessary to switch from grid power to battery power, although tiny, can cause some systems to crash. Second, many offline UPSs convert the DC (direct current) power from the battery to square wave AC, rather than the natural sine wave AC delivered by the power grid. This square wave power can cause many systems to freeze, and it damages any sensitive electronics over a sustained period of time. More advanced offline UPS devices attempt to deliver a "simulated sine wave" using many smaller square waves. These simulated sine waves reduce the potential for damage, but they don't totally eliminate the problem. See Figure 17.2 for an illustration of different types of AC. Any power filtration or surge/brownout protection provided by an offline UPS must be of the traditional type; most are no better at these tasks than a traditional, high-quality standalone surge protector.

FIGURE 17.2
*AC waveform
types.*

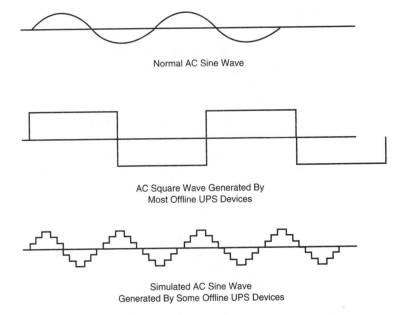

Normal AC Sine Wave

AC Square Wave Generated By
Most Offline UPS Devices

Simulated AC Sine Wave
Generated By Some Offline UPS Devices

The second type of UPS is the *online UPS*. An online UPS delivers all power to its loads from the battery and continuously keeps the battery charged with the AC power. Because the power being delivered to the loads comes from the battery rather than directly from the AC line, power delivery is constant, even if the AC mains power flickers on and off. The power delivered by the battery is clean, with no surges or brownouts. Online UPS devices are more expensive, are harder on batteries, and are more sensitive to environmental extremes of heat and humidity. Unless cost is the most important factor, however, online UPS devices are superior to offline devices.

Load Capacity

UPS devices are rated to deliver a certain maximum load in watts. Exceeding this load severely reduces battery life and can destroy the UPS. Make certain you purchase a device with enough capacity to not only maintain all the devices attached to your system but to also maintain enough additional capacity to give plenty of time for your system to gracefully shut down.

Signaling Capability

Most UPS devices have the capability to signal your system in order to log events, send alerts, and shut the system down. High-quality UPSs include their own custom software for monitoring UPS status and controlling your system; less expensive devices rely on the software included with your operating system (such as Windows NT's built-in UPS service). The custom software included with a higher-quality UPS is generally worth the extra money; it normally includes the necessary signaling cable and provides features that outstrip the operating system's own UPS software.

Battery Replacement

The battery in a UPS is generally a large, heavy, highly toxic item, requiring factory servicing to replace it at the end of its useful life. Some more modern UPS devices, however, have field-replaceable batteries, making your life less complex and reducing system downtime.

Additional Features

More expensive devices include even more features, such as the capability to monitor temperature both inside and outside the UPS, humidity monitoring, network configuration and management, and other such features.

Environmental Factors

Computing devices are also sensitive to the environment around them; extremes in humidity and temperature can be extremely detrimental to their functionality and can cause hardware freezes and device failure.

Modern hardware is, thankfully, far more resilient and less sensitive to environmental factors than it used to be; gone are the days when entire buildings could be heated with the excess heat generated by a company's computing devices. It's still important to keep temperature and humidity within acceptable limits, however.

Using a machine room gives you control over a number of factors. First, you can keep the room at a set temperature and humidity level. Second, you can keep your sensitive hardware and data more secure by restricting access to the room. Third, you can provide reliable power services by giving filtration and battery backup to the entire room, rather than relying on individual UPS devices. Fourth, you can centralize many of the major hardware administration tasks for your entire enterprise.

Machine rooms require a huge initial capital investment; however, for many enterprises, the protection provided is more than worth the cost.

Hardware Redundancy

As computers have evolved, they've become more and more reliable each year; hardware failure is no longer nearly as common as it used to be. However, it can still happen; hard drives fail, CPUs overheat and die, fans stop functioning, and network cards blow up. For most tasks, this risk is acceptable; if worse comes to worst and some piece of hardware dies, it and its lost data are replaced and the machine is restarted. However, some businesses have systems that cannot ever suffer downtime; for this reason, many server manufacturers have developed hardware with built-in redundancy features.

Some systems give you the capability to install multiple redundant hardware devices with automated fail-over switching to a working device in case one ceases functioning. Such redundancy can apply to cooling fans, power supplies, network cards—even hard disks and CPUs! (Redundant disk systems are discussed later in this chapter.) Although these systems are often quite expensive, many enterprises are willing to pay the price to ensure that downtime caused by hardware failure cannot happen.

Protecting User Data

Failure of some sort is destined to happen; whether caused by hardware giving up the ghost, a malicious attack, or simple bugs in the operating system resulting in a system crash, it's not only possible but likely that your system will eventually go down. In the process, you may lose the data your users store and manipulate on your systems. However, you can protect yourself from even these ugly facts of life with two different measures: sound backup strategies and redundant disk storage.

Backing Up Your Data

The concept behind data backup is simple: Keep a copy of critical data in case you suffer disk failure. You can back up your data to a number of different types of devices:

- *Online backup*. The term *online*, when used with respect to data storage, refers to a storage medium that's constantly, and instantly, available to the system. The disk storage normally used by your computer is online storage. Online backup, therefore, refers to simple, easy-to-implement backup measures, such as keeping a mirror copy of your disks (see "Redundant Disk Storage," later in this chapter). Online backup, although quick and easy, is also quite costly—you're really getting effective use of only half your online storage media, because half of your disk space is used to maintain an exact copy of your production data.

- *Nearline backup*. The term *nearline* refers to a storage medium that's not always kept online but can be made available quickly and easily. Nearline backup is traditionally implemented on removable media (ranging from floppy disk, for very small files, to large removable optical disks) or on large, custom jukebox devices using arrays of optical disks or tapes. Nearline storage is a powerful backup mechanism, providing not only rapid, reliable, and easily accessible backup but also the capability to store huge amounts of data not commonly used in a way that can still be accessed easily. Nearline storage, however, can be expensive and normally consumes large amounts of physical space, either with media storage or with large, bulky custom devices.

- *Offline backup*. Offline backup strategies are the type most commonly implemented. Offline backup involves copying data onto small, convenient, removable media, often using compression techniques. The most commonly used offline backup media is magnetic tape. Offline storage is relatively cost effective and simple to implement; however, it tends to be rather slow, and magnetic tape is notoriously unreliable, requiring careful handling and storage. The small size and reasonable cost of offline backup media make offline backup the most commonly used strategy by far; for this reason, the remainder of this section focuses on offline backup media.

Offline Backup Devices

You can find a number of different offline backup devices, each with its own advantages and disadvantages. These devices include the following:

- *Proprietary tape cartridges.* Proprietary devices, such as systems based on 3M's TRAVAN cartridge system, are most commonly found on workstations, rather than servers; they tend to be quite slow, with highly limited storage capacity. However, the low cost and ease of setup make them ideal for individual PCs not located on a local area network.

- *Digital Audio Tape (DAT) cartridges.* DAT is the most commonly found backup mechanism on small-to-medium-sized servers. DAT drives use a helical-scan mechanism (similar to the strategy used by VCRs) to store vast amounts of digital data on small tape cartridges. There are a number of standards for data storage on DAT tape. Most modern standards support only 4mm cassettes, although both 8mm and 4mm DAT drives were available originally. DAT tape capacities vary, depending on storage protocol and the compressibility of data. DDS-2, the most popular current standard, can store up to 4GB of raw data on a 120m-long 4mm DAT cartridge, with the potential of storing up to 8GB of compressed data. Most DDS-2 drives can back up data at rates approaching 20 to 30MB per minute, depending on server and SCSI controller load. Real-world rates tend to be much slower. Some newer DDS-2 drives can back up data much more quickly. DDS-3 drives improve on DDS-2, both in capacity (12GB native, 24GB potential compressed) and speed (potentially 50 to 60MB per minute). Jukeboxes are available to automatically swap DAT tapes for large backups. DAT drives are quite common and are well supported by various operating systems. The media is relatively cheap and widely available. However, backup rates are relatively slow, and DAT drives are notoriously quirky, requiring frequent cleaning and meticulous verification of each backup to ensure data integrity. Due to the constantly dropping cost and industry proliferation, however, DAT drives will continue to be a good solution for some time.

- *Digital Linear Tape (DLT).* DLT is a newer standard that uses larger tapes than DAT. DLT tapes are also much faster (potential speeds approaching 100MB per minute) and can store much more data (capacities of up to 40GB per tape) than DAT. DLT drives are quite expensive, as is DLT media; for large backups or time-critical backups, however, DLT is a superior solution. DLT backup solutions also tend to be more robust than DAT.

- *Advanced Intelligent Tape (AIT).* AIT is a recent backup solution and has little driver support in most operating systems. It is, nevertheless, a very attractive backup solution. AIT drives boast the capability to back up as much as 50GB of data on a single 8mm cartridge, at rates of up to 300MB per minute! Each cartridge includes onboard controller electronics to manage compression, storage, and cataloging, thus increasing throughput and reliability. The drives and media are quite expensive at the moment, however, and system support is likely to be sparse for some time.

Backup Software

Many operating systems, such as Windows NT, include some form of backup software; most of these packages are rudimentary, providing only limited management, cataloging, and timing options. Reliability is also somewhat of a factor with these built-in solutions.

A number of third-party software solutions for all major operating systems expand on the capabilities of those limited backup packages. Software such as Arcserve by Computer Associates and Backup Exec by Seagate include advanced scheduling, management, tape cataloging, and verification features as well as higher reliability and robustness. When choosing backup software, it's important to ensure that the software supports your back-up device, and it's also wise to ask around (on Usenet, for example) for opinions on usability and reliability.

Backup Types and Strategies

Now that you have both hardware and software, you need a manageable strategy for comprehensively backing up all your data.

First, it's important to understand the various types of backup most software can perform.

The first type is a *full backup*. A full backup backs up all the selected data to tape and sets the archive bit for each backed-up file to mark that the file has been backed up. A variation of the full backup is the *copy backup*, in which all data is backed up to tape but the status of the archive bit is not touched. Full backups capture all data to tape, but they can be time consuming.

The second type is the *differential backup*. Differential backups back up only those files whose archive bits are not set (that is, those files that have been modified since the last backup was run). The differential backup leaves the archive bit alone, however; subsequent differential backups include all changes made since the last reset of the archive bit, including the files backed up on the current differential backup. Differential backups are useful to provide additional coverage between periodic full backups; a strategy using full and differential backups requires only two tapes (the most recent full backup and the most recent differential backup) to restore all backed-up data. However, you pay for this convenience in media inefficiency (the same data is backed up multiple times) and in backup lengths that increase over the interval between full backups.

The third type of backup is the *incremental backup*. An incremental backup copies only those files whose archive bits are not set, just as a differential backup does. However, the incremental backup then resets the archive bits, as does a full backup. Subsequent incremental backups copy only the files that have changed since the most recent incremental backup. This makes faster, more efficient backups in between full backups. Restoring data becomes more complex, however, because both the most recent full backup and each subsequent incremental tape are required to restore all backed-up data.

In choosing a backup strategy, weigh the convenience of restoration against the time required for each backup cycle. Most backup strategies combine periodic full backups with daily backups, either differential or incremental. In some production environments, the benefit of being able to rapidly and easily recover from a system failure outweighs the inconvenience of the time needed for each backup; in other environments, there's little or no time in which you can lock out users to perform a backup, so the fastest, most efficient strategy is most important. In such an environment, you may even have to first copy data to a second drive or server that can be locked down and then perform the backup to tape.

Note: One factor not yet discussed is the capability to back up your workstations to tape. Many backup solutions have the capability to back up remote workstations to a server's backup drive. These solutions are extremely convenient, enabling administrators to centralize backup facilities; however, they can be complex to set up, often requiring client agent software on each workstation. Such strategies often also use tremendous amounts of network bandwidth.

It's also important to consider tape rotation schedules. The type of tape rotation schedule that's best for you depends on both your backup strategy and the length of time for which you want to maintain archived data.

If it's important to you to keep every backup archived safely away, your rotation schedule becomes simple: Use a new tape for each backup. The cataloging, storage, and fiscal investment in such a strategy can be prohibitive, however.

One common strategy is to have five daily tapes, which are reused, and one weekly tape, which is archived and replaced with a new tape each week. This enables you to keep weekly full backups stored safely away but economize on the use of smaller, daily backups.

Another strategy is to simply use 12 tapes over a two-week period: one tape per week for each week's full backup (a total of two tapes) and 10 tapes for the dailies. By rotating through these 12 tapes, you keep tape costs to a minimum. However, these tapes receive more wear and tear, and you have only two weeks' worth of data to fall back on.

Consider your long-term archival needs, as well as your needs for backup speed, convenience, and reliability, when developing a backup scheme.

Note: All these strategies and rotation schemes assume your data can all fit snugly on one tape; the same principles apply to multitape backups, but the complexity involved is greater.

Backup Scheduling

Another important factor to consider in your backup strategy is when to run the backups. Most businesses can safely run a backup overnight; in many 24-hour operations, however, this window of inactivity is not available. Open files are generally ignored (and therefore not backed up) by most backup software. In order to get the most reliable backup, you need to find some way to ensure the files you need to back up are closed (often by forcing logoff and file closure before the backup runs). On many systems, however, some files are kept open perpetually by software. In these situations, creative schemes (such as redundant disk storage and data replication across multiple servers) are required to ensure maximum data integrity.

Backup Reliability

Have you ever tried to restore a backup, only to find that the tape was bad or the data was corrupt? Make certain you monitor all verification logs to ensure that your backups are being made safely and consistently. Test your backup tapes from time to time by restoring a few files (which you've made copies of first!).

Backup Storage

Backups are intended to provide data integrity in case of disaster, including destruction of the backed-up system; if that same disaster can take out your backups, you haven't gained anything. For this reason, many enterprises rely on secure offsite storage. Many firms exist to provide this service, and they often include courier service to pick up your backups, cataloging services, and refreshing services (copying older tapes to newer tapes). Offsite storage can be expensive, but it may be worth it to a 24-hour, mission-critical system.

Backup Security

One thing many administrators don't consider is the security of the data on their tapes. Your server may be extremely secure to unauthorized access, but if someone can read your backup tapes, you're still vulnerable. This is a particular concern when using offsite backup; for this reason, use backup software that lets you encrypt or password-protect your backups.

Redundant Disk Storage

Data backup cannot address a few major data integrity concerns. First, there's the issue of backup scheduling itself: Any data modified since the most recent backup is lost in a catastrophic failure. Second, there's the issue of open files: It's generally impossible to back up open files, and many systems keep a number of files open as a matter of course. Third, recovery time is a problem: The several hours often necessary to recover from tape can be a major problem for some real-time work environments.

These problems can be addressed, however, by the use of RAID (Redundant Array of Inexpensive Disk) storage. The RAID concept is simple: Use multiple disks to provide disk hardware redundancy, thus greatly reducing the risk of data loss due to disk failure. The RAID concept has been expanded, as well, to provide for enhanced disk subsystem throughput through the use of multiple drives.

There are a number of different RAID levels; each provides different features, and each has its pros and cons.

The first, RAID 0, simply provides enhanced performance: RAID 0 stripes data across multiple disk drives. This system increases throughput by increasing the likelihood that the disk subsystem will be able to fetch different portions of the same file from multiple spindles at the same time. RAID 0 provides no additional fault-tolerance benefits; in fact, a RAID 0 system is more vulnerable to failure because it has more than one disk, any one of which can fail and ruin the volume.

RAID 1 consists of either disk mirroring (maintaining the same data on multiple disks) and/or disk duplexing (maintaining mirrors on separate disk controllers to eliminate the risk of controller failure). RAID 1 provides both fault tolerance and, in advanced systems, greater performance, because the same data can be read from multiple disks and/or controllers.

RAID 2, which is extremely uncommon, stripes data at a bit-by-bit level across disks.

RAID 3 stripes data at the byte level across all disks and uses an additional drive to store checksum/parity data. Should one drive fail, the parity data can be used to rebuild the RAID set on a fresh replacement disk with no data loss. RAID 3 sets often perform quite well, due to the striping of data, and also provide high fault tolerance. Fault tolerance can be improved by mirroring the parity drive so that there's no one single point of disk failure.

RAID 4 stripes at the block level and uses a parity drive like RAID 3. RAID 4 can potentially be more efficient than RAID 3, because data is fetched and stored in single read-write passes.

RAID 5 stripes at the block level, like RAID 4, but unlike RAID 3 and 4, it also stripes the parity data across all disks. This eliminates the performance bottleneck of maintaining parity data on one disk, thus enabling the system to perform write operations more quickly. However, this can make RAID set rebuilding slower.

RAID can be implemented either in software (such as the RAID solutions included with Windows NT, which can support RAID 0, RAID 1, or RAID 5) or in hardware, with special operating system–transparent RAID controllers. Hardware solutions generally perform far better but often cost a great deal. Hardware solutions, however, provide the additional capability to hot-swap drives: If a disk in a RAID set fails in a hot-swap set, you can simply replace the bad drive with a new one, thus eliminating system downtime. Some hot-swap systems even allow for the installation of a fail-over disk, which is instantly merged into the set in the event of a disk failure. You can then simply replace the bad disk with a fresh one, which then becomes the new fail-over disk.

Implementing Your Data Integrity Plan

We've looked at a vast array of options and techniques to make your data more secure. Most sites find it inappropriate or resource-prohibitive to implement all the strategies here. All are valuable, however, so which strategies should you use?

In developing your data integrity plan, evaluate the following factors:

- *Importance of data*. How important is your data? Is it critical that you lose none of it, or is simply keeping your server as reliable as possible sufficient because you can easily replace it? Is using backups enough or should you also use RAID? Can you afford a few hours of downtime, or do you lose money during each second that the system is unavailable?

- *Practicality*. Is administration of these systems your sole task, or do you have other responsibilities that limit the amount of time you can spend on data integrity? Do you have a staff of operators that can focus on these techniques? Can your company afford a machine room, or should you just use a UPS and keep an eye on the temperature and humidity?

- *Risk*. How at risk are you? Do you live in a major urban area or out in the boonies? Are you likely to suffer security attacks? How vulnerable are you to natural disaster or acts of God?

Tip: Are you trying to implement a sound, practical data integrity plan, but your management isn't willing to invest the resources? Make a business plan. List the costs and resources needed for your data integrity plan; weigh them against the costs of losing important data or suffering downtime. If the payback for your plan isn't enough to justify the expense, scale it back; if it is, a business plan helps convince management to back you up.

Planning for Network and Data Security

Let's now examine one of the most serious threats any network or user faces: the intentional threat. Although the threat from the outside is viewed by many to be the most ominous one, most studies show that the intentional threat usually comes from inside one's organization. In fact, almost 80 percent of all security breaches deemed to be intentional have come from insiders. One word that many people associate with this intentional threat is *hacker*. For the purposes of this chapter, however, a hacker is actually one of the good guys. Therefore, the bad guys will be known as *crackers*. Crackers are the persons who use hacking abilities for their own personal gain or some other malicious intent. Hackers do what they do to improve computer security and make programs and applications perform better.

Levels of Security

The first step to implementing security on any system is to develop an understanding of the security settings available for that particular system. With Microsoft networking, essentially three different types or "levels" of security can apply.

Microsoft networking uses a concept of sharing to enforce network security. Within Windows 95/98, the capability to "share" a resource means the capability to make it available for network use. If a resource has not been "shared," it's not available via the network. Although securing network resources through the careful use of sharing is a good start for security, it's also important for users to be able to secure the resources on their own computers. Windows NT/2000 users can secure network resources as well as their own local resources.

The level of security authorization a user has on a system is determined by the security granted to that user by the system administrator. The administrator of a particular system has a difficult job in determining what level of security to use, both for a particular resource and a particular user. For that reason, it's a wise move to always consider security before any installation or setup takes place. Additionally, the administrator should consider the use of a security policy (discussed later in this chapter) to help enforce security in an even and thorough manner.

The first step in enforcing any type of system security is to authenticate the user. Authentication is typically a process that consists of two steps: identification and verification.

Identification is the process whereby a user identifies who he is to the system, typically managed through the use of login names. To authenticate the user, the system typically challenges the user's claim by asking for the second part of the authentication process: verification.

Verification is the process the system follows in attempting to validate that the user attempting to log in is actually the person she says she is, normally by supplying a password. More and more, however, biometric verification is being used—fingerprint readers, retina scanners, and signature pads are finding their way onto many networks.

If the user is able to provide both identification (a valid login name) and verification (the correct password for that login name), she is given certain security clearances to use particular objects on that system.

To determine what the security clearances are for a given user, the security policies in effect must be examined.

> **Peter's Principle:** Lock it up!
>
> The one point I cannot emphasize too much is the absolute need for physical security. If your network servers are accessible to anyone other than network administrators, they're vulnerable. Passwords, encryption, UPSs, and redundant parts all are vulnerable to crackers and maintenance men if they can access your server.
>
> I well remember helping a network administrator discover why his server was re-booting every morning between midnight and 2 AM. At first, the backup software was suspected, but the re-boot occurred whether or not the backup was run. It also could occur before, during or after the backup. It took only one night of standing watch, though, to discover that building maintenance was unplugging the server to plug in a vacuum cleaner!
>
> A server belongs in a server room, under lock and key, available only to administrators and those in the company of administrators.

Security Policies

The term *security policies* actually has two different meanings in this chapter. The first meaning, the one discussed here, refers to a standard that's agreed upon by the administrative person or persons to enforce an agreed-upon security level throughout the enterprise. The second meaning refers to an administrative tool that became available with Windows NT version 4.0. That administrative tool is called the *Policy Editor* and is used to set up and enforce a particular environment for users of a system.

A security policy is an effective tool for ensuring that all the users in the enterprise conform to the security guidelines set up for the enterprise. An effective security policy has several parts, and each of those parts evolves from the information gathered during the first step in establishing a security policy: the risk assessment. A *risk assessment* is an evaluation of the enterprise and the risks it faces. A thorough risk assessment evaluates vulnerabilities, threats, and countermeasures.

Assessing Security Vulnerabilities

A good security policy begins with the administrator asking the question, "Where are we vulnerable?" A *vulnerability* is a point at which the system is potentially weak. Here are two examples of common points of vulnerability:

- *Backup system.* If the information is not being backed up to a tape drive or some other form of duplicate storage, the overall enterprise faces a weakness due to the possibility of data being lost if someone or something harms the data or the media on which the data is being kept. This is true whether the data loss is due to intentional or unintentional causes.

- *Users.* Users can be a vulnerability in two ways. First, if a user is not properly trained on the system or program he is using, he can make mistakes that lead to loss or damage of information. For example, a user who isn't trained on the proper use, storage, and creation of passwords could leave the system wide open to an intruder. Also, the untrained user could attempt to save data using the wrong procedure and actually overwrite or delete data accidentally. The second way a user can be a potential security risk is if he desires to intentionally harm the data in some way.

Assessing Security Threats

In addition to evaluating the potential vulnerabilities that an organization faces, authors of a security policy must consider the possible threats that endanger the enterprise as well. A *threat* is something that can take advantage of a particular vulnerability. Consider the following examples:

- *Cracker.* If one of the vulnerabilities is a back door or some other type of hole in the system itself, you can rest assured a cracker can find it and exploit it. A cracker looks for ways to infiltrate your system and is therefore a considerable threat to it.

- *Viruses.* Scanning for viruses is a necessity in every environment. Viruses show up in downloaded programs and files, email messages, and even off-the-shelf software. If one of the risk assessment's vulnerabilities is that no virus scanning is being done on the system, a virus should be considered a very real threat.

- *Environment.* Every regional area of the globe faces different kinds of environmental threats. Volcanoes, hurricanes, earthquakes, tornadoes, floods, and other potential disasters are some of the most difficult threats to protect against. In fact, sometimes the only countermeasure for this type of threat is to make sure that a backup copy exists and that there's some way to restore the backup elsewhere.

Establishing Security Countermeasures

After members of an organization have discussed, identified, and evaluated the potential vulnerabilities and threats their organization faces, they're ready to move on to the next step in the risk assessment and security policy process: countermeasures. A *countermeasure* is something that's done in an attempt to minimize the risk caused by a particular vulnerability or threat. Here are a few examples:

- *Backups.* Keeping a backup copy of the information contained in the computer systems is one of the best ways to ensure that the organization can get the data back if something happens. This type of countermeasure is very helpful against threats such as equipment failure and natural disasters.

- *Physical security.* Enforcing a rigid physical security policy is one way to help prevent attacks from outside intruders. Locked doors, electronic access badges, and removable hard drives that are locked in a safe every night are just a few ways to prevent someone from breaking in and gaining access to important information.

- *Cable Security.* Some organizations have to worry about the possibility that the signals that travel through their network cables might be tapped. If this is the case, you might consider using fiber-optic cable to transmit all information, because it's much more difficult to steal a signal from fiber-optic cable than it is from coaxial or some type of twisted pair.

Creating the Security Policy

After the risk assessment has been completed, the information gathered from it should be used to create a security plan specifically designed and tailored to the needs of the organization. The security policy should be very thorough and cover at least the following details:

- *Policies*. The security plan should state in detail exactly what the policies of the enterprise are regarding security and security-related issues. The policies should be explained to every individual within the organization, and each individual should be required to acknowledge his acceptance and understanding of, and compliance with the policies by signing a statement that indicates that fact. The policies should be very specific and not leave any information out.

- *Procedures*. Additionally, the security plan should list very detailed procedures that must be followed in order to enforce the security policies. Each individual who is responsible for a particular procedure should be made aware of the responsibility and the consequences of performing the procedure inadequately. It's a good idea to also have each responsible party sign the procedure(s) for which he is responsible to indicate approval and understanding of the tasks prescribed.

- *Updates*. A good security plan is only as good as the information contained within it. If that information becomes outdated, the security plan does also. It's a good idea to continually reevaluate your organization's vulnerabilities, the potential threats, and the available countermeasures, and to keep the security plan updated on a consistent basis.

Workgroups, Domains, and Trusts

One of the things that can affect the security policy of your enterprise is the implementation and configuration of your network. With Microsoft networking, a network may be implemented in essentially two ways. One method is called *workgroup networking*, and the other is called *domain networking*.

Workgroup networking enables users to find resources easily by categorizing them by location. Locations include both the devices on which resources are located and the workgroups in which they reside. The workgroup does not assist the security of the network directly, but it does make the network easier for users to use and therefore a little less prone to errors.

The only thing that determines to which workgroup a particular device belongs is how the device was configured. Users are not confined to browsing their workgroup; they can browse any workgroup they can see on their network. If the computers being used to form the workgroup are running Windows NT/2000, some additional security measures can be taken. Users can be authenticated by their usernames and passwords before they access a particular resource on the network. However, with Windows 95, Windows 98 and Windows for Workgroups, users can be verified only by means of a password, because a valid username is not required.

The only problem with using Windows NT systems in a workgroup to provide security is that to enforce rigid security, each user must have a valid username and password on every system he wants to access. This can lead to an administrative nightmare. With Windows NT, an administrator must ensure that every time a user wants to change a password, the change is made on all the systems on the network the user needs to access. If the user has a different password on each system, it's the user who has an ominous task to face. The user must then remember several different passwords, generally by writing them down or creating easily guessed passwords, which should be a violation of the security policy.

Microsoft's answer to this dilemma was to create an administrative tool called a *domain*. A domain is a collection of all the devices, users, and resources into one cohesive administrative unit.

> **Note:** Windows 2000 implements the Active Directory Service (ADS) which alleviates much of the complexity of the domain system used in Windows NT 3.5x and 4.0. However, ADS still contains domains and trust relationships, so this discussion should be considered background information if you're running Windows 2000 as your NOS. For more information on ADS, see chapter 18, "Directory Services."

When a user needs to have access to the domain, he simply logs in to the domain. After a user is authenticated, he automatically has access to all the domain resources that his security privileges give him access to without having to log in to each one separately.

A domain enables the administrator to effectively manage numerous users, resources, and devices while keeping the administrative tasks relatively simple. Having several thousand users or several thousand network resources can lead to administrative difficulties because there are more items to administer. If this happens, the first reaction of the administrative team is to start dividing up the tasks into different administrative groupings, which typically leads to the creation of multiple domains. If an enterprise makes the decision to create multiple domains, it's back to the original problem. Having multiple domains causes the users to need multiple login names and passwords. Alternatively, if the login names and passwords are the same, the administrative team must keep all the domains up-to-date.

To solve this dilemma, Microsoft created another administrative tool called a *trust*. A trust relationship is used to enable users to log in only once to their primary domain but then to give them the access (where security permits) to other resources in other domains. If the trust relationships are set up properly, a user can log in once and still use all the network resources he is authorized to use. When a trust relationship is created, the accounts domain (the domain with the user accounts in it) becomes the trusted domain and the resource domain (the domain with the resources to which the user needs access) becomes the trusting domain. See Figure 17.3 for an example of a trust relationship.

Figure 17.3

An example of a trust relationship.

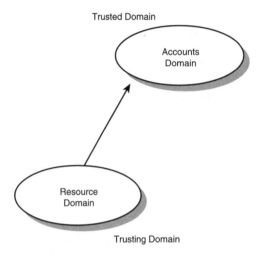

The Four Domain Models
======================

The Four Domain Models

Microsoft has created four different domain models that can be set up depending on the configuration of the organization. Figure 17.4 shows the Microsoft chart that helps an organization determine which domain model might be the best choice.

Figure 17.4

Choosing a domain model.

Domain Attribute	Single Domain	Master Domain	Multiple Master Domain	Complete Trust
Fewer than 40,000 users per domain	●	●		
More than 40,000 users per domain			●	
Centralized account management	●	●	●	
Centralized resource management	●			
Decentralized account management			●	●
Decentralized resource management		●	●	●
Central MIS	●	●	●	
No central MIS				●

The first domain model, the *single domain*, is relatively straightforward. The single domain model does not require any trust relationships and, as you can see from the chart in Figure 17.4, it works for up to 40,000 users in an environment that has a centralized MIS department and centralized resources and users.

The second domain model is called the *master domain model*. A master domain consists of two or more domains with one of the domains being the master domain. The master domain is also referred to as the *accounts domain* because the user accounts are typically set up only in the master domain. The master domain model works well for organizations with a centralized MIS department and centralized user management. The subordinate domains are normally set up around the resources they provide and are referred to as the *resource domains*.

In order for a true master domain model to exist, a one-way trust relationship must be set up between the resource domains and the master domain. Figure 17.5 shows an example of a master domain with two resource domains. Notice how the arrows are drawn in Figure 17.5. The arrow always points to the trusted domain. The reasoning for this is that the master domain is providing the authentication for all the users. The resource domains are saying to the master domain, "We trust you to provide login authentication for all the users." That way, the users have to log in to the network only once.

FIGURE 17.5
The Master Domain model.

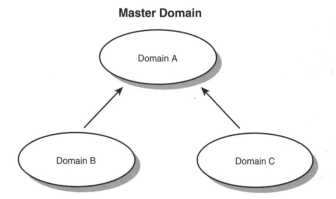

Master Domain

The third type of domain model is the *multiple master domain model*. In the multiple master model, at least two master domains have user accounts in them. There are normally two or more resource domains as well. Each resource domain must have a one-way trust relationship with each master domain. The master domains normally have a two-way trust relationship between themselves.

Figure 17.6 shows an example of the multiple master domain model with two master (accounts) domains and three subordinate (resource) domains. Multiple master models work best for organizations with more than 40,000 users that have centralized account management for different sites or regions. An example might be an enterprise that has corporate offices in the United States and Europe. There could be a master domain for each region and then several subordinate domains as necessary.

The last type of domain setup is the *complete trust model*. In the complete trust model, each of the domains forms a two-way trust relationship with each of the other domains. Although this involves plenty of trust relationships to manage, it can sometimes be the best method for an organization to employ. The complete trust model works for any number of users and is shown in Figure 17.7.

FIGURE 17.6
The multiple Master Domain model.

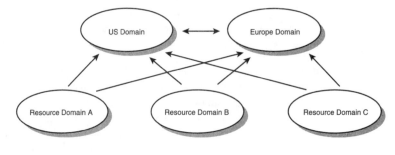

FIGURE 17.7
The complete trust model.

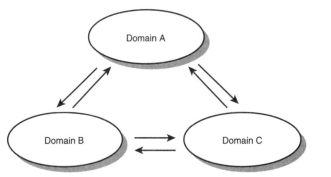

Security in Windows 95/Windows 98

Before beginning any discussion on security within Windows 9x (that is, Windows 95/98), it's important to note that Windows 9x offers only basic security for those who need to protect their systems against a casual browsing user, not against the diehard cracker. The login procedure of Windows 9x can be defeated without a lot of effort by someone with the know-how and desire. If you need more security than that, you should use Windows NT Workstation as your desktop operating system.

You can also enforce security with Windows 9x by enabling network users to browse shared resources on individual machines. Setting up shared resources on a Windows 9x machine enables the user or administrator to configure the resource with a password, if desired. Windows 9x offers the following three levels of access:

- *Read.* Read access enables the user to look at, run, or open a file or copy it to some other location. A user with Read access cannot change or delete the existing file or add new files.

- *Full.* Users with Full access can manipulate files and directories as they want.

- *None.* The only way to truly keep other users out of a network resource that has been shared on a Windows 9x machine is to require users to give a password to gain access to the share. Anyone who does not know the password cannot access the resource from the network. With Windows 9x, you can grant different passwords for Read access and Full access.

Password-Protected Shares

To set up a shared resource with Windows 9x, you must first have the proper Microsoft Networking components installed, which include file and printer sharing. The easiest way to share a directory (*folder* in Windows 9x terminology) is to browse for that directory using Windows Explorer or My Computer. After you find the folder that contains the files or folders you want to share, simply use the secondary mouse button to click once and bring up the context menu for that folder.

Select Sharing to get to the Share Properties box for that folder and then name the shared resource.

Here are some points to consider about the name of this shared resource:

- Who needs to access it? If you expect to have users on DOS-based machines trying to find the share, it's best to use eight-character names with no spaces or illegal characters so that the DOS users can gain access to the share more easily.

- What name you should use for the share? Obviously, a name such as *WORDDOCS* is a good way to describe a shared resource for Word documents. But a share name of *DOCS* might work just as well. You can give a more descriptive comment about the share in the box below the share name, so you don't need to get too complicated with the share name. Just remember that the more logical the share name, the easier it is for users to find and use it.

- What type of access should you assign to the share? Remember that three types of access can be assigned. Users can have Read permissions, full access to the folder and its contents, or no access at all.

Selecting the OK button when all the fields are filled in establishes the share and the associated settings for it.

Security in Windows NT

Windows NT/2000 gives users the same capability to share resources that Windows 9x does. The only difference between the share properties for a Windows 9x system and a Windows NT system is that additional types of access can be assigned. Windows NT also has the additional capability to assign access on a user-by-user basis. To assign security in the Windows NT environment, you use the same procedure outlined previously for Windows 9x.

Figure 17.8 gives an example of how to set up different types of access for different users and groups. You can see from this example that actually four types of access can be assigned to a Windows NT share:

- *No Access*. The No Access permission is not used for every user to block his access to a share. The No Access permission is a special revoking privilege that's used to take away rights from a user who might acquire rights indirectly from somewhere else. Users do not have rights to a share in Windows NT unless they've been given those rights. No Access is used when a user or group has access it does not need, but the administrator finds it easier to use the No Access capability to remove that user or group's permissions to this one share rather than completely rearrange the users and the groups to which it belongs.

- *Read*. Read permissions are essentially the same in Windows 9x and Windows NT. Individuals with Read permissions can look at a list of files, open files, read the contents, and copy the files.

- *Change*. Change permissions enable the users to do all the things that users with Read permissions can do. In addition, users with Change permissions can change and delete the contents of existing files and directories.

- *Full Control*. Users with Full Control permissions are not limited to what they can do with the shared directory or files.

FIGURE 17.8

An example of four types of share permissions in Windows NT.

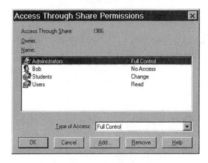

Windows NT also has the capability to protect local files in addition to the ones that are shared. To accomplish this, the files or directories must be located on a partition that has been formatted with NTFS (New Technology Filing System). NTFS has the capability to offer security for the files and directories stored on the partition.

To assign local permissions, you must access the Properties box for the directory or file and select the Security tab. The Permissions button on the Security tab enables the user or administrator to configure security settings for the files or directories even if the user is accessing them from the system on which they're located rather than from across the network. NTFS permissions apply even if no share is set up for the directory.

NTFS provides for very specific capabilities to be assigned to the users. In addition to providing additional settings, NTFS enables the user or administrator to set up "special access" and choose a unique configuration. Here are the settings (other than special-access configurations) under NTFS:

- *No Access*. Just like Windows NT share permissions, No Access is not a rights assignment, but a revoking capability.
- *List*. Provides the capability to see the files in the directory.
- *Read*. Basically the same as with Windows NT share permissions.
- *Add*. Enables users to add files (write) to a directory but not to a file.
- *Add & Read*. Just as it sounds, this setting gives users the read capability and the add capability.
- *Change*. Once again, this is very similar to the Windows NT share permissions. The only thing users do not get with the Change permission is the capability to take ownership of objects and change the permissions for the objects.
- *Full Control*. As the name implies, Full Control gives users full control of any objects for which they have this permission.

The individual permissions assigned are denoted by a letter. The list of possible choices includes the following:

- R: Read
- W: Write
- X: Execute
- D: Delete
- O: Take Ownership
- P: Change Permissions

Many more relevant issues surround the methods used to establish permissions for users. To be very effective, you must absolutely understand all pertinent issues related to how permissions are assigned and how the share permissions and local permissions interact with each other. Also, you must consider how to assign the rights most effectively so that users have the appropriate rights to carry out their tasks while making sure that no one user has any rights he doesn't need to have.

It's important to note that the network permissions a user gets from various assignments of rights are cumulative. The local permissions a user gets from various rights assignments are also cumulative. However, the relationship between local permissions and network permissions is not a cumulative one but rather relies on the most restrictive permission gained from the accumulation of network permissions and local permissions. Because this is rather confusing, an example is helpful.

In this example, a user, John, is a member of the Student group. He's attempting to use a resource on the network. The resource, referred to here as *FILES*, is a directory of files. Because this resource is a network resource, John must connect to the resource machine through a share that has been set up to enable users to get to FILES. This network share has two permission assignments allocated to it. The first assignment gives Read permission specifically to John. The second assignment gives the Student group the permission of Change. Because John is a member of the Student group, John also gets the Change permission.

As stated previously, the network permissions acquired are cumulative. This means John has both the Change permission and the Read permission. They add together to form the level of access that John gets to this network share. The highest level of access John can have to this network share is currently Change. Remember that the Change permission includes everything that Read provides, so it can simply be said that John has Change permission to the FILES resource.

Now imagine that the FILES resource is actually located on a disk that has been formatted with NTFS. This enables the system administrator to assign local permissions to the resource in addition to the network permissions that have already been assigned. For the purposes of this example, the FILES resource has a local permission assignment of Read for the user John. We'll also include a local permission assignment of Full Control for the group Student.

Because local permissions are cumulative, John has Full Control as his effective local permission assignment. Again, remember that Full Control includes the capability of Read. The caveat to remember here is that John is accessing this information from the network where his highest level of permission is Change. Therefore, when John tries to access the FILES resource from the network, he has Change permissions. The easiest way to remember this is that when comparing the total of all the network permissions assigned with the total of all the local permissions assigned to a user, the most restrictive total applies.

Because of this confusion, it's not uncommon to see most administrators set up all the network permissions for resources that lie on NTFS partitions as a share with Full Control permissions for Everyone. The administrator then goes back and gives specific permissions to users by implementing the local NTFS permissions. Remember, because the most restrictive permission applies when the local and network permissions are compared, the effective permission in this case is always the local (or NTFS) permission.

Auditing

One of the most powerful security features of the Windows NT platform is its capability to provide the administrator with a detailed tracking of almost any event that occurs while the system is running. An audit log can be a very useful tool for proving who or what did something to the Windows NT system and when it occurred.

Although auditing seems like a tool that every system should have running at all times, administrators and users need to consider an important performance issue. The easiest way to explain the performance issue is to examine it with an analogy. Pouring yourself a glass of water seems like a easy task that should take only a few moments to complete. However, think about how long it would take for you to complete that same task if you had to do the task and write down a detailed description of every step you took to complete the task. That would certainly take a lot longer. This is essentially the same issue faced when the auditing capabilities are turned on in most network operating systems.

For this reason, most administrators and users typically elect to use the auditing features on only the systems that require them most. They also tend to be rather selective about which items they want to audit. It should be noted that a newer, faster system that has been properly configured and not overloaded with other tasks should be able to handle most, if not all, the tasks required of it with very little performance degradation.

To use the auditing capabilities of Windows NT, open the User Manager or the User Manager for Domains applet and select Policy from the menu bar. From the drop-down Policy menu, select Auditing. Figure 17.9 shows the Audit Properties dialog box. To turn the auditing capabilities on, select the Audit These Events radio button and then select the appropriate success or failure items to monitor. After auditing has been turned on, you can select additional auditing settings for any files and directories on the system that are stored on an NTFS partition.

FIGURE 17.9
The Audit Policy dialog box.

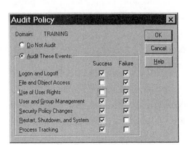

Diskless Workstations

One way to prevent users from copying information off the network systems and putting it on floppy disks or their local hard drives is to make sure they do not have a local hard drive or floppy disk drive. If the computer system does not have a hard drive or some other method of booting up from that workstation, the system can be a diskless workstation on the network.

Diskless workstations typically use a special network interface card that has a boot PROM (programmable read-only memory) chip on it. The PROM chip is used to load the network software into the machine's memory and enable it to attach to and boot up from operating system files stored on the network.

Encryption

As was stated earlier in this chapter, anyone who wants to get to your information badly enough can find a way to get to it. The last line of defense that administrators and users have is the capability to encrypt their data so that if someone does get to the information, he will still have a lot of work to do before he can read it or use it.

Encrypted data is transformed or "locked" into some other form that's not easily guessed or read but that can be retransformed or unlocked when necessary through the use of a key. The encryption process is basically the same as "locking" the data so that no unauthorized parties have access to it. The unlocking process is actually referred to as *decryption*. Essentially, only two methods are used to encrypt data: transposition and substitution.

With transposition, the order of the bits being sent is rearranged. For example, imagine that you want to send a message of "Hello" to another user. You and the other user agree that the key to your transposing is to move the first letter of each word to the back of the word, so you send "Elloh" as the message. If you use substitution as the method of encryption, you must find some other pattern or value to substitute for the message you're sending. If the key to your substitution is to use numerical values for the letters of the alphabet, the message becomes "8 5 12 12 15."

If you choose only one transposition or one type of substitution, someone can figure out the message without too much trouble. For that reason, most popular encryption methods in use today use a series of transpositions and substitutions. A mathematical formula is used to determine the key, which is used to encrypt and decrypt the message. When both parties know the same key used to encrypt or decrypt the message, the encryption technique is known as *symmetric cryptography*.

However, at times, encryption must be used between parties that do not share the same key. To do this, *asymmetric cryptography* must be used. Asymmetric cryptography requires each party to have both a public key and a private key. The public and private keys are related to each other using a mathematical function so that they become a set of keys used for encryption. The public key is made available to anyone who wants to send a message. The message is encrypted using the public key and can then be decrypted only by using the private key. Because the user to whom the message is being sent always retains the private key, he is the only one who can read the message sent to him.

Virus Shields

No discussion of network security would be complete without mentioning viruses, Trojan horses, logic bombs, and other sorts of electronic wildlife. A *virus* is a program that runs when an infected program is executed. It stands to reason then that only executable files with extensions such as .EXE, .BAT, .COM, and .SYS can become infected. As with a biological virus, computer viruses live to replicate and copy themselves to other systems and to other files.

Some viruses do nothing more than replicate and occupy space, but others can cause massive damage and even self-destruct when they're run. If anything harms the data or constricts the access to it, a security violation has occurred. Viruses are most definitely a concern for all systems. Viruses can be acquired from the network, from downloaded files, from shareware and freeware programs, and even from off-the-shelf software. To prevent these monsters from rearing their ugly heads and affecting your systems, you need to have some form of countermeasure.

Virus scanners and virus shields are two device types that can protect your systems. Each one provides a different type of protection. Virus scanners can be run any time a virus is suspected or on a scheduled basis. They do a thorough job of inspecting whatever files are selected and they attempt to find and remove any viruses that are detected. Virus-scanning programs typically use a database of sample virus code strings against which the files are compared. These database files are usually referred to as *virus definition files*. If a virus scanner locates a particular string of code, it has found a virus. Most virus scanners can also remove the viruses they find. To keep your system thoroughly protected, the virus definition files should be updated regularly.

A *virus shield* is a type of program that runs when the system boots and keeps running in memory the entire time the system is on. The virus shield constantly monitors all processing while attempting to locate a virus. The idea is for the virus to be caught before it gets on the system. A virus shield examines programs before they execute to attempt to catch the virus before it replicates or does any other type of damage. After they're caught, viruses can normally be removed before causing any harm, and normal execution of the program can continue.

Summary

Data and network integrity are always recognized as a good idea; however, the correct policies are rarely implemented properly, due either to insufficient resources (in capital, time, or equipment) or lack of knowledge about all vulnerabilities, or both. This chapter has given you the tools necessary to design and implement your own integrity plans, not only to keep your users happy and productive but also to keep your head on your shoulders when disaster strikes. With time, patience, knowledge, and the correct hardware and software tools, data can be secured and protected.

Directory Services

To understand modern networks, you need to understand Directory Services. To understand Directory Services, you need to understand the more basic concept of a *directory*.

In this chapter, we'll begin with a brief discussion of the purpose of a network directory, go on to survey the various aspects of the general directory concept, and then uses a telephone directory as an example to illustrate how these aspects can interact. We'll follow that with a discussion of the unique characteristics of a network directory and end with an overview of currently available directory service products.

The Purpose of a Network Directory

Network directories store and organize information about network resources such as computers, users, and printers. They can also be used to provide a variety of services, such as supplying users with information about system or application resources as well as controlling access to those resources. Don't confuse network directories with directories associated with file systems (now generally called *folders* in Windows and Macintosh operating systems). File system directories provide an organizational structure for files stored on a system, whereas network directories are used to organize information about network resources. Both of these directory types are applications of the more general directory concept that will be covered later in this chapter.

Many network directories are included with network operating systems or applications, and organizations with networks typically have multiple directories in place that are associated with the various systems or applications that exist in the network environment. In most cases, such directories operate independently of each other and require separate administrative procedures for maintenance. Users make use of those directories that provide information for or control access to the resources they use.

Some network directories are dedicated solely to providing information about system or application resources, but most directories are used to provide security services to control access to system or application resources. When a network directory is responsible for providing security services, it not only contains information about the resources being secured but also contains information about users or systems allowed to access those resources. In such cases, the information about users or systems contained in a network directory is used for authentication by a security service so that users or systems that are allowed access to secured resources cannot be impersonated.

Directory Framework

As a concept, network directories do not differ greatly from telephone directories or other organized lists that provide information. Network directories share certain aspects of the general directory concept with these more common forms of directories. These shared aspects explain the manner in which the information in directories is maintained and presented. The following sections explore the three major aspects of the general directory model:

- Scope
- Structure
- Presentation

Directory Scope

A directory is merely a type of database—one designed, built, and populated with data to allow users to locate objects using information associated with the objects. The directory can be further distinguished by its scope, defined as the types of objects it contains (its depth) combined with the portion of the real world it encompasses (its breadth). Like any database, a directory is a logically coherent collection of data with some inherent meaning. That is, the data are related in some way and have a useful purpose.

As an example, an employee directory for a company will include all employees of that company and certain types of information associated with those employees. All useful information must be systematically associated with the entry for each employee in the directory. As changes occur (new hires, terminations, promotions, job changes, and so on), the directory needs to be updated to reflect the changes.

Directory Structure

Once the scope of a directory has been defined, a structure needs to be established for the directory so that information within the directory can be maintained on an ongoing basis. This structure serves as the administrative aspect of a directory and fulfills two purposes:

- *Object identification*. Ensures that all objects within a directory can be uniquely identified so that they will map to an object unambiguously within the portion of the real world encompassed by the directory
- *Object organization*. Provides a framework that can be used to segment mainte- nance of logical subsets of the objects contained in the directory

Object Identification

Object identification is the means by which data elements within the directory can be uniquely identified. As an example, each employee in an organization could be identified by full name. However, because it's possible for employees to have identical names, it's often necessary to use some other characteristic, such as an employee code or Social Security number, to uniquely identify each employee.

The domain of identifiers available for assignment to data elements for unique identification within a directory is often referred to as the *namespace*. Assignment of identifiers from the namespace usually needs to be managed in some way to ensure that no two discrete objects represented in a directory are given the same identifier.

Namespaces in a directory can be specified in one of two ways: Each object type (that is, users, printers, servers, and so on) can have its own namespace (so that the same identifier can be used for different types of objects), or multiple object types can share a namespace. When each object type has its own namespace, the various object namespaces can still be mapped to a single namespace for the entire directory (meaning separate namespaces for each object type with another namespace encompassing all object types). Therefore, a unique identification for each object is achieved by combining identifiers for the objects within the namespace for the object class with an identifier for the object type.

As an example, an employee directory could be structured so that managers and staff are maintained separately. If the two types of objects—managers and staff—represented in the directory had separate namespaces, data elements representing both a manager and a staff member could use the same identifier. If the two types of objects shared the same namespace, it would not be possible for the same identifier to be used for both a manager and a staff member.

Let's say you create identifiers by using a person's first initial and last name. Furthermore, let's suppose the company employs a manager named Jean Smith and a staff member named Joe Smith. With only a single namespace for the organization, both would end up as *Jsmith*, which wouldn't work because the identifier must be unique. However, if managers and staff have separate namespaces, the identifiers might be Jsmith.MGR and Jsmith.STAFF, which are unique.

Object Organization

The other aspect of the directory structure is the organization of objects within the directory. If objects are grouped in some structured way within the directory, it might be possible to define separate namespaces for each group of objects, subordinate to the main namespace for the directory. The various group namespaces can then be mapped to a single namespace for the entire directory by combining identifiers for the objects within the subordinate namespace with an identifier for the group associated with that subordinate namespace.

Even though a large organization might have more than one employee named Paul Jones, it's less likely that a smaller unit within the organization (such as a department, division, or region) would have more than one employee named Paul Jones. If one Paul Jones is in the Eastern region and another Paul Jones is in the Midwest region, each employee would be known locally as just Paul Jones. Within the entire organization, the employees could be uniquely identified in the directory as Paul Jones in the Eastern region and Paul Jones in the Midwest region, respectively.

The organization of objects represented in a directory also serves to make access to information about the objects in the directory easier. This can also assist in the management of information in the directory through the grouping (or *partitioning*) of objects in some structured manner so that the groups of objects can be managed separately.

In the case of the employee directory example, a directory encompassing all employees in a large organization could grow too large to be managed effectively or to be convenient for users wishing to locate information about employees. You might address this problem by organizing the employee directory along divisions or regions within the organization so that each portion of the directory can be maintained independently.

Directory Presentation

Once the structure of a directory has been established, the directory is ready for presentation to users. This can be as simple as printing the contents of the directory and distributing copies to all users. Such a presentation of the directory is often not ideal; the results might be too voluminous or difficult to use because the directory is structured in the way it's actually maintained by the administrators.

Four objectives can influence the way in which a directory can be presented to users:

- *Completeness.* If a directory cannot be counted on to contain information about all the objects that inhabit its portion of the real world, it cannot be relied on. This is an obvious point when considering a directory presentation that includes all elements represented in a directory. When only a subset of a directory will be presented, completeness dictates that the subset contain all elements that can be expected to be included in the subset.

- *Accessibility.* This objective requires that a directory be available to users where and when they need to get information. Accessibility also requires that information presented from the directory be organized in a way that makes it easy for the user to locate what he or she is looking for. In the case of the employee directory, this could be accomplished by printing it on a sheet of paper or in a booklet and distributing copies to all employees. The resulting directory presentation could then be kept in desk drawers or posted in cubicles for easy reference by users. Other techniques for improving the accessibility of such an employee directory presentation might involve posting it on intranet Web sites that can be searched using an online database system such as Lotus Notes.

- *Accuracy.* If the directory information being presented to users cannot be relied on for accuracy, all information (including accurate information) will be considered suspect. Accuracy requires not only that information presented to the user be correct (accurately recorded in the directory) but also current (reasonably up-to-date or timely). Constant changes to objects and information in a directory will constrain the ways in which the directory can be presented to users, because some methods will be more difficult to keep up-to-date than others.

- *Efficiency.* Efficiency is what balances the often-conflicting objectives of completeness, accessibility, and accuracy. The quest for efficiency comes from the need to minimize the costs associated with presenting directories without sacrificing achievement of the other objectives.

These objectives act not only as goals but also as constraints, because each objective can influence the presentation of a directory in ways that seem to contradict other objectives. Deciding whether a particular presentation of a directory is effective requires that the interests of completeness, accessibility, accuracy, and efficiency be evaluated and then compared with the advantages of using other methods for presenting the directory. It's not uncommon for a directory to be presented using more than one method, each of which is chosen because it satisfies a particular objective more completely than the others.

In the employee directory example, printing the contents of the employee directory and distributing copies to users as a method of directory presentation might be considered inefficient if accuracy were a critical objective. This is because such a directory presentation would be inaccurate as soon as a change occurred in the organization, unless new editions were constantly being printed and distributed. Because this would be very costly, a method for directory presentation that would allow for online access to current information would more readily satisfy the efficiency objective. However, such a method could decrease accessibility for users who do not have access to resources through online connections.

Meeting the Objectives

The process of balancing the objectives of completeness, accessibility, accuracy, and efficiency is what determines the optimal methods for presenting information from a directory. Let's use the employee directory as an example once again. In this example, it's reasonable to expect that the directory could be presented in some static form (via a printed list or booklet) that's distributed to users.

The objective of completeness would be achieved by a printed directory as long as the intention is that all employees in the organization be included in the directory presentation. The objective of accessibility would be achieved as long as the information contained in the directory presentation made it easy to locate any desired information (printed directories are often convenient for users).

As has already been pointed out, the objective of accuracy would not likely be optimally achieved by such a method, because it's likely that the printed list would be out-of-date in a strict sense as soon as it's printed and distributed to users. But having a printed directory at one's fingertips is so convenient and the information in it is often "good enough" in aggregate terms to sacrifice some measure of accuracy. The objective of efficiency would limit the frequency of updates to the directory presentation because time and effort are required to print and distribute the employee directory to users. Efficiency would be measured in terms of balancing the need for accuracy of the directory presentation with the costs of printing and distribution.

An Illustration of the Directory Model

Because it's likely that everyone is familiar with the various forms of telephone directories, they provide a great opportunity to illustrate how the model can be applied to an actual implementation of a directory. This section describes a telephone directory using the directory model developed in the previous section.

Scope: What's in a Phone Book?

In its simplest form, a telephone directory is simply a database of telephone numbers that includes information about the individuals or entities to which the telephone numbers are assigned. In the largest sense possible, the portion of the real world encompassed by the telephone directory would be the collection of all telephone numbers that have been assigned to individuals or entities around the world. We quickly realize, though, that this would be inefficient due to the sheer number of entries needed. Therefore, we regionalize the directory to include only those phone numbers assigned within a particular geographical area. To put it another way, the scope of the typical white pages telephone directory is the collection of unique telephone numbers in a given area, along with the name of the person each number is assigned to (presented as an alphabetical listing of the names).

Telephone Directory Structure

Worldwide telephone service is facilitated by an interconnected network of telephone switches that allow connections to be established between most points on the globe. All these points are connected to local switches and can be uniquely identified via telephone numbers assigned by local telephone service providers. Each local telephone company is responsible for assigning telephone numbers to lines connected to switches under its control using a preallocated domain of numbers, which could be thought of as the namespace for the group of switches.

A large country will often have a number of these local administrative regions. In the United States, this partitioning occurs at a regional level using area codes that are administered by RBOCs (Regional Bell Operating Companies). For international communication, countries have been incorporated into a larger namespace through the creation of country codes based on agreed-upon conventions.

In this case, the structure of the telephone directory is managed by multiple local groups working independently. At the same time, the system ensures that all objects represented in the directory can be uniquely located using a combination of the country code, the area or local code, and the local phone number. This same telephone number is used as an address when establishing the telephone connection. The various parts of the telephone number are used as instructions that tell all intervening switches how to route the call.

Telephone Directory Presentation

The most common method for presenting a telephone directory is to print telephone books and distribute them to users of services in the areas they cover. Because of the sheer volume of information that comprises what could be described as the "global telephone directory," only a portion of this directory is presented to users in the form of telephone books. These portions of the global telephone directory contain information about people and organizations that have been assigned telephone numbers in the local area. This is acceptable in most cases because the majority of telephone communications occur between people and organizations in the same area.

Two different types of telephone books are usually distributed to users by telephone service providers: white pages and yellow pages. Both types of directory presentations are designed to make the information contained in the directory more accessible. White pages typically provide an alphabetized list of names that can be used for locating telephone numbers or addresses, whereas yellow pages present listings of businesses organized by categories that can also be used for locating telephone numbers or addresses. Such telephone books, although often rather bulky, are convenient and satisfy the accessibility objective of directory presentation by making telephone directory information available near most phones.

These telephone books also satisfy the completeness objective, as long as they include telephone numbers and other information about all people or organizations that have been assigned telephone numbers in the area covered by the telephone book. The objective that suffers with telephone books is accuracy because telephone books are only published periodically (typically once per year). Because changes occur frequently, some of the information in the telephone book will become outdated. The inaccuracy that grows over time is often considered acceptable for telephone books because they're so convenient and the vast majority of the information remains accurate.

Note: The objective of efficiency is the factor that partly explains why telephone books are not published more often. The publishing schedule for a telephone directory is determined by balancing publishing costs with the amount of information that changes over time.

Telephone service providers also maintain online telephone directory presentations that compensate for the shortcomings of the printed telephone book. Users can often call an operator or information line and obtain a telephone number by providing a name and, if necessary, some information about where the individual or entity might be located. Such a service is convenient for users, because it only requires picking up the phone and asking someone for the desired information. The service is also more accurate than a telephone book because the information provided by the operator will be more current than the information found in a telephone book.

The problem with such an online service is that it's very expensive to provide, and because many of the requests could just as easily be satisfied by referencing the published telephone book, it's necessary to discourage such "abuse" by charging for the service in some way. This allows the service to remain available for those who truly need the up-to-date information it provides.

Recent technological trends are also being exploited to improve the accuracy and efficiency of directory presentations. Web-based telephone directories that allow users to search for telephone numbers using a variety of criteria are being deployed by some telephone service providers. Web-based directories are advantageous because they provide the same level of accuracy available with a phone-based information service in a more efficient manner because they do not cost nearly as much to maintain. In cases where users have easy Internet access, such a service can also be more accessible than a telephone book.

The Network Directory's Special Features

Subjecting the phone directory to a more careful examination betrays its true identity: The telephone directory is, after all, a network directory.

What aspects of the telephone directory allow it to make its way into the territory of network directories? The first clue can be found in the definition of the scope, where the telephone system is characterized as an interconnected network of telephone switches. In addition, the key objects represented in the directory are telephone numbers, which act as addresses for establishing connections between points attached to switches over the telephone network. The primary purpose for presenting the directory is to allow users to locate telephone numbers using names or categories that are easier to remember than numbers.

Additional investigation of some of the details of telephone switch management and network routing would have revealed the integral role of the directory in the operation of the telephone network. This integration of the directory into the operation of the network is the critical factor that distinguishes network directories from the more general forms of directories (of which an employee directory is an example). The network directory acts as more than a simple listing of the resources available. By interacting with the user, the network directory can control access to the objects on the network and the directory itself. Aside from the presentation of network-related information to users, one of the more common purposes of a network directory is to provide a means by which system or application resources can be managed.

Access Control

Network directories have one unique characteristic: the role they play in controlling access to system or application resources on the network. A network directory's security role is defined as part of the directory's scope. Once a role is defined, it's necessary to specify the methods available for controlling access to resources within the scope as well.

Access to a network resource within the scope of a directory can be controlled simply by requiring a password before the resource can be accessed. This type of authentication is usually considered to be weak. For example, if every member of a group uses the same password to access the resource, there's no way to be sure which member is accessing it at any given time.

Methods exist for controlling access to resources that more adequately provide for individual accountability. They usually involve specifying methods for reliably determining the identity of users accessing secured resources. In order to identify users allowed to access system or application resources, the definition of the scope of the directory must incorporate user identification object types, such as system identifiers or user accounts. When system identifiers are used, a reasonable level of assurance is required that an unauthorized system cannot easily impersonate an authorized system by co-opting its identifier. When user accounts are used, a reasonably strong form of authentication needs to be performed so that an unauthorized user cannot easily impersonate an authorized user.

Multiple Network Directories

As systems and applications proliferate in a networking environment, the number of directories within that environment is also likely to increase. Because the directories often operate independently, this proliferation of directories places burdens on users as well as on the staff responsible for maintaining the directories associated with the systems and applications. These burdens are especially acute when multiple independent directories participate in securing access to network resources.

From an administrative perspective, the use of multiple independent directories requires redundant procedures to maintain the system identifiers or user accounts needed to identify authorized users. From a user's perspective, users are often responsible for maintaining several different user accounts and passwords.

The burdens introduced by the use of multiple independent network directories have led Directory Service vendors to invent the concept of the *metadirectory*—variously defined as a "directory of directories" or as an authoritative directory that controls changes to application-specific directories. We'll look at metadirectories later in this chapter when we examine the various directory offerings of the major operating system vendors. Right now, though, let's go back in time and look at some important milestones in the history of Directory Services.

The X.500 Specification

The Directory specifications described in this section (called simply the *Directory* in the standards documentation) represent an effort on the part of international standards groups to define a framework for directory services that would be useful for a variety of systems and applications. This framework is commonly referred to as *X.500* and is described in a series of documents developed in collaboration by the CCITT (Consultative Committee for International Telegraphy and Telephony), the ISO (International Standards Organization), and the IEC (International Electrotechnical Commission).

The most recent edition of the Directory specifications consists of two nearly identical sets of nine separate documents that were published in 1993 by the ITU-T (International Telecommunications Union, formerly the CCITT) and the ISO/IEC JTC1 (a joint technical committee of the ISO and IEC). The ITU-T version of the documents is referred to as the *X.500 Recommendations*, whereas the ISO/IEC version is known as *International Standard 9594*. The only differences between the ITU-T and ISO/IEC documents are minor variations in wording. The working documents are kept aligned by having common draft documents that combine both sets of wording.

> **Note:** Throughout this chapter, the terms *Directory* or *the Directory* (uppercase D) refer to the directory specified in the X.500 documents. The term *directory* (lowercase *d*) refers to a generic implementation of the standard or to nonspecific directories in general (such as, a telephone directory).

The X.500 specifications are extremely valuable as a conceptual framework for network directory services for a number of reasons. First, X.500 presents comprehensive specifications that have accumulated a high level of support within academia and the networking industry. They are now almost universally acknowledged as the prototypical framework for network directory services. In addition, the standards have benefited from a wealth of practical experience in the field, which has contributed to their ongoing development.

The Directory's Origins

The X.500 Directory specifications were developed originally to play a significant role in the OSI (Open Systems Interconnection) basic reference model for network communications. They were aimed specifically at addressing the requirement for an Electronic Directory Service (EDS) defined by the ISO for the OSI Application Layer. The documents that currently make up the ITU-T X.500 Recommendations combine to provide a comprehensive and detailed specification for a general-purpose directory service capable of allowing access to a variety of information. This directory information could be distributed widely and yet appear within a single logical framework.

The process of creating the first edition of the X.500 Directory standards required about six years, beginning in 1983, when both the CCITT and the ISO began work on proposals for a standard Directory specification. Finally in 1988, the Directory became a standard when the ISO ratified International Standard 9594, and the CCITT accepted the proposals as the X.500 Recommendations.

In the years following, X.500 steadily gained the support of other standards bodies, academic institutions, and network software developers. The Internet community was perhaps the area of the networking world where X.500 initially generated the most enthusiasm. Many recognized the potential for a directory to support global communications by defining a framework for a global service making information about network resources universally available (similar to the way the white pages of a telephone book work). The Internet community contributed a great deal of development and publicity to the evolution of X.500. Several RFCs (*Requests for Comments*, the semiofficial documentation for Internet standards and protocols) were written about various aspects of X.500 implementation. These RFCs provided implementation details as well as guidance for future development of the standards.

Despite all the interest in X.500 within the Internet community, the Directory has been unable to make the transition from technical journals, textbooks, and pilot projects to actual deployment of a global directory serving Internet users in the same way white pages directories serve telephone customers. Even so, the concepts and terminology associated with X.500 have become the framework for the development of network directories. Vendors, such as Novell and Microsoft, implementing directories for systems or applications routinely use the models codified within the X.500 Directory standards as integral parts of the design of their directories.

The initial 1988 standards presented the components of a distributed directory service that served as the basis of several pilot projects. These so-called *reference implementations* led to the development of the second edition of the standards, published in 1992 and 1993.

Scope of The Directory

The Directory specifications were designed to provide a framework for directory services, rather than a fully specified directory to support a predetermined set of applications. This arrangement required the introduction of a conceptual information model to allow those responsible for implementing directories to define a scope suitable for the environments and applications supported by their particular directories. The designers envisioned some generic applications for the Directory to provide examples of how the conceptual information model could be applied to define their scope. This section looks first at the generic applications described in the standards and then at the conceptual information model used to define the scope of a directory implementation.

Applications and the Directory

During the design process, several assumptions were made about the environment within which the Directory would provide services. First, it was assumed that the telecommunications networks for which the Directory would provide services could be arbitrarily large and subject to constant changes. Resources on the network could enter or leave at any time without warning, paths between resources could be added or removed, and various characteristics of these resources (such as addresses, availability, and physical locations) could change at any time. Second, although the overall rate of change of information associated with network resources might be rapid, the useful lifetime of such information would not be short. This meant that generally the information associated with a given resource would be accessed by users more often than the information would change. Finally, there was the assumption that resources involved in telecommunications services are typically identified by addresses or other identifiers selected for their ease of allocation or efficiency of processing, rather than for their ease of use by humans.

The designers envisioned the Directory as a tool with the primary role of allowing users to access information about network resources while providing for the maintenance, distribution, and security of that information. Users could include people and computer programs. Network resources could include servers providing network services, printers, and users.

The network information maintained in the Directory was intended to satisfy two needs of users: to be isolated from changes that occur to information associated with resources and to have access to a user-friendly view of the network and its resources. The introduction of a "level of indirection" between the users and the resources isolates users from changes to information associated with resources. This can be accomplished by associating names with resources. Allowing users to locate resources using a variety of characteristics associated with resources other than names or addresses provides a user-friendly view of the network and its resources.

Three generic applications for which the Directory would play an integral role were envisioned: interpersonal communications, intersystem communications, and authentication. The Directory would play the role in interpersonal communications applications (such as electronic mail) of providing humans or their agents with the information necessary to communicate with other humans or their agents. Intersystem communications applications would use the Directory to provide the information necessary for services to communicate with services running on other systems. Applications requiring authentication would use the Directory to verify identities by enabling users or resources taking part in communications to provide some proof of their identities.

Object Classes and Attributes

The Directory specifications introduced a conceptual information model to allow for a consistent definition of scope for directory implementations. As you learned earlier, applications drive the definition of scope for a directory implementation. Therefore, it was expected that the nature of the applications supported would govern the information contained in the Directory and the ways in which it would be accessed.

The generic applications defined for the Directory assume that certain types of information would be available within the directory. These might include the following:

- Information about people (such as electronic mail addresses, phone numbers, and public key identity certificates) that would be of interest to users attempting to establish communications with them

- Information about servers and services that could be used to learn their location and availability

- Operational information, such as access controls and internal consistency data, used to maintain the integrity of information in the directory

The information model was meant to generalize the constructs used to specify the way such information (and other types of information not envisioned by the Directory designers) would be represented in directory implementations.

The information model specifies a directory database consisting of a collection of entries (or *object instances*), each of which is associated with one or more attributes. Each attribute is defined with a data type and, optionally, can contain one or more values. Using standard database terms to describe this information model, the Directory database is analogous to a table, whereas objects and attributes are analogous to records and fields or rows and columns. The Directory, however, was not intended to be a general-purpose database, although it was conceivable that a directory implementation could be built on database systems.

Each instance of an object created in the Directory must contain attributes that define a name for the instance as well as the type of real-world object the instance represents. Names are used to uniquely identify each object instance in the Directory, and object classes are used to define the attributes available to hold information associated with each object instance. Typical object classes include people, computers, and network services, and each object class definition includes a predetermined set of attributes associated with it. The rules determining the attributes associated with object classes are defined in the directory schema established by whoever implements a directory and, optionally, by whoever has the responsibility for maintaining information in the directory implementation.

> **Note:** Individuals responsible for maintaining information in a directory implementation have the ability to modify the schema to define new object classes and attributes. This allows directory implementations to be useful for applications that were not anticipated by the directory implementation designers.

Attributes are defined independently of object classes, so it's possible that a given attribute could be used by more than one object class. Object classes are defined through *inheritance* (a new object class is built on the attributes of a base class) or *superclassing* (a new object class is defined by combining the attribute associations of one or more existing base classes with optional associations with additional attributes). The attributes associated with an object class are divided into mandatory and optional associations. An instance of an object class must have legal values for all mandatory attributes.

Defining the scope for a directory implementation consists of defining object classes and attributes to provide a framework for creating directory entries (object instances). For example, a directory implementation might define an object class of User that would be associated with the following attributes: Object Class, Common Name, Given Name, Middle Name, Surname, Description, Email Address, Telephone Number, and Fax Number. The Common Name field could be designated the distinguished attribute that's required for uniquely identifying each object instance. The mandatory attributes would then likely be the Object Class and Common Name attributes, with the rest of the attributes defined as optional.

Based on the generic applications envisioned for the Directory to support, a number of object classes and attribute types were defined in the Directory specifications that could be useful across a range of applications. The rules established for the default object classes, as well as their respective attribute definitions and assignments, make up the default schema for the Directory. The schema also defines permitted relationships between objects, a topic that's covered in the next section, because it's a structural concept.

Structure of The Directory

The Directory specifications provide a detailed framework for defining the structure of directory implementations that goes beyond fulfilling the two primary functions of the directory structure. Object identification and organization are addressed in the definition of the constructs and rules of the Directory Information Base (DIB), covered in the next section. Additional structural elements—such as provisions for distributed operation, replication, and access control—are also addressed in the Directory specifications through models and protocols and are examined in the following sections.

The Directory Information Base (DIB)

The information held in the directory database for entries and attributes, or *object instances*, is collectively known as the *Directory Information Base* (DIB). The entries correspond to resources in the network, and the associated attributes describe the properties of each resource.

The entries in the DIB are organized hierarchically as part of an inverted tree structure, known as the *Directory Information Tree* (DIT), that represents the logical organization of the directory's contents. Entries higher in the tree (nearer the root) often represent entities with an organizational purpose, such as countries, localities, organizations, or organizational units (such as divisions or departments). Such intermediate entries act as containers for additional subordinate entries that combine with those entries above them to form a *subtree*. Entries lower in the tree typically represent people, computers, or services and act as leaf entries instead of containers. They do not form subtrees because leaf entries are not allowed to have subordinate entries.

A mandatory attribute associated with every object class, referred to as the *distinguished attribute*, is the *relative distinguished name* (RDN) for the entry in the Directory Information Base, which uniquely identifies each object instance within the context of its location in the Directory Information Tree. Unique identification of every object instance in the DIT, independent of its location within the tree (called the *context*), is accomplished by combining the RDNs of every container between the root and the object instance to form the *distinguished name* (DN).

The Directory schema is maintained as part of the DIB to ensure that entries in the DIB remain well formed as modifications occur over time. The Directory schema serves two purposes. It defines the object classes, attributes, and allowable associations (mandatory and optional) between object classes and attributes (covered in the discussion of the information model) available in the Directory. It also defines the allowable superior and subordinate relationships, known as *name bindings*, between object instances within the DIT.

The Directory schema rules governing object classes, and attributes ensure that an object instance cannot be defined with the wrong attributes for its object class, with a missing mandatory attribute, or with the wrong type of data within an attribute value. The Directory schema rules governing name bindings between object classes ensure that the hierarchical structure of the DIT cannot be compromised by arbitrary superior or subordinate relationships between object instances, such as not allowing leaf entries to be used as intermediate entries.

The collection of RDNs that make up the Distinguished Name of an object instance provide information about the entry's relative location in the DIT. For example, the object instance for Mary Smith, a consultant for First National Bank Corp., might have a DN of {C=US, O=FBNC, L=Chicago, OU=Consultants, CN=Mary Smith}, which corresponds to a logical location in the DIT:

- *C*, which represents *Country*, is the highest grouping entry in the DIT. The Directory schema restricts such entries to appearing only below the root.

- *O*, which represents *Organization*, is the next highest grouping entry after Country. The Directory schema restricts such entries to appearing only below the root or directly below a Country entry.

- *L*, which represents *Locality*, is a grouping entry, which can occur at any point in the tree except directly under the root.

- *OU*, which represents *Organizational Unit*, is another grouping entry. The Directory schema restricts such entries to appearing only below an Organization entry.

- *CN*, which represents *Common Name*, is the distinguished attribute (or RDN) for an object instance—in this case, probably an instance of the object class User. CN is commonly used in full DNs to refer to the RDN of a leaf entry. The Directory schema usually restricts leaf entries to appearing only below certain container object instances, such as Organization or Organizational Unit.

The hierarchical structure of the logical directory embodied in the tree-like shape of the DIT is meant to provide for a multitiered structure so that maintenance of directory information can be divided and subdivided among multiple authorities. Local administrative authorities can be given authority for maintenance of directory information within a subtree. Administrative authorities responsible for a given subtree can subdivide authority within the subtree by delegating authority. Administrative authority over a subtree brings with it the responsibility to ensure, for example, that all the entries in the subtree have unambiguous DNs. Responsibility is passed down the tree from superior to subordinate authorities, with control being enforced by means of the schema.

Distribution and Replication

The Directory specifications take into account the fact that, in order to ensure efficient access to directory information, the contents of the DIB might need to be distributed or replicated to multiple locations in a network or internetwork. Distributing information in the DIB typically facilitates local management of local resources within a network-wide framework. When information in the directory is distributed, the DIT is still seen by users as an integrated whole.

Replication of information in the directory, called *shadowing* in the Directory standards, consists of maintaining multiple copies of the same information in different locations. Replication improves performance by allowing distributed network information held in the directory to be located near users so they don't have to traverse wide area network links (which are often slow or congested) to access the information. Replication improves availability by eliminating the impact of a single point of failure, because users can access information in a replica in the event that the original is unavailable. In the event of a system failure, replicated information can be used to reconstruct any directory information that was lost, as well.

Controlling Access to The Directory

The Directory specifications assume that the directory exists in an environment where various administrative authorities need to control access to certain elements of the directory information. Some of the Directory elements the designers identified as needing various levels of protection include information related to the DIT structure, directory user information, and directory operational information (including access control information). To help prevent unauthorized access to directory elements, it was determined that the identity of users should be verified so that access to directory information can be controlled adequately. An authentication framework was defined in the Directory specification consisting of two levels of authentication:

- *Simple authentication*. Requires just a password for verification of a user's identity
- *Strong authentication*. Based on credentials that are formed using public key cryptographic techniques

Although simple authentication is capable of providing some limited protection against unauthorized access, it was suggested that strong authentication was necessary for the directory to provide secure services. The Directory specifications also include guidelines for the use of digital signatures, public key certificates, and Certificate Revocation Lists (CRLs), including specification of how the information necessary for the operation of such systems may be stored and accessed in the directory.

An access control scheme, referred to as *basic access control*, is defined in the Directory specifications to provide the means by which local security policies are enforced through mechanisms within the directory that control access to directory information. Such control over access to directory information can be exercised to prevent unauthorized detection, disclosure, or modification of the information. When determining whether an authenticated user is allowed to access directory information, the access control mechanisms consider the following:

- The component within the directory being accessed
- The user requesting the operation
- The specific right required to complete the portions of the operation
- The defined security policy governing access to that information

Presentation of The Directory

The Directory specifications provide a well-defined set of access capabilities—known as the *abstract services* of the directory—for presenting directory information to users. Access to information in the directory is accomplished via a Directory User Agent

(DUA), which is an application process that acts on behalf of users. The DUA interacts with DSAs to allow simple modification and retrieval capabilities. At the time the specifications were developed, the designers expected that the basic access capabilities would be built upon in directory client implementations with local DUA functions to provide more advanced capabilities that might be required by end users.

Directory Access Protocol (DAP)

Several patterns of use of information or requests for information contained in the Directory were anticipated in support of the generic applications envisioned for it. They include the following:

- *Lookup.* The classic form of information retrieval, where users request specific information related to a known resource.

- *Name resolution.* Resources are located using names that can be easily predicted or remembered by users. This can be considered a special case of lookup.

- *Browsing.* Allowing users to select resources from a list when the name of the desired resource might not be known without seeing it.

- *Searching and filtering.* Information associated with resources is used to locate individual resources or groups of resources.

- *Authentication.* This is presented earlier as a generic application. It verifies the identity of users and resources.

The Directory Access Protocol (DAP) was designed to provide a standardized way for DUAs to interact with DSAs to access information in the directory. DAP specifies requests as functions allowing interrogation of the directory as well as allowing modification of directory information.

Five functions are included in DAP for interrogating the directory: Read, Compare, List, Search, and Abandon. They perform in the following manner:

- A *Read* request is aimed at a particular entry, and it causes the values of some or all of the attributes of that entry to be returned. When only some attributes are to be returned, the DUA supplies the list of attribute types of interest.

- A *Compare* request is aimed at a particular attribute of a particular entry and causes the directory to check whether a supplied value matches a value of that attribute. For example, this can be used to carry out password checking, where the password held in the directory might be inaccessible for Read but accessible for Compare.

- A *List* request causes the directory to return the list of immediate subordinates of a particular intermediate entry in the DIT.

- A *Search* request causes the directory to return information from all the entries within a certain portion of the DIT that satisfy some filter condition. The information that's returned from each entry consists of some or all of the attributes of that entry, as with Read.

- An *Abandon* request, as applied to an outstanding interrogation request, informs the directory that the originator of the request is no longer interested in the request being carried out. The directory may, for example, cease processing the request and may discard any results achieved so far.

Four functions are included in DAP for modifying information in the directory: Add Entry, Remove Entry, Modify Entry, and Modify Distinguished Name. They work as follows:

- An *Add Entry* request causes a new entry to be added to the DIT.

- A *Remove Entry* request causes an entry to be removed from the DIT.

- A *Modify Entry* request causes the directory to execute a sequence of changes to a particular entry. Either all or none of the changes are made, and the DIB is always left in a state consistent with the schema. The changes allowed include the addition, removal, or replacement of attribute values.

- A *Modify Distinguished Name* request is used to change the relative distinguished name (RDN) of an entry or to move an entry to a new container in the DIT. If an entry has subordinates, all subordinates are renamed or moved accordingly.

A number of controls can be applied to the various requests, primarily to allow the user to impose limits on the use of resources consumed by the directory when satisfying requests. Among the controls available are limits on the amount of time for an operation, limits on the size of the results set, scope limits for the search, and the priority of the request. Requests may be accompanied by security parameters that directory security mechanisms may need to control access to directory information. Filters may also be established to limit the entries that can be included in the result of a request that acts on multiple entries.

Lightweight Directory Access Protocol (LDAP)

Directory client software that implements DAP is subject to significant resource requirements due to the heavy overhead required to support the upper layers of the OSI stack and the complexity required to handle referrals when operating in a distributed environment. The resource requirements have made it difficult to deploy directory implementations because many client machines, especially PC and Macintosh systems, lack the resources necessary to properly support directory client software using DAP. This difficulty fostered the development of the Lightweight Directory Access Protocol (LDAP), which specifies a simpler client interface to the directory than was specified for DAP.

LDAP is not defined in the directory specifications but was developed (at the University of Michigan) to provide a client interface for directories conforming to the X.500 directory standards. The choice of attribute names and the hierarchical structure of LDAP are clearly derived from the X.500 directory specifications.

Note: It's important to remember that LDAP does not specify a directory structure but instead provides a protocol suitable for use by users interacting with any hierarchical, attribute-based directory similar to X.500.

LDAP has been adopted as an official Internet standard for a directory access protocol and has garnered the support of most influential network software developers. The current version, LDAPv3, addresses some limitations found during deployment of LDAPv2. It also adds new features, improves compatibility with the second edition (1993) of the Directory specifications, and better specifies how LDAP can be used with non-X.500 and standalone directories.

LDAP uses the same information model as that defined in the X.500 directory specifications as well as many of the functional client/server characteristics for interaction between users and the directory. When operating with directories conforming to the X.500 directory standards, an LDAP client interacts exclusively with LDAP providers (usually running as server processes) that are responsible for interacting with DSAs on behalf of the client. LDAP is used as the protocol governing communications between the LDAP client and the LDAP provider, and DAP is used as the protocol governing communications between the LDAP provider and the DSAs.

Note: When using LDAP to access information contained in non-X.500 directories, only the LDAP provider is different because that's the only component required to communicate natively with the directory. It's even possible to implement "native" LDAP directories, where the LDAP provider acts as the sole access point to information residing in the directory.

LDAP is simpler and less resource intensive to implement on client systems than DAP. In addition, because LDAP was designed with the objective of interacting with other (non-X.500) directories, it's finally feasible to build directory access capabilities into more applications. This is because adding LDAP support could allow interaction with a variety of directories.

The simplicity of LDAP is a result of a number of design considerations that were intended to reduce the protocol's resource requirements when compared with DAP. They include the following:

- The implementation of only a subset of the functions defined for DAP
- The offloading of complicated operations required in a distributed environment (such as referral handling) from the client to the LDAP provider
- Simplified encoding of attribute types and values using a lightweight form of BER (Basic Encoding Rules)
- Simplified encoding of protocol data elements (such as distinguished names) using ordinary strings
- The use of the TCP transport instead of the complex OSI protocols

Three operations are included in LDAP for interrogating the directory, whereas DAP includes five functions for this purpose. The functions in LDAP are Compare, Search, and Abandon:

- The *LDAP Compare* request is equivalent to its DAP counterpart, where the directory compares a client's assertion for an entry's attribute value with the value of the attribute for the entry in the directory.
- The *LDAP Search* request is similar to its DAP counterpart, where the directory returns all the entries consisting of all or some of the entry's attributes within a certain portion of the DIT that satisfy some filter condition. LDAP also uses the Search request to emulate the DAP Read and List functions through definition of filter conditions aimed at obtaining equivalent results.
- The *LDAP Abandon* request is equivalent to its DAP counterpart, where the client can inform the directory that it should abandon an outstanding interrogation request in the event that the client is no longer interested in the request being carried out.

LDAP includes four operations for modifying information in the directory. They're equivalent to the four functions included in DAP for this purpose. The LDAP functions are Modify, Add, Delete, and Modify RDN. They perform as follows:

- The *LDAP Modify* request is similar to its DAP counterpart, where the client can request that the directory modify an entry. LDAP defines simplified semantics for the Modify request by supporting three operations: Add Values, Delete Values, and Replace Values.
- The *LDAP Add* request is equivalent to its DAP counterpart, where a new entry can be added to the DIT.

- The *LDAP Delete* request is equivalent to its DAP counterpart, where an entry can be removed from the DIT.
- The *LDAP Modify RDN* request is similar to its DAP counterpart, where its functionality is limited to allowing changes to the last component of an entry's distinguished name.

LDAP provides a subset of the controls that can be applied to various requests, including those used to impose limits on the use of resources consumed by the directory when satisfying requests.

Network Name Resolution

We'll begin our discussion of specific network operating system (NOS) directory implementations with one of the simpler forms of network directories—those dedicated to performing the essential function of providing network name resolution services to simplify access to network resources. Network name resolution is a process that allows names to be associated with network resources. This means that resources can be accessed through names instead of network addresses, because names are more easily remembered than addresses. Three naming services are covered in this section: Domain Naming System (DNS) for TCP/IP, Windows Internet Naming Systems (WINS) for NetBIOS over TCP/IP, and Service Advertising Protocol (SAP) for IPX/SPX.

Domain Naming System (DNS)

The Domain Naming System (DNS) is without a doubt the most widely deployed network directory in use today. The Domain Naming System is a centralized naming service for the TCP/IP protocol suite that provides hostname-to-IP address resolution services to systems on private networks or on the Internet. Name resolution is used for the TCP/IP protocol suite to allow network hosts to be identified using names rather than numeric addresses, because names are usually easier for humans to remember.

The default way to provide hostname resolution services for the TCP/IP protocol suite is to use local hosts databases that map IP addresses to hostnames. On UNIX systems, the hosts database usually is a whitespace-delimited (that is, fields within a record are separated by blank spaces or simple punctuation—commas or semicolons) file called /etc/hosts. It consists of records (lines) containing IP addresses using dotted decimal notation and one or more names associated with each address. When a process attempts to contact a TCP/IP resource using a name instead of an address, the hosts database on the local workstation is automatically consulted to find the first IP address associated with the name. Once an address-to-name association is located, the associated IP address is used to contact the destination host. If no association can be found, the connection attempt fails, just as if an incorrect address had been provided.

There are several problems with using local hosts databases for name resolution that usually present themselves as network environments grow. First, when a node is added to a network or changes its location, the hosts databases for all systems that will initiate conversations with this node need to be updated in some way. Because it's usually difficult to predict the systems with which a given system will need to communicate, it's usually easier to distribute changes to all systems on a network. Such a scheme is manageable as long as there are not many systems that need to be updated, and as long as there's little or no communications occurring with systems on other networks. That's no longer feasible.

What's needed is a way to provide access to current hostname resolution information for systems connected to the Internet while allowing local administrative control over name resolution information related to local resources. The resulting design of the Domain Naming System, described in RFCs 1034 and 1035 and implemented in products such as the Berkeley Internet Name Domain (BIND), satisfied these requirements. DNS adopted a client/server model, where servers contain hostname-to-IP address mapping information about a portion of the network and make this information available to clients.

Nameservers

DNS servers, called *nameservers*, manage portions of a hierarchical namespace—a group of related objects contained within a small subset of the realm of the network. The entire namespace is hierarchical to allow for the unique identification by name of every system attached to the connected networks and registered in databases maintained by nameservers. The DNS hierarchy is divided into domains, or *zones*, that form an inverted tree that starts at the root and branches downward through independently managed domains. Authority to manage hostname-to-IP address mappings within a domain is delegated by an administrator of a domain holding a position in the hierarchy directly above the domain.

Any given nameserver knows only about the domains it's directly responsible for managing as well as the nameservers for any domains directly above and below its managed domains in the DNS hierarchy. Systems that are represented by entries in a domain database on a nameserver can be uniquely identified within the DNS hierarchy using a combination of hostname and domain name. For example, if a system has a hostname of "snoopy" within the domain database for foo.bar.com, it can be contacted by a client system outside the domain using the name snoopy.foo.bar.com, as long as the client system resolves names with a nameserver within the same hierarchy. This combination of hostname and domain name is sometimes referred to as an FQDN (fully qualified domain name).

Resolvers

Client systems, called *resolvers*, resolve names by interacting with nameservers using simple queries and responses. It's necessary for a client system to specify one or more nameservers that it will use to originate all hostname resolution operations. When multiple nameservers are specified, the resolver will use the first nameserver in the list as long as it's available—other nameservers often are used only when the first nameserver is unavailable. On UNIX systems, the nameservers used by a resolver usually are specified in the `/etc/resolv.conf` file, which contains a default domain name and the IP addresses of one or more nameservers.

Name resolution operations usually begin with the resolver sending a query containing a hostname that needs to be resolved to an address. The response that the nameserver sends to the resolver depends on a number of factors. If the name being requested is for a domain directly managed by the nameserver and the requested host has an entry in the local database, the nameserver will immediately send a response containing the requested host's IP address. The operation will be complete once the resolver receives the response. If the name being requested is for a domain that's not directly managed by the nameserver, the nameserver will do one of three things, depending on the configuration:

- The nameserver will usually first consult its cache that's used to hold the results of recent name resolution requests. The cache is used to cut down on name resolution traffic and to increase the speed with which responses can be provided to resolvers. If the requested information is not in cache, one of the traditional name resolution methods is used instead and the result is stored in cache.

- The nameserver will provide iterative name resolution by responding to the resolver with one or more referrals to other nameservers (either above or below the nameserver in the DNS hierarchy) that would better allow the host's DNS entry to be located. At this point, the resolver is responsible for contacting a referred nameserver in the same manner it contacted the previous nameserver. The resolver will continue chasing down referrals, as necessary, until the hostname can be resolved to an IP address, it runs out of referrals, or it receives a response that the host cannot be found.

- The nameserver will provide recursive name resolution by contacting another nameserver on behalf of the resolver and taking control of the name resolution process until it can provide a response to the resolver. In this case, the nameserver is responsible for chasing down referrals as necessary. The only response the resolver receives will be an IP address or a response that the host cannot be found.

When navigating the DNS hierarchy to resolve hostnames, a resolver could encounter nameservers that provide either iterative or recursive name resolution, although recursive name resolution is more commonly provided by nameservers.

Database Replication and Management

The information residing on a particular nameserver may be replicated to other servers that will provide identical name resolution services to resolvers for fault tolerance and load-balancing purposes. Administration of hostname-to-IP address mappings within a particular domain occurs at the primary nameserver for the domain, and copies of the

DNS database are downloaded periodically by replica nameservers in a process called *zone transfer*. As long as replication occurs frequently and consistently, resolvers can use any primary or replica nameserver for name resolution without worrying about whether the information is current or accurate.

Due to the cross-platform nature of DNS (numerous types of servers and clients can participate in DNS name resolution), there is no single method that's used to manage the DNS database. Depending on the operating system platform acting as a nameserver as well as the software used to provide name resolution services, the DNS database could be maintained directly through manipulation of the database tables or indirectly through utilities. Client name resolution operations are always performed using the protocols defined in the DNS specification.

DNS and the Internet

The Domain Naming System is important as a network directory due to its current status as an official Internet standard and its wide acceptance by users and organizations as the authoritative naming service for hosts and networks connected to the Internet. Even if a network is not connected to the Internet, DNS is still used by organizations with TCP/IP networks, because it provides a reasonably elegant method for management of name-to-address mappings for TCP/IP hosts on an intranet. DNS is also used as the basis for some electronic mail addressing systems to allow for the unique identification of users in the same way that systems are uniquely identified.

DNS primarily provides a single function: the resolution of hostnames to IP addresses. The problem with this is that users and organizations often would like to be able to access more information about systems, services, and other network resources, but doing so would require another directory to store this additional information. Because this other directory could also easily contain information about hostnames and IP addresses for name resolution, a separate DNS database would be tautological. The emergence of LDAP (Lightweight Directory Access Protocol) as an official Internet standard for accessing a variety of directories could make this scenario a reality.

Windows Internet Naming System (WINS)

Windows Internet Naming Service (WINS) is a name resolution service designed by Microsoft for network resources using the NetBIOS protocol. NetBIOS (originally developed by IBM), and its successor NetBEUI, has been the protocol of choice (rather than UNIX's TCP/IP or Novell's IPX/SPX) for Windows networking.

> **Note:** The use of NetBIOS/NetBEUI is dropping as Microsoft has encouraged the use of TCP/IP and NWLink (its implementation of IPX/SPX) for Windows networking, beginning with Windows 95 and Windows NT 4 and continuing with Windows 98 and Windows 2000. Nevertheless, WINS is still used in Windows peer-to-peer networks as well as for DHCP in Windows NT.

WINS is similar in function to the Domain Naming System, although it adds functionality through interaction with DHCP (Dynamic Host Control Protocol—see Chapter 13, "Remote Access Services (RAS)," for details) by ensuring that NetBIOS names are unique and by allowing the name resolution database to be maintained dynamically. The name resolution services provided by WINS are meant to replace the manual method of maintaining name resolution information for NetBIOS resources on TCP/IP networks that was first introduced with NetBIOS over TCP/IP for Microsoft's LAN Manager. This original method involved the use of lmhosts databases (actually a text file) stored on client workstations or servers that were similar in appearance to the hosts databases that can be used to allow for name resolution in the base IP protocol suite. Just as with the base IP protocol suite, it's possible to use DNS to provide name resolution for NetBIOS resources, but WINS is generally preferred due to its added functionality.

Updating WINS Databases: Push Partners and Pull Partners

WINS cooperates with the DHCP service running on a Windows NT Server, and this server is used for centralized administration and configuration of additional WINS servers, static name tables, and replication information. Additional WINS servers that contain replicas of the main WINS database are used to distribute NetBIOS name resolution services and traffic for fault tolerance and load balancing. Any given WINS server will be a push partner or pull partner with at least one other WINS server. Pull partners receive WINS database updates from other WINS servers, whereas push partners send information to other WINS servers. It's possible for a WINS server to be both push and pull partners with various other WINS servers.

Unless we're specifically referring to hardware, *server* is software. All NetBIOS name-to-IP address mapping records in the WINS database are assigned version numbers so that push and pull partners can determine which records need to be updated during replication. Both push and pull partners can initiate replication sessions based on a predefined replication threshold, which, in turn, is based on the time since the last replication. Push partners can also initiate replication once a threshold based on the number of updates has been exceeded.

When a pull partner initiates a replication session, it requests all records with a higher version number than the records it currently possesses from its partner. When a push partner initiates a replication session, it notifies its partners. They proceed as if they were initiating the replication session by requesting all records with a higher version number than those records they currently possess.

Service Advertising Protocol (SAP)

Service Advertising Protocol (SAP) is a naming service for the IPX/SPX protocol designed by Novell for its NetWare operating system. SAP allows systems (such as file servers, print servers, and gateway servers) to advertise their services and addresses so they can be located on the network using names instead of addresses.

SAP is typically implemented as a dynamic naming service where systems advertise their presence periodically while operating so that routers can build tables of available services. Routers dynamically remove services from the tables they maintain either when they're informed by an advertising service that it will stop functioning or when they do not hear from an advertising service for a specified period of time. The form of service information tables differs by systems; for example, NetWare servers (where routing is integral) store SAP entries in the bindery as dynamic objects.

Information about services is propagated to routers that maintain service information tables by service-providing systems and by other routers. Service-providing systems provide firsthand information about their services by periodically broadcasting IPX packets containing information about all services available on the system on their local network segments. Routers provide secondhand information about network services by periodically broadcasting all SAP information maintained in their tables on their local interfaces.

Each SAP packet contains one or more SAP entries, and each SAP entry consists of a type identifier, a service name, and an IPX network address. Type identifiers provide a standard numeric representation of the type of service being advertised, and each type identifier encompasses an independent flat namespace. For example, it's perfectly reasonable for the same name to be advertised with multiple SAP types as long as the same name is not advertised with the same SAP type. SAP has no way to prevent a service from using a name associated with a service that's already in use on a network, but establishing reliable communications when such a name clash occurs will be difficult.

Network clients use SAP to locate services by issuing queries for services either by sending a broadcast on the local network or by contacting a specific router. When a SAP query is sent to a specific router, the router will respond with all services from its service information tables that satisfy the query. When a SAP query is issued as a broadcast, all routers connected to the local network will respond with services that satisfy the query.

> **Note:** An example of a common broadcast request on a NetWare network is *Get Nearest Server*, which allows a client system to obtain the network address of the nearest server for its initial attachment to the network.

SAP is a highly effective name resolution service, and its simplicity has allowed it to remain in wide use in NetWare networks despite some serious problems with the way it operates on large networks. The most serious problem is that SAP can require a tremendous amount of broadcast traffic to propagate current service availability information that allows routers to keep their service information tables current. This characteristic has lead to the router broadcasts that occur on network segments being characterized as *freight trains* because hundreds of packets can be broadcast every minute on network segments throughout a network. In response to this, most organizations with large

NetWare networks implement SAP filtering to control the propagation throughout the network of information about certain types of services. This can lead to the unavailability of some services that might be needed occasionally, even though they would normally be reachable.

Several services have been developed by Novell to reduce the need for such broadcast traffic to maintain current service information that makes SAP much more manageable, such as NetWare Link Services Protocol (NLSP), NetWare/IP and its Domain SAP Services (DSS), and Novell Directory Services (NDS). However, SAP continues to play a role in IPX networks because many networks have older devices that require it and because it's still an effective way for client systems to learn about nearby services.

Kerberos

Kerberos is a network security system originally developed for Project Athena at MIT (Massachusetts Institute of Technology). It provides trusted third-party authentication and key management for secure communications between network nodes. With Kerberos, centralized key distribution hosts mediate the establishment of network sessions between systems in such a way that both ends of a session can authenticate to each other while agreeing on keys used for encryption or integrity validation of secure communications. Versions 4 and 5 of Kerberos (commonly referred to as Kerberos V4 and Kerberos V5, respectively) are the two most recent implementations of the Kerberos system and are the most common versions in use. Windows 2000 uses Kerberos V5 for authentication services.

Kerberos V4 and V5 Implementation

The implementation details of Kerberos V4 and V5 differ significantly, but the concepts behind the two versions are similar enough to allow them to be covered together. The key idea behind Kerberos is that a central host acts as the Key Distribution Center (KDC), which mediates communications between principals that trust it. As Kerberos views things, a *principal* is anything using the authentication system, be it a user or a network service running on a server. There may be more than one service being provided by a given server that uses Kerberos, just as there may be more than one user requesting a given service with the involvement of Kerberos.

The primary component of the Kerberos system is a master database residing on a server that maintains a list of each of its principals (users or services) and their private keys. Only the Kerberos servers and their principals know the private keys, and a Kerberos server uses these keys to create messages that are used to convince one principal that another is authentic. In Kerberos V4, each principal is assigned a three-part identifier that consists of a name, instance, and realm. Instances are somewhat redundant for normal users, but they're often used to identify services on a server that's identified by a name. Kerberos V5 dropped the instance component for principal identification, so each client is assigned only a two-part identifier that consists of a name and realm.

Realms are the administrative units of Kerberos: Each realm contains at least one KDC that holds the master copy of the Kerberos database to which all updates are made. Additional read-only copies of the Kerberos database can be replicated to additional KDCs within a realm so that authentication can continue in the event that the KDC holding the master copy of the Kerberos database is unavailable. When replicated KDCs for a realm are available on a network, the only operations that cannot be performed when the master copy of the Kerberos database is unavailable are adding and deleting users and changing passwords.

In Kerberos V4, principals can request sessions with other principals in different realms as long as the realm of the requested principal is directly registered as a principal in the requesting client's realm. Chaining of realms not directly related is not allowed in Kerberos V4, so in an environment with multiple realms, each realm must be registered as a principal in all other realms to support communications between all realms. In Kerberos V5, chaining of realms is allowed, but the ways that principals can use to discover a chain of realms is not specified. Implementations of Kerberos V5 usually create a hierarchy of realms (denoted by multipart realm names similar to DNS domain names) so that the hierarchy can be traversed to discover the required chain. In this case, it's not necessary for all realms to be registered as principals in all other realms because each realm only needs to be registered as a principal with realms directly above and below it.

The Authentication Process

Kerberos authentication uses two types of credentials: tickets and authenticators. Tickets are used to pass authoritative principal information between a KDC and a principal. Authenticators contain additional information that can be used to verify the information contained in a ticket and establish a session. Tickets and authenticators are issued during the authentication process when principals establish sessions with other principals. When a principal such as a user initially logs in, the user is assigned a ticket-granting ticket that's used to obtain additional tickets when it's necessary to establish sessions with other principals.

The Kerberos authentication process begins when a principal requests that a KDC provide it with the information necessary to establish a session with another principal. The KDC responds with a message encrypted with the requesting principal's key that contains another message encrypted with the requested principal's key. These messages are the tickets and authenticators. The requesting principal is then responsible for decrypting the message provided by the KDC with its key and sending the resulting message to the desired principal. This message contains information about the requesting principal, and because it's encrypted with the requested principal's key, the recipient can be assured that it originated from a trusted KDC once it's successfully decrypted and the requesting principal's information is validated. Once the authentication process is completed, both principals share a session key that can be used to ensure the confidentiality and integrity of communications between the clients.

Both Kerberos V4 and V5 represent major improvements over the ways security is normally handled in a UNIX environment, while also providing for centralized management of user, service, and resource naming. Although originally developed for UNIX, the Kerberos specifications, especially Kerberos V5, are generic enough to allow their use in environments outside of UNIX.

> **Note:** Because Kerberos is a radical departure from the ways in which security is usually provided on UNIX and Windows NT systems, deployment of Kerberos is often difficult because it requires "kerberized" utilities and services instead of the standard versions. These utilities and services replace most of the utilities and services provided with standard UNIX and Windows NT 4 implementations so that Kerberos services can be used.

Windows Networking: Workgroups and Domains

Microsoft's networking software before Windows 2000 (such as LAN Manager, Windows for Workgroups, Windows 95/98, and Windows NT) typically is capable of implementing either of two models for organizing networked systems into groups for administrative purposes. The simplest model is the *workgroup*, where all systems that are members of a workgroup are loosely related for the purpose of allowing shared resources, such as directories and printers, to be easily located. *Domains*, on the other hand, go beyond the resource-sharing aspects of workgroups by implementing a shared security service that can be used (by all systems in the domain that support security) to control access to local resources. This section focuses on directories implemented on Windows NT systems that support security services provided by individual systems and domains.

All Windows NT systems, regardless of whether they exist in a workgroup or a domain, provide security services to control access to resources and services located on the system. These security services allow for access to be controlled at the user and group levels and are enforced upon initial entry to the system.

Users typically can access Windows NT systems either locally or from across the network—in both cases, access to resources is controlled by the same security services. These security services use directories that contain information about users and groups that are identified by name and associated with internal object IDs that are assigned by the system. The names for users and groups share a common namespace, so it's not possible to have a user and group with the same name on a system.

Rights assignments for resources within the system are based on object IDs rather than names, and object IDs are not reused once an object is deleted. This means that if an object is renamed, its rights assignments will remain intact as long as the object ID has not changed. If an object is deleted and re-created with the same name, the object ID for the new object will be different and all previous rights assignments will be lost.

Domains implement a separate directory that contains information about machines, users, and groups that are part of the domain. Unlike workgroups, which systems can join at will and where they can advertise their services, systems must be added to a domain explicitly in order to participate in the domain's security services.

> **Note:** The privilege of adding machines to a domain is typically reserved for administrators, but it can be delegated to other users or groups as desired. It's not necessary, however, for a system to be a member of a domain to access most resources on systems within that domain.

The properties for users and groups defined in a domain's directory are similar to those for standalone systems, except that the domain's directory is shared by all systems that are members of the domain rather than being restricted to a single system.

The domain directory database is maintained on a server designated as a Primary Domain Controller (PDC), and additional copies of the domain directory database can be replicated to one or more Backup Domain Controllers (BDCs). Users can authenticate to any domain controller in the domain, so if the PDC is unavailable, user authentication can continue uninterrupted. All administrative activities for a domain must occur at the PDC because it contains the only read-write copy of the domain's directory database, and each domain can have only one PDC at any given time.

> **Note:** In the event that a domain's PDC is unavailable, activities such as adding and deleting users and groups or changing passwords cannot be performed. A BDC can be promoted to a PDC if the PDC cannot be returned to service in a reasonable amount of time.

All systems that are members of a domain and are not designated as domain controllers retain their local directories; this requires that a distinction be made between local and domain resources when assigning rights on each system in a domain. Domain users and group objects are identified by a two-part name that includes the domain name and the object name. System names are identified either by the object name itself (within the context of the system) or by a two-part name that includes the system name and the object name. This requires that domain names and system names be unique within the same namespace. This is enforced by the name resolution that's used for the network (which depends on the communication protocols being used).

Because the namespaces for users and groups within domain and local system directories are independent, different objects are allowed to have the same names within both the domain and local system directories. The local objects can be distinguished from domain objects through the two-part names, and it's possible for a domain user or group object to be a member of a local group residing on a system.

Implementing Trust Relationships

Any given system can be a member of only one domain. Allowing users defined in one domain to access resources located in another domain would be difficult without the concept of *trust* that exists in the domain security model. Without trust, separate accounts would need to be created in the directories for other systems or domains for users wishing to access those resources. Users would be required to authenticate each time they needed to access those resources even though they had already authenticated to their primary domain. This is not necessary because domains can be configured to trust other domains. Users in one domain can access resources in other domains using their existing domain credentials as long as the resource domains trust the users' domain. Domain trust relationships are directional, which means that trust relationships between domains need not be mutual.

Although the trust model allows for flexible access to resources across domain boundaries, managing trust relations can become quite difficult as networks grow and the number of domains increase. Part of the reason is that the trust model—as it's implemented up through Windows NT 4—does not allow chaining of trust relationships. It's not possible for a user to access resources in a domain that trusts a domain that trusts the user's domain unless the resource domain explicitly trusts the user's domain. If every domain in a network requires a two-way trust with every other domain on the network, the total number of required trust relationships would grow exponentially with each domain that's added to the network.

These problems are usually addressed by creating a distinction between authentication domains and resource domains. *Authentication domains* are dedicated to maintaining user and group accounts and do not trust any other domains (except perhaps each other). *Resource domains* are dedicated to providing resources and services for the network and are satisfied to leave the authentication tasks to the authentication domains that they trust. This configuration makes trusts much more manageable since authentication domains do not normally need to maintain trust relationships, and each resource domain needs only to maintain one-way trust relationships with the authentication domains.

Banyan StreetTalk

StreetTalk is a network naming service originally developed for Banyan's VINES (Virtual Networking System). Even though VINES itself has not experienced a great deal of success in the network industry, StreetTalk has achieved distinction as an innovative directory service due to the unique way it provides for globally identifying network resources (including services, users, and lists) in a loosely structured yet coherent manner. Due to the strength of StreetTalk, Banyan has extended its reach through its ENS (Enterprise Network Services) products to allow StreetTalk to coordinate access to services for network operating systems other than VINES, such as UNIX, NetWare, and Windows NT.

Every network resource associated with systems encompassed by a StreetTalk directory has a name and a set of attributes that allow it to be uniquely identified within the directory. The names of resources are independent of the particular network in which the server they reside on is located, making it possible for users to connect to services or resources attached to different servers without knowing where they reside. The names assigned to resources map to network addresses that are tracked by the StreetTalk directory, and all management activities use the StreetTalk names for resources rather than other identifiers. Attributes assigned to resources can also be used to assist with locating or categorizing them.

StreetTalk names consist of three components separated by the at (@) sign, and each component maps (moving left to right) to an item, group, and organization. Conceptually, items can be thought of as users or resources that belong to a group, which in turn belongs to an organization. As an example, the StreetTalk naming service for a server called "Quest" would be identified as ST@Quest@Servers, where Quest is a group created to contain all services associated with the server, and Servers is the default organization created to contain all servers. This three-part naming scheme is often viewed as mapping naturally to a hierarchical scheme. Such hierarchy is not rigidly defined for StreetTalk, although it's often the case in practice.

Certain types of resources, such as users, lists, and services, can be assigned one or more nicknames that allow the resources to be identified more easily than might be the case if full names were always required. Nicknames are little more than pointers to other resources that can be used interchangeably with the full names of the resources. Nicknames inhabit the same namespace that's used for full StreetTalk names. Usage of nicknames is sensitive to context with respect to default groups and organizations, but nicknames can refer to resource names that exist outside the group and organization containing the nickname.

Every StreetTalk service running on a server maintains a directory database on the server where the service is running, and this database is distributed among multiple servers when they're present. There are no centralized servers providing naming services for StreetTalk, as there are for other network directories, so there's no single point of failure for the naming service in a multiserver environment.

The directory databases maintained on servers contain detailed information about the items associated with groups on those servers, and each server maintains tables that map all known groups to servers. Organizations, in contrast, do not exist primarily in any single place but instead exist only as logical entities allowing groups to be associated with each other. Directory information is distributed among servers periodically at a fixed interval or when servers or groups are added or deleted.

Administrators are responsible for maintaining StreetTalk names and for managing the distribution of names throughout the network. Administrators gain their privileges through membership in special list items called "AdminList" that are associated with groups. Lists behave in the same manner as groups in most other directories with the added property of being able to contain names for multiple types of objects (including other lists).

Resource names can be located in a StreetTalk directory using a flexible set of search capabilities that allow searches based on parts of names or attributes associated with resources. Resource types (such as users, services, or groups) share a common set of attributes that have a name, type, and value. One of the interesting features of StreetTalk is that administrators can add custom attribute specifications for resource types to provide additional information about resources or to allow for additional associations between resources. For example, an attribute called "Location" could be added which would carry office number, floor number or building number information for the resource. This would make locating the resource easier, while groups of resources with the same value for "Location" could be grouped in a presentation.

StreetTalk is integrated with the security services of operating systems hosting StreetTalk naming services so that the StreetTalk directory can provide the information necessary to control initial entry to the system and access to system resources. Initial entry is controlled through the identification and authentication process, which typically involves a user presenting a StreetTalk name or nickname and a password to the login program that interacts with the security service. The security service uses the StreetTalk name to determine which server can provide the information necessary to validate the authentication request and then opens a connection with the StreetTalk service on that server to continue the authentication process.

Novell Directory Services (NDS)

Novell introduced a new concept in local area network naming and security services in 1991 when it released NetWare version 4 with NDS. This was a radical departure from the server-centric bindery system used in early versions of NetWare for authentication and name services.

Beginnings of NDS

NDS's designers began with the notion that the network and the server were not the same. The server was simply one more object in the network; therefore, the bindery's server-centric view had to be expanded to a network-centric view.

The designers learned that, even though NetWare 3's bindery allowed for over 16 million objects, there would always be networks that needed to have 17 million or more. NDS version 8 supports over 1 billion users, plus the other objects (printers, servers, and so on) needed for extremely large networks.

A fully relational database was needed to overcome the search-time penalty of the bindery. Furthermore, in a brilliant insight, the idea of a distributed database was included. This meant that parts of the database could be in different places, even multiple places, so that the loss of a single data repository (such as a server) would not totally crash the directory system.

For security reasons, as well as to further move the bindery/directory from server centric to network centric, the file system supervisor and the directory system supervisor were not necessarily the same person. Additionally, although some object needed all rights to a particular object and its properties, this ability might need to be held by different user objects for different parts of the network.

While the experience of NetWare's bindery formed a solid core of knowledge for the NDS designers, they also studied other directory systems to learn what was desirable and what should be avoided. for NDS.

LAN Manager's Domain system showed that a network-centric rather than server-centric view was desirable, as was the ability to have more than one instance of the directory's database. But the domain system still required the entire database to be present on a domain controller (the "head" server), so it wasn't completely divorced from being server centric. By making the server simply one more directory object, NDS immediately became more scalable to ever larger networks.

Banyan Systems' VINES network operating system had been known for years because of its naming service, in which each object within the network had a unique name as well as an alias (or *friendly name*) that users could use to access the object. Both concepts were incorporated into NDS.

The hierarchical structure of X.500, its tree-like design, and much of its nomenclature were used to create NDS. This foresight was well repaid in 1996 when LDAP (Light Directory Access Protocol), a protocol for quickly accessing an X.500 directory, became prominent as the best way to query directory databases across the Internet. Novell was able to quickly adapt an LDAP interface to NDS (released in early 1997), further distancing Novell from other network operating system vendors.

Today's NDS

NDS uses the basic X.500 structure and hierarchy, including most of the container and leaf objects defined in that standard. However, NDS provides functionality beyond the X.500 specification, offering a complete networking infrastructure that links users to network services, applications, and data.

Single Sign-On Service

With NDS, users and network supervisors only have to log in once with one password to be authenticated to the entire network, instead of logging into each file server and other network resources separately. Once authenticated, users have access to all the network resources to which they have rights, regardless of the size of the network and where the users or resources are physically located. Because NDS is cross platform (supporting NetWare, Solaris, Windows NT, OS/390, and Linux), this single sign on extends across multiple operating systems, resources, and data repositories.

Integrate Multiplatform Systems

NDS is access protocol independent (supporting both IPX/SPX and TCP/IP) and platform independent so that you can build networks or intranets with different hardware and operating systems. You can choose the hardware, server operating systems, and client operating systems that best suit your needs and still enjoy all the cost savings, ease of management, and other benefits of NDS. NDS is currently available on NetWare 5, NetWare 4, NT 4.0, NT 3.51, Solaris, and OS/390. It also supports legacy NetWare 3 servers as well as most current desktop operating systems (DOS, Windows 3.*x*, Windows 9*x*, Windows NT, Windows 2000, Linux, UnixWare and Macintosh).

NDS Security

NDS protects access to the network by requiring users to authenticate to it when they log in. NDS uses an authentication service based on the public/private key encryption technology developed by RSA Data Security, Inc., which relies on a private key and digital signature to verify the user's identity. Once the user is authenticated to the network, further authentication (which is required when a user makes a request to a different server) is handled in the background and is transparent to the user.

NDS also protects access to network resources once users are logged in to the network. Network supervisors control access to all network resources by assigning rights to objects that represent network resources, user groups, and individual users.

NDS Replication

With NDS, you can secure your network against data loss and downtime by replicating partitions to strategic locations on the network. This protects your network from problems caused by a single point of failure, such as a server going down or the temporary loss of a communication link. If a primary partition is lost, the network automatically reconfigures itself to use another copy, or *replica*, of the partition. In addition, you can restore a partition that has been lost from one server by using a replica on a different server. Novell has tested NDS replication with millions of objects replicated over multiple servers.

NDS allows you to implement a highly distributed directory model, where replicas of partitions are distributed to servers throughout the organization, or to store a large copy of the directory on a single server and replicate the entire database to a select number of servers. Because of NDS's massive scalability and replication model, you have the flexibility to deploy your directory without interruption and build the necessary infrastructure required for distributed or highly centralized directory applications, such as those required for electric commerce.

NDS Manageability

The hierarchical structure of NDS simplifies network administration by enabling network supervisors to arrange network resources in the directory tree according to the way they're used. With resources placed near the users who access them, network supervisors can grant access rights to entire branches of the tree at one time. They can give rights to complete groups of users and then deal with exceptions on an individual basis.

NDS Schema

NDS offers a flexible schema (that is, a rules system that defines how the NDS tree is structured). This schema includes what objects are defined, what attributes can be associated with objects, and what positions objects occupy in the directory tree.

NDS includes a default schema that contains all the base objects and attributes that many networks will ever need; nevertheless, you can extend the default schema to customize the database to fit your needs. For example, you can extend a user object by adding new attributes such as a Social Security number or an emergency contact name and telephone number. Independent software vendors (ISVs) can also integrate new services into the network by extending the NDS schema and creating new objects. For example, ISVs have added fax server functionality to the network by adding a fax server object to the directory tree.

NDS Single-Point of Administration

Because NDS supports multiple platforms and open standards such as LDAP, it provides a single, global directory that can contain information for all network applications. NDS maintains information about every resource on the network—including users, groups, printers, volumes, network devices, and any other customizable object—in a hierarchical tree structure. It provides a single point of administration for the entire network. Because NDS is a global directory, network supervisors can eliminate a number of redundant tasks. For example, to give a user access rights to all servers on the network, a network supervisor would normally have to give that user rights to each server individually. With NDS, however, you only need to create one user object. The one object gives the user the same user ID for every server on the network.

NDS's structure allows organizations to choose whether to centralize management and administration services that cross departmental boundaries or to delegate administration to the department or workgroup level.

Microsoft's Active Directory Service

Windows 2000 introduces an entirely new directory service to the world: Active Directory Service (ADS). ADS is built on the domain system used by Windows NT, with additions imported from X.500, DNS, and even NDS. ADS also introduces a new authentication scheme based on Kerberos V5.

ADS Naming

One of the most important changes in the Windows 2000 architecture is the use of UNIX-style DNS for name resolution. Windows NT 4.0 and earlier versions of Windows NT Server depended on NetBIOS names and the Microsoft-specific Windows Internet Name Service (WINS) to resolve computer names to IP (Internet protocol) addresses. With Windows 2000, DNS is introduced as the name resolution mechanism. Although Windows NT 4.0 will interoperate with and support DNS, it does not require integration with the DNS infrastructure in place in the enterprise. Because of this, it has been easy to install Windows NT in divisional or regional networks. At the enterprise level, Windows NT 4.0 can be rolled out with very little impact on, or concern for, the DNS infrastructure of the organization. It does increase the time spent managing name services, because both DNS and WINS need to be managed separately.

Because DNS is at the heart of Windows 2000 directory services, deploying Windows 2000 in an enterprise requires coordination at the highest enterprise level. Most organizations have DNS services already in place, and Windows 2000 Server must be configured to integrate within the existing namespace. The benefit, of course, is that name service will only need to be managed in one place—the DNS.

ADS and Domain Systems

The good news is that upgrading your network to Windows 2000 and ADS doesn't have to be a one-shot, all-or-nothing move. Windows 2000 supports a mixed environment of Active Directory domain controllers and Windows NT 4.0 domain controllers, so you can migrate at the pace that best fits your business needs. Clients won't notice the change and will think they're accessing Windows NT 4.0 domain controllers. Clients that don't have new ADS access software (such as Windows NT Workstation, Windows 95, Windows 3.1x, and DOS) can log on to Active Directory domain controllers by continuing to use Windows NT LAN Manager (NTLM) challenge/response authentication—just as they did with NT 3.51 servers.

This backward compatibility allows you to migrate domain controllers first and then migrate clients or to migrate a combination of servers and clients—whatever works best for you. The migration process does not require a mass migration to the new operating system version on either servers or clients. It's also not necessary to take a complete domain offline to migrate domain controllers or clients. Individual domain controllers are unavailable only during their operating system update. This allows you to migrate to the Active Directory without interrupting your business.

It is, however, important to remember that LAN Manager challenge/response authentication is less secure than NT Server's authentication, and it's much less secure than Active Directory's Kerberos-based authentication.

ADS Architecture

In the Active Directory, the concept of a *domain* remains, but domains are then further organized into trees. *Tree* is a standard directory services term derived from the branching structure of the organization of objects within the directory. The starting point is called the *root*. ADS trees can be viewed in two ways: as the division of the namespace for the domain tree (this is the physical architecture of the directory), and as the trust relationships between domains or trees (this is the logical architecture of the directory).

In ADS, a domain is a partition—the smallest replicable division of a tree—in the namespace. All domain controllers (DCs) in the same domain contain the entire directory for that domain, with identical databases. Objects are always replicated on the domain level. DCs never replicate objects to domain controllers in different domains. This makes a domain both a naming context and a partition in the namespace, thus defining the physical architecture of the tree.

An Active Directory tree, then, contains a hierarchy of domains that have trust relationships to each other. (This is a new concept: Windows NT 4 domains are all peers, and there is no hierarchy.) Within a domain, you can further implement a hierarchy of organizational units. This creates two levels of hierarchies inside the tree: the hierarchy of the domains and the hierarchies of OUs (organizational unit) within the domains. The OU hierarchy inside a domain is independent—each domain can implement its own OU hierarchy.

This two-tiered hierarchical structure allows a great deal of flexibility in administrating domain trees. For example, an entire domain tree can be owned and administered by a central IT team. The IT team can create the same OUs in all domains—such as an IT OU where local IT user accounts reside or a technical support OU for support employees. Additional OUs can be formed to meet users' needs in the particular domain.

In the headquarters domain, a human resources and a finance OU can be created. For a regional office domain, an OU for the office sales team can be created. Administrative rights for these particular OUs can be delegated to specific users or groups so that these users can administer their own areas without involving IT. What's more, because these users have administrative rights only on their own OUs, they can never interfere with IT's global rights and responsibilities.

The flexibility in this logical architecture allows organizations to create an environment that mirrors the business's organization. ADS supports either a centralized or decentralized business model as well as any combination of the two. For example, you can use the domain structure to provide a centralized framework, and then you can use the OU structure within domains to support decentralized operations.

ADS implements a DNS-based naming style (the familiar `name@domain` style of email addresses) that's founded on the LDAP proposals. In this naming hierarchy, the single components of the DNS domain names are expanded to DC (domain component) entries. For example, if the user John is in the OU "Boston," which in turn is in the OU "Sales," and both OUs are in the domain `microsoft.com`, the ADS unique name of the user would be `john@boston.sales.microsoft.com`.

ADS Domains

Simply put, a Windows 2000 domain is a partition (that is, a subset) of the namespace—the entire directory tree—where a common security policy applies. A domain's security policy defines how strong the passwords have to be (that is, length, case, and character set allowed); the password history (which defines the degree of "uniqueness" required); the lifetime of Kerberos tickets; account lockouts; and more. When a user account is created in a domain, it's assigned a security ID (SID). A portion of the SID always contains an identifier of the domain where the SID was originally issued. This makes it easy to find out which domain contains a user or group and to determine whether to grant access to resources. A domain is a physical security boundary. Full administrative control is contained within a domain.

ADS Organizational Units

An organizational unit (OU) is a container within a domain that can hold other objects. Within the domain, an OU is similar to a folder in a file system: a container that holds files or other directories. In like manner, a Windows 2000 OU is a container that holds other objects or other OUs. OUs are used for grouping objects (in many ways, they're similar to Windows NT 4 groups) and for delegating administrative rights. Objects that are typically stored in OUs are users, groups, printers, and distributed file system (DFS) shares. The permission to create these objects and change attributes on these objects can be assigned to specific users and groups. This results in an improved granularity of administration.

The ADS Schema

The schema in the Active Directory database defines objects and properties that can be created in the directory. When the Active Directory is installed on the first domain controller in a forest (a set of directory trees that share a common schema, configuration, and global catalog), a default schema is created. This includes all objects and properties that are required for the directory service to work and is replicated to all domain controllers that join the forest later.

Because the directory service is pervasive throughout the network, the directory is a great place to store information that can be used by directory-aware applications. One example is a Human Resources (HR) application. The directory already includes a great deal of information about users, such as their first and last names, their office numbers, their phone numbers, and perhaps their home addresses. Although all this information is useful to a Human Resources application, additional information would have to be added, such as the employees' salaries, Social Security numbers, tax withholding information, and health insurance information.

ADS allows you to extend the schema to create new properties and classes for all the information you may want to add. New classes can be derived from existing classes and can inherit all properties from the previous classes. New properties can be created, and these properties can be added to classes. Properties can be created as either required or optional. Required properties are required to obtain a value when a new object is created. These properties can later be changed, but they cannot be deleted. For example, a user object must contain a common name (CN), a SamAccountName (used for backward compatibility with NT's Security Account Manager), and a password.

Optional properties can be added or changed at any time. These properties are not required for the directory service to work, but they hold additional information that's useful for system administration or for other users in the enterprise. Examples include phone numbers, office numbers, and a manager attribute.

For example, suppose you need to distinguish between employees and contractors who need network access. You derive a new user class, Employee, specifically for full-time employees. You also determine that to support your HR application, you need to add salary and Social Security number properties to the schema. You then add the newly defined salary and Social Security properties to the Employee class as "may" attributes. The security granularity of Windows 2000 allows you to grant read and write access to these properties to members of the HR department while granting the individual user only read access to his or her data.

An extensible schema also allows third-party applications to store information they need in the directory for ready access throughout the network. However, be sure that the same schema is used in every domain throughout your trees and forest; otherwise, odd (and unpleasant) things could happen.

The ADS Database

Active Directory uses the new Extensible Storage Engine (ESE) as the basis for its database. ESE is an improved version of the Jet database, which was used in Microsoft Exchange 4.0 and 5.0, and is the same database engine that will also be used for the new versions of Microsoft Exchange. This improved storage engine allows you to create a database of up to 17 terabytes in size (if you've got the disk space—and RAM—to support it). The database can hold up to 10 million objects. This doesn't mean that your database will necessarily be huge, however. ESE reserves storage only for those properties that actually have a value. As an example, the default schema predefines approximately 50 properties for a user object. If you create a user, and you set only four properties—such as first name, last name, common name, and password—the database uses space for these four attributes only. If you add more values later, the database dynamically allocates storage for the data.

ESE can also store properties with multiple values—for example, the database can store multiple phone numbers for a single user without requiring multiple phone number attributes.

ADS Replication

Windows NT domains were based on a machine called the Primary Domain Controller (PDC), which held the database of all network objects within the domain. For fault tolerance, it was recommended that there be at least one (and preferably more) Backup Domain Controllers (BDC), which could offload some of the authentication traffic from the PDC as well as be ready to take over as PDC should the primary's machine fail. Unfortunately, the network traffic needed to keep a BDC synchronized to a PDC was enormous. Having a BDC and PDC connected by a slow WAN link could bring activity to a crawl during replication.

Windows 2000's Active Directory has an improved replication engine that allows you to differentiate between replication that happens using a local network connection and replication that happens over a slow WAN connection. It introduces the concept of *Sites*—an administrator-defined group of IP subnets with good connectivity. Within the same Site, replication starts after a specified deferral time. Between Sites, replication is scheduled and uses WAN network bandwidth only at specified times or time intervals.

In general, replication traffic in the Active Directory is reduced when compared with the same number of objects in Windows NT 4.0. Although the Active Directory defines more objects and more properties per object, the replication traffic is reduced, because replication in the Active Directory is done at the individual property level (instead of the entire user account). If you change only one property on an object, only this property is replicated to the replication partners, not the object as a whole.

Replication in ADS is not based on time but rather on a unique identification code called an *Update Sequence Number* (USN). Each domain controller holds a table containing entries for its own USN and the USNs of its replication partners. During replication, the domain controller compares the last-known USN of its replication partner (saved in the table) with the current USN that the replication partner provides. If there have been recent changes (that is, if the replication partner provides a higher USN), the data store requests all changes from the replication partner (called a *pull replication*). After receiving the data, the directory store sets the USN to the same value as that of the replication partner.

If properties of the same object are changed on different domain controllers, the domain controllers reconcile the data according to rules using the following priorities:

- *Version number*. All properties carry a version number, which is used to determine which property should be declared as the correct one. The Active Directory always uses the higher version. Although this does not guarantee the correct solution, the use of an unequivocal algorithm ensures that reconciliation can be performed locally without negotiating with the replication partner and that it always results in the same data being used on all domain controllers.

- *Timestamp*. If the version numbers on the changed property are the same, the domain controller uses a timestamp to reconcile the data. The property and the version number are always created with a timestamp. The attribute with the latest timestamp is used. Domain controllers assume that time information is accurate, although they do not negotiate the time. Again, this is not always the correct solution. However, the use of this algorithm ensures that the domain controllers continue serving the clients rather than performing lengthy time negotiations.

- *Buffer size*. If both the version number and the timestamp are the same, the domain controller performs a binary memory copy operation and compares the buffer size. It arbitrarily chooses the one with the higher buffer size. If the two buffers are equal, the attributes are binarily the same, so it makes no difference which is chosen.

Because none of these options guarantees that the correct choice will be made, all reconciliation operations are logged, and administrators have the option of recovering and using the rejected values.

Peter's Principle: Metadirectories: What's Up with That?

In mid-1999, Microsoft acquired Zoomit, the creator of VIA, the most prominent of the so-called *metadirectories*. Then Novell announced its dirXML technology, which incorporates an XML (extensible markup language) engine to create a virtual metadirectory in NDS.

Now in my world, a metadirectory is one that holds metadata—not actual objects but rather descriptions of those objects and where to find them in other, physical directories. Unfortunately, some vendors (such as Zoomit) took the term *metadirectory* and redefined it so that it could be used to describe what I'd call an *uber directory*—a directory that gathers up and holds all the data from all your other directories.

The problem with uber directories is that they must become the authoritative source of all directory changes throughout the myriad directories within your organization in order to maintain synchronization. This presents a number of objections, not the least of which is the political problem—IS wants to control the network directory, HR wants to control the personnel directory, and every other department wants sole control of its directory. No one wants to give up control.

Real metadirectories (which I'll call *virtual directories* to differentiate them from uber directories) consist, for the most part, of database views of the directory objects throughout the enterprise. Each department can continue to maintain its own directory and choose to expose to the virtual directory only the information it wants to disseminate.

Add to this the problems of size (an uber directory would be huge compared to a virtual directory for the same data) and the concomitant use of bandwidth for synchronization and its easy to see that a virtual directory is by far the preferable way to go.

Novell chose to add virtual directory features to NDS, whereas (it would seem) Microsoft wants to make ADS an uber directory.

Both companies should incorporate the new technologies into their directory products early in the year 2000, and a lot can happen between now and then (when the metadirectory features are deployed). Let's hope that Microsoft follows Novell's lead toward a virtual metadirectory.

Summary

In this chapter, you've been introduced to the directory concept as a general purpose listing through the example of an employee directory. By looking at the generally understood concept of a telephone directory, which was expanded to a generic definition of a network directory, you got an idea of some of the principles behind a directory. A directory is defined by its scope—the collection of objects it contains, their unique identifiers, and the directory's access methods.

We then looked closely at the X.500 specification. Even though directories completely conforming to the X.500 Directory standards are rare, directories implementing important conceptual or functional elements of the Directory have been around for a long time. For example, the Domain Naming System (DNS), Novell Directory Services (NDS), and Microsoft's Active Directory Service (ADS) provide services similar to those defined in the X.500 Directory standards. Such directory or naming services usually adopt the X.500 architecture (entries and attributes organized in a tree structure) and some amount of the X.500 functionality. Implementation of directories based on the X.500 Directory specifications has been slow due in part to the complexity and resource requirements of directory client software. These problems have been addressed with the emergence of the Lightweight Directory Access Protocol (LDAP).

The chapter closed with a more detailed look at particular Naming Services and Directory Services in use today on networks both large and small. UNIX's DNS is still the backbone naming system for the Internet, and it has a strong influence on current Directory Services. Banyan Vines' StreetTalk, although not directly a predecessor of NDS and ADS, strongly influenced their development through its ease of use for both administrators and users. Novell's bindery system and Windows NT's domain system—although adequate for small, departmental networks—could not scale efficiently to the enterprise.

This brought us to Novell Directory Services (NDS), first implemented in NetWare 4, and Microsoft Active Directory Service (ADS), introduced with Windows 2000. Although it's too soon to tell if either will become the dominant Directory Service for networks, they contain enough similarities that learning one is a good preparation for using the other.

Troubleshooting and Preventing Problems

The complex networks of today require a proactive, forward-thinking management system, which takes into account all aspects of the computing environment. The difficult task of ongoing maintenance often takes up all the available time of the network staff. Obviously, it can be very hard for an organization to break from the reactive mode and begin to plan and analyze the day-to-day issues.

Network Control Operations and Disaster Operations are two essential processes that must be considered, analyzed, and planned for in order to keep a network running optimally. This chapter starts by discussing specific applications of these operations throughout several environments.

An additional proactive strategy that, unfortunately, too few organizations deploy is a disaster-recovery strategy. This chapter discusses methods for implementing and testing a disaster-recovery strategy and plan. Strategies for testing and refining the network disaster operations are also discussed.

Even if you follow all these strategies, however, the dreaded phone call or the visit by a distraught user, informing you the network is down, can still turn your relatively calm day into a mass of confusion and concern. No matter how well your network planning and implementation has gone, you'll eventually be faced with solving a network-related problem. These problems can occur for a variety of reasons. Unfortunately for the network administrator, they are often highly visible events, which need to be resolved as quickly as possible to keep your organization functioning at its peak.

If you follow the advice and directions in the section "Proactive Network Control Operations," you'll document your network's architecture and its systems configuration as well as establish an operational performance baseline. This information can be a great help in the diagnosis and resolution of network difficulties, because it provides a reference "checkpoint" from which deviations that may have caused the problem to identify.

The key to resolving network problems is to develop a logical, structured analysis approach toward problem identification and correction, and the final part of this chapter will help you do just that.

Proactive Network Control Operations

The discussion surrounding proactive network control operations takes on a different, more serious connotation when linked to overall network problem prevention. It's common to hear other employees talking about the sensitivity of certain functions and their criticality to the daily operations of an organization. The discussion centers on the failure of the organization to closely monitor these operations or to provide adequate maintenance. This lack of action almost always causes extra problems for these operations as time passes.

These functions are the "easy-to-talk-about" and "hard-to-implement" operations that almost always receive a lower level of priority than they should. This section of the chapter talks about the importance of standardization, documentation, and network management as well as their significance in maintaining the health of the network.

Most operational groups tend to be satisfied with less-than-perfect solutions just because they work. Most organizations, when utilizing the best software and hardware solutions available today, should realize extremely desirable benefits and features that work very well. What keeps this from happening? Quite simply, it's the lack of time, the shortage of staff, or the difficulty of the specific operation that causes proactive tools to get lower priority and attention. Determining standards and proactive procedures can be an exhausting, never-ending process. Documenting these standards as well as documenting the network information is extremely time consuming. However, this investment of time is well spent! All pertinent user information as well as the inventory and configurations of network hardware should be recorded and stored. Inventory information for both desktop hardware and software is essential to managing system upgrades and ongoing maintenance.

Of course, there's a whole array of less glamorous functions, too. Necessary evils such as tape backup routines and rotations, uninterruptible power systems and battery maintenance, and software licensing have to be implemented and completed. Day-to-day upkeep of databases for mail lists and server maintenance force Information Systems personnel to keep moving all the time. The luxury of proactive network control operations loses a lot of luster during the day while routine business fires are being extinguished.

From a technical perspective, network management devices are among the most underused tools available to network managers today. These management devices include such functions as the setting of threshold levels on critical hardware components. Monitoring these settings, adjusting them to be more useful, and paying attention to their details all pay excellent dividends during times of crisis.

A discussion concerning proactive network control operations would not be complete without some linkage to the Internet and all the business-based intranets springing up throughout the world. The key concept in proactive network control and management within these environments is *security*. A recent study has shown that network managers consider security to be the single most important factor concerning them within their own networks today. The multitudes of antivirus software and organizations bringing security products to market also point to the increase in awareness of these security requirements.

Note: The "recent study" refers to a marketing presentation report published by 3Com Corporation that ranked the concerns of network management personnel. In this presentation, which was developed to market the features of a new class of switching product, security was cited as the number one concern for network managers today.

Internet access has increased significantly over the last few years. Not too long ago, most organizations had very few requirements for Internet access and therefore didn't offer it to their employees. Lately, no organization can keep their employees from spending some time on the Internet every day of the week. The arguments occur daily as to whether this is a good or bad thing for corporate America, but the consensus is that Internet access is a good thing. The downside to this very high level of external access is that it provides a greater number of openings for the unscrupulous people in networking to attempt to gain illegal access.

What makes a network secure? The answer is not as difficult as you may guess. Strong security policies that are rigidly enforced are the foundation for a secure network. Complete knowledge of the user community—including those using dial-up access and all after-hours activities—gives administrators an awareness of significant details that may indicate attempted intrusions as well as the tools to create an accurate and secure authentication database. Strict requirements for desktop modems, which are sometimes the openings hackers use to gain network access, and password privacy alleviate most of the means of gaining illegal entry. Some of the articles about network intrusions state that the great majority of break-ins are from internal employees. Stressing the importance of prudent computer usage and alerting all users to potential openings into the network go a long way toward tightening the deadbolts on the network.

Gifted programmers and unauthorized crackers can wreak immense havoc with great ease in many of today's networks. This is not only through the access they may gain to critical information but also through the development and circulation of virus software. These viruses can destroy months and years of work. Policies that address the manual passing of software between computers as well as governing downloads of software from the Internet are necessary to screen as much harm as possible away from the network.

Many virus-scanning software packages are available today. From high-end, server-based packages to low-end, down-and-dirty shareware, this software can be very important to protecting the health of a network. Even more important is the actual execution of the software and maintenance of the virus database. Generally, these databases are updated monthly, but can change daily as new viruses are discovered. Fortunately, most vendors support sending email notification when new updates are available. Of course, the whole argument about who is benefiting from these virus alerts can fill another book, so for the purposes of this discussion, just consider it wise to seek out and run the most appropriate software for your situation.

Applications for Proactive Network Control Operations

Although proactive network control operations are talked about more often than actually deployed, a certain amount of work really should be done to ensure highly reliable network access to both the local user community and the remote user community. First, we'll address these critical operations (and many others) as they pertain more specifically to the larger, enterprisewide networks.

Following that, we'll talk about certain other operations that have a better fit within the small-sized to medium-sized organizations. The funding and staffing is generally much smaller and less skilled at this level. That fact points to a need for better utilization of the available resources. Many times the network administrator happens to be simply the person who understood computers the best. These people mean well but just don't have an overall understanding of how computers and systems work. The frailty of computer systems, if not properly understood, eventually brings everything down.

The point at which networks outgrow the "small-to-medium" classification is generally considered to be when they're required to support more than 1,000 users. These networks typically are the ones that are accustomed to remaining somewhat stable and unchanged for long periods of time. The sheer number of users and the potential for 24-hour uptime requirements force network mangers to put off standard maintenance and upgrades. This network stability is normally good except that the deployed technology tends to become outdated and the network upgrade becomes a big project. Avoiding these big projects is another byproduct of systematic and timely maintenance and upkeep.

The final section under this topic discusses the needs of the smaller, remote user community. The needs of this environment are certainly not as great as those of the previously discussed environments. The health of the remote users, though, can be just as critical to the overall health of the corporate network, if analyzed as a whole, when a high number of similarly sized environments exist. Often central site talent supports these remote networks over some wide-area connection. This factor obviously makes it more difficult to quickly troubleshoot and solve problems within the remote environment and can also lead to an unhealthy corporate network.

The Enterprise Environment

The high-end complexities of networking equipment, which are essential to supporting the enterprisewide requirements of the largest organizations, can be both exciting and frustrating for the people who are charged with keeping the network running well. The best hardware and software solutions are often accompanied by appropriate training required to keep this equipment maintained correctly. This training can be parceled out to the staff, keeping network personnel skills at sharp levels and providing fields for individuals to specialize in while adding value to their organizations. On the other hand, many sleepless nights and ruined weekends occur because the networks can't be changed or upgraded during operational hours.

Many large organizations also have detailed change-management operations, which allow for discussion and anticipation of network changes and outages. This proactive tool often finds the shortcomings in back-out plans and provides other departments with advanced notice of network outages. Because there are times when off-hours work has to be accomplished—such as by the accounting department during tax season—open discussion of planned outages avoids missing deadlines. Certainly, an outage during this time would be a costly mistake and might end up costing some employee her current job.

There are also the other departments in Information Systems (IS), such as the mainframe group or minicomputer operators, that are linked to the network and to specific servers. Typically, these environments host users from the wide-area side of the network and may have to support different time zones and availability requirements. The types of proactive functions and routines that have been run for years in mainframe systems have been finely tuned to provide better than 99 percent uptimes. Certainly, the client/server world is not at that level yet, but it's fast approaching it. The hardware is improving tremendously as the software keeps gradually getting smarter. This combination will enable failures to be avoided and bypassed quickly. The perception that the network is always there and performing well is a hard ideal to live up to, but it can be done!

Email, voice mail, and other network communications are additional areas that routinely require and usually enough proactive maintenance required to perform effectively for long periods of time. The main reason organizations have been successful at proactive management with these systems is that they have staffed sufficient numbers of people and trained them adequately to do their jobs. These very expensive systems are important to the daily functioning of the entire organization. In many cases, a high-ranking executive may get immediately on the phone to IS if he has a problem with his electronic or voice mail.

How can these different environments be supported proactively in an enterprisewide network? The answer is relatively straightforward here. Personnel correctly trained and procedures correctly applied are the keys to a reliable network.

An often overlooked but effective proactive function is membership by staff personnel in user groups and attendance at trade shows. The large corporations that finance these networks usually have the capability to fund fault-tolerant, redundant infrastructures that can withstand many types of minor outages. Furthermore, these funds should be spent on education of staff technical people to properly configure and maintain the network components.

Because the environment spreads out over a wide area, it's usually difficult to get to some portions of it. This is another good reason for strong and accurate documentation. As sites are installed and upgraded, records should be updated also. These records, if accurate, go a long way toward helping central site people solve remote problems. Of course, if the environment is very large, these tasks become more difficult. That reason alone is why regular upkeep of documentation is important. Never letting the tasks get too far out of hand helps ensure that they will get done. When a job gets to the point that it requires a week of dedicated time to update some records, the job simply does not get done. The result is inaccurate and therefore worthless documentation.

Another very useful function is known as *standardization*. With standardization, after the most appropriate hardware and software solution is chosen for the job, this same solution is implemented throughout the environment so as to establish a level of consistency. This consistency is the key to effective proactive management. Standardizing makes ongoing maintenance and support easier. Having personnel proficient in many software packages is nearly impossible. Having a strong person in one application is very common, though. This is a direct result of standardization and training.

The Small-to-Medium Environment

The largest percentage of business organizations probably resides within the loose boundaries of this classification. Groups of more than 10 and less than 1,000 users can be considered "small to medium." Typically, users' needs and skills are varied and create extra confusion for network support staffs. Some users have strong computer skills and have the ability to find wonderful pieces of software throughout the Internet. These users can very easily download virus-infected code and spread it within the corporation instantly.

To satisfy a need for certain location presence, some organizations must deal with a shortage or a complete lack of good support people. These companies very often cannot afford strong talent and may even try to educate internal people. If internal education works, the newly trained employee is likely to take his skills on to the open market and improve his spot in the pecking order of life. What does this shortage of adequate staff do to hurt the network and its components? History suggests that, in situations with minimal staff, personnel tend to avoid most of the tedious operations. Proactive maintenance such as tape backups are not being routinely done and maintained. Little fault tolerance and power backup capabilities are usually incorporated into these environments. Financing these "luxuries" is difficult, and often organizations have to make a conscious trade-off: susceptibility to business downtime for reduced overhead expenses.

What proactive functions are so important that they just have to get done in the small and medium environments? Again, the answer here is documentation and standardization. These tools maximize the efficiency of the limited resources. Regular tape backup procedures can scarcely be considered a luxury in any environment anymore, so having someone take responsibility for backups and their proper storage is crucial. Making sure tapes are rotated and stored correctly is important to ensure that, when data is needed off a backup tape, it can be found easily and restored.

The typical obstacles to protecting information within a network can become even greater in the smaller network environments. Small-to-medium organizations tend to have a higher proliferation of modems and modem access and therefore a higher vulnerability to penetration by crackers. Employee turnover also tends to be a little higher, making it easier to loosen password security. Procedures that address these types of vulnerabilities must be deployed correctly to help in securing the overall network.

The Remote User Environment

Unfortunately, the remote user environment provides almost insurmountable complications for proactive management. Remote users rarely have local access to adequately trained people for any kind of computer hardware or software maintenance. In fact, knowing how to use a word processing application is often enough to make someone the computer guru for the office! Historically, central site support staff have found these users hard to work with. Although they have a level of knowledge that makes them *think* they know what's going on, they don't have a view of the overall network and how their piece interacts with it. This is why small acts—such as reconfiguring a server to broadcast extra data or a router to filter something—can affect the wider enterprise network.

What are some of the basic requirements for proactive control in these environments? The answer is to have some set standard for the types of devices that can be deployed at these locations. In order for remote managers to correctly diagnose problems through their understanding of the correct operation of these devices, some standard set of procedures must also be followed.

It can be very costly to deploy network hardware that's capable of remote management and that can also act as an intermediary system for larger, more powerful systems in an overall network management solution. The simpler solution that usually gets deployed involves less intelligent equipment and the keeping of spare parts at the central location. Again, proactive maintenance and reliability is exchanged for cost savings.

Network Testing, Baselining, and Monitoring

The purpose of this section is to demonstrate the importance of network testing, baselining, and monitoring as well as to tie them together through an overall proactive strategy—a strategy that acknowledges the importance of proactive management. A byproduct of all this proactive network control is accurate documentation. The strategic importance of accurate documentation can be summed up easily: The managers of the network know what is supposed to be going on. The relevance of this fact is that they should also know when the network is *not* performing correctly or when it is even a little out of whack.

A *very popular* term in the networking industry is *baselining*. There are many variations on what the term actually means, but in general, it defines the performance level of the network at some point in time. Compare this to what a doctor does for his patients by performing physical examinations over a period of time. The doctor knows how things have been and can note the changes. These changes are indicative of something good or bad, and it's the responsibility of the doctor to figure out what those changes mean. When you apply this same idea to the network, it's easy to see how accurate knowledge of performance, high usage times, and other utilization statistics provide excellent insight into the efficient operation and management of the network.

How is baselining accomplished? Typically, an organization with a larger network already owns the types of tools necessary to perform the baselining service. Protocol analyzers and servers with big hard drives help to capture current utilization statistics and store them for future manipulation. Smaller organizations often rent this type of equipment or hire a consulting firm to do this work. Again, the byproduct of performing this function again is good, accurate documentation. From this documentation, managers can assess areas of weakness and begin to provide for improvements. This improvement process might mean setting up a larger budget or redeploying existing equipment. The good news here is that the network's condition is being evaluated before a crisis occurs.

What does network testing provide for proactive network management? In large organizations that can provide a nonproduction lab environment, testing enables administrators to evaluate the results of implementing new software and hardware without interfering with normal information flows. This luxury may not be available in medium-sized groups or may not be the best option for some large groups, so off-hours testing of upgrades and changes has to be done. Many times the complete impact of a change is not witnessed until the network load of the whole organization is brought to bear on the change. This is the reason for well-conceived back-out plans. These plans describe the steps required to restore the network to the previous functioning state.

Other functions require regular testing also. Regular tests need to be performed on backup tapes using features such as searching and selective restore. Weekends are often a great time to kill the power and evaluate the effectiveness of the UPS systems. The larger companies may even have diesel-generated power. Successful startup of the backup generator, after losing total power to a facility, can keep a company in business through some rough times. Whether this function will deploy as expected can be determined only through a scheduled and implemented proactive testing process.

One area discussed throughout this chapter is security. It's important to focus on two aspects of security: monitoring the licensing of software and periodic and random security checks. These types of functions are rarely done in any environment outside of the larger enterprise network. Proactive monitoring of software licensing can keep an organization from being fined for software piracy. These fines are generally very large and can be just as damaging to an organization as a security breach. Random security checks can verify system security integrity and also identify improper usage of software licenses. Although security is often not a major concern in smaller organizations, they are just as vulnerable to security breaches. Corporate spying goes on in today's world. Attacking the supplier of piece parts to a large organization can often yield valuable information. For meeting a spy's goals, this might be as effective as breaking into the large organization's network and host systems.

Refining Existing Network Control Operations

Although the level of hardware redundancy and network management skills usually declines as the size of the network shrinks, it's still very possible to develop a solid workable proactive network control plan with reduced resources. Many of the barest necessities—such as backup routines—can be automated now. The level of computer literacy is advancing quickly and even the smallest groups usually have at least one person who can change a tape from a backup drive.

If organizations establish and stick to a clear-cut strategy, they are in a position to resolve problems or overcome failures quickly and easily. Monitoring and testing enable administrators to develop improvement schedules and plans, which are essential to constantly improving the capabilities of the environment. This is similar to the process of continual improvement being deployed in the manufacturing sector today.

Fault-tolerant hardware platforms such as mainframes, minicomputers, and desktop computers all come with a certain high price tag. It may seem easy to choose less-expensive items early in the decision process. This may not always be the best decision, though, if the cost of ongoing operations becomes high. Expensive equipment with a high level of fault tolerance is often deployed within high-end organizations at the central locations. This same high cost, however, often keeps redundancy options from being implemented in the networks of smaller and remote groups.

Additionally, strategies that encompass routine tape backup procedures, use of uninterrupted power supply equipment, and proper backup and rotation of all software media prove to be the most effective at providing enduring uptime and network stability. Legal usage of licensed software and policing of the end-user community are also recommended policies that tend to get overlooked at many organizations. Clear-cut processes that are well documented make all these rigorous duties much easier. Taking the time to perform these functions correctly is very important in avoiding time and money losses down the road. It's always less expensive to pay the price required to do the job correctly in the first place than it is to repair the resulting problems later.

The last piece of a solid overall proactive strategy—and often the most overlooked portion—is the personnel on staff and the brainpower they bring to the team. Participation in user group activities provides outstanding education and an additional reference for staff members to develop proactive network control strategies. Early exposure to hardware and software bugs via group membership and documents can prevent users from having to personally experience faults in their own networks. Additionally, exposure to good resources can help them troubleshoot and resolve problems quickly. Timeliness is the key to effective management and for strengthening the perception of a highly reliable, stable, networking environment.

Proactive Network Disaster Operations

This section of the chapter discusses the set of operations known collectively as *disaster recovery*. These are the proactive operations used to define and test the plan for restoration and recovery of the network following a serious disaster. It's interesting to note that these operations are less likely to be implemented in any network that isn't enterprisewide and that doesn't support large amounts of mission-critical data. The loss of data can be just as damaging to a small organization as a larger one, but the willingness to take the risk is much higher. Many times "willingness" is nothing more than a reaction to the fact that the necessary dollars are simply not available.

So what are proactive network disaster operations? It would seem that they are the operations that most network managers never want to have to implement. No matter how hard you try to build in the tolerance to fault and disaster, it's not possible to account for everything. In environments where money is not a major issue, practically all possible disaster scenarios can be accounted for. Most organizations, though, have limited finances available and must evaluate and prioritize resources.

Prioritizing the resources necessary to salvage the operations of the business has to come first in the planning of network recoveries. This plan must include plans for staff members to relocate or do whatever is necessary to complete their regular jobs despite the network problem.

Fortunately, several major organizations today specialize in customizing disaster-recovery strategies for other organizations. They often have locations with hardware and software available to back up most types of data centers. Of course, the types of hardware and software systems that need to be recovered are defined during contract negotiation and it becomes the responsibility of the service provider to have your company's functional areas ready to go on a moment's notice.

The major "disaster recovery" service firms provide a good answer for very large companies, but after the largest thousand or so organizations, the overall size of the potential client companies starts to get smaller. How do these less-than-major organizations support their networks and business requirements during times of crisis? They—just as every other organization—must think about their business needs and determine solutions in advance. Spending the time necessary to figure out what could go wrong and what can be done to make that as painless as possible is very important.

Focus on the little things that can be done to help avoid big problems during troubled times. Persistent application of difficult processes enables a company to be ready to resolve a crisis. Paying attention to the needs of the business in disaster plans is important, also. Trying to guess what the priorities of a business are can be a career-ending decision. Leaving out a piece of the business that is less known can easily spell trouble for some senior IS manager.

Applications for Proactive Network Disaster Operations

Several alternative applications for proactive network disaster operations are available. The large, enterprisewide networks encompassing many cities and individual locations are the first networks analyzed. Because these are the glamorous, mainframe-based networks on which all large companies run their businesses, it makes sense to give them top billing here. These enterprisewide networks also contain bits and pieces of all the smaller environments. Many of these larger network environments also have some minicomputer functionality to support along with buildings full of desktop computers.

The small-to-medium organizations with less than a thousand users are analyzed second. Many assumptions are made about the subtle differences between medium organizations and large ones. For the purpose of this chapter, a medium organization probably has less extensive network requirements and a limited geographic area of exposure.

Finally, the small remote workgroup encompassing only handfuls of users is discussed. This prototypical environment is part of each of the previous two environments but is discussed alone because so many workgroups such as these don't have the corporate big brother to lend them a hand. The importance of good network management techniques and philosophy is stressed, because good network management provides a higher level of safety when network downtime is directly connected to lost revenue.

The Enterprise-Wide Disaster Recovery

The term *enterprise* is used often today to describe most large networks. Although it's true that enterprise networks are large, it's possible for a large network to not be enterprisewide. For this chapter, the term *enterprisewide* describes a network of networks. These individual subnetworks generally fall under the ownership of one organization. Fortune 1000 companies build these types of networks and support mainframe-based computing, minicomputer-based computing, and microcomputer networks. Although the means of communication and levels of technology differ greatly, all these environments require specialized talents and skills. Only the very large organizations can afford to support all these functions.

Because network disaster operations also require dedicated and expensive personnel, it's often an area that's allowed to "run in place," so to speak. Typically, these staffs are charged with operating regular network monitoring and security procedures, also. These are some of the reasons medium-sized organizations don't build enterprise networks.

How do these big companies plan for and execute their disaster-recovery operations? For the most part, staffs assigned within their Information Systems groups take year-round responsibility for these tasks. These groups plan the tests that occur two to four times a year. They schedule the meetings and produce the reports. The business units typically choose their own level of cooperation. Senior management usually provides some prodding to be onboard with the testing and has plans for support in times of trouble.

As was mentioned earlier in this chapter, there are third-party organizations that handle the disaster-recovery operations for many large companies. Typically, they offer some large computing center that has a high level of communications capabilities. These capabilities are taxed as each new customer brings its own unique network design to the center for failure security. The wide area communication that's a big part of enterprisewide computing has to be transferred to these disaster facilities. This is where special arrangements with the long distance carriers come in. Most of the bigger nationwide carriers have capabilities to "swing" a network from one point of focus to another. As expected, the cost of these services is enormous and is something companies avoid using if at all possible.

These enormous computing centers can also do the same magic in support of midsize computing networks. One of the innate benefits of the minicomputer technology is its capability to spread or distribute information across several locations. This feature lends itself very nicely to workable disaster-recovery scenarios. Because only one center is typically knocked out at any time, that center can easily be relocated to another location within the local organization. Organizations never like to lose business, but comparing the productivity loss of only a single location to that of an entire organization is something to consider during planning.

The Small-to-Medium Network and Disaster Recovery

For the purposes of this chapter, small-to-medium networks are considered to be those built around minicomputers and microcomputers. These constructs have many plusses and minuses. The advantage of this environment is its distributive capabilities. This keeps failures at any single point from being disruptive to the entire organization. These environments usually allow for some delay between the processing of information and the use of the printed reports. This less-than-real-time functionality enables services such as the regular mail and some overnight delivery services to act as workable substitutes during many types of computing outages.

Where do disaster-recovery operations fit within these networks? They exist as part of many people's everyday routine. The analysts within several departments should be expected to meet two times a year and establish some functional plan for resolving things in the event of some disaster. Ideally, at least one time each year, an actual test should be executed. The list of areas to fix is usually very large, and after the test is done, the planning receives less than the necessary attention. This is the downside for organizations that already have stretched budgets and staffs.

The benefit of having several locations within a limited geographical area is apparent when it comes to personnel relocation. This physical relocation alone can keep a business running during extended outages. In the case of microcomputers, the equipment can be moved around fairly easily, also. In addition, people tend to pull together during a disaster. The group's synergy provides for significant productivity improvements. These improvements can make up for the loss of routines and normal resources.

Turning more specifically to microcomputer networks or LANs, much of the necessary functionality can be easily moved or redeployed. Users may be forced to give up some performance and ease of use but should still be able to accomplish their jobs. A good maintenance plan includes regular server backups with rotated storage of the tapes. This plan ensures easy restoration of servers and functionality in remote locations. The ease of dial-up functions in today's network environments enables users to have quick and somewhat easy connectivity to distant locations. This connection should be adequate to accomplish many business functions.

The Remote User and Disaster Recovery

Believe it or not, remote users are usually accommodated fairly well in normal disaster-recovery scenarios. Because most enterprisewide networks contain these remote user communities, it makes sense for them to be supported during disaster outages as well. The ease of changing the direction of dial-up facilities, such as analog telephone and ISDN, enables these small groups of users to adjust quickly to the network changes.

The unfortunate side for these smaller workgroups is that they usually lose the regular support and the level of resource access to which they have been accustomed. It's during these times that the field users appreciate the corporate teams. The rest of the year the corporate folks are underappreciated and referred to by many loving nicknames.

Testing Disaster-Recovery Operations and Strategies

In some very large corporations, network disaster operations and disaster-recovery tests are a regular part of the corporate culture. As many as four times a year, a disaster is simulated and the recovery plan is allowed to unfold. All the problems created during the drill are usually recorded, analyzed, and fixed for the next test. Whole departments may be instituted to monitor and analyze the ongoing performance of the network. These same groups may also be tasked with designing and analyzing disaster-recovery tests.

Over the course of several years, a very sound and stable plan emerges. This plan encompasses support for all the major computing platforms and identifies areas of risk as they exist today. The plan discusses the deployment of resources and facilities for changing communication requirements. Experience suggests that these plans are very wide in scope but often get deployed during times of disaster in some smaller scenario. The techniques and lessons learned are the same. The fortunate organizations that have proactively planned and tested and made the necessary changes are ready to adapt. Having the capability to react is a distinct advantage in the business community, and the cost/benefit analysis of its price tag should be seriously considered during planning sessions by senior managers.

Refining Existing Network Disaster Operations

Executing disaster drills over the course of a year enables a forward-thinking organization to discuss the strengths and weaknesses of its disaster-recovery strategy. Such an organization usually has internal workgroups and departments that schedule and manage these disaster-recovery operations.

These "disaster-recovery" or "network planning" groups always get the attention of the individual business units because they typically can help out a recovery analysis project with financing. These groups also get a high level of attention from the Information Systems people because IS staffs are required to participate and make the disaster-recovery tests successful.

Generally speaking, these tests are very expensive with high travel costs. Using the relevant information and learning from these tests enables the company to fix weak areas in its recovery plan and maybe even retest the revised plan in a future scenario.

It's hard to make the follow-up sessions successful. A company that has experienced a rather stressful disaster test and will typically begin to settle back into normal routines. The meetings and reports required to do a thorough follow-up just require more time. It's important, however, to follow such exercises with prompt attention. As in any good project, there must be closure. The closure from a good disaster test is discussion of benefits and weaknesses. These discussions lead to good ideas for the next round of testing, and a new project can unfold as the old one is put to rest.

Logical Fault Isolation

Because you're reading this book, you're probably either in charge of a network or at work in an Information Systems department supporting a network environment. This means that you probably have already had some experience, good or bad, diagnosing computer problems.

Structured analysis has been used in many disciplines as a way to define a step-by-step, logical, and repeatable process toward an end. In this case, the desired end is the accurate identification of both a network problem and its cause, leading to the selection of the appropriate resolution.

Using this technique to isolate the specific problem, or *fault*, is called *logical fault isolation* and is the most effective means for finding the correct solution, the first time. The tactic of applying solutions randomly is potentially dangerous, often introduces additional problems into the mix, and results in the expenditure of large amounts of time and resources. Time and resources mean money—money better spent on more worthwhile projects.

The isolation process has six steps, which eventually lead to the proper resolution of a network problem. Used together, these steps can be easily remembered as the "ADJUST" method:

- **A**ssess the priority.
- **D**iscover pertinent information.
- **J**ustify probable causes.
- **U**nit test and isolate.
- **S**tudy and evaluate results.
- **T**ranscribe results and processes.

Following these six steps provides a consistent approach toward problem determination, even in the most difficult of situations. The following sections examine each of these steps in greater detail to give you a better understanding of their purposes and benefits.

Assess the Priority

Some might suggest that this is the most important step in the ADJUST methodology. The user community places constant demands on people in any network-support position—demands that require the efficient allocation of available resources. Being able to quickly assess the impact of a reported problem is a key competency for those tasked with keeping an organization's network infrastructure afloat.

Every user thinks that his problem is the most important. The reality is that everything cannot be resolved at once. In fact, attempting to do so can lead to further complications if changes to the network architecture are not done in a coordinated fashion.

Not every problem is a true emergency. It's essential that reported problems be classified into a priority queue that shows each problem in its order of necessity. Network support staff should address the most immediate problems on the list, even if they're not the most appealing.

Fight the temptation to "knock out the easy ones first." The time spent on those problems is better spent focused on the critical concerns. Responding to a user request for access to the new color laser printer may be easier than solving a routing problem on your network, but the impact of that routing problem is more deserving of your attention.

Discover Pertinent Information

Information discovery is the first step in the process of resolving any network problem. The initial communication you receive notifying you of a network problem is not likely to contain all the pertinent information. As you work through the process of problem identification, information is power and can make it easier for you to arrive at an accurate determination.

Your two major sources of information are your users and the reports generated by network monitoring tools and utilities. Collect as much information regarding symptoms, operating environment, software, hardware, error messages, and other results as you can. Try not to filter out information at this stage.

Interview Your Users

Most network problems have an impact on your user community. Don't ignore this large source of information. Besides, users are always willing to offer any information that might help you solve their problems.

Many technicians are reluctant to do this because of the impression that users do not have sufficient technical expertise to provide useful analysis. In reality, users often have very helpful input to offer but are not being questioned correctly. As with all things, "Garbage in, garbage out."

You need to understand your users' terminology and technical skill levels. Ask them for their observations, not their assessment. Find out what they *expected* to happen, and what *actually* happened.

Here are some questions to ask your users:

- Can you describe the problem you experienced?
- Which software application(s) were you using at the time?
- Has anyone else experienced this problem?
- What was the exact error message you received?
- Were you using a network resource such as a hard disk or printer?
- Are you still connected to the network?
- Did you have to restart your workstation after the problem occurred?

Interviews of this kind can offer insights into network and application behavior. These insights can, in turn, lead you in the correct direction and help narrow the list of potential problem areas.

Analyze Network Activity

The other information resource is the reports generated by the various network monitoring utilities available for your network operating system. The information in these reports should be compared against your baseline configuration and performance characteristics.

Deviations between your baseline information and the current network reports should be investigated. They may indicate where possible causes lie.

Check the history of changes made to either the network, the affected workstation(s), or software applications involved. A quick review of this log may show whether this problem has occurred before and what was done to resolve it.

Implementing *System Change Control*—the process of tracking the history of changes made to the network's infrastructure (devices, workstations, servers, printers, system configuration, software, and so forth)—can be a real plus. System Change Control is a process that was originally defined by the Project Management Institute of Carnegie-Mellon University. It's a process by which organizations can track problems and solutions for historical reference and documentation. It helps you track any configuration and software changes made to network devices. Knowing how, when, and why a network modification was made can often provide the key to solving an unexpected side effect of that change.

> **Tip:** For medium-to-large network installations, it's highly recommended that a network management system be implemented to inventory all network devices and workstations attached to the network. Microsoft's System Management Server v1.2 can integrate this functionality into a Windows NT Server network solution.

Create a checklist of questions that your interview process should cover before moving on to the problem determination phase. This document should be a "living document," changing as you gain more experience in network troubleshooting and learn more about the unique combination of software and hardware in your specific network environment.

Basic questions on this form might include the following:

- How many users were affected by the problem?
- Were they all on the same network segment?
- Was the entire network affected?
- Can the problem be reproduced?
- Is the problem application related or network related?
- Has any equipment been moved, modified, or replaced recently?
- What other software was involved (include version numbers)?
- Has anyone else attempted to fix this problem in the past?
- Was a new application recently installed on this workstation?

After you've collected all the available feedback related to the problem at hand, you're ready to begin the process of determining what caused it.

Justify Probable Causes

The next step is to analyze all the information gathered in the discovery process and to develop a list of possible causes of the problem.

Ask yourself these questions:

- Does the data suggest that a particular segment or component of the network is involved?
- Does the problem seem to be localized to just one workstation?
- Are common components involved (network adapters, vendors, software drivers, software versions)?

In the previous step (discover pertinent information), you were advised to not eliminate any piece of information provided by your various sources. Now is the time to examine all the information you've accumulated and evaluate it based on your experience, the technical reference materials at your disposal, and the results of your baseline comparisons. Look for common patterns in the symptoms or results. As you come up with your list of possible causes for the network problem, questions such as those listed previously can help you narrow your list down to the most likely culprits and give you justification for making your selections.

Try to rank the list, showing the most likely candidates first. The more experience you acquire, the easier it is to assess where the problem lies.

Unit Test and Isolate

This is the moment of truth. You've taken the time to gather the pertinent information. You've taken the time to organize and analyze that information into a set of potential causes. You've ranked those possible scenarios from most likely to least likely. Now it's time to come up with *solutions*!

After your list is complete, an iterative process of "test, evaluate, and isolate" is used to narrow the list of potential causes down until you find the real problem.

Starting with the most likely candidate from your list, determine the solution that you expect to best rectify the situation.

> **Tip:** Many resources can help with the identification process. For Windows NT Server networks, two highly regarded resources are available.
>
> The first resource is Microsoft's Hardware and Software Compatibility Lists. These two lists show all the hardware devices and software packages that are proven to be compatible with the Hardware Abstraction Layer (HAL) of NT's network operating system. The other resource is the Microsoft Technical Information Network (TechNet) CD-ROM and its online subset, the Microsoft Knowledgebase.

For example, if the problem involves the inability of a workstation to recognize a file server, you might come up with the following set of causes:

- Bad physical connection (cable, connectors, hub, terminators)
- Incorrect or obsolete network client or protocol(s)
- Bad or incorrectly configured network interface card (NIC)

Always apply solutions one at a time. This makes it easier to undo each solution and reduces the possibility of one change impacting the success of another. By applying each solution individually, you're utilizing an isolation technique that increases the probability of a successful result. Applying multiple changes in hopes of solving a problem often results in unexpected side effects that may only exacerbate the situation.

Test the solution to determine whether it resolved the problem. If it did not, back out the changes you made and determine a solution for the next probable cause on your list.

> **Tip:** If you can back up the files and/or configuration information for the components on which you're working before beginning this "test, evaluate, and isolate" process, do it. Always have a fallback position in case things get too complicated to roll back.

It's very important to remember (that means "document") the changes you make so that you can record them for later archives or undo them if those changes are ineffective (or make things worse). You never know whether a change you make may cause the problem to worsen rather than improve. Failure to document has come back to haunt many administrators, when a supposed solution has unexpected consequences and the administrator is unable to undo the changes.

Study and Evaluate Results

If your test solves the network problem, you have succeeded! If the problem persists, continue with the next possible cause on your list. If you exhaust all the items on your list, you need to start the ADJUST process again, back at the discovery step—there's obviously a piece of information that your gathering process has failed to produce.

If you find yourself at this point, don't be afraid to ask for help from more senior people—they may be other individuals in your organization, or they may be from the firm that installed your backbone. They may also be professional contacts you've made outside the organization.

Find them. Engineers are often reluctant to do this because they take so much pride in solving problems on their own. However, this can sometimes be counterproductive. It pays to take advantage of all available sources of knowledge.

There are many newsgroups and mailing lists on the Internet that respond to inquiries from engineers looking for solutions to problems. The best network analysts develop a network of professionals to whom they can go for ideas and feedback. Aspire to be that kind of network analyst.

Transcribe Results and Processes

After ensuring that the problem has been successfully resolved (ask your users—they can tell you), it's time to document the problem—its symptoms, the cause, the resolution that was applied, and how you figured everything out. It may also be necessary to update your network architecture, infrastructure, and system configuration parameter information if your resolution required changes in those areas.

Following System Change Control methodologies ensures that you continually update and publish the adjusted baseline each time it's modified. This history can then become a useful tool the next time a problem has to be researched.

This information should be stored in a problem-resolution database, which becomes your best resource for future problem solving. It also becomes an important training resource for new staff and provides the organization with a knowledge base customized to its networking environment.

This structured method for problem resolution can take time when you're faced with a complex networking anomaly. But keep in mind that, if you do it correctly, you need go through this process only once. What's more, with the gradual development of your own knowledge base, the process becomes more and more streamlined.

Common Networking Problems

This section lists some of the more common networking problems that administrators face on a day-to-day basis. Although every network has its own unique configuration and characteristics, many of the issues here are certain to have some relevancy to your environment.

Physical Media

The physical media of a network (the cables, connectors, hubs, network adapter cards, and so on) are vulnerable to breakage and should be the first things checked when a network connectivity problem occurs. A short or break in a cable can cause one workstation, or an entire network segment, to fail to connect to a server or recognize other network devices.

Administrators need to develop a method for determining whether a connectivity problem is located within the affected workstations or the physical media connecting them. This should be the first step before taking more invasive actions (such as reconfiguring computers, swapping adapter cards, and removing/updating drivers) on a workstation.

If you have a spare machine with a working network interface card, it can be used to test the cable. If the spare machine connects to the network resource in question, the problem is in the workstation rather than the cable.

Here are some likely areas to investigate:

- Make sure the cable is firmly connected to the workstation and that connectors are not frayed or weakly attached. This is especially true with coaxial cable plants.

- Make sure you haven't exceeded the recommended cable lengths for the type of cabling being used (see Table 19.1). Each cable type has very detailed specifications for length, number of extents, and impedance.

- Use a time-domain reflectometer (TDR) to determine whether you have a short or break in the cabling. This is a must when tracking down problems in cable runs inside walls and cabinets.

- Make sure you're using the same type of cable throughout the network. Special equipment is necessary to support multiple cable types in a network (routers, bridges, and so forth). Make sure they're operating correctly.

- Check your terminators to make sure the network is not experiencing infinite resistance problems.

Table 19.1 Cable Specifications

Cable Type	Maximum Length
Thinnet coaxial	185 meters
Thicknet coaxial	500 meters
Unshielded twisted pair (UTP)	100 meters
Shielded twisted pair (STP)	100 meters
Fiber optic	2 kilometers

Network Interface Cards (NIC)

Another frequent culprit causing networking woes is the infamous network interface card (or *network adapter*). The successful operation of this card requires that two things be done correctly:

- The adapter card must be firmly seated in a slot on the workstation's motherboard.

- The proper drivers must be installed and configured to match the network architecture.

Sometimes network cards just stop functioning, due to age, environmental agents, quality, or amount of continuous use. Often, however, a network adapter fails to work because of configuration errors or compatibility problems with the workstation or its operating system.

Here are some likely areas to investigate:

- Are there lights on at the back of the card? There should normally be one or two LEDs on the back end of a network card. One is a *link light*, which shows that the card has established connectivity with the network at the Data Link Layer of the OSI model. The second light is a *transmission light*, which blinks as the card receives/sends information across the network. (No lights means no connection.)

- Have any new network-aware applications been installed on the workstation recently? Some applications install their own drivers, which may not be compatible with your network or the OS version on that workstation.

- Check the date of the existing network drivers installed from the Network Control Panel. (Perhaps the vendor has newer drivers that would resolve the problem.)

NIC Configuration Parameters

Every network card has its own configuration parameters, but the primary areas that cause headaches are interrupt request (IRQ) settings, the base I/O port address, and the base memory address for the adapter. If any of these is incorrect or in conflict with another device in the workstation, the NIC does not operate consistently, if at all.

An Intel machine has 16 IRQ values (0–15, see Table 19.2). These are assigned to various devices and serve to alert the processor when the device needs attention.

Table 19.2 Interrupt Request Numbers

IRQ	Device
0	System timer
1	Keyboard
2	Programmable interrupt controller
3	Communications port 2 or 4
4	Communications port 1 or 3
5	Printer port 2 (LPT2) or "open"
6	Floppy disk controller
7	Printer port 1 (LPT1)
8	Real-time clock
9	Redirect from IRQ 2 or "open"
10	Open
11	Open
12	PS/2 mouse port or "open"
13	Math coprocessor
14	IDE hard drive controller
15	IDE hard drive controller or "open"

The *base I/O port address* serves as the "doorway" through which all communication between the processor and the device is channeled.

The *base memory address* is a memory location where a buffer is kept for data being transmitted to and from the network. This address is often hexadecimal D8000.

Here are some likely areas to investigate:

- Has the workstation's network configuration been changed recently? If so, find out why and what the previous settings were.

- Does the configuration process attempt an "autoconfiguration" mode? Sometimes these do not work. Try setting the card manually.

- Are any of the three primary parameters in use by another device? If so, reconfigure the adapter to ones that are open. If there are no available values, or if the adapter does not offer a wide-enough selection, you may need to reconfigure or remove existing devices.

Network Protocol Mismatch

For a workstation to communicate across the network, its network adapter card must share a common set of protocols with the network devices the workstation needs to access. The configuration for each protocol is different.

In many cases, several network protocols must be transmitted across a single network adapter card. This process of "binding" several protocols to one network adapter is accomplished by using either the Network Device Interface Specification (NDIS) or Open Data-Link Interface (ODI) protocol stacks.

If all other network adapter checklists show no configuration or mechanical problems, protocol mismatch is the next thing to check. A workstation configured for Novell's IPX/SPX protocol (called *NWLink* in Microsoft networks) can never successfully communicate with a file server configured for TCP/IP.

This problem is common in networking environments that have multiple server platforms (such as UNIX, NetWare, and Windows NT Server).

Here are some likely areas to investigate:

- Has this workstation accessed the server in the past and lost that capability, or has it never successfully connected?

- Check the Network Control Panel and see which protocols have been installed on the workstation. Are they all correctly bound to the network adapter?

- For each protocol installed, are all its configuration parameters correctly filled in? For example, the TCP/IP protocol suite requires an IP address, subnet mask, and default gateway address. Are they filled in properly?

- If this is a TCP/IP network, is the workstation getting its IP dynamically (via DHCP or BOOTP)? Is that assignment process working?

- If this is a TCP/IP network, is the DNS IP address entered correctly for this segment?
- If this is an IPX/SPX network, is the correct frame type being used?

Network Congestion

The primary symptom of congestion is poor network performance within a segment of your network or across the entire network. This may occur only occasionally, during times of high usage. In other cases, this can build up slowly over a period of weeks or months until the level of performance degradation is intolerable.

The causes for this can be varied. You need a network monitor to determine the level of bandwidth being used across the network, the times of peak usage, and the types of packets being transmitted. A protocol analyzer can give you more information regarding the segments having the highest amount of traffic and any bottlenecks across the network.

Here are some likely areas to investigate:

- Is this a recent problem or is it commonplace? Congestion may be an indication of poor network design and can be resolved only by revamping the network backbone.
- Check for high numbers of packets from one IP address. A malfunctioning network adapter card could be "chattering" and sending lots of unnecessary packets.
- Check to see whether any new applications have been installed on the network. Perhaps a client/server application is generating lots of packet traffic.
- Has the user community increased significantly? Perhaps the network needs to be augmented to handle the natural growth of your organization.
- Which protocols are being transmitted across the network? How many protocols are being used in your network? To keep traffic to a minimum, the fewer the number of protocols the better.
- Is NetBEUI running across the network? NetBEUI is a broadcast-intensive protocol. Try utilizing WINS servers to reduce NetBEUI broadcasts, or you can tunnel NetBIOS through TCP/IP or IPX and eliminate NetBEUI entirely.

Broadcast Storms

A *broadcast storm* describes a scenario in which a network's bandwidth is literally filled to capacity due to an excessive number of broadcast packets. When this occurs, network performance slows to a crawl.

Broadcast storms often result from malfunctioning network adapter cards and hubs. They can also be caused by excessive broadcasts across NetBEUI-based networks.

To diagnose a malfunctioning device, you need the help of a protocol analyzer to isolate that device so you can replace it. If you use internal routers and routable protocols, you might be able to lessen the impact of a broadcast storm because routers do not route broadcast traffic.

Power Problems

When the power in a building goes out, even for just a few seconds, it can have an unpredictable (and often negative) impact on network and other electronic components. Power coming back on can also cause problems due to the initial "surge." Machines need to be protected against the sudden outage of power and the sudden surge of returning power.

An uninterruptible power supply (UPS) unit can provide sufficient power to servers and other computer equipment to give them time to execute their normal shutdown procedures. In fact, some UPS units can interface with servers to initiate a system shutdown in the event of a power outage. This is a very useful feature given that no one may be in the office when the outage occurs.

Look for UPS units that also provide *line conditioning*. This feature keeps the current flowing constantly and evenly to the servers. This eliminates or lessens the normal dips and spikes in power. Power fluctuations can eventually cause premature failures in power supplies, hard drives, and motherboards.

Although most organizations are wise enough to protect their servers with a UPS, other components (printers, hubs, routers, firewalls, user workstations, and so forth) may not be so equipped.

Server Problems

Here are the biggest server-based problems that impact a network:

- Lack of sufficient processing power
- Lack of sufficient memory capacity
- Loss of information due to hard drive crashes

The more services, user sessions, authentication, and I/O requests a server has to handle, the larger the need for raw CPU processing power. Network performance can suffer when network usage increases beyond the capacity of the servers that run the network. A performance monitor can monitor the drain on CPU resources and identify when a server may need to be upgraded to multiple processors or have its workload distributed among other machines.

Another resource that's closely related to the overall throughput a network is the amount of memory (RAM) to which the operating system, services, and applications have access. Memory is especially important for database servers and servers that process system authentication and security requests. When in doubt, add more memory.

A server disk crash can be a catastrophic event to an organization if certain safeguards have not been put in place. Solutions such as implementing RAID Level 5 (disk striping with parity) fault tolerance can reduce the impact of an individual drive going bad. However, a larger plan needs to be implemented to handle larger failure scenarios. Many organizations have mirrored drive and server farms in place so that if one server goes down, sufficient redundancy is available for immediate or engineer-assisted transition to a backup solution.

This is less of a troubleshooting concern than it is a consideration during the initial planning of your network design. Based on the value of your organization's data, a comparable data backup and recovery plan, including an offsite data-storage rotation, should be part of any network implementation.

Tools for Gathering Information

A variety of tools is available, at both the hardware and software levels, to help you gather real-time information from your network. This information, in turn, helps you diagnose network problems and provides clues that can point you toward resolutions.

The previous section mentioned several of these tools, which are explained in more detail in the following sections.

Digital Volt Meters

A *digital volt meter*, commonly referred to as a *DVM*, is a basic electronic measuring device, which in simple terms measures the amount of voltage passing through a resistance. Many of us know it as a device to measure the voltage of batteries or electrical outlets.

In a networking environment, its primary use is for continuity testing. In nontechnical terms, it's used to determine whether current from one end of a cable reaches the other end. If there is no *resistance*, the current is flowing through the cable unimpeded. If there is resistance, there may be a break in the cable.

You can also use a DVM to test for a "short" in a length of cable by placing one lead on the inside "core" of the cable and the other lead on the shielding layer. If any current registers, the shielding and the core are touching somewhere in the cable, thus causing a short.

Time-Domain Reflectometers

A *time-domain reflectometer*, or *TDR*, sends pulses along the cable at regular intervals. This device looks for breaks or other imperfections in the cable that might prevent it from carrying a signal across the network. The difference between this device and a DVM is that a TDR estimates the distance to the break.

The TDR analyzes the pulse readings and displays a result indicating where along the cable the break might be. A good TDR should be able to locate a break in a cable within a few feet. It does this by measuring the amount of time it takes for a pulse to reach the break (or short) and bounce back to the device.

TDRs can be used for both electrical and fiber-based cabling.

Oscilloscopes

An *oscilloscope* is an electronic device that measures the amount of signal voltage per unit of time. It has a display to show the results of its readings. When used in conjunction with a TDR, it can display shorts, breaks, attenuation (loss of signal strength), and bends and crimps in the cable.

Advanced Cable Testers

These testers go beyond just looking for cable breaks and imperfections. They can display information about resistance, impedance, and attenuation.

These devices can provide real-time information on the following areas:

- Error frame counts
- Message frame counts
- Beaconing
- Congestion errors
- Excess collisions
- Late collisions

Advanced testers can monitor network traffic and can even be focused to follow the traffic between two specific computers or devices. They can provide information about a particular cable or network adapter card that you suspect may be causing problems.

Protocol Analyzers

A protocol analyzer, like an advanced cable tester, performs a number of functions during real-time analysis of network traffic. But it goes even further. It can actually transmit, capture, and decode packets. It also can provide statistics based on real-time network traffic.

This is probably the most popular analytical tool of network engineers because it covers the entire gamut of testing needs. With the capabilities of a protocol analyzer, you can detect the following:

- Network bottlenecks
- Failing network adapter cards
- Connection errors

- Faulty network components (hubs, repeaters, and so forth)
- Protocol problems
- Broadcast storms

A hardware protocol analyzer usually contains a built-in TDR so it can locate cable breaks. But its strength is to take that analysis all the way up the OSI Reference Model. This means it can analyze traffic at all levels of the OSI model.

A hardware protocol analyzer can therefore be used to evaluate the effectiveness of a segment and measure the traffic to and from a computer on that segment. It can be used to track the protocols moving along wide area networks and the Internet.

Network Monitors

Microsoft Windows NT Server comes with a *network monitor*, which is a software implementation of a protocol analyzer. This software enables a workstation to capture and monitor network traffic going to and from the machine on which it's being executed.

When the monitor is executed from a promiscuous modem, traffic can be monitored even if it's not directed to the monitoring machine. (A standard modem does not provide access to packets not destined for the machine in which it is located.)

Monitors can capture, decode, analyze, and provide statistics about packet types, errors, and traffic to and from any computer on the network. Microsoft's Network Monitor can generate charts of network traffic at various intervals and can be run to get "snapshots" throughout the day (with information being saved to disk for later review).

It's very important to use network monitors to determine baseline performance statistics. These statistics can then be used in the troubleshooting process to identify abnormal traffic/activity.

Performance Monitors

The Windows NT Performance Monitor is a general-purpose software tool that can monitor all activities taking place within a file server. It can monitor the activities of all services and devices in the server. Network traffic that's processed by the server can also be tracked. This tool can give a good profile of a server's workload over a period of time— information that can be very helpful when assessing deviations from normal activity.

Helpful Resources

Many sources of technical and advisory information are available to help you make the best decisions regarding network maintenance and to help you troubleshoot network difficulties. Some resources are available in the public domain; others require a subscription or other fee.

Some of these resources are described in the following sections.

Vendor Technical Support

The most obvious resources available to network engineers are the companies from which they purchased their network hardware, software, and connectivity. If these companies offer technical support, take advantage of it—even if it's for only one year. You're sure to find it to be worth the money when you're installing and maintaining a complex network environment.

In addition, many of these companies have users groups around the country made up of real people, working in real network shops, and encountering the same pitfalls and challenges that you are. Find a users' group in your area; these people often end up being your best peer consultants and they can give you "real-world" answers to your problems.

Internet Newsgroups and Mailing Lists

The Internet can be a treasure chest of technical information. Several NT and networking mailing lists and newsgroups provide a forum where questions and scenarios of all kinds can be posted. People seem more than willing to show others that they are knowledgeable.

Obviously, you have to test out these suggestions for validity, but I have found people to be genuinely motivated to help out a fellow engineer.

Download Sites

Vendors post bug fixes, software patches, updated device drivers, maintenance utilities, and other tools on their company sites to help facilitate the successful implementation of their products. Most of these vendors provide file servers, running the File Transfer Protocol (FTP), for access via the Internet. Others provide a Bulletin Board Service (BBS) for their customers to access.

Magazines and Technical Journals

There are literally hundreds of magazines, newspapers, and technical journals, both printed and online. These publications are full of technical tips, hints, and reviews of software and hardware products and services. These can often be solid resources of troubleshooting information.

Technology changes so rapidly now that you need to keep yourself current on upcoming trends and technologies. Books are a wonderful resource but they can quickly become outdated given the pace at which this industry is changing.

Subscribe to magazines such as *LAN Magazine*, *NT Magazine*, *Data Communications*, and *Network World*. Consider subscribing to online news services such as NEWS.COM on the Internet, which sends an email each day with technology headlines. There are even online newspapers that you can configure to present only the subjects in which you're interested.

> **Peter's Principle:** Where to Go For Help
>
> After you've tried the methods outlined in this chapter and after you've con-
> sulted the printed and online documentation and help for your network oper-
> ating system, it's still possible you might be having trouble. Fortunately, both
> Microsoft and Novell provide online newsgroups where you can ask questions
> and get prompt replies from very knowledgeable volunteers—people who run
> their own networks and take the time to help out folks in trouble. Both
> Internet Explorer and Netscape include news readers to read these groups. To
> get started, point your browser to `http://support.novell.com/forums/` (for
> NetWare) or `http://www.microsoft.com/technet/discuss/support.htm` for
> Windows NT and then follow the instructions to set up a newsreader, post ques-
> tions, and find the answers you need.

Microsoft Windows NT Hardware/Software Compatibility Lists

Microsoft maintains a list of vendors who have gone through a certification process to have their products "certified" to operate under the Windows NT Server/Workstation environments. Many network problems have been traced to a network adapter or hard drive controller card that was not certified to be compatible with NT Server.

The Hardware Compatibility List (HCL) and the Software Compatibility List (SCL) can be found on Microsoft's Web site at `http://www.microsoft.com/ntserver/info`.

Microsoft Technical Information Network

TechNet is a CD-ROM of technical information, software drivers, patches, service packs, and tools that focus on aspects of networking across all of Microsoft's product offerings. This subscription service distributes two CD-ROMs on a monthly basis. Contact Microsoft at 800-344-2121 for more information.

The Microsoft Online Knowledgebase

The Microsoft Knowledgebase is a searchable index of technical reports. It can be found on Microsoft's Web site at `http://www.microsoft.com/ntserversupport`.

Windows NT Server Resource Kit

This is a wonderful collection of utilities, documentation, and other resources for NT net-work administrators. This CD-ROM includes resources for both NT Server and NT Workstation. Consider this a "must have" for NT-based networks.

Summary

Problem prevention—trying to identify and eliminate problems before they get out of control—and troubleshooting—solving problems that do get out of control—take up much of the time of a network administrator.

This chapter focused on environments of several different sizes and discussed the trade-offs involved with each within network disaster operational functions. The chapter presented information on many of the different proactive operations that can be carried out within a network management organization. This discussion recognized that these operations become low-priority responsibilities for all members of the network team and many pieces fall through the cracks.

This chapter provided insight into effective network disaster operations. Although it seems that only the high-end organizations can afford to implement these procedures, all organizations can use some level of planning and deployment. Many ideas were presented to help all sizes of organizations develop some plan for improvement.

Finally, we looked at troubleshooting techniques that are developed through a structured, repeatable, documented process that improves with use. It involves collecting information, analyzing that information, and pursuing a course of action based on that analysis.

Taking a methodical approach helps take the "art" of troubleshooting and turn it into a science. Following a step-by-step process of elimination, you reduce the potential for key information to get lost in the chaos of the knee-jerk reaction.

PART V

Appendix

Glossary

AAL (ATM Adaptation Layer)   ATM contains an adaptation layer that's responsible for creating the 48-octet datagrams that become the payloads of ATM cells. There are five different AALs, numbered 1 through 5, designed to support one of ATM's four different classes of service. These are known as classes A, B, C, and D. The first four AALs support the analogous class (1 with A, 2 with B, 3 with C and 4 with D) while AAL 5 can be used with either class 4 or class 5. Each class supports transmissions in different ways and, consequently, requires a separate set of protocols at the end stations.

Access Control List (ACL)   Objects in a Directory Service contain a property called an ACL, which lists objects that have been assigned trustee rights to an object.

Active Directory Service (ADS)   ADS is an advanced Directory Service native to Microsoft's Windows NT release 5.0 that's designed to facilitate the scaling of intranets. All networked resources are catalogued as "objects" into a central directory. This centralization makes all networked resources much easier to manage and access. The user is relieved of the burden of finding resources: They're all in the Active Directory of ADS.

Active Monitor (AM)   Token Ring's many rules are enforced by a single station. This station, known as the *Active Monitor* (AM), can be any of the stations in the ring. Usually, the AM is the first station to become active. Ownership of AM responsibilities can be contested and passed to other stations, after more stations activate. The AM monitors all traffic, ensures that the ring's protocol rules are adhered to, and is responsible for initiating any actions that might be necessary to overcome protocol violations or failures.

ANSI (American National Standards Institute)   ANSI is a private, nonprofit organization. Its charter is to facilitate the development, coordination, and publication of voluntary national standards.

API (application programming interface)   An *application programming interface* is a standardized software interface that an application program uses to access lower-level services.

Application Layer   The top layer in the seven-layer OSI Reference Model. Despite its name, the Application Layer does not include user applications. Rather, it provides the interface between those applications and the network's services.

ATM (Asynchronous Transfer Mode)   ATM is an evolving switched network technology known for scalability and consistency. ATM technologies can be used in both wide and local area networks.

attenuation   A decrease in the strength of a transmitted signal.

attributes   Each Directory Service's object has attributes assigned to it that describe properties associated with the object. File and directory attributes exist that affect the actions a user may take on network files and directories. An object's attributes can vary depending on the type of object it is. Typically, DS objects' attributes are called *properties* so that they're not confused with file attributes.

backbone   A LAN's "backbone" is the portion of its facilities used to interconnect all the hubs.

BGP (Border Gateway Protocol)   A modern routing protocol used between systems.

bindery   Versions of NetWare through 2.15 rely on a flat-file database called the *bindery*. The bindery consists of entries that control a user's access to files and directories, workstations, printers, and applications. A bindery exists on each server. In NetWare 4 and 5, the bindery has been replaced by Novell Directory Services (NDS).

bps   The bandwidth of a data communications frequency, as well as the physical media that supports its transmission, is measured using the number of bits per second (bps).

Categories of Performance   Performance ratings of unshielded twisted pair is rated by a series of performance thresholds defined by the EIA. Categories 3 and 5 remain the only two commonly encountered performance levels.

Category 3 UTP   Category 3 (Cat 3) UTP offers 16MHz of bandwidth, which translates into signaling speeds of up to 10Mbps at 100 meters.

Category 5 UTP   Category 5 UTP can support transmissions of up to 100MHz for up to 100 meters.

CCITT (International Consulting Committee for Telephone and Telegraph)   The CCITT was the organization responsible for setting many of Europe's telecommunications standards. It has reorganized itself and changed its name to the International Telecommunications Union (ITU).

chaining   A method of name resolution in which a server requests information about an object from other servers. In chaining, Server 1 will ask Server 2 for information on the object. If Server 2 does not have the information, it will report back to Server 1 and keep looking. It will ask Server 3, Server 3 will ask Server 4, and so on until Server 1 has an answer.

checksum   A forward error-correction mechanism used in the data transmission. Checksum values are created by adding together the binary value of each alphanumeric character in a block of data.

CIR (Committed Information Rate)   A term used for Frame Relay to describe the guaranteed minimum amount of bandwidth available at any given time.

circuit   The electrical or optical connection that forms the physical connection between any two points in a wide area network.

circuit switched network   A network that features packetized data that travels through the same series of switches to reach its final destination.

CISC (Complex Instruction Set Computing)   Refers to a microprocessor architecture that features a robust instruction set that attempts to perform as much work as possible with each instruction, as opposed to emphasizing the speed with which individual instructions can be executed. CISC instructions do not execute as quickly as instructions in a RISC architecture, but each instruction accomplishes more work than a RISC instruction.

client   Any computer that accesses resources stored on servers via the LAN.

cluster   A loosely coupled set of computers that function as a single computer. Clusters can take a seemingly infinite variety of topologies, each tailored to extract a different combination of benefits from the distributed redundancy of the cluster's resources.

CN   See *Common Name*.

coaxial cable   Coaxial cable, almost always referred to as *coax*, has two concentric conductors. It is, quite literally, coaxial in that both conductors share a common axis. The most common version of this cable type consists of a single conducting copper wire that's insulated by dielectric material. This dielectric material is then wrapped in another cylindrical conductor. This cylindrical conductor can be either a solid or braided wire. The conductor is then wrapped in another layer of insulation and the whole assembly is covered with a protective outer jacket of either polyvinyl chloride (PVC) or Teflon.

Common Name (CN)   Every Directory Service object has a name that's unique within its context in the directory structure. This is called the *Common Name* when it refers to users, nodes, or servers.

container objects   An instance of a class used to organize the directory tree. Container objects may contain other containers as well as leaf objects. Organizations, Countries, and Organizational Units are examples of container objects.

CPE (Customer Premises Equipment)   Hardware used to connect to a WAN circuit that's physically located at the customer's site.

CRC (Cyclical Redundancy Check)   CRC is a more robust error-detection algorithm than checksum. It's also used to determine whether an error has occurred during transmission. However, the CRC character's value is derived in a much more rigorous manner than is a checksum. The data is read as a binary string: This "number" is divided by another predetermined binary number to form the CRC value.

CSMA (Carrier Sense, Multiple Access)   CSMA is the primitive contention-based media access arbitration mechanism used by Ethernet I.

CSMA/CD (Carrier Sense, Multiple Access with Collision Detection)   CSMA/CD is an improvement over the CSMA media-access arbitration method. It, too, is contention based, but it provides mechanisms to prevent, detect, and automatically recover from collisions that inevitably occur. CSMA/CD first appeared in Ethernet II and was retained by the IEEE's 802.3 version of Ethernet.

CSU/DSU (Channel Service Unit/Data Service Unit)   The device that connects a network node to a WAN link.

DAS (dual-attached stations)   FDDI provides for dual-attached stations. Such stations feature two sets of media interfaces: one for each of FDDI's two rings.

Data Link Layer   The second layer of the OSI Reference Model. Like all the layers, the Data Link Layer has two sets of responsibilities: transmit and receive. It's responsible for providing end-to-end validity of the data being transmitted. On the transmit side, the Data Link Layer is responsible for packing instructions, data, and so forth into frames. A *frame* is a structure indigenous to the Data Link Layer that contains enough information to make sure that the data can be successfully sent across a LAN to its destination. The Data Link Layer is responsible for detecting and correcting any and all errors. The Data Link Layer is also responsible for reassembling any binary streams received from the Physical Layer back into frames. Given that both the structure and content of a frame are transmitted, the Data Link Layer isn't really rebuilding a frame. Rather, it's buffering the incoming bits until it has a complete frame.

DCE (Data Communications Equipment)   A defined interface for multiconductor copper cabling. This interface provides a pairing of transmit and receive conductors that's complementary to the Data Terminal Equipment (DTE) interface. A DCE interface can only be cabled to a DTE interface; otherwise, communications fail.

demarcation   The point from which the customer takes responsibility from the phone company for a WAN connection.

demultiplexing   Separating multiple types of data from a single link into their original components. See *multiplexing*.

directory tree   See *tree*.

Distinguished Name (DN)   Each object in a Directory Service has a unique name that identifies it, based on its location in the directory tree. This is a combination of the object's Common Name and the Distinguished Name of its container.

distortion   The unwanted modification of signals in transit. Distortion may be caused by either electromagnetic interference (EMI) or radio-frequency interference (RFI).

DIX Ethernet   See *Ethernet I*.

DLCI (Data Link Control Interface)   The address used to identify a particular PVC in a Frame Relay network.

DLM (Distributed Lock Manager)   DLM is an essential technique for controlling the modification of data in databases that are shared across multiple CPUs.

DN   See *Distinguished Name*.

DPAM (Demand-Priority Access Method)   A round-robin arbitration method in which a central repeater (also known as a *hub*) regularly polls the ports connected to it. This polling is performed in port order and is conducted to identify ports that have transmission requests. After the need to transmit is established, the repeater determines whether the priority is high or normal. These priorities are designed to service time-sensitive requests before servicing "normal" requests for bandwidth.

DTE (Data Terminal Equipment)   A defined interface for multiconductor copper cabling. This interface provides a pairing of transmit and receive conductors that's complementary to the Data Communications Equipment (DCE) interface. A DCE interface can only be cabled to a DTE interface; otherwise, communications fail.

EGP (Exterior Gateway Protocol)   An aging routing protocol used between autonomous systems.

ELAN (emulated local area network)   The emulated LAN in a local area network emulation (LANE) environment.

EMI (electromagnetic interface)   A low-frequency induction that can distort transmitted data.

encapsulation   A method of carrying packetized data from one protocol across a link in the data portion of another protocol's packet.

Ethernet   Ethernet describes the many forms of a LAN protocol that features Carrier Sense, Multiple Access with Collision Detection. This protocol was standardized by the IEEE in its 802.3 specification.

Ethernet I   The world's first LAN was Xerox's PARC Ethernet. This technology originated as an intra-office, baseband transmission technology for interconnecting workstations. It was cobbled together by researchers at Xerox's famed Palo Alto Research Center (PARC) for their own use as a superior alternative to using floppy disks for sharing information. Later, after the more self-contained and well-behaved version (known as Ethernet II) was created, PARC Ethernet became known as *Ethernet I*.

Ethernet II   The second-generation LAN technology from Xerox PARC. Ethernet II is also referred to as *DIX Ethernet*, in acknowledgment of its triumvirate of corporate sponsors: Digital, Intel, and Xerox.

FDDI (Fiber Distributed Data Interface)   FDDI is a 100Mbps token-passing LAN that was standardized via ANSI's X3T9.5 specification.

fiber-optic cable   Fiber-optic cables are capable of carrying the higher frequencies of the Electromagnetic Spectrum—that is, light. Fiber-optic cables come in a wide variety of shapes, sizes, and wavelength ratings.

frame   A structure that contains enough information to make sure data can be sent across a network, either a LAN or WAN, to its destination.

Frame Relay   A type of switched WAN transmission facility. Frame Relay enables the definition of multiple, logical permanent virtual circuits, each with their own minimum amount of bandwidth over a single transmission facility.

frequency   The electromagnetic wave continuously oscillates in a somewhat symmetrical pattern, from positive to negative, as it travels. The rate at which this oscillation occurs is called *frequency*. Frequency is measured in hertz (Hz).

Gbps   The abbreviation for billions of bits per second.

GHz   The abbreviation for billions of hertz per second.

GUI (graphical user interface)   Operating systems, such as the Microsoft Windows family of products, utilize a visually oriented environment that enables the user to access resources with a pointing device. This visually oriented environment is known as a *graphical user interface*.

hertz   See *Hz*.

Hz (hertz)   The number of oscillations in the electromagnetic wave, per second. One cycle, or *hertz*, represents a 360 degree change in one second.

IAB (Internet Architecture Board)   The IAB, formerly known as the *Internet Activities Board*, governs the technical development of the Internet. It contains two working committees: the Internet Engineering Task Force (IETF) and the Internet Research Task Force (IRTF).

IEC (International Electrotechnical Commission)   Founded in 1909, the IEC is headquartered in Geneva, Switzerland and sets international standards for anything electrical and electronic.

IEEE (Institute of Electrical and Electronic Engineers)   The IEEE is responsible for defining and publishing telecommunications and data communications standards. Its most significant effort has been the definition of the standards for local and metropolitan area networks (LANs and MANs). These standards, embodied in a large and complex series of technical standards, are generically referred to as *Project 802* or the *802 series of standards*.

IEEE 802.1   802.1 defines the overview and architecture for interoperability between LANs and MANs. This is the basis for all the 802 initiatives and includes standards for LAN/MAN management and bridging between 802-compliant networks.

IEEE 802.2   802.2 defines the Data Link Layer (Layer 2) standard for telecommunications and information exchange between systems, both LAN and MAN based. This specification provided the backward compatibility required to support a transition from the pre-standard versions of Ethernet to the 802.3 standardized version.

IEEE 802.3   802.3 establishes the new standard for a LAN that features a Carrier Sense, Multiple Access with Collision Detection. This "new" LAN is properly referred to as *CSMA/CD* but is popularly known as *Ethernet*.

IEEE 802.4   802.4 defines a Physical Layer standard for a bus topology LAN with a token-passing, media-access method. This LAN is called *Token Bus* and can support 1, 2, 5, or 10Mbps data rates.

IEEE 802.5   802.5 establishes the standards for Token Ring's access methods and physical signaling techniques.

IETF (Internet Engineering Task Force)   The IETF is responsible for setting the technical standards for the Internet as well as the defining new standards for Internet technologies.

IGRP (Interior Gateway Routing Protocol)   A widely used link-state routing protocol developed by Cisco Systems. IGRP is proprietary and only supported on Cisco routers.

IP (Internet Protocol)   IP was originally designed for a military wide area network. It has risen to prominence as the Network Layer protocol for the Internet and for intranets.

IPX (Internet Packet Exchange)   Novell's proprietary Network Layer protocol suite. IPX is almost always referenced in conjunction with Novell's proprietary Transport Layer protocol: Sequenced Packet Exchange (SPX). The combined protocol suite is called *IPX/SPX*.

IRTF (Internet Research Task Force)   The IRTF researches new technologies that may be of value to or have any impact on the Internet. Technologies deemed to be of potential value are referred to the Internet Engineering Task Force for further investigation.

IS-IS (Intermediate System to Intermediate System)   An OSI-based protocol.

ISO (International Organization for Standardization)   The ISO was founded in 1946 and is headquartered in Geneva, Switzerland. It's a voluntary, nontreaty organization that's chartered by the United Nations to define international standards. Its charter includes literally all fields, except for anything electrical or electronic. One of the more significant standards (for networking) produced by the ISO is the OSI Reference Model. ISO is actually a mnemonic designed to facilitate the organization's recognition in multiple languages. ISO is derived from the Greek word *isos*, meaning *equal* or *standard*. ISO is not an acronym for the name.

ITU (International Telecommunications Union)   Formerly the CCITT. The ITU is the organization responsible for setting many of Europe's telecommunications standards.

Kbps   The abbreviation for thousands of bits per second.

kHz   The abbreviation for thousands of hertz per second.

LAN   *See* local area network.

LANE (local area network emulation)   LANE enables ATM LAN clients to access and use existing LAN applications through a software layer added to the emulating devices. This software layer becomes an integral part of that device's ATM protocol stack.

laser   "LASER" has come into common usage as a noun, but it's actually an acronym. This acronym describes the physical process by which the concentrated energy associated with lasers is created. The acronym stands for Light Amplification through Stimulated Emission of Radiation.

leaf object   In a Directory Service, a leaf object represents entities on the network such as nodes, users, printers, or groups. Leaf objects are organized in containers. Some of the more common leaf objects are Computer, Group, File Server, Print Server, User, and Volume.

LEC (LANE Emulation Client)   Each client in a LANE ELAN is known as a *LAN Emulation client*. The individual LECs are addressed via their MAC address.

LES (LANE Emulation Server)   Each ELAN must have a single LAN Emulation Server (LES). The LES may be contained within a switch, a client computer, or a server computer.

LGN, LCN (Logical Group Number, Logical Channel Number)   These numbers are used to uniquely identify a virtual circuit in X.25 networks.

LLC (Logical Link Control)   The LLC provides addressing and control of the data link. It specifies which mechanisms are to be used for addressing stations over the transmission medium and for controlling the data exchanged between the originator and recipient machines.

local area network (LAN)   LANs are used to interconnect devices that are in relatively close proximity. The basis for LANs is defined in the IEEE's Project 802 family of specifications.

local loop   The last section of a circuit that spans from a telephony carrier's central office to the customer's premises. Often referred to as the *last mile*.

LUNI (LANE User to Network Interface)   ATM's LANE necessitated the development of a new interface—the LUNI. This interface is used by LANE clients to access the LANE server, where the actual emulation occurs.

MAC (Media Access Control)   Although putting ones and zeros onto the physical media is a function of the first layer of the OSI Reference Model, regulating access to that media for transmission is a function of the Data Link Layer. As standardized by the IEEE, this regulation is known as *Media Access Control* (MAC). The IEEE recognizes three methods for regulating media access: contention, demand priority, and token passing.

MAN   See *metropolitan area network*.

Mbps (megabits per second)   The abbreviation for millions of bits per second. The lowercase *b* denotes bits per second, not bytes. Mbps is used to measure throughput.

MBps (megabytes per second)   This is a metric of throughput, expressed in millions of bytes per second. The capitalization of the letter *B* designates bytes, as opposed to bits.

metropolitan area network (MAN)   Metropolitan area networks are defined through the IEEE's Project 802, the same initiative that standardized LANs. MANs are more closely related to WANs than LANs, because they're used to interconnect limited geographic areas. They remain relatively obscure and seldom used.

MHz   The abbreviation for millions of hertz per second.

MPPP (Multilink Point to Point Protocol)   This protocol enables a dial-up connection to utilize multiple links.

multiplexing   Combining multiple types of data onto a single link.

Network Layer   The Network Layer, Layer 3 of the OSI Reference Model, is responsible for establishing the route to be used between the originating and destination computers. This layer lacks any native transmission error detection/correction mechanisms and, consequently, is forced to rely on the end-to-end reliable transmission service of the Data Link Layer. This layer is used to establish communications with computer systems that lie beyond the local LAN segment.

NIC (network interface card)   A printed circuit board that's installed in a vacant slot in a computer's I/O bus. The back of the card contains a physical interface for a specific connector type, which is designed for a specific transmission media. This card provides the connectivity between a computer's internal system resources and the external resources connected to the network. It embodies the logic of the LAN's Data Link and Physical Layers.

NDS   The global naming system used in NetWare 4 and 5. NDS has been ported to other systems, such as Windows NT, Solaris, Linux, and OS/360. It contains information about the network, including the objects in the network.

NNI (Network-to-Network Interface)   A connection between networks.

OSI Reference Model   The Open Systems Interconnection (OSI) Reference Model was developed to facilitate the open interconnection of computer systems. The OSI model categorizes the various processes needed in a communications session into seven distinct functional layers. The layers are organized based on the natural sequence of events that occur during a communications session.

OSPF (Open Shortest Path First)   OSPF is an open-standard, link-state routing protocol.

packet switched network   A network that features packetized traffic, forwarded through a series of switches to its destination.

partition (1)   A demarked section of a fixed disk system formatted to a particular operating system.

partition (2)   A logical part of a Directory Services tree used to provide better management, security, or access.

peer-to-peer network   A peer-to-peer network supports unstructured access to network-attached resources. Each device in a peer-to-peer network can be simultaneously a client and a server. All devices are capable of directly accessing data, software, and other network resources. In other words, each networked computer is a peer of every other networked computer—there is no hierarchy.

permanent virtual circuit   A software-defined connection across a circuit switched or packet switched network. After they're defined, PVCs are always online.

Physical Layer   The bottom layer of the OSI Reference Model. The Physical Layer is responsible for the transmission of the bitstream. It accepts frames of data from Layer 2, the Data Link Layer, and transmits their structure and content serially, one bit at a time. This layer is also responsible for the reception of incoming streams of data, one bit at a time. These streams are then passed on to the Data Link Layer for reframing.

POTS (Plain Old Telephone Service)   The abbreviation for plain old telephone service. This jocular expression describes the voice-grade services of the Public Switched Telephone Network.

PPP (Point-to-Point Protocol)   PPP is the newest packet-framing protocol. It provides self-configuring, full-duplex, bidirectional, peer-to-peer connections to a wide range of hosts.

PPP Multilink Protocol   A feature of PPP that makes possible the combination of several data pipelines into one large pipe for faster transmission speeds.

PPTP (Point-to-Point Tunneling Protocol)   The creation of a virtual client/server link that's tunneled through an IP network. Tunneling enables clients to use a WAN as their virtual network.

PPTP control connection   The control connection is responsible for the creation, management, and termination of its corresponding PPTP tunnel.

Presentation Layer   The Presentation Layer is Layer 6 of the OSI Reference Model. It's responsible for managing the way data is encoded. Not every computer system uses the same data-encoding scheme, and the Presentation Layer is responsible for providing the translation between otherwise incompatible data-encoding schemes.

PSTN (public switched telephone network)   The abbreviation for the technical description of the global, voice-grade telephony infrastructure. The service provided across this infrastructure is often referred to as *POTS* (Plain Old Telephone Service).

Quality of Service (QoS)   Any means of identifying the time value and/or priority of a given packet as it traverses a network.

RAID (Redundant Array of Inexpensive Disks)   RAID started out as a simple idea for developing autorecovering, fault-tolerant, large, logical disk drives from small, inexpensive drives. The multiple drives are housed in a common chassis. Data is written redundantly to multiple drives, thereby providing protection from the loss of a disk drive. When a drive is lost and then replaced, the surviving RAID devices automatically detect the broken file system and reconstruct it. The rapidity with which this recovery is effected depends on the level of protection implemented. RAID support now has seven separate levels: RAID 0 through RAID 6. The first five were originally defined RAID 1 through RAID 5 at the University of Berkeley. These levels represent different combinations of cost and protection from failure. RAID 0 and RAID 6 are products of the marketplace. It's important to note that RAID is not a formal standard. Consequently, there's tremendous disparity between the levels of support provided at any given RAID level across vendor products. Many vendors recognize only the original five Berkeley RAID specifications, numbered 1 through 5.

- *RAID 0 (Redundant Array of Inexpensive Disks, Level 0)*. Data is striped across multiple disks, without any error correction or redundancy.

- *RAID 1 (Redundant Array of Inexpensive Disks, Level 1)*. Data is mirrored. One drive serves as the operational drive, with "live" contents. The second drive is an online backup of the first drive that's automatically updated: Every write operation performed on the first disk is automatically duplicated on the second.

- *RAID 2 (Redundant Array of Inexpensive Disks, Level 2)*. RAID 2 is a more robust implementation of RAID 0 that includes error checking and correcting codes (ECC). Data is striped across multiple disks. This facilitates recovery from damaged data.

- *RAID 3 (Redundant Array of Inexpensive Disks, Level 3)*. RAID 3 stripes data, in bytes, across multiple disks. One disk is used exclusively to record parity data.

- *RAID 4 (Redundant Array of Inexpensive Disks, Level 4)*. Stripes data in blocks, not bytes, across multiple disks. One disk is exclusively reserved for the recording of parity data.

- *RAID 5 (Redundant Array of Inexpensive Disks, Level 5).* This level of support is the most commonly used of the seven variants. Like RAID 4, it stripes data in blocks across multiple disks. The difference is that RAID 5 writes its parity data across multiple disks.

- *RAID 6 (Redundant Array of Inexpensive Disks, Level 6).* This variant provides all the functions of RAID 5 but also implements redundant disk controllers, cabinet fans, and buses.

RAS (Remote Access Server)   Microsoft's software module for the Windows environment that manages remote access to LAN-attached resources.

repeater   A device that accepts transmitted signals, amplifies them, and puts them back on the network. In a LAN, a repeater—more popularly referred to as a *hub*—enables multiple devices to be networked together by providing multiple ingress points to the network.

RDN   See *Relative Distinguished Name.*

Relative Distinguished Name (RDN)   Because it's often tedious to refer to Directory Service objects by their Distinguished Names, a Relative Distinguished Name (RDN) is used. The RDN is a partial name that identifies an object by its relationship within the current context.

RIP (Routing Information Protocol)   An older distance-vector routing protocol.

RISC (Reduced Instruction Set Computer)   A microprocessor architecture that features a relatively small set of simple instructions that execute more quickly, but perform less work, than a CISC instruction. Historically, RISC computers have been reserved for computationally intensive applications.

RFI (Radio Frequency Interference)   A high-frequency induction that can distort transmitted data.

RMON (Remote Network Monitoring Specification)   An updated version of SNMP. RMON is designed to provide interoperability between network monitoring and management devices from different vendors.

routed protocol   A network protocol, such as TCP/IP or IPX/SPX, that can pass data through different network segments to reach a destination.

routing protocol   Routing protocols are used by routers to communicate with other routers. The purpose of such communications is to develop and maintain tabular information about potential paths through the routed network to any given destination.

SAR (Segmentation and Reassembly)   ATM contains a protocol suite that segments outbound data into a protocol data unit. These units are used to create cells. Inbound data must be reassembled before it can be passed up to the next higher-level protocol.

SAR-PDU (Segmentation and Reassembly Protocol Data Unit)   Each AAL places the data it receives from the SAR into a precellular structure known as a *Segmentation and Reassembly Protocol Data Unit* (SAR-PDU). SAR-PDUs are passed to the ATM Layer, where they have five-octet headers grafted onto them to form the familiar 53-octet ATM cells.

SAS (single-attached stations)   FDDI provides for single-attached stations. Such stations feature one set of media interfaces that can be used to connect to a ring-with-trees topology.

schema   The definition of the structure of a Directory Services database.

SCSI (Small Computer Systems Interface)   SCSI (pronounced *scuzzy*) is a hardware interface that's used to interconnect hosts and peripheral devices. SCSI has been extended into multiple specifications. These specifications can support anywhere from 7 peripherals up to 15, and data rates from 5 to 40MBps. The SCSI specifications are:

- *SCSI-1*. The original small computer systems interface. This was more of a concept than a product and was quickly superseded by SCSI-2.

- *SCSI-2*. The first standardized form of SCSI. This specification features an 8-bit bus that supports a total of eight devices (including the adapter card) and has a data rate of 5MBps. Single-ended cabling is limited to 19.7 feet. Differential cabling can extend to 25 meters.

- *Fast SCSI-2*. Fast SCSI-2 increased the data rate to 10MBps. Maximum supported single-ended cable length decreased to 9.8 feet.

- *Fast Wide SCSI-2*. Fast Wide SCSI-2 was a further improvement in the SCSI-2 specification. It features a 16-bit bus. This enables 16 devices (including the adapter card) to be interconnected, with a data rate that can range from 10MBps to 20MBps.

- *8-bit Ultra SCSI-3*. The 8-bit Ultra SCSI-3 specification was, as the name implies, a new variant based on an 8-bit bus. The improvement came in a 20MBps data rate for the eight devices. Maximum length of single-ended cables depended on the number of devices: 9.8 feet could be used for four or fewer devices; otherwise, the cable had to be no greater than 4.9 feet.

- *16-bit Ultra SCSI-3*. This 16-bit version of the SCSI-3 specification features a 16-bit bus, with a commensurate number of devices, and a 20 to 40MBps data rate. The same cable length limitations for the 8-bit version apply.

server   Any LAN-attached computer that hosts resources that are shared by other LAN-attached devices.

server-based networks   Server-based networks introduce a hierarchy that's designed to improve the manageability of a network's various supported functions as the size of the network scales upward. Often, server-based networks are referred to as *client/server networks*.

Session Layer   The fifth layer of the OSI Model. The Session Layer is relatively unused: Many protocols bundle this layer's functionality into their transport layers. The function of the OSI Session Layer is to manage the flow of communications during a connection between two computer systems. It determines whether communications can be unidirectional or bidirectional. It also ensures that one request is completed before a new one is accepted.

shielded twisted pair (STP)   Twisted pair wiring with a layer of either foil or braided metallic wire that envelops the twisted pairs. This shielding lies directly below the surface of the jacketing. Its purpose, ostensibly, is to enable the twisted pairs to operate in environments that are prone to electromagnetic interference (EMI) and/or radio frequency interference (RFI). In practice, it actually impedes the normal functioning of the twisted pairs.

SLIP (Serial Line Interface Protocol)   A packet framing protocol that uses serial lines to transmit data. This protocol was never standardized and did not support many of the advanced functions needed in this type of connection. It was the forerunner of PPP.

SNMP (Simple Network Management Protocol)   A protocol that gathers information from networking hardware to monitor its performance.

SPAP (Shiva Proprietary Authentication Protocol)   A proprietary version of PAP made by Shiva, Inc. to support its remote access product.

SPX (Sequenced Packet Exchange)   Novell's proprietary Transport Layer protocol suite.

statistical multiplexing   Dividing a single circuit into multiple connections based on a bandwidth-sharing scheme.

STP   See *shielded twisted pair*.

striping   A technique that simultaneously writes redundantly to multiple disks with a single write instruction. This technique makes it possible for any given file to be read faster, because multiple devices are simultaneously retrieving it.

switched virtual circuit   A connection across a packet switched network that forwards packets individually, rather than via a predetermined path.

TCP (Transmission Control Protocol)   TCP is a Transport Layer protocol that's frequently used in conjunction with IP. These two protocols are frequently mistaken for a single protocol, because they're almost always referenced together as *TCP/IP*.

TDM (time-division multiplexing)   Dividing a single circuit into multiple connections based on a time-sharing scheme.

transmission facilities   The media used to transport a network's signals to their destinations. Media types can include coaxial cables, twisted pair, and even fiber-optic cabling.

Transport Layer   The fourth layer of the OSI Reference Model. The Transport Layer provides a similar service to the Data Link Layer, in that it's responsible for the end-to-end integrity of transmissions. Unlike the Data Link Layer, the Transport Layer is capable of providing this function beyond the local LAN segment. It can detect packets that are discarded by routers and automatically generate a retransmit request. Another significant function of the Transport Layer is the resequencing of packets that may have arrived out of order.

tree   A Directory Services database is often called a *directory tree* because of its shape—branches of containers that can be traced back to an origin (called the *root*).

twisted pair wire   Twisted pair wiring, used to support voice communications, has become the *de facto* standard wiring technology for LANs. A twisted pair consists of two relatively thin wires—18 to 24 American Wire Gauge (AWG), or 0.016 to 0.035 inches in diameter. These wires are coated with a thin layer of polyvinyl chloride (PVC) and spiraled around each other. This twist is highly functional: It helps cancel out any EMI that would otherwise be inducted into the copper by providing a balanced radiation of energy between the two wires.

UDP (User Datagram Protocol)   UDP is another Transport Layer protocol that's used in conjunction with IP.

UNI (User-to-Network Interface)   A connection between an end node and a network switch.

VCC (virtual channel connection)   The proper term that describes the type of logical connection that's established between the LECs and the LES in an ATM ELAN. The VCC is a virtual channel connection, and separate connections are required for ATM's control and user planes.

virtual private network (VPN)   A private network that's connected across a public network through the use of tunneling and/or encryption.

WAN   See *wide area network*.

wavelength   A metric used to measure the intensity of electromagnetic energy. A *wavelength* is the distance from the top of one wave's crest to the top of the next wave's crest. This metric is reserved for the higher-frequency phenomena, such as light, X-rays, and gamma rays.

wide area network (WAN)   WANs are used to interconnect LANs across geographic distances.

X.121   The protocol that X.25 relies on for its network addressing.

X.25   An aging network specification for transporting packets across a public switched network.

X.500   A specification for a standardized directory service promulgated by the ITU in 1988 and updated in 1993.

Peter Norton

Index

SYMBOLS

A

F

FREE Personal Bookshelf ONLINE
MACMILLAN

Get **FREE** books and more...when you register this book online for our Personal Bookshelf Program

http://register.samspublishing.com/

SAMS

Register online and you can sign up for our *FREE Personal Bookshelf Program...*unlimited access to the electronic version of more than 200 complete computer books—immediately! That means you'll have 100,000 pages of valuable information onscreen, at your fingertips!

Plus, you can access product support, including complimentary downloads, technical support files, book-focused links, companion Web sites, author sites, and more!

And you'll be automatically registered to receive a *FREE subscription to a weekly email newsletter* to help you stay current with news, announcements, sample book chapters, and special events, including sweepstakes, contests, and various product giveaways!

We value your comments! Best of all, the entire registration process takes only a few minutes to complete, so go online and get the greatest value going—absolutely FREE!

Don't Miss Out On This Great Opportunity!

Sams is a brand of Macmillan Computer Publishing USA.

For more information, please visit *www.mcp.com*